Child Abuse Interventions

LONDON: HMSO

Applications for reproduction should be made to HMSO
First published 1993

ISBN 0 11 321642 4

Contents

Preface

The previous version of this review of the research literature on child abuse interventions first appeared as a report to the Department of Health in 1988 (Gough, Taylor, and Boddy, 1988). Since this time, a large number of further research studies have appeared in the literature and so the report has been revised and updated for publication in the current form.

I am very grateful to several people who have helped make this project possible. First of all, Jeremy Taylor who was employed on the original project and worked with me to devise coding schedules, search the literature, and code and summarize studies. Later, Bridget Rothwell and Rowena Primrose spent several months providing further help in tracking down and coding studies. Also Hedi Argent provided helpful editorial advice on the text, though she bears no responsibility for the subsequent revisions that were necessary due to the appearance of a large number of new studies in the early 1990s.

Thanks also to Irene Young for her hard work in typing successive drafts of the report and to Andrew Boddy, Director of the Public Health Research Unit, and joint grant holder on the project, for his continued support.

Finally, I am grateful to the Department of Health for the financial support that made this review possible.

The work for this review was mainly undertaken at the University of Glasgow, but was completed at Japan Women's University, Tokyo, where I moved to in 1992.

Overview

This review examines the research literature on the efficacy of interventions to prevent or to react to cases of child maltreatment. Despite the very high number of publications on child abuse, only a small proportion are formal evaluations of the efficacy of interventive services. A search of the literature from 1980 to early 1992 revealed 225 studies, though the search was not exhaustive and some studies will have been overlooked.

There are many reasons for individual studies to be undertaken and the research literature does not necessarily reflect the pattern of routine or specialist provision offered in practice to children, parents, and families. Nor do the studies fit into neat theoretical categories. For the purposes of this review, therefore, the studies have been grouped into chapters on purely heuristic grounds. The first chapter introduces the review. Chapters Two to Six consider preventive approaches, whilst Chapters Seven to Eleven consider reactive interventions once maltreatment has been identified. The final Chapter (Twelve) discusses the research issues raised by the review.

The methodological limitations of many of the studies, the lack of clear findings, and the lack of replication studies makes it difficult to draw firm conclusions about the relative efficacy of different intervention strategies. This literature review limits itself, therefore, to only drawing tentative conclusions from the research and suggesting ways forward for future studies. These conclusions are listed at the end of each chapter and repeated in this overview. At the end of each chapter of the report there are standardized summaries of all the studies to allow readers to make their own assessment of the research and to choose which studies to follow up in more detail. The review aims to be a ground clearing exercise to help inform the planning of future intervention studies.

Educating Children (Chapter Two)

Preventive educational programmes directed at children mostly concern teaching skills to enable potential victims to avoid child sexual abuse.

1. There is evidence that educational programmes can increase the conceptual awareness of school age children about child sexual abuse and teach them how to report actual or potential abuse. Apart from the studies of stranger abduction, it is not clear whether the knowledge generalises to actual behaviour.
2. Other studies show that pre-school children can be taught behavioural responses designed to avoid potentially abusive situations from strangers. These behaviours are not necessarily relevant to intrafamilial abuse.
3. There is some evidence that the educational programmes have a differential impact, protecting those children most, who are less likely to be exposed to potentially abusive situations, and who are, in any case, better able to protect themselves from abuse.
4. Future research needs to examine the differential impact of the programmes on different children with different levels of pre-test skills and at varying degrees of risk rather than contrasting grouped data. This should include children of all ages (not just younger children as at present), from different social backgrounds, and with different abilities and disabilities.

5. It is not clear what effects the programmes have on the coping strategies of children who are subsequently unable to avoid being abused.

6. The studies report few negative effects of the programmes or of the test measures used such as simulation testing. However, these issues have not been addressed in any detail and great care needs to be taken before embarking on such programmes.

7. As well as indirect negative effects, the programmes may have indirect positive effects. They could increase the knowledge and ability of individual adults to protect children, raise community awareness and lead to reporting of abuse. One strategy would be to introduce the programmes within a wider policy of educating children about personal rights, human relationships and sexuality.

8. Attention needs to be given to the likely positive and negative effects on potential adolescent sex offenders. The ways in which children might be prevented from growing up into adolescent abusers needs to be more fully explored.

9. The research studies are strong on the use of experimental designs, but weak on the development of appropriate and valid dependent measures to assess reduction in the actual risk of abuse, the effects of coping with actual abuse, and the potential negative effects of the educational interventions.

10. The research studies would be more profitable if more of them compared and contrasted the impact of several techniques rather than being isolated evaluations of individual programmes. Currently it is the behavioural studies that provide the best examples of testing of programmes, including the use of parents as trainers.

11. There seems to be no information available on the type and range of programmes currently being implemented and to what effect in Britain. It is likely that there is a lack of provision in particular geographic areas, for children with special needs, and for children of secondary school age. A survey of programmes in use would identify gaps in current provision and inform future policy. A study of actual practice could identify the quality and quantity of current provision.

There is clearly considerable potential for programmes that enable children to avoid sexual abuse. Future research needs to clarify the differential impact of the programmes on different children, the generalisability of the skills learned and effects on coping strategies when children are unable to avoid abuse. The potential for programmes to enable protection against other forms of abuse has not been fully explored, although this may more directly challenge implicit values and power relations in families and so raise fundamental issues about the rights of children in our society. Educational programmes for parenthood have been introduced, but there is also potential for more focused work, particularly for preventing young males becoming perpetrators of child sexual abuse.

Educating Adults and the Community (Chapter Three)

Many of the educational programmes directed at children have an indirect effect at educating adults and the community. Other programmes have this as their main purpose. In some cases this can extend to the involvement of the local community in local child protection policies.

1. There are few studies of adult and community education programmes in the literature. Those that do exist are concerned with targeted training for

groups of adults to increase the level of education of child abuse issues in the general population, and develop local services and their integration into the local community. Most of these studies described interventions for ethnic minorities.

2. The studies do not use focused experimental designs or sufficiently specific outcome measures to allow conclusions to be drawn about the relative efficacy of the programmes or their different components.

3. The strength of the studies is in their demonstration of a range of approaches to adult and community development, and the favourable responses of users and workers.

4. Future studies would be more profitable if located within the research literature in similar fields of adult and community education. The experience gained in these other areas could be usefully applied to child abuse education.

5. There has been little development of these programmes in Britain. This leaves public debate to media discussions of particular cases, including the problems of investigation and response to suspected child sexual abuse. The need to develop community education and involvement in child abuse and child protection is probably more pressing than the need for intervention studies to assess the effectiveness of various approaches.

6. Programmes developed in Britain could usefully focus on the large number of professional workers who have daily contact with children and their parents, but still only receive little training about child abuse.

7. New programmes in Britain could also focus on developing knowledge and skills such as in (i) general parenting and child care, (ii) awareness of the nature of child abuse and agency responsibilities in child protection.

8. Other programmes could focus on developing community involvement in child care and child protection such as in (i) the integration of local services into the community to encourage positive preventive work rather than only responses to perceived inadequate care, (ii) development of community awareness and responsibility for providing appropriate child care environments, (iii) developing community participation in local child protection policy and practice.

9. Any programmes developed in Britain will need to take account of covert as well as stated variations in beliefs about child care and the role of the family.

10. Surveys of current knowledge and attitudes in respect of child care and of child protection would provide a good starting point for further debate in community education in child abuse and protection.

There is little research experience available to assess the value of broad educational programmes. However, the lack of such provision suggests that there is much scope for the development of various educational strategies in Britain. These strategies could simply be knowledge and skill based or more radically involve community participation in service provision.

Volunteers and Parent Aides (Chapter Four)

Many of the studies of the use of lay or less highly trained staff have concerned preventive work with individuals who may commit abuse – that is, in circumstances where parenting difficulties are identified. (The use of such programmes in the neonatal period are considered in Chapter Five).

1. The studies examined preventive schemes that use volunteers and parent-aides to develop parents' own resources and abilities to cope. The projects were based in different organizational and professional contexts and used

a variety of approaches. The preventive strategies and techniques can be understood within a classification of social support.

2.	The studies all reported improvements and the interventions were positively perceived by both users and workers. The lack of independent measures makes it difficult to assess whether there were improvements in actual behaviour and functioning. Perceptions of change could have been influenced by many factors including the level of co-operation and satisfaction expressed by the parents.

3.	There were few experimental controls in the studies, and so any improvements in functioning could have been due to the interventions applied or due to other factors. The general lack of specification of the different aims, techniques and outcomes of emotional support, make it difficult to assess the relative efficacy of techniques, both between and within studies, and how they relate to different client groups.

4.	Benefits of the schemes include low cost, enablement rather than treatment, and the lack of stigma and freedom from statutory responsibilities, though it is unclear whether the support is best offered separate, in addition to, or as part of statutory provision. There is a need to distinguish the benefits and costs of different types of social support offered in different ways to those with different needs. Some clients may benefit from tangible material aid, others may benefit more from advice or from the sense of self worth arising from personal relationships. The latter may be fostered by aides or volunteers or by a membership model of social support.

5.	Most of the improvements reported in the studies concerned maternal mental state or mothers' positive views of the programme. That there was little evidence of change in children or mother-child interactions suggests that different extra techniques are necessary for these areas. This conclusion is supported by separate studies of maternal depression.

6.	There are many volunteer and befriending schemes or similar supportive groups in existence that are not directly concerned with child abuse. The task for future research is to isolate those components of social supports that are most effective for different clients in different situations. This requires clearer specification of these components, controlled research designs, and independent measures of assessment of outcome. The studies could be more productive if they were more directly based upon the existing research literature on social supports and coping strategies, as well as on a greater specification of the components of support offered by volunteer and parent aides.

The low cost, and the acceptability of lay services by clients, suggests that they offer considerable potential for development. Some support for this view is provided by the outcomes of programmes for cases of actual abuse (Chapters Seven to Eleven). Empirical evidence of their effectiveness will depend on further clarification of the nature of the support offered by the lay services and their organisational context, particularly in relation to statutory services.

Ante Natal and Post Natal Services (Chapter Five)

The preventive services in the neonatal period examined in the research literature are directed at new parents in general, parents possessing general risk characteristics, or those identified individually as being likely to experience serious problems in the care of their children.

1.	The studies examined interventions that use a variety of techniques to support families (mostly mothers) in the ante and post-natal periods. The techniques used included training in skills, provision of tangible aid, cognitive guidance, and emotional support. The users of these services were first-time mothers from normal or demographically at risk populations, or mothers who had been specifically referred with potential parenting problems.

2. The studies revealed some positive programme effects but these are difficult to confirm because of problems in research design. The research was also not able to specify in detail which of the techniques and resources used were most effective for which clients. The main difficulties were:
   - lack of independent measures of outcome;
   - multiple comparisons attempting to isolate effects of specific components of intervention, resulted in small cell sizes in some of the more experimentally controlled designs;
   - a lack of explicit theoretical base and clear hypotheses that would allow specificity of research designs and appropriate measures of outcome.

3. Positive results of programmes on parental functioning were not matched by improvements in child functioning or child-parent interactions. The conclusion is that either the children's needs should be directly targeted or preventive interventions with parents should start prenatally.

4. There is some evidence of programmes having differential effects on different groups of subjects and that these effects were sometimes negative. There is thus an even greater need for future studies to specify the components of the aims of interventions and the manner in which these are achieved.

5. Some interventions were successful in identifying families at future risk. As such screening produces many false positives and negatives, it is important to consider the negative effects of a wrong prediction. Screening for general need for help and support has fewer negative consequences, than screening specifically for child abuse, but there is still the potential for negative effects of special interventions.

6. The costs of the interventions are high considering the weak evidence of the modest results received. On the other hand, several of the services and resources could be provided to improve the quality of pre and post-natal care for consumers of these services even without proven effects on parental or child functioning.

The argument for intervening in the neonatal period is clear; this is a sensitive period in the development of relationships between the parents and the child. There are practical benefits of access to the family which may include their willingness to accept services. It may be possible to identify the children most at risk and the families in whom intervention is appropriate. The studies demonstrated some support for the possibility of identifying children at risk – unfortunately, despite the attractiveness of the philosophy of early intervention there were few clear results of these programmes having an impact on the later circumstances of the families.

Adult and Child Groups (Chapter Six)

Many of the programmes considered in the review included some form of group work. Those that were principally associated with more general educational programmes, with the use of volunteers or parent aides, or with prevention in the antenatal or neonatal periods, are considered elsewhere. This chapter is concerned with the few studies of group work that did not fall into these categories. All the studies were about the use of groups for parents thought to have parenting problems and being at risk of abusing their children.

1. Research studies on groups developed in order to reduce the risk of child abuse all involved subjects individually identified as at risk. The groups had a variety of aims and utilized a range of different techniques that fell broadly into the categories of social activities and mutual support, education, behavioural training, and psychotherapy. Some groups included several of these approaches and one group was created by a residential facility for young single mothers experiencing problems.

2. There was not sufficient research evidence from the studies to distinguish which general approach or specific technique was most effective and in what circumstances. Most groups seemed to provide benefits for the psychological and social functioning of the mothers and their children, but there were also indications of reductions in the mothers previous sources of social support.

3. The limitations of the research designs were similar in kind but often greater in magnitude to those reported in other chapters. This is probably due to the lack of research in the area rather than any intrinsic difficulty in undertaking such research. Studies in this area are comparatively straightforward as they can be time limited and it is relatively easy to randomly assign subjects to more than one treatment condition.

4. The research to date provides a basis for hypotheses about which types of group are indicated for different people presenting with different problems; hypotheses that can be explored by future studies.

5. Further research is required because groups have obvious potential for providing emotional support, education, and behavioural and psycho therapy. Groups are relatively inexpensive compared to other forms of provision and may be a more acceptable form of service delivery than conventional one to one client-worker relationships.

6. Research on groups as a preventive approach to child abuse needs to take into account the rapid growth of family centres using diverse methods of work within a range of different models of care.

The potential of parent groups is similar to that suggested for lay services for at risk families. There is some empirical support for the positive influence of groups for children but empirical evidence for the efficacy of these methods will only be forthcoming when there is clearer specification of the context and content of these activities.

Behavioural Approaches to Physical Abuse (Chapter Seven)

Behavioural interventions for the treatment of physical abuse of children is one of the most developed areas of research.

1. There is evidence that behavioural techniques are effective within the acknowledged limits of changing the ratio of positive and negative interactions. There is some evidence of some techniques being more effective in changing different aspects of parenting and that some parents may be more easily helped than others.

2. There is evidence that the improvements accruing from the interventions can be provided in a relatively short period, usually in well under six months.

3. Some of the studies had the disadvantage of not involving the children in either the treatment or the research measures of baseline and outcome data.

4. The need for future research, is not to prove the efficacy of the behavioural model, but to determine the best method for its application in child abuse

cases, and its potential scope. Research on these unresolved issues would clarify which is the most appropriate context for behavioural programmes.

5. Unresolved issues include:
   - the relative efficacy of different techniques with different individuals with different presenting problems
   - the necessity of client motivation for success
   - the case types most available and most suitable for treatment
   - the advantages and disadvantages of court ordered treatment
   - the effects of families having additional problems and the difficulties and the necessity of working with these additional problems (with behavioural or other methods)
   - the degree to which success depends on integration of treatment within supportive casework
   - the length of treatment and possible repeat interventions.

6. The studies reviewed generally had the methodological virtues of (a) providing detailed baseline descriptions of their cases, (b) specifying the treatment, and (c) specifying outcome in operational terms and with obvious and direct relevance to the problem and the treatment.

7. Although many methodological problems remain, the behavioural studies stand out in the child abuse literature, as being more likely to test explicit hypotheses developed from previous theoretically based work, often drawing on the wider behavioural literature which considers other client groups. They also use more appropriate outcome measures of behavioural change, rather than self-report data or global measures such as known incidence of re-abuse. Studies of child abuse interventions based on very different theoretical approaches, could benefit from employing the hypothesis testing strategy of the behavioural studies.

8. Currently, behavioural approaches are restricted to a few special treatment centres and to clinics with psychologists on the staff. Not many children placed on child abuse registers or their families, are likely to benefit from these programmes. Policy decisions are required about how best to include more behavioural programmes within the child protective services.

Although there are many issues requiring clarification, there is evidence that behavioural interventions are effective in cases of physical abuse. The relatively infrequent use of these methods suggests that there is considerable scope for the development of behavioural work in the provision of routine services.

Special Projects for Children and Families (Chapter Eight)

There are many special programmes for intervening in identified cases of abuse and many of these have attracted research interest.

1. Studies of special treatment not included in chapters on behavioural approaches to physical abuse, multi component programmes, and sexual abuse involved the following types of programmes:
   - educational or skilled based programmes for parents and families
   - psycho-therapeutic and supportive group work
   - direct therapeutic work with individuals
   - child focused services
   - projects for non organic failure to thrive.

2. Educational and skill based programmes seemed to show encouraging results. Three studies were experimentally controlled and reported greater improvements

compared to controls on cognitive development, behavioural, or knowledge scores.

3.   Studies of group services for parents, revealed many imaginative programmes. The results were mostly based on clinical scoring and reported improvements in self esteem and social functioning and none of the studies were experimentally controlled. The studies were able to illustrate methods of work rather than to determine their effectiveness.

4.   Studies of direct individual work with adults and families ranged from intense psychotherapy to the use of lay home visitors and volunteers. Positive improvements were reported, but only three of the studies were experimentally controlled and only one used consistent independent measures.

5.   The child focused studies examined interventions offering children psychotherapy, extra stimulation and care, and practice in initiating social interactions. These studies were most likely to use independent measures of outcome and they also reported significant improvements in child functioning. However, this did not always reduce the risks to the children and allow them to remain in, or return to, their original family. Also, the lack of experimental controls in all but two studies make it difficult to determine the cause of any post-test improvements. There were few projects that directly addressed the needs of children. Some facilities may have been made available for children in parent focused programmes but these were often of secondary importance and went no further than normal day care principles.

6.   Studies of non organic failure to thrive described interventions ranging from support and advice to individual therapy to rigorous behavioural programmes. The studies demonstrated marked improvements at post-test on the independent outcome measure of weight gain. Few studies used control groups, and the one study that did, found considerable catch up growth in controls. However, the other controlled studies mostly confirmed the findings of uncontrolled studies.

7.   Many of the studies in this chapter had the same methodological problems, which limit the interpretation of results as discussed in other chapters. Some of the most encouraging results were in the child focused studies. These were relatively well designed, and thus went against the trend of many child abuse studies where the most rigorous experimental designs report the least encouraging results.

In sum, many of the studies reported encouraging results, but without a greater focus on how and why they were achieved, it is difficult to interpret this research. A particular problem is the lack of comparability; how are policy makers to choose between programmes when considering useful directions for service development? One general conclusion was a demonstration of the value of child directed services; an activity that is relatively rare in routinely provided services.

Multi-component Interventions   (Chapter Nine)

Multicomponent interventions in specialist centres provide only a small proportion of routine service provision but form the basis of a large proportion of the major research studies.

1.   A series of studies were identified that evaluated multi-component therapeutic interventions for child abuse. The components of these interventions were similar to those in more narrowly focused projects discussed in other reactive interventions described in this volume.

2. The multi-component nature of the projects added to the methodological problems discussed in the previous chapters. These problems were heightened by the greater number of variables involved in multi-component interventions. Only very large scale studies are able to use multivariate methods to distinguish the interacting effects of different intervention components.
3. The size of the two large North American research studies allowed the statistical comparison of the effects of different project components, although the results were limited by the use of clinical outcome measures.
4. The results of the two American large scale studies supported the use of lay therapy services, group counselling, educational groups, and direct services for children.
5. The studies did not report positive interaction effects between the components of the large programmes. This is worthy of further study as it is one of the main potential benefits of multi-component projects.
6. Although the studies reported encouraging treatment effects including a reduced propensity for abuse, the actual outcomes were not encouraging. There were still re-incidence rates of between 30% and 47%.
7. Small scale specialist multi-component interventions often attract research interest. These studies have value in describing specialist work, but are often not effective in determining the efficacy of different interventions. These studies might be more productive if they concentrated upon analysing the processes of intervention rather than attempting and failing to assess their efficacy.

Methodological problems have limited the contribution of these studies. Most report a complex of techniques provided for small populations which do not permit the use of adequate methods of analysis although they do have experiential value. From the standpoint of research methods, it is important to distinguish between the value of one component of the intervention and the more complex interactions that may occur as one component influences the value of another. An important feature of the large American studies (which allowed these distinctions to be explored) was that there were few interactional effects. The clearest results were of the independent value of lay therapy, educational and counselling groups, and direct services for children. These services are probably uncommon in routine services.

Routine Services and Special Initiatives (Chapter Ten)

The majority of identified cases of child abuse are provided with routine rather than specialist services – though the latter have attracted more research interest.

1. There have been few studies which examine the efficacy of routine casework or simply describe the content, process, and outcome of this work.
2. There is a great need for this data for at least the following reasons: (a) To provide information on current practice and its effect on case outcomes; (b) To understand the context and influence of procedural and legal systems on therapeutic interventions; (c) To clarify the definitions, and processes of child protection work for the development of more coherent studies of therapeutic interventions. If these are not clear, it is unlikely that research hypothesis can be articulated and tested out.
3. The descriptive data available on routine practice, reveals that there is little use of specialist social work or of referral to other disciplines such as child psychology, psychiatry or paediatrics. Any additional services are provided directly by social work departments or through resources under their control. This contrasts with the fact that most research effort has been invested in evaluating specialist services.

4. Descriptive studies reveal that many abused children are removed into long term care and that this is a protracted exercise. Most of the children received into care come from families in deprived areas without the physical or emotional resources to cope unaided with child care responsibilities. Non compliance with court ordered services is associated with removal of children into care.

5. Studies of case outcome have suggested that outcome can be predicted from case presentation, such as substance abuse by the parents. Other studies indicate the importance of examining both service and case variables in predicting outcome.

6. Child protection cases have relatively high rates of re-referral. There is little evidence that child protection services improve outcomes for children or reduces re-referral rates (except when children are permanently removed). Abused children have worse long term outcomes than control children, but this may be due more to continuing adverse aspects of their lives rather than specific attributes of the abuse or child protection responses.

7. Systems to provide routine child protection management information are in their infancy, but confirm significant variation in practice. These new systems offer much potential for providing feedback to professionals and policy makers and to provide data to inform future micro studies of practice.

8. A few studies have examined the effects of special developments on routine services. These report encouraging results, but their methodological limitations restrict them to being mostly descriptions of innovatory practice.

Too few studies have attempted to evaluate routine services; one difficulty is the overlay of legal and other measures of child protection which may cloud attempts to assess the effectiveness of the "therapeutic" activities that are also included in them. Data currently available suggests that child protection has little impact on re-referral rates or on long term outcomes for the children. Further research should elaborate the nature of child protection, the content and efficacy of routine work, and the potential for implementing the techniques developed by special programmes. The recent development of child protection management information systems will provide a major stimulus and source of data for such studies.

Child Sexual Abuse (Chapter Eleven)

The short history of widespread awareness about sexual abuse means that there are few well designed studies of intervention efficacy. The research that has been undertaken can be distinguished by whether it is primarily concerned with the child protection system, the perpetrator, victim, or the whole family system. Few studies formally assess the impact of services on non abusing parents.

1. Research studies have reported that some interventions have been associated with improved scores on research measures at post-test, but the lack of many controlled studies or comparative studies limits the conclusions that can be drawn.

2. The research data that are available, differ in emphasis from data for other forms of child abuse. There is a greater focus on individual treatment for perpetrators, on group treatment for victims and adult survivors, and on the causative effect of certain family systems. There is also more explicit regard for the effects of the statutory child protection process.

3. Four causal factors have been described for perpetrators of sexual abuse. There is evidence that one of these, inappropriate sexual orientation, has been successfully treated by behavioural interventions. The studies can be criticised

for their reliance on measures of sexual arousal and recidivism, but the results are relatively strong compared to most child abuse intervention studies and the methodology can be commended for testing of specific hypotheses.

4. There are indications that other factors regarding perpetrators including sexual blockage, emotional congruence and social inhibitions, are suitable for treatment and could provide a basis for future research.

5. There is an impression that treatment for perpetrators is one of the least available services, despite having the strongest empirical support for efficacy.

6. Research data on treatment for victims and survivors is very limited. There is some research support for the benefits of groups and of some individual therapies, but little data to suggest that one approach is superior to another or that a particular approach is indicated for particular types of case. There are few research reports on interventions with male victims or on extra compared to intra familial abuse.

7. Multi-component programmes for whole families in cases of incest, report high rates of success, but there are uncertainties about the independence of the outcome measures used. Evaluation is particularly complex because, (a) many treatments are used in parallel and (b) the interactive effects of routine field services, child protection agencies, and the criminal justice system.

8. The reported success of multi-component programmes in reducing recidivism, is similar to the success reported by behavioural programmes for perpetrators, despite very different methods of intervention. This may be due to equal efficacy, experimental error, or different client populations. Neither finding is supported by large scale retrospective outcome studies of all sexual offenders.

9. Future research is unlikely to be productive unless individual studies limit themselves to testing narrow hypotheses regarding specific treatments and/or specific agency and legal processes. The current literature is well able to provide details of the individual issues that this research could address. Many approaches to treatment are suggested by (a) the clinical work reported in the literature and detailed in recent reviews, (b) new studies of the process and outcome of routine case management, and (c) the sequelae of child sexual abuse indicated by clinical records and retrospective studies, and recently confirmed by prospective studies.

Research on perpetrators has shown some success in re-orientating sexual age preferences, but little attention has been given to examining other causal factors such as social inhibition, sexual blockage, and emotional congruence. There is a lack of well designed research on treating and preventing the effects of sexual assault. Studies mapping the short and long term consequences of abuse are assisting to identify specific aspects of the causal pathways and suggest bases for intervention that can be tested by focused experimental studies. Studies on treating the child and the family are more problematic. The analysis of causal sequences and the effects of abuse are more complex when examining families rather than individuals and these processes are overlaid by the legal and other measures of child protection. It is therefore unsurprising that there is little clear data on the efficacy of programmes for the treatment of child sexual abuse, particularly multicomponent programmes, despite optimistic clinical reports.

Overview of Research Issues (Chapter Twelve)

Furthering the empirical evidence for the relative efficacy of different child abuse interventions will be achieved only by overcoming the serious methodological limitations of the current literature.

1. The literature evaluating the efficacy of child abuse interventions covers a wide range of techniques applied at different levels, theories and strategies of work.

2. Several gaps in the literature exist and these often relate to gaps in service provision. There is also still a relative lack of reference to routine child protection services and the legal and procedural aspects of child protection which constitute the context of reactive interventions. A distinction needs to be made between studies of the dynamics of child maltreatment and the processes and outcomes of child protection interventions.

3. The majority of studies were limited by their lack of reference to a wider research and practice base of related but non-child abuse work; for example, the research literature and service developments in family support programmes.

4. Most studies were limited by methodological problems arising from a lack of specification of their sample, focus, objectives, methods, design, measures and results, and the inter-relationship between them.

5. Despite methodological weaknesses, many of the studies provided useful descriptions of the process of the innovative interventions. It is suggested that the studies would therefore be more productive if this analysis of process were the main initial purpose, rather than a by-product of unsuccessful outcome studies.

6. The most successful studies were narrowly focused evaluations of specific interventions, where research was primary, or at least equal to the service, component.

7. Other successful studies were large demonstration projects with large enough sample sizes to allow multivariate analysis. The expense of these studies restricts their general use.

8. Treatment outcome studies are necessary but should only be attempted with highly specified research designs. Narrowly focused designs have been the most successful to date and provide the most sensible model for future research. This results in an incremental model for developing research knowledge and will probably be best achieved by comparative research designs.

9. Related research would also contribute to the study of the efficacy of child abuse interventions. This could include studies of the natural history of childhood adversities in the population; the description of routine child protection practice and outcome; and related, but non-child abuse, health, welfare and educational services.

10. The development of computerized service management systems, particularly child protection management information systems, should have a dramatic effect on our knowledge of the content and outcome of service provision.

Improvements in the methodology and thus the relevance of research to the efficacy of child abuse interventions will be achieved when studies are sufficiently disciplined to focus on testable hypotheses that contribute to specific aspects of knowledge about methods of intervention. This is an important requirement because of the diversity of the interventions that are possible; there is thus a need for coherence in the theoretical assumptions that different programmes employ. Other requirements are, first, that studies should assess the interaction between activities directed towards child protection and those concerned with therapeutic change and should be clear about the implications of this interaction for the research and, second, that both case definition and the content of the intervention should be precisely stated and controlled. Improved data on current practice from management information systems should aid this process.

CHAPTER ONE
Introduction

Scope and Purpose

The concept of child maltreatment is not new, but it is only since the 1950's that it has grown to be a major area of health, welfare, and legal practice. The growth in the number of identified cases has been matched by an exponential growth in writings on child abuse and child protection. A substantial component of this literature is research on the nature, extent, outcome, and possible intervention strategies for child maltreatment. The purpose of the current volume is to review that part of the research literature concerned with evaluating the efficacy of different interventions that have been developed as either reactive responses to abuse or as strategies to prevent abuse occurring in the first place.

In order to make such a review practicable a number of limits on the extent of the review have inevitably been necessary. From a conceptual point of view many of these limits are rather arbitrary, but they are determined by the main purposes of the review which is to make the research more accessible by summarizing the studies in one volume.

One important boundary of the review is that it only addresses interventions whose outcome has been evaluated in some formal way. The review does not attempt to consider all the intervention strategies that have been attempted in the field or described or suggested in the literature. There are other publications, often written by experienced practitioners, that fulfil the need to describe the possibilities of child abuse work. The purpose of the current review is to bring together the diverse literature of completed research studies. It is not intended as a text on intervention strategies in child abuse.

A second limitation of the review is that it does not attempt to describe the research literature in related areas of work. It could be argued that the study of child abuse and child protection should be within a broader framework of the causes and consequences of problems in parenting and child development (see, for example, Cichetti and Carlson, 1989) and that intervention should be seen within the context of services for children and families (Stevenson, 1992). A therapeutic programme for families at risk of abusing their children, for example, is not that different from studies of therapeutic programmes for non coping or dysfunctional families. These arguments are probably correct, but there are a variety of different research fields that might be considered the most central. Extensive research literatures exist on the causes and treatment of psychiatric disorder, stress, parenting difficulties, violence and aggression, and sexual offending. Each of these literatures contains articles reviewing current research knowledge and practice dilemmas. What is less available are reviews of the variety of different studies that can be subsumed under the heading of child abuse. Although there are conceptual problems in distinguishing child abuse from other areas, the review has a practical purpose. It aims to be a resource for those with an interest and purpose in being informed about child abuse intervention studies, yet who are unable for reasons of time or availability to access this information directly themselves. There is a pressing need to integrate the related areas of work concerned with the health, welfare, and protection of children, but this ideal is beyond the scope of the present text.

A third boundary to the review is created by the nature of the studies identified. Most of the reactive interventions that have been subject to research evaluation are at the individual or family level of analysis (Gough and Boddy, 1986). The studies do not typically examine the effects of intervention on the level of the community or society, even though these macro level interventions may be just as, if not more, effective at reducing the incidence and negative effects of child maltreatment. Studies of preventive intervention sometimes take a broader approach, but they are still largely concerned with individuals, parent-child dyads, or whole families. Furthermore, interventions based at the individual or family level predominantly take either a medical model of diagnosis and treatment or a social welfare model of the state intervening to mitigate inequalities in society. There is little research evaluating child abuse interventions based upon changing such inequalities (for example, developmental and radical models of welfare, see Hardiker et al 1991, Gough, 1993). The research emphasis on medical or social welfare models of intervention is necessarily reflected in this review.

The volume is divided into two main parts. In the first part preventive studies are discussed. The second part then addresses studies of reactive interventions after child maltreatment has occurred (sometimes described as tertiary prevention). This division is also rather arbitrary. The concept of abuse is based on social interpretations of events. The definition of abuse depends upon some event or experience being considered harmful to a child (including the infringement of the child's rights) and someone or something being considered responsible for that harm (whether or not the harm was intended by those perceived as responsible). These distinctions are difficult to make. People do not agree as to what is harmful and even if they do agree on this, they may not agree about responsibility for the harm and whether it is abusive. In practice the distinctions are even more difficult because the full details of what occurred to a child and how and why it occurred are often only partially known and so the distinction between risk of abuse and actual abuse are relative. What is important in practice are operational definitions of abuse provided by the actions of health, welfare, and legal agencies. In other words, the agencies define a situation as one of child abuse or possible child abuse with all the practical consequences of child protection that this may entail. Child abuse research, with the exception of population studies on incidence, virtually always recruits its samples from health, welfare, and legal agencies. The result is that the research subjects are subsamples from these agency child protection systems. This is far from an ideal basis on which to define research samples, unless of course the focus is upon the decision making practices and outcomes of these systems (Chapter 10). The use of agency samples and agency definitions is, however, the reality of most child abuse research.

The prevention cases are mainly made up from individuals and families who have been identified clinically as being at risk of abusing their children, though some studies examine those who may be at risk on purely demographic grounds, and some prevention projects are targeted at the whole population. A number of research projects involve a mix of subjects or are unclear about whether children are thought to have been abused. These studies were allocated to different sections of the review according to whether their approach is predominantly preventive or reactive.

Arbitrary decisions also had to be made in order to group studies into individual chapters for discussion. As the purpose of the review was to examine the research that had been undertaken rather than review all possible interventions, the grouping of studies could not be sensibly achieved on an a priori basis. Instead the studies were grouped into the chapters on the basis of their similarity with each other. The divisions are not ideal. Many studies use a variety of techniques on a range of different subjects, but it is not practical to consider all the studies together. Instead studies were divided between chapters on the basis of similarity of purpose rather than on the techniques that were applied in the intervention. Inevitably, there are some studies that do not fit so well into their group and some chapters represent a broader range of approaches than others. The division of studies into chapters was done on heuristic grounds. As the research literature grows and develops in the future other methods of classifying studies are likely to become more relevant.

The review makes only limited interpretations and conclusions from the research results presented. This again reflects the current state of the research. Child abuse is a difficult area within which to conduct research and many of the studies to date do not reach the level of methodological rigour that allows firm conclusions to be drawn. Even where well designed studies have been successfully completed, these have rarely been replicated. If another study has been undertaken it may have reported results at variance with the first study. It is therefore premature to make more than a few tentative conclusions from the research. Readers will undoubtedly be disappointed if they are in search of clear answers to the question as to what or what does not work in therapy. Where firm conclusions are possible, this is mostly in terms of suggesting further research to follow up the tentative findings of the current knowledge base.

Instead of providing firm conclusions that would quickly become outdated and subject to revision, the review concentrates on describing the research studies and the findings. The review follows the standard practice of listing the research studies in tabular form (in each chapter). In addition, more detailed summaries of each study are presented at the end of each of the main chapters. This allows readers to determine for themselves the relevance of any particular study. It must be stressed that the research summaries can not do full justice to the individual research projects which are often reported in lengthy articles, research reports, or even whole books. There is also the possibility of errors in transcription or interpretation, so the reader is strongly advised to seek out the original references on any study that is of particular interest. The summaries should, however, be able to indicate to readers which studies would be of most interest to them.

To a large extent the review is a ground clearing exercise on the vast literature that exists in the field. The review can provide some coherence to the field and a means by which others can negotiate a way in and out of the literature. Other authors may then have the ability and energy to fully assess the extent that non-child abuse interventions could be usefully applied to child abuse and child protection research and practice.

Identification of Studies

The philosophy of only including studies that were overtly concerned with child abuse and child protection has already been discussed. The second criteria for inclusion was that the study was attempting to evaluate the efficacy or outcome of an intervention, whether preventive or reactive. A report was not included if it merely described an intervention and suggested that it might or might not be useful. Studies were only included if there was some specific assessment of outcome. The outcome measures did not have to be complex, but had to show some systematic recording of outcome and this rule was applied more stringently for case studies as there are so many individual case descriptions within the literature. The criteria of outcome assessment was not applied so strictly if there were few studies meeting the review criteria in a particular area of study.

Several strategies were taken to ensure that relevant research evaluations would be included in the review. The first strategy of computer line searches of databases held by the Medline, Psychinfo, and the National Center on Child Abuse and Neglect in Washington produced surprisingly few references of the right kind. On the whole, this was because searches based on titles are an inefficient way of identifying studies meeting certain criteria. For example, 'Evaluating a behavioural intervention in child abuse' might be a discussion of methodological research issues rather than an intervention study. Many of the articles listed in the computer searches turned out to be of the wrong kind. Conversely, the computer searches often did not locate important articles identified by other means.

Other strategies of study identification proved to be more productive. There were:

1. Reviews of publication lists and reference lists from centres and organisations specializing in child abuse work such as the American Association for Protecting Children; Child Welfare League of America; C. Henry Kempe National Center in Denver, Colorado; National Center on Child Abuse and Neglect, Washington; National Clearing House on Family Violence, Ottawa; National Committee for Prevention of Child Abuse, Chicago; National Resource Center on Family Based Services, University of Iowa; National Society for the Prevention of Cruelty to Children, London.
2. Papers presented at major national and international child abuse congresses.
3. A search of over fifty journals concerned with child abuse, social work, psychology, psychiatry, medicine, nursing, paediatrics, sociology, and other subjects. Journals were searched manually for the years 1980 to early 1992. Follow up of references identified from journal articles.

The most productive source of material was from personal knowledge of the field and from the journal search. Most intervention studies are published as reports or journal articles and the few that are published as books are likely to have journal articles associated with them. Most of the studies identified came from the United States, followed by Great Britain, and with a few studies from Australia, New Zealand and other countries. The review was not exhaustive and it is likely that a number of important studies have been overlooked. The search was only undertaken on work published in English, so important work published only in other languages will also have been missed.

Structure of the Report

The report consists of ten main chapters each describing a group of intervention studies, the first five chapters consider prevention studies on:
Educating children
Educating Adults and the Community
Volunteers and Parent Aides
Ante-natal and Post-Natal Services
Adult and Child Groups (plus reference to other preventive strategies)
    The second five chapters are concerned with reactive interventions. That is interventions subsequent to cases being identified as ones of child abuse. The chapters are titled:
Behavioural Approaches to Physical Abuse
Special Projects for Children and Parents
Multi-Component Interventions
Routine Services and Special Service Initiatives
Child Sexual Abuse
    Each of the chapters has four main sections. First is a Background section which provides an introduction to the nature of the area under consideration. This might include some historical background, reference to studies in a related field, or a discussion of the theoretical background to the studies. The purpose is merely to

provide some background and introduction to the studies rather than to provide a comprehensive review of the type of interventions being considered.

The second section is entitled Research Studies which introduces the research studies identified by the review.

Third is the Discussion section, the length of which depends upon the extent that findings of the studies have already been discussed in the Research Studies section. In Chapter Eight on Special Projects for Adults and Children the discussion is totally subsumed within the Research Studies section.

The fourth and final section of the chapter is a summary listing the main points that have been raised in the chapter. Each of the main chapters are followed by a Research Summaries appendix providing standardized summaries of all the studies considered in the chapter. At the end of the report (before the references) there is an appendix listing the main authors and date of all the studies and indicating in which chapter they have been discussed.

Research Summaries

After each of the main chapters the research studies are described systematically under standard headings of Sample, Focus, Objectives, Programme, Design, Measures, Results, and Notes. These headings were developed from a rigorous coding system that was applied to approximately three quarters of the studies reviewed. The coding schedule involved over one hundred questions used to 'interrogate' each research report. The method was more detailed than required for this review, but ensured a rigorous approach to summarizing cases. It also ensured that important distinctions between samples and methods of studies were less likely to be overlooked (Gough, Taylor, and Boddy, 1988).

The standard headings used in the summaries were designed on the basis that most studies would be of interventions that were already in place on a permanent or trial basis, rather than interventions applied temporarily as part of a research experiment. The headings of Focus, Objectives, and Programme, therefore referred to the purposes and content of the intervention and not to the purposes or content of the research. The explanations of the full list of headings are as follows:

TITLE

The full or abbreviated title of the research paper is used and sometimes this includes American spelling of words such as 'behavioral', 'program', and 'center'.

SAMPLE

Where the clients are drawn from, to what extent the sample is a sub sample of all cases treated, the nature of the child adversity (if any) and responsibility for this, other sample characteristics.

FOCUS

The level at which the intervention is focused, whether this be the individual adult or child, family, neighbourhood, or society. Whether the intervention is aimed at the causes, the effects, or other aspects of abuse.

OBJECTIVES

What the intervention is aiming to achieve, including the target recipients of these objectives. This does not necessarily refer to the objectives of the research. It only concerns the intervention programme.

PROGRAMME

The context of the intervention including the setting, the staffing, and intensity of service; the general approach, theory, or philosophy of the intervention; the specific methods and techniques used.

DESIGN

The methodology used to assess the outcome of the intervention.

MEASURES

The variables used to measure change, the method used to collect this data, and the independence of the measures from the intervention programme.

RESULTS

The measures or changes in measures revealed by the research design.

NOTES

Any extra comment by the author of the research or the author of this review that might qualify or throw extra light upon the meaning of the results.

The extent that these categories could be adequately described in the review depended upon the information available in the research papers. In some cases, a wealth of information was provided that could not all be included in the summary. In other cases, it was difficult to ascertain certain basic details about the research such as the composition of the sample used. This lack of basic data on methodology even occurred in long research papers providing much detail about other aspects of the study. There were also complications when aspects of the same study were published in different locations. Some authors were consistent across articles in their study descriptions, but others were less consistent or less than clear in indicating that different papers referred to the same study.

It is also important to state that the research summaries attempt to convey the views of the authors of individual studies and these, of course, do not necessarily reflect the views of the author of this review.

Finally, it must be emphasized again that the summaries can not do full justice to the original research reports that may describe years of detailed research. Also, it was not possible to send all the summaries to the original authors to check for accuracy in interpretation or transcription. Readers are therefore strongly advised to locate the original references of any study of particular interest, or of any study of which they wish to quote.

CHAPTER TWO
Educating Children

Background

The educational programmes developed to date are primarily concerned with child sexual abuse and are mainly targeted at children from the general population, although some have been developed for specific risk groups including children with disabilities. There is less discussion in the literature of attempts to educate children to protect themselves from other forms of abuse and hardly any of this has been formally evaluated. This is probably because the other forms of abuse more overtly challenge concepts of parenting. There is more ambivalence about, for example, physical chastisement of children than about child sexual abuse. Empowering children to resist punishment would be a more direct attack on parents' rights to control and punish their children.

The aim of most existing programmes is to increase the level of awareness of sexual abuse and to offer methods of avoiding it throughout the child population so that children are better able to avoid and deal with potentially abusive situations. Some programmes take a broader remit and are more overtly concerned to enable children to express their personal rights (for example, Doherty and Barratt, 1989), whilst others, such as Kidscape have developed programmes to help protect children from bullying.

This area of work has developed rapidly in the last ten years alongside the growing awareness of the extent of child sexual abuse in the general population. In particular, Finkelhor (1986), cites:

- the high rates of child sexual abuse in the community for both males and females including very young children,
- the low rates of identification of abuse by adults with few children revealing that they are being abused or else revealing it in a way that it is not understood or believed by adults.

In North America there has been a rapid development of preventive programmes and there are now over forty plays and hundreds of colouring and other books for children (Trudell & Whatley, 1988). Several states have made the use of these programmes obligatory in publicly funded schools. For example, at one point of time the state of California mandated prevention training for children in each of the four stages of school education at a cost of over ten million U.S. dollars per annum (Berrick, 1989; Gilbert et al, 1989).

In Britain there has been much less activity with only one programme (Kidscape) being widely known and used, though other programmes are slowly being introduced as more education authorities employ staff specifically to monitor and develop this form of training.

The programmes available world-wide differ in length, content and presentation (see Nelson and Clark, 1986; Gilbert et al, 1989; Berrick and Gilbert, 1991). Some are single half hour sessions and others last several days or weeks (Wurtele, 1987). Despite these variations the programmes share the same general philosophies and specific aims outlined by Finkelhor (1986):

General Aims

- to educate children about the responsibilities and boundaries of parental care, of other caretakers, and of other adults.

- to educate them about their own bodies and the nature and appropriateness of different relationships.
- to teach them the extent and nature of their own rights and self worth.
- to develop their self confidence, knowledge, and skills in order to empower them to assert and protect their rights and seek the assistance of others when necessary.

Specific aims

- to teach children about the existence and nature of child sexual abuse.
- to broaden children's awareness of who potential abusers may be, including people that they may know and like and members of their own family.
- to arm children with strategies to avoid abuse or to receive assistance if they are abused or at risk of abuse. To encourage them to have confidence in taking such action.

Although these aims are in themselves laudable, the programmes have been criticised for putting too much emphasis on children protecting themselves. Self protection by children is only one of the many possible methods of reducing the availability of potential victims to perpetrators. Other methods include imprisonment of offenders, the screening of persons employed in child care activities, and care by parents of whom they allow to have contact with children. The difficulty is that potential offenders against children are so numerous (see discussion on sexual abuse offenders in introduction to Chapter 11) and the obstacles against proving guilt so high that these strategies would not alone protect children.

Reducing the availability of victims is only one limited strategy for preventing child sexual abuse (Trudell & Whatley, 1988). The long term goal is to try to prevent people from becoming offenders. Finkelhor (1986, discussed in Chapter 11) has classified the preconditions for sexual abuse into the four categories of (1) the emotional gratification from such acts, (2) sexual arousal to children, (3) blocks to other forms of sexual and emotional gratification, and (4) why normal social inhibitions against such acts do not deter the abuse. To intervene to prevent these four preconditions could be achieved by treating the individuals who display these characteristics or by making social changes in society that reduce the risk of the characteristics developing. Either strategy, even if effective, would take a considerable time to significantly reduce the number of individuals who pose a threat to children. In these circumstances it may be unethical not to forewarn children of these risks and provide them with at least some techniques with which to protect themselves or to seek help.

Research Studies

The growth of educational programmes has been matched by increases in evaluative research. This has not been the case for other forms of child abuse intervention. The result is that evaluations of educational programmes have been one of the major growth areas in child abuse research (see reviews by Wurtele, 1987; Berrick, 1989; Conte and Fogarty, 1989; Doherty and Barratt, 1989; Berrick and Gilbert, 1991; Finkelhor and Strapko, 1992). One reason for this may be the funding arrangements and commercial aspects of some programmes. Another reason may be the relative ease with which it is possible to undertake proper controlled experimental designs on these programmes.

The majority of studies (listed in Table 2.1) have used questionnaire or interview outcome measures to assess the impact of the interventions. The programmes were attempting to change the children's knowledge, attitudes, and skills and so the outcome measures were tailored to assess the degree of appropriate or 'correct' test responses made by the children. (Responses were considered to be correct or incorrect according to the evaluators' theoretical framework; which might be open to question).

TABLE 2.1

Educating Children Research Studies

Study	Programme	Age	Sample	Design	Main Measures
Adams (In preparation), Armitage (1989)	Puppet Gang Video	x=3.6	n=19	RPM+C	recall, touching
Adams and Llewellyn (1991)	Puppet Gang Video	3–5 years 6–7 years	n=21 n=10	RPM	Intelligence, recall, touching
Binder and McNeil (1987)	CAP	5–12 years	n=88	RPM	Coping strategies
Blumberg et al (1991)	STOP! & CCAPP	x=7 years	n=264	RPM+C	Touch discrimination, knowledge, fears
Borkin and Frank (1986)	A Puppet Show	3–5 years	n=83	Post	Touching
Conte et al (1985)	Deputy Sheriff Instruction	4–5 years	n=20	RPM+C	Prevention concepts
Doherty and Barrat (1989)	Personal Safety Programme	6–7 years 8–9 years 10–11 years	n=20 n=20 n=28	RPM+C	Role play, prevention concepts
Fryer et al (1987A, 1987B) Kraizer et al (1988)	Role play and instruction	1st & 2nd grade	n=44	RPM+C	Intelligence, stranger abduction simulation
Gilbert et al (1989)	Seven programmes	3–5 years	n=118	RPM+PC	Care series
Hamilton (1989)	Feeling Yes, Feeling No	10–11 years	n=44	RPM	Touching, feelings, personal safety
Harvey et al (1988)	Good Touch – Bad Touch	x=6 years	n=71	RPM+C	Response to vignettes, knowledge, coping
Hazzard et al (1991)	Feeling Yes, Feeling No	3rd–4th grade	n=399	RPM+C	WIKATS, WWYD
Jones (1990)	Puppet Gang Video	5–6 years	n=30	RPM+C	Recall, appropriate behaviour
Kolko, Moser, and Hughes (1989)	Red Flag, Green Flag Better Safe than Sorry II	7–10 years	n=213	RPM+C	Concepts of abuse & prevention, disclosure
Mayes et al (1991a, 1991b)	Kidscape	6 years	n=30	RPM+C	Safety, danger of picture story scenarios
Miltenberger & Thiesse Duffy (1988)	Red Flag/Green Flag	4–5 years 6–7 years	n=13 n=11	RPM+C	Touch & danger discrimination, stranger abduction simulation

Peraino (1990)	We Help Ourselves	x=4 years	n=46	RPM+C	Appropriate touch, appropriate chastisement
Poche et al (1981)	A Behavioural programme	3–5 years	n=3	RPM	Stranger abduction simulation
Poche et al (1988)	Instruction+/− rehearsal	5–7 years −Behavioural	n=24	POST+C	Stranger abduction simulation
Sigurdson et al (1986)	Feeling Yes, Feeling No	9–13 years	n=13 yrs	RPM	Personal safety questionnaire
Stillwell et al (1988)	SAPP	3–4 years	n=4	RPM	Touching and safety knowledge
Suphi (1990)	Puppet Gang Video	x=4.4 years	n=24	RPM	Languages, recall, secrets
Swann et al (1985)	Bubbylonian Encounter play	8–11 years	n=63	RPM	Knowledge of safety concepts
Wolfe et al (1986)	'Skits' + discussion	9–12 years	n=290	POST+C	Knowledge of safety concepts
Wurtele et al (1986)	'Touch' film vs BST	x=6 years x=11 years	n=28 n=43	RPM+PC	PSQ, WIST
Wurtele et al (1987)	Participant vs Symbolic modelling	kindergarten	n=26	RPM+C	PSQ, WIST, FATS
Wurtele et al (1989)	Behavioural vs Feelings Programme	4–6 years	n=100	RPM+C	PSQ, WIST, FATS
Wurtele (1990)	Behavioural skills	x=4 years	n=24	RPM+C	WIST, PSQ, TPQ, PPQ
Wurtele et al (1991)	Parent implemented	x=4 years x=5 years	n=52	RPM+C	WIST, PSQ, TPQ
Wurtele et al (1992)	Behavioural skills by teachers or parents	x=5 years	n=61	RPM+C	WIST, PSQ, TPQ, PPQ

BST = Behavioural Skills Training Program; CAP = Child Abuse Prevention Project;
CCAP = Child Abuse Primary Prevention Program; FATS = Fear Assessment Thermometer Scale;
PPQ = Parents' Perception Questionnaire; PSQ = Personal Safety Questionnaire;
SAAP = Sexual Abuse Prevention Program for Preschoolers;
STOP! = Stop, Tell Someone, Own Your Body, Protect Yourself Role Play; WIKATS = What I know about Touching Scale;
WIST = 'What if' Situation Test; WWYD = What Would You Do Scale

Design
POST = post-test only; RPM = Repeated Measures including pre-test; PRPM = Repeated Measures post-test only;
+C = Control or comparison groups; +PC = Control or comparison group but at post-test only

The most common feature of these studies beyond the general aims of the interventions and the type of outcome measures was the sampling of children from educational establishments so that they represented the local child population. The study by Conte et al (1985) was unusual in sampling children from a privately operated day care centre and it is unclear how representative this sample was of the local child population. There may also have been cultural differences between the areas chosen in the studies. These were predominantly urban city areas in North America with the exceptions of one sub-sample in Swann's study (Swann et al, 1985) and the use of a smaller urban areas by Sigurdson et al (1986) and by several studies by Wurtele. The studies differed in age ranges, size of samples, and in the nature of the educational programmes and their evaluation.

Preschool

Several studies have attempted to train preventive skills to young children through instruction about appropriate touches and feelings and how to respond and seek help if they are approached in an inappropriate way. Many of these studies have reported disappointing results; a study by Peraino (1990) being an exception.

Borkin and Frank (1986) evaluated a puppet show followed by discussion and colouring activities designed to teach children about appropriate touching and how to react to advances of sexual abuse. At follow-up, just over a month after the intervention, nearly half of the 100 four and five year old children responded correctly to the test question of how they would react to a touch that did not feel good. The responses of the three year old children were significantly less correct than those of the older children. The authors suggest this could have been because three year olds were too young to learn the rules or that they were more reticent in producing the required responses to the test. But it is difficult to evaluate the results without pre-test to measure prior knowledge and understanding of the concepts under study.

The parents and teachers were also asked to rate the programme on its efficacy and age suitability. The adults rated it highly which is important even if the intervention was not too effective at inducing learning. There is a great need to have parental cooperation when introducing these educational materials. Also, there is a potential bonus if parents learn indirectly from the programme about the risks of sexual abuse and how best to protect their children.

Another non controlled repeated measures design was carried out by Stillwell et al (1988). They found that preschool children taught a curriculum on touch and telling improved upon their verbal responses at pre-test, but these improvements quickly decayed at two and four weeks follow up despite booster training. Only one child showed any decrease in the target safety behaviours.

Disappointing results have also been reported by studies attempting full experimental designs. Conte et al (1985) undertook a study of personal safety skills teaching to twenty children, half of whom were aged between four or five and half of whom were aged six to ten years. Training was for one hour per day for three consecutive days. There was a control group of a further twenty children who were 'wait listed' and included in the programme later. Allocation to experimental and control groups was random. A pre-test showed that there was no difference between the groups in prior knowledge on experience of abuse and that any difference at outcome was more likely to be due to the intervention. The post-test was a questionnaire administered by students who did not know to which group each of the children had been allocated. The results showed a significant increase in the knowledge of the experimental group compared to the control group, but the authors felt that it was still not particularly encouraging. The improved performance of the experimental group was greatest for the older children and depended on more concrete rather than abstract concepts. In the authors' view this gave the children only 50% of the concepts they required to protect themselves sufficiently from abuse.

A much larger study has been reported by Gilbert et al (1989) on 118 children receiving different prevention curriculums at seven preschools in California. Significant improvements on some measures were reported, but the children's scores were still very low and led the authors to argue that the programmes were only minimally effective and should be reserved for older children who have the necessary cognitive abilities to benefit.

The studies indicate that the more abstract concepts within programmes are more difficult for children to learn (Conte & Fogarty, 1989) and that pre-school children find these particularly difficult. This view is also supported by recent unpublished studies on preschool children reviewed by Berrick (1989). It has been argued (De Young, 1988; Gilbert et al, 1989; Berrick and Gilbert, 1991) that the developmental level of the younger children prevents them from understanding the type of conceptual abstractions being taught. For example, within Piaget's theory of cognitive and moral development young children would interpret the morality of actions such as inappropriate touches on the basis of their outcome rather than their abusive intent (De Young 1988). Berrick and Gilbert (1991) have used this approach to critically examine the relevance of a range of different prevention programmes for preschool, and first and second grade children in California.

This pessimistic view of prevention programmes for young children has been challenged by studies employing behavioural strategies. The argument is that it is preferable and more effective to teach children how to react in certain circumstances than to try and teach imprecise concepts such as appropriate touch or good and bad feeling.

Miltenberger and Thiesse–Duffy (1988) compared the interventions of parent instruction with the Red Flag/Green Flag colouring book (with and without verbal rehearsal) and a behavioural training package. At pre-test children seemed to be able to identify dangerous situations, but not to have the appropriate behaviours to respond and only behavioural training improved these responses.

Poche (1988) compared three prevention strategies and reported that an instructional video plus behavioural rehearsal was more effective than the video alone and both were more effective than a traditional verbal school programme. A similar finding has been reported in a series of experiments by Adams and colleagues (Jones, 19990; Suphi, 1990; Adams and Llewellyn, 1991; Adams, in preparation). A video of puppets displaying appropriate and inappropriate touches was more effective when linked with some form of role play (Armitage, 1990; Jones, 1990).

Some of the stronger evidence in support of the behavioural approach has also arisen from a series of studies by Wurtele (1986, 1987, 1989, 1990, 1991, 1992). These indicate that behavioural programmes are more effective than other methods (Wurtele, 1989), that participant modelling was more effective than symbolic modelling (Wurtele, 1987), and that behavioural programmes can be effectively taught by parents in the home (Wurtele et al, 1991) even with economically disadvantaged children attending a Head Start nursery (Wurtele et al, 1991). Wurtele does, however, acknowledge that the increase in mean scores conceals the fact that there are some children who still continue to score poorly after behavioural training (Wurtele, 1992).

Primary School Children

A large number of preventive programmes for primary school aged children have been evaluated. Some programmes have used drama to project their message. Swann et al (1985) studied the efficacy of a thirty minute play, the "Bubbylonian Encounter" presented by a children's theatre company. This is a series of vignettes which deal with issues of touch and assault and act out strategies of resistance. Outcome for the 63 children was assessed from oral responses to questions by their teacher and from video tapes of responses to test vignettes. A pre and post-test design was used, with some children only receiving a post-test to assess the learning effect of seeing the test vignettes. The results showed an increase in the experimental group's awareness of intrafamilial abuse and what to do in abusive situations. However, the post-test only group, performed well on all measures without having seen the original play. The parents reported no bad reactions to the play and were in favour of its use as was a group of professionals which also saw the play.

The intervention studied by Wolfe and his colleagues (1986) involved two five minute 'skits' followed by a structured discussion on potential abusers, children's feelings, what they can do about abusive situations, the responsibility for abuse and the importance of seeking help immediately. A 7 item post-test questionnaire was used on the 145 children involved and on the random control group of a further 145 children. The experimental group performed significantly better on tests for responses to abusive situations and attitudes to culpability of children for abuse. There were no group differences for several individual items, including uncertainty about whether a child would be believed if seeking help. The control groups also showed low levels of awareness in tests for passive exposure, self blame and realistic portrayal of abusers. The authors conclude that these are the areas requiring most elucidation.

Three other studies examined the "Feeling Yes, Feeling No" programme which involves a series of video presentations with classroom teaching and discussion. The programme can take several weeks to complete as, in addition to the video film, there are 9 hours of class exercises.

Sigurdson et al (1986) provided a pre and post-test questionnaire with twenty nine items. A significant improvement on eight of the questionnaire items was reported, for female children only. Why the girls should perform better is unclear, but the authors suggest that at this age the boys may be less mature and so less able to cope with the more abstract concepts involved.

Despite the recorded improvement, the results of the intervention are generally disappointing considering the effort and time invested. One explanation suggested by examining the scores of individual items is a 'ceiling' effect caused by a high pre-test knowledge of the 'correct' answers to some test items. Other items not subject to this effect may have concerned more abstract concepts which the children were too young to learn effectively.

Hamilton, in another non controlled study of the same intervention programme (Hamilton, 1989) reported much more encouraging results with large increases in appropriate responses at post-test. Hamilton reported that the highest increases were found for female children and three high ability children. Further support for the programme comes from Hazzard et al's (1991) study that found highly significant post test scores compared to controls on safety discrimination scores, though not for prevention skill scores.

Nearly all the studies reviewed have shown that brief interventions can increase children's knowledge about prevention concepts. There is decay of knowledge at later follow up but several studies have shown that this can be avoided by using booster training sessions (see review by Conte & Fogarty, 1989).

Other programmes that have been evaluated include the Red Flag/Green Flag colouring book (Kolko et al, 1989), Kidscape (Mayes et al, 1991) and various combinations of instruction (Doherty and Barratt, 1989) discussion and role play (Binder and McNeil, 1987; Fryer et al, 1987 a, b; Kraizer et al, 1988; Harvey et al 1988; Blumberg et al, 1991) and direct behavioural programmes (Wurtele, 1986).

In the Binder and McNeill (1987) study there was a significant increase in knowledge after only two hour workshops. They also found that parents significantly underestimated the knowledge of their children at pre-test and of the younger children at post-test.

These studies vary in their research design, their research measures, and the programmes they were evaluating, but they virtually all report success in increasing children's scores from pre to post-test and that this was significantly greater than any change in control group scores (where applicable). The one exception is the evaluation of Kidscape, where the intervention group scores increased, but no more than the control group, suggesting that the experimental process (probably the test questions) had as great an impact as the training programme. Alternately there could have been bias from sampling as there was not random allocation to groups. Children received training only if their schools had agreed to the programme.

Although most of the programmes seem to be effective in teaching prevention concepts to school age children, these findings do not specify which aspects of the programmes are most effective. Several studies, however, compare different programme strategies. The finding is that behavioural approaches are particularly effective as was reported by studies of preschool children.

Wurtele et al (1986) attempted to compare the efficacy of a film presentation with behavioural skills training. They found, that with both a younger (6 years) and older (11 years) group of subjects, only the behavioural skills training showed a significant effect compared to controls. Blumberg et al (1991) also found that behavioural training was more effective than a more abstract multi media programme.

The certainty in interpreting differences between interventions at post-test is complicated by indirect effects of interventions. Kolko et al (1989), for example, found that parental knowledge increased at post-test despite parents receiving no training. Similar results have been reported by Miltenberger and Thiesse–Duffy (1988) and by unpublished studies reviewed by Finkelhor & Strapko (1992). In one of Wurtele's studies (1986) the scores of the film group at a later follow up test improved, suggesting a 'sleeper' effect that may have been mediated by peer and family discussion of sexual abuse.

Outcome Measures

The finding that behavioural skills training has a greater impact compared to more passive forms of training and that concepts are more difficult to teach than skills, has also fed into the debate about the best measures for assessing improvements in children's ability to protect themselves. There is an increasing awareness of the limitations of measures requiring subjects to feed back the conceptual knowledge that they have been taught (Conte & Fogarty, 1989). Instead the conceptual and skills knowledge are tested by children having to respond to novel hypothetical situations such as in the 'What If' Situation Test (Wurtele et al, 1986) or in safety discrimination tasks (Mayes et al, 1991), or by requiring children to role play responses as in Doherty and Barratt's (1989) study. These approaches are probably a better estimate of the knowledge that children could apply to a high risk situation, but this does not mean that the children are able to apply this knowledge in real life situations. To meet this criticism some evaluation studies have adopted applied behavioural outcome measures.

A study by Poche, Brouer and Swearington (1981) used modelling, rehearsal and instruction to teach three pre-school children how to respond to strangers. The children were pre-tested by coding their responses to an approach by a stranger in a school playground. The children were unaware that they were being tested. None of them responded with the preferred response of their parents which was a polite verbal rejection followed by movement away from the stranger. After the teaching sessions, which totalled 90 minutes per child, all of the children responded appropriately to a re-test, set this time in a street. Two of the three children were re-tested twelve weeks later. One child responded appropriately and the other said appropriate words but did not move away from the stranger.

These results are encouraging. The study shows that even young children can be taught how to respond in a way that is likely to protect them from being lured away by a stranger and being sexually abused. This is an important finding, because molestation by strangers is thought to be often opportunistic and not to involve violence, at least in the abduction. In a later study (already discussed under preschool studies) Poche and colleagues (1988) compared three treatment programmes on young children. The proportion of children displaying criterion correct response to the real life simulation probes were 58% for video plus behavioural rehearsal, 47% for the video alone, but 0% for those receiving a standard programme or no programme at all. The authors argue that this shows the high vulnerability of young children to abduction.

Another programme that used a real life simulation to test children's learning is reported by Fryer, Kraizer and Miyoshi (1987a, 1987b) and Kraizer et al (1988). The intervention is similar to the first Poche et al (1981) study. It offers concrete rules and responses for interactions with strangers to children in kindergarten or the first and second grades of elementary school. The four main rules and the criteria for their application were taught in daily 20 minute presentations over an 8 day period. The effect of the intervention on 23 children was assessed using a random control design with a pre-test and with immediate and delayed post-tests using measures similar to those used by Poche and her colleagues. These involved the staging of a potential abuse situation to test the children's degree of vulnerability to abuse. Fryer et al (1987a) added important additional pre-test measures of language ability, self esteem and cognitive awareness and understanding of issues associated with risk and prevention.

The results of the initial post-test in this study showed a significant improvement compared to the control group in the proportion of children responding appropriately in the simulation test. At the further post-test, 6 months later, this learning was maintained. The control group was not given the initial intervention training, but they were provided with the same instruction before the second post-test at six months and the 'pass rate' of these children went up from 52% to 100% (although only 14 of the original 21 children were available at the six month follow up). These are encouraging findings, considering the decay over time in awareness of concepts of self protection reported by Plummer (1984, cited by Finkelhor, 1986). Less positive results were achieved for the four children in the experimental group who failed the initial post-test. These children were given the programme a second time and only two of the four then passed the simulation test.

The failure of two of the children on the post-test led the authors to suggest that there may be a minority of children who do not profit from preventive education. The relationship between the study findings and the psychological tests applied before the educational programme therefore bear examination. These tests did not predict which children would pass the pre-intervention simulation, but the self esteem test did predict which children in the experimental group would improve from fail to pass on the simulation test. In addition, those children who were successful on the immediate simulation post-test had significantly higher scores in a post-test of knowledge and understanding of risk and prevention.

The conclusion therefore is that the children who benefited most from the intervention were those with higher self esteem, and that their appropriate behaviour on the simulation test was matched by an increased understanding and awareness of the issues involved. This could lead us to question the value of widespread programmes as they may only be effective for those groups most able to protect themselves, and less likely to be exposed to risk. Interventions may only speed up the learning skills and concepts, which the more able children, are about to learn anyway.

Because the study showed that there was a small core who did not improve in response after two interventions, the question is, whether this kind of teaching is only relevant for a group of children with at least medium levels of self-esteem and at no more than medium levels of risk. For example, low self esteem is associated with a lack of stable supportive relationships, which is in turn associated with intrafamilial abuse. The issue of variable receptivity is a central question for the development of widespread programmes. It could suggest that children should be pre-tested to determine which form of training programme would be most appropriate. Alternatively, pre-testing could be used to screen high risk groups to receive training.

Discussion

Generalisation of Results

The main drawback of the research studies is that they fail to establish that the effects of preventive education on children can be generalised. There are several aspects of this problem of generalisation.

Firstly, apart from the stranger abduction studies, it is not clear if the increased knowledge displayed by the children receiving the programmes generalizes to changes in actual behaviour.

There is only limited evidence that the concepts taught to children are retained for more than the short term. Indeed, Plummer (1984, cited in Finkelhor and Strapko, 1992) reports that children are particularly likely to have lost two crucial concepts at follow up: that abusers may not be strangers and that secrets should sometimes be told. Even assuming that concepts can be held for long periods, there is only limited evidence that they bear any valid relation to the central resources children need in practice to protect themselves from abuse.

Plummer's findings concerning strangers leads to a second problem of generalization – whether the resources children may gain to resist abuse by strangers will generalize to protecting them from family members or other people known to them. This problem particularly concerns the studies done by Poche, Fryer and colleagues which were behavioural in approach. Poche et al emphasised teaching the correct response to potentially abusive situations, rather than conceptual awareness of child sexual abuse and potential perpetrators. They then used real life simulations to test the rules learned. In one sense, this seems a more appropriate measure, given that it is relatively easy to train young children to exhibit certain behaviours and that it can be very difficult to teach them concepts. But would children know that these responses could also be used with their father or uncle? The message that abusers are strangers may well be reinforced by using strangers in real-life simulations. The children have not been made so aware of the distinction between good and bad touches or that abusers can be friends or relatives. Fryer et al (1987a) reported an increased conceptual awareness that might generalize to intrafamilial situations but this was not re-tested at the 6 months follow-up. There is thus little evidence that behavioural approaches of this kind really equip children to resist intrafamilial abuse.

A third problem of generalisation is whether the programmes have a differential effect on different children. The studies do not usually relate their outcome measures to the social or psychological characteristics of the subjects. Some children may be both more at risk of abuse and also less able to benefit from the training programmes that aim to assist them protect themselves. Few of the studies have tested the children on psychological measures of intelligence, personality and behaviour. These variables are currently being explored by Hamilton, whose preliminary findings suggest that children with behavioural problems may be more vulnerable to abduction. They were more likely to go with a stranger in a stranger abduction simulation test (Hamilton, personal communication).

A related issue is the effect that the training packages have upon those who have already been sexually assaulted. Those involved in training programmes are sensitive that some children may disclose abuse, but there is little data on how the programmes effect the way in which these children cope with their victimization (Finkelhor and Strapko, 1992). Little is also known about the effects on those who unfortunately can not avoid abuse in the future (though a study of the preventive programme histories of abuse victims is underway at the Family Research Laboratory, University of New Hampshire). It is not known if the programmes help the children to adjust and cope with the abuse. Most studies examining the impact of sexual abuse are retrospective, which makes it difficult to determine which variables, if any, distinguish between those who are worse affected by the experience. One study that has attempted this (Conte and Schuerman, 1987) has found that the strategies adopted by children during the assaults were related to the impact of the abuse. The two incompatible responses of passively submitting and actively resisting abuse were both associated with reduced impact. The authors speculate that the potential adaptability of these responses may relate to the children's general coping strategies in their lives. This initial study can not answer the questions that need to be asked, but the potential relevance of such work for preventive education is obvious.

Relevance of Programmes

Underpinning all this discussion about the intervention programmes is their relevance to the realities of sexual assault on children. It is necessary to understand which individuals assault which children, and in what ways, in order to determine how best to arm children to defend themselves (accepting that this can only be one small part of an overall prevention strategy). Until recently most data on the nature of sexual abuse was restricted to the type of abuse, age of child, and relationship to the offender. Little was known about the actual social context in which abuse occurred.

Two recent studies have interviewed perpetrators, to determine how they chose their victims, and how they engaged their children in sexual activities (Budin & Johnson, 1989; Conte, Wolf and Smith, 1989). Both studies indicate that offenders have conscious strategies for manipulating children into becoming victims and not disclosing the abuse to others. They choose children who seem vulnerable in some way and are likely to respond to the friendly attention of the offender. The offender then 'grooms' the child by developing the child's trust and dependency and initiates abuse through non sexual physical contact that gradually becomes sexual. Once abuse has taken place children are controlled and coerced with gifts and social and physical threats to keep the abuse secret.

These findings are supported by a study of children's accounts of becoming victims. Berliner & Conte (1990) report that the children often felt positive towards the perpetrator and dependent on him, that the shift to abuse was usually gradual, that the child was led to feel responsible for the offender's happiness and for initiating the sexual activities. The findings of all these studies suggest that self-protection from sexual abuse is more complex than learning to resist an aggressive assault. The subtle shifts between what has and has not been consented to and between appropriate and inappropriate behaviour are difficult to specify, particularly when they involve unequal power and needs in socially vulnerable children. Conte, Wolfe and Smith (1989) argue that children's concept of consent requires detailed study and that children should be taught that they can withdraw consent. The findings also suggest that sexual abuse prevention should be seen within the wider perspective of each child's social development. Children who receive inadequate or inappropriate love and care are also more likely to encounter risk situations, to fall victim to such risks, and to be more vulnerable to the effects of such abuse.

Little is known about how children could be helped to re-act differently to manipulative approaches by offenders. Yarmey & Rosenstein (1988) have shown that parents do not even have a very accurate idea of their children's conceptual knowledge of sexual abuse. It is clear however that prevention is not simply a matter of knowledge. As Conte & Fogarty (1989) point out, knowledge is not usually an effective means of changing people's social and health related behaviour.

Another fundamental issue is the reality of the power differential between adults and children. Adults usually have greater physical strength, financial and other material resources, and knowledge of the world. Also the views and wishes of adults have more legitimacy within the adult run world. Some therefore argue that it is not sensible to put so much of the preventive responsibility on to children (Melton, 1992) and that it is dangerous and dishonest to suggest that children can be sufficiently empowered to protect themselves (Kitzinger, 1990). Kitzinger (1990) also argues that the whole response of adults to the problem of sexual abuse is often stated in adult terms. The abuse is often portrayed as being wrong because it robs children of the innocence of childhood, rather than that the children have a right not to be sexually exploited. A similar issue is raised by the literature on the adverse psychological effects of sexual abuse, because sexual abuse would still be considered wrong even if there were no lasting effects (see Finkelhor, 1979).

Even when children are older and possess much of the knowledge contained in preventive programmes they are unable to protect themselves and feel unable to seek assistance from others. It is interesting to note, therefore, the dearth of programmes aimed at teenagers despite the high frequency of sexual assault in this age group including assault by peers and date rapes. It suggests that in addition to knowledge and skill based programmes, a change is required in the message that society gives to young children and adults about their respective rights and how these may or may not be enforced. In retrospect it may be that one of the most powerful effects of educational programmes may be the indirect messages about sexuality and individual rights. The message would be stronger if the programmes did not avoid issues of sexuality, rights and power differentials, and were also targeted more frequently at older as well as younger children.

A final issue is the role of training programmes in preventing children from becoming perpetrators themselves. Many reports now confirm that many perpetrators start offending when they are themselves children (see introduction to chapter 11). Research, describing the nature of offences by children on other children is only just beginning (for example, Johnson, 1988). Such information is essential for developing programmes to enable children to come forward for help before they offend, as well as for them to realise that their peers are able to protect themselves and will disclose attempts to abuse them.

All these points suggest that sexual abuse prevention programmes need to be studied within a wider context than at present. One way of achieving this is to teach different but related programmes. It may, for example, be more useful to teach children general social skills or assertiveness skills. Children of all ages might then be empowered to be more resilient to manipulation. Similar arguments can be used for broader education in sexuality and personal relationships. Unfortunately, many sexual assault prevention programmes are only acceptable to schools because they minimise the sexual education content.

Future Research

There is much scope for research to clarify the potential benefits of sexual abuse prevention training and to help maximise such benefits. The following broad approaches are suggested.

1. A clarification of the purposes of the interventions leading to the development of more specific and explicit measures to assess the success of these programmes. This is already happening with the studies of behavioural

programmes, but it should be more evident in all of the evaluations. It would enable the measures to become more sophisticated and more relevant to the prevention of child sexual abuse. It is clear that paper and pencil tests of knowledge have limitations, and yet there are ethical and other dangers in simulation testing. One way forward is to further develop the use of vignettes, and of games in which hypothetical situations can be discussed or acted out to both teach children and test their learning.

2. The outcomes measures developed also need to be informed by a better knowledge of what is effective in minimizing risk of abuse. This requires additional studies to isolate the factors that seem to protect children in practice. This could be achieved by retrospective studies of the histories of children who avoided abuse, and prospective studies of the effectiveness of interventions in reducing the incidence of abuse, either in individual children or in the whole community, measured by general reporting rates.

3. Comparative testing of intervention programmes tailored by content and style of presentation for different recipients or target groups. Studies are increasingly comparing different intervention programmes, but not contrasting the differential effects on different subjects. Subjects could be distinguished with respect to age, ethnicity, local culture, abuse status such as high risk, or victims of previous abuse, and psychological variables such as self esteem, and coping styles.

4. Assessment of variable risk to being abused and variable receptivity to preventive education. It may be that those children most at risk of abuse are the least able to benefit from current prevention programmes. It is therefore essential that this possibility becomes a focus of research in this area. That may require a total re-assessment of the research designs employed, but at the very least it is important for evaluative studies to present data on the characteristics of less successful outcomes in addition to presenting statistical analyses of grouped subject data.

It is unlikely that much will be achieved by examining the impact of individual interventions on single or undifferentiated target groups. Researchers would be better to contrast the effect of different strategies on the same target group or of one approach on various target groups. For example, the study by Fryer et al (1987a, 1987b) was particularly important because of its examination of the relevance of self-esteem to the impact of preventive education.

A final research issue is the current use of programmes in Britain. There are likely to be gaps in educational provision, both geographically and in the age and type of pupils receiving programmes. Children with special needs and older pupils are probably significantly under represented on these programmes in Britain. It is also not clear which programmes are being employed. Kidscape is probably the most widely used programme in Britain, but this is one of the few programmes not to have shown a learning effect in formal research studies (Mayes, 1991a, b). Even if programmes are relevant and effective, there is a potential problem from programmes not being implemented in the best possible way, with consequent harm to children and families and to relationships between and within public agencies. We do not know with what skill, with what prior negotiations and precautions, and with what effects programmes are currently being implemented.

Further Use of Programmes

Even without strong research evidence about the effects of preventive interventions in reducing risks to children in a direct or influential manner, there are still persuasive arguments for continuing these programmes.

Firstly programmes may have an impact on the adults (including professionals) who hear about or are involved in the preventive work, and so increase their understanding and awareness of child sexual abuse.

Secondly programmes may raise the community awareness of abuse, increase the possibilities of identification of cases, and lead to an increase in the social unacceptability of sexual exploitation of children. Sexual exploitation of children is, in some senses, already generally unacceptable, but there have been cases in which mitigating circumstances were proposed or where a child was portrayed as being at least partly responsible.

Programmes to prevent child sexual abuse can be more broadly based than in school educational training. For example, there are other programmes which use dramatic performances to allow children and adults to understand social issues and to initiate conversations on difficult topics. Particularly well known is the 'Kids on the Block' series which uses puppets to present scripts on topics such as teenage pregnancy, child physical abuse, deafness and cerebral palsy.

Even more broadly based interventions are possible. There is a children's board game (Safely Home), that is largely built upon concepts of personal safety and several special editions of the children's comic 'Spiderman' that examines the same issues. The first comic was issued in 1985 by Marvel Comics in collaboration with the United States National Committee for Prevention of Child Abuse and at least 16 million copies have been distributed (Garbarino, 1987).

Thirdly, these programmes could be considered as an important part of children's general education about society and sexuality, just as teenage pregnancy might be considered a suitable topic for discussion in schools. But this may not always be feasible because of opposition by some individuals and groups to sex education in the curriculum (Finkelhor, 1986). The people who work against child sexual abuse come from very differing ideological standpoints some of which are extremely conservative about sex education.

Fourthly, and related to the issue of general sex education, is the potential for education programmes to prevent children becoming adolescent sex offenders. There is evidence that adolescents make up a considerable proportion of child sexual abusers (Abel et al, 1985), which makes them an obvious target for preventive interventions (Bagley & Thurston, 1988). It is to be hoped that the increased awareness of child sexual abuse will have a positive effect in inhibiting its occurrence and in making society put more emphasis on children's rights and children's safety.

There are also potential adverse effects of preventive programmes, that need to be considered. Although few fears have emerged so far children may become scared or upset by the content of some of the programmes (Kraizer, 1988; Leventhal, 1987) and their relationship with parents and other significant adults may become disturbed, particularly if the children have already been victims of abuse. Also by possibly fostering a spirit of distrust between adults and children, these interventions could also result in adults being less prepared to help children in trouble in the streets, and children being unreceptive to offers of assistance even if they were genuinely in need. Undermining spontaneous interaction between adults and children may be a high price to pay for preventive strategies, but on the other hand, it is evident that children are at high risk of abuse.

There may also be particular dangers from interventions using special techniques such as risk simulations. These could make children more, rather than less, vulnerable, as they have no unpleasant consequence for the children and so could take the threat out of potentially abusive encounters. The use of simulation tests, which can only be experimentally valid if undertaken without the children's consent, may also infringe the children's rights.

Programmes which only hint that they are about sexual abuse or which over-emphasize extra familial in contrast to intrafamilial abuse, are likely to do more to confuse than enlighten children. It would be preferable to promote a clearer understanding by children and adults of personal rights, the value of different forms of human relationships and the place of sexual relationships within these. Constrained as we are by our current lack of clarity and openness about sexuality and about the rights of children generally, we need to actively consider the potential adverse effects of educative programmes that are introduced.

A final risk to consider, is that information on the avoidance of sexual assault, can be useful to offenders in making them more sophisticated in their strategies. Sexual abusers of children can be found in all social classes and occupations, including teaching and child care, and so may be well aware of preventive training. Similarly, adolescents who develop deviant patterns of sexual arousal may have received preventive education on child sexual abuse as children. If this is a danger of preventive programmes, it also shows their potential for broader preventive education examining issues of appropriate and inappropriate sexual relationships.

Summary

1. There is evidence that education programmes can increase the conceptual awareness of school age children about child sexual abuse and teach them how to report actual or potential abuse. Apart from the studies of stranger abduction, it is not clear whether the knowledge generalises to actual behaviour.

2. Other studies show that pre-school children can be taught behavioural responses designed to avoid potentially abusive situations from strangers. These behaviours are not necessarily relevant to intrafamilial abuse.

3. There is some evidence that the educational programmes have a differential impact, protecting those children most, who are less likely to be exposed to potentially abusive situations, and who are, in any case, better able to protect themselves from abuse.

4. Future research needs to examine the differential impact of the programmes on different children with different levels of pre-test skills and at varying degrees of risk rather than contrasting grouped data. This should include children of all ages (not just younger children as at present), from different social backgrounds, and with different abilities and disabilities.

5. It is not clear what effects the programmes have on the coping strategies of children who are subsequently unable to avoid being abused.

6. The studies report few negative effects of the programmes or of the test measures used such as simulation testing. However, these issues have not been addressed in any detail and great care needs to be taken before embarking on such programmes.

7. As well as indirect negative effects, the programmes may have indirect positive effects. They could increase the knowledge and ability of individual adults to protect children, raise community awareness and lead to reporting of abuse. One strategy would be to introduce the programmes within a wider policy of educating children about personal rights, human relationships and sexuality.

8. Attention needs to be given to the likely positive and negative effects on potential adolescent sex offenders. The ways in which children might be prevented from growing up into adolescent abusers needs to be more fully explored.

9. The research studies are strong on the use of experimental designs, but weak on the development of appropriate and valid dependent measures to assess reduction in the actual risk of abuse, the effects of coping with actual abuse, and the potential negative effects of the educational interventions.

10. The research studies would be more profitable if more of them compared and contrasted the impact of several techniques rather than being isolated evaluations of individual programmes. Currently it is the behavioural studies that provide the best examples of testing of programmes, including the use of parents as trainers.

11. There seems to be no information available on the type and range of programmes currently being implemented and to what effect in Britain. It is likely that there is a lack of provision in particular geographic areas, for children with special needs, and for children of secondary school age. A survey of programmes in use would identify gaps in current provision and inform future policy. A study of actual practice could identify the quality and quantity of current provision.

Chapter Two Research Summaries

1. Adams and Llewellyn (1991), 2. Adams (In preparation), Armitage (1989), 3. Suphi (1990), 4. Jones (1990)

TAKING CARE WITH TOBY: A PUPPET VIDEO TO PREVENT SEXUAL ABUSE IN CHILDREN

Four studies numbered according to references in heading. For all studies the focus of the intervention programme is the child for primary prevention of abuse. Objective of training children in personal safety to enable them to take care of themselves. Intervention first developed for sexual abuse, then broadened so that now contains eleven separate scenes or modules.

Project 1

Sample: 21 children (12 boys and 9 girls), 11 aged 3 to 5 years (mean 3.9) and 10 aged 6 to 7 years (mean 6.6 years).

Programme: 10 minute video 'The Puppet Gang' examining good and bad touches. Good: nappy change, bathing, kisses and cuddles. Bad: girl touched on bottom by male adult friend. In video girl told friend of bad touch who reported similar experience. Both disclose to girl's parent and are believed.

Design: Repeated measures (pre, post and 2 week follow up) on intervention group only (2 age levels).

Measures: Recall of video, description of good/bad touching.

Results: Recall of video: at immediate post test older children performed significantly better than younger children for both total content and central events. Best remembered were 'Frank touching Jayne's bottom' (76%), 'Jayne was good to tell her mother' (43%). Worst remembered were 'John's mother bathing him – good touching' (23%), 'Frank tells Jayne a bad secret' (49%). View of good/bad touches: significant improvement in views of bad touch for older and younger children. Follow up achieved for 52% of children (mean age 6.1 years) with significant decreases compared to immediate post test in recall of total content and numbers of puppets names, but significant improvement in recall of central events and in description of good and bad touches.

Project 2

Sample: 19 children, 9 boys, 10 girls, average age of 3.6 years.

Programme: Three groups (1) Puppet Gang video modules on good/bad secrets and good/bad touching (2) video plus role play session 2 weeks later (3) Control group view Tom and Jerry cartoon.

Design: Repeated measures (pretest, immediate post test – 2 week and 6 week follow up) experimental design with random allocation to 2 experimental and one control condition.

Measures: British Ability Scales (pretest only), description of good/bad touching (all but immediate post test), recall of video (all but pretest).

Results: Recall of video (i) video only: significant reduction in scores between immediate post test $\times$ 2 week follow up, but not between 2 week and 6 week follow up, (ii) video + role play: significant increase in scores from post test (before play session) to 2 week follow up (after play session). At immediate post test no difference between experimental groups but at 2 week (after role play session) 6 week follow up video + role play group showed significantly greater recall. Significant correlation between IQ and scores on video recall.

Descriptions of good/bad touches and secrets: significant correlation between scores of controls across pretest and follow up tests, and for video only group between 2 and 6 week follow ups. No other associations on the 3 tests for each group, i.e. improvement in scores for both experimental conditions.

Project 3

Sample: 24 children, mean age 52 months.

Programme: Puppet Gang video with modules on good/bad secrets, touches and surprises.

Design: Repeated measures on intervention group only.

Measures: British Picture Vocabulary Scale (BPVS) – pretest only, knowledge about good/bad secrets and surprises (pre and post test) recall of video (post test only).

Results: Recall of video: central events of 'surprise of party' and 'bad secret of touching' often recalled, but 'saying no' and whether protagonist believed or not less often recalled. All children reported enjoying the video and said that it made them happy (42%) confused (33%), sad (8%), or neither (17%). Significant increase in knowledge about good/bad secrets at post test. Increases correlated with BPVS scores but not correlated with age or sex of children (though girls scored higher at both pre and post test).

Project 4

Sample: 30 children aged 5 to 6 years.

Programme: (1) Puppet Gang Video with module on bullying (2) video plus activity cards and role play (3) control group videos Tom and Jerry cartoon.

Design: Repeated measures (pre test, post test, and 2 week follow up) experimental design with random allocation to 2 experimental and 1 control condition.

Measures: Behaviour questionnaire (all tests) recall of video (all but pretest).

Results: Significantly better recall of video at immediate post test and follow up for video plus activity cards and role play compared to video only conditions. No pretest difference in knowledge of appropriate behaviour but higher post test and follow up scores for both experimental conditions compared to control group.

Notes: (to all 4 projects): authors state that no indication of children lying / fabricating answers, they were more likely to leave out information or decline to answer questions. Also that knowledge of children displayed in class not always captured by formal testing. Authors conclude from that videos plus active learning is an effective training technique for young children. Reference also made to pilot work using programmes therapeutically and to aid recall with children who had been victims of sexual abuse.

Binder and McNeil (1987)

EVALUATION OF A SCHOOL-BASED SEXUAL ABUSE PREVENTION PROGRAMME: COGNITIVE AND EMOTIONAL EFFECTS.

Sample: 88 children aged between 5 and 12 years participated in a programme in a suburban area of the Western United States. Parental permission for the study was granted.

Focus: The child for primary prevention of child sexual abuse.

Objectives: To teach children skills of self assertion, in order to protect themselves and each other, to enlighten parents and teacher about sexual abuse and about the programme.

Programme: Programme (Child Assault Prevention Project) administered by trained facilitators. Teacher,

parents, and children participated in separate 2 hour workshops. The children's workshop involved guided group discussion with 3 role plays of (1) theft by a school bully, (2) being grabbed by a stranger, (3) being asked for a kiss or touched by a trusted adult.

Design: Repeated measures on intervention group using multiple baselines.

Measures: (1) 13 item questionnaire (pre and 2–4 weeks post test) with hypothetical scenarios to test knowledge of coping strategy and self defence techniques presented orally to younger children (5 to 8 years) and in written form with Likert type scales for older children (9 to 12 years). (2) Parents' predictions of their children's responses to the questionnaire (pre and post test). (3) Parent's reports of their children's previous knowledge of topic. (4) Parental assessment of their children's emotional distress on an 18 item scale (pre and post test). (5) Teachers' rating of changes in the children's behaviour (within 2 weeks post test). (6) Children's rating of progress.

Results: (1) Significant increases in children's scores on questionnaire. 5 individual items were significant for younger children and 3 for older children. (2) Parents significantly underestimated their children's knowledge at pre-test. Under rating declined significantly but was still significant for parents of younger children at post test. 43% of children had prior information on sexual assault, at least 10% had received prior specific prevention training. (4) Parents report small but significant increase in emotional distress in children. (5) Most teachers report no change in children's behaviour. (6) Majority of children reported that the programme made them less scared and more able to protect themselves.

Blumberg et al (1991)

THE TOUCH DISCRIMINATION COMPONENT OF SEXUAL ABUSE PREVENTION TRAINING.

Sample: 264 primary school children (139 male, 125 female) from kindergarten to 3rd grade (mean age of 7 years) from three schools in San Diego. 51% Caucasian, 18% Black, 17% Hispanic, 7% Asian, 7% other. Parents on average had approximately 12 years of education and annual income of $30,000.

Focus: Education of children re primary prevention of child abuse and personal safety.

Objectives: (1) Both intervention programmes: To provide sexual abuse and basic safety skills training. (2) Multimedia programme only: physical and emotional abuse also addressed.

Programme: All 3 groups received 1 hour of training from unfamiliar adults. Whole school classes received training whether or not they were all subjects of study.

(1) Stop. Tell Someone, Own Your Body, Protect Yourself (STOP!) role play (RP) programme. Specific elements of presentation varied for different ages of children, but means of instruction essentially the same. (a) Presentations by volunteers led by experienced social worker. (b) Role play, modelling, rehearsal, and discussion and sharing of feelings and ideas in order to teach prevention concepts. (c) Concepts include body ownership/nights, body openings that needed protection, touch discrimination, safety rules of saying no and telling, inappropriate secrets, that perpetrators are usually known to child, that sexual abuse is never the child's fault. (d) Definition of sexual abuse in terms of concrete behaviours.

(2) Child Abuse Primary Prevention Program (CCAPP) multimedia (MM) programme: (a) Presentations by educators: a district counsellor, school nurse, and 4 teachers. (b) MM programme used more abstract methods of presentation. Younger children taught concepts using a teddy bear with changeable expressions and a film on keeping safe in dangerous situations (sexual abuse, strangers, general safety). Older children taught through discussion and a puppet show about incest. (c) Concepts similar to RP programme, but in addition also taught to discriminate touch on basis of feelings. (d) Definition of sexual abuse referred to bad feelings from some touches and so less concrete than RP definition.

(3) Control group received fire prevention training.

Design: Repeated measures (pre and post-test) experimental design with random allocation to two treatment and one control condition. Random allocation of whole school class containing any study subjects. Interviews with children by psychology graduate students that lasted 20 to 30 minutes and undertaken an average of 34 days post-test (range 3 to 94 days).

Measures: (1) Touch Discrimination Task (TDT) to evaluate child's understanding/ability to discriminate OK and not OK touches and to measure over sensitization to appropriate touch. Children rated appropriateness (OK or not) of 7 vignettes, 5 concerned touches to private parts of the body (2 appropriate, 3 or not), 2 concerned appropriate touches to other parts of the body. (2) A fear survey. (3) A sexual abuse knowledge index. (4) A measure of behavioural skill acquisition.

Results: (1) No pretest differences found between groups on demographic data or TDT scores. (2) ANOVA showed significant main effect for school grade at pre-test. (3) Significant main effect for treatment with a significant difference between the RP and the control group. No effect of school grade on pre to post-test change in scores. (4) Analysis of individual TDT vignettes showed significant improvements in scores for RP groups for 3 of the appropriate and 1 of the inappropriate touch vignettes. Pretest scores on the inappropriate touches high for all groups.

Notes: Authors note that improvement in scores by role play group were mostly in distinguishing appropriate touches indicating potential of programmes to make children less suspicious and more realistic re nurturing touch.

Borkin and Frank (1986)

SEXUAL ABUSE PREVENTION FOR PRE-SCHOOLERS: A PILOT PROGRAM

Sample: Subsample of 83 out of 100 pre-school children aged three, four and five who have participated in programme. The larger sample was drawn from a normal population of children attending one day care centre and three nursery schools in Greater Cincinnati.

Focus: The child, for primary prevention of child sexual abuse.

Objectives: To protect pre-school children by teaching appropriate touches and methods of responses to abuse approaches. To inform parents and teachers about child sexual abuse and ways to discuss it with the children.

Programme: Children: puppet show, demonstrations, discussions, colouring activities. Adults: attend performance and are given leaflet on child sexual abuse.

Design: 4–6 week post test on whole treatment group. No pre-test or comparison group.

Measures: 'Correct' or 'Incorrect' response of children to a question on how to react to touches that do not feel good; adult rating on efficacy and age suitability of programme.

Results: Only one three year old spontaneously offered the correct rule, compared to 13 of the four year olds (43%) and 12 of five year olds (43%). Chi Square analysis showed the performance of the three year olds to be significantly poorer than the older children. Adults reasonably satisfied with efficacy of the intervention.

Notes: Authors suggest the use of reported child abuse statistics as an outcome measure in research of this kind.

Conte et al (1985)

PROGRAM TO PREVENT THE SEXUAL VICTIMISATION OF YOUNGER CHILDREN

Sample: 20 male and female children sampled from a normal population attending a day care centre in a suburb of Chicago. Half the children were aged four or five, half were aged between six and ten years. All had at least one working parent.

Focus: The child, for primary prevention of child sexual abuse.

Objectives: To provide pre-school children with knowledge about child sexual abuse: parts of the body, appropriate touches and secrets, skills in assertiveness and help seeking.

Programme: Teaching by trained Deputy Sheriffs for one hour per day for 3 consecutive days.

Design: Repeated measures (pre and post tests), experimentally controlled design with random allocation to experimental and control groups (a wait list control group provided with the prevention programme at a later date); multivariate analysis of data.

Measures: Questionnaire on concepts taught. Administered by experimentally blind social work students.

Results: Significant increase in knowledge of children, but of only about half the concepts: these were the more concrete rather than abstract concepts. Older children learnt more, notwithstanding their higher level of knowledge at pre-test.

Notes: The authors raise many issues including: the relevance of skills and concepts to the reality of preventing sexually abusive assaults; variable receptivity of individual children to training; the importance of detailed training of instructors; the need for vigilance over the unintended consequences of interventions. The latter two points related to the observed deviation from the 'model programme' by the Deputy Sheriff instructors, which included the unplanned use of 'horror stories' by the instructors to reinforce the message of danger to the children.

Doherty and Barrat (1989)

PERSONAL SAFETY PROGRAMME

Sample: 20 children aged 6 to 7 years plus 17 controls, 20 children aged 8 to 9 years with no controls; 28 children aged 10–11 years plus 27 controls. Total 68 experimental and 44 control children. The experimental groups came from 3 schools in Cambridgeshire that participated in the programme. Controls recruited from 3 further schools matched to others by school type and socio-economic composi-tion. Approximately equal sex ratio, but boys over represented in experimental group.

Objectives: To increase children's knowledge about potentially dangerous situations (including child sexual abuse), to encourage them to value their bodies and to trust their own feelings about appropriate touch, to teach strategies to respond to risk including the identification and development of their potential personal supports.

Programme: (1) Teacher awareness programme: (a) Comprehensive 9 hour programme on procedures, managing disclosure, definition, myths, case studies, causes of abuse, feelings, listening, skills, signs and symptoms. (b) observe mock case conference (c) training in undertaking the children's programme.

(2) Children's Programme: Class room lesson of 20 to 30 minutes involving discussion, activities, stories, modelling rehearsal and role play. Programme taught in 7 units of 'General Safety'. 'My body', touches and feelings, 'dealing with a bully', 'dangerous situations with people you don't know'. 'Dangerous situations with people you do know'. Telling an adult'. The programme covers many aspects of personal safety of which sexual abuse is one part.

Design: Repeated measures (pre and post test) of children with matched controls. Post test of parents and teachers.

Measures: (1) Teacher Awareness Programme: Teacher's evaluation by questionnaire on the content of the programme, a general assessment of the course, the value of the course to the teachers personally. Trainers evaluation of each part of the programme.

(2) Children's Programme: (a) Teachers' feedback at meetings or on written forms. (b) Parents' feedback at meetings (c) 19 item questionnaire to test children's knowledge of preventive concepts and skills adjusted for each age group. (d) Role play scenarios of resisting a bully using hand puppets for youngest children and PSP worker for the other children – role plays coded for use of safety measures and assertiveness, also follow up questions to test for knowledge of skills. These behavioural measures were only applied to a subsample of 40 children made up of 10 experimental and 10 control children from both the 6–7 age group and 10–11 age groups.

Results: (1) Teacher's Awareness Programme: Teachers gave high assessment to each separate part of the programme. PSP workers reported that each of the sessions worked well and to their specific purpose.

(2) Children's programme: (a) Teacher's feedback: common responses about the programme included: was a valuable experience for the teachers; suitable, enjoyable and beneficial for the children; important central component of role play, though maybe too difficult for youngest children; insufficient time for whole programme, for use of worksheets and for

role play dislike of one particular story; difficulties experienced by children in saying 'no' to an adult and telling an adult about an abusive situation; the need to include the programmes as part of the curriculum.

(b) Parents' feedback: Responses included: children showed no signs of stress or disturbance; examples of children displaying new knowledge/skills; request for information to help parents reinforce the programme; sadness that the programme was necessary; some concern about naming of genitals; general support for programme.

(c) Children's knowledge: (i) 6 to 7 years old: At pretest children poor on knowledge of bad secrets, dangers from adults, and strategies if refused help by an adult. No pretest differences but at post test the experimental group had improved significantly compared to controls. 94% of experimental group improved overall scores, but poor improvement on several items, particularly dangers from known adults and obedience to adults. (ii) 8 to 9 year olds: significant increase in scores (no controls). Difficulties on similar items to younger children at pretest and continuing reluctance to disobey adults at post-test. 80% improved overall scores. (iii) 10 to 11 year olds: High pretest knowledge, but still significant improvement in scores compared to controls with 69% improved overall scores. Continuing difficulty with items on self blame for abuse at post test.

(d) Role play: For 6–7 year olds and for 10–11 year olds there were significantly greater individual improvements on the use of safety measures and of assertiveness in the role plays. There were similar improvements in the knowledge component except that there was a ceiling effect for the 10–11 year olds with high pretest knowledge. No significant correlation found between the behavioural measure and the questionnaire or knowledge measures.

Notes: Results of teacher questionnaire leads authors to recommend that whole day sessions preferable for teacher awareness programme. Authors argue for the importance of the role plays for both educating children and evaluating impact of programme.

Fryer et al (1987a, 1987b); Kraizer et al (1988)

MEASURING ACTUAL REDUCTION OF RISK OF CHILD ABUSE; MEASURING CHILDREN'S RETENTION OF SKILLS TO RESIST STRANGER ABDUCTION.

Sample: 44 male and female children in the first and second grades of kindergarten of a midtown elementary school.

Focus: The child, for primary prevention of child sexual abuse.

Objectives: To provide pre-school children with knowledge and skills leading to actual behaviour change to reduce vulnerability.

Programme: An 8 day classroom programme with twenty minute presentations per day. Sessions include role play and instructions in personal safety when not in the presence of caretaking adults.

Design: Repeated measures (pre and post-test and 6 months follow up) experimental design with a randomized wait list control. Follow up six months later for 29 of the 44 subjects all of whom had, by age ten, participated in the programme. The intervention was repeated a second time for 4 children at follow-up who had failed the first post-test in the initial experimental group.

Measures: Pre-test only: receptive vocabulary (Peabody Picture Vocabulary Test); Pre and post-test self esteem (Hartex Perceived Competence Scale), cognitive awareness (The Children Need to Know Knowledge – Attitude Test), simulation of unsupervised children's responses to approaches from strangers.

Results: A significant effect (chi-square) of the simulation test. Approximately half of the experimental and control groups passed the pre-test but this increased at post-test only for the experimental group (to over three-quarters). Higher self esteem at pre-test and knowledge of concepts at post-test was only positively correlated with simulation success in the experimental group. At follow-up only 2 of 29 failed the simulation, and these were 2 of the 4 who had failed after they received the programme twice. Subject attention at delayed post-test was associated with children who had performed well initially.

Notes: The authors discuss the importance of simulation tests and of discriminate analysis to locate the characteristics of those children who may not profit from preventive education.

Gilbert et al (1989)

PROTECTING YOUNG CHILDREN FROM SEXUAL ABUSE. DOES PRESCHOOL TRAINING WORK?

Sample: (1) Children: 118 preschool children aged between 3 years 4 months and 5 years and 6 months recruited from 7 preschools in California with a range of urban/rural settings. 52% of the children were white, 25% black. Three sites had predominantly white, and three sites had predominantly black children participating. Even sex ratio. 93 children in experimental groups and 25 in post test control. (2) Parents: Parents of 116 children. 97% were women with an average age of 33 years of whom 31% were single mothers.

Focus: The child for primary prevention of sexual abuse.

Objectives: To teach children concepts and actions for self protection against sexual abuse.

Progamme: Seven prevention programmes aimed at parents and their children. Parents curicula include information on sexual abuse and explanation of child programmes. Children's curicula all include concepts of stranger danger, verbal assertiveness. Many include concepts of types of touch, secrets, children's rights, and guilt and blame.

1. Child Assault Prevention Project (CAPP) from CAP Training Center of Northern California based on feminist rape prevention theory that stresses community responsibility for stopping violence against women and children. Major goals of building women and children's strength and power to prevent abuse. Children's curriculum of 3 half hour daily sessions.

2. Children's Self Help Project. (CSHP) developed by San Francisco Child Abuse Council. Belief that sexual abuse is a manifestation of adult/child power imbalances and that children have right not to be abused. Curriculum used child sized puppets, lasts half an hour presented over 2 days.

3. Touch Safety Program (TSP) from Marin Child Sexual Abuse Treatment Program. Goals of reducing vulnerability and to prevent abuse through curriculum of 3 half hour workshops over a week. Includes animal puppets. Also red, yellow, and green faces to illustrate the Touch Continuum.

4. Talking About Touching (TAT) from the Child Advocacy Council. Curriculum developed by Seattle Committee for Children. Depends on teacher participation. Includes prevention of accidents and physical and sexual abuse. Sexual abuse concepts include the right to say no, body ownership, the importance of telling. 27 lessons of 20 minutes over 3 to 6 week period. Each lesson consists of a story plus class discussion.

5. Child Abuse Prevention, Intervention and Education (CAPIE). Based on Family Service Agency of San Bernardino which believes in strengthening positive values of family life. Contains aspects of rape crisis movement broadened to a community education perspective. Curriculum lasts up to half an hour in one presentation.

6. Stop Abuse Through Family Education. (SAFE) from the El Cajon Unified School District. Aims to actively involve schools, stresses the importance of adult responsibility for child safety. Children's curriculum is a single half hour presentation.

In addition to the children's workshop parents were invited to meetings to discuss the programmes and other aspects of sexual abuse. Also, teachers were given training about the programme.

Design: Repeated measures (pre test and post test 4 to 6 weeks after training) on 7 pre existing intervention groups in 7 preschools (non random allocation) with post test only control group.

Measures: (1) Children: The Child Abuse Researchers' Evaluation Series (CARE Series) taking 20 minutes to complete and administered individually to children. A quarter of the interview was an anxiety scale. The children were presented with 10 hypothetical situations and the child moved the arms of a cardboard rabbit to indicate the bunny's level of anxiety. Half of the interview used a "Bunny Book" to assess responses to different types of touch: the continuing touch, secrets, support system, and self assertion. Children were asked to choose the rabbits depicting the emotional reaction to different touches and to guess the touch that resulted in an expressed emotion of a rabbit. The final quarter of the interview assessed stranger wariness and self assertion by movement of wooden rabbits in various risk scenarios. (2) Parents: Person to person pretest interview on demographic data, parents' wariness of child carers, children's exposure to abuse prevention and safety concepts, and judgements to how the children would act in different circumstances. Telephone post test interviews on parents knowledge and understanding of sexual abuse and their assessment of their children's safety at post test. (3) Teachers: Pretest interview with administrators, post test interview with teachers.

Results: (1) Children: (a) Anxiety: No significant effect of intervention. (b) Touch: Some evidence that at post test children held a more negative view of common interactions and that they were more able to associate different touches with different emotions particularly with mixed up and sad emotions (but some evidence of pretest effects). Even at post test only half of the children could explain their responses. (c) Secrets: significant increase in response of must tell an adult, but half of children still responded that should not tell. A quarter did not recognise what was a secret. (d) Support systems: most children able to identify sources of help and this increased significantly at post test for the depiction of the sad bunny. (e) Strangers: statistically significant increase in wariness from pretest, but scores remained low.

(2) Parents: Parents reported that 26% of children had participated in a previous prevention training mostly one year prior to the study and 61% had seen some television concerned with prevention (public service announcements, commercials. Sesame Street puppets). Many parents themselves taught children safety rules particularly concerning strangers, but

children rarely meet strangers unsupervised. Many parents reported careful screening of education/day care services (60% of parents) and baby-sitters (50% of parents). Parents believed their children to have names for their private parts (87%), to be good at following safety rules and predicted that would protest if attacked by a stranger. There was low attendance at parents meetings (34%) and little evidence of parental knowledge gain at post test.

(3) Teachers: Administrators reported recent changes in operating procedures with multi teacher supervision of children. Teachers were generally supportive of the programmes though had some specific criticisms.

Notes: The research is reported in a book with detailed discussion about the relevance of preventive educational programmes. The authors argue that preschool training should be phased out and emphasis instead placed upon training parents, teachers, and older children with the necessary cognitive abilities.

Hamilton (1989)

PREVENTION IN CHILD SEXUAL ABUSE – AN EVALUATION OF A PROGRAMME

Sample: (1) A random subsample of 32 children out of 172 children aged 10–11 years who participated in the programme at three schools in East Scotland. (2) A further 12 children who participated in the programme and were considered above (n=4) below (n=4) average ability by their teachers. Full data was only available on 8 of these children. Approximately equal numbers of male and female children in the total sample of 44 children.

Focus: The child, for primary prevention of child sexual Abuse.

Objectives: To increase children's knowledge of prevention concepts and their skills for avoiding sexual assaults.

Programme: A sexual assault preventive education programme (Feeling Yes, Feeling No). Programme contains 3 fifteen minute video films presented with 9 hours of classroom exercises such as role play and drama. Includes identification and communication of one's feelings, the meaning of sexual assault and ways to avoid it, body terms. Both intra and extra familial abuse addressed. Administered by regular teachers (after training) in six weekly classes. Parents saw videos in advance and gave permission for children's involvement.

Design: Repeated measures on intervention sample only.

Measures: (1) Random subsample: Pre and post semi-structured questionnaire on good/bad feelings and touches, responses to scenarios on personal safety, meaning of sexual assault. (2) Small non random subsample: Post test interview on children's experience of the programme, teacher assessment of children's ability level, the semi-structured questionnaire (8 children only).

Results: Considerable increase in appropriate responses to the definition of a stranger (0% to 69%), strategies for keeping safe from a stranger (23% to 49%), and from a neighbour (6% to 40%). Self attribution of fault by the child reduced for assaults by a stranger (74% to 8%) by a neighbour (67% to 17%) and by a family member (25% to 0%). Belief that risks from an adult could include sexual abuse increased for stranger (19% to 50%), neighbour (6% to 34%) and father (9% to 34%). Very little retention of set of 3 questions for children to ask themselves if approached by a stranger. Female children and the 3 high ability children had greatest improvements with the 3 high ability children scoring well in all except for the three stranger questions, 6 to 10% of children showed deterioration. Sources of assistance and names of body parts had high pre-test scores. 3 children disclosed abuse. Interview data: programme important/useful/enjoyable despite frightening aspects; embarrassment at body parts but not about sexual assault; no negative feelings about appropriate touches; difficulty in remembering taught cognitive strategies.

Notes: Importance of inter agency collaboration emphasized because some agencies limited the directness of the questionnaire.

Harvey et al (1988)

THE PREVENTION OF SEXUAL ABUSE: EXAMINATION OF THE EFFECTIVENESS OF A PROGRAM WITH KINDERGARTEN-AGED CHILDREN

Sample: 71 kindergarten children from 4 schools in a rural area of mid Georgia, USA, age range from 61–80 months; mean 70 months. There were 33 boys (13 black, 20 Caucasian) 38 girls (18 black, 20 Caucasian) from a low and lower middle class environment.

Focus: Child for primary prevention of sexual abuse.

Objectives: To protect pre-school children from child abuse by teaching appropriate touches and methods of responding to abusive approaches.

Programme: Both groups received 3 half hour sessions on consecutive days.

Experimental group: The Good Touch – Bad Touch Program consisting of: defining sexual abuse, differentiating between good, bad and sexually abusive touches, delineating safety roles to prevent abuse and identifying who can abuse children. Methods included instruction, modeling, rehearsal and social reinforcement. Session 1: concepts taught by instruction; stories and a simple game. Session 2: review of Session 1 plus a film and a song. Session 3: review and further stories.

Design: Repeated measures (pretest, 3 week and 7 week post tests) with random allocation (controlled for sex and race) to control and experimental groups.

Measures: Children's judgements on whether 10 pictures of adult-child touch were good or sexually abusive. 5 questions about coping with abuse. 6 questions on appropriate responses to both a vignette of abuse included in the training (Direct Test) and a new vignette (Generalization Test).

Results: No socio-economic or race effects. The experimental group performed significantly better than the control group for all variables at post test and follow up except for the Direct Test at post test.

Notes: The authors conclude that kindergarten children can be taught these skills, that they are maintained at follow up, and can be generalized to novel vignettes.

Hazzard et al (1991)

CHILD SEXUAL ABUSE PREVENTION: EVALUATION AND ONE YEAR FOLLOW-UP

Sample: Eight schools in middle income neighbourhoods chosen from 21 volunteering to participate from suburban area in a large city in S.E. United States. Schools grouped in to 2 sets of 4 schools matched on ethnic composition and achievement level. Complete data obtained from 399 children from 3rd and 4th grade classes. 68% Caucasian, 23% Black, 4% Hispanic, 3% Asian, 2% other. Equal sex ratio. Sample for 1 year follow up of 103 children from two schools in condition 1 and one school in condition 2.

Focus: Education of children as primary prevention of sexual abuse.

Objectives: To teach children the knowledge to avoid abuse and to teach and encourage them to seek assistance if abused.

Programme: Four experimental conditions of (1) teacher and child training, (2) child training, (3) teacher training, (4) delayed child training control.

Child training consisted of a 3 session adaption of Feeling Yes, Feeling No curriculum. Sessions included a 15 minute videotape, group discussion and role plays. Also prevention poster displayed. Concepts included touches and feelings, saying no and telling, what is sexual abuse, problem solving to avoid dangerous situations, sexual abuse is sometimes by 'known' others, keep telling if not believed, sexual abuse is never fault of child. Silent question box in classroom for anonymous questions for trainer to answer the following day. Trainer also available for individual discussions with children. Disclosures referred to school social worker.

Sub-sample of treatment children at one year follow up received 1 hour booster session of video 'Yes, You Can Say No' about a child sexually abused by uncle who discloses to parents after support from friends. Also discussion and crossword puzzle covering concepts in original training.

Condition 4 controls received a 1-session fire safety or water safety programme and then received sexual abuse training 6 weeks later after 1st follow up tests.

Teacher training consisted of a 6 hour workshop on child sexual abuse. Workshops led by 2 experienced psychologist and used didactic presentations, videotapes, experimental exercises, water plays, group discussions, and discussions with child protective services worker. Issues addressed included incidence, dynamics, indicators, short and long term effects, basic interviewing techniques, reporting, treatment resources, and primary prevention.

Design: Repeated measures, (pre and post-test, 6 week follow-up, one year follow up on sub sample) experimental design with block randomized allocation to 3 intervention and one delayed intervention control condition. The one year follow up on sub sample consisted of a pre and post-test to a booster child training session.

Measures: (1) Demographic data at pre-test, (2) What I Know about Touching Scale (WIKATS) – a 25 item scale at pre, post and 1st follow up test. (3) State Trait Anxiety Inventory for Children (STAIC) at pre, post, and 1st follow up test. (4) What Would You Do? (WWYD) A videotape of six 30 second vignettes, 4 potentially abusive, 2 not obviously a risk. Video presented as an individual structured interview by a trained research assistant (not experimentally blind). Children asked whether the situations were safe/unsafe and reason for this and what they would say and do in these situations. Responses coded into a Safety Discrimination score and a Prevention Skills score. Children also rated the extent that they would have different positive and negative feelings in each of these situations. WWYD measure used at post-test on block random selection of 85 treatment subjects and 38 control subjects, and at 6 week follow up on block random selection of 78 treatment subjects. At the 1 year follow up, half the children completed the measure pre the booster session and half post the session. (5) Feedback forms from staff including data on disclosures. (6) Parental postal questionnaire at post-test on perception of programme and 16 behaviour check-list to identify negative reactions of children.

Results: (1) Previous education: Proportion of children reporting that parents had discussed sexual abuse with them at least once was 68%, at least three times was 33%. Proportion reporting viewing at least one television programme on this was 53%, and reporting reading one book, magazine, or comic was 32%.

(2) WIKATS: Data analyzed by ANOVAs. No differences between cases with complete or incomplete data. No differences between Conditions 1 and 2 so combined and contrasted with controls. Significant effect grade with 3rd grades scoring lower than 4th graders. Effects of Treatment Conditions and Treatment Condition × Time were both highly significant. Treatment subjects increase in scores was highly significant with only slight increase in scores of controls. Time × sex interaction also significant with girls scores being slightly higher at post-test and 1st follow up for all conditions. No effects or interactions found for race or school achievement.

(3) Anxiety: No effects or interactions shown by analysis of covariance.

(4) WWYD: At post-test treatment children had significantly better Discrimination scores but similar Prevention Skills scores compared to controls. Treatment scores were maintained at 1st follow up. These Discrimination and Prevention scores were not significantly correlated with anxiety or knowledge scores. Children's emotional reactions to unsafe scenes was negative but did not differ between treatment and controls. For safe scenes treatment children had stronger positive and weaker negative reactions than control children. At 1st follow up there was no change in treatment children's reactions to safe scenes, but their reactions to unsafe scenes had become less negative.

(5) Disclosures: 8 (1.5%) of on-going sexual abuse, 20 (3.8%) of past sexual abuse, 5 (0.9%) of on-going physical abuse, 1 case (0.2%) of past physical abuse. Not possible to distinguish data between treatment and control groups.

(6) Parental questionnaires returned by 46%. Only significant difference in child behaviour was that controls talked more about fires or fire safety. Significantly more treatment parents reported their children talking to them about the programme. 69% of treatment parents stated programmes had good effect overall, remainder said that no effect. 95% stated they would agree to participate in a similar programme.

(7) One year follow up: (a) No effect found for booster session in WIKATS, but significant Time effect suggesting improvements for all children from 6 weeks to 1 year follow up. (b) WWYD Safety Discrimination scores significantly better than at 1st

follow up for children tested post booster session but not significantly higher than those tested pre-booster session. (c) WWYD Prevention skills scores were not significantly different from 1st follow up and no effect shown for booster sessions. (d) WWYD Emotional reactions: only difference was more negative reactions to unsafe scenes than at 1st follow up for children tested post-booster session, but not significantly more negative than those tested pre-booster session. Analysis showed that effect due to increased ratings of anger and sadness, but not fear.

Notes: (1) Authors argue that results show that a programme with affective and concrete and behavioural rehearsal components can be effective (on all measures except Prevention Skills) with mid-elementary children, and that equally effective for all children and treatment conditions, and effects maintained at follow up. (2) Authors surprised that no effect on children's anxiety levels or from whether teachers had been trained. (3) Despite lack of effect of booster sessions, repeat training through school career is advocated because children's abilities and needs change. (4) No data presented on the effects of teacher training in the absence of child training (Condition 3). That teacher training was effective in increasing teachers' knowledge and ability is reported in an earlier paper (Kleemeier et al, 1988) which compared teachers in conditions 2 (child training + teacher training) and Condition 3 (teacher training only) with teachers in Condition 1 (child training only) and Condition 4 (controls). The results showed teachers receiving training improved compared to controls in knowledge of abuse, ability to identify specific indicators of abuse, and appropriateness and support in responses to vignettes of possible sexual abuse situations.

Kolko, Moser, and Hughes (1989)

CLASSROOM TRAINING IN SEXUAL VICTIMIZATION AWARENESS AND PREVENTION SKILLS: AN EXTENSION OF THE RED FLAG/GREEN FLAG PROGRAM.

Sample: Intervention group: 213 children from 6 schools in Washington County. Controls: 35 children from another school. Children were aged between 7 and 10 years with approximately equal sex ratio. Parents were mostly in their mid 30's. Teachers were mainly female.

Focus: The child, for primary prevention of child sexual abuse.

Objectives: To increase children's preventive skills and ability to disclose incidents of inappropriate touching/abuse.

Programme: 14 formally trained staff volunteers taught prevention rules and concepts of good/bad love and touching with RF/GF Colouring Book and 'Better Safe than Sorry II' film in two consecutive weekly sessions. Programme help line, repeat visits by trainers to assist and reassure children that child not at fault if unable to avoid abuse. Parents did not participate in the programme.

Design: Repeated measures (pre and post-test and follow up) experimental design with one intervention and one control group.

Measures: Self report questionnaire at pre test, 2 week post test, and 6 month follow up. Factor analysis of Likert Scale type items at pre-test. Children: factors of awareness of problem, subjective disturbance re potential abuse, likelihood of talking about abuse. Also non Likert items of concepts/skills and correct preventive responses. Post test and follow up item on change in likelihood of disclosure. (2) Parents: factors of awareness, preparedness to respond, utility of information given, and a post test and follow up item on change in understanding. (3) Teachers: measures as for parents, but focused on whole class. (4) Reports of inappropriate touches from children, parents, teachers, and school guidance counsellors. Also demographic data.

Results: (1) Children: at post test and follow up had a significantly greater increase in awareness and correct preventive responses compared to controls but no significant difference in likelihood of disclosure. At follow up also significantly greater increase in use of programme concepts/skills. (2) Parents at post test: significant change in understanding. At follow up significant difference in awareness, preparedness, use of information, and change in understanding (but due to decreases scores in controls – except for preparedness). (3) Teachers: significant increase in use of information and change in understanding at post test and follow up. (4) More self reports than parent reports of abuse. Intervention group had less self reports at follow up but more known to school counsellors. No gender differences found.

Notes: The authors note that different strategy used to elicit reports of abuse from children and from parents. Also that availability of staff post training may be crucial support for disclosure.

Mayes et al (1991a, 1991b)

AN EVALUATION OF THE KIDSCAPE TRAINING PROGRAMME

Sample: 120 children, with equal sex ratio, 10 from each of 2 primary classes (Primary 2 aged 6 years and Primary 6 aged 10/11 years) in 6 schools in Glasgow.

3 schools using Kidscape programme plus 3 others (not using this or similar programmes) matched for religious denomination and size of school, and socio-economic status of families.

Focus: Child for primary prevention of abuse.

Objectives: To teach children skills and concepts to keep safe in 4 types of situation (1) bullying, (2) approaches by strangers, (3) inappropriate intimacy, (4) pressure to keep 'bad secrets'.

Programme: Lesson in 4 sections of feeling safe, dealing with bullies, dealing with strangers, and dealing with known adults. Themes taught through 6 paired role plays (and/or stories): one of a pair describing a situation and the other describing appropriate responses. A 7th role play demonstrates seeking help from an adult. Role play involve both teachers and children. Keep safe posters for children to complete with their parents. Also materials for follow up lessons or projects.

Design: Repeated measures (pre-test, immediate post test, and 2 month follow up) natural experimental design with one experimental and one control condition. Matched groups. Two age levels per condition.

Measures: (1) Picture-story technique with children making judgements of the safety/danger of different situations portrayed in black and white line drawings. Response by green (safe), yellow (uncertain), or red (unsafe) coloured discs. Average of 13 drawings per child on the 4 key themes of bullying, strangers, intimacy, and secrets. Half involved Kidscape and half non Kidscape situations. Also variations in scenarios by presence of bystanders in pictures. (2) Children's explanations of what would be appropriate responses to the situations (and why) rated blind by experts on 5 point scale of safety.

Results: 1. Children's judgements of safety of situations across all 3 tests: (a) Experimental subjects significantly more likely than controls to (i) rate stranger situations as unsafe and (ii) to rate all situations as unsafe rather than uncertain. Younger children are more likely than older children to (i) rate bullying and intimacy as unsafe and (ii) to rate all situations (particularly strangers) as safe or unsafe rather than uncertain. Older children more likely than younger children to rate secrets as unsafe (though still less unsafe than bullying or strangers). (b) Bullying: rated more safe for (i) presence of mother, (ii) presence of unknown adult male onlooker; rated more unsafe for lone child with single group of bullies. (c) Strangers: rated more safe for presence of mother; rated more unsafe for (i) presence of 2 strangers, man and woman (experimental group only), and (ii) male strangers plus same sex child friend (control group only). (d) Secrets and intimacy: rated more safe by controls and more unsafe by experimental groups for most scenarios at pre-test and post test and for child alone at follow up test.

2. Safety of Children's responses. For all 3 tests the responses of older children were safer than younger children and those of experimental subjects were safer than those of control subjects (indicating significant pretest differences between groups). No effects of sex of subject or of Kidscape/novel type situations. All groups made safer responses to bullying and stranger themes and to mother present scenario. Least safe responses by younger children to secrets theme. Both experimental and control groups showed a significant improvement in safety responses at post test. Controls showed the greatest improvement and therefore the significant pretest differences between the groups became reduced at post test. Few effects of themes and scenarios except that the experimental group perform better than control group for (i) the older children on stranger theme (pre and post test only), (ii) for older children on intimacy theme (all 3 tests), and (iii) for younger children on secrets theme (pre and post test only).

Notes: Authors conclude that pretest differences and significant improvements for both groups suggest (i) cultural differences between schools choosing or not choosing to use the programmes and (ii) greater experimenter (from testing procedures) than programme (Kidscape) effects on children's awareness of safety (and these effects maintained at 2/3 month follow up). Much emphasis of results on what situations children perceive as safe or dangerous. Also that children, particularly younger children, perform badly and learn least on themes of secrets and intimacy.

Miltenberger and Thiesse–Duffy (1988)

AN EVALUATION OF HOME BASED PROGRAMS FOR TEACHING PERSONAL SAFETY SKILLS TO CHILDREN

Sample: 24 children in 15 families (12 two-parent, 3 single-parent) from a Midwest metropolitan area of 100,000 people. Thirteen 4 to 5 year olds' and eleven 6 to 7 year olds' participated. All families were of middle to upper middle class socio-economic status.

Focus: Child for primary prevention of sexual abuse.

Objectives: To teach personal safety skills to 4–7 year old children.

Programme: Three groups. (1) Parent instruction with Red Flag/Green Flag prevention colouring book followed by behavioural assessment and training by researcher; (2) As group 1 but parent told to emphasize key points and to orally rehearse prevention responses with child; (3) Behavioural assessment/ training only.

Design: Repeated measures (2 pre-tests, 1 post test, 2 to 3 follow up assessments, 1 follow up probe) experimental design with allocation to three intervention groups.

Measures: Picture discrimination: experimenter described picture showing good (n = 2) and bad (n = 3) touches which the child rated as good or bad. Verbal scenarios: descriptions of 3 scenarios (1 with doll as visual aid) of dangerous situations and child given 10 sessions to describe how he/she would react. Role plays: 2 role plays of potentially dangerous situations with known research assistant playing potential perpetrator. Real life probe: (2 month past post test) when child alone unknown research assistant uses incentive to attempt to lure the child away. Parental views, telephone interview (1 day past post test) and anonymous questionnaire (2 weeks post follow up probe) on parental satisfaction with study and changes in their children's behaviour.

Results: (1) Picture discrimination: high baseline and post test scores for most children. (2) Verbal scenarios and role plays: low baseline scores indicating children able to identify dangerous situations but not to exhibit protective behaviour. (3) Training with the prevention book did not produce criteria performance in any subjects (whether or not additional instructions and verbal rehearsal). (4) Criteria (or near) achieved for all subject following behavioural training. At the 2 month real life follow up probe nearly all children said no to the potential perpetrator (score of 1), many left the scene (score of 2) but only the older children left the scene and told a parent (score of 3). Parents said that they were happy with the study and reported no lasting behavioural problems, though 2 children visibly upset at the follow up probe.

Notes: Authors argue that only behavioural training and not prevention book effective on variables tested. Also argue that criterion performance only maintained for older children but follow up probe of real life test possibly was more difficult than other role plays. Data presented for each subject. No statistical analysis.

Peraino (1990)

EVALUATION OF A PRESCHOOL ANTIVICTIMIZATION PREVENTION PROGRAM.

Sample: 46 preschoolers of average age of 50 months (S.D.5.3) selected as either middle income (from one YMCA preschool) or lower income (from 5 schools in the Houston Independent School District).

Focus: Education of children for primary prevention of victimization.

Objectives: An antivictimization education project that seeks to prevent child victimization and ensuing mental health problems.

Programme: We Help Ourselves (WHO) preschool programme of three 15 minute classroom presentations approximately 1 week apart. Trained volunteer meets with small groups including class teacher and introduces one topic per week using puppets and stories to facilitate discussion (and encouragement to report any victimization). Topics are strangers, physical and emotional hurts, and touches. Class teachers receive a one hour presentation plus follow up materials to reinforce concepts with children. Parents receive one hour presentation post programme, and taught how to respond to disclosure by a child. Also self-help resources.

Design: Repeated measures for Program Group (post-test and follow up) and for No Program Group (pre-test and follow up) with random allocation to Program and No Program Group. Resultant four-factor design of Group, Sex, Income Level, and Race (White vs Black vs Hispanic). Follow-up 1 to 2 months post-test planned for 23 subjects but achieved for 19 subjects (10 from Program Group).

Measures: Interview questionnaire using three unisex monkey puppets representing the child, a familiar adult, and an adult stranger. Three questions concerned requests to leave a playground with familiar or unfamiliar adults or enter the car of an unfamiliar adult. Three questions concerned physical abuse, chastisement, and injury. Five questions asked about good/bad touch, identifying 'private parts', appropriateness of medical examinations, appropriateness of genital contact with familiar adult during play, and appropriate responses to inappropriate touches. Interviews of 5 to 10 minutes undertaken and scored by non blind interviewers with high inter rater reliability.

Results: Only significant main effect from ANOVA was for Group with Program Group scoring significantly higher (post-test) than No Program Group (pre-test). Program Group scores particularly higher for not going with stranger who offers to buy a toy, what to do if physically abused, that genital contact from familiar person may be inappropriate, and what to do if sexually abused. No significant effects for sex, race, or income. At follow up non parametric tests revealed a significant improvement for the No Program Group but not for the Program Group.

Notes: Study hypotheses of higher scores for Program Group compared to Non Program Group and for females compared to males. Ny hypotheses about race or income. Author discusses relevance of trends in data re sex, race, and income. Author suggests that sex differences in knowledge about abuse may develop with age from females being socialized about an increased potential for victimization.

Poche et al (1981)

TEACHING SELF PROTECTION TO YOUNG CHILDREN

Sample: Three pre-school children (1 male, 2 female) aged between three and five years.

Focus: Child, for primary prevention of child sexual abuse.

Objectives: To provide pre-school children with skills to protect themselves from sexual abuse and to assess the necessity of giving reasons for the responses taught.

Programme: Instruction, modelling, behaviour rehearsal and social reinforcement of appropriate reactions (verbal and physical) to three 'lures' commonly used for child molesters. The training took place in outdoor locations near to the school. Fifteen minute sessions ended when a child correctly responded at least once to each of the three lures over three days.

Design: Repeated measures (pre-test, post-test and twelve week delayed post-test) on intervention group only.

Measures: Responses to simulated lures in a community setting.

Results: At pre-test all 3 subjects exhibited high risk, inappropriate responses. Training to the level of correct response took five or six sessions per child. All 3 subjects responded appropriately to the post-training lure in the community and there was no variation in response to the three different lures. Only 2 of the children were tested at the 12 week follow-up, both children produced the correct verbal responses, but only 1 child moved away as trained. All of the children seemed motivated to perform the responses without a detailed explanation of the potential dangers of being abducted.

Notes: The authors suggest the use of booster training sessions to maintain the taught safe responses.

Poche et al (1988)

TEACHING SELF-PROTECTION TO CHILDREN USING TELEVISION TECHNIQUES.

Sample: 74 children (29 in Kindergarten, 45 in first grade) aged 5–7 years; 33 girls, 4 boys; 19 black, 55 white. The children were randomly selected from the total children in each of 5 classes receiving one of the experimental conditions. The 3 schools were located in low, middle and upper income neighbourhoods in Kalamazoo, Michigan.

Focus: Child for primary prevention of sexual abuse.

Objectives: To teach young children self-protective skills against abduction.

Programme: Four separate groups (1) Instructional 20 minute colour videotape in which young adult males attempted to lure children away with enticement and the child actors demonstrated the safety rules of saying no and running to parent or teacher. Video was interactive in asking questions of the audience, leaving pauses for replies, and indicated the minimum differences between correct and incorrect responses. Total duration of 25 minutes. The trainer prompted the children to make the interactive responses. (2) Same video instruction as group 1 plus individual behavioural rehearsal where trainer role played a friendly abduction and attempted to lure the child. If child responded incorrectly then told correct response and repeated until correct criterion achieved. Total duration of 45 minutes. (3) Children presented with standard school programme including verbal instructions of correct responses to potential abduction plus a short film warning about strangers. Total duration of 60 minutes. (4) Control group of delayed training. After the post training tests all children were debriefed and the control group shown training videotape.

Design: A post-test experimental design with random allocation (of the 5 school classes) to 3 experimental an 1 control conditions.

Measures: Post training real life simulation probes in which adult male attempted to lure child with enticements. Verbal refusal and/or running away to an advance from a stranger was rated by observers as: 'O' if went with abductor regardless of response, '1' if stayed near with no refusal, if '2' stayed near but used any refusal '3' if ran away with no refusal, '4' if ran away with any refusal. Children not responding correctly given immediate extra training. Children scoring '4' were given 1 month follow up real life probe.

Results: On all measures order of successful results (statistically significant in analysis of variance) were: video plus rehearsal, video only, standard programme, and control group. Proportion of children displaying criterion verbal and motor responses were video plus rehearsal 58%, video only 47%, standard programme 0%, control 0%. At 1 month follow up these children maintained their criterion scores. 75% of children in the control group and 11% in video plus rehearsal group agreed to go with the abductor. 91% of children using criterion verbal referral also ran away. Only 17% of those using other verbal referral ran away.

Notes: The authors argue that the results show the high susceptibility of young children to abduction, the effectiveness and durability of video training compared to standard programmes, the benefits of teaching a descriptive criterion verbal response that occasions an escape response, that there is no need to have a rationale of harm to teach these skills.

Sigurdson et al (1986)

WHAT DO CHILDREN KNOW ABOUT PREVENTING SEXUAL ASSAULT?

Sample: 137 children from a possible 158 children in two classes, in grades, 4, 5 and 6 (ages 9 to 13 years) from a Vancouver school, covering an urban and rural population with varied socio-economic backgrounds.

Focus: The child, for primary prevention of child sexual abuse.

Objectives: To increase children's level of awareness and assertiveness about self protection, enabling them to identify and communicate their feelings, to recognise potentially dangerous situations, and to develop skills and practice in obtaining effective assistance.

Programme: A structured video course with classroom inter-action, (Feeling Yes, Feeling No). The programme took 4 weeks to complete and involved 3 video presentations in conjunction with over 9 hours of classroom exercises and discussion.

Design: Repeated measures (pre and post-tests) on intervention sample only, with repeated measures providing multiple baselines.

Measures: Pre and post-test: a personal safety questionnaire that included 29 'yes', 'no', 'don't know' questions about current knowledge and attitudes related to self protection. Post-test only: a written evaluation of the classroom programme by the children.

Results: Between a quarter and half of the children gave appropriate answers at pre-test, which is no better than chance. At post-test there was a significant improvement (mainly from the female students), in answers to 8 of 29 questions; 97% of the children reported that they enjoyed the programme.

Notes: Data on each questionnaire item is presented in the study.

Stillwell et al (1988)

EVALUATION OF A SEXUAL ABUSE PREVENTION
PROGRAM FOR PRESCHOOLERS.

Sample: 4 out of the 20 children aged between 3 and 4 years attending preschool at Southern Illinois University. Children chosen on basis of availability and of having no previous experience of prevention programme.

Focus: The child, for primary prevention of sexual abuse.

Objectives: To teach children concepts and actions for self protection against sexual abuse.

Programme: Sexual Abuse Prevention Program for Preschoolers (SAPPP) developed from 'Talking about Touch with Preschoolers'. Children were taught to identify different types of touch, to say 'no', and to 'tell others' in 6 lessons. Each lesson included a topic introduction, stories related to the topic, target behaviour rehearsal, and class discussion.

Design: Repeated measures, (pretest, within test probes, post test, and 2 × 4 week follow up) to allow a multiple probe technique to demonstrate changes dependent upon the intervention.

Measures: At pretest, post test and two follow ups child presented with three stories followed by questions requiring yes/no answers and demonstration of knowledge of appropriate target behaviours. A fourth probe question was used that required only yes/no answers and related to novel situations to test for generalization of learning. A probe question was asked on its own after lessons, 2, 4 & 6 and included with the three other questions at pre, post and follow up tests.

Results: The children scored significantly higher scores at post-test on verbal responses, though there was a decay in these scores at 2 and 4 week follow-up despite a booster session being given to three of the four children. Only one child showed any increase in target behaviours from pretest scores.

Notes: The authors suggest a number of variables that may have affected the results including too few lessons and that the probe test was brief and limited to verbal responses and not including actual target behaviours.

Swann et al (1985)

CHILD SEXUAL ABUSE PREVENTION: DOES IT WORK?

Sample: (1) all 63 children in grades 2 to 5 (ages 8 to 11) in an urban school in a mid-western state of the United States; (2) 56 parents from a rural community whose children had seen the play; (3) 225 parents and professionals who had seen the play.

Focus: Child, for primary prevention of child sexual abuse.

Objectives: Use of entertaining drama to educate children to discriminate appropriate from abusive touching, to be aware of the range of possible abuse, and to seek assistance if they are abused.

Programme: A 30 minute play (Bubbylonian Encounter), performed by adult professional actors, describing the experiences and education of a character from another planet about appropriate and inappropriate touch. The presentation includes vignettes to demonstrate correct responses to sexual approaches.

Design: Children: repeated measures (pre and post-test) producing multiple baseline for 44 subjects; post-test only for 19 subjects to assess effect of repeated measure.

Measures: Pre and Post-Test on Children: multiple choice plus written responses of children to five video taped vignettes. Post-Test only for all 3 samples: written, spoken and questionnaire responses to reactions to the play.

Results: High pre-test knowledge of abusive touching and no evidence of effect of intervention; significant increases in awareness of potential perpetrators within the family and in the number of appropriate responses to sexual approaches. The post-test only group produced near perfect responses on all the measures. 65% of children reported they enjoyed the play, most parents were positive about their children seeing the play, and nearly all the parents and professionals were positive about the programme.

Wolfe et al (1986)

BRIEF INTERVENTION FOR EDUCATING CHILDREN IN
AWARENESS OF PHYSICAL AND SEXUAL ABUSE

Sample: 290 children in 4th and 5th grades (ages 9 to 12) from 3 representative inner city United States schools.

Focus: Child, for primary prevention of child sexual and physical abuse.

Objectives: To increase children's awareness of physical and sexual abuse including the development of appropriate attitudes about adults and about self-blame.

Programme: Presentation of 2 five minutes "skits" in the classroom, followed by a discussion around 5 main areas: potential abusers, children's feelings, responsibility for abuse, the range of possible child responses, and the importance of seeking help immediately.

Design: Post-test only with random allocation to control and intervention groups.

Measures: 7 item true/false questionnaire on responses to abuse, seeking help, attitudes to responsibility, likelihood of being believed, and recognition of potential abusers.

Results: Analysis of variance showed no main or interaction effects for sex or grade. Chi-square showed significant differences between groups for 3 of the 7 test questions, although the differences in the raw data were small. The control and intervention groups both scored highly on the 3 help seeking items and both groups scored relatively few correct answers on the item whether they would be believed.

Notes: The authors discuss methodological issues and recommend greater targeting of preventive programmes.

Wurtele et al (1986)

TEACHING PERSONAL SAFETY SKILLS FOR PREVENTION OF SEXUAL ABUSE: A COMPARISON OF TREATMENTS.

Sample: Younger group of 28 children in kindergarten and 1st grade with mean age of 6 years. Older group of 43 children in 5th and 6th grades with mean age of 11 years. Near equal sex ratio and all attending public school in lower to middle class district in small town in eastern Washington.

Focus: The child, for primary prevention of sexual abuse.

Objectives: To teach personal safety skills to children in order to identify, avoid risks, and request help if necessary.

Programme: Subjects assigned to one of 4 groups (1) control: 50 minute discussion on self concept and personal values. (2) Film: 35 minute film 'Touch' with modelling of saying no, calling for help, getting away, telling someone until believed. 15 minute discussion of skills learnt, feelings aroused. (3) BST Behavioural Skills Training of modelling, rehearsal, social reinforcement, shaping, and feedback of skills re body terms, okay/not okay touches of 'private parts', oral response of 'no', evading abuse, seeking help. (4) Combined film and BST reduced to 60 minutes. Training by graduate students.

Design: Repeated measures (post test and 3 month follow up for intervention group and post-test only for controls) experimental design with random allo-

cation (balanced for sex) to 3 treatment and 1 control group for both younger and other subjects (i.e. 8 groups in all).

Measures: Personal Safety Questionnaire (PSQ) of 13 hypothetical questions (scored 0 to 13). 'What If' Situations Test (WIST) involving 4 vignettes of abusive touches with questions about when to resist, when to escape, names of who to tell. Possible scores of 8 per vignette and so a maximum of 32 points.

Results: At post-test BST and BST + Film showed significant improvement compared to controls on PSQ. Only BST presented on its own showed an effect on the WIST. At follow up there was a general increase in scores. The Film Group scores increased to the level of the other intervention groups. Older children had greater knowledge but did not show greater learning than controls.

Notes: Saslawsky and Wurtele (1986) used a similar sample to compare a wait list control with viewing and discussing the film 'Touch' (i.e. comparison of groups 1 and 4 in Wurtele et al 1986). Children who viewed the film demonstrated significantly greater knowledge about abuse on the PSQ and enhanced personal safety skills on the WIST. The gains were maintained at 3 month follow up. No evidence of a sensitizing effect of pre-testing could be found.

Wurtele et al (1987)

PRACTICE MAKES PERFECT? THE ROLE OF PARTICIPANT MODELING IN SEXUAL ABUSE PREVENTION PROGRAMS

Sample: 26 white children (12 boys, 14 girls) attending a kindergarten in two public schools serving a largely lower to middle class population in a rural area of Eastern Washington.

Focus: Children for primary prevention of sexual abuse.

Objectives: To effectively and safely increase children's knowledge about sexual abuse and to enhance their acquisition of personal safety skills.

Programme: Subjects assigned to either Participant Modeling (PM) or Symbolic Modeling (SM). Both consisted of a 50 minute presentation concerned with the self-protective skills of: understanding the location of private parts and the concept of appropriate touch and having appropriate verbal and motoric responses to attempted abuse. PM group used methods of instruction, modeling, rehearsal, social reinforcement, shaping and feedback. The experimenter modelled the skill, and each child had to practice it. In the SM group: the experimenter modelled the skills and the children watched.

Design: Repeated measures (pre-test, 2 post-tests and 6 week follow up) experimental design; allocation to 2 treatment groups by rank order.

Measures: Personal Safety Questionnaire (PSQ), "What If" Situations Test (WIST) Fear Assessment Thermometer Scale (FATS). Interviews with the children whose responses were recorded verbatim. Audio-taping of the programmes. See Wurtele et al (1986) for descriptions of measures.

Results: No significant differences at pretest on PSQ and WIST for sex, school or programme. The PM group showed a significantly greater increase in WIST scores than the SM group at both post tests. Treatment effects for both groups maintained at follow up but with no significant differences between the groups. No effects on PSQ. At pretest 85% of all the children stated that medical touches of private parts were appropriate and this increased to 92% at follow up. Children in both groups enjoyed the training programmes.

Notes: The authors argue the results indicate greater efficacy of the PM Programme and that this was not due to differential knowledge gain (i.e. PSQ scores) or enjoyment of the programme.

Wurtele et al (1989)

COMPARISON OF PROGRAMS FOR TEACHING PERSONAL SAFETY SKILLS TO PRESCHOOLERS.

Sample: 100 children attending two Headstart pre-schools serving a low income predominantly white population in a north western U.S. community of 50,000 people. 49 boys and 51 girls. Age range of 4.4 to 6.3 years with a mean of 5.0 years.

Focus: The child, for primary prevention of sexual abuse.

Objectives: To teach personal safety skills to preschoolers.

Programme: Subject assigned to (1) Behavioural skills training program (BST), (2) Feelings program. (3) Control Programmes presented simultaneously in 30 minute sessions on three consecutive days.

In both programmes (1) and (2) instructors taught children that: (a) they are bosses of their bodies (b) the location of 'private parts', (c) appropriate touches of private parts, (d) and (e) nature of inappropriate touches, (f) children's right to say no and to tell others (g) inappropriate touches not the child's fault. In both groups children also taught by instruction, mod-elling, rehearsal, praise and feedback, to discriminate touches to react verbally, to escape and to tell if inap-propriately touched. Rehearsal of responses to stories of potentially dangerous situations used to enhance

generalization. Movement through the programme dependent upon group mastery of each skill.

BST and feeling groups differed in definition of inappropriate touch. BST children taught that 'it is not OK for a bigger person to touch or look at my private parts' (except for health/hygiene reasons). Feelings group taught that some touches make you feel good, others make you feel bad, others are con-fusing. Rule taught: 'If a touch makes me feel bad or confused, then it's not OK'.

(3) Control group: instructor taught children vari-ous safety skills related to fire prevention, crossing the street, playground safety, etc.

Design: Repeated measures (pre-test, post-test, and one month follow up) experimental design with random allocation to 2 treatment and 1 control group.

Measures: (1) 'What if' Situations Test – III (WIST III): questions on appropriateness and child's response to 6 vignettes of adult requesting to touch private parts. (2) Personal Safety Questionnaire (PSQ): 8 questions on knowledge of sexual abuse and personal safety (post-test only). (3) Fear Assessment Thermometer Scale (FATS): rating scale of fear of objects, people, and situations. (4) Program Enjoyment Rating Scale. (5) Parent's Perceptions Questionnaire (PPQ): par-ents rating of their children's fear of FATS items. (6) Teacher's Perceptions Questionnaire (TPQ); check-list of positive and negative reactions of the child to the training.

Results: (1) WIST III appropriateness of touches: No pretest differences. At post test BST sample signifi-cantly more likely than controls to correctly identify inappropriate requests. The Feelings sample were significantly more likely than controls to consider as inappropriate the appropriate requests that made them feel bad. (This effect was the only effect maintained at follow up). The Feelings sample were significantly more likely than the BST sample to consider as appropriate the inappropriate requests that made them feel good. (2) WIST III prevention skills: significant increase in skills in both BST and Feelings groups at post test, but only maintained for BST group at follow up. (3) PSQ: significantly higher scores compared to controls for both BST and Feelings Groups. (4) Programme enjoyment: All groups indicated high levels of enjoyment. (5) FATS: No significant main or interaction effects between groups. (6) PPQ: Only 50% of question-naires returned. No significant differences between groups in reports of other personal self educational opportunities nor in children's fear levels to the three interventions. There was poor correspondence between the PPQ and FATS with parents often underestimating their children's fears. Significantly more parents rated the BST as producing 'a good effect overall' compared to the Feelings group.

(7) TPQ: Pretest sex differences. No significant main effects between groups or over time.

Wurtele (1990)

TEACHING PERSONAL SAFETY SKILLS TO FOUR YEAR OLD CHILDREN. A BEHAVIORAL APPROACH

Sample: 24 children (17 boys, 7 girls), 92% White, mean age of 4.2 years, attending a YMCA school in Colorado. All came from two parent families with modal income between $30,000–$40,000.

Focus: Primary prevention of child sexual abuse.

Objectives: To teach pre-school children from low socio-economic backgrounds knowledge and skills to make them more able to protect themselves from the risk of sexual abuse.

Programme: (1) Behavioural Skills Training Program (BST) – see Wurtele, 1992, for description. (2) Attention Control Program in which children taught safety skills related to fire, roads, playgrounds, etc, but not sexual abuse.

Design: Repeated measures (pre, post, and one month follow up) experimental design with random allocation to one experimental and one control condition.

Measures: 'What If' Situations Test (WIST); Personal Safety Questionnaire (PSQ); Child rating of program enjoyment and whether they liked their private parts (post-test only); Teacher's Perception Questionnaire (TPQ); Parent's Perception Questionnaire (PPQ) (post-test only). See Wurtele, 1992, for description of measures.

Results: (1) No pre-test between group differences found. (2) Significant Group X Time effect on PSQ and WIST indicated by repeated measures MANOVA. Univariate analysis indicated significant increase for BST group in correctly identifying inappropriate requests and skills in telling and reporting (but the children still had difficulty with these skills and did not retain them well over time). (3) No differences in children's liking of programme or of their private parts. (4) No group differences in teachers questionnaire, but a Time effect for child assertiveness. (5) Parents ratings showed no between group differences in behaviour or fears. Significantly more BST than controls had discussed training with parents. No parents reported bad effects of programme and 74% reported good effects. All would agree to repeat of similar programme in future.

Notes: Author discusses the vulnerability of control groups who had difficulty in identifying inappropriate adult requests.

Wurtele et al (1991)

THE EFFICACY OF PARENT-IMPLEMENTED PROGRAM FOR TEACHING PRESCHOOLERS PERSONAL SAFETY

Sample: 52 children (29 boys, 23 girls), 94% White, mean age of younger group (3.5–4.5 years) 49.3 months, of older group (4.5–5.5 years) 59.5 months. Over 95% families had annual income over $20,000. 37% mothers and 42% fathers had 4 year college degree. Children were attending a YMCA school in Colorado. Sample were the 89% of parents approached who agreed to participate minus 7 children who did not complete the programme.

Focus: Primary prevention of child sexual abuse.

Objectives: To teach pre-school children knowledge and skills to make them more able to protect themselves from the risk of sexual abuse.

Programme: (1) Behavioral Skills Training Program (BST) implemented by parents in the home – see Wurtele, 1992, for description. (2) Wait list controls.

Design: Repeated measures (pre, post, and one month follow up) experimental design with random allocation to one experimental and one wait list control condition.

Measures: 'What If' Situations Test (WIST); Personal Safety Questionnnaire (PSQ); Child rating of program enjoyment and whether they liked their private parts (post-test only); Parent's Perception Questionnaire (PPQ) (post-test only). See Wurtele, 1992, for description of measures.

Results: (1) MANOVA on pre-test scores only found effect for age. (2) Significant Group X Time effect on PSQ and WIST indicated by repeated measures MANOVA. Univariate analysis indicated significant increase for treatment group in correctly identifying inappropriate requests and in all four skills of Say, Do, Tell and Report. (3) 94% of children reported liking the programme. No between group differences in this or in their liking of their private parts. (4) No loss of knowledge and skills at follow up. Younger children scored better at 2 month follow up, older children scored better at 1 month follow up. (5) Parents ratings showed no between group differences in behaviour or fears. 78% of parents had previously discussed the dangers of sexual abuse with their children. No parents reported bad effects of programme. 86% reported good effects. 99% would agree to the use of a similar programme in the future.

Notes: Authors discuss the concepts children had most difficulty learning: what to report when telling someone of abuse and who might be a perpetrator.

Despite these difficulties the authors conclude that children as young as 3.5 years can be successfully taught important prevention concepts and behaviours in the home.

Wurtele et al (1992)

A COMPARISON OF TEACHER VS PARENTS AS INSTRUCTORS OF A PERSONAL SAFETY PROGRAM FOR PRESCHOOLERS.

Sample: 61 children (33 boys, 28 girls) with a mean age of 57 months attending a Head Start preschool in Colorado. 46% were White, 31% Hispanic, 16% Black, 2% Asian, 2% Native American, 2% other. Families were two parent, 56%; single mothers, 33%; or other such as headed by grandparent, 11%. Income levels were below $10,000 for 56%, below $30,000 for remainder. 97% of parents approached consented to participate.

Focus: Primary prevention of child sexual abuse.

Objectives: To teach pre-school children from low socio-economic backgrounds knowledge and skills to make them more able to protect themselves from the risk of sexual abuse.

Programme: (1) Behavioural Skills Training Program (BST) taught by teachers in small groups (4 to 7 children) for 30 minutes per day for 3 days. Children taught that they are bosses of their own bodies; to locate own private parts, that appropriate for parents and health professionals to touch their private parts for health or hygiene reasons; not appropriate for others to touch private parts (especially if it is meant to be a secret) or be forced to touch those of an other, that it is never the child's fault if these things occur. Programme included stories of both appropriate and potentially dangerous situations and children practiced discrimination between the two. Also taught verbal and motor responses to inappropriate situations by modelling, rehearsal, praise, and feedback.

(2) BST taught by parents. Parents version included a Token Time packet with 29 programme objectives to be marked off as completed for positive reinforcement for child and for parent to track progress. Students acted as caseworkers to advise, support, and monitor parental progress. Parents took average total of 88 minutes to complete programme.

(3) Control group of teacher instruction on safety skills such as fire prevention, pedestrian safety, safety about poisons.

Design: Repeated measures (pre and post-test and follow up) experimental design with random allocation to two experimental and one control condition.

Measures: (1) 'What if' Situations Test (WIST) of 6 brief vignettes of appropriate and inappropriate requests to test ability to discriminate and make appropriate responses. (2) The Personal Safety Questionnaire (PSQ) of 11 questions on knowledge of sexual abuse. (3) Programme enjoyment and attitude toward their private parts rated by children pointing to pictures of smiling and frowning faces. (4) Parent Perception Questionnaire (PPQ) at post-test to rate how fearful their children were in 9 situations. Also parents' rating of global effect of programme and whether they would allow child to participate again in similar programme. (5) Teacher Perception Questionnaire (TPQ) on reactions of child of training, at post-test only.

Results: (1) MANOVA on pre-test scores revealed no main or interaction effects on between group differences. (2) Children in both experimental groups performed significantly better than controls on all 3 child measures at post-test and follow up. At follow up only, parent trained children scored significantly better than controls on specific skill of reporting abuse. (3) Children indicated that they liked the programme and liked their private parts and no between group differences found. 4 children disclosed abuse: 3 on-going, 1 in past. (4) Teacher ratings showed no between group differences. (5) Only 43% of parental questionnaires returned. No significant differences in fears or problem behaviours, but parent group children as more likely to cry easily than controls, and teacher group more likely to make physical complaints than other groups. 67% of parents rated the programme as having a good effect and would agree to repeat of similar in future.

Notes: Authors argue that results show that low SES preschool children can be taught sexual abuse safety skills and that this can be accomplished by parents, who were interested and willing to do this, though the support, advice, and monitoring by the students may have been crucial. Authors discuss the problem that despite the improvement on group scores, some trained children were not scoring highly. Also parent training may not be appropriate for some families, particularly abusing or otherwise dysfunctional families.

CHAPTER THREE

Educating Adults and the Community

Background

This chapter considers educational approaches for the prevention of abuse aimed at parents and families, neighbourhoods and communities, and society at large. As in the previous chapter, the emphasis is on primary prevention. Interventions more specifically aimed at groups considered to be at risk of abusing their children, are described in Chapters 4 to 6. Educational approaches to identified cases are discussed in the first section of Chapter Eight.

The education of parents and the community could be achieved indirectly through the use of educational interventions aimed at children; either through the direct involvement of adults, or from the general shift in society's awareness and priorities that the programmes for children reflect and reinforce. Many child focused programmes explicitly use materials to serve the twofold function of educating the adults and helping them, as parents and teachers, to educate the children (for example, Elliott, 1986). The importance of these materials is emphasized by Finkelhor (1986), who cites evidence that without the structure provided by such materials, parents often fail to discuss sexuality, personal rights and safety with their children, and tend instead to focus on the physical risks of being approached by dangerous strangers. Thus, educational materials used in programmes, aimed at children, may enable adults to overcome the embarrassment of discussing these issues and provide them with techniques and information to aid these discussions. The 'Kids on the Block' series is a good example of this, as the puppets portray individual characters, whose plight can be discussed with parents and teachers.

The discussion of educational measures for children in Chapter 2 referred to the narrow focus of these programmes: the prevention of child sexual abuse only, rather than a consideration of other types of abuse, of wider knowledge and skills, or of the social context in which abuse occurs. Educational approaches could take a more open brief and be concerned with all aspects of abuse, child care practice, and parental responsibility in both individual and social terms.

This chapter is concerned with programmes more directly focused on adults and the community. It does not include reference to all parent education programmes (see, for example, Dangel and Polster, 1984; Hodgkinson, 1991), but only those with a more overt reference to child abuse. The potential aims of the programmes for parents and communities discussed in this chapter include:

Parents:

1. To encourage parents to recognise their own problems and to seek advice and support before situations deteriorate and become self compounding.
2. To increase parents' understanding of the realities of child abuse (particularly child sexual abuse) so that they are better able to protect their own children.

Adults generally:

3. To increase adults' awareness of the incidence of child abuse so that they are better able to support those at risk of becoming either perpetrator or victim, as well as better able to identify and involve statutory agencies if abuse occurs or is likely to occur. Increased sensitivity to abuse means: (i) awareness of one's

own inability to cope and potential for abuse; (ii) greater receptivity to children seeking help.

Professionals:

4.   To increase professionals' knowledge of: (i) the existence of abuse and its complex nature, (ii) issues of child protection, (iii) the responsibilities to act to protect children, and (iv) to liaise with the relevant other agencies. Educational programmes directed at children often involve the assistance of professionals who may not be familiar with the problems of child abuse. In some cases the educational interventions can lead to the identification of specific cases of abuse.

5.   To promote specific approaches to child protection work such as to be locally community based to encourage: (i) good inter-professional collaboration, (ii) a joint collaborative approach with members of the community; (iii) the use of supportive interventions to families in contrast to interventions deemed punitive such as legal sanctions or mandatory reporting.

The Community:

6.   To increase the importance given to: (i) child abuse issues in the community, (ii) to the community's responsibility for child abuse and child protection, and (iii) the accountability of child protection agencies to the local community.

7.   To promote the needs and rights of: (i) children, (ii) of parents, or of (iii) traditional family values.

Educational programmes vary in the extent that they focus on these different aims. Many of the programmes aimed at parents tend to be directed at 'at risk' groups and are therefore secondary prevention measures (considered in later chapters). Other programmes may be aimed at increasing general awareness of child abuse issues to adults in the community or may be directed to specific aspects of parent training (Perkins, 1980; Dowling, 1983; Dangel & Polster, 1984) or forms of interaction such as in developing non violent relationships (New South Wales, 1984). Alternatively programmes may develop from child protection agencies wishing to develop public and professional attitudes and collaboration (teaching programmes directed only at professionals, such as McGrath et al, 1987, are not considered in this review).

Sometimes the agencies are wishing to develop the concept of child protection in the community so that it becomes child protection as community action. This may arise from a range of different ideological viewpoints concerning the care of children and the appropriate aims and methods of welfare services. Some programmes, for example, are targeted at promoting inter-professional relationships and team cohesion at the local level with good communication and education in the local community (Morreale, 1986) and accountability to that community (Tipton, 1986). Others consider child abuse to be a product of negative societal factors, and so argue for the relief of isolation and stress in the community (Spokes and Digby, 1986). The aim of this strategy is to assist parents to cope in contrast to child protection responses that are considered by some to be over negative and unhelpful (Crow, 1985; Spokes and Digby, 1986). These approaches relate to wider ideological debates about the need for legal powers in child protection cases with some workers arguing that the use of courts or the police is punitive and destructive and prevents parents coming forward for help (Wolff, 1990; Marneffe, 1991). This leads on to wider issues about the relevant role and responsibilities of professional workers. In the absence of democratically established legal measures the workers could be servants of the local community or could take on themselves a policing role of adjudicating between appropriate and inappropriate parenting (see Hardiker et al, 1991, for discussion of ideologies of welfare).

Research Studies

Although the education of adults is discussed in the child focused research literature, there are very few research studies of adult or community education programmes. The majority of studies identified for this review (listed in Table 3.1), were part of a series of 11 demonstration projects funded by National Committee for Child Abuse and Neglect (NCCAN) and published by National Committee for the Prevention of Child Abuse (NCPCA) in Chicago (Gray et al, 1983) and aimed at developing initiatives for rural and minority populations in the United States. Another study is concerned with a similar initiative in a village in the Philippines (Del Castillo, 1985). Only one study examined the impact of a community approach in an economically prosperous area with well developed child protection services (Crow, 1985).

The study by Crow (1985) contrasted the child protection services in an area of Melbourne that had developed a community response to child maltreatment with

TABLE 3.1

Research Studies on Educating Adults and the Community

Study	Programme Aims	Sample	Design	Main Measures
Crow 1985	Local responsibilities	Two areas of Melbourne	Descriptive	Participation, coordination, flexibility of services
Del Castillo (1985)	Community awareness	500 families in Filipino village	POST	Rates of abuse
Gray E. et al (1983)				
1. Blackfeet project	Community awareness	6,700 residents of Indian reservations	POST	Co-ordination of services, awareness of child abuse issues
2. Television mini series	Knowledge & attitudes of child rearing	102 high risk cases in Chicago	POST + C	Parenting inventory, impact of film
3. Mexican-American	Parent education	70 young low income	RPM + C	Child care knowledge and attitudes
4. Education, Information, & Referral	Local knowledge & systems for child protection	4 counties in N.W. Washington	RPM	Rates of abuse
5. Inter Act Street Theatre	Preventive education	'Hard to reach' parents	RPM	Child rearing attitudes, anger control
6. Pan Asian Project	Preventive education,	224 oriental women, cross cultural attitudes San Diego	RPM	Child rearing attitudes
7. Project Network	Community awareness and prevention	800 of low SES, Atlanta	POST	Awareness of child abuse issues

Design
POST = post-test only; RPM = Repeated Measures including pre-test; PRPM = Repeated Measures post-test only;
+ C = Control or comparison groups; + PC = Control or comparison group but at post-test only

a matched area without such an initiative. The findings showed that workers in the initiative areas had greater knowledge of child protection issues including methods of response and of services and resources available. In addition, workers in these areas had closer links with other services and were more likely to make use of the community in responding to child maltreatment. The effect of the community response was therefore on both knowledge of child protection and in the practice of its implementation, though the latter was probably a reflection of the ideology of those workers who chose to take a community approach.

The other studies on special initiatives were all based in rural and underdeveloped areas. They were also concerned with raising the level of awareness of child abuse within professional services, but were starting from a lower baseline in more socially disadvantaged areas. The aim was not merely to educate members of the public, so that they could better use the resources of local agencies, but also to help develop these agencies and bring the service providers and their potential clients closer together. In doing this, the projects were sometimes involved in identifying and providing education or even a direct service for 'at risk' groups.

The techniques used by the projects varied considerably. Several used dramatic presentations. The 'Inter-Act Street Theatre for Parents' involved the performance of a number of theatrical 'skits' by actors in various settings (Gray et al, 1983). Drama was used to show in an entertaining and non-threatening manner, skills and positive attitudes in child care and control. The impact of the drama was followed up with an information pack that summarised the messages in the performance and included crisis telephone numbers.

Community settings were here used to provide, otherwise hard-to-reach parents, with information and practical advice for coping with stress. The aim was to provide alternatives to potentially dysfunctional behaviour, by modelling anger control, stress control and child control skills. The purpose was also to increase parents' self-help abilities by developing the concept of natural support and assertiveness and by offering realistic expectations in child care. The achievement of all these objectives was assessed by asking a proportion of the audience at the performances to complete both pre and post-test attitude questionnaires.

The study found significantly more appropriate responses in the post-test for all groups on at least some attitude questions. Between three and four thousand people were tested from broadly defined social groups: professional, general public and 'high risk' (those in poor housing schemes, social work clients, etc). The greatest degree of improvement was observed in the 'general public' groups, but little detail was given about how responses between groups varied to specific attitude questions.

A second demonstration project using drama was 'Close to Home: A Television Mini Series for Parents' (Gray et al, 1983). Three half-hour television films about real-life situations were shown to 102 low income 'high risk' subjects. The aim was to change ideas and feelings about child rearing. The films covered coping as a single parent, the stress of life changes and the problems of parental expectations of children and their behaviour.

The stated objectives of the films were to prevent child abuse before it occurred, to provide knowledge and skills for parents, to develop adult education materials and programmes, and to develop the potential of television as a preventive tool. Assessment of the programmes was by a post-test questionnaire and group discussion. The lack of any pre-test made it possible only to contrast the reactions to the three films. The film on parental expectations gave the most direct message and so an acceptance of this message was easiest to measure. The more diffuse messages of the other films made it difficult to assess, whether or not, the respondents views had been directly influenced. Probably the strongest evidence of affect, was that some subjects were emotionally upset by watching the films.

Most of the projects did not rely on presentations to large open meetings, but instead, recruited parents into groups for discussion and teaching. A particularly interesting project with an emphasis on a non-directive approach was the 'Pan Asian Parent Education Project' (Gray et al, 1983). Groups of parents from Vietnamese, Samoan, Japanese, and Filipino backgrounds were actively recruited in San Diego County, California, through local publicity and community workers. A total of 224 participants were recruited into 25 parent groups and a subset of 6 of these groups was formally evaluated in the assessment.

The programme consisted of small group discussions, led and facilitated by community workers, who came from the same ethnic background as the parents, and who were specially trained for the purposes of the project, in child development, crisis intervention, parenting skills, adolescence, nutrition and group dynamics. The groups met for five to twelve weeks. The educational content centred upon exploring the similarities or differences in child rearing and socialisation between the mainstream and ethnic minority cultures. During the second half of the groups' existence the emphasis changed to examining the appropriateness and acceptability of different child rearing practices and coping skills.

The stated objectives of these programmes were: to provide a preventive service by reducing isolation and increasing self esteem, to develop referral processes for solving environmental problems, and to explore the values and attitudes of child care practice and possible alternative models. The aim was also to develop a guide for use by other groups and agencies in the future and to train bilingual agency workers in prevention.

Due to various practical difficulties the researchers pre and post-tested less than one quarter of participants and it was not possible to undertake relevant statistical tests on the data. The results did, however, show an improvement in the knowledge of the tested groups of Vietnamese and Filipino on child development and United States Law, although there was less change in their views about child rearing. In the Samoan groups there was little learning on other issues, but some softening of their attitudes about child rearing. The participants and the trained leaders of all the groups, gave a high rating to their personal experience of the sessions.

Several projects took a more direct educational approach. The 'Comprehensive Programme for Young Mexican American Families' (Gray et al, 1983) provided an intensive programme of preventive intervention with three main components. The first involved classes on topics such as child care and development, nutrition and birth control. The second involved home visits to check and monitor progress of parent-child interaction. The workers gave immediate feedback to the parents, and also drew on these observed interactions as a basis for later class discussion. The third component was a child care centre that encouraged creative play and child care practice.

The goals of these interventions were only stated in the broadest of terms but the outcomes were assessed using a repeated measures controlled design. The control and experiment groups (total n = 67) were pre and post-tested on knowledge, attitudes and practices in child care. An analysis of co-variance indicated a significant experimental effect. These results are encouraging, but the report gave little detail of the actual interventions, or of the problems being experienced by the families in the sample, or the ways in which they were helped by the programme. Although the programme affected parents' responses to a questionnaire it is not clear how this relates to the parents' ability to provide for their children.

Another multi-component project that included education of targeted groups was 'Project Network: Child Abuse Prevention in Inner City Atlanta' (Gray et al, 1983). The programme consisted of education workshops, parenting skills groups, supportive counselling for those at risk of referral for child abuse, and an informal consultation and advocacy service for clients and service providers. The target population was a deprived inner city black population of about 7,000 people.

The broad purpose of the project was to increase community awareness of child abuse and to strengthen families to reduce its occurrence. The underlying theory was that child abuse was multicausal and so should be tackled at various levels. The project started with a didactic emphasis, but as it progressed, it became more inter-active, and moved away from a professional model to encouraging self-help and the use of volunteers.

Although the project is presented as primarily educational, the outcome as measured by the self-reports of members of the community and the service providers is seen very much in terms of the effect on the workings of the social welfare system. Families were seen as making better use of external resources and workers felt that the project filled a gap in service provision particularly in acting as a link between the welfare system and families. Those welfare workers who had directly used the services were particularly positive in their responses. Administrators and others felt that the project had been successful in increasing community awareness. No hard evidence was given to support this view, although the community education sessions were rated positively by attenders.

It can be seen that multicomponent interventions, which aim at increasing community awareness of child abuse issues, may sometimes offer more direct education or support for targeted groups. In addition, they may develop contacts between service providers and clients and so develop the social welfare system. This approach is particularly evident in the final three studies reviewed. The first, 'Primary Prevention Partnership: Education, Information and Referral in Northwestern Washington' (Gray et al, 1983) was a project with three main components of intervention. The first component was the education of the public at large, of 'at risk' groups, and of service providers, through meetings, media presentations, distribution of written materials, and training classes or workshops. Secondly, task forces were established to promote information and referrals to prevention and treatment programmes. Thirdly, moves were made to institutionalise the new information and referral systems, in order that the various community organisations would continued beyond the life of the project. These three components of the intervention were designed to achieve the three major goals of increasing awareness of child abuse as a symptom of stress, increasing the accessibility of community resources, and ensuring continuity through the promotion of community ownership of the new developments.

The impact of the programme was assessed in various ways. Firstly, the reporting rates of child abuse were monitored. An increase in reports following closely upon the implementation of the project, was at least partly attributed to the programme. Secondly, interviews were held with workshop participants, who were on the whole, very satisfied with the programme. The third measure was the impact on community awareness as assessed by interviewing representatives of major social services. These workers found that there had been a positive impact, except in one geographical area, where there had been difficulties in implementing the project. Similar results were obtained for the perceived usefulness of the different information and retrieval systems that had been set up. The 25 service activities, which the programmes had helped to create and support, were also seen as an important measure of success. The evaluators believed that the project acted as a catalyst in helping the community to develop a more aware, responsive and cohesive system.

The 'Blackfeet Child Abuse Prevention Project' (Gray et al, 1983) was planned as a two year demonstration project to improve community awareness and service provision on an American Indian reservation with approximately 7,000 residents. The intervention included educational presentations to service providers, outreach activities such as home visits and educational picnics involving over 2,000 people, and leaflets for the whole population. The interventions aimed more directly at service development, included the compilation of a resource directory (but not distributed), a manual to assist workers in dealing with telephone inquiries, and membership of various service committees, in order to develop service organisation and delivery.

The evaluators felt that repeated measures of impact on community members would be intrusive and contrary to the aims of the project. The evaluation therefore depended upon interviews with selected service providers at the end of the programme. The interviewees believed that there had been an improvement in both community awareness of child abuse and service delivery, but most of them did not consider the project responsible for these improvements. Many were even unaware of the outreach aspects of the project. These results could represent either a failure of the project or a lack of contact between service providers and their community. The issues are difficult to address when there is so little pre-specification of the project's aims and no independent outcome measure to allow a priori hypotheses to be tested.

The 'Neighborhood Protective Strategy for Children with Special Reference to the Philippines' (Del Castillo, 1985) was an intense public education programme with talks, broadcasts and widely distributed leaflets in a Filipino village. The project also involved the training of volunteers in the management of identified cases of child abuse. Volunteers were considered useful, because they were less likely to be seen as part of 'the authorities' by the families, and because they filled gaps in an underdeveloped structure of local welfare services. Each volunteer worked in a small patch in order to foster a community orientated response to the problem.

There was no formal research design to assess the outcome of this project but there were some indicators of success, mainly the identification of 77 cases of abuse in a population of 500 families. These were seemingly cases of a relatively mild nature, but the volunteers' response provided a supportive outreach service. The author reports that there was no recidivism, but the meaning of this term is not defined and no figures are given for the number of cases identified and managed prior to the project.

Discussion

The adult and community projects demonstrate a variety of techniques for achieving different though related aims. Frequently, one intervention had several aims and thus several components.

The most general aim was to make the whole community more aware of child abuse. This component included various educational approaches to highlight the issues for parents and to demonstrate how to overcome potential problems. The Pan Asian Parent Education Project took a broader approach in also examining cross cultural attitudes to child care. The projects were able to offer various techniques for improving community awareness but could not clearly show them to be effective. This is not surprising, considering the difficulties in specifying the aims of broadly based projects in sufficient detail, to allow appropriate outcome measures to be employed.

There are also difficulties concerning the practical relevance of measures of awareness of child abuse issues. Respondents can be tested to see if the messages of the intervention, have been sufficiently well received and understood, to be reported back in questionnaires and open ended interviews, but we do not know if this indicates real changes in behaviour towards children.

In addition to not having appropriate and well specified measures of outcome, the studies did not use sufficiently focused research designs to allow any experimental effect on awareness to be clearly demonstrated.

The second aim of these projects was the more targeted training of specific individuals in the community. This component could have been more easily assessed by using standard experimental designs and highly focused outcome measures, but few of the studies exploited this possibility to the full. However, the evaluations still provided some of the most convincing results of change. One project, the 'Comprehensive Program for Young Mexican-American Families' used an experimental design and recorded significant improvements in the parents' knowledge and attitudes in child care following the intervention.

A third aim, of at least some of the projects, was the development of local services and their links with community organisations and with potential clients. Although there was a concern to identify cases of abuse, the emphasis was on increasing the community's involvement with existing or newly formed services. The philosophy was of rejecting or at least limiting the control aspects of child protection intervention. The project personnel did not see their role as policing neighbourhoods to identify 'the child abusers'.

It is again difficult to evaluate the success of these programmes. Crow (1985) assessed the knowledge of workers and the extent that they professed to have close relationships with other services and to involve the community in child protection cases. Most of the other studies used the perceptions of parents and service providers as an outcome measure. Although these are reasonable indications of some aspects of the impact made by projects, direct measures of behavioural change could have offered more convincing evidence of changes in practice.

One such measure, used for several projects, was the number of new cases referred in a specified period. Although changes in the local situation were probably caused by the intervention of the projects, child abuse referral rates are an extremely difficult statistic to interpret. Referrals are often only retrospectively defined as being child abuse cases. They are thus the product of a series of unknown agency processes, rather than a true reflection of the number of real referrals. Both increases and decreases in referrals can be interpreted as evidence that an intervention has been successful. An increased rate does, however, at least show an increase in service activity, whether or not this activity is appropriate.

Research Issues

The studies reviewed were virtually all very positive about the projects. On the one hand this is encouraging, on the other hand the presence of so few negative and critical findings does not help policy makers who are trying to decide on the most useful strategies to adopt. The only report that contained serious, critical comments, concerned the 'Blackfeet Child Abuse Prevention Project' (Gray et al, 1983). Here problems were described regarding the management and the focus of the project. In most other studies the evaluators seemed to be acting as advocates for the projects. Weak and uncritical assessments are a particular problem with multicomponent interventions, as they do not help to isolate the most useful and beneficial components.

The studies can therefore suggest options but can not distinguish between the relative merits of particular strategies except in a few particular cases. (For example, clear lessons can be learned from the Partnership Project in Washington State (Gray et al, 1983) which had problems in developing a programme in a county where well established services were already, to some degree, in competition with each other).

The studies reviewed vary between narrow programmes of parent training and support, wider programmes aimed at community awareness and the integration of services and approaches advocating the ideology of child protection being anchored in and accountable to local communities. Future research on the more narrowly focused programmes might be better directed to the assessment of the skills needed to prevent abuse, and acquired by the individual as a result of intervention. Or these skills could be assessed on a wider community basis. At present the studies fail to meet the necessary criteria to evaluate either of these approaches. They have a diffuseness and breadth of purpose which does not lead to a focused assessment. Research on programmes with broader aims of community participation and accountability are more likely to use active research methods to demonstrate and to develop the viability of this approach. Such studies could, however, also benefit from adopting dependent variables that provide objective criteria of these potential effects of the programmes.

New studies could use an assortment of methods to achieve their aims. As there is little research evidence in the child abuse literature to support particular methods, it would be preferable to draw on other topic areas in the existing literature on community education and service development. This should be done for each of the potential aims of educational/developmental strategies listed at the beginning of the chapter. This strategy would introduce a wealth of knowledge that could be applied to child abuse and child protection though there may of course be some particular aspects of child abuse that need to be taken into account. The task is to attempt to examine carefully what these differences might be, rather than to initiate research on child abuse, that would operate in a relative vacuum and confound different levels of evaluation. Practice would be better informed from being located in an already developed research field. Furthermore, the restriction to a narrow focus of the interventions, would be more likely to lead research to develop specific aims and preferred outcomes, that could be more easily measured and assessed.

The need for more research may be evident, but this is complicated by the ideological differences between different approaches to community and service development. Without research, however, it is not possible to disentangle the empirical and ideological issues which is necessary for rational service planning.

The need for research is not only in assessing the efficacy of preventive educational programmes. There is also a need to survey the current knowledge, skills, and attitudes in society. There are remarkably few studies of the range of parenting methods in society (Newson and Newson, 1976; Straus and Gelles, 1986), or understanding of the concept of abuse (Giovannoni and Beccera, 1979; Stainton Rogers and Stainton Rogers, 1989; Davenport, Browne, and Palmer, submitted). The National Committee for the Prevention of Child Abuse (NCPA) in Chicago have undertaken annual surveys to assess broad changes in public behaviour and knowledge related to child abuse (Daro, 1991). Over the five years from 1986 to 1991, the number of respondents who consider that physical punishment of children never harm children has fallen from 24% to 18%. Concern over physical punishment was particularly high amongst young, Black, non high school graduate respondents. The response to questions about actual discipline practices showed a 11% decrease in the use of yelling and swearing at children and a 12% decrease in the use of spanking. Spanking was most common amongst Blacks, those with moderate to low incomes, and respondents living in the South of the United States. More serious forms of physical punishment were found among older respondents and those with incomes of below $15,000 or above $50,000. Fewer parents with high incomes reported using physical punishment, but those who did seemed to use the more serious forms.

The NCPA survey of 1991 included additional questions on the causes of maltreatment. The most frequently reported causes were violence between husbands and wives and poverty, reported by 58% and 45% of respondents respectively. Older respondents more often reported concern with violence in the media, toy guns, and poverty. Minorities, particularly Blacks, were concerned with these issues plus racism and contact sports. Younger respondents more often reported concern with teachers hitting students, parents hitting children, the use of the death penalty, and racism. Women were concerned with both intra familial violence and violence in the media. Low income families with less formal education more often stated concern over teachers hitting children, the use of the death penalty, media violence, toy games, and sexism. Higher income families with more formal education gave greater emphasis to spouse abuse, racism, and poverty.

The final issue examined by the NCPA survey was the belief that people had in their ability to prevent child abuse. Since 1987 there has been a steady slow decline in people's belief that they could have a moderate or large effect on prevention. Young adults, Blacks and Hispanics, those living in the West of the United States, and respondents with a low income were the most optimistic. Despite the general decrease in optimism over time there has been a slight increase in those reporting that they had taken some personal action to prevent child abuse with a third of parents and a quarter of other adults reporting taking such actions in the preceding year.

Practice Issues

The majority of the projects reviewed, were part of a programme funded by the Federal Government in the United States. There are many other programmes directed at developing community services, but relatively few of these are aimed at community awareness and education, nor have many been formally evaluated.

The National Committee for the Prevention of Child Abuse and Neglect produces a variety of prevention materials. These include booklets to arm professionals with advice about prevention projects and about public awareness. There are also materials for the general public, such as the car bumper sticker and the slogan 'Take time out – Don't take it out on your kid', a message displayed and carried throughout North America. They also use television commercials containing the same message. The commercials show common examples of when parents might react to stress by over-chastising a child. A similar approach is used with children such as the distribution of many million copies of Spiderman comics on sexual, physical and verbal abuse.

Australia also has many examples of attempts to increase public knowledge and awareness. Both the Queensland Centre for Prevention of Child Abuse in Brisbane and the Children's Interest Bureau in Adelaide provide information and resource materials aimed at children, families and professionals. These include brightly coloured fact sheets with straightforward explanations about child abuse and sources of further information about the different types of abuse and about personal safety programmes.

In Britain there is little adult and community education in child abuse. There may be local projects exploring these issues, and courses are offered by the Open University and local adult education institutes, but until very recently, most public information on child abuse was provided by mass media reports on specific cases, when children have suffered at the hands of their parents or from state intervention in their lives.

The way in which cases receiving media coverage are presented to the public usually fall into three main categories of: (i) depraved or evil parents whose children are left unprotected by incompetent and naive professionals, (ii) 'good' parents persecuted by professionals with dubious expertise and motives who attempt to remove their children and break up their families, (iii) multiple abuse of children in institutions run by agencies with a remit to care and protect children. There are several common features of the cases. Firstly they are often unusual cases and therefore not necessarily representative of routine cases seen by agencies. Each new case in the media is often more extreme than the last and so feed the moral panics (Parton, 1985) and the stereotyping of issues that surround child abuse. The new more extreme cases confirm the stereotypes of the breakdown of family values, or the panic from the evil of some new form of abuse, whether this be baby battering or satanic sexual abuse. There are also serious criticisms of the agencies involved on the basis that they were unnecessarily over protective or neglectfully under protective in their efforts to protect the child.

A problem with the media coverage of these cases is their tendency to simplify and polarise issues and misrepresent routine child protection and so do not educate the public about the dilemmas of child protection. On the other hand, it is probably these dilemmas that fuel the media interests. The cases that receive coverage become a focus for the political struggle about the respective roles of family and state in social regulation and protection of children (Dingwall, 1992). When the cases involve sexual rights and roles then the political tension is heightened further. Over the past few years, the increased concern about child sexual abuse, has led to a broader discussion of the social issues involved in these cases in the media. In particular, television programmes such as 'Childwatch' have promoted discussion on the adequacy of the current legal and agency responses to child abuse cases. Also many radio phone in programmes and magazine articles have allowed a wide range of people to discuss their views and experience of child abuse.

Voluntary organisations, have also recently become more active in the area of child abuse. The National Society for the Prevention of Cruelty to Children (NSPCC) and the Royal Scottish Society for Prevention of Cruelty to Children (RSSPCC) were created specifically to combat child abuse, but other charities, such as Barnardo's, the Children's Society and National Children's Homes, have also begun to take a more active role in these issues. All of these organisations publicise the extent of the problem of child abuse and advertise the services that they are able to offer. They have also taken an educative role in explaining the nature and problems of child abuse. The NSPCC, for example, distribute many relevant leaflets free to the public. Despite these recent developments, the main issue for development in this area is not the difficulty of deciding which public education programmes are the most appropriate or successful in the United Kingdom, but rather the lack of such programmes.

There are several different targets or aims for community education programmes which might be developed in Britain. Some of these would involve professional staff as well as ordinary members of the community. These programmes could include the following levels or foci:

- development of *knowledge* and skills in child care, problems in parenting and how these can be resolved or mitigated. Such programmes could grow out of general education in child care and human development;
- campaigns to raise *awareness* of the needs and rights of children and of the phenomena of child abuse; awareness of the roles and responsibilities of members of the public, professional staff, and government agencies;
- promotion of community involvement and *responsibility* for ensuring that children's rights are protected including the provision of physically and emotionally supportive environments; communities accepting (and sharing with agencies) responsibility for the dilemmas of child protection.
- development of *network* or links between professional staff and the public including community organisations and cultural or ethnic subgroups in order to optimise the provision of preventive services. Such development work cannot easily be separated from the other foci listed above or from the training of staff in child abuse work.

In considering such programmes, two issues must be addressed. Firstly, an important component of community awareness is the development of shared views in society, about what is appropriate childcare, which methods for supporting parents and children are acceptable, and when it is necessary to intervene with legal sanctions. Beliefs about what is harmful and necessary for children, and who holds responsibility for ensuring that these responsibilities for provision and protection are met, underpin our concepts of child abuse (Gough et al, 1987). The use of legal powers of intervention in family life is a particularly sensitive topic when there are cultural variations in child care or inequality of power within different subgroups in society. Cooperation between agencies and the community is therefore essential in areas with substantial ethnic minority populations. Cross-cultural differences of attitudes about appropriate child rearing, are likely to exacerbate tension or lack of contact between families and services in these areas. Similarly, the gender issues involved in many aspects of the power differentials in families are bound to affect the acceptability and appropriateness of different forms of intervention to different family members.

Secondly, there is an urgent need to educate a very wide range of professional staff about child abuse; not only key practitioners from social and health services, but also the many nursery staff and teachers who work with children on a daily basis. Staff training is a vital part of practice that cannot be separated from educational programmes in the community. At present, child abuse makes up a very small proportion of the training given to even those professionals, likely to be involved in direct child abuse work. It is therefore unlikely that the general staff working within education, health, social work and legal agencies will be given much significant teaching on this topic. In North America there are a substantial number of written curricula on child abuse for a wide range of disciplines. Such resources are not widespread in Britain, but the new Open University course on child abuse could meet at least some of the training needs.

Building up knowledge and skills will be the central component of any community/ professional programme, but it is also important to deal with the high levels of anxiety that exist about child abuse. The anxiety arises from the intrinsic complexity of these cases, the emotive issues that are raised, and the publicity surrounding individual cases that end unhappily. The danger is, that the anxiety can inhibit the professionals from effectively employing the skills that they have acquired in their other work, and this de-skilling can be perpetuated by training that suggests that all the answers are known by experts. The belief in such a level of expertise may imply that practice decisions can always be made that will be judged as 'correct' both prospectively and retrospectively.

One further aspect of community and professional education, is the potential for misunderstanding and conflict between professional groups, because of their different responsibilities and priorities in child care. It would be helpful if trainees in one profession learned about the perspectives on child abuse of other professionals, before they become entangled in case management involving various agencies and legal responses to family members. This is not an argument for a blurring of roles and lines of responsibility between disciplines, but rather that these distinctions be better known, understood and accepted.

Summary

1. There are few studies of adult and community education programmes in the literature. Those that do exist are concerned with targeted training for groups of adults to increase the level of education of child abuse issues in the general population, and develop local services and their integration into

the local community. Most of these studies described interventions for ethnic minorities.

2. The studies do not use focused experimental designs or sufficiently specific outcome measures to allow conclusions to be drawn about the relative efficacy of the programmes or their different components.

3. The strength of the studies is in their demonstration of a range of approaches to adult and community development, and the favourable responses of users and workers.

4. Future studies would be more profitable if located within the research literature in similar fields of adult and community education. The experience gained in these other areas could be usefully applied to child abuse education.

5. There has been little development of these programmes in Britain. This leaves public debate to media discussions of particular cases, including the problems of investigation and response to suspected child sexual abuse. The need to develop community education and involvement in child abuse and child protection is probably more pressing than the need for intervention studies to assess the effectiveness of various approaches.

6. Programmes developed in Britain could usefully focus on the large number of professional workers who have daily contact with children and their parents, but still only receive little training about child abuse.

7. New programmes in Britain could also focus on developing knowledge and skills such as in (i) general parenting and child care, (ii) awareness of the nature of child abuse and agency responsibilities in child protection.

8. Other programmes could focus on developing community involvement in child care and child protection such as in (i) the integration of local services into the community to encourage positive preventive work rather than only responses to perceived inadequate care, (ii) development of community awareness and responsibility for providing appropriate child care environments, (iii) developing community participation in local child protection policy and practice.

9. Any programmes developed in Britain will need to take account of covert as well as stated variations in beliefs about child care and the role of the family.

10. Surveys of current knowledge and attitudes in respect of child care and of child protection would provide a good starting point for further debate in community education in child abuse and protection.

Chapter Three: Research Summaries

Crow 1985

COMMUNITY RESPONSES TO CHILD MALTREATMENT

Sample: Two areas in Melbourne: one that had developed a community response to child maltreatment and a second larger area with similar demographic features.

Focus: The community in terms of primary, secondary, and tertiary prevention of child maltreatment.

Objectives: The development of a community's ability to take responsibility for the prevention, identification, and management of child maltreatment.

Programme: Philosophy that services should be locally based, be developed in conjunction with the community, be culturally relevant, be available to all residents, encourage mutual support, involve and deal honestly with clients. Development of a preventive strategy though (1) a protocol for protective services from consultation with professionals and parents in the community, and (2) community education through training for parents and professionals.

Design: Descriptive comparative study.

Measures: (1) Parents and professionals self report data from interviews on parent participation in services, flexibility of services to individual needs, whether services encourage mutual support between families, coordination and cooperation between services, attitudes towards and responses to suspected child maltreatment, other services required. (2) Documents on local services.

Results: Children's service workers in both areas concerned to help families under stress, many involve parents in the services, and are flexible to individual needs. In the area that had developed a community response the workers had a broader understanding of maltreatment, would use the community to respond to child maltreatment, and had closer links and knowledge of other services/resources. In the area that had not developed a community response more of the workers did not know how to respond to child maltreatment.

Notes: Study undertaken by the Coalition for Community Action on Child Abuse whose initial aims were to identify and publicise community based programmes, to oppose the introduction of mandatory reporting, and to increase awareness of the complex issues of child abuse. Philosophy that need to enable families and communities to protect their own children. The report contains much descriptive data.

Del Castillo (1985)

NEIGHBORHOOD PROTECTIVE STRATEGY FOR CHILDREN IN THE PHILIPPINES

Sample: 500 families in a Filipino village in which part of the population is economically depressed.

Focus: Community awareness and service provision to prevent child abuse.

Objectives: To promote community awareness of child care and possible difficulties. To improve outreach to children 'at risk'.

Programme: Intense public education, involving talks, broadcasts, and leafleting. Collection of children found in local bars. Direct intervention and referrals of identified cases of child abuse. Programme implemented through the creation of a village council for the protection of children. Volunteers were trained to scan the community and connect abused children with the relevant agencies. Training was on-going, with the emphasis on liaison between the agencies and the volunteers. Few details about counselling were available.

Design: Outcome measures only.

Measures: Few details given. Mainly the numbers of child abuse cases identified, plus the perceived usefulness of the project.

Results: 77 cases of child abuse were identified. The cases were thought to be responsive to the intervention with little recidivism, though the author is cautious about such conclusions considering the minimal follow-up. Author is more confident about effects of the project on the community, including raised consciousness about child abuse issues.

Gray E. et al (1983)

BLACKFEET CHILD ABUSE PREVENTION PROJECT

Sample: Population of 6,700 residents of an Indian reservation with widespread low income, poor housing, unemployment, physical isolation, alcohol abuse, and fragmented services. No research sub-samples.

Focus: Community awareness and service provision as primary and secondary prevention of child abuse.

Objectives: To develop community awareness and to enlist community agents to help maintain awareness and sustain prevention activities. Main emphasis on community education, networking agencies, and changing existing systems.

Programme: Presentations (×19) to service providers (n = 357). Outreach activities including presentations, home visits and community activities (n = 2000+). Pamphlets distributed to all residents and posters displayed. Resource directory compiled (but not distributed). Guidance manual for service providers. Workers participation in committees to develop local child care systems. There was a staff of 5.

Design: Post-test assessments of impact.

Measures: Interviews with social welfare agency personnel about public knowledge of child abuse issues, and about any improvement in co-ordination of services. Direct impact measures were considered to be too intrusive.

Results: Between a half and two-thirds of the 12 respondents believed that their own knowledge, community awareness, and inter-agency co-ordination had increased. However, very few attributed this to the project, even though the majority had been involved with it. Evaluator believed project to have made a substantial contribution.

Notes: There were criticisms that the project was not sufficiently well focused or managed and the programme funding was suspended after only 9 months of operation.

Gray E. et al (1983)

CLOSE TO HOME. A TELEVISION MINI SERIES FOR PARENTS

Sample: 102 low income 'high risk' subjects and service providers in Chicago and San Antonio. Research sample drawn from this population. Few details given.

Focus: Education of parents as primary prevention of child abuse.

Objectives: To provide knowledge, skills, and encourage appropriate attitudes to child rearing. To develop parent education materials and to develop television as a medium for prevention.

Methods: 3 half hour television films about real life situations designed to change ideas and feelings by helping parents to relate to the feelings of their children. The film 'High Hopes' concerns parents' high expectations of their children. 'Hard Times' explains the problems of teenage single parents. 'Changes' examines the stress of life changes. Few details given on the showing of the films.

Design: Post-test comparison between films.

Measures: Parenting Inventory (Bavolek), questionnaire, and group discussions on film content, emotional impact, effect on attitudes and if in contrast with own experiences.

Results: No differences between films on parenting inventory. The film on parental expectations had the clearest message and so a concordance with this message was easier to assess. The more diffuse nature of the other films made it more difficult to ascertain their effects on the audience. Some subjects, however, were upset by the films.

Gray E. et al (1983)

COMPREHENSIVE PROGRAM FOR YOUNG MEXICAN-AMERICAN FAMILIES

Sample: Approximately 70 Hispanic women at risk of maltreating children by virtue of low income and locality. Details on sampling population such as the association of low income with parental use of punishment. Few details on research sample. Control group recruited from a comparable neighbourhood.

Focus: Education of parents as primary prevention of child abuse.

Objectives: A parent education curriculum aimed at a low income ethnic group with the aim of enabling parents to help children to overcome problems and thereby reduce the level of child abuse in the population.

Programme: Classes involving toy making, educational demonstrations and discussion. Topics included child care and development, illness, first aid, nutrition, and birth control. Home visits to monitor parent-child interaction with monthly video filming to provide feedback. Child care centre for children's activities and for parents to improve child care practice.

Design: Repeated measures (pre and post-test) experimental design with one treatment and one control comparison group.

Measures: Questionnaire completed by parents on their knowledge of child care and development and their attitudes to touching, punishment, and social support. Parental self-report of their child care including the use of physical and emotional support.

Results: Significant post-test difference between treatment and control groups on most measures. Differences in the use of punishment were not quite significant, though in the expected direction. Data including analysis of co-variance suggests no confounding of pre-test differences or sample drop-outs, except for differences in parental age between the groups.

Gray E. et al (1983)

EDUCATION, INFORMATION AND REFERRAL IN NORTH WESTERN WASHINGTON

Sample: Catchment area of 4 counties. For the most part, sparsely populated rural areas with a third of the population in poverty sub areas, including Hispanic migrants and Indian reservations. The areas were seen as lacking in effective child protection resources.

Focus: Community and professional knowledge as primary and secondary prevention of child abuse.

Objectives: (1) To improve community and professional knowledge about child abuse, particularly as a symptom of stress; (2) to develop information and referral systems in order to increase the accessibility and use of community resources; (3) to ensure continuity of project developments.

Programme: For each objective: (1) education through public meetings, media presentations, training for pre and post-natal classes, 16 workshops or conferences for service providers, resource directories, brochures and a library; (2) task forces to promote prevention and treatment programmes; (3) task force to sponsor training and develop groups to continue beyond life of project grant. Programme had 2 principal workers who attempted to achieve change through local community advisory boards.

Design: Repeated measures with pre and post-test measures on both the service providers and the whole community.

Measures: Child abuse reporting rates, service providers' knowledge of child abuse, assessment of the co-ordination of services, interviews with service providers to assess perceived usefulness/impact of project.

Results: Large increase in reported cases of child abuse. Impact of project and increased knowledge of child abuse in 3 of the 4 counties (in the fourth county services were already available and co-existed competitively with the demonstration project for which there seemed to be some resentment). Workshop participants were very satisfied. Regional administration judged project to have improved co-ordination and referral. Directory of services was well received.

More than 25 services were aided in their formation by the project. No statistical analyses.

Gray E. et al (1983)

INTER-ACT STREET THEATRE FOR PARENTS

Sample: Approximately one-third of the 11,000 people who saw the presentation were either professionals, general public, or 'high risk' groups.

Focus: Education of parents as primary prevention of child abuse.

Objectives: Preventive education to promote attitude changes. To target 'hard to reach' parents through the use of natural settings and information that helps people to cope with stress. Aim to increase ability for self help and to provide alternatives to dysfunctional behaviour.

Programme: Presentation of "skits" by a troupe of actors in a variety of settings, at meetings, in public places such as shops, parks, housing schemes and social waiting rooms. Information packs containing messages of skits and crisis telephone numbers were distributed after the performances.

Design: Split half pre-test, post-test. Data only collected on one "skit" from each respondent. Each data item analysed separately for each "skit".

Measures: Different sets of 3 or 4 questions about attitudes, anger control, or other aspects of child rearing for each "skit".

Results: For all "skits" post-test scores were higher than the pre-test scores (from other respondents) for at least some items. Post-test differences were more often significant for the general public audiences.

Notes: Difficult to interpret the relevance of the findings reported.

Gray E. et al (1983)

PAN ASIAN PARENT EDUCATION PROJECT

Sample: Typical participants were non working Vietnamese, Samoan, Japanese or Filipino mothers. They were mainly between thirty and forty years of age with 2–3 children under ten. Approximately half were married to US servicemen, were not fluent in English and were on low incomes. The participants were actively recruited in San Diego through local publicity and the project's community aid workers. Some parents were referred by child protection services. There were 224 participants in 25 parent groups, 6 of which were formally evaluated.

Focus: Community and professional knowledge, attitudes, and agency services.

Objectives: To provide a small group preventive service, by developing awareness of cross cultural differences in values and attitudes towards child rearing, by decreasing isolation, and increasing self esteem of mothers. To develop referral processes for solving environmental needs through work with the parents and with the relevant agencies and their personnel.

Programme: Discussion of culture and experience of the parents in small groups (6–15 parents) that met for 5 to 8 weeks and which were facilitated by trained community aides from a similar background. Training of social welfare agency personnel, including information guides prepared from the parent groups.

Design: Repeated measures (pre and post-test) for 6 of the 25 groups.

Measures: Questionnaires on parents attitudes to child rearing, perceptions of differences between the values of own and dominant U.S. culture, knowledge of child development and child abuse law. Group facilitators (from more than the six evaluated groups) on participants reactions and responses to programme. No stated measures of isolation and self esteem.

Results: Participants and facilitators both rated the groups highly. Participants from most of the ethnic groups showed an improvement in knowledge of child development and child abuse law. The Samoan group showed the least change, although there was some softening in ideas about child rearing. The ethnic groups varied in the extent of their prior knowledge and learning of US mainstream practices. The Vietnamese participants, for example, showed little increase in knowledge of this, despite facilitators reporting it as a main area of change. No statistical analyses performed.

Gray E. et al (1983)

PROJECT NETWORK: CHILD ABUSE PREVENTION IN
INNER CITY ATLANTA

Sample: 800 participants recruited from a 7,000 (approx) low socio-economic status black population in inner city area of Atlanta with few social services. Some participants recruited through community surveys, some through other agencies.

Focus: Education and supports as primary prevention and to provide and/or co-ordinate services as secondary prevention of child abuse.

Objectives: To increase community awareness of child abuse and to strengthen families, to reduce risk of abuse, using methods of education, liaison between clients and agencies and direct counselling. As child abuse and neglect has multiple causes, the interventions were at a number of different levels.

Programme: Education workshops (n = 401), parenting skills groups (n =335+), direct work (n = 35) through advocacy and consultation for users and service providers, referral to appropriate resources, and supportive counselling. Also other publicity and inter-agency work.

Design: Data collected cross-sectionally from different sub-samples at various times throughout the project.

Measures: Various questionnaires and open interviews to test the awareness of various professionals about child abuse issues, the impact of project on routine services, and the ability of the families to cope with their problems.

Results: The majority of participants in parent training rated it at least as high as 'good' and 'very relevant'. In four cases of direct work (preventive counselling) examined there were improvements within the families and in their use of resources and in their relationships with key workers. Most professionals interviewed thought that the project had been of benefit to the families and to the service providers and had increased general community awareness about child abuse. Particularly useful was the linking between providers and users.

Notes: Authors discuss the problem of continuing the developmental work at the end of the project.

CHAPTER FOUR

Volunteers and Parent Aides

Background

Volunteers and para professionals such as parent-aides, as they are sometimes called in the United States, are a popular method for the prevention of all forms of family difficulties including child abuse.

Parent-aides are paid for their work, but are not usually professional staff of the health or welfare agencies. They do not require any formal qualifications and are chosen on the basis of their personal qualities and experience. They are given training before and during their involvement. Some experimental projects have used recently qualified professionals in this role. In some cases the aides and volunteers are essentially providing emotional support. In others the emphasis is on general informal helping (Ballew, 1985), on providing advice and being a mentor for the parent (Withey et al, 1980), or helping to find solutions to temporary crises (Baker et al, 1981).

Parent-aides are recruited to provide an individual and personally committed service. They are likely to have small caseloads and they do not have the statutory and bureaucratic responsibilities of social work professionals. They can thus have more direct contact time with clients. In addition, the lack of statutory control, which is inherent in much professional social work, allows the aides to have a more personal relationship with clients, however professionally they perform their tasks. Another advantage of volunteer and parent aides are their cheapness compared to fully professional workers. This is not to argue for a method of reducing the costs of welfare provision, but rather that low cost provision can be offered on a more widespread basis than intensive professional services. This has at least two distinct advantages. Firstly, there is less need for precision in identifying high risk cases requiring intervention. The service can be offered to all who might benefit and with less stigma than associated with professional services. Secondly, the low cost service can be more of a community resource with adults providing support to their fellow residents. The help provided can be within a community rather than a medical or legal model of provision. The parent-aide and volunteer services can, however, also be a resource available to professional workers (Miller and Whittaker, 1988). The way in which this is exercised will determine the extent that the community resource is offered within a community versus a medico-legal deficiency model of provision.

Research on volunteers and parent aides are particularly concerned with providing social support, so it is helpful to consider what the concept of social support includes. Gottlieb (1985) has suggested the following five categories of social support through informal help by individuals or by social networks:

a) emotional support.
b) tangible aid.
c) cognitive guidance actions that help individuals appraise their situation and the effect of the attributions that they make about it.
d) socializing and companionship.
e) milieu reliability – the belief in an individual's group or group's commitment and support in times of need, even without evidence that such support would be forthcoming. An example is the belief in the ability to call on the support of close relations whether or not much contact is maintained.

All of these five categories were evident in the intervention projects reviewed, and they provide a useful basis for examining other aspects and components of the projects (see discussion section).

Research studies

Several of the studies on ante and post-natal prevention projects include volunteers, and these are considered in Chapter Five. A few further studies where parent aides have been employed in cases already identified as child abuse are discussed in the third section of Chapter Eight. This chapter concentrates on studies which examine the use of volunteers and parent-aides in preventive work with families who already have children (listed in Table 4.1). In the first of these studies (Baker, 1981), 6 parent-aides provided long term support to 30 mothers. The aides were carefully matched to the parents (mostly mothers) and provided a long-term, supportive relationship to foster self-esteem and independence, the ability to love and care for their children and other life skills. The relationship enabled the aides to provide role models and often guidance. At post-test both the aides and the parents reported improvements in parent-child relations.

In the second study, (Miller et al, 1984, 1985) parent-aides provided a more time limited intervention. The aides and clients (mothers) agreed on specific objectives to be achieved within a 12 week period. The aides' task was to establish the trust and confidence of the mothers to be a supportive model and adviser, and to enable the mothers to develop their own abilities. As long as the goals were realistic, the programme allowed for a focused intervention with positive feedback on progress for both the aides and clients. The authors were concerned about the dependency and the reinforcement of incompetence, that could arise from more long-term supports. Most of the goals were related to parenting problems and the aides reported an average modest improvement over the twelve week period.

A similar time limited goal focused approach was adopted in the Child Parent Enrichment Project evaluated by Barth (1989). This took a social ecological model

TABLE 4.1

Research Studies on Volunteers and Parent Aides

Study	Programme	Sample Size	Population	Design	Main Measures
Baker et al (1981)	Parent aides	n=30	SSD referrals	POST	Self reports
Barth (1989)	Child parent enrichment	n=97	Agency referrals	RPM	Goal attainments, CAPI
Cox et al (1990)	Newpin befriending	n=19	Health Visitor referrals	RPM+C	Mental state, mother-child interactions
Gibbons and Thorpe (1989)	Home Start volunteers Social work	n=55 n=105	Vulnerable families	POST+C	Social disadvantages, family problems, services provided
Miller et al (1984, 1985)	Time limited parent aides	n=37	Risk of abuse	RPM	Goal attainment
Rosenstein (1978)	Telephone & home counselling	n=329	Risk of abuse	RPM	Level of programme activity
Van der Eyken (1982)	Home Start volunteers	n=30	Stressed families	POST	Perceptions of change

CAPI=Child Abuse Potential Inventory

Design

POST=post-test only; RPM=Repeated Measures including pre-test; PRPM=Repeated Measures post-test only;

+C=Control or comparison groups; +PC=Control or comparison group but at post-test only

with trained parenting consultants and mothers (perceived as high risk) agreeing on goals to be achieved within six months. Goals were related to parenting style and skills and use and access to resources. After six months there was a significant increase in the mother's goal attainment level particularly in goals related to the family environment. In addition there was a significant decrease in scores on child abuse potential scales.

Three further studies examined the use of volunteers who would be in a supportive and befriending role similar to parent-aides. The major difference between them is that volunteers are even more free of statutory and bureaucratic responsibilities than parent-aides.

Rosenstein (1978) studied a telephone and home visiting service. Volunteers were provided with 25 hours of training, which included parenting skills, and they then acted as friends and helpers to their clients. The volunteers' task was to nurture parents and to encourage them to make use of community resources. The purpose was to fill a gap in services by providing help to those families who were known to be at some risk of abusing their children, but whose problems were not sufficiently serious for statutory services. Another aim of the programme, was to raise community awareness about child abuse, in a similar manner to the community projects discussed in the previous chapter. The author did not try to evaluate the direct impact of the programme on the clients, but instead, used measures of service uptake. These measures can obviously be affected by many factors, but the results showed an encouraging large increase in self-referrals.

The most well known volunteer scheme in Britain is Home Start. The original scheme was started in Leicester by Margaret Harrison and is now in operation in many parts of Britain and overseas. A descriptive evaluation was carried out by William Van Der Eyken in 1982. The volunteers in this scheme enter into long-term supportive relationships with mothers experiencing a variety of often quite severe problems, including the risk of child abuse. They offer practical help, advice and encouragement, but the significant factor is the committed nature of the nurturing relationship, for clients who may have missed out on such relationships in childhood. Because they are not professionals, and are also mothers themselves, these volunteers are regarded as having moral authority. This is underscored by the philosophy of the project of 'being with' rather than 'doing to' clients.

Van Der Eyken's (1982) research on Leicester Home Start concentrated on the philosophy and processes of the scheme, but also included outcome data of family change as assessed by the co-ordinator, the volunteer, the family and social workers and health visitors who might also be involved. Positive change was reported in nearly all cases and this was more often described as a considerable rather than minor change. Although the data are not controlled or independently assessed they are encouraging, particularly in view of the range of problems experienced by the client group.

In a later study, Gibbons and Thorpe (1989) contrasted the clients of a Home Start unit with families receiving routine preventive Social Work. They found that Home Start was involved with families experiencing nearly as many social, economic, family and personal difficulties, as the clients of social work departments. The nature of the two services differed most obviously in the number of weekly home visits, – very few being offered by Social Services. Home Start volunteers also reported the use of many more family support activities than social workers, whilst Home Start users reported a much higher rate of general usefulness and satisfaction than social work clients. What is not clear, however, is whether the higher appreciation of Home Start was the result of more personal contact with the volunteers or other aspects of the service, or the context in which it is offered to families. Also, positive client perceptions of services, do not necessarily suggest greater efficiency at reducing family problems in the long term. An important point noted by Gibbons and Thorpe, is that the social services have a statutory responsibility to support families and to protect children, which leads them to discuss whether the role of voluntary support, such as Home Start, should be seen as separate, complementary, or a 'top up' to the local authority provision.

A more recent development has been the Newpin project in South London (Jenkins, 1984; Pounds and Mills, 1985; Mills and Pound, 1986; Pound, 1987; Cox et al, 1990). This project also uses volunteers to befriend and support mothers, but in a different way from Home Start. The befrienders are mostly recruited by health visitors or are introduced by those already in the project. There is a declared attempt to match volunteers with mothers from the same neighbourhoods and communities. They therefore share similar conditions and this not only engenders empathy between the two parties but also allows a much more reciprocal relationship where the befriended can act as a resource for the befriender.

Another feature of this project is the combination of using home visiting volunteers with activities at the Newpin Centre. The Centre has only a few modest rooms, but provides a creche where mothers can leave their children, and a drop-in centre where they can come for a chat with other mothers or for pre-arranged activities such as special talks. The Centre also provides a place for volunteers and clients to meet outside their own homes. The befrienders are all trained before they are allocated to a client mother, at the Centre, in which the volunteers can explore their own needs and problems. The programme therefore offers much more than training on how to help the project users. The befrienders are in a way clients themselves, and part of the 'Newpin Family'.

A pilot evaluation of Newpin (Pound and Mills, 1985) collected data by interviewing users about the changes in their lives since joining the project and the mothers reported marked increases in self-esteem, less depression, and better personal relationships starting from the new befriending relationship with the volunteer. The project was therefore greatly appreciated by the clients.

These findings have been confirmed by a fuller repeated measures evaluation contrasting control and experimental and volunteer and referral mothers (Cox et al, 1990). The results show that the experimental groups improved more than controls on maternal mental state. Within the experimental group those most actively involved improved the most on maternal mental state, mother's perception of change, and bath time interactions. In the control group the mother's relationship with partner deteriorated at post-test, which is of concern because of the highly significant association found in the whole sample at pre-test between this variable and maternal mental state.

Discussion

The studies reviewed in this section examined experimental projects which provided a preventive service at a very much reduced cost compared to the use of permanent paid agency staff. The question is, whether these inexpensive projects are effective, and whether they provide a useful strategy for child abuse prevention.

All of the studies found an improvement in the functioning of the parents and their relationships with their children. Although the authors were careful to qualify their results, it is clear that they believed the programmes to have made an important impact. It is a pity that only few studies used experimental controls or independent measures of assessment. Control groups would have demonstrated whether any improvement was due to the intervention rather than spontaneous remission of problems or the influence of other uncontrolled factors. Independent measures would have ensured that there was no 'halo effect', whereby the interventions subtly influenced the users' or workers' assessments of change.

Some of the studies argued that the existence of a few results, which showed a worsening of family problems indicated an objective research evaluation of family problems. But this could be due to a few cases clearly and dramatically reaching a crisis, whether or not the remaining assessments were free of bias. Furthermore, there could be positive and negative labelling of families at the outset which might influence the perception of later progress. For example, it is known that in some child abuse cases, the client's acceptance of responsibility or of the need for a social work service, is seen as a predictor for treatment and improvement. A rejection of the need for a service, could then pre-dispose workers to assume that there was no real progress, despite recognisable change. Similarly, clients thus negatively perceived, would not be pre-disposed to recognise improvement following intervention. This is an argument against the use of correlations between workers' and clients' scores as evidence of the objectivity and independence of measures.

These points may seem unduly critical of research reports that offer convincing arguments for the practical and human value of non-professional services. The problem is, that the evidence does not allow us to distinguish sufficiently between projects, or to single out within projects, which components are the most useful and in what circumstances.

What the programmes have in common, is the aim of enabling parents to develop and use their own skills, through the use of informal services. The helpers are thus freed, to greater or lesser extents, from some of the rules of more formal services, and are able to make more committed and personal relationships. Professionals are committed too, of course, but they are providing a service based on statutory duty and professional responsibility which contrasts with the more personal involvement of aides and volunteers and their careful matching with clients on the basis of particular characteristics. This personal commitment seems essential, even if the relationship is short-term, contractual and task orientated as in the Miller study (Miller et al, 1984, 1985).

Despite the common characteristics of the programmes, a wide range of approaches was used. In contrast to many studies reported in other chapters, the programme descriptions were usually informative about their philosophies and why they had, for example, chosen a particular type of volunteer. The studies were less clear about the specific outcomes desired for families. Many of the approaches were attempting to assist and encourage parents in a broad range of areas so that they could be better able to help themselves in the future. The breadth of these aims meant that the outcome measures also had to be broad. Most of the positive results related to the mother's general functioning, mental state and relationships with partner rather than in relationship or interactions with their children or the functioning of their children. Studies of maternal depression have shown that intervention programmes can produce improvements in maternal mental state, but without any significant change in the mother-infant relationship or in developmental deficits in the child (Bailey, 1986; Cooper et al, 1991; Eliot, 1989; Murray, 1992; Leverton, 1991). It may be that the studies reviewed in this chapter are effective in providing social support to improve maternal mental state and the quality of their lives, but that additional services are required to assist the mother child relationship and the development of the child.

Even if the parent aide and volunteer studies are principally concerned with social support this still needs to be differentiated into its component parts before it is possible to establish which interventions are successful in achieving different benefits. Social support is an extremely broad concept (Alloway & Bebbington, 1987; Barrera, 1988) and Gottlieb's (1985) categories, described in the introduction to this chapter, provide a useful way of dealing with this variety.

Emotional support was an important constituent of all the projects, but differed according to the volunteers or aides. The extent of these differences is not always clear from the research reports, but nature of the helping relationship varied from a maternal form of nurturing to a more reciprocal friendship. Advocates of the nurturing model put the emphasis on parents' need to be parented themselves, whilst the reciprocal model argues for mutual support and empathy resulting from shared experience. Reciprocal friendship has elsewhere been found to be an important element of social support (Antionucci, 1985).

There are many strands to emotional support, and their relative efficacy may depend on the problems being experienced. Some theorists (Thoits, 1985), suggest that stress threatens a person's identity or self-esteem, and that social support will be effective to the extent that it matches the perceived threat. For example, a support strategy that was appropriate for a particular person in one set of circumstances might be inappropriate or even damaging in a different case.

Tangible aid other than material help and referral to other resources, is to provide information or skills training which enable people to have more power over their lives. Information can vary from details of state benefits and approaches to household management, to theories of child development and family systems. Training can be concerned with child care, social skills, or the learning of workplace skills. The volunteer and aide schemes differed in the extent and in the form that these supports were offered. For instance, child care skills were sometimes formally taught, sometimes discussed more informally and in other programmes were supposed to be learnt from role modelling.

Tangible Aid varies between programmes, depending on whether the emphasis is more upon social and psychological resources or on material help. But parent-aides, who emphasise befriending, will also have access to the material resources of the local professional health and welfare agencies. On the other hand, volunteers may more easily gain access to informal sources of material help available within local communities. There is similar variation in the tangible aid of referral, access, and negotiation with other services. An added dimension, here, is when the user also has an allocated worker, and the volunteer or aide may have a role as negotiator between the two parties. Any such action is bound to be affected by the organizational context in which the aide or volunteer is working.

Cognitive Guidance or appraisal is difficult to disentangle from some of the other categories of social support. Whether guidance offers alternatives, supports decisions, suggests courses of action, or sets limits, will depend on the nature of the befriending relationship as well as the organizational context in which the volunteer or aide works. These issues are highly relevant to the development of services in Britain, as social workers move towards the management of service provision with less time for direct casework (Goldberg and Sinclair, 1986).

Socializing and Companionship is also closely related to the reciprocal nature of the helping relationship, but there are some further significant factors in the programmes reviewed. One is the deliberate provision of enjoyable activities for the parents as described in the Baker study (Baker et al, 1981). Other programmes emphasized the importance of friendship and some were also explicit about the need for creches so that parents could have some relaxation and freedom from the 24 hour one-to-one responsibility for their children, and opportunities to mix socially with other parents. Apart from the better quality of life provided by these resources, the social activities may improve self-esteem and sense of identity and buffer people against stress (Thoits, 1985). In addition, researchers have found that social isolation and loneliness are related to poor social skills (Thoits 1985) which in turn, mitigate against the development of social supports. Providing or encouraging social activities might therefore reverse negative downward trends, in which lack of normal support, itself prevents normal supports being offered (Thoits, 1985).

Milieu Reliability is acknowledged as an important factor in the growing literature on relationships (Hinde, 1979) and in recent studies of parenting (Quinton & Rutter, 1988) and of children in the 'care system' (Millham et al, 1986). The danger is that the security children obtain from milieu reliability is often lost when they are received into care by local authorities (Millham et al, 1986).

Although the social support of milieu reliability is based upon perceptions and beliefs rather than visible behaviour, it is probably one of the most important contributions to peoples' sense of identity, self esteem, and sense of control or mastery (Thoits, 1985). Similarly, it has been proposed by some child development studies, that the basic trust and attachment that infants develop for their caretakers is essential for appropriate social adjustment in adult life (Bowlby, 1969); this includes the ability to become caring parents in turn and to provide attachment figures for the next generation of infants. It is therefore not surprising that attachment has been used as an explanatory variable in child abuse (Ainsworth, 1980, Crittenden and Ainsworth, 1989). Milieu reliability may then be a crucial part of the commitment offered in the parent aide and volunteer schemes, and makes any qualifications or limits imposed on the support an important issue for any particular project.

Unfortunately, the studies reviewed, did not detail the level of personal commitment made or received, in the different schemes. Thus it is only possible to speculate that the short-term interventions had less milieu reliability than longer term programmes. The Newpin experiment stands out through its emphasis on the importance of attachment (Pound, 1987) and the support to users of both their matched volunteer and the whole 'Newpin Family' so that parents have a sense of belonging to a caring group.

In sum, Gottlieb's (1985) categories reveal that the projects reviewed had social support components, but that they were not sufficiently detailed in the programme descriptions or experimental designs, to allow an assessment of the relative worth of these components and their sub-types. The research studies made little reference to the literature on social supports and coping.

A related criticism of the studies, is the failure to address the question of whether the five categories of support are more effective when delivered within a single relationship or within a supportive network of close ties (Gottlieb, 1985). The volunteer and aide programmes provide an individual relationship, but several of the programmes were overtly concerned with developing the users' own social network; in some cases, through individual support to raise self-esteem, sense of identity, and mastery and so increase the chances of making friends and starting a positive cycle of improvement in their lives. In other programmes there were more direct efforts to link similar individuals together. Support would then be provided by the artificially constructed group or through the network that may develop from contacts made within the group. Alternatively membership of a long standing supportive service may provide a feeling of belonging and self worth that some people can not attain alone in the community.

As with other forms of intervention discussed, there is the possibility that offering social supports can have adverse effects. This is most clearly illustrated by the fact that families themselves as well as being a primary source of support are also one of the major causes of stress to individuals (Fosson, 1988). Child abuse researchers are aware that individual relationships and social support networks may have a detrimental effect on parents' functioning and the caring environment that they can offer their child (Van Meter, 1986). The parent-aide and volunteer programmes attempt to counter such influences by enabling the user to be less dependent on adverse social contacts, and by developing new and more positive relationships. Some of the studies reported a few cases which deteriorated during the intervention programmes, but there was a general assumption that this was due to problems within the families which the projects were unable to tackle. It was not suggested that the interventions could themselves have had adverse effects when properly applied. However, such outcomes have been documented within the stress research literature. Although it is true, that bringing together people who share similar backgrounds may encourage empathy, the reciprocal sharing of problems and the realisation that one is not alone in having certain experiences is not necessarily beneficial, as it can foster feelings of helplessness within the clients (Wortman and Lehman, 1985). Evidence of detrimental effects of supportive services is also discussed in Chapter Five.

The research studies show, that parent-aides and volunteers have the potential of offering an extremely useful preventive service. Despite the lack of clear cut data the research here provides better evidence of success, than many other areas of child abuse intervention.

There are several reasons why these services can be implemented on a wide scale. Firstly, there is the extremely low cost in comparison with routine professional services. The programmes harness the resources of the community rather than teach skills to a few professionals. This is not only efficient, but fosters social integration at the neighbourhood level.

A second reason for wide-scale informal programmes, is the lack of stigma attached to volunteer schemes in comparison to health and welfare services which have connotations of illness or of social inadequacy. The projects can be seen as a positive response to family problems, rather than as a consequence of failure, with all the attendant divisive labelling. Furthermore, the programmes can reach families which might otherwise be hard to reach and may even be deliberately avoiding the health and welfare services.

Summary

1. The studies examined preventive schemes that use volunteers and parent-aides to develop parents' own resources and abilities to cope. The projects were based in different organizational and professional contexts and used a variety of approaches. The preventive strategies and techniques can be understood within a classification of social support.

2. The studies all reported improvements and the interventions were positively perceived by both users and workers. The lack of independent measures makes it difficult to assess whether there were improvements in actual behaviour and functioning. Perceptions of change could have been influenced by many factors including the level of co-operation and satisfaction expressed by the parents.

3. There were few experimental controls in the studies, which makes it difficult to assess whether improvements in functioning were due to the interventions applied or due to other factors. The general lack of specification of the different aims, techniques and outcomes of emotional support, make it difficult to assess the relative efficacy of techniques, both between and within studies, and how they relate to different client groups.

4. Benefits of the schemes include low cost, enablement rather than treatment, and the lack of stigma and freedom from statutory responsibilities, though it is unclear whether the support is best offered separate, in addition to, or as part of statutory provision. There is a need to distinguish the benefits and costs of different types of social support offered in different ways to those with different needs. Some clients may benefit from tangible material aid, others may benefit more from advice or from the sense of self worth arising from personal relationships. The latter may be fostered by aides or volunteers or by a membership model of social support.

5. Most of the improvements reported in the studies concerned maternal mental state or mothers' positive views of the programme. That there was little evidence of change in children or mother-child interactions suggests that

different extra techniques are necessary for these areas. This conclusion is supported by separate studies of maternal depression.

6.   There are many volunteer and befriending schemes or similar supportive groups in existence that are not directly concerned with child abuse. The task for future research is to isolate those components of social supports that are most effective for different clients in different situations. This requires clearer specification of these components, controlled research designs, and independent measures of assessment of outcome. The studies could be more productive if they were more directly based upon the existing research literature on social supports and coping strategies, as well as on a greater specification of the components of support offered by volunteer and parent aides.

Chapter Four Research Summaries

Baker et al (1981)

PARENT AIDES AS A PREVENTIVE INTERVENTION STRATEGY

Sample: 30 families receiving parent-aide service in Oswego County in upstate New York. Most cases referred by social services for risk or the actual occurrence of child abuse or neglect and similar problems. Acceptance on basis of need and availability of aides.

Focus: Parenting by families at risk of abuse.

Objectives: To provide supportive role models for parents to enable them to act as independent nurturing parents to their children.

Programme: 5 parent-aides each with a case load of 6 families. Careful matching of aides to families. The length of the service varied from 6 months to 2 years and ended by mutual agreement. Aides acted as a role model for handling children, offered teaching and guidance on practical skills, self control and decision making, engaged in enjoyable shared activities and gave general support to parents. A 24 hour service provided by telephone. Regular team meetings included aides programme co-ordinator and any workers from other agencies involved.

Design: Post-test of intervention sample.

Measures: Interviews with clients and parent aides.

Results: 90% of parents would recommend programme and 77% felt that accepting the aide was their choice. Aides' role seen particularly in terms of supportive listening and caring. 80% of parents reported some improvement in relations with their children. Parent-aides saw their task as fostering independence, self control and decision making. Parent-aides reported a decrease in risk of abuse or actual abuse incidents in 90% of the families and improvements in child care, coping with stress and home management in over 60% of families. The aides felt that this avoided reception into care or facilitated the return home of some of the children. Aides said that parental attitudes to child rearing and discipline were the hardest to change.

Notes: The study is a retrospective assessment of a service and is examining the processes and content of the service. Because of this, the goals and methods are to a large extent a finding of the interviews, rather than a priori categories for the research. The similarity in perception of the aides' role between workers and users is therefore an interesting result. The authors see the interviews of aides and clients as cross validating each other and note a positive relation between parents and aides reporting success. Few details provided on relationship of programme with other social work.

Barth (1989)

EVALUATION OF A TASK-CENTRED CHILD ABUSE PREVENTION PROGRAMME

Sample: Clients were referred by public health social workers, social services, teen parent programmes and a total of 17 different agencies serving high risk mothers and pregnant women. 97 out of the 144 participants included in the evaluation. Age range of 14–38 years, with a median of 22 years. 44% were white, 32% Latino, 18% black, 3% Asian and 1% Native American.

Focus: Education of parents (mothers) for primary and secondary prevention of child abuse and/or neglect.

Objectives: To teach and devise individual coping strategies for stress and childcare in the home setting by working at specific tasks and developing personal coping styles for handling new or additional parenting responsibilities; to help clients change their social environment by building formal and informal resource networks.

Programme: The Child Parent Enrichment Project Programme (CPEP) that takes a social ecological model of child maltreatment. Trained parenting consultants offer suggestions for changes in parenting style, give demonstrations of parenting techniques and help clients to obtain community services that offer food, shelter and financial assistance. Parenting consultants, in consultation with the mothers, decide on a minimum of three goals to pursue for the next six months. Each goal is divided into manageable tasks detailed on task sheets, and the parenting consultants visit the home bi-weekly.

Design: Repeated measures (pre and post test) on intervention group only.

Measures: Child Abuse Potential Inventory (CAPI). Goal Attainment Scales were completed by clients and parenting consultants. Consumer satisfaction forms completed by clients. Success in preventing child abuse was estimated by identifying child abuse reports to social services.

Results: 17.15 tasks were accomplished per client (approximately one task per visit). 49% were accomplished by the Parenting Consultant, 41% by the client alone and 9% together. Significant increase in mean goal attainment level, with the greatest goal gains being related to improvements in the environment of the mother and child. Pre-test CAPI scores averaged 108.9 indicating very high risk, but fell significantly at post test to 96.8 (p < 0.05). Improvement in CAPI scores more strongly associated with tasks undertaken by client rather than by staff. During or after the programme there were few child abuse reports to Social Services, but there was no evidence that these were fewer than clients not receiving programme. Clients evaluated the services favourably. Greatest satisfaction was with their relationship with the parenting consultant and the practical help provided. Dissatisfaction expressed that programme too short.

Notes: See also Barth (1991) in Chapter Four.

Cox et al (1990)

Newpin: The Evaluation of a Home Visiting and Befriending Scheme in South London

Sample: Mothers referred primarily by Health Visitors to service and, if accepted, by Newpin then allocated as a 'referral' or as a 'volunteer' who receives training to befriend a 'referral' case. Mothers commonly had poor relationship with partners had adverse experiences in their own childhoods. The experimental group (n = 40, 19 volunteers and 21 referrals) recruited to original Newpin programme in Walworth. The control group (n = 24, 14 volunteers and 10 clients) recruited for planned new programme in Tower Hamlets. Both groups from deprived inner city areas of London.

Focus: Functioning of mothers with parenting and relationship problems.

Objectives: To ameliorate emotional stresses, depression, low self-esteem and to improve parent child relationships. The scheme aims to help both the volunteers and the referral mothers. Ethos of mutual support and development.

Programme: New Parent-Infant Network (Newpin) professionally led volunteer scheme using befriending volunteers to provide mutual emotional support, friendship, and practical help to mothers. Also a client group or individual counselling or therapy plus a drop in facility for mothers at Centre and an open creche facility for children. The befriending

volunteers are also local mothers of young children, recruited in various ways and including mothers originally referred to the scheme for help. Volunteers are provided with training once a week for six months consisting of (i) lectures on children, parenting, relationships, (ii) a self development group to explore past and current relationships, loss and trauma. After training, continuation of supportive group plus supervision of befriending role. Befrienders and befriended enter into a contract to do things together which is terminated when problems are concluded or mother joins wider network of Newpin services. Contact between volunteers and the other mothers is variable, but is usually several times per week and volunteers are encouraged to bring mothers to the drop in centre. The centre is staffed by a centre co-ordinator and a secretary.

Design: Repeated measures (pre-test and 6 months post test) of design with non random allocation to two experimental and two control conditions.

Measures: (1) Maternal interviews for demographic data, own early experiences, current mental state, quality of relationships with partner, emotional and behavioural disturbance in index child (closest to 2 years of age/causing most parenting difficulties), mother's perception of change. (2) 1 hour video recording of bath times and meal times (not yet analysed) with coding of mini sequences on the 7 dimensions of warmth to child, stimulation, mutual cooperation and negotiation, structural anticipation of child's needs, autonomy for child, control and conflict, emotional containment and distress in child. (3) Developmental assessment of index child. (4) Length and level of involvement in service (exptal groups only).

Results: (1) Pre-test differences: (a) Experimental group had (compared to controls) smaller families, fewer histories of psychiatric disorder lasting more than 2 years, worse housing, less preschool provision, more social work content, and more reported that they had injured their child at some time. (b) Some volunteers had experience of Newpin pre-test and the longer this experience the less psychiatric disorder at pre-test. (c) Volunteers (compared to referrals) less likely to have current psychiatric disorder and more likely to be cohabiting, but no differences in background data. (d) Highly significant association between mental state and quality of relationship with partner.

(2) Mental state: significant improvement for all groups but greater for experimental group (p < 0.07). Well involved subjects improved more than poorly involved for subsample of depressed mothers. Greatest improvement was in referrals who had 6–12 months experience of Newpin. Volunteers had better mental state at pre-test but changed less during the study.

(3) Relationship with partner and symptoms in child: Improvement for all groups on all measures except deterioration in relationship with partner for control referrals. No significance between group differences found.

(4) Mother's perception of change: significantly greater improvement for experimental group compared to controls and for well involved compared to poorly involved. Most common change was in confidence and feeling in charge of own life. Perceived improvement associated with maintenance of good mental state or improvement from bad mental state.

(5) Bathtime interactions: Improvements for all groups. Well involved experimental subjects improved most but only significant for dimension of anticipation. Well involved deteriorated on dimensions of control and distress. Those with intermediate experience of Newpin were worst at pre-test and improved the most. No differences in improvement between volunteers and referrals.

In sum, well involved performed best and poorly involved and controls performed worst at post test, but results not always significant. Deteriorations in performance reported for (a) control volunteers for mental state, (b) control referrals for relationship with partner, (c) low involved for 5 of 7 dimensions of bathtime interactions, (d) low involved volunteers for child emotional behaviour problems.

Notes: 9 volunteers had more than 6 months experience of Newpin prior to pre-test and authors argue that they may have already improved on study measures. Authors suggest that a longer term follow up is necessary to evaluate programme. They also refer to a contrast group of depressed mothers from another study. See also prior publications on pilot study (Pound and Mills 1985, Pound et al 1985). Currently there are 5 Newpins with plans for further expansion.

Gibbons and Thorpe (1989)

CAN VOLUNTARY SUPPORT PROJECTS HELP
VULNERABLE FAMILIES? THE WORK OF HOME START

Sample: (1) 55 families from one Home Start unit of whom 28 were interviewed. (2) 105 families with children under 14 newly referred to Social Services. (3) 21 families already receiving social work.

Focus: Coping of vulnerable families.

Objectives: To prevent and reduce family difficulties (within a statutory context for social services).

Programme: (1) Home Start: Person to person emotional and practical support by trained volunteers individually matched to each parent. (2) Preventive social work. (3) Routine social service provision to families with difficulties.

Design: Comparison of programmes based on service offered, clients serviced, client perception of services.

Measures: Objective indicator of social disadvantage (on all 55 Home Start families). Family Problem Scales and Malaise Inventory completed by parents. Parental accounts of services received and their usefulness. Workers' reports of services provided.

Results: Allocated social service cases had most indicators of social disadvantage and of risk/vulnerability. Referral cases had more indicators of vulnerability than Home Start families but mostly less indicators of social disadvantage except for violence to spouse. 22% of Home Start families had been at high risk of state intervention for child protection. Home Start high risk families reported greater satisfaction and more general help received than low risk families, whilst the reverse was reported by allocated social service families. Malaise scores were similar for allocated social services and Home Start families. Where there were parent-child problems most Home Start families received weekly visits from the volunteers (86% of high risk and 79% of low risk families) whilst few social work families received such frequent visits (8% for high risk and 0% for low risk families). In general, volunteers were seen as providing more help than social workers. More families were very satisfied with Home Start (50% for high risk and 36% for low risk), than the social work service (8% for high risk and 22% for low risk). Home Start volunteers reported an average of 15.9 family support activities compared to 11.5 reported by Social Workers.

Notes: The authors stress that the sample is small, that the cause of the differences reported are not clear, and also discuss the different roles of voluntary and statutory social-work services. More details of the Home Start scheme is given in the summary of Van Der Eyken (1982).

Miller et al (1984, 1985)

A TIME LIMITED, GOAL FOCUSED PARENT-AIDE
PROGRAM

Sample: 37 families seen by service in first 2 years of operation. Referred by social services as being at risk of abuse or other problems. The main criteria for acceptance to programme were risk of abuse and acceptance of the programme. The families were predominantly single parent families and many were isolated, depressed, and dependent on state benefits. Two thirds of sample were white and one third black. The families had problems with parent-child relations.

Focus: Functioning of parents at risk of abuse.

Objectives: To enable children to remain with their parents by improving the context and practice of parenting through mobilizing the parents own resources.

Programme: Goal focused and 12 week time limited programme using trained parent-aides. Aides matched with parents by programme co-ordinator. Goals for each case determined at outset and assessed after 9 weeks of services. If goals not achieved, then a second contract can be drawn up. Aides carefully selected on basis of human qualities, knowledge of community resources, and child rearing. Aides given a month's training followed by twice weekly seminars one of which was a support group. Aides developed trust with parents, provided emotional support and nurture, offered an appropriate model, and taught parenting skills. The intervention was complementary to normal social services casework.

Design: Repeated measures (pre and post test) on intervention sample.

Measures: Achievement of goals on a 5 point scale from −10 to +10 as assessed by aides and caseworkers. Programme records of the interventions completed under one contract. Programme records of requests for the service.

Results: There were 128 target goals, 41% related to parenting problems, 16% to personal or mental state problems, 16% to problems in daily living, 12% to accessing community resources, 8% to social resources, and 8% to other problems. The average goal achievement rating was +5.6 with increases of +5.2 for parenting problems, +5.6 for personal problems, +5.4 for problems in daily living, +4.6 for community resources, +6.0 for social resources, +9.9 for other problems (only 8% of all goals). 54% of cases were terminated after the 1st contract. Demand for the service increased over time.

Notes: The authors see the service as definitely effective and state that the recording of some individual negative results indicates that the goal rating process was objective. Authors also discuss some multiple crises cases where short term goals were achieved, but where crises re-occurred and where the aides services were again needed. The second paper stresses the importance of keeping records, of clarifying roles when giving the workers direction, and feedback to make them mindful of the time limits and focus of the work. This encourages effectiveness and efficiency of service, but depends on the setting of specific and realistic goals.

Rosenstein (1978)

FAMILY OUTREACH: A PROGRAM FOR PREVENTION OF CHILD ABUSE AND NEGLECT

Sample: 329 families provided with assistance by the project over a 5 year period. Criteria for acceptance included risk of child abuse, school problems, and neglect of children. Severe problems were referred on to other agencies. Self-referrals increased and constituted about 50% of referrals at the end of study period.

Focus: Functioning of families at risk of abuse. Also community awareness of child abuse.

Objectives: To inform public about child abuse and neglect and raise awareness of public responsibility. To prevent child abuse through work with families. The philosophy of the project is to help those whose problems fall short of the criteria for acceptance by other agencies, yet who still need assistance. Also to help the statutory agencies find foster and adoptive homes in the local community.

Programme: (1) Community: providing information through the mass media and public talks. (2) Families: telephone and home counselling by 16 trained volunteers supervised by one professional caseworker. The main training block is 25 hours of skill training including parenting skills. Volunteers act as friends and helpers to the parents in solving problems and making use of community resources. Volunteer's role is of a 'nurturing parent'.

Design: Repeated measures on intervention sample.

Measures: Agency records of total numbers of referrals, self referrals and actual clients. Number of speaking engagements.

Results: Self-referral increases from 8.5% of all referrals at end of first year to 51% at end of fifth year. Total referrals increased by 350% from first to second year. A total of 329 clients accepted to programme. 350 public presentations were given to an audience of 8,400.

Notes: Author argues for 'use of services' as an outcome measure because of the difficulties in assessing the extent that abuse has been prevented. Article provides details of the training for volunteers.

Van Der Eyken (1982)

HOME START: A FOUR YEAR EVALUATION

Sample: 30 families selected randomly from 156 in contact with the service. Data also available on over 300 referrals to the project over a four year period. All the families had pre-school children, 90% had low incomes, 40% were single parents, 25% had children on the local child abuse risk register. Families also characterized by poor housing, social isolation, poor physical and mental health, spouse abuse, low intelligence and rejection by close relatives. Most referrals to project are from social workers and health visitors and are often due to concern about levels of stress and potential loss of control by the mothers.

Focus: Functioning of vulnerable families.

Objectives: Restoring control to mother and family, to create a healthy environment for child rearing.

Programme: Use of trained volunteers carefully matched with parents in order to offer them a supportive and committed 'mothering' relationship. Volunteers provide emotional support, teach budgeting and cooking skills, direct play and stimulation of children and offer practical help, including limited material supports, at times of crisis. The volunteer-client relationship is growth orientated and, although there is some limit setting, this is within a reciprocal relationship based on 'being with' rather than 'doing to' clients. Volunteers are all mothers themselves and receive support from the project organizer.

Design: Post-test on intervention sub-sample.

Measures: Perceptions of social worker, health visitor, co-ordinator, volunteer and client, of changes in the family situation; agency records of children taken into care and the co-ordinator's assessment of changes in circumstances of all Home Start clients.

Results: Between 80% and 90% of each respondent group indicated change in the families. For the health visitors and the families themselves, this was nearly always coded as a considerable change. For the co-ordinator three-quarters of the changes were considerable. For the social workers and volunteers just over half of the families were seen as having changed considerably. From the 132 children of all Home Start clients on the local child at risk of abuse register, only 18 were taken into care.

Notes: The author does not present his study as a full evaluation, but argues that it indicates a strong likelihood that the intervention had important effects. The book discusses the theory and practice of Home Start and includes case study material. Emphasis is put upon the importance of the parent being accepted as a person in their own right rather than just as an agent for changing their child's circumstances. By not being paid, the volunteers have greater moral authority than professional staff and can present the families in a more sympathetic light to the professionals. Volunteer involvement may have to be more long-term but can result in parents outgrowing the need for a service, whilst professional intervention may reinforce sense of loss of control. Author suggests that the service is particularly useful for families with inner resources and without severe psychological problems, but who are overwhelmed by immediate stress factors.

This evaluation was published in 1982. In 1991 there were 141 Home Start schemes in operation worldwide. An average scheme has one full time organizer, 27 volunteers, and 66 families being served. Average costs in U.K. are £417 per family or £179 per child per year (or part of). Volunteers are trained for one day per week for 10 weeks and then receive further support and training. Families receive an average of 14 months support.

CHAPTER FIVE
Ante Natal and Post-Natal Services

Background

As intrafamilial child abuse is so closely linked to the total parenting relationship, some prevention programmes have focused their intervention programmes on the very beginning of this relationship in the neonatal period. The appeal of intervening during the ante-natal and post-natal period is clear. It is not surprising that many intervention programmes concentrate on first time mothers who will have had only indirect experience of parenthood. By logical extension, there is an argument for education, even before a first pregnancy, so that the choice to have children may be well informed and the development of useful skills and knowledge can start very early. However, the discussion in Chapter Three, on educational interventions, noted that although there has been a development of parent education in schools, this has not always been linked to the literature on child abuse prevention.

In addition to its position in this life cycle, the neonatal period is thought by many, to be a particularly important and formative period. The influential works of John Bowlby (1972) and Donald Winnicott (1973) both stress the importance of a good early start to parenting and suggest the existence of a short, sensitive period, in which the mother is most open to developing a positive bond and attachment to her child. More recently, professional views have changed (Rapoport, 1977) and less stress is put upon the biological relationship of mother and child or on the negative effects of early separation (Rutter, 1981). It is thought that adverse effects on children are often reversible (Clarke and Clarke, 1984) and that when problems persist, these are due to continuing negative influences (Richman et al, 1982). This may particularly be the case, when other adversities affect the family or child (Richards, 1979) or when positive experiences for the child, which could possibly mitigate earlier damage are lacking (Sameroff and Chandler, 1975).

Alongside these changes in theory, there has been a growing movement to change the policy and practice of maternity care: parents should have the right to choose the care arrangements (Oakley, 1984) and ante-natal and post-natal clinics should offer a more personal service.

There has also been a growing concern about child abuse and other indicators of what are considered to be general inadequacies in parenting. These problems are often attributed to the parents' own poor upbringing which, it is argued, renders them less likely to create secure social environments for children, and less able and perhaps less motivated to cope adequately with childrearing. The interpretations vary, according to their emphasis on the psychological, material or cultural perpetuation of poor parenting. In the last chapter, for example, reference was made to the importance of early attachments in relation to adult functioning, parenting, and child maltreatment (Crittenden and Ainsworth, 1989; Pound, 1987).

Whatever the explanations, all the theories imply at least a weak form, of a cycle of deprivation, in which successive generations are unable or unlikely to escape the disadvantages of the previous generation. This has led to compensatory programmes, many of which are directed at children and infants (Hunt, 1975), but many are also directed at parents and families (Beller, 1979; Huntingdon, 1979). This implies a deficit model of parental functioning, which is used in most forms of screening, including risk schedules for child abuse. Recently, there have been some moves to re-orientate services to be more positive: a philosophy of empowering parents to be able and confident rather than pursuing their perceived deficiencies (Cochran, 1985; Barker and Anderson, 1988).

There is still the issue of whether any extra services should be generally available or should be rationed and directed at those considered to be most in need. The need can be assessed by the existence of general risk factors or from a more individualized assessment of risk in respect of the parents ability to care for their child. This relies on the methods of risk assessment having some validity. Despite many methodological problems in the measure of risk factors (Leventhal, 1982) and professional workers assessment of parenting (Dingwall et al, 1983; Leventhal et al, 1986) the assessments do have some predictive power statistically. The risk assessments produce many false positive and false negative predictions of outcome and so are not sufficiently accurate to predict outcomes on individuals (Leventhal, 1988).

Research studies

In the child abuse literature several studies have examined the potential preventive effect of extra ante-natal and post-natal services, but they differ in the type of sample used (studies listed in Table 5.1).

The first group of studies target mothers generally or, more often, first time mothers. These mothers could be living in urban areas with few material resources and with low levels of existing services, but the research samples are not defined according to any detailed risk category. A second group of studies recruits samples according to some very general risk factors, such as single parenthood, low socio-economic status, or social isolation. A third group of studies also lists risk factors, but to a much greater degree, so that the mothers who are referred for inclusion in the research samples, have been identified as having potential parenting problems. The three types of studies are considered in turn.

Several of the intervention schemes use volunteer workers and could have been considered in Chapter Four. They are included here because the volunteers are used to support mothers in parenting new born infants.

1. General Population including First Time Mothers and Low Income Groups

Many studies examined the effect of additional perinatal support on a broad range of families attending maternity hospitals. The supplementary services provided in the programmes included discussion groups, counselling groups, extra post-partum contact, supportive follow-up through home visiting and telephone calls from professional workers or volunteers, and educational classes including instruction in infant care for fathers.

Four studies used random allocation of parent-child dyads into experimental and control treatment conditions, to assess the effects of the interventions. For the 'Rural Family Support Project' (Gray et al, 1983), internal comparisons were used, principally length of treatment, to assess the impact of the interventions, but the emphasis of this study was on the demonstration of a programme and the development of local services.

The experimental results were variable, but in general treatment effects were small. Siegal and his colleagues (Siegal et al, 1980) used a variety of treatment groups, in order to distinguish between the effect of different components of the programme, and found a positive effect from extra post-partum contact on parental behaviour at 4 and 12 months post delivery. This is impressive considering the timescale, even though there was a greater effect from background factors. But the failure to find any effect of the home visiting component is disappointing. The

TABLE 5.1

Research Studies on Ante Natal and Post Natal Services

Study	Programme	Sample Size	Population	Design	Main Measures
Barnard et al (1988) Booth et al (1989)	Home visits: skill vs information models	n=147	Low social support	RPM+C	Maternal competences mental state, parenting
Barth (1991)	Child Parent Enrichment	n=191	High risk factors	RPM+C	Social supports, mental state, CAPI
Chapman and Reynolds (1982)	Post natal groups	n=5	Health Visitor referrals	RPM	Appropriateness of parenting behaviour
Dachman et al (1986)	Infant care training	n=6	1st time fathers	RPM	Observation of child care skills
Gabinet (1979)	Dynamic personality theory therapy	n=77	Risk of abuse	RPM	Parent adjustment coping, child care
Gray E. et al (1983) 1. Perinatal Positive Parenting	Volunteer visits	n=252	No identified problems	RPM+C	HOME Inventory, parenting inventory
2. Pride in Parenthood	Family Friends	n=28	Socially isolated mothers	RPM+C	Parental beliefs about child, punishment
3. Rural Family Support	Develop services	n=1622	Mothers in Indiana	POST	Parental & professional perceptions of services
Gray J.D. et al (1977, 1979)	Intensive services + lay visitor	n=150	High & low risk mothers	POST+C	Developmental assessment
Larson C.P. (1980)	Pre natal and/ or post natal visits	n=115	Low SES & education	RPM+C	Maternal health & behaviour, HOME
Lealman et al (1983)	Social work + drop in centre	n=103	At Risk	RPM+C	Children's growth, rates of child abuse
Monaghan and Buckfield (1981)	Neonatal clinic supports	n=200	New Zealand mothers	POST+C	RIC, hospital admission
O'Connor et al (1980)	Rooming in	n=143	Low income mothers	POST+C	Hospital admissions, child abuse
Olds et al (1986a, 1986b, 1988)	Home visiting	n=400	Single, low SES	RPM+C	Parenting observations, child development
Ounstead et al (1982)	Additional health service supports	n=110	At risk parenting	POST	Child development, professional concern
Quitquit et al (1986)	Home visits & supports	?	At risk mothers	POST	Client satisfaction
Siegal et al (1980)	Extra post-partum contact	n=321	Poor urban area	POST+C	Attachment
Soumenkoff et al (1982)	Support, therapy	n=91	At risk mothers	Descriptive	Prematurity, outcome for child in family
Stevenson and Bailey (1988)	Post natal support group	n=85	London mothers	RPM+C	Development/ behaviour, maternal supports, mental health
Taylor and Beauchamp (1988)	Extra after care	n=30	Primaparous	PRPM+C	Parenting attitudes/ behaviour

RIC = Removal of children into care; CAPI = Child Abuse Potential Inventory; HOME = Home Observation & Living Scale
Design: POST = post-test only; RPM = Repeated Measures including pre-test; PRPM = Repeated Measures post-test only;
+C = Control or comparison groups; +PC = Control or comparison group but at post-test only

authors suggest that home visiting might have had an effect if it had been started earlier, but there is no real evidence to support this hypothesis.

Taylor and Beauchamp (1988) did find a significant effect from hospital and home visitation. Significant effects were reported on all measures, which is another impressive finding considering the programme only consisted of one month of weekly ninety minute visits. A limitation of the study is that the results were from post-test measures only. There were no pre-tests to ensure that there were not prior differences between intervention and control groups.

In the O'Connor study (O'Connor et al, 1980) extra post-partum contact and a generally more liberal maternity care regime, was significantly related to less adverse outcomes in agency records, compared to controls. This is surprising as Siegal found no impact on these records. O'Connor's results are hopeful but the use of agency records raises problems. Records are not independent measures of functioning, because they can be so greatly influenced by social factors (Gough et al, 1987). Firstly, an agencies' perceptions of families may be affected by the knowledge that these families are participating in a special programme. Secondly, even if agency perceptions are objective, the awareness of special interventions may also affect the actions it considers appropriate for such families. Social factors shape agencies' perceptions as well as actions, which is well illustrated by evidence that the identification of social welfare cases varies geographically by as much as a factor of 10, and only a proportion of this variation is likely to be due to variations in incidence (Gough 1987, 1988, 1992; Gough et al, 1987).

Several studies did not restrict their samples to socially or economically deprived groups. Taylor and Beauchamp (1988) included a broad range of high and low income families. 'Perinatal Positive Parenting' in the Ellen Gray series (Gray et al, 1983) examined a mainly middle class sample. She and her colleagues reported a treatment effect from the joint parent-volunteer led discussion groups, but unfortunately the high rate of sample attrition calls these results into question.

Stevenson and Bailey (1988) undertook an experimental study of a post natal mothers support group recruiting mothers from six general medical practices in London. Mothers were randomly assigned to the intervention groups but there was differential uptake of this offer. Attenders were of higher social class and had received more formal education than non attenders. At three year follow up attenders scored higher on a test of physical and mental health than non attenders, but only if they had been experiencing adversity. If they had not been experiencing adversity the attenders scored worse than non attenders. Attenders who attended frequently improved more than those attending infrequently. It seems that the outcome depended upon who the attenders were and their reasons for attending. Research therefore needs to become more detailed and sophisticated in the hypotheses being tested and in the variables being controlled in the research design and analysis.

In the final study, Dachman and colleagues (1986) attempted to teach fathers skills in infant care. The programme had a dramatic effect on fathers' scores of the correct steps to take in caring for their infant and in the number of stimulation activities that they engaged in with their infant. Stimulation scores only increased when the fathers were observed handling their own child. Fathers did not engage in stimulation activities when demonstrating their care behaviour with a doll.

In sum, the studies provided some evidence in favour of instruction of fathers in infant care, extra post-natal contact between mother and child, and increased involvement of parents. However, much could be argued for, on purely democratic and humanitarian grounds. For example, the amount of immediate post-natal contact of mother and child in the control groups of both the O'Connor and Siegal studies, are well below what would be considered acceptable practice in Britain in the 1990's. Only minimal mother-infant contact was allowed immediately post-partum and later contact was restricted feed times. Practice in the USA may also have changed since these studies were carried out.

2. General Risk Groups

Another group of studies were more specific in targeting their interventions on families who might be at greater risk of parenting problems on the basis of their social and economic background, including young or single parents.

89

The Pride in Parenthood project, similar to others in the Ellen Gray series (Gray et al, 1983), demonstrated the feasibility of an innovation while using it to develop local community services. The intervention formally evaluated, concerned the use of volunteer 'Family Friends' to support isolated first time mothers. No significant effects were found, although considerable client satisfaction was reported.

Lealman (1983) investigated the effect of extra health visiting and social work support on mothers in a wide range of risk situations. A large sample was used, which allowed random allocation of high and low risk groups to normal and extra services. Several positive effects of the programme were reported, but these results were not convincing in view of the type of measures used. Of more interest, is the finding of worse outcomes for the high risk group and much worse outcomes for the few families that were already receiving social work services before the intervention of the project. These findings suggest that we may be able to predict who is most at risk, but not be able to prevent poor outcomes.

More optimistic results have been reported by Olds and his colleagues (Olds et al, 1986a, 1986b, 1988), from a randomized controlled experiment design to assess the impact of various combinations of education and support on potentially at risk mothers. It was difficult to find differences between the treatment groups, but for single teenage mothers on low incomes there was significantly less infant crying, punitive restrictive maternal behaviour, emergency hospital care, and significantly greater infant intelligence in the targeted groups than in the controls. In addition, inclusion in the programmes was associated with completion of education by mothers and with return to work and fewer or later further pregnancies by single mothers on low incomes. Some of the measures arose from maternal self reports, and although these are not independent measures, they may still act as indicators of the project impact on maternal attitudes or levels of coping. For example, a mother's report of reduced infant crying may mean that the baby actually cries less or that the mother is less affected by the crying or both. Unfortunately, the study was not able to define whether the long term nature of the project was crucial to the positive effects that were recorded.

Another study of increased service support was conducted by Larson (1980). Mothers considered to be at risk as assessed by demographic factors were randomly allocated to three groups of pre and post-natal visiting by home visitor, post-natal visits only, and a no visit control group. The mothers with pre and post natal visiting scored significantly better on immunization rates, the environment for the child in the home, scores of maternal behaviour, feeding and interaction problems, and for participation of fathers. On most measures the group with post-natal visits only did better than controls, though not as well as those also receiving pre-natal visits.

The final study in this group was an experiment contrasting two different models of extra support for mothers considered at risk on a measure of low social supports (Barnard et al, 1988; Booth et al, 1989). The first model (MH) encouraged the mothers interpersonal skills and problem solving through the home visiting nurse's relationship and active participation with the mother. The second model (IR) was based on more traditional approach of community nursing offering advice and assisting with referrals to other agencies. The MH model was associated with greater contact and involvement with the nurse, less maternal depression, higher scores on the home environment and parenting competency. However the effect of group membership on depression, education, social skills, and security of attachment of child were all affected by the abilities of the mother. Less able mothers fared better in the MH group and the more able fared better in the IR group. The conclusion must again be that the efficacy of a programme depends upon the clients and their needs. Research will have to examine these processes in more detail.

Another finding was that despite mothers in the MH group accepting a more positive view of their world and showing improved scores on parenting, home environment and depression scales, the security of child attachment was poor across all groups. A result that confirms the conclusion that improving parental mental state and home environment does not necessarily translate into improvements in the functioning of the child.

3. *Parents referred as individually at risk*

The final group of studies examined interventions targeted at families identified on an individual basis as being at risk – rather than on general demographic characteristics as in the previous group.

Most of the studies were concerned with similar support services to those in the previous two sections. Two studies did use different methods or outcome measures to those already considered and both these studies reported positive results, although neither study was sufficiently precise in design for this to be accepted uncritically.

Gabinet (1979) used trained supervised students to apply psycho-therapy to help clients to work through painful experiences and increase self awareness of parenting. Outcome measures were ratings of parental functioning and parental behaviour. Both measures increased at post test and improvement was correlated with length of treatment. The problem with the results is, that the codings were completed by the therapists and were therefore open to experimental error.

Soumenkoff and colleagues (1982, 1986) used an unspecified form of psycho-social care within the hospital during the antenatal period, in order to lower rates of prematurity. This seemed to be achieved when results were compared to average levels of prematurity for the hospital. Ounstead et al (1982), however, found no effect of extra ante natal support on birth weights.

The other studies in this group used a variety of supportive and educational techniques and a similar assortment of methods and measures for evaluation. Chapman and Reynolds (1982) reported improved maternal behaviours subsequent to a post-natal support group for at risk mothers. Quitiquit et al (1986) reported high parental satisfaction of a preventive home visiting scheme for high risk mothers attending a military hospital in Hawaii. Monaghan and Buckfield (1981) evaluated the impact of a broad package of child care, education and advice, and other social supports on a large sample of high risk mothers and reported an effect on the proportion of children received into care. The results are difficult to interpret because the comparison figures were derived from a previous study and there may not have been consistency in agency decisions to remove children from their homes.

Two other studies applied more rigorous controlled experimental designs and, interestingly, these were the least optimistic about the effects of the interventions (Gray J.D., 1979; Barth, 1991). Gray examined a scheme of increased paediatric and community nurse service plus emotional support from a lay visitor. Barth (1991) reported on a scheme of task centred support from approximately eleven home visits by trained parenting consultants. Although some positive effects of intervention reported by the studies, the main finding was the continued problems of these families, thus vindicating the screening methods at referral. May be the families' problems were too pervasive to be significantly modified by time limited interventions of this kind.

A positive outcome reported by Gray J.D. et al (1979), was that where injury occurred to children in the experimental group, it tended to be of a less serious nature than in the control group. This shows a subtle positive effect of therapy and suggests that simple outcome measures such as child abuse or aggression towards the child abuse may be too crude a measure to register improvements. As already stated, child abuse is not a precise concept, is very susceptible to variation in its identification, and is but one of many possible adverse outcomes for children and families (Gough et al, 1987).

Discussion

The components of the programmes examined in these studies, were similar for all the sample groups and for both the antenatal and post-natal periods. They included material and educational resources, emotional and social support, increased opportunities for bonding in what may be sensitive periods for mothers and infants with more liberal maternity ward and medical monitoring regimes, and extra routine services from medical, nursing and social work staff.

The evaluations varied to the extent in which experimental designs were employed. Two studies were more concerned with exploring new approaches to service delivery and in developing local services, than with assessment of particular techniques, and this was reflected in their research methodologies. Other studies did attempt experimental designs, but without replication studies or other confirming evidence, they were not precise enough to allow great credence to be given to any significant results.

Studies which did employ greater precision in experimental design and which used independent outcome measures, fell prey to a different problem. In an attempt to distinguish the various components of the interventions, they adopted complex designs with several experimental and control groups. The importance of comparing the relative impact of different aspects of multicomponent interventions cannot be overestimated, but the use of multiple groups weakened the research designs in two ways. Firstly, the reduced sample in each group made it more difficult to identify any experimental effects. Secondly, in the absence of highly specified hypotheses, there was no basis for distinguishing between the relative importance of different outcome measures or between different experimental and control groups. There were so many potential comparisons, that the significant findings reported were less convincing than if these particular findings had been specifically predicted in advance.

Generally, there is a need for explicit theoretical bases for the interventions, which should clarify what was being attempted and thus inform experimental hypotheses, the selection of specific outcome measures, and the analysis of results. A common problem was that outcome measures were not independent. For example: parents' opinions of their children or of the helpfulness of the service may be useful measures depending on what the intervention was aiming to achieve. Parents' opinions of their children could be sensibly used to reflect attitude changes, but not to assess changes in parental behaviour without some additional evidence or justification (which was usually lacking). Similarly, parental opinion of the service may be a useful indication of consumer response including motivation and likelihood of service uptake, but may not accurately measure the degree of service impact on parenting.

Many of the interventions were based on concepts of social support discussed in Chapter Four, and similar criticisms apply to the absence of specification about how particular supports relate to particular problems and how these are assessed in the studies. However, some of the programmes also had a more specific training role which is easier to evaluate.

Several studies reported positive effects of the intervention programmes for all three types of risk population. Most of the outcome measures were of parental behaviour or mental state and few studies made direct independent measures of the children or their interactions with their parents. Those studies that did use such measures found that they did not improve in line with improvements in the parental measures (Barnard et al, 1988; Booth et al, 1989; Gabinet, 1979). It may therefore be dangerous to rely on parental measures and parental assessments of children's progress. Studies of post natal depression have also reported that interventions effective at alleviating depression do not always improve child functioning or child-parent interactions (Leverton, 1991; Murray et al, 1991). The existence of maternal depression is, however, associated with the occurrence of problems for the children (Cutrona and Troutman, 1986; Stein et al, 1991; Murray, 1992). It may therefore be important to initiate preventive programmes ante natally so that they can help prevent the depression that leads to the seemingly more intractable child and child-parent interaction problems. Alternatively more direct work involving the children is called for. The potential for a prevention ante natal approach is supported by Larson's (1980) finding that pre-natal plus post-natal visiting was more effective than post natal visiting only. Soumenkoff et al (1982) also report that extra pre-natal supports for at risk mothers was associated with reduced prematurity rates, but other studies of social support in pregnancy report no effect on birth outcomes, though they do indicate effects on maternal anxiety, satisfaction with obstetric care, involvement of fathers in care of the child, and health problems in the children (Simpson, 1989).

Another important finding of the studies reviewed in this chapter is the differential effects reported for sub-groups within some of the study samples (Barnes et al, 1988; Booth et al, 1989; Stevenson, 1988). For example, the report that more intelligent mothers or those not experiencing adversity did not benefit or even regressed after receiving a programme benefiting other mothers. A study by Affleck et al (1989) in families with infants in special care baby units found similar results. Mothers with low needs for support had lower outcome scores on sense of competence, perceived control, and responsiveness, whilst those with high needs for support improved on those measures at post-test. The support offered to those already coping seems to have been disruptive. May be mothers would have benefited from supports of a different kind or offered in a different way. Just as perceptions of negative events mitigate their psychological effect, perceptions and reactions to supportive interventions will also mediate their efficacy.

A third finding of the studies reviewed is the confirmation of the screening procedures. Many parents identified at risk did have later parenting problems notwithstanding the interventions offered (Gray, J.D., 1977, 1979; Lealman et al, 1983; Ounstead et al, 1982). The predictive risk assessments were well below 100% effective and so only provide a basis for targeting resources rather than labelling as at risk of child abuse. This strategy of targeting resources is only appropriate if the interventions do not have adverse effects on some subjects. The studies showing differential effects on sample sub-groups suggest that stigma of labelling and possibly wasted resources are not the only costs of inaccurate targeting policies.

The impact of the intervention programmes reviewed was not dramatic, and it could be argued that the cost of the extra preventive resources required, are not justified by the degree of prevention achieved. However they could be justified purely on grounds of improving pre and post-natal services for the benefit of all mothers, not just those targeted by social agencies as being in some way deficient. In this context it is worth noting that only a few studies reviewed used consumer satisfaction measures to assess programme success, in contrast to the common use of this measure in the programmes to develop community awareness (Chapter 3) and the provision of support by aides and volunteers (Chapter 4). If services were provided on the basis of parents' needs or parents' rights then the research studies might need to select different outcome measures that may only correlate with child outcomes in the long term.

Summary

1. The studies examined interventions that use a variety of techniques to support families (mostly mothers) in the ante and post-natal periods. The techniques used included training in skills, provision of tangible aid, cognitive guidance, and emotional support. The users of these services were first-time mothers from normal or demographically at risk populations, or mothers who had been specifically referred with potential parenting problems.

2. The studies revealed some positive programme effects but these are difficult to confirm because of problems in research design. The research was also not able to specify in detail which of the techniques and resources used were most effective for which clients. The main difficulties were:
    – lack of independent measures of outcome;
    – multiple comparisons attempting to isolate effects of specific components of intervention, resulted in small cell sizes in some of the more experimentally controlled designs;
    – a lack of explicit theoretical base and clear hypotheses that would allow specificity of research designs and appropriate measures of outcome.

3. Positive results of programmes on parental functioning were not matched by improvements in child functioning or child-parent interactions. The conclusion is that either the children's needs should be directly targeted or preventive interventions with parents should start prenatally.

4. There is some evidence of programmes having differential effects on different groups of subjects and that these effects were sometimes negative. There is thus an even greater need for future studies to specify the components of the aims of interventions and the manner in which these are achieved.

5. Some interventions were successful in identifying families at future risk. As such screening produces many false positives and negatives, it is important to consider the negative effects of a wrong prediction. Screening for general need for help and support has fewer negative consequences, than screening specifically for child abuse, but there is still the potential for negative effects of special interventions.

6. The costs of the interventions are high considering the weak evidence of the modest results achieved. On the other hand, several of the services and resources could be provided to improve the quality of pre and post-natal care for consumers of these services even without proven effects on parental or child functioning.

Chapter Five Research Summaries

Barnard et al (1988), Booth et al (1989)

PREVENTION OF PARENTING ALTERATIONS FOR WOMEN WITH LOW SOCIAL SUPPORT

Sample: 147 mothers (reduced to 95 at post-test) in the third trimester of pregnancy recruited from clinics in King County Washington. Criteria of low social support (clinical rating from interview) and less than 23 weeks pregnant. Women tended to live in crowded conditions, to move frequently, to have little stability, high marital discord, and little medical care. Mothers had mean age of 21 years, 70% were single, and most were not high school graduates.

Focus: Social competence and parenting of young at risk mothers with low social support.

Objectives: To prevent socio-emotional disturbances and developmental delay in the children.

Programme: Treatment for approximately 18 months from mid pregnancy to child age of 1 year. Home visits by a single consistent caregiver with written protocols and specific objectives. An average of 16 contacts of a total of 18 hours per client. Two methods: (1) Mental Health (MH) Model. The nurse demonstrated interpersonal skills and problem solving through her relationship with the mother, involving the mother as an active participant, and structuring the environment to help the mother to be more effective. (2) Information/Resource (IR) model that approximated to traditional infant community nursing services. It focused on the physical and developmental health of the mother and child with the nurse providing information plus making and co-ordinating referrals to other agencies.

Design: Measures collected by experimentally blind staff including rating of video taped interventions. (1) Maternal competencies: Beck Depression Inventory (BDI); Personal Resources Questionnaire; Community Life Skills Scale, a 32 item scale completed by researcher; Social Skills Scale, a 63 item observational record of conversations with the researcher; Life Experiences Survey, and Difficult Life Circumstances Scale; (2) Parenting Competency: The Nursing Child Assessment Teaching Scale (NCATS); Nursing Child Assessment Feeding Scale: Home Observation for Measurement of the Environment (HOME). (3) Child's Competency: Bayley Developmental Scales; Mastery Motivation Tests; Achenbach Child Behaviour Checklist (at 2–3 years); Ainsworth Strange Situation (at 13 and 20 months). (4) Record of interventions of monitoring, informing, support, therapy, and of achievement of programme goals.

Results: (1) Drop out: 65% of sample retained at child age of 1 year, but made up of 80% remaining in MH group and 53% remaining in IR group. Drop out was mostly due to subject refusal (12%), geographical moves (10%), death or adoption of infant or foetus (8%). Drop out cases did not differ on demographic variables, but the mothers were less socially competent. Only differences found between remaining treatment groups were that IR group had more children over 6 years and fewer Caesarian deliveries. (2) Nurse contact, attained treatment goals, and relative frequency of 'therapy' nursing acts were significantly higher in the MH group. The IR group had significantly greater relative frequency of 'informing' nursing acts. (3) MH group had less maternal depression at child age of 1 and 2 years compared to the IR group. MH group also perceived that in receipt of more support, had a more positive view of their world, had more mothers whose social competencies had increased, and had higher HOME and NCATS scores. However, no post-test differences in social skills or mother-child interaction. (4) Only 45% securely attached, but no gross between group differences in attachment at 13 months. (5) Two way ANOVA (group and maternal characteristics) showed that for lower IQ mothers there was significantly greater attachment, parent-child interaction, and HOME scores in the MH group. For higher IQ mothers there was greater security and stability of security of attachment in the IR group. For maternal characteristics of depression, education, and social skills there was the same pattern of less competent mothers having better outcomes in the MH group and the more competent mothers faring better in the IR group.

(6) Multiple regression indicated that attainment of treatment goals predicted post-treatment social skills and that these skills predicted the quality of mother-child interactions. Path analysis indicated the strong association between attainment of treatment goals and mother-child interactions (both direct and indirectly through post-treatment social skills) was due only to mothers with low initial skills. For mothers with high initial skills there was only the association between post-treatment skills and mother-child interactions. (7) Correlational analyses showed that for the low initial skills mothers, the nurses used more therapy when they had more client contact, when the number of household members was small, and when the subject had more than one child.

Notes: The two papers seem to be on the same study yet the sample criteria in Booth et al (1989) include broader risk categories than low social support. The authors argue that (a) interpersonal relationships are important in maintaining clients in intervention, (b) MH group effective for women with low initial skills, (c) the effect of the MH treatment on maternal depression important as it may allow mother to function sufficiently to seek support that in turn enables her to nurture her child, (d) the poor child attachments in both groups suggests that it is insufficient to only work with the parent (e.g. depression) in very vulnerable families, (e) the success of mothers with high initial skills was more strongly related to their internal and external resources than to the treatment.

Barth (1991)

AN EXPERIMENTAL EVALUATION OF IN-HOME CHILD ABUSE PREVENTION SERVICES

Sample: 191 pregnant women identified by agencies as possessing at least two of a range of risk factors including under use of services, psychiatric, criminal, or abuse record, low self-esteem, chaotic lifestyle, lack of social support, poor health, unwanted pregnancy. Many had at least 4 factors, the most common being low esteem/depressed/isolated, under use of needed services, lack of available supports. 11% of referrals could not be contacted. 12% refused to participate, 16% could not be contacted for post test, resulting in 61% of referrals fully completing study.

Focus: Parenting effectiveness of mother at risk of abuse.

Objectives: To enable effective parenting and minimise risk of abuse through developing mothers' abilities, social support, bonding, and goal setting and problem solving.

Programme: Child Parent Enrichment Project (CPEP). Trained parenting consultants assigned to parents on basis of geography and ethnicity provided an average of 11 home visits (range 5 to 20). Task centred approach with agreed tasks recorded on sheets for review of task achievement. Tasks included attending prenatal care, regular meals, and preparing home for new baby. An average of 17 tasks per client were completed. Consultants also provided material assistance, advice, and modelling of appropriate child care and home care skills. Service lasted approximately 6 months. The control group mothers were referred to health or social services as indicated by a 2 hour assessment interview.

Design: Repeated measures (pre-test, post-test at child age 4 months, and follow up at average of 3 years) with random allocation to one experimental and one control condition.

Measures: 1. Pre and post test measures: (a) shortened version of Child Abuse Potential Inventory (CAPI), (b) Centre for Epidemiologic Studies Depression Scale (CES-D), (c) State-Trait Anxiety Inventory (STAI), (d) Pearlin Mastery Scale on locus of responsibility, (e) Community Resources Use Scale (CRUS), (f) Social Supports and Preparation Scale (SSP) on the availability of helping resources and preparation for birth of child, (g) Inventory of Social Supportive Behaviours (ISSB), (h) Social Support Inventory (SSI).

2. Post test only measures all from mothers' reports: (a) Prenatal care of visiting doctor, (b) Whether followed healthy or unhealthy diet during pregnancy, (c) Summary score of birth problems, (d) Length of hospital stay, (e) Birthweight, (f) Comparison between expected and experienced discomfort in childbirth, (g) Worries re care of child, (h) Infant Temperament Questionnaire (ITQ), (i) Need Care: care of child by others due to lack of care by mother, (j) Health: child illness, (k) Emergency Care: frequency of emergency medical care, (l) Baby Care: frequency of routine medical child assessment and immunization.

3. Follow up of involvement in child welfare services: (a) non investigated reports, (b) non substantiated investigations, (c) investigated and substantiated reports.

Results: (1) No pre-test differences between groups except for greater proportion of child abuse referrals in CPEP group. (2) Effectiveness of screening indicated by low levels of supportive relationships for mothers and high CAPI scores. (3) No significant between group differences identified by multivariate analysis of covariance or analysis of variance. (4) Parents reported satisfaction with the programme. (5) Few differences in subsequent child abuse reports. More unsubstantiated reports in control group. Also a trend of CPEP mothers not previously reported to have fewer reports than controls.

Notes: Authors suggests that some evidence of a prevention effect from the fewer child abuse reports in the intervention group, but that the families' difficulties were may be too great for a short duration para professional programme. The intervention was helpful and worthwhile for some families.

Chapman and Reynolds (1982)

POST-NATAL GROUP FOR MOTHERS WITH SERIOUS MOTHERING PROBLEMS

Sample: Post-natal; 5 mothers and 6 infants referred by health visitors; concern because of poor understanding, expectations, or satisfaction with maternal role. All had husbands in the armed forces or professions and were not materially deprived. Most births had complications.

Focus: Secondary prevention for mothers at risk of child abuse.

Objectives: To modify behaviour patterns; to increase awareness of relationship problems; to increase confidence and to decrease dependence on health visitor; to develop realistic expectations of children and awareness of their needs.

Programme: 6 weekly, 1 hour group sessions, consisting of video presentations of the Open University 'First Year of Life Course', talks by child psychologists and a pre-school adviser on child handling and play. Homework diary for attempting new child care techniques. Discussions with health visitor or behavioural nurse therapist of videos and homework tasks.

Design: Repeated measures (pre and post-test) on treatment group.

Measures: Rating scales of parenting behaviour on basis of appropriateness and whether enjoyed by parents. Mothers' perceptions of the service.

Results: All but one child improved, measured on the appropriateness of their mothers' behaviour, including a child subsequently placed on the child abuse register. The registered child was one of two for which there was a slight drop in ratings of parental enjoyment. Overall there was an improvement on both measures. The majority of the mothers were positive about the opportunity to share experiences and gain information and about the size of the group. They would have liked more practical demonstrations and information on feeding and illness.

Dachman et al (1986)

INFANT CARE TRAINING PROGRAMME WITH FIRST TIME FATHERS

Sample: Experiment 1: three fathers (aged 24, 26 and 34) whose wives were pregnant for the 1st time. Experiment 2: three fathers (aged 24, 26 and 29) whose wives were pregnant for the first time.

Focus: Infant care by fathers.

Objectives: To develop fathers' skills in infant care. To evaluate a hospital based (Expt. 1) and a home based (Expt. 2) training programme.

Programme: Sequence of sessions for both experiments: (1) Instruction manual with self administered test questions, review of items with trainer and observational test (Expt. 1 only). (2) Training session: modelling of skills not meeting criterion, observational test and corrective feedback. (3) Repeat training session: retest and modelling of skills not meeting criterion.

First session lasted approximately 90 minutes, further sessions of 30 to 60 minutes. Mean of 2.2 training sessions per subject. Experiment 1 used a baby doll for training most testing. Experiment 2 used only the fathers' infants at home.

Design: Repeated measures on intervention sample only.

Measures: Observation of father performing a set of care procedures with baby doll. Interval observation and per cent occurrence of 10 care skills by trained observer. Direct observation of father's skills with newborn infants at home. Consumer satisfaction questionnaire.

Results: Parents in both experiments approved of the intervention procedures and treatment outcomes.

Experiment 1: Baseline correct infant care step scores of 22% to 33% increased after instruction manual to scores of 60% to 73% and increased after training sessions to scores of 88% to 91%. At follow up direct observation in the home scores were from 87% to 99%. Infant stimulation activities were zero at baseline and hardly increased after the instruction manual, but increased to between 23 and 50 activities at post training and to 29 to 35 activities at follow up in the home.

Experiment 2: Baseline scores of correct infant care steps with doll of 22% to 33% and with their infant at home of 31% to 59%. After post training scores increased from 80% to 92%. The number of stimulation activities were zero at baseline with doll, but were from 9 to 43 for their infant at home, and increased to between 41 and 43 at post training, with a large increase in non verbal stimulation.

Gabinet (1979)

PREVENTION OF CHILD ABUSE AND NEGLECT IN AN INNER CITY POPULATION

Sample: 77 out of 180 pregnant women or recent mothers referred by obstetricians or paediatricians as being at risk of abuse on basis of past abuse, ambivalence re either their pregnancy or their child. Sample had personality problems such as tendency to depression, paranoia, and schizophrenia (as measured by MMPI scales). There were also social and financial problems. Sample selection on basis of availability due to referral on to other services or not sufficient co-operation.

Focus: Secondary prevention for mothers at risk of child abuse and neglect.

Objectives: To change parental behaviour, to increase awareness of feelings, to help meet parents' emotional needs, to improve their coping, and to prevent deterioration in parents' lives which could lead to child abuse.

Programme: Therapy based on dynamic personality theory as developed by Fraihberg (1975) administered in the home by trained college graduates and a social worker. Treatment involves working through painful experiences to increase self awareness, impulse control, and stress reduction and is tailored for each client following initial assessment. Each mother received at least six visits. There was also a weekly group to increase social skills and contacts.

Design: Repeated measures (pre and post-tests) to allow internal comparisons through contrasting improvement with base level of functioning and with degree of intervention.

Measure: Pre-test of personality (MMPI), post test of worker ratings of improvement on 14 scales that include child handling, coping with crisis, parental adjustment, and exercise of their household and parental responsibilities.

Results: Mean improvements of 30% to 50% on all variables and these were significantly related to length of time in programme. Parent factors increased faster than child or parent-child interaction factors.

Notes: Possible confounding effects of (1) sample selection in terms of the selection of the 77 sample from the 180 referred; (2) sample selection in terms of the length of time in therapy; (3) use of workers' ratings of change. Article discusses the need for initial support for parent before child care issues can be usefully addressed, the problems of reconciling supportive prevention with the occasional necessity for crisis intervention, and problems of outreach families.

Gray E. et al (1983)

PERINATAL POSITIVE PARENTING

Sample: 252 first time mothers living in a certain geographical area being seen by a particular paediatrician in one hospital during one year without identified problems. Sample was notable for being predominantly white, middle class, well educated, and married. Measures collected on sub-samples varying in size from n = 97 to n = 139 depending on post-test instrument.

Focus: Parenting of first time mothers. Primary prevention.

Objectives: To provide subjects with personal supports and information to assist them in their new roles as parents.

Programme: Hospital visit from volunteers who discuss and show videos and written materials on child care; follow-up 'phone calls to the family home; follow-up visit to check everything was all right and to offer modelling of caretaking skills and information on community resources. If a problem manifested itself, volunteer could call a meeting of the project to assess situation. If family referred to another agency, then project contact ceased. Also groups co-led by a volunteer and a parent, were held in a variety of settings and discussed aspects of child care. Volunteers were recruited by advertising and from community organizations and received 24 hours training.

Design: Repeated measures (post-test and follow up) design with random allocation to treatment and a smaller control group. Different sub-samples tested.

Measures: Parenting inventory on role reversal, lack of empathy, unrealistic expectations, beliefs re physical punishment (Bavolek Adult/Adolescent Parenting Inventory); mothers' idealization of child (Broussard Neonatal Perception Inventory). At 12–15 month follow-up: inventory on nurturing (H.O.M.E. Inventory) and home observation of parent-child interactions.

Results: No significance between group differences on parenting inventory or measure of neonatal perception at immediate or later follow-up. At later follow-up significant treatment differences in maternal involvement and nurturing. Process evaluation showed relatively low rate of project interventions in the sample.

Notes: Large sample drop out on many outcome measures.

Gray E. et al (1983)

PRIDE IN PARENTHOOD

Sample: The treatment sample consisted of 28 socially isolated first-time mothers in the last trimester of pregnancy referred by obstetricians from 4 hospitals in Norfolk, Virginia. Norfolk contains many military families and has relatively high reporting rates for child abuse. The sample was fairly young, on low incomes, and resided in inner city areas. There was also a similar control group containing at least 27 expectant mothers.

Focus: Parents potentially at risk of child abuse and neglect.

Objectives: To increase nurturing capacity, coping skills, self-concept, support networks, and reduce stress of young, socially isolated first time mothers.

Methods: Use of Family Friends, 5 women (3 white, 2 black) 4 of whom were grandmothers. Family Friends were selected for personal qualities and were given training. Contacts were through home visits (20%), telephone calls (45%), outings (18%) including accompanying parents to welfare agencies. Some Family Friends also helped with physical resources and educational resources. Twice monthly meeting of all participants including infants and male partners with discussions on parenting and child development.

Design: Repeated measures (pre and post-test) experimental design with random allocation to experimental and control groups. Samples divided in half with the two main measures only applied to one half.

Measures: Inventories of parental expectations, empathy, belief about punishment (Adult/Adolescent Parenting Inventory) and parents' idealization of child (Broussard Neonatal Perception Inventory), client satisfaction questionnaires (post-test to treatment group).

Results: Control group had higher pre-test baseline on both perceptions of, and attitudes towards, infants. No significant treatment/control differences associated with intervention. Mothers in the treatment programme all rated it very favourably. Many friendships developed in the group and there was a high level of father involvement.

Notes: Large sample drop out in pre and post-test measures making any intervention effects difficult to detect. Few numerical details given in the report. The development of community services was a major objective of the programme but was not formally evaluated in the report.

Gray E. et al (1983)

RURAL FAMILY SUPPORT PROJECT

Sample: (1) 1622 mothers giving birth in the first two years of the intervention project in any of the 5 rural counties covered by the project that was based in Columbus, Indiana, (2) 29 of the service providers who received training in awareness of child abuse. (3) 13 representatives of local service agencies and institutions.

Focus: Parent-child bonding. Primary prevention.

Objectives: To establish: pre-natal classes, bonding experiences for parents, hospital procedures for prolonged post-natal contact, sibling visits in hospital, support and referral services for high risk families, guidance for developing post-natal peer support groups, home visiting services, parenting and child development classes for school children, model programmes for community based parent education and a model for project replication.

Programme: Adapting old services, implementing new services, training old staff, consultation on service development and service delivery, and publicity. Project staff of 4 set up initial planning groups to promote programme and to achieve the listed objectives. They then withdrew from leadership function to act as enablers for the tasks taken on by the local services and community.

Design: (1) Post-test on a sample of service recipients with statistical comparisons based on whether new or old services experienced. (2) Post-test on a sample of service representatives. (3) Repeated measures (pre and post test) on a sample of service providers who underwent training.

Measures: (1) Post-test for mothers: questionnaire on the services, adult-child relationship and confidence in caring for child plus a follow-up interview on those willing to participate (n = 270) about their experience of the birth. (2) Post-test for representatives: opinions as to the impact of the programme on adults preparation for parenthood, on service providers' awareness and ability to intervene with parenting problems. (3) Pre and post-test of in-service training, awareness of child abuse and neglect and intervening in problems of parenting using responses to vignettes.

Results: (1) Post-test for mothers: high scores, but these correlated with experience of post partum contact. Those who were already mothers were particularly confident with children. Separate analysis of first time mothers showed no effects from changes in the hospital programmes, though there was a significant negative effect of attendance at ante-natal classes. The further follow-up recorded positive experiences of the birth but the sub-sample consisted of those most confident in child care. (2) Post-test for representatives: positive in terms of the provision of new services except for parent education resources. They did not believe that there had been a drop in the number of dysfunctional families. (3) In-service training: the only pre to post-test significant change was in the proportion who stated that they would discuss noted parenting problems directly with the parent rather than with someone else. The overall picture is of a change in service provision but no clear impact recorded on the individual or family level.

Notes: Authors emphasize the deliberate rejection of intrusive research methods as they would violate the relationships developed by the project. Community ownership of new initiatives was seen as crucial to their being useful and to their being maintained in the long term.

Gray J.D. et al (1977, 1979)

PREDICTION AND PREVENTION OF CHILD ABUSE AND NEGLECT

Sample: 150 mothers randomly sampled from 350 first and second time mothers who did not receive neonatal intensive care in early 1970's in one hospital. Sample screened through interviews, questionnaires, and neonatal observations and placed into a high risk group of 100 and a low risk group of 50 on basis of circumstances, expectations, feelings, and neonatal interactions. Research groups consisted of 75 mothers with 25 each in (1) high risk group plus intervention (2) high risk without intervention (3) low risk.

Focus: Secondary prevention for mothers at risk of child abuse in the post-natal period.

Objectives: To alleviate social pressure, foster attachments and prevent child abuse. Also to examine feasibility of prediction of abnormal parenting.

Programme: Paediatric check-up with bi-monthly clinic visits, telephone calls at regular intervals and times of crisis by paediatrician, weekly visits from public health nurse, emotional support from lay visitor, and referral to other agencies as appropriate.

Design: Post-test comparisons with random allocation to high risk treatment group and high risk control groups. Also low risk control group to evaluate screening technique.

Measures: Agency records of resources provided, physical growth, immunisations and accidents; indicators of abnormal parenting; developmental assessment (Denver Development Screening Test).

Results: No statistically significant difference between intervention and control groups on rates of development, accidents or child abuse. Significant difference in expected direction on number of cases with serious injuries requiring hospitalization. Also found screening was effective because designed high risk groups produced significantly more child abuse reports, accidents, out of home placements, marital problems, post partum depression, poor feelings of attachment and likelihood of bottle feeding. Correct prediction rate of 79% claimed.

Notes: Few details on the interventions or which components most useful.

Larson C.P. (1980)

EFFICACY OF PRENATAL AND POST-PARTUM HOME VISITS ON CHILD HEALTH AND DEVELOPMENT

Sample: 115 mother infant pairs from total of 936 meeting study criteria of French or English Canadian ethnicity, age between 18–35 years, below poverty line income, no tertiary education, no significant illness in pregnancy nor prior history of psychiatric hospitalization, delivery of healthy full-term infant, agreement to participate (43 fitting pre-birth criteria declined). Subjects recruited from private offices of obstetricians of large urban teaching hospital in Montreal.

Focus: Parenting of mothers with demographic risk factors.

Objectives: Preventive approach to child health. To facilitate early experiences of at risk children and improve specific health outcomes.

Programme: Group A: (1) Prenatal-visit during 7th month of pregnancy in order to meet home visitor, review visits, review anticipated delivery, post partum, preparation for new child at home. (2) Hospital visit on 2nd post partum day to involve mother in care of child and maximize opportunities for interaction. (3) Post natal visits: 4 in first 6 weeks, plus a further 5 by 15 months of age. Visits followed prearranged protocol appropriate to age of child with counselling and advice on general caretaking, mother-infant interaction, social context and supports and child development. Group B: Post-natal visits only: 7 in weeks 6 to 36, plus a further 3 by 15 months of age. Group C: no intervention control group.

Design: Repeated measures (during and post-treatment) random allocation to two treatment and one control condition.

Measures: Independent experimentally blind assessments in the home at 6 weeks and 6, 12, and 18 months of age of (1) health status inventory on use of services, (2) HOME, a home environment and stimulation inventory, (3) a maternal behaviour rating scale.

Results: (1) No significant pre-test differences between groups. (2) Both intervention groups made adequate use of well child clinics, but significantly more in Group A had up to date immunizations. No group differences in emergency room visits, but significantly higher accident rates in Group C. Group B perceived by home visitors to have greater problems than Group A, indicated by significantly longer average visits. (3) HOME Scale: significantly better scores for Group A compared to Groups B and C at each assessment. Provision of play materials and variety in daily routine seemed to be most affected.

Across groups, primiparous mothers scored high for organization of environment and multiparous scored high for avoidance of restriction and punishment. (3) Maternal Behaviour: Group A scored higher than other groups at each assessment, and statistically significant except at 12 months. Across groups, primiparous tended to be more responsive with higher quality and frequency of contact. (4) At follow up, Group A had significantly fewer feeding problems, mother-infant interaction problems, and non participant fathers.

Notes: The author concludes that the intervention was effective but only if started prenatally.

Lealman et al (1983)

PREDICTION AND PREVENTION OF CHILD ABUSE – AN EMPTY HOPE?

Sample: 2802 maternity cases in Bradford in 1979, 511 (18%) of which were deemed to be at risk as teenage single parents with little ante-natal support. Sample divided into four groups: (1) 103 at risk plus intervention (2) 209 at risk without intervention (3) 199 at risk but already using social work (4) 2291 not at risk. All Asians excluded.

Focus: Secondary prevention in the ante and post-natal period for mothers at risk of child abuse and neglect.

Objectives: To screen cases at risk of child abuse and other problems. To prevent these problems with a programme of extra support services.

Programme: Social work service from project worker plus drop-in centre and extra health visiting from isolated mothers.

Design: Controlled experimental design with random allocation to groups. Additional comparisons with a naturally occurring treatment group and with non risk cases.

Measures: Children's growth, immunisation, admission to hospital, casualties, deaths, placement on child abuse at risk register, worker's assessments of family.

Results: At risk cases had fewer immunisations, more medical and social admissions to hospital, placements on the child abuse register, and more deaths. These figures were worst for risk cases receiving routine social work, followed by risk cases receiving no intervention, followed by at risk cases receiving project intervention. An exception was failure to thrive, which had the highest rate in the risk cases

with routine social work, followed by at risk with project intervention, followed by a much lower rate for at risk without intervention and lastly, the not at risk cases. Two thirds of identified abuse occurred in the 18% of cases deemed at risk, which vindicated screening measures even including many false positives.

Notes: Few details of the interventions provided. Manner in which routine social work cases were different from other at risk cases not specified.

Monaghan and Buckfield (1981)

IDENTIFICATION OF MOTHERS AT RISK OF PARENTING FAILURE AND METHODS OF SUPPORT

Sample: 200 mothers offered support in the neonatal clinic in a hospital in Dunedin, New Zealand of which 75 were rated as high risk. High risk mothers had emotional and material deprivation including poor housing and finance, poor relations and experiences with own parents, a sense of failure and low expectations of child. Few details on comparison high risk sample from a previous research project.

Focus: Secondary prevention for mothers in the post-natal period at risk of child abuse. Also the ability to predict at risk cases.

Objectives: To provide emotional, material and educational resources; to prevent parenting difficulties that could lead to child abuse and the removal of a child from the parental home.

Programme: Assessment; professional meetings to co-ordinate service; neighbourhood centre; Family Day Support Unit staffed by nurses and providing practical help with the child management; centre for advice for disadvantaged or disabled children; Director of Community Services; 24 hour 'phone line; 'Acorn Club' weekly discussion groups on child rearing in relaxed setting staffed by hospital and community workers; use of hospital swimming pool to encourage physical play and contacts. Comparison group from previous research offered referrals to general practitioners and routine social work.

Design: Comparison of outcomes of high risk group with outcomes of another high risk sample from previous research.

Measures: Loss (removal) of children from maternal care at 1 year of age; admission to paediatric ward for social or management reasons; self awareness and confidence of mothers attending Acorn Club; promptness of parents in seeking help; attachment and commitment to children.

Results: Statistically significant fewer removals of children from the present sample of high risk mothers compared to the previous project. The reduction is in part due to fewer crisis situations in the new sample. Article states that there was also an improvement on all other measures in contrast to previous research sample.

Notes: Few details on many of the outcome measures. The measure of removal of children is precise, but the policies and practice of the local services may have changed between the two pieces of research that are contrasted. The article does acknowledge the possible differences between the two high risk samples in the two pieces of research. Further details of part of the intervention are described in Egan (1986) and the development of the new screening methods are described in Monaghan et al (1986a, 1986b).

O'Connor et al (1980)

REDUCED INCIDENCE OF PARENTING INADEQUACY FOLLOWING 'ROOMING-IN'

Sample: Low income mothers giving birth in a hospital over a nine month period were selected randomly for 'rooming-in'. Research sample were the 143 'roomed in' who were first time mothers and who had normal healthy pregnancies and deliveries.

Focus: Parenting ability of low income first time mothers. Primary prevention of parenting inadequacy.

Objectives: Test of hypothesis that increasing post-partum mother infant contact increases early bonding and so reduces subsequent parenting inadequacy.

Programme: 'Rooming in' allowed up to 8 hours per day of mother infant contact with unlimited visiting of either the child's father or maternal grandmother following the initial post-partum separation of between 7 and 21 hours. Controls had at least 12 hours post-partum separation with subsequent contact restricted to feeding times.

Design: Post-test experimental design with random allocation (based on room availability) to one experimental and to one control group. No significant differences found between experimental and control subjects on race, age, intention to breastfeed, education, or welfare status.

Measures: Agency records of hospitalization, failure to thrive and abnormal development, physical abuse and substantiated maltreatment, voluntary or involuntary relinquishment of parental care, pathology in family relationships.

Results: Significantly more control families recorded as experiencing parenting inadequacy and significantly more of the children hospitalized because of this. However, there were also significantly more non-parent caretakers in the control group.

Notes: Sample unaware of hypothesis, but they may have been able to guess the general nature of the study. Also agency records not independent measures of outcome.

Olds et al (1986a, 1986b, 1988)

A RANDOMIZED TRIAL OF NURSE HOME VISITATION

Sample: 400 mothers recruited by 30th week of pregnancy. Recruited from 500 referred by a range of clinics on basis of primiparous plus risk characteristics of greater than 19 years old, single parents, or of low socio-economic status. 85% of the 400 met at least one criteria, 23% met all three criteria, and 15% not in risk groups. Author believes that most of the eligible subjects in the county were recruited, but 10% missed through late registration at clinics, and 10% missed by some non referrals by private obstetricians. County was a semi-rural area in Appalachian Region of New York State with 100,000 inhabitants.

Focus: Parenting by mothers with socio-demographic indicators of risk.

Objectives: To prevent a wide range of child health and developmental problems including child abuse.

Programme: Dependent on research groups (1) DS: no intervention, developmental screening at 12 and 24 months. (2) DS+T Developmental screening plus free transport for pre-natal and well child care. (3) DS+T+HV: Developmental screening plus free transport plus nurse home visitor during pregnancy, (4) DS+T+HV plus continuing home visiting up to two years post-partum. Home visiting programme was concerned with establishing rapport with families and in identifying and reinforcing family strengths. There were three main components: education of parent in child development and health education, involvement of family members and friends in child care and support of mother, linking mother with other services.

Design: Repeated measures (pre and post-test) experimental design with random allocation to groups stratified by race, marital status and geographic location.

Measures: Agency records of resources provided, length of gestation, birth weight, subsequent hospital visits; tests of intelligence at 12 months (Bayley Scales) and 24 months (Cattell); parental report of conflict, punishment, night waking, crying, eating problems and temperament; 'blind' observations (using checklist) of punishment, restriction, and provision of play materials.

Results: No treatment differences between groups (1) and (2) so these were combined to act as a comparison group for treatment groups (3) and (4). Treatment groups showed no overall effect on birth weight and length of gestation, but there were significantly heavier birth weights for the home visited young adolescent mothers. There were also significant effects on improved diets and support system and levels of smoking and kidney infections. At post-natal assessment there were slight significant differences in the expected direction for poor teenage single mothers: parental reports of infant crying, conflict and scolding, and observed restrictions, punishment and play material provision, and infant intelligence at 6 and 12 months. Treatment groups also had significantly fewer hospital visits. In the comparison groups there was an association between both hospital visits and abusive behaviour to infant, and reduced maternal sense of control. Treatment groups had no such observed relation. For women who had not completed high school there was a treatment effect on rapidity of returning to school. For poor unmarried women the treatment group subjects were employed 82% more of the time, had 43% fewer pregnancies and delayed the birth of their second child twelve months longer.

Notes: Few distinctions made between the 2 treatment groups. Very many potential comparisons possible because of number of measures and groups used.

Ounstead et al (1982)

FOURTH GOAL OF PERINATAL MEDICINE

Sample: 110 mother-child pairs referred by midwives because of concern about parenting ability, psychiatric history, disturbed behaviour in hospital, or other social or behavioural concerns. Cases referred from a total of 5365 births. 20% of babies admitted to Special Care Baby Unit compared to population rate of 7%. 37% of parents were currently single compared to a population rate of 8%.

Focus: High risk mother-child pairs for secondary prevention of bonding failure.

Objectives: To provide extra help and support to mother-child pairs identified as at risk of bonding failures and future parenting and developmental problems.

Programme: Additional support provided by general practitioner and health visitor to 60% of families.

Supportive and informative relationship with consultant paediatrician to 33% of families. Reminder received more intensive support.

Design: Post-test on intervention group only.

Measures: Questionnaire to health visitors and general practitioners to ascertain child's weight, health, placement, and professional concern about child at one to two years of age.

Results: Weight not different to general population, hospital admissions slightly higher than average, concerns about welfare of 25% of children, 6 children placed away from natural parents. Also 7 cases not identified by screening exercise were causing concern at one year of age.

Quitiquit et al (1986)

EARLY IDENTIFICATION OF HIGH RISK FAMILIES IN THE MILITARY

Sample: Mothers attending ante-natal services at a military hospital in Hawaii who are coded as at risk from a self report questionnaire and from an open-ended interview with the programmes Public Health Nurse.

Focus: Secondary prevention. Mothers in ante-natal period at risk of child abuse and neglect.

Objectives: To identify, prenatally, those mothers at risk and to enable them to adequately care for their children by reducing family stress, parent isolation, and by increasing their knowledge and skills and autonomy.

Programme: The Within the Home Visitor Program (W.I.T.H.) run by the Parent and Child Center of Hawaii (P.C.C.H.) as part of the Services Assisting Family Environments Project (Project S.A.F.E.) funded by the Department of Defence. The W.I.T.H. programme involves home visits assisting with material needs and transport, networking the family with other families and organizations, providing emotional support, and modelling and teaching appropriate child care.

Design: Post-test only.

Measures: Client satisfaction.

Results: Over 95% positive reports from parents involved in the programme.

Notes: A fuller evaluation was being considered.

Siegal et al (1980)

HOSPITAL AND HOME SUPPORT DURING INFANCY

Sample: 321 women willing and able to participate in the study from the 520 women attending a hospital in a poor urban area who met the study criteria. The criteria were an uncomplicated pregnancy, no twins predicted, no previous foetal deaths, no family members in study, an expectation that the mothers would be remaining in the area for the next year. The sample was divided into 6 groups: 3 experimental groups and 1 control group for those experiencing normal deliveries and 1 experimental group and 1 control group for those experiencing difficult pregnancies.

Focus: Mother infant relationships in low income families as primary prevention of child abuse.

Objectives: To assess the extent to which extra post-partum contact and home visits to low income families increase attachment and health care and reduce child abuse.

Programme: Early post-partum (E) contact of over 45 minutes in first 3 hours. Extended contact (EC) of over seven and a half hours per day for each subsequent day in hospital. Home visiting (HV) for 3 months to provide support in coping with situational stresses and to promote maternal involvement with infant. Control groups received only brief post-partum contact followed by two and a half hours daily contact in hospital and no home visiting.

Design: Post-test (×2) experimental design with random allocation into 4 experimental and 2 control groups. These were (1) normal delivery +E+EC; (2) normal delivery +E+EC+HV; (3) normal delivery +HV; (4) normal delivery control; (5) difficult delivery +EC+HV; (6) difficult delivery control. There were no significant differences between experimental and control groups in age, race, parity, years of education, marital status, vocabulary pre-test.

Measures: Maternal interviews and home observations at 4 and 12 months post partum used to develop 92 item ratings of attachment behaviour. Factor analysis on the attachment items produced 4 factors of acceptance, interaction/stimulation, consoling of infant, and infant positive/negative behaviours. Other measures included clinic, hospital admissions and hospital records; child protection records and central State Register.

Results: For the uncomplicated deliveries at 4 months early plus extended contact (group 1) was significantly associated with 'acceptance' and 'consoling'. Background factors were related to most outcomes and accounted for a major part of the variance. At 12 months the only intervention effect was early and extended contact (group 1) on infant positive/nega-

tive behaviour. For the complicated deliveries there was no statistically significant differences for the interventions at either 4 or 12 months, though there were some effects from background factors. No relationship was found between the interventions and the service records for either the complicated or uncomplicated deliveries.

Notes: The authors conclude that the results justify intervention but that it should be combined with other interventions in order to produce sustained effects. They argue that the lack of home visiting effects was due to it starting too late. If it had started during pregnancy, better rapport would have been established.

Soumenkoff et al (1982)

PREVENTION OF CHILD ABUSE AT THE ANTE-NATAL CARE LEVEL

Sample: 91 mothers attending a hospital in Brussels for ante-natal care referred to the project as being at risk by the departments of obstetrics, ante-natal care or child psychiatry. Mothers were referred on criteria associated with child abuse such as denial of pregnancy or background of abuse. Majority were single, socially isolated, and in low socio economic group. Many either did not want pregnancy or showed no anticipation of the birth. Sub-sample of 19 mothers whom the obstetric department considered to be in need of psychiatric help. They displayed psychopathological behaviour, ambivalent relationships or were violent.

Focus: Parenting by mothers considered to be at risk of abusing their children.

Objectives: To correct socio-economic and/or emotional maladjustment of mothers in order to prevent premature births and abuse of the infants. Same for sub-sample, but to a greater degree including changing self image, negative feelings, and social relationships in order to lessen chance of pathological parenting.

Programme: Various planned psycho-social interventions including hospitalization for those in acute stress, post-natal support and contraceptive advice. Also longer than usual assessments and interviews with the obstetrician plus greater general availability to the mothers. The sub-sample provided with long term intensive therapy that included social support, psycho-analysis, crisis intervention, family guidance and other forms of psychotherapy, and liaison with other agencies. Staff were social nurses and social workers.

Design: On-going longitudinal descriptive design.

Measures: Prematurity, evaluation of the child in the family at 6 months. For sub-sample: patients response to treatment and assessment of child's situation after birth.

Results: Only 57 of 91 mothers given full intervention and had a prematurity rate of 3.5% which contrasts with a hospital average rate of 7.6%. For intensive sub-sample there was 'success' for 16 of the 19 cases although only 9 children actually remained with their mothers. One success concerned twins who were abused, but parents protected them against further abuse by taking them to hospital.

Notes: Few details on methods of intervention or assessment of outcome beyond prematurity. Authors' comment on beneficial effect of programme on the approach of the Obstetrics Department. Further data on the programme can be found in Soumenkoff and Marneffe (1986), Marneffe et al (1986). These papers present data showing the potential of these prevention programmes, but illustrate the difficulties in ensuring long term follow-up support for the at risk families.

Stevenson and Bailey (1988)

CONTROLLED TRIAL OF POST NATAL MOTHERS' GROUPS AND PSYCHOSOCIAL PRIMARY PREVENTION

Sample: All 613 mothers giving birth in 6 general medical practices in London were randomly assigned to experimental (n=420) and control (n=193) samples. The experimental sample were invited to attend a mothers' group, some did not attend (non attenders). 150 attended at least once (attenders), but due to practical difficulties outcome data were not collected on 2 of the practices. Outcome data available on 85 attenders of groups, 112 non-attenders and 98 controls.

Focus: Mothers as primary prevention of psycho-social problems

Objectives: To provide social support as a practical intervention to prevent psychosocial problems in mothers and their children

Programme: A post natal mothers support group in each general medical practice usually conducted by a health visitor and general practitioner. Groups run along counselling lines with a client centred approach. Group leaders were given 2 introductory training lessons and then fortnightly and then monthly supervision sessions. No extra services offered to control group.

Design: Repeated measures (pre-test at 10 days after birth, post-test at eight months after birth) with random allocation to one experimental and one control

condition but non random uptake of offer of experimental intervention.

Measures: (1) Pre-test: Maternal interview by Health Visitor for demographic data, contact with agencies, perinatal complications, contact with own mother, type of ante natal care, journey time to group. (2) Post test at 8 months: Developmental examination by clinical medical officer plus information from mother. Maternal interview on use of services, usefulness of their support network, plus other psychosocial variables. Maternal rating of different sources of social support. General Health Questionnaire (GHQ) self administered to identify non psychotic mental illness including depression. (3) At 3 year follow up: GHQ, Behaviour Screening Questionnaire (BSQ), English Picture Vocabulary Test (EPVT), semi-structured interview for psycho social data including use of services, relationship with spouse (rated both by mother and interviewer), recent worries, education and employment, checklist of child's developmental milestones, mothers' rating of availability and adequacy of social support.

Results: (1) Psychosocial factors: high rates of behaviour problems and poor language development of the children and maternal psychiatric disorder all related to situation adversity such as stress, worries, poor social support, education, and housing. (2) Uptake: attenders significantly more likely than non attenders to be of higher social class, be married, be homeowners, have had longer full time education, be a primiparous birth with perinatal complications, and have infrequent contact with their own mother. (3) Outcome: having controlled for psychosocial variables, attenders who had mild worries or who rated social support as insufficient were more likely than similar non attenders and controls to be depressed at 3 year follow up. Attenders had better scores than non attenders on the GHQ if experiencing adverse conditions but scored worse than non attenders if conditions not so adverse. Mothers with high GHQ scores at 8 months post test who attended frequently showed a significant improvement (drop) in scores compared to those attending only once. Few other significant results.

Notes: Authors report that mothers report subjective benefit of groups, but conclude that there is little objective evidence that the groups were effective in preventing behaviour problems, language delay, or maternal psychiatric disorder.

Taylor and Beauchamp (1988)

HOSPITAL BASED PRIMARY PREVENTION STRATEGY

Sample: 30 mothers in maternity ward from 48 asked to participate and meeting criteria of over 18 years, in good health, and primaparous. Average age of 24 years, 57% married, 53% White and 47% Black, 53% high and 43% low income, 47% Jehovah's Witnesses, 40% Protestant, 13% Catholic. 70% gave birth to female infants.

Focus: Parenting strengths as primary prevention of maltreatment.

Objectives: To enable parents to have a greater understanding of their child's development, to adopt more liberal views of child rearing, to be more aware and responsive to the child's potential for interaction, to be more confident and competent at parenting.

Programme: Additional after care from student nurse volunteer whilst mother still in hospital plus home visits at 1, 2, and 3 weeks post partum. Visits of approximately 90 minutes. Topics included stress management, family adjustment, parenting problems, use of community resources, child care and child management. Parents active rather than passive participants. Visits audiotaped for purposes of supervision and monitoring progress. Control subjects received routine services including an infant bath demonstration and attendance at a mothers' breakfast discussion group where a nurse provided information on early infant medical care and on contraception.

Design: Repeated measures (post-test and 2 month follow up) with random allocation to one experimental and one control condition.

Measures: (1) Expectancy scale in which parents stated age at which child would achieve a range of physical and social behaviours. (2) Child rearing attitude rating scale of 60 items. (3) Behavioural rating of 10 minute video of parent's caretaking (post-test only). (4) Open ended questionnaire of parental competence re confidence and problem solving (follow up only).

Results: (1) Experimental subjects had significantly greater knowledge of social development than controls at post-test and follow up, and significantly greater knowledge of physical development at follow up only. (2) Experimental subjects displayed significantly greater liberal attitudes to child discipline at post-test and follow up and significantly more liberal attitudes to nurturing care at post-test only. (3) Observational data showed experimental subjects using significantly more verbal stimulation than controls. (4) Questionnaire data revealed that experimental subjects offered a greater number of responses to hypothetical child rearing problems than controls.

Adult and Child Groups

Background

Group work is a popular method of intervention. It is cost effective in reaching many clients at the same time. Also, participants can benefit from each other by learning of others experiences, watching how others learn and benefit (or not) from the intervention, and from the mutual support and learning from others participants. In addition, the group may possess a particular dynamic which can not be produced in one to one work.

Therapeutic group work is a highly specialized field with a variety of theories about the mechanism and purposes of groups. This chapter is not concerned with such therapies. Rather, the chapter groups together the few studies that have evaluated preventive strategies using a group format. All of the studies involved families identified as experiencing parenting problems that might, if unchecked, lead to abuse of some of the children. The concern arose because the parents' life styles and social situation created stresses that could lead to abuse, or because the parents were finding it difficult to manage their children or relate to them appropriately. The programmes aimed to increase parenting abilities, sometimes by direct instruction, in other cases by behavioural methods, whilst other studies examined groups adopting a more psychotherapeutic model. This chapter considers preventive group work, but being the last chapter on prevention it ends with a brief discussion of some other forms of preventive work with families.

Research studies

The studies reviewed in this chapter are listed in Table 6.1. A few further studies where groups were used for identified cases of abuse are discussed in later chapters, particularly in the second section of Chapter Eight. The groups included in these research studies tended to be time limited with regular weekly or twice weekly meetings. Sometimes the groups consisted of adults and children together, sometimes there were separate adult and child groups.

Most of the groups encouraged a sense of nurturing and reciprocal support. For some projects this was the primary focus. Welbourn and Mazuryk (1980), for example, describe a weekly group consisting largely of joint activities such as outings and classes that created a structure for social activities. The aim was to decrease the social isolation and increase the level of communication and help seeking in the mothers, who were considered to have psychological problems that put their children at potential risk. The group lasted nine months and the authors report that there were changes in whom the parents socialized with, but no change in the absolute level of social activity. The workers also reported an increase in maternal functioning but this finding was not supported by external ratings of the workers' assessments.

Social contact was achieved in a very different way by the three groups studied by Palfreeman (1982). The groups contained both 'at risk' and not at risk mothers. The first group was based in a mother's home and consisted of discussion between four mothers studying an Open University course on child development. The second group was based in a church hall and allowed discussion between the mothers and observation of the play and interaction of the children. The third group was

TABLE 6.1

Research Studies on Adult and Child Groups

Study	Programme	Sample Size	Population	Design	Main Measures
Armstrong (1981) Armstrong & Fraley (1985)	Counselling, Family School, Peer support	n=46	Stressed families	RPM	Child development HOME, stress, peer support
Galdston (1971, 1975)	Therapeutic day care unit	n=46	Violent families	RPM	Worker ratings of child and adult behaviour
Howlett et al (1985)	Behavioural training groups	n=30	Child behaviour, at risk families	RPM	Child behaviour
Ounstead et al (1974)	Mother & child groups	n=24	At risk of abuse	POST	Worker ratings of child and adult behaviour
Palfreeman (1982)	Mother & toddler groups	n=26	Low incomes	RPM	Client satisfaction, impact of groups
Philips et al (1981)	Weekly group	?	Parenting problems in deprived urban area	POST	Worker ratings of mothers child care & social behaviour
Pillai et al (1982)	Family Walk in Centre	n=50	Social & child care problems	RPM	Worker ratings of mothers child care and social behaviour
Resnick (1985)	Weekly groups	n=18	Low SES, parenting skills	PRPM+C	Maternal attitudes, mental state, child behaviour
Roberts et al (1977)	Weekly group	n=6	Parenting & relationship problems	RPM	Worker ratings of child and adult behaviour
Roth (1985)	Parents Anonymous	n=22	Risk groups	RPM	Worker ratings of child behaviour
Scaife and Frith (1988)	Behaviour management course	n=6	Family problems	RPM	Child behaviour
Schellenbach and Guerney (1987)	Parenting course	n=19	High & low risk	POST	Client reports
Schinke et al (1986)	Problem solving groups	n=35	Adolescent mothers & stress	RPM+C	Parenting skills, mental state
Scott (1986)	Programme for independent living	n=70	Young single mothers	POST	Worker ratings of mothers' & children's progress
Telleen et al (1989)	Mother's support group, Parent Education class	n=10 n=22	Urban deprived area	RPM+C	Social supports, stresses, mental state
Thomasson et al (1981a, 1981b)	Family Life Discussion Group	n=49	At risk factors	RPM	CAPI
Welbourne and Mazuryk (1980)	Lunch, hairdresser & instruction group	n=8	At risk of abuse	RPM	Goal attainment, social activity check list

CAPI = Child Abuse Potential Inventory; HOME = Home Environment and Living Scale
Design
POST = Post-test only; RPM = Repeated Measures including Pre-Test; PRPM = Repeated Measures post-test only;
+C = Control or comparison groups; +PC = Control or comparison group but at post-test only

similar but smaller and based in a college of further education. The groups were well received by the mothers and demonstrate the feasibility of mixing the skill levels of parents in the groups with the intention that those less skilled could benefit from those more skilled.

The use of teaching to provide a focus for groups as well as a means of increasing the skills of the mothers was a technique used by several of the groups. Pillai (1982) studied a group that was one part of a wider service provided by a walk-in centre. In addition to groups for teaching parenting and social skills, parents were offered counselling, liaison with other services, and in some cases home visits. In contrast, the groups described by Thomasson and colleagues (1981 a,b) provided education and the opportunity for discussion. Both studies reported improvements in repeated measures of parental care. In Pillai's study the measures were workers' ratings, whilst Thomasson used the Child Abuse Potential Inventory (CAPI) with a lie subscale. Finally, Telleen et al (1989) evaluated The Family Support Program that combined parental education with a mothers' self help discussion group. The study was experimentally controlled but the measures were dependent on parental self report. At post test the parents reported that they felt more able to obtain assistance about their child, that they felt less isolated, but the number of their social supports and social participation decreased significantly. A finding that indicates the dangers of professionally based supports reducing parents' own support networks. Even if the parents feel less isolated at post-test, this may not endure in the long term.

Another educational strategy was investigated by Schellenbach and Guerney (1987). In contrast to most of the other studies that were concerned with the care of relatively young children, this programme was concerned with parenting of adolescents. The programme addressed two aspects of parenting. Firstly, the parents ability to empathize with the adolescents changing needs. Secondly, issues of conflict and control between parents and adolescents. The only results presented concerned the parents' appreciation of the programme and levels of attendance at the course, but the study is included for its description of a different type of preventive group.

Resnick undertook a study to contrast two types of educational group (Resnick, 1985). One group attempted to improve parenting skills by teaching life skills, whilst the other group used a behavioural training programme to achieve the same end. The study used an experimental controlled design and found no real improvements in either treatment group compared to controls. In addition to this disappointing finding, increases in appropriate child care (such as maternal play) were associated with fewer social supports and less goal setting of the parents. The authors suggest that interventions can have a negative effect as increased levels of child care may reduce social contacts. This complements the finding by Welbourn and Mazuryk (1980) and Telleen (1989) that the encouragement of new social contacts can result in a decrease in the use of previous social contacts. Furthermore, there is evidence from the studies on neonatal programmes that certain interventions may be disruptive for certain subjects (see for example, Stevenson and Bailey, 1988).

The use of behavioural techniques was the major component of several studies. Schinke and colleagues (1986) used a mixture of instruction, practice, and modelling of communication skills. The approach was similar to the life skills group reported by Resnick in that reductions in the stresses of daily life and the increase of social supports was the strategy for increasing the parents' ability to cope and provide better child care. The theory was that the minor stresses of daily life can cumulatively be as disruptive as major life events. Schinke reported improvements on test scores (including behavioural role plays) of parents' social esteem and functioning compared to controls.

Phillips and colleagues (1981) described a one year weekly group that attempted to reinforce parents successful interactions with their children. The parents came from a deprived inner city area and were thought unable to meet their children's needs because of their own emotional deprivation. By stressing the positives of what the parents could do, including positive video feedback, the project aimed to develop parental skills and confidence. The results were dependent upon workers' ratings and showed increasing socialization and social skills in the parents. The authors argue that an important component of the intervention was the nurturing positive atmosphere and pre-existing friendships between group members. This is in contrast to most other projects with no pre-existing relationships between participants.

Wolfe et al (1988, summarized in Chapter Nine) have described one of the most rigorous behavioural studies that was experimentally controlled and used independent outcome measures (Wolfe et al, 1988). Mothers were trained in child management through instruction, modelling, and behavioural rehearsal. Also by in-vivo-desensitization where mothers learned to relax and cope with their child. The results showed that the intervention group improved more than controls on child abuse potential scores, maternal depression, and number of reported child behaviour problems. No effect was found on the home observation measures.

Other studies using behavioural approaches attempted to teach the principles of response contingencies and techniques of behavioural intervention so that parents would be better able to understand the patterns of interaction in their own families and so better manage their children. Scaife and Frith (1988) evaluated a group of ten sessions lasting ninety minutes each in which there were talks about child development and behavioural norms, methods for dealing with problem behaviour, and the use of observation techniques and diaries. Parents were given advice and feedback about any specific problems that they were experiencing. The programme also aimed to teach health visitors about the use of behavioural techniques. The outcome measures showed that the mothers did learn the behavioural techniques, that their perceptions of their children's behaviour became more positive, and that the need for intensive health visiting was reduced.

A similar approach has been described by Howlett et al (1985). Parents were given their own programme of behaviour modification for dealing with child management problems such as tantrums. Children often attended group sessions, but were not invited to sessions involving teaching of techniques, or health education or welfare advice. Sessions with the children allowed free interaction of mothers and children, and mothers could be encouraged to successfully handle any crises that developed with their children. The authors reported improvements on child behaviour problems but these results were not experimentally blind so may only indicate improved perceptions of behaviour.

In contrast to the educational and behavioural approaches some studies were more concerned with the emotional worlds of the parents and were thus more psychotherapeutic in style. The working through of ambivalent feelings that mothers had about their children would, for example, be considered an appropriate component of therapy. In the study by Roth (1985) parents attending a Parents Anonymous programme were exposed to models of good child care and were encouraged to examine the feelings that interfere with their ability to parent. Roth reported a strong association between parental attendance at the programme and improvements in child behaviour.

Other studies concerned with the affective aspects of parenting also reported improvements at post test (Galdston, 1971, 1975; Ounstead et al, 1974, Roberts et al, 1977), but did not use sufficiently independent measures of outcome to make definite judgements about the efficacy of the interventions. Two studies, however, did specify that there were more marked changes in the behaviour in the children than in their parents (Galdston, 1971, 1975; Roberts et al, 1977).

Two studies did not fit well into the educational, behavioural or affective therapeutic categories. One intervention used a combination of advice, nurturance and education provided through home based counselling, a family school with group work, and a neighbourhood peer support group (Armstrong, 1981; Armstrong and Fraley, 1985). The study was not experimentally controlled but did use many independent research measures and the authors reported decreases in the stressors of depression, isolation, and over harsh child punishment. Less improvement was achieved in general parenting and child health, and single parents did least well. There was progress in most planned goals of intervention, but only a quarter of aims were achieved.

The final study describes a residential group home for young mothers thought to be at risk of parenting problems (Scott, 1986). Each mother had a bedroom that they shared with their child and were linked up with seven other mother-child pairs to make a mutually supporting group. Mothers also were provided with individual or group therapy and training in job skills. The project was not formally evaluated, though the author reports that 80% of the clients left the centre with a good chance of successful independent living. The study is included in this review as an example of group work different to the standard time limited weekly group.

Discussion

There are few well designed research evaluations of preventive groups. The methodological limitations of these studies are the same as reported in other chapters, but exist to a greater degree with the group studies. This is probably because it is a relatively under researched area. Research on preventive groups is not intrinsically problematic. Groups are normally time limited, are well structured which enables research measures to be taken, and there are few ethical problems in randomly assigning subjects to different treatment conditions.

The majority of studies reported improvements, but few of these results can be relied upon as definite evidence of programme success. The overall impression from the studies is that the programmes can increase the self esteem of parents and their perceptions of their children's behaviour. The one study that reported both home observations and parental reports of behaviour only found a programme effect on parental reports (Wolfe et al, 1988). Some studies also report agency records of child abuse, but these are notoriously unreliable measures of the extent of child maltreatment in the population.

The results concerning parents' (usually mothers') social behaviour is even more problematic. The studies report that parents feel better in themselves and less isolated yet also report decreased numbers of social contacts. Similar findings in studies of neonatal interventions suggest that research should evaluate the relative effects of interventions on other social supports. Other social supports may not always be helpful and may sometimes be destructive (Van Meter, 1986), but there is more possibility of continuity with previous supports than in searching for new sources of support. Phillips et al's (1981) study indicates that it is possible to organize groups with people known to each other before, but there may be difficulties for group members in discussing the behavioural contingencies pertaining in their families or other private and sensitive aspects of family life. A compromise may be to ensure that participants come from the same area and social context (as in the Newpin volunteer support scheme). Currently many researchers recruit subjects from similar social backgrounds, but the similarity is usually in terms of social disadvantage rather than arising from a community approach to prevention.

The research reviewed serves a useful function in illustrating some of the range of possible preventive groups and raising research issues that further studies can explore. The relative lack of studies is unfortunate considering the potential that groups have to offer. They are relatively easy to organize and are modest in their use of resources. They provide skills, supports, and therapy, in contexts that might be both more acceptable than more conventional services. Research is necessary to determine which types of groups are beneficial for different people with different problems and to ensure that any negative effects of groups are avoided.

A form of group intervention that is often a part of child abuse interventions but rarely evaluated separately is family centres. In Britain, the development of family centres has been one of the most evident new prevention resources of the last twenty years. The family centres have been created by a range of agencies such as education and social service departments and voluntary agencies in order to fulfil different needs. It is therefore unsurprising that they should employ different methods and techniques. What is not clear is the extent that the aims and purposes are clearly articulated and, if so, whether they are likely to be achieved by the methods employed on a daily basis in the centres. The diversity of family centres has led several researchers to classify their components and philosophies of care (Phelan, 1983; Holman, 1988; Warren cited in Walker, 1991).

Walker (1991) lists the methods employed in family centres as including psychotherapy, family therapy, group work, individual counselling, skills training/education, and parent toddler group play sessions. Walker also lists the different orientations of the centres ranging from a child health focus, to a child development focus, to supporting the parents' (usually the mother's) needs so that they are better able to care for their children. Some centres may adopt all these approaches. In family centres in child abuse special units, for example, there has often been a concern to nurture the parents and to teach them child care skills and yet to also ensure that the child is receiving appropriate care and stimulation, that they are healthy, and that they are achieving their developmental milestones. Other family centres may be less professionally directed and controlled with different philosophies of service provision.

Holman (1988) lists three different models of family centre. The first is client focused with the clients being referred by statutory agencies as with a child abuse special unit. Even if parents are not obliged to attend there may be pressure on them to do so and the work of the centre is likely to be based on concepts of professional roles and tasks rather than by participation by the clients in decision making within the centre. The second, neighbourhood model, has a broader range of activities and more open access to local families who are likely to be encouraged to participate in the centre, and with staff roles being flexible to accommodate this. In the third, community development, model the emphasis is on the centre being a resource for local community action. The staff do not undertake professional casework on referrals. The management is under local community control allowing the centre to undertake local collective action. These distinctions by Holman mirror the models of welfare described by Hardiker et al (1991). The client focused family centre fits the residual model of services organised to provide therapy for the few families that do not achieve the basic minimum. The neighbourhood family centre is providing a local resource and thus fulfilling the institutional model's responsibility of meeting local needs. The community development family centre allows citizens to exert more control over resources and state systems and to achieve their rights as in the developmental model of welfare. In some cases this may operate within a radical/conflict view where the aim is to change society by whatever means possible (Hardiker et al, 1991).

Finally, brief mention needs to be made of other special preventive services that could include but do not always include groups, and may not be specifically aimed at child abuse. In reviewing support services for families, Goldberg and Sinclair (1986) listed the four categories of support to individual families, relevant day care, services for groups of families or family members, and multiple approaches (see also study of support services by Gibbons, 1990). In the United States there is also a considerable number of special programmes for families many of which are listed in 'National Resource' Center on Family Based Services (1986) and in Zigler et al (1986).

In the United States the focus of interest on preventive services has recently been upon the prevention of children being taken into care because of concerns about child protection or about unacceptable behaviour of older children. There is particular interest in home based or family centred services, currently labelled family preservation services. Nelson, Landsman, and Deutelbaum describe three sub-types of crisis intervention, home based models, and family treatment models (Nelson et al, 1990). Crisis intervention is currently the main focus of interest particularly in relation to the Homebuilders programme (Whittaker et al, 1990; Wells and Biegel, 1991). Families are only accepted into the programme if at least one family member wishes to keep the family together and this plan is not opposed by any other key family member. The programme attempts to resolve the family crisis and to teach the family the skills necessary for them to stay together. Services are crisis orientated and intense and offer counselling, advocacy, training, and material services with a twenty four hour on call service. The emphasis is on promoting client independence and the service is short term, preferably no longer than ninety days and usually for only four weeks (Pecora et al, 1991). The indications from early evaluation is that the programme does increase the number of children who are not removed or who, if removed, are quickly reunited with their families (Spaid & Fraser, 1991; Wells & Biegel, 1991). The fundamental issue, though, is whether the families should or should not be preserved and who should decide this and on what basis. Families can provide a supporting, caring, environment for children, but this is not always the case. Despite the risks of removing children it is dangerous to assume that family preservation should be the only criteria for success.

Summary

1. Research studies on groups developed in order to reduce the risk of child abuse all involved subjects individually identified as at risk. The groups had a variety of aims and utilized a range of different techniques that fell broadly into the categories of social activities and mutual support, education, behavioural training, and psychotherapy. Some groups included several of these approaches and one group was created by a residential facility for young single mothers experiencing problems.

2. There was not sufficient research evidence from the studies to distinguish which general approach or specific technique was most effective and in what circumstances. Most groups seemed to provide benefits for the psychological and social functioning of the mothers and their children, but there were also indications of reductions in the mothers previous sources of social support.

3. The limitations of the research designs were similar in kind but often of greater magnitude to those reported in other chapters. This is probably due to the lack of research in the area rather than any intrinsic difficulty in undertaking such research. Studies in this area are comparatively straightforward as it is relatively easy to randomly assign subjects to more than one treatment condition.

4. The research to date provides a basis for hypotheses about which types of group are indicated for different people presenting with different problems; hypotheses that can be explored by future studies.

5. Further research is required because groups have obvious potential for providing emotional support, education, and behavioural and psycho therapy. Groups are relatively inexpensive compared to other forms of provision and may be a more acceptable form of service delivery than conventional one to one client-worker relationships.

6. Research on groups as a preventive approach to child abuse needs to take into account the rapid growth of family centres using diverse methods of work within a range of different models of care.

Chapter Six Research Summaries

Armstrong (1981), Armstrong & Fraley (1985)

A TREATMENT AND EDUCATION PROGRAM FOR PARENTS AND CHILDREN WHO ARE AT RISK OF ABUSE AND NEGLECT

Sample: 46 families with 74 children for whom data were available from over 200 families receiving the services of a Family Support Centre since 1977. Referral to the centre was from various agencies and included self-referral. Only families with at least 5 identified areas of stress were accepted. The sample came from a 'blue collar population' close to Philadelphia. The average age of the mothers and children were 27 years and 2 years respectively. 35 families were seen at the follow-up assessment.

Focus: Functioning of parents, children and parent-child interactions. At risk groups.

Objectives: For the 3 components of the programme. (1) To reduce the parents' needs and stresses. (2) To develop children's self image, trust in adults, and physical, cognitive and social development. (3) To develop independence.

Programme: 3 components. (1) Home Based counselling, nurture and education of parents plus referral to other services as appropriate. (2) Family School, with groupwork including preschool children, to develop communication, self care, maternal skills and problem solving. Children with developmental delay offered individual education plan. Group work with parents to develop parenting techniques. Interaction sessions with children to work on specific goals such as limit setting, discipline and positive reinforcement. (3) Neighbourhood Peer Support Group for discussion and social activities with help of a resource aide worker.

The Home Based Service lasted for 10 months. The twice weekly Family School started after 3 months and lasted for 3 months, finishing before the Home Based Service. The Peer Support Group ran for 1 year with the resource worker and the parents were then encouraged to meet on their own.

Design: Repeated measures (pre and post test and 3 year follow up) on intervention samples only.

Measures: Child development (Bayley Scales of Infant Development, McCarthy Scales of Children's Abilities), parent-child interaction (subscales from Home Observation for Measurement of the Environment and Childhood Level of Living Scale), an index of

stress from within the individual's characteristics, the environment and past life events.

Results: Fewer children abused (p<0.05) than in similar group reported by researchers. There was a significant fall in the number of stresses per family, particularly regarding isolation, depression, and harsh child punishment. Least improvement for single parent stresses, and child health. Parent-child interactions increased and a quarter of planned goals achieved with some progress in most aims. Not all families managed to participate in all components and measures. Success was correlated with participation in all 3 components of programme. At follow-up 3 years later, the families showed an improvement in comparison to their state at initial referral, but they had lost some of the improvement measured immediately following the programme. There were no reports of child abuse or removals to foster placements although other negative life events had been experienced. The families reported satisfaction with the programme.

Notes: Authors argue that effectiveness was demonstrated, although they note the lack of control, the existence of other services to the families, and the effect of family crises on service delivery. Correlation of success with programme participation does not necessarily represent a causal effect of the intervention.

Galdston (1971, 1975)

THE PARENTS' CENTRE PROJECT FOR THE STUDY AND PREVENTION OF CHILD ABUSE

Sample: 46 families from Greater Boston, referred by health and welfare agencies for child abuse and violently ambivalent relations with their children, arising from difficulties with their own parents, marital discord, and sexual dissatisfaction. Some families on welfare, but the sample included middle class families who could not be described as deprived. Children shown paucity of effect, violence, and poor co-ordination. Attenders at project were mostly mothers.

Focus: Functioning of parents and parent-child relationships in at risk groups.

Objectives: To restore and maintain parent-child relationships and prevent the break up of the family.

Programme: Attendance of children at therapeutic day care unit. Attendance of parents at a weekly group led by a male and female social worker where personal experiences were discussed. Psycho-analytic approach elucidating the ambivalent emotions of parents towards their children in order to avoid these emotions being expressed too directly on to the child. Project staff do not provide individual casework but are available to discuss and offer advice to families. The project is in addition to other services. Programme length varied but was over 7 months on average.

Design: Repeated measures (pre and post-test) on treatment sample only.

Measures: Service providers' assessments: of children's tolerance of anxiety and of disturbed adult behaviour, capacity to relate to others, toilet training, violent behaviour, language use, and motor organization. Similar assessment of parents' capacity to express pleasure in relation to their children.

Results: Abrupt and marked changes in children's behaviour, emotional expression and purpose after 2 weeks at centre. Also very quick marked improvements in children's growth. Improvements for parents but less clear and not correlated with progress in children. Only 2 reports of abuse after involvement in programme.

Notes: Author states that progress of children would not have been achieved without treatment of parents, even if the parents did not improve. The author also notes impressive ability of children to withstand chaotic parental environment without regression. Few details given about referral criteria or contents of child therapy.

Howlett et al (1985)

SAVE THE CHILDREN PROJECT 1981–1984

Sample: 30 mothers of pre-school children referred by health visitors in Aberdeen. Criteria for acceptance included concerns about safety of child, mother-child interaction and child behaviour as measured by the B.S.Q. Behavioural Screening Questionnaire (BSQ). An important additional criteria was the acceptance of home observation visits, which required parental motivation. The families often had multiple problems in relation to finance, housing and marriages.

Focus: Skills of mothers' from at risk group.

Objectives: To develop positive mother-child relationships by increasing self-confidence, by encouraging mutual support, and by developing new child care skills. Belief in the importance of reciprocity.

Programme: Initial home observation followed by mothers and children joining new group. There were 5 groups, meeting twice a week for 6 months. Groups overlapped so that new comers could gain positive impression from those finishing a group. Groups included free interaction of parents and children with worker interventions to suggest changes. Mothers encouraged to handle crises such as tantrums with advice and support. Each mother had own programme of behaviour modification to be attempted at the centre and at home with diaries for monitoring progress. Also sessions without the children for discussion of progress, teaching of techniques, health education, and welfare rights advice. Referrals made to other agencies.

Design: Repeated measures (pre and post) on intervention sample only.

Measures: Behavioural Screening Questionnaire.

Results: 25 of the 30 children had significantly reduced B.S.Q. scores (Wilcoxon matched pairs test) at post-test. (Wilcoxon's matched pairs test). Analysis of individual behaviour (using McNemas test) showed greatest change ($p<0.001$) for tantrums, eating, concentration and attention seeking followed by sleeping ($p<0.05$). No effect for sorting, activity, moods, sociability, fears, or worries. Mothers expressed satisfaction with increased social contact and confidence in child care.

Notes: Authors qualify results because of lack of an independent researcher and their doubts as to the general application and long term effects of the intervention. Authors also list the components they consider important for success: belief of staff in techniques, non-judgemental climate, preparedness to nurture parents, and flexibility of intervention, close staff relations, structure to the groups, supportive role of mothers' groups, motivation of parents, and clear progress. In future authors would put more emphasis on play skills, as imaginative play was noticeably lacking in sample children.

Ounstead et al (1974)

ASPECTS OF BONDING FAILURE

Sample: 24 mothers referred by general practitioners because at risk of abuse in Oxfordshire. Criteria for both referral and acceptance specified. Children were maximum age of four. Most cases had history of disturbed mother-infant interactions, two thirds had history of puerperal depression, two thirds of children on sedative for sleep/crying problems. Many had asthma or eczema. Many mothers reported sexual problems.

Focus: Functioning of mothers from at risk group.

Objectives: To help mothers with their own problems and to cope in a more constructive way with their children.

Programme: Individual social work at home for mothers who join mothers' group when 'ready'. Children have own group in adjoining room with play activities and 'cuddling live' for the smaller children. Free access between mothers' and children's groups which allowed mothers to see their children being handled 'cheerfully'. Mothers' groups contained 5 to 8 mothers plus one therapist. Few details except for mothers' daily diaries of explosive situations at home. Mothers encouraged to telephone social work at times of crisis.

Design: Post-test assessment of intervention sample.

Measures: Workers' assessment of functioning of mothers and of children including learning to play and explore their environment.

Results: Improvement for all mothers who were able to receive support from each other and to cope with problems. Even the strategy of thinking about telephoning for support was often sufficient to control a crisis. Children's play and exploration increased. These activities were thought to be associated with a sense of safety and with the presence of mother.

Notes: Authors emphasize the selected nature of sample that restricts general application of results. The evaluation is only one part of an article discussing a treatment centre in Oxford.

Palfreeman (1982)

'At Risk' Families in Mother and Toddler Groups

Sample: 26 mothers and their 52 mostly pre-school children from approximately 46 mothers attending the groups. The mothers were married, lived in a depressed urban area of Widnes in Cheshire, virtually all had left school before the age of 16, two thirds had their first child by the age of 22 years, few were integrated socially into their neighbourhood and they relied on their own parents for social contact and support. Families were on low incomes, but not severely deprived materially. Some parents recruited through advertising, some introduced to groups by health visitors, 7 of whom were considered as at risk by social services.

Focus: Functioning of mothers from both at risk and non at risk groups.

Objectives: To overcome feelings of isolation and uncertainty experienced by mothers and to promote a positive attitude towards their mothering role. To provide a better understanding of child behaviour

and development, child rearing, and health education.

Programme: Three different mother and toddler groups started by a health visitor. (1) Home based group for 4 mothers who had been sponsored by health visitors on an Open University Child Development course. (2) Group held in a church hall for 30 mothers and their children. The group was advertised and was open to all. 8 mothers considered at risk by social services were introduced to the group by health visitors. The group was run by a play leader plus adult helpers. (3) Group held in a college of further education. 7 mothers were introduced to the group by health visitors and 2 of these had children on the local 'at risk' register. A further 5 mothers were invited to join the group to make a total of 12. The group was run by a play leader plus two local mothers. The health visitor often attended the groups, which included discussion between mothers and the health visitor, observation of the children, and play for the children.

Design: Repeated measures (pre and post-test) on intervention sample.

Measures: Pre-test: interview with mothers on their social background and expectation of group. Post-test: interview with mothers on usefulness of group and its impact.

Results: Pre-test showed that mothers desired social contact for both themselves and their children. They saw the groups as having succeeded in this though some felt there could have been more activities for the children. Other benefits perceived by mothers were the sharing of experiences and ideas for child care. These responses of the mothers indicate that the aims of the intervention were to some degree achieved.

Notes: The responses of the mothers fit well with the aims of the intervention and the author concludes that given the right opportunities mothers can 'learn from each other's experiences and be supportive towards each other'. The purpose of the research was also to demonstrate the feasibility of forming such groups with a mix of 'at risk' and other local mothers.

Philips et al (1981)

High Risk Infants and Mothers in Groups

Sample: Self-referrals and referrals from friends and professionals of children under 3 years for day care or counselling; selection on basis of problems particularly disturbed mother child relationship. Selection also on basis of balance of personalities in groups. Sample from upper west side of New

York city which is a deprived inner city area with many black/hispanic families. Membership of group changed throughout the existence of the group.

Focus: Functioning and parenting of mothers from at risk group.

Objectives: Reduction of social isolation and prevention/correction of socio-emotional problems in mother and mother and child relationship within a 'health orientated' rather than problem or sickness orientated philosophy. Mothers seem unable to respond to children's needs because of own emotional deprivation.

Programme: A one year weekly group for mothers and children run by the infant care centre of a family agency with play and discussion and lunch when mothers attend to their own children. Mothers encouraged to invite fathers and other family members and to 'share' these loved ones with the group. Group techniques included positive reinforcement of mothers and children with use of (a) video feedback of successful interactions, (b) modelling, (c) teaching of interactional behaviour, (d) helping mothers to identify problems and to request help when necessary, and (e) an atmosphere of nurture. Co-leaders of group were a social worker and a teacher/therapist. The co-leaders avoided acting as advocates for children which might have undermined support and trust of mothers.

Design: Post-test assessment of intervention sample.

Measures: Workers' assessments of mothers' awareness of children's needs, and methods of care and control of child, social skills and socialization with other mothers, and maternal aggression and reaction to separation.

Results: Increased social skills and socialization of mothers and reduced aggression, mothers turned to peers rather than own children for support and thus reduced mutual dependence. Pre-existing friendship between group members was an important component of success.

Notes: Mothers note that the development of the group was hindered by irregular attendance and changing membership. Article included detailed description of group. Outcome measures were areas where change was noted rather than predetermined categories.

Pillai et al (1982)

Family Walk-in Centre – Eaton Socon: Evaluation of a Project on Preventive Intervention Based in the Community

Sample: 50 parents and children who were in contact for the first time with the centre over a seven month period. Approximately half were referred by agencies and half by volunteers or self referred. Main presenting problems were social isolation, child care problems, marital difficulties and depression. There were no child abuse cases. The centre is located within a community of 3,000 families in Cambridgeshire.

Focus: Functioning of mothers with problems.

Objectives: To assist vulnerable families who can not cope with stressful transition states and who lack self-esteem and motivation.

Programme: Parents offered counselling, discussion, and groups for teaching parenting and social skills; there were also relaxation sessions. Children joined a therapeutic group. Service provided by caseworker, play therapist, and trained volunteers (mostly young mothers trained and supported by caseworker). Home visits undertaken in some cases. Liaison also provided with other agencies and services.

Design: Repeated measures on treatment sample.

Measures: Workers' assessments of parents' child care and adult child relationships. Agency records of rates of attendance at centre and registration on local Child Abuse Risk Register.

Results: Approximately half the families were still attending after 3 months and there was an improvement in 40% of the sample on the family variables. Rates of attendance increased throughout the study period. The size of the local At Risk Register decreased. Volunteers self-esteem increased.

Notes: The authors emphasize the value of volunteers in effective outreach both in reaching families and in need and in developing trusting relationships with the community. Few details provided about the contents of individual or group work or about the families having only cursory contact with the centre. The article discusses vulnerable families and the preventive aim of remoulding dynamic functions of family life, but the focus of work seems to be principally with the mothers.

Resnick (1985)

Enhancing Parental Competencies for High Risk Mothers

Sample: 18 mothers from each of 2 programmes in urban areas of Ontario that were under study, plus a group of volunteer controls with similar characteristics. Mothers were poor and collecting welfare benefits and there was possible risk of disturbed mother-child relationship. Pre-tests revealed high rates of depression (52%) and risk of child abuse (Michigan Screening Profile for Parenting).

Focus: Functioning of mothers from risk groups.

Objectives: To increase mothers' self esteem, goal setting and planning, parenting competence, and to create networks of social support. Longer term objectives of reducing psychopathology in mothers and children.

Programme: Two types of groups. Both types of groups contained approximately 12 mothers and ran for 14 weekly meetings. (1) Opportunity for Advancement (OFA) was run by a community organization using a socio-educational model with the intentions of improving parenting skills by developing life skills. This included group discussion and experimental exercises directed at self-esteem and goal setting. (2) New Direction for Mothers (NDM) was run by a mental health centre and used a training and behavioural model to improve parenting. This included group discussion and role modelling.

Design: Repeated measures (post test and 1 year follow up) design with 2 treatment conditions and 1 comparison or control group. Sampling from clients of two service programmes and with special recruitment of a similar comparison group from volunteers.

Measures: Mothers' parenting attitudes (Parenting Attitudes Research Instrument), self esteem (The Way I See It), maternal depression (CES – Depression Scale), questionnaire on goal setting abilities, blind coding of video taped parent child interactions, social isolation (Social Network Analysis), behavioural problems in children (Child Behavioural Checklist), parent or child pathology further assessed by reported utilization of treatment facilities.

Results: No evidence of impact of either programme in contrast to controls on social esteem, social supports and goal setting. Some immediate reduction in maternal hostility immediately post both programmes, but difference not maintained at follow-up. In contrast to the experimental hypothesis, increase in maternal play was associated with reduced social supports and goal-setting by the mothers. There was a significant decrease in depression but this was across all groups. No differences in child behaviour problems was recorded. There was under 50% average attendance at treatment sessions and a 25% drop-out in the comparison group.

Notes: The authors suggest that the minimum effect of the interventions may be due to the limited treatment exposure. They also suggest that encouraging child care skills, in mothers ambivalent towards

work and family life, may decrease external contacts as found in the study data. Few details of the programmes but article specific about experimental hypotheses and relevance of the dependent measures.

Roberts et al (1977)

PREVENTION OF CHILD ABUSE: GROUP THERAPY FOR MOTHERS AND CHILDREN

Sample: 6 families of pre-school children with parenting problems in the Oxford area, selected by group therapists. Parents characterised by poor self-respect, isolation, relationship problems, unrealistic expectations of child. Children exhibited behaviour and developmental problems. Most of sample already receiving support services.

Focus: Functioning of mothers with parenting problems.

Objectives: To increase parents' confidence and self-esteem particularly in relation to child rearing; to extend their social supports and ability to offer mutual support; to provide therapy for the children.

Programme: Parents' group for 1 hour 15 mins per week for 6 months with a doctor and a social worker as co-therapists. Group interaction encouraged, one to one discussions avoided, co-therapists sat apart. Mothers allowed to proceed at own pace and not challenged with reality too soon. Children's group involved constructive play and individual help including specific referrals where necessary. Before and after groups mothers and children were together to allow play, discussions with play therapists, and work on relationship problems.

Design: Repeated measures (pre and post test and 3 month follow up) of intervention sample.

Measures: Workers' assessment of mothers' self esteem, ability to relate, trust and maintain regular contact and friendship with others. Workers' assessment of children's attachment, constructive play, social skills, and physical and emotional development. Independent social workers assessment of tension in the home.

Results: Increase in mothers' self-esteem, rapid increase in children's development, decrease in tension in the home. At 3 months follow-up the mothers were making fewer demands on local services. The intervention was associated with an increase in the morale and confidence of health and social service teams.

Notes: The authors judged the success to be due to the following components: careful preparation, back-up of experienced staff for consultation, confidence of staff, and the interaction between the mothers' and children's groups to allow work on the relationship problems.

Roth (1985)

RELATIONSHIP BETWEEN ATTENDANCE AT A PARENTS ANONYMOUS ADULT PROGRAM AND CHILDREN'S BEHAVIOUR AT THE PARENTS' ANONYMOUS CHILD CARE PROGRAM

Sample: 22 children over 4 years of age and their parents from a larger number who have attended the programme.

Focus: Functioning of parents from risk groups.

Objectives: To increase parenting skills and ability.

Programme: Attendance at Parents Anonymous Adult Program where parents are exposed to parenting skills, can verbalise the pressures they experience, and can work through the feelings that interfere with their ability to be effective to parents. Children attend child care programme.

Design: Repeated measures on treatment sample with internal comparison by analysis of covariance.

Measures: Child care workers' pre and post-test ratings of children's behaviour, including behaviour in structured activities, interactions with staff, interactions with peers and 'meaningful participation' in children's groups. Measure of parental attendance at Parents' Group over a 12 month period.

Results: Significant effect of parental attendance on child behaviour ratings (p<0.0009): children of parents with greater than 50% attendance had behavioural rating of 7.98 compared to a rating of 4.61 for parents attending less than <50% of their programme.

Notes: Author concludes that the adult programme benefits child behaviour. Suggestion made that compulsory attendance might be useful for some mothers. Effect of child programme and motivational differences between parents not examined. Few details.

Scaife and Frith (1988)

A BEHAVIOUR MANAGEMENT AND LIFE STRESS COURSE FOR A GROUP OF MOTHERS INCORPORATING TRAINING FOR HEALTH VISITORS

Sample: Six mothers of pre-school children presenting behaviour problems referred by community health services. Acceptance criteria was at least one of: high frequency of health visits, high frequency behaviour problems, chronic family factors contributing to problems and limited social support available. All families came from villages, 7–10 miles from an urban conurbation.

Focus: Child behaviour and family problems.

Objectives: To teach parents the principles of behaviour technology by which they may bring about changes in their child's behaviour; to encourage the development of friendship networks between the parents in the group; to teach a strategy (progressive relaxation) which would assist mothers in coping with their own tension and anxiety as it contributed to child management problems; to facilitate the isolation of marital, social and economic difficulties; to enable parents to reclassify their child's behaviour as deviant or non-deviant; and to train health visitors in the application of behavioural principles to childhood development disorders.

Programme: Ten one and a half hour sessions each focusing on a different aspect of child management. Methods included group exercises, observation techniques, diaries, videos, talks about child behaviour, motor development and behavioural norms. 'homework' for mothers, strategies for dealing with misbehaviour, long-term goals, feedback on specific problems.

Design: Repeated measures (pre-test, post-test and follow up) design on intervention group only.

Measures: Behaviour Problem Checklist derived from Rutter Scales Principles of Learning Theory Questionnaire. Evaluation questionnaire (follow up only). Frequency of requests from the parents for health visitor advice on child management problems recorded 6 months prior and subsequent to the group sessions.

Results: Significant increase in the mothers' comprehension of behavioural techniques. Maternal rating of child behaviour changed in the desired direction for four out of five children for whom data available. Health visiting content also reduced. Mothers generally positive about course. Mothers experiencing general family problems and whose children's behaviour improved were more likely to perceive the course as having been helpful.

Notes: Authors discuss the efficiency of the intervention in terms of (1) groups being a more efficient use of psychologists' time than individual work, (2) the reduction in Health Visitors workload, and (3) the advantages of training primary care staff in behavioural methods.

Schellenbach and Guerney (1987)

IDENTIFICATION OF ADOLESCENT ABUSE AND FUTURE INTERVENTION PROSPECTS

Sample: Nineteen parents from eleven families who were involved in a research project about the identification of adolescent abuse. Both high and low risk parents took part.

Focus: Education of parents for primary prevention of child maltreatment.

Objectives: To increase the use of positive discipline techniques as opposed to negative techniques, to provide information to parents on the kind of parenting challenges which they could expect during adolescence, and to provide training in skills for enhancing communication during adolescence.

Programme: Family Interaction Project (FIP) a parenting course that addressed two separate but complementary dimensions of the parent-adolescent relationship. (1) The affective dimension or the ability to empathize and understand the changing needs of the adolescent, (2) the control dimensions of the conflict-resolution dimension between parents and adolescents.

The programme contained information on adolescent development, skills training in effective communication between parents and adolescents and training on conflict resolution. Listening and expressive skills were taught, with positive skills always introduced first. Role-plays, homework assignments and demonstrations used.

Design: Post-test on intervention group only.

Measures: Preliminary pilot study so data limited to anonymous self-reports from participants, feedback from graduate student observers and leaders' judgements.

Results: Parents considered the content of the course appropriate and would recommend it to friends. More focus on discipline preferred. 85% attendance.

Schinke et al (1986)

STRESS MANAGEMENT INTERVENTION TO PREVENT FAMILY VIOLENCE

Sample: 35 mothers recruited from a population of 70 adolescent mothers in a public school continuation programme, who had given birth within the last two years, were mostly single, had a mean age of 16.5 years and were at risk from stress.

Focus: Psychological state of 'at risk' mothers.

Objectives: Stress management by teenage mothers.

Programme: Groups ran for 12 sessions and included group instruction and practice of problem solving, modelling communication skills by workers, role play of communication skills in twos and threes, teaching of relaxation skills, and feedback by workers in all areas. Approach based on view that psychological stress is cognitively mediated and arises as much from small everyday traumas as from more dramatic life events.

Design: Repeated measures (pre, post, and delayed post test) experimental controlled design with one experimental and one control group.

Measures: Various scales of self-esteem, depression, social and personal support, parenting skills and sense of competence, attitudes and mastery; various social skills from blind ratings of video tape of interaction in role plays.

Results: Analysis of co-variance using pre-test scores. No statistical pre-test differences. At post-test the treatment group scored significantly better than controls on social supports, on generating options, and on component skills from the behavioural role plays. At delayed post-test, the intervention subjects had more positive scores on self esteem, generating options, personal support, parenting competence, and good care of child. These group members also reported high rates of satisfaction with the value of the intervention and the future applicability of stress management services.

Notes: Authors suggest results offer optimism, though they admit lack of external validation. Few details about the many measures and the bases of the statistical results presented. The authors work in a school of social work and implemented the programme as well as its evaluation.

Scott (1986)

AND MOTHER MAKES TWO

Sample: 70 young, single mothers who have lived in a residential centre to date. Referrals predominantly from social services; selection on basis of assessment of ability to use and benefit from the centre with others in groups; drug abusers not accepted. Problems presented by mothers including parenting, a history of unsuccessful relationships with violent men, and in some cases, disturbed behaviour and low intelligence.

Focus: Potentially 'at risk' mothers.

Objectives: To help mothers to adjust to new role of parent and to break the potential cycle of abuse in these 'at risk' single, young, mothers.

121

Programme: A residential programme (Dartmouth House Centre) with training for independent living. Each mother shares a bedroom with their child and 8 rooms form a core group which is encouraged to be mutually supportive by multi-disciplinary staff. Mothers require permission to go out on their own and must make baby sitting arrangements. During normal working hours there is a developmental training programme tailored to individual needs and interests. Counselling, intensive psychotherapy, group therapy and training in office skills is provided. Mothers are encouraged to care as much as possible for their children, but other activities are provided.

Design: Treatment sample post-test only.

Measures: Workers' description of capability for independent living, progress in training and development of the children. Agency records of enquiries about the centre.

Results: At least 80% of 'trainees' leave with a high chance of successful independent living. The children developed well in the centre. The increasing number of referrals to the centre indicated a growing reputation within the local Social Work Department.

Notes: Article provides information on referrals, structure, and living arrangements, but few details on some parts of the treatment programme. Article discusses the problems of young single mothers and the importance of user selection to the success of the centre.

Telleen et al (1989)

IMPACT OF A FAMILY SUPPORT PROGRAM ON MOTHERS' SOCIAL SUPPORT AND PARENTING STRESS

Sample: Self referred mothers with children under age seven who remained with the mothers support group for three months (n=10), and mothers participating in a parent education class for three months (n=22). Also control group (n=23) recruited from private routine paediatric clinic. 95% were white, median age 30 years, 90% married, 60% with two children. No parents had been reported for child abuse. Programme developed to reach parents in a city with increased rates of child abuse and high levels of unemployment.

Focus: Education of parents as primary prevention of child abuse.

Objectives: Education and support of mothers to increase their social support network and reduce parenting stress.

Programme: The family support programme including a mothers' self help discussion group twice a week during the day and a parent education programme for mothers and fathers once a week in the evening. Education programme used the Systematic Training for Effective Parenting (SFEP) curriculum focusing on parent-child communication, child management techniques, alternatives to physical punishment and other methods of coping with annoying child behaviour. Lectures, parent readings, group discussion and role playing used for solving problems of child management. An early childhood specialist provided activities for children while parents were attending the class.

Design: Repeated measures (pre and post tests) experimental design with non random allocation to 1 treatment and 1 control group condition.

Measures: All parent self report measures: The Parenting Social Support Index with three scales of Resource Size, Support Satisfaction and Support Need. Depression measured by the Centre for Epidemiologic Studies Depression Scale (CES-D) based on frequency in previous week of 20 symptoms on a four point scale. Parenting stresses and child perception assessed using both the Parent and the Child Domain Scales of the Parenting Stress Index – a screening and diagnostic assessment designed to yield a measure of the relative magnitude of stress in the parent-child relationship.

Results: Compared to the control group, programme participants felt they had others with whom they could talk to get help and advice about their child, and they felt less alone after programme participation. The number of informal sources of support, positive feedback, childcare and social participation decreased significantly for the experimental group, but the sense of social isolation was significantly less, particularly for those mothers participating in both the support group and education programme. Only significant pre-test differences were experimental group mothers reporting greater child behaviour stresses, and these improved significantly compared to the control group. At post-test the children liked their parents, wanted to be close and play, did not fuss and cry as much as before, and were not as moody or easily upset. Parents found the children less demanding and less irritating. No programme participants were reported for child abuse or neglect during the intervention.

Thomasson et al (1981a, 1981b)

EVALUATION OF A FAMILY LIFE EDUCATION PROGRAM FOR RURAL 'HIGH RISK' FAMILIES

Sample: 49 adults who attended at least 10 of the 16 sessions of the programme from the 79 original participants referred by child protection workers and recruited from the community. Criteria for acceptance was the possession of at least one characteristic of populations at high risk for child abuse. 90% of participants were below the poverty line.

Focus: Parenting skills as secondary prevention of child abuse.

Objectives: To improve child care and prevent child abuse by increasing parents' knowledge about child development and community resources, and on increasing communication skills, problem sharing, and solving abilities. The programme was based on an ecological model of child abuse as proposed by Garbarino (1976).

Programme: The Family Life Discussion Group (FLDG) programme consisted of 16 weekly group sessions. 9 of these involved educational presentations, 7 were small group discussions on topics including child development, behaviour management, parenting, sex education, communication skills social issues, and local resources. Child care and transport was provided for meetings and $184 was paid to members attending all sessions to encourage attendance and to provide some respite from financial stress. To encourage an award was presented at the 7 week follow-up when a further fee was paid.

Design: Repeated measures (pre-test, post-test and follow-up) on treatment sample only.

Measures: Child Abuse Potential Inventory (CAPI) a self administered screening service of child abuse potential. Consumer evaluation questionnaire of programme.

Results: Significant reduction in CAPI inventory scores from pre-test to post-test and from pre-test to follow-up. No decrease in scores from post test to follow up, participants with highest initial scores changed the least. Analysis of the pre-test CAPI scores of those who did not complete the programme showed these individuals to represent the highest risk group. No significant differences in scores from the CAPI 'lie sub-scale' were recorded. Participants reported that they enjoyed the programme, but 60% would not have attended without the fee and 43% would not enrol again without a fee.

Notes: Authors state that the results support the ecological model of child abuse. They list the criteria that contributed to the programmes success and the areas requiring improvement. Article discusses the development of the CAPI inventory.

Welbourn and Mazuryk (1980)

INTER-AGENCY INTERVENTION: AN INNOVATIVE THERAPEUTIC PROGRAM FOR MOTHERS LIKELY TO BECOME ABUSERS

Sample: 8 mothers of children aged between 1 and 4 years in Toronto, characterised by previous psychiatric/psychological problems, considered in danger of child abuse because of mental state and inability to care and protect their children. Few details of sample selection and whether child abused in past.

Focus: Functioning of mothers from at risk group.

Objectives: To reduce social isolation and increase communication and ability to seek help. To provide positive developmental experiences for children.

Programme: 9 month programme with weekly lunch, visit to hairdresser and group discussion. Also instruction in cooking, child handling and nutrition, relaxation exercises, outings and arts and crafts activities. Child care provided to enable mothers to attend and to allow children to be monitored in relation to child abuse and neglect, and to provide them with stimulation. Also some individual work with mothers.

Design: Pre and post-assessment of intervention group.

Measures: Social Activity Check List completed by workers and mothers; Standardised Goal Attainment Behaviour Scale completed by workers and external raters; worker ratings of priority areas for each mother; external raters' codings of worker descriptions of parents' help seeking and child care; worker descriptions of mothers' progress; Denver Developmental Screening Test.

Results: (1) Social activity: no significant difference but an increase in reaching out and going out with new friends and a reduction in interaction with old friends and visits to doctor. (2) Goal Attainment: workers reported a significant increase in maternal functioning, but external raters were not in agreement with this assessment. (3) Descriptive data: workers reported the growth of a strong cohesive group and the development of positive change in the lives of individual mothers. (4) Developmental test: no evidence of delay before or after intervention.

Notes: Authors report no involvement of spouses. Few details given as to content of specific interventions or which components had most impact.

CHAPTER SEVEN

Behavioural Approaches to Physical Abuse

Background

A behavioural approach has been favoured to deal with physical maltreatment of children, because physical abuse is often considered to be an interactional problem or a response to stress or anger. The problem is not seen simply as adult pathology, and the majority of known perpetrators are not considered to be seriously mentally ill or psychotic. Neither are perpetrators seen as sadists who enjoy physically abusing children, unlike sexual abusers, who may be regarded as seeking, sexual gratification. When the abuse is physical, it is generally assumed, that both parents and children would prefer to interact in more positive ways.

Within a behavioural model, physically abusing parents, adopt unproductive responses to child control problems or to stresses from other parts of their lives. There is some evidence of cycles of physical abuse across generations, so that these parental responses may well have been learned in childhood, by living in aggressive families. This kind of behaviour is then both a physical risk for children, and a model for them, to learn aggressive responses, which not only carries forward to the next generation, but has a more immediate effect within family interaction patterns. If children learn to respond aggressively to harsh forms of parental control, then a downward spiral can occur, resulting in extreme parental anger and severe physical abuse.

Behavioural treatment is also considered appropriate, because physical abuse is associated with high levels of material and emotional stress. There are benefits in removing these stresses, but as this can prove extremely difficult in practice, a more realistic option is to enable people to develop other strategies of coping, including anger control and relaxation. This option has been informed by the research of Kadushin & Martin (1981) who identified some of the events immediately preceding abusive incidents. Parents living in stressful circumstances, may include a high proportion of people who have had unsettled childhoods, and who may be more vulnerable and less able to cope with the stresses that present.

A final reason for the adoption of behavioural therapy, is its successful application in related areas of work. It has been shown that behavioural interventions can change the aggressive behaviour of adults and of children (Stuart, 1981) and that parents can be trained to be effective in changing their children's behaviour (Johnson & Katz, 1973). It is therefore a small logical step from trying to change behaviour in order to improve the quality of parenting, child behaviour and family interaction, to intervening to reduce the risks of children being re-abused.

Research Studies

Other reviews of the literature have argued for the benefits of a behavioural approach and have illustrated the lack of good experimental studies (Isaacs, cited in Conger and Lahey, 1982; Smith & Rachman, 1984). There are many case studies and before and after studies of treatment groups, but relatively few controlled experimental designs. This is surprising, considering the relative ease of investigating the efficacy of behavioural interventions, compared to less well defined treatment strategies. The sensitive nature of child abuse work, does make random allocation designs difficult to implement, but the publication of several such studies shows that it is possible.

Conger, Lahey and Smith (1981) have usefully outlined the main directions taken by the behavioural programmes described in the literature. These are (1) to teach parents methods of child control that do not require physical punishment, (2) to reduce their averse reactions to the children's behaviour, (3) to teach child development so that parents can be more realistic in their expectations of their children, (4) to encourage positive rather than negative family interactions. Although the aim is to change both parent and child behaviours, the intervention is usually focused on the parents, and it is common for the children not to be directly involved in the programmes.

The studies are based upon standard principles of social learning theory: the identification of inappropriate interactions, the reinforcement of positive interactions and ignoring of negative behaviour. Although the actual help given to each family will be based on individual assessment, the therapy will be within the range of behavioural theory and practice. Many of the studies are based on the work of Patterson, Reid, and their associates in Oregon (Reid et al., 1981). Their work on coercive interaction patterns within families, provided an obvious basis for dealing with physical abuse, particularly as measures such as 'Total Aversion Behaviours' developed by Reid et al could be used as dependent variables.

The findings of all the studies identified in this review (listed in Table 7.1) were encouraging, particularly the reduction of negative and coercive behaviour in parents and children within a matter of weeks or months, and maintained at later follow up. It seemed easier to reduce negative behaviour than to increase positive behaviour. However, even small increases in positive behaviour could represent a more significant change in interactions patterns, than the absence of negative interactions.

Fourteen of the studies reviewed had research samples of three or less cases and were predominantly case studies with pre and post-tests to assess progress over treatment. Three of these studies used multiple baselines (Owen Scott et al., 1984; Sandler et al, 1978; Sandford and Tustin, 1973), but only Denicola and Sandler (1980) adopted a withdrawal design to assess if outcome measures were systematically associated to the two treatment interventions of parent training and coping skills. Although both families in the study showed decreases in negative behaviours that were maintained at follow up, no systematic association was found between timing of treatments and outcomes.

Nine of the studies employed experimental controlled designs, six of which included random (Nicol et al, 1988; Syzkula and Fleischman, 1985; Whiteman et al 1987; Wolfe et al, 1988), block order (Wolfe et al, 1981), or block geographic allocation (Smith and Rachman, 1984) to treatment and control conditions. One study employed a non random control group (Barth et al, 1983), another used matched controls (Conger et al, 1981), and another was a meta analysis of three previously reported studies (Reid et al, 1981).

These nine more formal evaluations confirmed the positive results of the case study designs. Improvements compared to controls included perceptions of self and of the children and anger control (Barth et al, 1983, Whiteman et al, 1987); maternal depression (Conger et al, 1981; Wolfe et al, 1988); aversive and coercive behaviours (Nicol et al, 1988; Reid et al, 1981); parenting skills (Wolfe et al, 1981); and ratings of the home environment and of the potential for child abuse (Wolfe et al, 1988). There were few reports of measures not improving in response to treatment.

Only one of the studies reviewed experimentally contrasted the efficacy of different techniques. Whiteman et al (1987), contrasted cognitive restructuring, relaxation, problem solving, and a mix of these three techniques. The authors report that all of the techniques except relaxation were related to improvements

TABLE 7.1

Behavioural Approaches to Physical Abuse Research Studies

Study	Programme	Sample size	Population	Design	Main measures
Barth et al (1983)	Self control training	n = 6	CPS referrals/ maltreatment	RPM = C	Role play of child care, marital relationships
Bunyan (1987)	New coping techniques	n = 1	Overchastisement	RPM	Observation, self report, behavioural records
Conger et al (1981)	Child management, stress management	n = 5	Physical child abuse	RPM + C	Observation of parental behaviour, child compliance
Crimmins et al (1984)	Skill training	n = 1	Abuse & neglect	RPM	Observation in clinic and at home
Crozier and Katz (1979)	Parent child interaction training	n = 2	CPS cases	RPM	Observation of positive & aversive interactions
De Bortali-Tregerthan (1979)	Behavioural training	n = 2	Abuse/aggression	RPM	Abuse of child, use of 'time out'
Denicola and Sandler (1980)	Parent training, coping skills	n = 2	CPS referral/ overchastisement	RPM	TAB
Hutchings et al (1981)	Child care skills	n = 1	Physical abuse, poor child control	Descriptive	Child care strategies
Mastria et al (1979)	Behavioural training	n = 1	Overchastisement	RPM	Positive/negative interactions
McAuley (1980)	Child management training	n = 2	Psychiatric referrals, abuse	Descriptive	Clinical observations
Murphy and Davis (1979)	Child management training	n = 1	Verbal abuse	RPM	Positive/negative interactions
Nicol et al (1988)	Focused behavioural case work	n = 38	Physical abuse	RPM + C	Family Interaction Coding system
Owen Scott et al (1984)	Behavioural skill training	n = 1	Physical abuse	RPM	Role play of child management, anger control
Reid et al (1981)	Social interactional training	n = 27	Child conduct disorder	Meta analysis	TAB
Sandford and Tustin (1973)	Behavioural treatment	n = 1	Violence to child	RPM	Aversive behaviours
Sandler et al (1978)	Positive reinforcement training	n = 2	Overchastisement	RPM	Positive/aversive interactions
Smith and Rachman (1984)	Social interactional treatment	n = 16	Physical abuse	RPM + C	Marital relationships, clinical rating of parenting
Szykula and Fleischman (1985)	Child management training	n = 24	CPS cases	RPM + C	Removal of children into care
Whiteman et al (1987)	Cognitive behavioural training	n = 55	Abuse/anger control	RPM + C	Anger control, child care attitudes
Wolfe and Sandler (1981)	Child management training	n = 3	CPS referrals/abuse	RPM	TAB, child compliance
Wolfe et al (1981)	Home based training	n = 16	Physical abuse	RPM + C	Parent-child interactions
Wolfe et al (1982)	Intensive behavioural training	n = 1	Physical abuse	RPM	Positive/aversive interactions
Wolfe et al (1988)	Child management training	n = 30	CPS Cases	RPM + C	CAPS, HOME, parent-child interactions

CPS = Child Protection Services; CAPI = Child Abuse Potential Inventory; HOME = Home Environment & Living Scale; TAB = Total Aversive Behaviour.

Design
POST = Post-test only; RPM = Repeated Measures including pre-test; PRPM = Repeated Measures post-test only; + C = Control or comparison group; + PC = Control or comparison group but at post-test only.

in attitudes towards the child and child rearing methods, but only problem solving and the mix of methods was effective in increasing anger control.

Discussion

The results of the behavioural studies are impressive. Many of the experimentally controlled studies experienced methodological problems such as subject attrition, but the studies are still more rigourous than many other studies considered in this review. The results also counter the trend reported in several other chapters that the more rigourous the evaluation the less positive the findings reported.

The studies raise several issues that need to be considered when future research is undertaken in order to develop behavioural interventions. One issue is the motivation of parents to be involved. Several studies reported very high rates of subject drop out, which undermined the experimental design (Smith & Rachman, 1984; Nicol et al, 1988), as drop outs are unlikely to be random between the treatment groups.

This point is related to the source of client referrals. Some studies relied on referrals by court order or under threat of court action (Crimmins et al, 1984; Wolfe et al, 1981). The danger here is, that the clients may not be motivated to change, and simple attendance and basic cooperation may not be sufficient to induce changes in behaviour and family interactions. For example, McAuley (1980) argues that successful treatment results, when families build on their existing skills, and if they do not have the motivation, or if they are entrenched in maladaptive interaction patterns, then change is difficult to achieve. De Bortali – Tregarthen (1979) also stresses the importance of the voluntary and committed involvement of the client. Sutton (1992) found that behavioural programmes to change problem child behaviour were almost doomed to fail if undermined by the mother's husband or other partner.

These views may be too pessimistic as a requirement to accept therapy may substitute for genuine client motivation. Both Crimmins et al (1984) and Wolfe et al (1982) reported positive results for subjects who were obliged to accept treatment. Furthermore, Maletzkey (1980, 1991) found no significant difference in positive behavioural outcomes, between self and court referred perpetrators of child sexual abuse (see Chapter 13). The structure afforded by the threat of official sanctions and control, may provide the context that some families need for constructive change. It has been argued that many physically abusive families resist the idea that they lack parenting skills. (Sandler et al, 1978) and that perpetrators of sexual abuse also see no need for treatment (Becker 1991, Li, 1991). Even if parents do accept the need for change, they may not understand or accept the methods of behavioural techniques. Court ordered treatment might provide the necessary motivation to commence treatment to allow the client to appreciate the need and benefits of the service.

Client motivation and actual or threatened court powers are not the only client characteristics which might effect treatment outcome. Most of the studies were concerned with maladaptive parent child interaction patterns, but they varied in the extent to which they were prepared to tackle other problems. Some studies made explicit statements that other aspects of the families' lives required help before there was a possibility of behavioural change. In other studies there is mention of families receiving routine social casework support, which was probably addressing more general problems in the family's lives, but was not necessarily keyed into the behavioural interventions. Nicol (1988) studied a treatment programme designed as a focused behavioural addition to the intensive support the families were already receiving from a Special Treatment Unit. In other study reports, there was little mention of services being offered, but it is likely that all families were receiving some form of child protection service.

A further and related issue is how strictly specified criteria for inclusion in the treatment programmes were applied. Some, like Smith and Rachman's (1984), accepted all cases of physical abuse and specifically excluded failure to thrive and child sexual abuse. Such a broad criterion would result in a large variation of physically abusive situations, extent and type of other family problems, and motivation towards the special programme. Predictably there were many difficulties in applying an experimental controlled design. Other programmes were more specific about choosing a behavioural intervention for families displaying particular characteristics which might be amenable to such treatment; particularly the authors of the many single case studies reviewed.

One major advantage of the behavioural studies is, that even if they were not specific about the case referral routes, they did provide standardised information about the families. This allows Syzukula and Fleischman (1985) to contrast outcome and report evidence of improvement in only the less severe cases. The approach of these studies, lends itself to behavioural assessments of the families at both pre and post-test. Studies discussed in other chapters, often did not specify the problem to be changed or how the outcome measures related to this aim. The behavioural studies showed the greatest awareness of methodological limitations and the least hesitancy in making these explicit (see for example, Smith and Rachman, 1984).

The specification of family functioning, not only allows for more focused programme evaluation, but also provides case descriptions which might lead eventually, to knowledge about which cases are not amenable to change. Such knowledge could help caseworkers and courts to decide whether a child has, or does not have, a safe future in their original family. Some therapeutic interventions depend upon long term work, and it is therefore important to know as soon as possible, whether such work is a viable option, so that the child kept at home is not unnecessarily at risk.

In the main, the behavioural projects covered a short period of between one month (for example, Reid et al, 1981) and six months (for example, Owen Scott et al, 1984). There were usually weekly or biweekly meetings, though one programme (Hutchings et al, 1981), used an initial period of intense daily work, which slowly decreased to thrice and twice weekly and eventually to monthly sessions. Several of the interventions with relatively short treatments of four to eight weeks, were assessed with experimentally controlled designs that found associations between treatment and improved outcome (Barth, 1983; Nicol et al, 1988; Whiteman et al, 1987). These studies did not provide adequate follow-up data to judge maintenance of the new behavioural interactions. Better follow up data showing maintenance effects over time were shown by Wolfe et al (1988) and by some of the individual case studies.

The dangers of too short an intervention, are illustrated by two studies where there was a considerable drop or regression, at a mid data point, for one or more subjects (De Bortali-Tregarthen, 1979; Syzkula & Fleischman, 1985). It is not clear what brought on this reversal, but if the intervention had happened to end at this point, there may have been no possibility of recovery in the levels of behaviour. Smith & Rachman (1984) also stress the importance of lengthy interventions. Their programme lasted six to eight months and they concluded that a lengthy behavioural intervention was a useful component of longer supporting relationships. This view fits well with Smith and Rachman's other observations about the breadth of the families' problems and the services they require.

There is evidence that behavioural therapy is a successful component of interventions in some child abuse cases, but there are still questions about how best to apply it and to whom. Syzukula and Fleischman's (1985) study was unusual in contrasting the effects of intervention on different case presentations and Whiteman et al's (1987) study was atypical in contrasting the efficacy of different therapeutic interventions. These are major issues that have to be faced by future research, but despite these unresolved issues and the many remaining practical methodological problems (Smith & Rachman 1984), the behavioural studies stand out as evaluations of child abuse interventions. Compared to the rest of the literature, these studies have shown more willingness to specify the nature of the treatment and outcome variables, and they are more likely to test out specific hypothesis. In particular, the use of behavioural outcome measures, is much to be preferred to the global and imprecise measures of recidivism (re-abuse), found in many other research reports. However, some behavioural studies over rely on self-report data. Furthermore, many of them are single case studies, and are mostly A-B designs, which cannot distinguish the effects of treatment from other factors that may lead to improvement.

The relative superiority of the behavioural studies, is not simply an argument for the sole use of experimentally controlled research, but implies that all studies would benefit from greater clarification of the variables and hypothesis being considered. Similarly, future research would benefit from drawing on the wider literature in which behavioural treatment models are based.

At present, behavioural therapy is usually practised by psychologists who, in the main, work within National Health Service Clinics, in the Schools Psychological Service, or in special treatment centres. Current information suggests, that only few of the identified cases of child abuse, are referred to these services (Gough et al, 1987). Child abuse literature in general and intervention studies in particular tend to concentrate on describing special provision, rather than routine practice, and so the studies reviewed in this chapter may give a distorted view of the numbers likely to be offered behavioural techniques. The review of the intervention studies showed that behavioural therapy can be effective. It is therefore necessary to assess how best to organize services so that it could be more widely offered. For example, behavioural programmes could be used by health visitors (Stevenson, 1987; Association for Child Psychology and Psychiatry, 1990), social workers, or by psychologists attached to family centres (Pritchard & Appleton, 1986). It has also been reported that telephone based behavioural interventions for child behaviour problems are virtually as effective as more intensive home visit or group based interventions (Sutton, 1992). This may not be effective with all child abuse cases, many of which involve multi problem families with few resources and no telephone. It does suggest, though, that treating individual behavioural problems may be an effective, quick, and affordable component of help to be offered to families not coping with child care.

Summary

1.   There is evidence that behavioural techniques are effective within the acknowledged limits of changing the ratio of positive and negative interactions. There is some evidence of some techniques being more effective in changing different aspects of parenting and that some parents may be more easily helped than others.

2.   There is evidence that the improvements accruing from the interventions can be provided in a relatively short period, usually in well under six months.

3.   Some of the studies had the disadvantage of not involving the children in either the treatment or the research measures of baseline and outcome data.

4.   The need for future research, is not to prove the efficacy of the behavioural model, but to determine the best method for its application in child abuse

cases, and its potential scope. Research on these unresolved issues would clarify which is the most appropriate context for behavioural programmes.

5. Unresolved issues include:
   - the relative efficacy of different techniques with different individuals with different presenting problems
   - the necessity of client motivation for success
   - the case types most available and most suitable for treatment
   - the advantages and disadvantages of court ordered treatment
   - the effects of families having additional problems and the difficulties and the necessity of working with these additional problems (with behavioural or other methods).
   - the degree to which success depends on integration of treatment within supportive casework
   - the length of treatment and possible repeat interventions.

6. The studies reviewed generally had the methodological virtues of (a) providing detailed baseline descriptions of their cases, (b) specifying the treatment, and (c) specifying outcome in operational terms and with obvious and direct relevance to the problem and the treatment.

7. Although many methodological problems remain, the behavioural studies stand out in the child abuse literature, as being more likely to test explicit hypotheses developed from previous theoretically based work, often drawing on the wider behavioural literature which considers other client groups. They also use more appropriate outcome measures of behavioural change, rather than self-report data or global measures such as known incidence of re-abuse. Studies of child abuse interventions based on very different theoretical approaches, could benefit from employing the hypothesis testing strategy of the behavioural studies.

8. Currently, behavioural approaches are restricted to a few special treatment centres and to clinics with psychologists on the staff. Not many children placed on child abuse registers, or their families, are likely to benefit from these programmes. Policy decisions are required about how best to include more behavioural programmes within the child protective services.

Chapter Seven Research Summaries

Barth et al (1983)

Self Control Training with Maltreating Parents

Sample: Four couples and two single parents referred by children's protective services for 'diminished mental capacity and anger control'. The parents were deficient in parenting and self control skills and had low levels of marital adjustment, common in maltreating families. Most families were unemployed. Children were of various ages and had emotional and behavioural problems. A control group was recruited from a well baby clinic. The controls had greater levels of education and all their children were under five years of age.

Focus: Improve parental functioning and child management.

Objectives: To allow access to models of effective parenting, to provide feedback in parenting skills, to build parents' social skills, to develop awareness of cognitive precursors of anger, to increase interpersonal contact in group.

Programme: Training in self control through the use of calming self statements, impulse delay, alternative action plans or scripts, relaxation and improved parent-child communication. Training in communication involved the use of a calm voice and steady eye and statements of wish, rather than of directives or orders. For all skills demonstrations, modelling, role play, feedback, and homework assignments were used. Group leaders emphasized the need for the parents to identify their own stressors and to self praise and reinforce the successful use of alternative strategies and resources. Group cohesion was encouraged by sharing of tasks and eating together. Parents met for 8 twice weekly group sessions led by graduate social work students.

Design: Repeated measures (pre and post-test) design with non random allocation to one treatment and one control condition.

Measures: Client assessments of the programme; self reports of relatives and friends; questionnaires on interpersonal behaviour, behaviour in hypothetical interaction situations, and marital relationships (Locke Wallace Inventory); observer ratings of negative commands, positive commands, approval and disapproval in role play. The role plays involved a young woman acting as a non compliant and often hostile child.

Results: Compared to controls, the treatment group showed significant improvements in positive self statements, self perceived anger control, nervousness, calm, and irritability. There were no significant changes in perceived parent-child conflict and marital relationships. In the role plays there were significant improvements compared to controls in 'I statements', and in effective commands. The mean inter-rater reliability of scores was 0.76. At follow up parents reported continued use of the trained skills, particularly relaxation and self talk. The parents were very positive about the group and its effect on their lives.

Notes: Articles discusses the use of the group as a means of reducing social isolation. Also methodological problems of not working directly with the children.

Bunyan (1987)

Behavioural Approach to the Treatment of a Conducted Disordered Child in the Natural Home Setting

Sample: A family who had been referred to Social Services due to father's overchastisement of son aged $4\frac{1}{2}$ with acute behavioural problems. Also daughter aged $2\frac{1}{2}$ years, father 28 years old, mother 26 years.

Focus: Behavioural treatment of a family with child at risk of abuse.

Objectives: To provide assistance for parents in the management of the child's problematic behaviour by reducing the frequency and strength of the child's excessive behaviour, to encourage a more acceptable sleep routine, and to increase his socially appropriate behaviour.

Programme: A behavioural programme of intervention with emphasis on the parents learning new coping techniques based on the application of the operant model, Sheldon, 1982. Parents taught via modeling to adopt a more commanding style and to use the strategies of extinction, time out and positive reinforcement. After 15 weeks positive reinforcements were changed from continuous to intermittent and from material to more social.

Design: Repeated measures (for 5 weeks of pre-assessment, for 15 weeks of treatment, and 6 month follow up) single case study.

Measures: Parental self report, direct observation and video recording by social workers, behavioural records such as charts and diaries and rating scales. Measures included incidence of defiance, demanding, physical aggression, destruction, nocturnal demanding, out of bed behaviour. Also pre and post test parental evaluation questionnaire.

Results: Defiance, demanding and physical aggression decreased markedly in frequency in first 5 weeks of treatment. The parents were more confident and authoritative in their approach to child management. Problem behaviours briefly recurred between weeks 10–14. The child's sleep irregularity was resolved within 5 days of treatment, though nocturnal demands and out of bed behaviour continued for 40 days. Quantitative results confirmed by parental questionnaire. Six month follow-up demonstrated that improvements had been maintained with no recurrence of target behaviours.

Notes: The author emphasizes the importance of these methods in helping parents to help themselves and to restore their self confidence, dignity, and prosocial interactions with their children.

Conger et al (1981)

An Intervention Programme for Child Abuse: Modifying Maternal Depression and Behaviour

Sample: 5 abusive mothers (4 black, 1 white) referred to programme by Department of Family & Children's Services for physical child abuse. Average age of the children was 3.7 years. Most children had received injuries and 3 required hospitalization. All families were economically stressed and most lived in public housing. Controls were 5 black single female parent families.

Focus: Parent-child interactions.

Objectives: To teach abusive parents to maintain control of children without physical punishment, increase positive and reduce negative exchanges within families, improve marital relationship, improve parental coping skills.

Programme: Improving child management by verbal instruction, modelling, role play, information on child behaviour and development. Developing stress management by cognitive restructuring, prompting, reinforcement, leading to assertiveness in handling environmental stressors. Helping parents to cope by increasing relaxation skills through Bensonian relaxation training and by therapy for couples using Jacobson's behavioural approach. The average length of treatment was weekly or twice weekly sessions for three months and carried out by graduate and post-doctorate clinical psychologists.

Design: Repeated measures (pre and post-test) matched control design.

Measures: Observational coding, using event recorders in the home, of negative and positive physical behaviours to children and of child compliance from Burgess & Conger, 1978. Median inter-rater reliability varied from 0.88 to 0.97. Emotional and physical distress were assessed by the Cornell Medical Index and the Beck Depression Inventory.

Results: There were significant baseline differences between abuse and control groups in positive and negative physical behaviours, in rates of child compliance to commands, in maternal depression, and emotional and physical distress. Improvements in the treatment sample but not in the control group in negative behaviours, positive behaviours and maternal depression. Both groups showed compliance, but this was most stable in the control group. No mothers were reported to protective services for abuse after their involvement in the treatment programme.

Notes: Authors state that results are tentative because of small sample, lack of precision in matching, and little follow up data, but general impression is favourable. The removal of a subject from each group to achieve a statistically significant result for changes and compliance means results need to be interpreted with care.

Crimmins et al (1984)

A Training Technique for Improving Parent-Child Interaction Skills of an Abusive Neglectful Mother

Sample: A 21 year old unemployed single parent, living with her mother and siblings, diagnosed as lacking the skills to enable positive interaction with her child. No hostility to child but mother had been court ordered to attend outpatient clinic because of abuse and neglect. Child was four years old with some evidence of malnutrition and injury.

Focus: Mother-child interaction.

Objectives: To increase the mother's positive verbal and physical behaviours.

Programme: The psychologist therapist taught target skills to mother. Mother practised cooperation through playing with son and compliance by asking child to do things in 5 minute interaction sessions. Immediate feedback was provided by the hidden trainer using a 'bug in ear' device.

Design: Repeated measures (pre and post-test and 2 follow ups) on single case.

Measures: Ratings of observed behaviour in clinic and at home. Target behaviours included positive verbal and physical behaviours. There was also general assessment of mother's active involvement and interactions and also the mother rated own perception of her child's behaviour.

Results: Improvement on all measures. Some loss of these improvements at a 4 month follow up, though scores were still above baseline. No re-abuse recorded at 18 months post-test.

Notes: Many of the frequencies in the results are low, making interpretation difficult.

Crozier and Katz (1979)

SOCIAL LEARNING TREATMENT OF CHILD ABUSE

Sample: Two families referred by Child Protective Services. Family 1: a two parent family with three children. The 4½ year old daughter was hyperactive and her parents used extreme physical punishments as a means of control. Family 2: a single parent with a 4½ year old male child. The mother self referred because of her fears over excessive physical chastisement that had already resulted in welts and bruises.

Focus: Parental behaviour and parent-child interactions.

Objectives: To train parents in the use of more adaptive child management techniques in order to reduce conflict and physical chastisement of the children.

Programme: Short intensive course of 8 sessions over 2½ weeks by the first author, a graduate student in psychology. Parents read literature on living with children, were involved in role playing sessions, in the use of contingent positive reinforcement, and ignoring or using time out for aversive child behaviours. Parental consistency and the inefficiency of punitive techniques were emphasized. The parents were also taught how to identify problem areas which resided in both their own and their children's behaviour. Anger control was taught through various self control and thought stopping procedures. A crisis hotline was provided.

Design: Repeated measures (pre- and post-test and follow up) on small treatment sample.

Measures: Rates of positive and aversive parent-child interactions observed in the home at baseline and post-test by trained observers. Behavioural codings were taken from Patterson's Manual for Coding Family Interactions and were coded in 90 consecutive 20 second intervals. Inter rater reliability was over 90%.

Results: In Family 1 aversive behaviours by all family members halved and this was maintained at 6 month follow up. There was a corresponding but weaker increase in positive behaviours, including the behaviour of a sibling of the target child. In Family 2 there were relatively low rates of both positive and aversive behaviours by the child, which did not alter much over treatment. The mother had high baseline rates of aversive behaviour which statistically reduced over treatment and this was maintained at follow up. No new episodes of abusive behaviour were reported in either family within the treatment or follow up period.

Notes: Authors argue that both child and parent behaviours improved despite treatment being directed at parents and that this is supporting evidence of the functioning relationship between the behaviours of different family members.

De Bortali-Tregerthan (1979)

A BEHAVIOURAL TREATMENT OF CHILD ABUSE: A CASE REPORT

Sample: An 18 year old unmarried mother of two children (15 months and 3 years) who bore bruises and scars. The mother requested help at the end of a probation order for abuse. She felt that she could not control her aggression towards her two children. Mother had material stresses and low income.

Focus: Mother-child interaction.

Objectives: Reduce mother's negative behaviours, promote positive behaviour, improve cognition and social and practical competence.

Programme: Children's behaviours to be eliminated were discussed and defined and included tantrums, whining, disobedience and aggression. Mother was trained to use time out procedures for worst behaviour and to ignore less aversive behaviours. Foster home placement was available if mother felt unable to control her aggression, but she was trained to 'thought-stop' aggressive thoughts and was trained in child development so that her expectations of the children would be more realistic. Control stimuli for feelings of depression and frustration were discussed and defined. Ways of increasing her sources of positive reinforcement were explored. There were 16 sessions over 3 months.

Design: Continuous measures on single case.

Measures: Instances of abuse, use of 'time out', bruises on child, and client self reports.

Results: Abuse and time outs decreased, except for a crisis period 6 months into treatment. Apart from the crisis, the client reported that she had thought stopped consistently on negative thoughts about her children and had engaged in activities incompatible with abuse. Both home and clinic visits indicated that the mother was using the trained technique appropriately. At 18 month follow up there was no evidence of re-abuse. The mother declared that she now loved both her children and although she could become impatient under stress, she is able to keep these feelings under control. The mother has overcome various stresses since treatment and is successfully developing her life.

Notes: The author states that the success of the technique depends on the voluntary and committed involvement of the client.

Denicola and Sandler (1980)

TRAINING ABUSIVE PARENTS IN CHILD MANAGEMENT AND SELF CONTROL SKILLS

Sample: Two families referred to Child Management Programme. Both families had poor management skills and there was evidence of bruising or over-chastisement of the children. One family contained a mother, three preschool girls, and partially absent father and there were financial, legal and interpersonal stress, and poor impulse control. Both families were court ordered to be under the supervision of child protection services and one of the families was court ordered to attend the programme. Both families were motivated for treatment.

Focus: Functioning of parents and parent-child interactions.

Objectives: To improve child management and coping skills including anger control of the parents. Sub-objectives specified by the behavioural approach involved.

Programme: (1) Parent training: reading materials, exercises and discussion taken from Becker's 'Parents and Teachers'. Videotapes of problem situations and discussion of their resolution. Modelling and role play with constant feedback. 'Contingency Contracting Procedure' used to reward parents for completion of tasks. Rewards were games and materials for children. (2) Coping Skills: relaxation, learning to change arousing self talk, plus strategies for coping with arousal that did occur. Training in problem solving skills with alternate solutions to aggressive, and 'stress inoculation procedures' in order to provide opportunities to practice coping skills. Training session lasted 60 to 90 minutes.

Design: Repeated measures (pre and post-test) on small intervention sample within a two variable withdrawal design, to allow individual assessment of the impact of each of the two intervention procedures.

Measures: Based upon Patterson's Coding Framework. Parental ratings of Total Aversion Behaviour (TAB), attention, non deviant behaviour, and questionnaire on child rearing attitudes of the mother. Child ratings of Total Aversion Behaviour, non deviant behaviour and child conduct.

Results: Family 1, showed improvements in TAB, approval and non deviant behaviour that were maintained or continuing to improve at follow up. Family 2 showed similar but more marked improvements. The children in the families showed a slight improvement in TAB and non deviant behaviour. None of the changes were systematically related to the mode of treatment as assessed by the variable withdrawal design. In general, reductions in negative behaviour were greater than increase in positive behaviour.

Notes: The authors state that measures of coping skill attainment would have improved the study.

Hutchings et al (1981)

CHILDREN AT RISK: WORKING WITH THE FAMILY

Sample: Divorced mother of two children, one of whom was a 4 year old boy on the child abuse register. Main problem was the boy's behaviour and mother's inability to handle him. Relationship problem from birth. There had been social service involvement for five years. Child had tantrums, demanded attention and was overactive. He was locked up at night to restrain him, had poor spoken language, and had occasionally been physical abused.

Focus: Maternal skills in child management.

Objectives: To provide mother with training to make up skill deficit and so improve mother child interactions and child behaviour.

Programme: Interview and observation of interactions to identify nine main problems including child night time behaviour and financial problems. Development of more constructive strategies including good night routines of reading and cuddling, and non response to child tantrums. New strategies modelled and practised and feedback given. Initial intensive work over three days then three times weekly to two times weekly and eventually once a month.

Design: Descriptive case study.

Measures: Defined by problems identified at start of therapy group addressed by therapist.

Results: 'All problems resolved'.

Notes: Authors believe that many families could benefit from this structured approach, but do not indicate which case types would benefit most.

Mastria et al (1979)

TREATMENT OF CHILD ABUSE BY BEHAVIOURAL INTERVENTION: A CASE REPORT

Sample: Mother and child self referred on recommendation of school. The mother was a 29 year old high school graduate, unemployed and receiving alimony, and described as immature, isolated and depressed. Child was aged 7 with slight behavioural and developmental problems and evidence of being physically over chastised or abused.

Focus: Maternal functioning and mother-child interactions.

Objectives: To teach and enable mother to control her child effectively and so reduce the chronic conflict between mother and child.

Programme: Video taping of mother-child interactions to feed back to mother, plus modelling of more effective strategies to reinforce positive child behaviours and reduce negative behaviours, which included distracting child when aggressive. Also use of self time out of conflict at home. Treatment consisted of ten 90 minute sessions with a therapist in a mental health centre.

Design: Repeated measures (pre and post-test) on single case.

Measures: Assessed positive and negative behaviours of mother and child in interactions. Some ratings by independent observer to ensure reliability of measures. Also self reports of mother and child.

Results: Therapist ratings indicated mother to be more confident, mature, in control, less self centred, hostile and manipulative. Child more tolerant of frustration and more friendly with peers. Mother reported similar findings plus that she felt closer to child who was more affectionate and cooperative. Child reported that he was less angry, more confident and felt liked and closer to his mother who was less angry and violent, more consistent and more fun to be with. The changes were maintained at a three month follow up.

McAuley (1980)

SUCCESS AND FAILURE IN APPLYING BEHAVIOURAL ANALYSIS

Sample: Case 1: 4½ year old boy referred to psychiatrist for advice on management. Problems of violent father, physical abuse of child and wife, aggressive child, poor mother-child interaction, social isolation. Case 2: 5 year old boy with conduct problems referred to psychiatrist, mother with psychological problems and anxious and upset at having abused

child. Fairly supportive marital relationship though recent marital rows and social withdrawal related to child's behaviour.

Focus: Mother-child interactions.

Objectives: To provide material training to enable mother-child interactions to improve and thus lessen child behaviour problems.

Programme: Three week child management training in psychiatric in-patient unit. Treatment involved the establishment of simple home rules, training in assertiveness and reinforcement techniques and management of behaviour to pre-empt escalation of conflicts. Emphasis on facilitative rather than directive behaviour. Attempts to involve fathers before and after in-patient treatment. Follow up work with Case 2.

Design: Descriptive case studies.

Measures: Clinical observation of attitude and behaviour to children, use of taught techniques and behaviours of children.

Results: Case 1: Mother slow to learn techniques, especially, those involving positive interactions. Sometimes she performed well, but seemed to lack motivation. Attempts to involve father failed. Behaviour problems persisted though at a reduced intensity. Case 2: Rapid progress in the unit resulting in warm interactions. Progress on the whole maintained, though marked deterioration occurred twice, but was overcome by extra training during extended case follow up. Some involvement of the father who was supportive of mother if not directly involved himself.

Notes: Author suggests that the differential outcome is due to Case 1 having long standing multiple problems, whilst Case 2 had short term and child related problems. In successful cases, it is the enhancing of existing skills that seem to work – partly because of motivation to use them. Author speculates that in long standing cases, any positive child behaviour is dissonant with established coercive interaction patterns.

Murphy and Davis (1979)

MODIFICATION OF A MOTHER'S VERBAL ABUSE

Sample: 31 year old college educated, intelligent, verbally abusive mother and bright 6 year old daughter. Clients selected because of affiliation with Parents' Anonymous and willingness to participate.

Focus: Mother's behaviour and mother-child interactions.

Objectives: To reduce negative behaviours of verbal abuse by mother and interruptions by daughter.

Programme: Three weeks of observations in the home with the experimenter talking to mother to allow a situation in which child interruptions could occur. Operant conditioning explained to mother, followed by eight weeks of observations with delayed feedback and positive reinforcement for successful child management.

Design: Repeated measures (pre and post-test) on single case.

Measures: Live observational scoring by trained volunteers plus video taping of some sessions. Coding is of negative child behaviour and negative and positive mother behaviours. Inter rater reliability of 0.8 to 1.0.

Results: No change in child interruptions, slight increase in mother ignoring interruptions and in positive reinforcement. Video tapes showed an improvement in positive categories of interactions. Mother reported as inconsistent in applying techniques.

Notes: Authors attribute improvement to experimenter presence, but not clear why video tapes showed improvement. Little data provided on mother's negative behaviours.

Nicol et al (1988)

A FOCUSED CASEWORK APPROACH TO THE TREATMENT OF CHILD ABUSE

Sample: 38 families in which actual physical abuse had occurred and who experienced coercive family conflicts. Cases were referred from statutory or voluntary social service agencies and no cases of known sexual abuse or current family crises were included. The majority of the parents were single and most were unemployed and from low socio-economic backgrounds. The childrens' ages varied, with a mean of 4.8 years.

Focus: Family interaction patterns.

Objectives: To intervene in the coercive interaction patterns of the families using a broad framework of intervention, necessary because of the advanced and entrenched negative interaction patterns of the families.

Programme: Focused case work which used behavioural modification principles, but within a broader framework of support. Sequence of treatment was: supportive work to establish a trusting relationship between worker and client; analysis by the team of the family problem and the development of a

dynamic hypothesis and strategies for changing this situation; negotiation of this analysis and plan with family; treatment 3 times per week for 6 to 8 weeks. The control group was assigned to a child focused service of play sessions. This consisted of treatment of the target child 2 times per week for 10 weeks by a clinical psychologist. Negative behaviours were ignored and positive behaviours reinforced. Discussions and other forms of exploring the child's problems and needs were also included.

Design: Repeated measures (pre and post-test) experimental design with random allocation to one experimental and one control condition.

Measures: Observation of family interaction in the home, with the Family Interaction Coding System that contains 21 clearly defined behavioural categories, particularly prosocial and aggressive behaviours grouped as Total Aversive Behaviours. Individuals are targeted for 5 minutes observation with behaviours and the accompanying response of others noted over 6 seconds. Inter-rater reliability was consistently over 75%.

Results: Post-tests were only possible on 55% of cases due to a high drop out rate. The results showed focused case work to be associated with a statistically more significant decrease in coercive behaviour, than in the control group. In comparing outcomes, focused casework was associated with significantly more positive behaviour. These effects were only significant when data on children and parents were grouped in families. The significant differences disappeared when subjects were examined separately.

Notes: More detail of the therapeutic approach and discussion of individual cases in Nicol et al (1985).

Owen Scott et al (1984)

USE OF SKILLS TRAINING PROCEDURES IN THE TREATMENT OF A CHILD ABUSIVE PARENT

Sample: 36 year old mother of an 11 year old son, referred to child psychology clinic by social services, because of incidents of physical abuse, including harsh spanking and one stabbing incident.

Focus: Skills of mother.

Objectives: To solve target problems identified in interviews with mother. These included skill deficits in assertiveness, child management, problem solving, and anger control.

Programme: Behavioural approach of instruction, modeling, role playing and rehearsal, and written activities on four main target skill areas. Also feedback and discussion and relaxation to develop anger control. There were 23 weekly sessions of 45 minutes and there was one male and one female therapist.

Design: Repeated measures (multiple baselines) on single case.

Measures: Video of role play coded for assertiveness, formal test of child management, coding of home observations on interaction problems, self reports of problems, self report questionnaire on anger control, self report assertion and fear of negative evaluation scale. Measures deliberately broader than targets of intervention. High inter-rater reliability reported.

Results: Improvement on all measures. Least improvement on self reports of assertion, anger, and fear of disapproval. Improvements were mainly associated in time with their focus in treatment and were maintained at 4 month follow up. At 10 month follow up there was a positive mother child relationship, there had been no re-abuse and the child was no longer considered at risk.

Notes: Little indication given of the significance of improvements or of the effects of continual re-testing.

Reid et al (1981)

A SOCIAL INTERACTIONAL APPROACH TO THE
TREATMENT OF ABUSIVE FAMILIES

Sample: 27 abusive families identified retrospectively, from records of 898 distressed families with child conduct disorder problems, involved in three treatment studies. Child abuse was not always evident before referral to the treatment studies. The index children were of an average age of $7\frac{3}{4}$ years with a range of three to twelve years. The average birth order was 2.8 years. The families were of average social class and 63% were 'intact' family groups.

Focus: Parent-child interactions that could lead to child abuse.

Objectives: To teach parents to improve their child management skills, particularly in handling confrontation, in order to reduce, (1) aversive behaviour of parent and child, (2) child conduct disorders and, (3) the risk of physical abuse of the children by the parents.

Programme: Intervention based on the work of Patterson and Reid and their colleagues, 1975, on coercive interaction patterns. Treatment included the teaching of social learning theory with films, discussion, and the modelling of techniques. Parents were taught to pinpoint, observe, and record child behaviours and respond appropriately to these behav-

iours. New reinforcement and punishment contingencies were negotiated with parents and children. Treatment lasted at least for four weeks and was at the Oregan Learning Centre and Home.

Design: Meta analysis of the results of three studies of child conduct disorder.

Measures: An index of total aversive behaviour (TAB) – a composite measure from the rate per minute of 14 observed aversive behaviours. Aversive behaviours include cry, whine, ignore, disappear, tease, non comply.

Results: A significant (P<0.5%, 1 tailed test) reduction in aversive behaviours of mothers and children was recorded over the treatment period. Only a small average improvement was recorded for fathers, but there were also no significant baseline differences between fathers from abusive and non abusive distressed families.

Notes: Authors suggest that results should be regarded tentatively as (1) some of the non abuse groups may in fact be abusive and, (2) abusive families with conduct disorders, may not be representative of abused families generally. Authors argue that treatment must include specific work on parental aversive behaviour, but be combined with other intervention techniques, for other family problems, such as social isolation. Much of the article is concerned with contrasting the nature of the abusing and non abusing families.

Sandford and Tustin (1973)

BEHAVIOURAL TREATMENT OF PARENTAL ASSAULT ON
A CHILD

Sample: A family consisting of a mother aged 21, father aged 31, and a 13 month old daughter. The child had spent most of her life in hospital due to feeding difficulties. After three weeks at home the mother approached the local services because of concern that the father would injure the child who already had bruises. The father could not tolerate his child's cries and hitting her brought about a temporary cessation. The child was removed to foster care, where she displayed a healthy appetite.

Focus: Father's behaviour and interactions with child.

Objectives: To intervene in the conditioned responses that had developed between the father and child. In particular to reinforce the father, for tolerating the child's crying and to make the child herself reinforcing for the father.

Programme: (1) Aversive sounds of children crying and a tin party hooter were presented to assess a baseline of tolerance. (2) Presentations of aversive stimuli were followed by reinforcing stimuli of pleasant sounds and by a picture of the daughter as a conditioned reinforcer. The level of aversive stimuli was gradually raised from low to high levels through 7 sessions. (3) As phase 2 but four sessions with sharp increases in the criterion for reinforcement (the aversive stimuli).

Design: Repeated measures (multiple baseline) on single case.

Measures: Extent of aversive stimuli to produce escape response.

Results: Aversive stimuli only tolerated for one minute at baseline, but no escape response after 16 minutes in last treatment session. No abuse of child in first two weeks home, but the child returned to foster care as the mother wishes to continue her employment and the foster mother wished to adopt the child.

Sandler et al (1978)

TRAINING CHILD ABUSERS IN THE USE OF POSITIVE REINFORCEMENT PRACTICE

Sample: Two single mothers referred for use of excessive physical punishment. Problem seen as a lack of effective social reinforcement. Five female children between the ages of 4 and 8 years.

Focus: Mothers' parenting skills.

Objectives: To improve parents' social reinforcement of their children. Specific sub-objectives arose from baseline observation sessions.

Programme: Between 9 and 11 sessions over 3 months. First session provided an opportunity for observation to reveal inconsistent pattern of behaviours. Treatment involved training materials and home assignments, role play, and tangible positive reinforcers such as free meals and 'movie passes'.

Design: Repeated measures (multiple baseline) of small intervention sample.

Measures: Selected from Patterson Coding System. Case 1: Approval, physical, positive commands, laugh, talk, laugh (child), talk (child). Case 2: Talking to child, attention to child, approval towards child, laughing with child. All coded separately for target and other child. Codings made over 6 seconds in 5 minute blocks. Inter-observer reliability of 92% and 85% for the two cases.

Results: Case 1: Approval, child compliance and negative commands all improved substantially and this

was maintained at a 4 month follow up. Physical positive behaviours also increased but returned to baseline at follow up. There were fluctuations in ratings of 'talk' and 'laugh' and no large increases in positive commands. Case 2: Attention to target and to other child increased and was maintained. 'Approval' and 'laugh' also increased but fluctuated and were not maintained. In both cases there were constructive changes that were maintained 5 months post-treatment. There were also improvements in some pro-social behaviours that were not specifically taught, but these improvements were not as consistent.

Notes: The authors suggest that the low ratings of child aversive behaviour, indicate a need for targeting efforts at parents, who may project their own lack of skills on to their children and be resistant to the idea that they require skills training. The article gave little data on the psycho-social characteristics of the parents.

Smith and Rachman (1984)

NON ACCIDENTAL INJURY: A CONTROLLED EVALUATION OF A BEHAVIOURAL MANAGEMENT PROGRAMME

Sample: 16 new child abuse cases referred to the projects from 3 social service departments. There were initially a further 11 cases that dropped out before pre-test assessment and another three cases were rejected for not meeting study criteria. The criteria included risk of or actual physical abuse, in the absence of specific failure to thrive or child sexual abuse. Only 10 families remained in the sample at post-test: 6 in a treatment group and 4 in the control group. Children were aged from 3 months to 8 years in the treatment group and 7 months to 3 years in the control group. Treatment families were nuclear, of average social class and there was some maternal depression. The main difference between treatment and control cases was that control children had more injuries.

Focus: Parental skills and parent-child interactions.

Objectives: To teach parents more appropriate, non violent ways of handling their children.

Programme: Treatment was by a child psychologist who worked out individual treatment plans with the social worker involved. Treatment devised from social learning theory and the work of Patterson on coercive family interactions. Parents were taught and modelled differential reinforcement, use of time out, and token system for child management. Parents also taught relaxation and assertion, given behavioural treatment for depression, and structured approaches to job hunting, family planning, and negotiating with various agencies. Treatment was approximately weekly for 6 to 8 months. Controls received routine social work help that included counselling, material and practical help, and case monitoring.

Design: Repeated measures (pre and post-test) experimental design with allocation to one treatment and one control condition on basis of geographical area.

Measures: Independent (mostly blind) clinical assessment of parenting, quality of marital relationships, and other social relations, and social isolation. Agency records of resources provided, and changes in family. Parental ratings of 3 target problems, considered important by psychologist and family.

Results: No re-abuse and general improvement in both groups, where data was available. Few changes in marital quality when family state good at pre-test. Few changes in social isolation or depression. A three year follow up of agency records showed that some cases were still open and one treatment group child and two control group children were in care.

Notes: Authors discuss the problems in reaching conclusions because of loss of experimental blindness, sample drop out, uneven level of child injury in treatment and control groups, shortness of treatment, and adequacy of measures. The article is very detailed on the methodological issues and difficulties experienced. Conclusion is that the treatment probably provides a useful contribution within a long term supportive relationship. Also the treatment involves detailed assessments necessary to determine whether family capable of change.

Szykula and Fleischman (1985)

REDUCING OUT OF HOME PLACEMENTS: TWO
CONTROLLED FIELD STUDIES

Sample: Study 1: families with children under threat of removal because of risk of child abuse. All were clients of special social learning programme, referred from routine child abuse services, and accepted as being suitable, in having less than severe problems, and some coping resources. Children aged between 3 and 12 years. Study 2: Similar to Study 1 except 24 treatment cases and 24 controls. The families were split into 13 'less difficult' and 11 'more difficult' cases.

Focus: Parent-child interactions.

Objectives: To intervene to change parents' child care skills, the interactional patterns with their children, and their practical life skills.

Programme: In both studies, parents were taught to observe and discriminate child behaviours. Then to use token system and praise as contingent reinforcements for positive behaviours and 5 minutes of isolation in response to negative behaviours. Also training in shaping behaviour, general problem solving, and self control procedure. In study no. 2 the control group received an unspecified range of services from limited supervision to participation in individual and family therapy.

Design: Study 1: Repeated measures (pre and post-test) on treatment sample. Study 2: Repeated measures (pre and post-test) experimental design with random allocation to one treatment and one control condition.

Measures: Placement of children away from their parents.

Results: Study No. 1: Sharp reduction of placements away from home after implementation of programme. Study No. 2: In the less difficult group 1 of the 13 in the treatment group and 5 of the 13 in the control group were received into care, which is a significant effect. In the more difficult group the receptions into care were 7/11 and 5/11 for the treatment and control groups respectively, which is not a significant difference.

Notes: Receptions into care are seen as a crucial outcome variable, although not an independent measure.

Whiteman et al (1987)

AN EXPERIMENTAL COMPARISON OF COGNITIVE
BEHAVIOURAL INTERVENTIONS AIMED AT ANGER OF
PARENTS AT RISK OF CHILD ABUSE

Sample: 55 subjects drawn from two agencies in New York City; 15 clients were child abuse cases from a public agency; 40 clients were from a private agency considered at risk of child maltreatment. Referral criteria were mainly problems in anger control not associated with psychotism or the effects of drugs or alcohol. Mean age was 33 years. Ethnicity was white (22%), Hispanic (24%), and black (50%). A third were married, a third divorced, a third separated, and a third had never married. Half were on public assistance.

Focus: Parents and parent-child interactions.

Objectives: To reduce parental anger in the face of provocations by children that may lead to physical maltreatment of children.

Programme: Treatment was guided by two main principles of establishing a learning process and facilitating a sense of anger control for parents. One of four specific methods was used on subsamples:

(1) cognitive restructuring, to change the perceptions of the child and of the stress that the parents encountered, (2) relaxation procedures to alleviate states of arousal triggering and accompanying anger responses. (3) development of problem solving skills to replace the previous hostile responses, (4) a combination of the strategies in (1), (2) and (3). The therapists were four social work doctoral students who worked on an individual basis, through 6 weekly sessions in the home.

Design: Repeated measures (pre and post-test) experimental design with random allocation to four experimental and one control condition.

Measures: (1) Coding on a parental anger scale on the basis of (a) hypothetical situations in which there is provocation by another adult, (b) client role playing of a script with child provocations, (c) self descriptions of proneness to anger. (2) Coding of parental child rearing attitudes and reactions to children's behaviour on the basis of (a), affection such as hugging and praising, (b) discipline, (c) empathy such as sensitivity to child's feelings and moods and, (d) behaviours irritating or troublesome to parents.

Results: No significant inter group differences at pre-test. At post-test, the greatest significant effect for anger control measures, was achieved by the combined therapeutic intervention, followed by the problem solving programme. Neither cognitive restructuring nor relaxation techniques were significantly associated with anger control measures. On the child rearing measures, there was a significant change in empathy and perceptions of the children as troublesome, for the subgroups concerned with problem solving, cognitive restructuring, and the combined therapeutic intervention. The scores of the relaxation group increased but did not become significant. A more conservative statistical analysis indicated that the greatest association occurred in the cognitive restructuring group.

Notes: The authors discuss possible reasons why composite measures and problem solving were associated with improved anger measures whilst cognitive restructuring seemed important for parental perceptions and empathy. The possible causal links between anger and child rearing are also discussed.

Wolfe and Sandler (1981)

Training Abusive Parents in Effective Child Management

Sample: Three family units: one mother and son; one mother and daughter; one mother, stepfather, and two children. Families referred on the basis of at least one incident of abuse as defined by the child protection services. The four children were

of nursery school age and developmental delay was noted in one child. All three families were in receipt of welfare benefits. Participation in the programme was voluntary, but within the context of threatened removal of children from the home. Two families agreed to participate in order to keep their children at home.

Focus: Parent child interactions that could lead to child abuse.

Objectives: To reduce negative behaviours of parents and promote positive behaviour and child care skills.

Programme: A work book was used to identify, with the parents, specific child behaviour problems and appropriate management techniques. The techniques were demonstrated to the parents through role playing and were practiced by the parents with their children, with experimenter feedback. There was also a contingency contracting procedure by which parents were reinforced for completing agreed assignments of taught child management techniques.

Design: Repeated measures (pre and post-test) on small intervention sample with a two variable withdrawal design to isolate the impact of both intervention procedures.

Measures: Two specific measures were used. Firstly, the percentage of parental commands followed by child compliance and, secondly, a composite measure of total aversive behaviour (TAB) made up from rates of aversive behaviours such as disapprove, ignore, tease, cry, yell. Measures were coded by trained blind observers. There was also a post-test parental questionnaire, on whether the programme met their expectations and case worker evaluations of progress.

Results: There was a rapid and consistent reduction in the total aversive behaviours of the parents and this was maintained for many months post treatment. There were similar improvements for child aversive behaviours, except for one child, who had a low stable baseline score on the TAB. Fluctuations in rates were more pronounced for children than parents. The command/compliance rates increased from a baseline of 24% in two families to post treatment rates of 63% and 80%. The third family contained the child with the low TAB rate where compliance was initially 91% and rose to 100%. None of these results seemed to be functionally related to either experimental procedure, but rather to the continuous effects of intervention. Parents and caseworkers reported both satisfaction with the programme and reduced risk to the children.

Notes: The authors suggest, that although abuse is typically 'private', the range of measures in the study are sufficiently valid to indicate a reduced risk for children.

Wolfe et al (1981)

PARENT TRAINING FOR CHILD ABUSERS

Sample: 16 cases of physical child abuse under a court order or threat of order to have therapy. Mean age of children was 4½ years. Most families were on low incomes.

Focus: Parental behaviour and parent-child interactions.

Objectives: To improve parents' child care skills and thus improve parent-child interactions and the risk of future physical abuse.

Programme: Individualized home based weekly training that was 'criteria based' so that problems were resolved before new ones could be addressed. Also training of skills in weekly parent group. Techniques included positive reinforcement, time out, modelling, shaping, problem solving vignettes, and films teaching human development. Also deep muscle relaxation techniques. Treatment lasted 8 weeks. Control group provided with routine child abuse services that included bi-weekly monitoring.

Design: Repeated measures (pre and post-test) experimental design with block allocations to one treatment and one control condition (by order of referral with first 8 cases in treatment groups and next 8 cases in control group).

Measures: Home observations using a Parent/Child Interaction Form to rate positive reinforcements, and use of commands and appropriate punishments. Coders were experimentally blind, at least at pre-test. Parent ratings of problem behaviours with the Eyberg Child Behaviour Inventory. Caseworker ratings of families' treatment needs, anger control, and child development on an Agency Referral Questionnaire. Agency records of abuse.

Results: Multivariate analysis of co-variance revealed a significant treatment effect on all measures, but mainly on increased parenting skills. At ten week follow up, 5 of the 8 treatment families showed maintenance of effect. At one year no abusive incidents had been reported in 14 of the 16 families. By this time some of the control group had received some treatment.

Notes: Authors emphasize the speed at which clients develop skills through special programmes, in contrast to routine services. Few details of sample provided.

Wolfe et al (1982)

INTENSIVE BEHAVIOURAL PARENT TRAINING FOR AN ABUSIVE MOTHER

Sample: A single epileptic mother of low I.Q. with three children. Two 9 year old male twins had cuts and welts on faces and bodies, were non compliant, overactive, socially unresponsive, and intellectually delayed. The 2 year old girl had a low I.Q. There were multiple instances of neglectful parenting and the family was court ordered to attend behavioural psychology clinic. The mother had been a child welfare client for five years prior to court order and was financially supported by welfare benefits.

Focus: Maternal parenting skills.

Objectives: To decrease physical and verbal hostile parenting and increase positive parenting behaviour.

Programme: Weekly sessions for 3 months. Treatment involved providing feedback to mother, whilst she undertook compliance and cooperation tasks with her children, behind a one way screen. Mother instructed to employ non aggressive control strategies and immediate feedback was provided through a 'bug in ear' device. There were also discussions with the mother about the implementation of these newly learnt strategies in the home.

Design: Repeated measures (pre and post-test) single case design.

Measures: Observer coding of negative and positive verbal and physical parenting and child behaviour in the clinic and in the home.

Results: Negative behaviour rate of 2.5 per minute decreased to zero. For physical behaviour there was a significant increase in compliance, but not in the cooperative task. For verbal behaviour there was a significant increase in both tasks, that was maintained after 'bug in ear' feedback ended.

Notes: Article stresses the success achieved with this challenging case. Little information provided on parents motivation or other services being offered.

Wolfe et al (1988)

EARLY INTERVENTION FOR PARENTS AT RISK OF CHILD ABUSE AND NEGLECT

Sample: 30 women who fully participated and for whom full data available from target group of 53 meeting study criteria. Criteria were younger than 25, child aged between 9 and 60 months, major problems in parenting, at risk on Child Abuse Potential Inventory, no evidence of psychopathology or higher intervention priorities, under supervision of Child

Protection Agency and no involvement in other community treatment services. 16 parents in experimental group and 14 in control group. Median age of women 21 years and of children 24 months. Agency supervision of average of 6 months. Children mildly delayed in physical, perceptual, and cognitive development (approx 4 months). Only 3 women married or involved in relationships though some male companions.

Focus: Education of at risk parents as secondary prevention of child abuse.

Objectives: Parent training to actively involve parents as behaviour change agents for their children.

Programme: (1) Experimental group: Mothers and children were interviewed by the agency psychologist to discuss the nature of the treatment. Parent training intervention was based on a social learning approach to child abuse that was specifically aimed at emergent problems in child management and development. Phase 1 provided instruction, modeling, and rehearsal procedures. Phase 2 taught parents to give clear concise commands, to reward compliance and to implement a time-out procedure. Therapists focused on problems raised or observed at the clinic and training was competency based using criterion referenced Parent-Child Interaction Form. Therapist and video feedback with discussion. In vivo-desensitisation, relaxation, diversion and coping skills with the child present. Also information meetings and standard agency home visits from caseworkers.

(2) Control group only received information groups and standard case worker visits. Information groups (2 hours twice weekly) included social activities and informal discussion of family and health topics, while children attended day care activities.

Design: Repeated measures (pretest, post test, and 3 month follow up) experimental design with random allocation to treatment and 1 control condition.

Measures: (1) Self-report measures: The Child Abuse Potential Inventory (CAPI) at pretest and follow up only. Beck Depression Inventory (2) (BDI). Observational measures of child-rearing: Dyadic Parent-Child Interaction Coding System (Robinson & Eyberg 1981), and the Home Observation and Measurement of the Environment Scale (Home). (3) Measures of child behaviour: The Pyramid Scales of adaptive behaviour (not at post test) and the Behaviour Rating Scale (BRS). Parent and Worker ratings of the programmes and progress.

Results: (1) No pretest differences. Experimental group dropouts from treatment differed only on greater parental stress on CAPI. (2) Parenting: Analysis of variance of CAPI and BDI scores revealed a significant main effect for time qualified by a significant treatment × time interaction. The CAPI scores of experimental group were reduced more (to within normal range) than control group at follow up. The significant effect on the BDI was due to greater reductions in scores for the experimental group at post test. At follow up, experimental group scores were higher than controls but still below pretest levels. No significant effects on home observation. Both groups improved significantly on Home scores. (3) Child Behaviour: significant main effects for group and time and a significant group × time interaction. The experimental group reported fewer problems during treatment and the control group reported more. This effect maintained or increased at follow up. Univariate analysis revealed significant group effects for the number of behaviour problems and their intensity, but not for other child behaviour problems. (4) Subjective ratings: 85% of parents stated that interventions were enjoyable and helpful. Workers rated experimental group mothers to be managing significantly better than controls at post test.

Notes: Authors suggest that lack of improvements on home observation scores might be due to narrowness of variables and unnatural situation.

CHAPTER EIGHT
Special Projects for Children and Families

Background

This chapter examines studies that have evaluated reactive interventions aimed at children, parents and whole families, that are not covered by the chapters on the behavioural programmes for physical abusing parents, multi-component demonstration programmes or child abuse special units, or child sexual abuse (see also the brief discussion of preventive programmes for family preservation at the end of Chapter Six).

Behavioural approaches considered in Chapter Seven are only one type of possible intervention, for increasing parental skills or levels of functioning. Other programmes may be less narrowly focused on specific behaviours or child care. They may address the parents' emotional state, their material and emotional supports and stresses, their vulnerability to such stresses and their coping skills.

A distinction can be made between interventions aimed at the initial causes of abusive behaviour by the parents and interventions aimed at the effects or consequences of such abuse. Such a distinction may seen marginal, but it is important. The actual act of abuse may totally change the interpersonal context in which the abuse occurred. This may not be as true for less time specific abuses, such as neglect, but many families will experience a major qualitative change in relationships. Within the wider community, they will suffer the reaction of others, such as health, welfare and legal agencies. Once the abuse has become known or suspected, agency procedures and legal processes may be initiated, which could have far reaching consequences on vulnerable abusing parents who are caring for children after and during child abuse investigations. The investigations may be stressful in themselves, and could be followed by the absence of an abusing parent, who may have been central to the family's previous functioning, as well as the temporary or permanent removal of their child.

With interventions directed at children, rather than at adults or the whole family, there is a clearer distinction between the strategies aimed at behaviour that may be considered to have increased the probability of abuse, and attempts to mitigate the effects of abuse. A focus on child causal effects, does not necessarily imply blame or responsibility. It may simply be an understanding of the complexity or interactions which could put some children at greater risk of abuse than others. Whatever the focus of the child directed interventions, the techniques employed are the same as far adults, but with a greater emphasis on the developmental aspects.

Research Studies/Discussion

Despite the many forms of re-active interventions possible, the literature reveals relatively few formal evaluations of different models of work. This chapter therefore also includes a few of the many more descriptive studies that exist (see listing of studies in Tables 8.1 to 8.5). The programmes aimed principally at parents, fell into the following main categories: predominantly education or skill-based projects, psychotherapeutic and supportive strategies with groups, and interventions based upon individual work, child focused projects, and non organic failure to thrive. As these studies are so diverse, they are discussed under these respective headings rather than under a separate discussion section as in other chapters.

Education, Skills, and Training

The projects with an educational or training approach dealt with child care, child management, skills in relationships with children and adults, life skills, and home based skills (Table 8.1). The emphasis varied between projects, as did the degree of formal instructions and task orientated teaching in relation to more open discussion.

In the project evaluated by Stephenson (1977), the parents were taught self esteem and practical home based skills. Children improved rapidly compared to controls on teacher assessment measures and general indicators of functioning and these were supported by increases in the more independent measure of cognitive development.

Bell and colleagues (1983) studied a child care programme for teenage single mothers, with group sessions which concentrated upon parenting and achieving independence. The emphasis was on achieving attainable goals and included parental monitoring of these goals, while the children also received their own service, through age appropriate groups. In the study by Parish and colleagues (Parish et al, 1985) the project included parent groups to teach skills such as anger control, but most emphasis was on a service for children.

Brunk et al (1987) undertook a comparative study of parent training and multisystemic therapy. Parent training was in groups and focused on human development and child management techniques, particularly the benefits of positive rather than negative and positive methods. Although the training was in groups, the problems of each individual family were identified and monitored during training. Parent training was associated with outcomes of decreased parental stress and social problems on self report measures. There were also some improvements

TABLE 8.1

Education, Skills, Training Research Studies

Study	Programme	Sample size	Population	Design	Main measures
Bell et al (1983)	Parent Effectiveness training	n = 29	Teenage mothers & abused children	POST + C	Independence, employment, abuse
Brunk et al (1987)	Parent training, Multi systemic therapy	n = 17 n = 16	Physical abuse/ neglect	RPM + C	Parent mental state, child behaviour interactions
Burch and Mohr (1980)	Educational Parenting groups	n = 65	Child Abuse	RPM + C	Child care knowledge, knowledge and attitudes
Dawson et al (1986)	Problem solving training	n = 3	Neglect	RPM	Child care strategies
Feldman et al (1986)	Parent training	n = 7	Mothers with low IQ	RPM	Stimulation of child
Feldman et al (1992)	Child care training	n = 11	Mothers with low IQ	RPM	Child care skills
Kruger et al (1979)	Parent education group	n = 5	Abuse/neglect	POST	Workers' assessments
Peters and Carswell (1984)	Parenting skills	n = 717	CPS cases	Descriptive	Parental competence
Stephenson (1977)	Child enrichment, parent training	n = 24	Child abuse/neglect	RPM + C	Social and cognitive development, family functioning

Design
POST = Post-test only; RPM = Repeated Measures including Pre-test; PRPM = Repeated Measures post-test only;
+ C = Control or comparison groups; + PC = Control or comparison group but at post-test only.

on observational measures of parent-child interactions, but these were greater in the multisystemic group where therapists could more directly target problematic interaction patterns.

Peters and Carswell (1984) examined a parent education group which was part of a wider programme that included home visits by a parent assistant. The weekly classes discussed children's needs and home based skills and were led by a home economist. During the home visits, the parent assistants both taught the parents specific skills and provided a model for the development of other skills in the home, according to a contract negotiated with the parents.

In the study by Burch and Mohr (1980) another personal service was provided. Parents were given weekly educational presentations but also took part in smaller groups, where individual problems could be dealt with in more detail. Improvements were assessed by a checklist of statements about child care and parenthood, which parents had to code as true or false. A similar focus on specific skills and abilities is evident in the report by Dawson and colleagues (1986). In this project three parents were encouraged to develop strategies for solving problem vignettes. Improvements over the course of the intervention were assessed by coding the solutions proposed. Such focused approaches are in contrast to some of the other educational strategies that took a more open or discursive approach. For example, the six week educational discussion group examined by Kruger (Kruger et al, 1979) which was extended for a further seven weeks at the parents' instigation.

A focused training strategy was also studied by Feldman et al (1986, 1992). He reported substantial improvements in child care skills by mothers with limited intellectual abilities. The mothers had very low baseline levels of skill, but these quickly increased during training even though the mothers were experiencing multiple social problems. The authors argue that this shows that the social problems do not prevent parents from learning appropriate skills, though additional interventions may be necessary in order to allow the parents to exercise these new skills.

The educational intervention projects varied in emphasis on different topics, educational methods employed, and the degree of professional control and management. This raises the question about which approaches are most effective or have other types of advantages. All of the studies report an improvement over the length of the interventions, but these results are difficult to interpret for familiar reasons. The first problem is that only three of the studies are experimentally controlled (Burch and Mohr, 1980; Stephenson 1979; Brunk et al, 1987). The results of Burch and Mohr (1980) are particularly strong because the study was controlled and used a formal instrument for assessing parents' knowledge and attitudes towards child care using a true/false choice question. The instrument may have been subject to a learning effect and may not equate with actual parental behaviour, but at least the results show that parents can be taught what is considered appropriate for children. In the Stephenson (1979) study, the most objective measures were for children, who did show improvements. The improvements in family functioning were derived from broader general indicators and it is less easy to be confident that these could not be influenced by workers' views and expectations. The Brunk study (Brunk et al, 1987) found that parents reported parent training to be more effective (for social problems) and therapists thought that multi systemic therapy was more effective (for restructuring parent-child relations). Both sets of respondents might be correct, but there are obvious dangers of respondent bias. Data from home observations showed that behaviour patterns had changed in both groups, but to a greater degree in the multisystemic group.

The other studies were not controlled and used repeated measures on the treatment group. The measures used were, with the exceptions of the Feldman studies (Feldman et al, 1986, 1992) and the problem solving rating in Dawson's study (Dawson et al, 1986), primarily based upon non independent assessments of improvement. The possible bias resulting from this, makes it difficult to be certain that improvements actually occurred. Even if there were improvements, it is not clear if they were due to the therapeutic value of the specific techniques applied, or to other experimental effects. The question is not whether the projects were, or were not, beneficial to their clients, but whether there is a basis for choosing between them. Burch and Mohr (1980) and Stephenson (1979) and Brunk et al (1987) all showed an experimental effect, but the other projects may well have been equally successful. It is therefore necessary to rely on clinical judgement and experience, to decide which aspects of which programme, are valuable for which clients.

Supportive or Psycho-therapeutic Groups

The therapeutic group interventions (Table 8.2) most clinical in approach, were reported by Belluci (1972), Paulson et al (1974), and by Justice and Justice (1978). Belluci examined the impact on ten mothers of group sessions based on psycho-dynamic principles, and reported many improvements in the areas of self awareness and self esteem, in social interactions and in relationships with significant others. There was no improvement in degrees of social isolation. The results were based on therapist assessments. Similarly, Paulson and colleagues (1974) described their experience of eclectic psychodynamic group psychotherapy. The study was not intended as a formal evaluation, but half of the children who had been in care were returned home, though it is unclear how many would have returned home without parental treatment.

Justice and Justice (1978) studied the effect on thirty couples of a group with a maximum membership of five couples at any one time. The group was eclectic

TABLE 8.2

Psycho-Therapeutic Groups Research Studies

Study	Programme	Sample size	Population	Design	Main measures
Behaviour Associates (1977) Lieber and Baker (1977)	Parents Anonymous	n = 613	Members of P.A.	RPM	Self report of knowledge, behaviour
Belluci (1972)	Psycho dynamic group	n = 10	CPS referrals	Descriptive	Therapist assessment
Breton (1979)	The Hairdressing Group	n = 7	Deprived mothers, physical abuse	Descriptive	Therapist assessment
Justice and Justice (1978)	Group therapy	n = 30	Child abuse	RPM	Goal attainment
Kitchen (1980)	Family Centre	?	Physical abuse	Descriptive	None
Land (1986)	Multi-component	n = 89	Physical abuse/ neglect	POST	Parent-child relations
Paulson et al (1974)	Group psychotherapy	n = 54	Neglect/ maltreatment	RPM	Workers' assessments
Prodgers and Bannister (1983)	Psycho drama group	n = 8	Physical abuse	Descriptive	Clients insights/self esteem
Rogowski and McGrath (1986)	Discussion group	n = 6	Child abuse	POST	Client satisfaction/ understanding

Design
POST = Post-test only; RPM = Repeated Measures including Pre-test; PRPM = Repeated Measures post-test only;
+ C = Control or comparison groups; + PC = Control or comparison group but at post-test only.

in adopting a variety of therapeutic techniques including transactional analysis and rational emotive therapy. Improvement was assessed according to a scoring system of goal attainment. This provided a focused basis for assessment but still relied upon therapist ratings. A third of the couples achieved sufficiently high scores to indicate that therapists considered them to have successfully completed the programme. Four couples, who dropped out of the group, had their children permanently placed in care.

Prodgers and Bannister (1983) used the family centre of a child abuse special unit as a basis for forming a psychodrama group involving eight mothers. Role play and sculpting was used to allow the mothers to explore their relationships, particularly between them and their children and how and why these had become difficult. An attempt was made to involve mothers with differing levels of ability on different dimensions so that they could share and learn from each others different strengths. Outcome measures were limited to therapists' assessments, which indicated increases in the mothers' insights and self esteem.

Two studies which concentrated on parent child interactions and modelling in supervised child care situations, were reported by Kitchen (1980) and Land (1986). Kitchen's is a descriptive study of a family centre, where parents were given positive care and shown that they would be able to learn appropriate skills to care for their own children by following the example of the centre staff. Land's study was on two programmes for court ordered cases of child abuse, which used supervised parent-child interaction, specific therapeutic techniques, home visits and social supports. Improvements were assessed by a programme administrator, who is reported not to have been directly involved in treatment, but may not have been experimentally blind. The results report significantly greater improvements for families who were in the programme for more than four months and who also received more than twelve hours treatment per week.

Other programmes studied, were less clinical. For example, Breton (1979) examined a 'Hairdressing Group' where the physical care involved in hairdressing, was used as a focus for a working family group. The descriptive evaluation revealed that the parents very slowly developed self esteem and competence, from an initial level of dependency when they were only able to receive and not to offer nurture. Even further from a professional clinical model, were the Parents Anonymous groups (Behaviour Associates, 1977; Lieber and Baker, 1977). They used psychotherapeutic techniques, but were self help treatment groups, with a volunteer professional consultant. The evaluation was made from a United States nationwide postal survey, and the investigators found a significant association between length of group attendance and self reports on attitudes to parenthood and children. Whether this result is due to changes in behaviour, in presentation of self, or reflects a sampling effect, in either attendance at Parents Anonymous or responding to the survey, is unclear.

The final study in this section concerns a group with the focus not upon psychological difficulties, but upon the stresses that reveal or create such problems (Rogowski and Stempler, 1986). It included a discussion group with local agency managers about housing, welfare rights, and the child protection system: how it works and what people fear. The parents reported both satisfaction with the group and improvements in their understanding, ability, and confidence in managing stresses.

All the groups discussed in this section provided a useful and interesting service, but their relative efficacy is unknown. The studies were not controlled and many only used worker assessments of outcome, which are not sufficiently independent or consistent to be used to determine the relative efficacy of different strategies. The study by Justice and Justice (1978) did use the precise outcome of non return of children from care, but this is not an independent or consistent measure. Couples who are considered not to be successfully using or benefiting from the groups, may have less support from workers and therefore less opportunity to make requests for children to be returned.

Individual Work

These projects, like the group and educational initiatives, varied both in psycho-therapeutic models used, and in the professional control of the interventions (Table 8.3). Two clinic centred projects, took particularly focused approaches. Argyles (1980) presented a case study in which the therapist explored the parents' and children's feelings and past experiences, within a trusting therapeutic relationship. The trust, security and self awareness resulting from this long-term therapy, led (according to the therapist's assessments) to improved individual functioning and thus a more stable family. The children became more securely attached as well as more independent, and were therefore able to develop appropriately. The second study by Zastrow (1981) described a very different technique. This addressed the 'self talk' used by abusing parents to justify abuse of their children before and after the event. Rational Therapy was used to make the parents more aware of these strategies and to change them accordingly, but no data were presented on whether the actual behaviour of the parents changed.

Other studies in this section were principally concerned with services provided in the parents' homes. Leeds (1984) reports the use of intensive casework made possible through reduced caseloads and a 24 hour crisis service. Project objectives were related to service objectives of closing resolved cases and preventing placements of children in care. This was achieved but took longer than originally hoped. Similarly, Stempler and Stempler (1981) report a case where a homemaker and caseworker teamed together, produced progress in a family which had previously

TABLE 8.3

Individual Work Research Studies

Study	Programme	Sample size	Population	Design	Main measures
Argyles (1980)	Attachment therapy	n = 1	Physical abuse	RPM	Self report of knowledge, behaviour
Brown (1985)	Parent aides	n = 24	Child abuse	RPM	Therapist assessment
Hornick and Clarke (1986)	Lay therapy	n = 55	Abuse/risk of	RPM + C	Self reports of parenting
Lane and Van Dyke (1978)	Lay therapy	n = 27	Physical abuse	POST	Marital status, child placement
Leeds (1984)	Intensive social work	n = 37	Neglect/abuse	RPM	Goal attainment
Lines (1986)	Parent aides	n = 36	Physical abuse/ neglect	POST	Goals, abuse
Press-Rigler et al (1990)	Parent aides	?	Child abuse/neglect	Descriptive	Descriptive
Stempler and Stempler (1981)	Homemaker-caseworker teams	n = 1	Neglect/emotional abuse	Descriptive	Parental competence
Tracy and Clark (1974) Tracy et al (1975)	Behavioural outreach	n = 37	Physical abuse/ risk of	RPM	Goal attainment
Zastrow (1981)	Rational therapy	n = 2	Physical abuse/ sexual abuse	Descriptive	Descriptive
Zimrin (1984)	Volunteers	n = 20	Physical abuse	RPM + C	Coping, interactions

Design
POST = Post-test only; RPM = Repeated Measures including Pre-test; PRPM = Repeated Measures post-test only; + C = Control or comparison groups; + PC = Control or comparison group but at post-test only.

shown no improvement. Mention has already been made (in Section 8.1) of Brunk et al's study that reported greater improvements on interaction patterns for subjects receiving multisystemic therapy rather than group based parent education.

The largest number of studies in this section refer to the use of lay therapists, lay visitors, and outreach workers (Brown, 1985; Hornick & Clarke, 1986; Lane & Van Dyke, 1978; Lines, 1986; Press-Rigler et al, 1980; Tracy and Clark, 1974; Tracy et al, 1975; Zimrin, 1984). All of the programmes were concerned with providing social and emotional support, and modelling of appropriate child care and home based skills, but vary in emphasis. For example, Tracy and colleagues (1974, 1975) examined practical advice and advocacy, while at the other extreme, Zimrin (1984) reported a controlled study of the use of volunteers to provide friendship and 'mere human contact' in addition to routine social services casework.

Most of these studies report an intervention effect, but the research summaries show that these were rarely based on independent measures. A common negative result, however, is a high rate of client drop-out from non statutory provision. Two of the studies used control groups and found some encouraging results. Hornick and Clarke (1986) found that target parents scored significantly higher than controls, in worker and parent measures of empathizing with children, enjoying parent-child interactions, and in believing that parents influenced children. In Zimrin's (1984) study, worker ratings were also used but with a check for inter rater reliability. Zimrin found a significant increase in maternal coping compared to controls, but this effect had disappeared at a three month follow-up. Only the study by Brunk et al (1987) used both a controlled design and independent measures of outcome to conclude that the intervention of multisystemic therapy had been effective.

Child Focused Interventions

Several of the studies already considered involved interventions including direct work with children. The studies by Bell et al (1983), Stephenson (1977), and Parish et al (1985) dealt with projects which offered extra stimulation and enriched environments to children. Bell's study also reported skill training. Both Bell and Stephenson's studies used experimentally controlled designs and reported significant improvement in child functioning compared to controls, though it is not clear how independent the measures or the control sample were in the Bell study.

Other studies concerned with children are listed in Table 8.4. Culp and colleagues (1987) used a repeated measures design on the intervention group of a therapeutic day treatment programme. Children were offered a range of therapies, education, counselling, and crisis services. Improvements were greater for children who had been abused rather than neglected or at risk and also greater for female compared to male children.

Another repeated measures non controlled design was reported by Parish and colleagues (1985). Children were enrolled in a special pre-school class, with some parental participation and separate parent groups. Experimentally blind assessments showed significant increases in a range of social, linguistic, and motor skills.

Another study of services offered to both children and parents, was undertaken by Elmer and associates (Elmer, 1986; Schultz et al, 1979; Sankey et al, 1985). It was a last chance for parents to benefit from the help offered, and to show ability and motivation to care appropriately for their children, before final decisions were made on the permanent placement of the children. The children were very young and stayed in a residential centre, where they received mothering and stimulation from a nurse. Parents visited three or four days per week and were trained in child care. It was hoped that the stimulation of the infants, would make interaction easier with their parents. The results showed that the children did improve significantly compared to the controls, on most measures as assessed

TABLE 8.4

Child Focused Research Studies

Study	Programme	Sample size	Population	Design	Main measures
Culp et al (1987)	Therapeutic day treatment	n = 109	Neglected/abused children	RPM	Child development
Elmer (1986), Sankey et al (1985), Schultz et al (1979)	Residential treatment	n = 31	Abused children	RPM + C	Child development, interactions
Fantuzzo et al (1987)	Peer social initiation	n = 6	Maltreated children	RPM	Peer initiations
Fantuzzo et al (1988)	Peer vs adult initiations	n = 39	Maltreated children	RPM + C	Positive social behaviours
Green (1978)	Psychodynamic treatment	n = 20	Abused children	POST	Therapists assessments
Harling and Haines (1980)	Specialised foster homes	n = 43	Abused/neglected children	POST	Emotional/physical development
Kunkel (1981)	Residential treatment	n = 18	Abused/neglected	POST	Child placements, family functioning
Parish et al (1985)	Family orientated treatment	n = 53	Physically abused children	RPM	Social & cognitive

Design

POST = Post-test only; RPM = Repeated Measures including Pre-test; PRPM = Repeated Measures post-test only;
+ C = Control or comparison groups; + PC = Control or comparison group but at post-test only.

by formal coding instruments, but only 10% of the children were allowed to return home.

Other studies have examined interventions directed solely at children. Fantuzzo et al (1987) trained socially able children to act as experimental confederates and to make play overtures to socially withdrawn children. The withdrawn children showed increases in their own play initiations with the confederates and some of this increased social behaviour was generalized to the regular classroom. In a follow up study, Fantuzzo et al (1988) contrasted the efficacy of child and adult confederates with a control group. The results confirmed the effectiveness of the peer confederates at increasing social behaviour in withdrawn children with no effect being reported from the intervention by the adult confederates or by the control condition. The authors suggest that children are wary of unknown adults and that peers are preferred confederate therapists.

A very different approach is reported by Green (1978). The treatment for the children was based upon psycho-dynamic concepts, as well as more skill based theories of impulse control. The therapist reported improvements in fifteen out of sixteen cases, but this was not independently assessed. A psycho-therapeutic approach was also evident in Kunkel's (1981) study of residential treatment for abused children. Counsellors provided a nurturing and consistent relationship for the children, so that they could work through unmet dependency needs and yet be taught the boundaries of acceptable behaviours. The children were placed in permanent substitute families and fourteen out of sixteen of these placements were working at a one year follow-up.

The final study (Harling & Haines, 1980) in this section, examined another project concerned with child placements, in this case, attempts at rehabilitation with their families of origin. The programme involved the use of specialist foster homes for severely mistreated children, with practical support from homemakers and with student volunteers as siblings and role models for the children. Again, few children were able to return home in practice, even though they had improved on all measures. The intervention was therefore unsuccessful in relation to placement but the children seemed to have benefited.

The gains in the studies of child centred services were often in objective measures of weight and cognitive development, and thus less open to bias than more psychological or social measures, although only the studies by Elmer and Fantuzzo were experimentally controlled. Also there was little emphasis on direct work with children in most of the treatment programmes. The studies by Fantuzzo were an exception and provide evidence of the importance of working directly with children and the efficacy of using other children in this role. Many other studies with a child therapy component only made passing reference to these child services. It may be that this pattern reflects the reality of service provision where child services may have a day care or a monitoring role, rather than specific objectives of child treatment or training (Corby, 1987; Gough et al, 1987).

Failure to Thrive

Schmidt and Mauro (1989) distinguish four types of non organic failure to thrive (NOFT).

1. Neglectful where the mother (or other carer) spends insufficient time or attention to feeding their child because they are preoccupied with other responsibilities such as work or caring for other children, or because they are preoccupied with psychological difficulties such as depression, low self esteem, or marital problems.
2. Accidental due to ignorance concerning required foods or methods of feeding.
3. Poverty making food unavailable (which, as Schmidt and Mauro point out, is the main cause of malnutrition in the world).
4. Intentional restriction of food to the child

Much of the child abuse literature on failure to thrive is concerned with parents falling into the first two of Mauro and Schmidt's categories of neglectful and accidental (studies listed in Table 8.5). In many cases neglect and ignorance are interwoven resulting in a lack of nutrition for the infant.

Iwaniec (1991) in a study of seventeen NOFT children described four different interactional caretaker styles of (1) forceful, anxious, and impatient; (2) chaotic and unconcerned; (3) angry and hostile, but indifferent; determined and coaxing, but anxious. Other authors have provided longer category lists of interactional problems between the caregiver and the child (see Drotar et al, 1990, for a review).

Despite the interest and concern with parent-child interaction patterns it is thought that the primary problem for the child is the effect of these interaction difficulties on preventing the child receiving sufficient nutrition. This is in contrast to the view that the children do not thrive because of emotional deprivation. Research has shown that nutrition does usually result in weight gain.

Moore (1982) undertook a study of a nurturing, supportive casework service offered by student social workers. All families seemed to benefit and the children's weights increased. Haynes et al (1984) reported on a lay visiting service for hospitalized infants who received extra stimulation. The study found no effect of the service on measures of the children's cognitive and physical development, though the mothers did keep in more contact with the services, compared to controls.

More overtly psychological interventions have been reported by Hanks et al (1988) and Iwaniec et al (1985). Hanks and colleagues provided mothers of six infants

TABLE 8.5

Failure to Thrive Research Studies

Study	Programme	Sample size	Population	Design	Main measures
Hanks (1987) Hanks et al (1988)	Poor feeding practices	n = 6	FTT children	RPM	Growth measures
Haynes et al (1984)	Lay hospital visitor	n = 20	FTT children	RPM + C	Growth measures
Iwaniec et al (1985)	Multi component social work	n = 17	FTT children	RPM	Growth, parent & child behaviour
Larson et al (1987)	Behavioural feeding programme	n = 3	FTT children	RPM	Food acceptance
Moore (1982)	Supportive treatment	n = 28	FTT children	RPM	Growth, family progress
Ramey et al 1975	Response contingent	n = 9	FTT infants	RPM + C	Growth, IQ, rate of learning
Sturm and Drotar (1989)	Family centred	n = 19	FTT children	RPM + C	Growth, HOME

HOME = Home and environment living scale

Design

RPM = Repeated Measures including Pre-test; PRPM = Repeated Measures post-test only; + C = Control or comparison group

with five fortnightly individual therapy sessions. The therapy addressed not only the dietary and feeding issues but also other child care problems and the wider context in which this was occurring. The wider context could be the psychological functioning of the whole family or simply the family feeding styles. In one family, for example, the mother was ambivalent about the child's weight gains as she herself wished to lose weight. Another family revealed that they had no cooker and ate all meals cold from tins. Hanks et al found that the individual therapy provided to these families was associated with significant gains in the children's weights compared to population norms.

Iwaniec and colleagues (1985) provided a longer term programme with crisis intervention for parental stress reduction and stimulation for children, followed by three stages of intervention to structure and manage feeding sessions using instruction and behavioural techniques such as modelling and counselling of the mothers. Workers' and parents' assessments showed significant positive changes in child and parental behaviours and interactions, and in the children's feeding patterns. No children had to be re-admitted for non organic failure to thrive.

An important issue raised by the effectiveness of these studies is which components are necessary for success. Even though all the intervention are relatively brief and time limited, may be even more limited interventions would be successful. Fryer (1988) in a meta analysis of eight outcome studies of hospital admission for NOFT (including the study by Haynes et al, 1984) found a significant improvement in physical growth but not for psychosocial development. Sturm and Drotar (1989) found no significant differences in the effects of three interventions of family centred or parent centred therapy or a low key advisory service. All three groups showed significant growth gains over the twelve months of the interventions, though there was a sub-group of children presenting with chronic NOFT who failed to show early improvement and who continued to be well below normal weight three years after treatment.

For theoretical and practical reasons some authors have moved away from broad based approaches that enable the parent to cope better with their child's feeding. Instead they have more directly addressed the child's ability to control his or her environment. Ramey et al (1975), for example, evaluated an intervention programme involving home based training of the infant's contingent stimulation. The children's weight increased markedly but no more than controls, who received a daily food delivery and food use monitoring service. The intervention group did improve more than controls on psychomotor and rate of vocalization scores.

In another study, Larson (1987) applied a rigourous behavioural programme to three infants. Each therapy session commenced with play and music, then play stopped and feeding was gently introduced whilst the music continued. Acceptance of food was praised, but rejection resulted in the cessation of the music, child being told 'No', being put in crib, and being ignored by mother. After three minutes the cycle was repeated. The programme was associated with rapid increases in food acceptance.

The findings of these studies support Schmidt and Mauro's (1989) and Hobb et al's (1993) contention that the previous practice of treating NOFT children as inpatients is not necessary except for the seriously ill children or children requiring admission for other reasons. Diagnoses can be made at outpatient clinics and clinic and home based services can achieve marked increases in growth in most cases. What is not clear is the content or extent of service required. Brief behavioural interventions can achieve weight gains, but is this sufficient to change the response contingent stimulation or is separate extra work required with the caretakers to facilitate their care practices to assist with wider contextual problems?

Summary

1. Studies of special treatment not included in chapters on behavioural approaches to physical abuse, multi component programmes, and sexual abuse involved the following types of programmes:
   - educational or skilled based programmes for parents and families
   - psycho-therapeutic and supportive group work
   - direct therapeutic work with individuals
   - child focused services
   - projects for non organic failure to thrive.
2. Educational and skill based programmes seemed to show encouraging results. Three studies were experimentally controlled and reported greater improvements compared to controls on cognitive development, behavioural, or knowledge scores.
3. Studies of group services for parents, revealed many imaginative programmes. The results were mostly based on clinical scoring and reported improvements in self esteem and social functioning and none of the studies were experimentally controlled. The studies were able to illustrate methods of work rather than to determine their effectiveness.
4. Studies of direct individual work with adults and families ranged from intense psychotherapy to the use of lay home visitors and volunteers. Positive improvements were reported, but only three of the studies were experimentally controlled and only one used consistent independent measures.
5. The child focused studies examined interventions offering children psycho-therapy, extra stimulation and care, and practice in initiating social interactions. These studies were most likely to use independent measures of outcome and they also reported significant improvements in child functioning. However, this did not always reduce the risks to the children and allow them to remain in, or return to, their original family. Also, the lack of experimental controls in all but two studies make it difficult to determine the cause of any post-test improvements. There were few projects that directly addressed the needs of children. Some facilities may have been made available for children in parent

focused programmes but these were often of secondary importance and went no further than normal day care principles.

6. Studies of non organic failure to thrive described interventions ranging from support and advice to individual therapy to rigourous behavioural programmes. The studies demonstrated marked improvements at post-test on the independent outcome measure of weight gain. Few studies used control groups and the one study that did found considerable catch up growth in controls. However, the other controlled studies mostly confirmed the findings of uncontrolled studies. Future research needs to examine which aspects of these different programmes made them successful and which programmes are best suited to different case presentations.

7. Many of the studies in this chapter had the same methodological problems, which limit the interpretation of results as discussed in other chapters. Some of the most encouraging results were in the child focused studies. These were relatively well designed, and thus went against the trend of many child abuse studies where the most rigorous experimental designs report the least encouraging results.

Chapter Eight: Research Summaries

Argyles (1980)

ATTACHMENT AND CHILD ABUSE

Sample: A family of a mother and five children aged from 6 to 16 years. Frequent bruising of 4 younger children and accusations against mother. Mother alcoholic, abused as child and beaten by boyfriend. Eldest child forced to assume many child care responsibilities.

Focus: Mother's capacity for attachment.

Objectives: To improve mother-child relationship as this will be more effective than directly addressing abuse.

Programme: Therapist encourages ventilation of children's fears and worries about family separation and mother's own experiences of being abused. Therapist looks for, and builds upon evidence of mother's capacity for attachment. Therapist provides a secure base for exploring anxieties and voicing feelings. Therapy lasts 3 years.

Design: Descriptive outcome of treatment case.

Measure: Therapists assessment of exchange of positive feelings in family. Children's behaviour (anxious, clinging, etc.), mother's determination to preserve family, mother's drinking and neglect of children, family stability.

Results: After several sessions there were improvements: mother moved to a new house and took a less violent lover, but mother continued to drink and leave children although she did begin to make baby sitting arrangements. Therapy ended with increased family stability and more independence being shown by youngest child.

Notes: Article stresses importance of damaged capacity for attachment, to being an adequate parent.

Behaviour Associates (1977), Lieber and Baker (1977)

PARENTS ANONYMOUS-SELF HELP TREATMENT FOR CHILD ABUSIVE PARENTS

Sample: The 613 members who responded to the questionnaire sent to all those attending Parents Anonymous in April 1976. Range of types of abuse in sample.

Focus: Parents.

Objectives: Prevention of child abuse and its recurrence through development of sense of self and more positive family relationships.

Programme: Weekly 2 hour group meetings that provide a safe setting for parents to share current issues. Use of Parent Effectiveness Training, Gestalt Therapy, and other psychotherapeutic techniques. Groups are consumer run with a parent chair person. There is a volunteer professional consultant who represents a positive image of authority and who refers to other services available.

Design: Repeated measures on intervention sample. Regression analysis of time in project and outcome.

Measures: Self reports of self esteem, social interaction, knowledge about child development and behaviour, feelings about parenthood, ability to handle child abuse problems, benefits of project. Child abuse referrals.

Results: Significant association between length of time in project and all self report variables, except for attitudes to parenthood and children, but these started at high levels so possible ceiling effect. Large drop in child abuse referral rate on entry to programme and no significant reduction thereafter, but possible floor effect.

Notes: Not clear how representative Parents Anonymous Members are of child protection cases. Also possible response bias on sample completing questionnaires.

Bell et al (1983)

AMELIORATING THE IMPACT OF TEEN-AGE PPREGNANCY ON PARENT AND CHILD

Sample: 29 single mothers included in first 2 years of project. All mothers met at least 4 of the criteria of: single and isolated, referred by court or social services, victims of abuse, less than 18, poor, illegitimate births, health problems, children in care, substance abuse. Children additionally required to meet 2 of the criteria of: low birthweight, traumatic birth, lack of pre-natal care, victim of abuse, developmental delay, behaviour problems, failure to thrive.

Focus: Children's development, functioning of mothers.

Objectives: To improve the children's social and cognitive skills and reduce negative behaviours. To develop the mothers child care skills, sense of independence, and viable support systems.

Programme: Parents had group sessions based upon material from 'Parent Effectiveness Training' and the 'Head Start Program'. Emphasis on achieving independence, on parenting, and teaching parents an intervention programme to carry out with their children at home. Emphasis was on attaining goals, and mothers were trained to collect measurable data on their children. Children received home based intervention from parents. There was also children's groups divided according to age, which included age appropriate stimulation (infants), skill development in pre-academic skills (pre-school), behaviour modification and training social skills (school age).

Design: Post-test on treatment sample compared with unspecified controls.

Measures: Independence, employment, referral for abuse.

Results: 'Significant' difference in improvement of treatment sample compared to controls. Child abuse referrals were 1/29 for treatment group and 6/83 for controls.

Notes: A more vigorous evaluation promised.

Belluci (1972)

GROUP TREATMENT OF MOTHERS IN CHILD PROTECTION CASES

Sample: 10 mothers of 48 children from child protection cases of social services department. Apparent preference in sample recruitment for more severe cases with court involvement and for mothers with motivation and ability to discuss feelings. Therapists saw the women's early marriages and frequent pregnancies as attempts to achieve fulfilment when they lack self esteem.

Focus: Mother's emotional needs and strengths.

Objectives: To improve emotional functioning of mothers.

Programme: A weekly group based on psycho-dynamic principles, with a male and female therapist to provide positive model of male-female relationships, that could be non sexual and where disagreement could be non violent. Also co-therapy thought to dilute strain of coping with so much need, to avoid potential for collusion, and provide consistency of care. Homemaker service which offered mothering to mothers. Volunteers organised activities for chil-

dren in their holidays. Most members still in therapy two years after start of group.

Design: Descriptive post-tests.

Measures: Therapists assessments of mothers' self esteem, relationships with partner, mothers' behaviour and general functioning, child functioning; child placement.

Results: Increased self esteem of children. For mothers there were increases in self esteem, assertiveness, self awareness, resolution of material imbalance, ability to relate non sexually to men, ability to express anger without fear of rejection. Also fewer placements of children, away from home than usual. No success in reducing isolation of families and increasing their use of community resources.

Breton (1979)

NURTURING ABUSED AND ABUSIVE MOTHERS: THE HAIRDRESSING GROUP

Sample: 7 mothers of physically abused children selected because of their social, emotional, and financial deprivation.

Focus: Functioning of mothers.

Objectives: To provide a nurturing environment to improve self esteem, social skills and competence, and problem solving ability including the ability to ask for help when needed.

Methods: Mothers met as a group for a weekly 4 hour session in a specially procured flat. The group was like a family that could provide nurture, teach skills and solve problems. Nurture was given through food and shelter and by hairdressing, which offered a socially acceptable form of touching and physical care. Mothers were encouraged to be initially dependent and to explore feelings, and were taught problem solving on non threatening topics.

Design: Descriptive outcomes of treatment group.

Measures: Description of the progress of the group.

Results: After a year of sustained nurturing and re-parenting, the mothers started to be able to give more of themselves. Although progress was very slow the women made impressive gains and they were able to cope with problems that beset the group and were able to develop and move the group forward.

Brown (1985)

JOINING TWO SOCIAL INSTITUTIONS TO COUNTER RURAL ALASKAN CHILD ABUSE

Sample: 24 cases of various types of child abuse. Wide age range of the 53 children in the families. Variety of parental problems including alcohol abuse (n = 6) and maternal depression (n = 5). The families had single parents.

Focus: Parents.

Objectives: To create change by the provision of social support.

Programme: Parent aides most of whom have received training, visit over an average of 11 months. Aides are caring listeners rather than therapists. The recruitment, training and supervision of volunteers closely follows the model of a child abuse team described by Kempe and Helfer in 'Helping the Battered Child and His Family', Lippincott, 1982.

Design: Repeated measures (pre and post-test) on treatment group.

Measures: Unspecified general assessment.

Results: 70% of families showed a clear improvement. Case outlines include comments such as a 'family thriving', parents 'quit drinking', and 'accepted psycho-therapy'.

Notes: Few details on evaluation. Article emphasises the social isolation in Alaska and the community based aspect of the services.

Brunk et al (1987)

COMPARISON OF MULTISYSTEMIC THERAPY AND PARENT TRAINING IN THE BRIEF TREATMENT OF CHILD ABUSE AND NEGLECT

Sample: 18 cases of physical abuse and 15 cases of neglect (total n = 33) from an original total of 43 who completed pre-tests recruited from social services cases of child abuse or neglect. 55% of children male, 45% female; 57% white and 43% black. Cases of sexual abuse and parents with history of psychosis or retardation excluded.

Focus: Skills, ability, or functioning of parents in order to prevent the recurrences of child abuse or neglect.

Objectives: Both programmes arrived to improve parenting by addressing (1) parenting skills or (2) the systemic context of the families.

Programme: Two programmes. Both involved weekly 1½ hour session for 8 weeks. (1) Parent training (n = 10 abuse and 7 neglect families) groups in human development and child management techniques (Wolfe et al, 1981). Topics included contingent positive reinforcement, nonpunitive techniques, the need for parental consistency, the negative effects of punitive methods of discipline, and the importance of developing more positive parent-child interactions. Specific problems identified in each family and individual program developed and monitored during subsequent sessions. One therapist to each of 4 groups with average of 7 parents from 5 families per group. (2) Multisystemic therapy (n = 8 abuse + 8 neglect families) conducted with each family in their own homes. Therapists used techniques of joining, reframing, and prescribing tasks to change interaction patterns. Neglectful parents learned to perform executive functions and abusive parents developed greater flexibility. 25% of cases provided with therapy on marital relations, 25% on mother's relations with extended family, 31% on parent child relations, and 19% on peer relations. Therapist also offered improved parent education (88% of cases) and advocacy with outside agencies (50% of cases).

Design: Repeated measures (pre-test and post-test) experimental design with random allocation (counter balanced for abuse/neglect case) to 2 treatment conditions.

Measures: (1) Self report measures: Individual system: The Symptom Checklist – 90 (SCL) for parents' psychiatric functioning and Behaviour Problem Checklist (BCL) for children's behaviour. (b) Family system: Family Environment Scale (FES) on relationships, personal growth, and system maintenance. (c) Social system: The Family Inventory of Life Events and Changes (FILE) on parental stress. (2) Treatment Outcome Questionnaire (TOQ) for parents' therapists' perceptions of treatment needs. (3) Observation of parent-child interaction: 10 minute videotape of semi-structured task of parent teaching child to complete block designs of increasing difficulty. Coding of parental controls (verbal/non verbal, action/attention), child antecedent behaviours (orientated/not orientated/in contact), child consequent behaviours (orientated/in contact/task completion). Also coding of sequential behaviour of parental effectiveness, child passive non-compliance, and parental unresponsiveness.

Results: (1) Self report measures: significant pre to post-test effect on global indices. Univariate effects on psychiatric symptoms (SCL) and parental stress (FILE).

(2) Treatment Outcome Questionnaire: univariate pre to post test decrease for all groups on both parents and therapists reports of individual problems and family problems and therapists reports of social system problems. There was a significantly greater effect for parent training group on client ratings of improvements in social problems and for multisystemic group for therapists ratings of

improvement in family problems. Also a significant treatment group effect revealed by MANOVA.

(3) Observational measures: Inter rater reliability of between 65% and 84% on different sequences. MANOVA revealed a significant pre/post by treatment group effect. Significant improvements on the following sequences: (a) Parental effectiveness – attention, (i) not oriented child – parental verbal attention – child oriented : neglect families in multisystemic group, and abuse family in parent training group, (ii) in contact – non verbal parental attention – child orientated : multisystemic group only (iii) child not orientated – non verbal attention – child orientated : all from pre-test to post test. (b) Parental effectiveness – action (i) child orientated – verbal action – task completion + in contact – verbal or non verbal action – task completion : multisystemic group only. (c) Child passive non compliance, (i) contact – parental verbal attention – in contact : multisystemic group for abusive families only (ii) child orientated – verbal action – child orientated : multisystemic group only. (d) Parental unresponsiveness, (i) child orientated – parental verbal attention – child orientated : multisystemic group particularly for neglectful families only, (ii) child orientated – verbal attention – task completion: all groups.

Notes: Authors conclude that (1) both treatments associated with reduced parental stress, problems, and psychiatric symptoms, (2) that multisystemic therapy more effective at restructuring parent-child relations, (3) that parent training more effective at reducing identified social problems, maybe because the training groups provided social supports. Need to note possible respondent bias on self report and treatment outcome questionnaire, the low inter rater reliability on some observation measures, that multisystemic therapy was in the family home and parent training in a clinic.

Burch and Mohr (1980)

EVALUATING A CHILD ABUSE IINTERVENTION PROGRAMME

Sample: The 65 abusing (or risk of) parents enrolled in programme at pre-test and the 20 of them still in programme at post-test 4 months later. The families tended to have many children, to be of low socio economic status; a third were Catholic. Control families recruited from Child Protection Services.

Focus: Parenting attitudes/skills.

Objectives: To change attitudes to parenting, to increase ability to deal with child management problems and knowledge of child development. To provide nurturing experience and social support and to teach problem solving abilities.

Programme: Groups with 20 minute socialization period, followed by 25 minute educational presentation. Also similar groups for discussion and intensified training or to work on personal problems. Children provided with individual and group activities.

Design: Repeated measures (pre and post-test) with one treatment group and one control condition. Cross sectional comparison of treatment length with outcome.

Measures: Research instrument of 24 correct/false statements developed by staff. Statements refer to knowledge, attitudes, and values in parenthood and child care.

Results: Treatment group had a significantly greater increase in scores compared to controls. In the cross sectional analysis comparison, first time participants scored higher than controls or more experienced programme clients.

Notes: Article addresses the issue of the relationship between evaluators and programme staff.

Culp et al (1987)

DIFFERENTIAL DEVELOPMENTAL PROGRESS OF MALTREATED CHILDREN IN DAY TREATMENT

Sample: Subjects were 109 children enrolled in a therapeutic day treatment centre, 61 male and 48 female, 55 black and 54 white. The mean age was 2.8 years (range 6 weeks to 6.2 years). The children were mainly from lower socio-economic families with 83% of families earning less than $5,000 per year and the remaining 17% earning between $5–10,000 per year. Children were referred to the treatment programme by protective service workers because of physical abuse (32%), neglect (53%), or as a preventive measure because of maltreatment of a sibling (15%).

Focus: Developmental status of maltreated children and functioning of parents.

Objectives: To enhance the developmental progress of the children.

Programme: A centre – based therapeutic day treatment programme based on a cognitive – developmental model. Different group settings for age groups of infants, toddlers and preschoolers. Groups were for 6 hours per day and included individual treatment and special education including play therapy, speech therapy, and occupational therapy. Transportation and nutritious breakfasts, lunches, and snacks provided. Parents provided with family and individual therapy, support group counselling, parent education, volunteer parent aides, 24 hour crisis helpline, emergency aid, and a clothing and toy exchange. Also parent – child interaction training. Foster parents received ongoing consultation. Periodic assessment and 3 monthly review with other agencies.

Design: Repeated measures (pre and post-test) on intervention group only.

Measures: (1) Early Intervention Developmental Profile (Michigan Profile) with 6 scales of perceptual – fine motor, cognition, language, socio-emotional, self-care (feeding, toileting, dressing, hygiene) and gross motor development. (2) Sex and race of child and reason for referral.

Results: No interaction effects. No associations between sex, race, or reason for referral and progress on language or gross motor scales. (1) Race of child: no effects. (2) Sex of child: girls made greater gains than boys on all 6 developmental scales, statistically significant for all but language and gross motor scales. (3) Reason for referral: significant effect on cognitive and socio-emotional scales with abused children making the greatest gains and prevention cases making the smallest gains. No interaction effects.

Notes: The authors suggest that, (1) lack of progress of neglected children may be due to distractability and other ways in which they are unable to cope with a teaching environment, (2) the relative lack of progress of prevention cases is an argument against using such programmes for these children. Group means not provided.

Dawson et al (1986)

COGNITIVE PROBLEM-SOLVING TRAINING TO IMPROVE CHILD-CARE JUDGEMENT OF CHILD NEGLECTING PARENTS

Sample: 3 mothers of neglected pre-school children, referred to psychology clinics by Child Protection Service as part of a contract to retain custody of children. Mothers had a deficit of cognitive problem solving skills. All had financial problems. There was no record of physical abuse, criminality or serious psychological disturbance.

Focus: Competence of mothers.

Objectives: Improve parents' competence in problem-solving and child care.

Programmes: Use of 15 problem vignettes; parents encouraged to think of multiple ways of handling the problem. Therapists discussed parental strategies and alternative solutions during following

session. Also discussions of child development. Treatment was provided by 2 psychology doctoral students. Each mother offered approximately 8 weekly sessions.

Design: Repeated measures for each subject.

Measures: Ratings of transcripts of the mothers' strategies and obstacles to problem solving and effectiveness of solutions suggested. Reliability of codings checked by blind rater with reliability of between 0.74 and 0.87. Also social work assessments of performance on child care, daily living tasks, and emotional attachment to child. Agency records of subsequent reports of neglect and parental custody.

Results: Problem solving of vignettes improved for all 3 subjects and this was maintained at follow up for the one parent tested. Family lifestyle and quality improved for all mothers in 8 out of 9 areas. Performance of daily responsibilities was the only measure unchanged. Greatest improvements were for solutions to life problems, emotional attachment, solution to child rearing problems, and global assessment of being a 'good' parent.

Notes: No direct data on the parents' problem solving behaviour.

Elmer (1986), Schultz et al (1979), Sankey et al (1985)

RESIDENTIAL AND IN-HOME TREATMENT FOR ABUSED CHILDREN

Sample: Child protection service cases, court adjudicated, with recommendation for referral to programme in centre located in Pittsburgh. This was usually the last chance for the parents to show their ability to care for their children. N = 31 infants under 6 months of age, 10 of whom had been abused and 21 of whom were at high risk. Subjects matched with two comparison groups: (1) 'PC' who were similar to experimental group but not admitted to centre and, (2) 'NC' who were 'normal' families. Subjects matched individually on basis of age, race, sex, SES, birth weight and birth order.

Focus: Development status of children; child care by parents.

Objectives: Increase parental abilities and confidence in child care and develop more realistic expectations of children. To increase parental self esteem, and support networks. Also to stimulate and enhance the progress of children, which could facilitate parents' attempts to improve their interactions with their children.

Programme: A short term treatment and residential assessment centre for children, with parents attending three or four days per week for 3 months, before recommendations are made on placement, to court. Children receive stimulations and mothering from a nurse. Parents encouraged to play and care for child and provided with role models and training in positive reinforcement and child development.

Design: Repeated measures (pre and post-tests) experimental design with matched experimental and control groups.

Measures: Children's height, weight, cognitive development (Bayley Scales). Parent child interaction scales (Bernard Scales). A follow up post-test when children reached one year of age.

Results: Treatment group had significantly greater improvements in weight, height, and on most of the interaction scales. At one year of age, treatment group mostly still doing well, but scores were similar across groups. Socio-economic status was significantly related to outcomes on scores across all groups. Only 3 of treatment group remained at home, so improvements achieved for children but little success in reuniting families.

Notes: The Parental Stress Centre was formed by the Juvenile Court, the Children's Hospital, Child Guidance and Child Welfare. Residential programme had 5 beds in a children's home at any one time.

Fantuzzo et al (1987)

THE EFFECTS OF PEER SOCIAL INITIATION ON THE SOCIAL BEHAVIOUR OF WITHDRAWN MALTREATED PRESCHOOL CHILDREN

Sample: Six children (2 three year olds, 4 four year olds) of low to average intellectual ability referred to Mt. Hope Family Center by social services due to risk or actual maltreatment. Four of the children were the lowest functioning socially in the centre and had multiple reports for child neglect. Two of the children had high social functioning and were chosen to act as research confederates by being peer social initiators for the 4 withdrawn children.

Focus: Social functioning of maltreated children.

Objectives: To train socially withdrawn maltreated children to increase the frequency of their positive social responses and social initiations.

Programme: Children taken out of their class to play with toys in playroom. (1) The 6 children divided into 2 groups each consisting of 1 confederate child and 2 withdrawn children. (2) Baseline observations of all 6 children in free play. (3) Confederates trained

to make play overtures to the withdrawn children through demonstration, role play, and practice in presence of investigator. (4) Training session before which confederate reminded of task and after which he received praise and also a tangible reinforcer if achieved at least 10 positive social initiations. (5) Return to baseline with confederates requested to play normally (6) Repeat of training and baseline sequences (7) Two weeks later follow up.

Design: A reversal multiprobe ABAB design plus follow up.

Measures: Observation system by Strain et al (1976) using continuous event recording of positive motor-gestural and vocal-verbal behaviours and whether these were responses or initiations. Data collected in treatment setting and also in classroom setting to test for generalization. In both settings 6 minutes of a 15 minute session coded. Interobserver agreement of codings averaged 91% (range 83–98). Teachers also questioned about changes in behaviour of children over treatment.

Results: Interventions resulted in increase in peer initiations for all 4 withdrawn children in the treatment setting. Some of this increase generalized to the classroom setting and this was maintained for 2 children at follow up. The children showed increases in both initiations and positive social responses. The ABABA sequence was only well mirrored in positive social responses in the generalization classroom setting. For initiation behaviours the second set of training sessions seemed to have the strongest effect. Classroom teachers reported that the confederates and the withdrawn children were more social in both structured and unstructured classroom activities.

Notes: The authors state that other research has shown the effectiveness of peer social initiations. The current study extends this finding to a maltreated population.

Fantuzzo et al (1988)

EFFECTS OF ADULT AND PEER SOCIAL INITIATIONS ON THE SOCIAL BEHAVIOUR OF WITHDRAWN, MALTREATED PRESCHOOL CHILDREN

Sample: 39 maltreated preschool children (28 boys, 11 girls) enrolled in the Mount Hope Family Center Day Services Program. 46% were white, 54% were black, mean age of 4.3 years. The children came from families who were receiving public assistance funds. All cases were defined by social services as documented abuse or risk (9 physically abused, 18 neglected, 9 at risk preventive cases). Three further children scoring highly on tests of social initiation acted as confederates providing peer social initiation.

Focus: Social behaviour of children.

Objectives: To increase the positive social behaviour of withdrawn, maltreated preschool children.

Programme: Each child received two consecutive 15 minute play sessions per day for 4 days spread over up to 3/4 weeks. Children went to the play sessions in pairs, one of whom was a high social initiator and one whom was a low social initiator at pre-test. The first session per day was a generalization session with an adult present, but only to provide supervision. The type of second play session each day depended on the treatment or control condition to which they had been assigned: (1) Peer initiator: 3 high initiating children trained to be confederate social initiators. (2) Adult initiator: teachers' aides taught to use same number of initiators as matched peer confederates. (3) Non initiating adult or peer: confederate peer or teachers' aide joined play session but did not make social initiations only responded positively to initiations, by the child dyads.

Design: Repeated measures (multiple) experimental design with random allocation (counter balanced for pre-test social initiation) to 2 treatment and 1 control condition.

Measures: (1) Positive social behaviours (verbal/motor and initiations/responses) coded blind from 6 minute videos of behaviour pre and post each of the 8 play sessions. (2) Preschool Behaviour Questionnaire (PBQ) to assess psychological adjustment (for n = 19) and Brigance Diagnostic Inventory of Early Development for pre-academic progress (for n = 32).

Results: (1) Positive social behaviours: For treatment settings there was no significant main effect, but significant interaction effect on Group × Time MANOVA. ANOVA's and post hoc comparisons revealed the following significant effects for the 3 treatment conditions (i) peer: improvement in oral initiation, oral and motor responses (ii) adult: decrease in oral and motor responses, (iii) Control: no effects. For the generalization settings there was also a significant Group × Time interaction but only a significant univariate effect for oral initiations in the peer condition. (2) Psychological adjustment (PBQ) showed no effect for group, but an effect for Time and Group × Time interaction. Mean scores improved for peer condition and worsened for the adult and control conditions with the peer condition scores being significantly lower than the 2 other conditions at post test. For academic progress (Brigance) all groups improved significantly at post test.

Notes: The authors suggest that it is the social initiations rather than mere presence of peers that is important as the adult conditions scored worse at post test. They also state that such findings are in line with other studies reporting that socially deprived children may become wary and avoidant of novel adults.

Feldman et al (1986)

INCREASING STIMULATING INTERACTIONS OF DEVELOPMENTALLY HANDICAPPED MOTHERS

This is the second of 2 studies reported in the paper. Study 1 (not summarized here) showed that the parents with intellectual disabilities generally interacted much less with their children, and were particularly less likely to praise appropriate child behaviour or to initiate child vocalizations.

Sample: 7 developmentally handicapped mothers and their children. Mean IQ of mothers was 71 (range 64–77). All were unemployed, 3 received welfare and 4 lived in government housing. 5 were married, 2 were single, 4 of the 5 fathers were employed in blue collar jobs and at least 2 were considered retarded. Children's average was 14 months (range 4–22). 4 of the mothers had participated in the first study reported in the paper that compared mother-child interactions with control mothers.

Focus: Mother-child interactions of mothers with an intellectual disability.

Objectives: To train mothers with intellectual disabilities to interact with and stimulate their infants.

Programme: Baseline test of 5 types of interaction known to stimulate child language and cognitive development. Mothers only trained on interactions for which they fell below a criteria calculated from mean scores of parents without an intellectual disability (from Study 1 not summarized here). The following skills were trained (a) Praise – all 7 mothers, (b) Imitation of child vocalizations – all 7, (c) Talking to the child – 2 mothers, (d) looking at the child – 3 mothers. Two children received training in the home only, 3 in a group setting only, and 2 trained at both home and group settings. The training sessions involved (1) a brief discussion on mother – child play, (2) the trainers then focused on the particular target behaviour, discussed its importance, and gave examples of when it should be used, (3) Mothers requested to provide their own examples and ask questions, (4) Trainer models the behaviour with the child (home setting) or children (group setting) for about 10 minutes, (5) Mothers practised the interactions with their child with observation, prompting, praise, and some repeat modelling from trainer. Generalization was facilitated by (a) training within the naturally occurring event of play, (b) showing the mothers how to evoke appropriate play in their children, (c) teaching them to 'cue in'

161

to the child's behaviour so that this could prompt parental behaviour, (d) the use of multiple exemplars during training. Five to 10 follow up sessions over the next 10 months in the mothers' homes. Occasionally test questions to mothers who were prompted if necessary. Maintenance also through mothers' self recording on chart for first 2 months.

Design: Repeated measures (multiple probe) on experimental group only. Measures at baseline, during training, to test for generalization at follow up.

Measures: 10 second observations, 10 second record procedures of target behaviours. Kappa reliability coefficients above 0.85 except for talking (0.78) and looking (0.58). Observations over 10 months at (1) Baseline: 3 to 12 observations, (2) Training: within 30 minutes of each session, (3) Generalizations in the home, (4) Follow up: 5 to 10 observations over the next 10 months.

Results: All mothers showed increases in target skills and maintained these at or above the mean performance of control mothers from Study 1. (1) Praise: baseline mean of 5%, rising to 30% in training, & 33% in maintenance, though minimal improvement in one mother and variable performance in 2 others. Also praise from other mothers was often excessive. (2) Imitation of child vocalizations: baseline mean of 17% rising to 75% in training, and 56% in maintenance. (3) Talking to child: increased substantially in both parents concerned, (4) Looking at child: increased for 1 of 2 mothers concerned. Generalization successful with homescores as good as in group training. All children increased their vocalizations, but only 4 substantially. Also reports of general improvement in the richness and responsiveness of mother-child interactions.

Notes: The authors conclude that relatively brief non didactic behavioural instruction can be effective, be generalized to new contexts, and be maintained at follow up despite intellectual disabilities of parents. Authors also note the high rate of deficit in praise and imitation interactions compared to controls (Study 1) and thus the importance of these behaviours in assessment and curriculum provision for these parents.

Feldman et al (1992)

TEACHING CHILD-CARE SKILLS TO MOTHERS WITH DEVELOPMENTAL DISABILITIES

This is the second of 2 studies reported in the paper. Study 1 (not summarized here) showed that the parents with intellectual disabilities made significantly more errors in performing crucial child care skills compared to controls.

Sample: 11 mothers diagnosed as mentally regarded with mean IQ of 74 (range 68–79), mean age of

26 years (range 21–39), 8 were married, 7 received welfare, 3 lived in subsidized housing. All but one family were monitored by child protection agencies. Children had mean age of 9 months (range 3–36) and 8 showed delays in cognitive development.

Focus: Child care skills of mothers with intellectual disabilities and at risk of providing insufficient care to their children.

Objectives: To train child care skills to mothers with intellectual disabilities.

Programme: (1) Child care skills chosen for baseline observation were chosen on basis of workers' concerns, parents' requests, and informal observations. Each mother then received training in the 1,2, or 3 skills in which she had a mean baseline score below 80% of the control group (not intellectually disabled) in Study 1. In total, 21 skills taught to the 11 mothers. Skills included bathing child, washing child's hair, cleaning baby bottles, preparing feed, and toilet training. (2) Training sessions were conducted weekly in the mother's home and consisted of verbal instructions, pictorial manuals, modelling, physical guidance, feedback of specific verbal praise or correction, and reinforcement. Immediately after each session the mother was given coupon if she scored higher than the proceeding session or over 80% if this criterion had already been reached. The coupon was exchangeable for items such as toys, nappies and perfume, previously selected by the mother. (3) Intensive training ceased when a criterion of 100% on the safety steps and 80% of other steps were achieved for 3 consecutive sessions. Follow up to probe for maintenance was then continued for an average of 31 weeks (range 4–74) depending on availability to observe and continued developmental relevance of the skill. A sub group of 7 mothers (the lottery group) chosen at random received a reinforced maintenance procedure where criteria performance was rewarded with the chance of receiving a coupon by guessing the number of a rolled dice with the number of guesses allowed being slowly decreased until the reinforcement was stopped.

Design: Repeated measures (multiple probe) on experimental group only. Data analysis across subjects and within subjects for 4 mothers.

Measures: Correct performance, on each step of each skill and for necessary safety steps, recorded through direct observation. For a few steps not readily observed (such as treating nappy rash) verbal responses of mothers used. Scores calculated as percentage of steps in process correctly executed. Mean interobserver agreement was for skill steps 90% (range 69–100) and for safety steps 87% (range 83–94). Presence of diaper rash, cradle cap, weight gain, and for older children, their toileting skills.

Observations made at baseline, throughout training, and for follow up. At later follow up at an average of 17 months after training (range 3–38) 6 mothers questioned about the usefulness of the programme.

Results: Across all 21 skills mean correct performance was 58% at baseline, rising to 90% in training, and 91% in follow up with 100% performance on safety steps. High levels of maintenance was observed in both the lottery and the no lottery group. Training in treating nappy rash or cradle cap in 3 children was associated with the elimination of these conditions. Training in feed preparation was associated with increased rate of weight gain in a failure to thrive infant. Also quick success for 1 of 2 mothers trained in toilet training. All 6 parents contacted at later follow up stated that the programme had been useful for them and their child, they liked the therapist, and they would recommend the programme to other parents.

Notes: Authors conclude that the results counter other studies reporting non responsiveness of these parents to training. They suggest further studies to assess if different parenting skills have different levels of maintenance and may require maintenance reinforcement such as the lottery method. Authors also emphasize that these parents have multiple problems and that other concurrent interventions may be necessary.

Green (1978)

PSYCHIATRIC TREATMENT OF ABUSED CHILDREN

Sample: 20 abused children (14 girls and 6 boys) with a mode age of 7 years, referred by paediatric department and Child Welfare Bureau. Children had emotional behavioural problems and came from impoverished inner city families.

Focus: Effects of child abuse on children.

Objectives: To improve children's psychological functioning including 'ego functioning'.

Programme: Psychodynamic treatment of symbolic re-enactment, ego strengthening, impulse control thinking, and support of self esteem. Treatment was often for 2 to 3 years.

Design: Post-test on treatment group.

Measures: Therapist's assessment of children's psychological functioning and number of negative behaviours.

Results: 15 of the 16 children remaining in treatment for at least 9 months showed improvements in cognitive functioning and academic achievement, impulse control and more satisfactory object relations.

Notes: The author stresses the importance of early interventions to mitigate the effects of abuse.

Hanks (1987), Hanks et al (1988)

INFANTS WHO FAIL TO THRIVE: AN INTERVENTION FOR POOR FEEDING PRACTICES

Sample: 6 children who completed study from a deprived area in northern England. Criteria of under 4 years; below 3rd centile for growth and development; no physical ill health, handicap or developmental delay; no other current treatment; informed consent of parents. Age range of 11 to 18 months at entry to study.

Focus: Feeding and caretaking of infants failing to thrive.

Objectives: To enable mothers to provide their children with adequate nutrition.

Programme: 5 fortnightly sessions for each mother infant dyad. At first session discussion of problem and mother's acceptance of this. Parents asked to keep a dietary record and this plus parents' ability to control children's behavioural problems and other parenting problems were main themes of sessions. Also discussion of mother's role in her family and her own experiences of being parented.

Design: Repeated measures (multiple from pre test to 2 month follow up) on intervention group only.

Measures: (1) Infant's height, weight, mid-upper arm circumference (MUAC) as standard deviations from population norms. (2) Denver Developmental Screening Inventory (DDSI) at pre-test only. (3) Parental measures at pre-test of General Health Questionnaire (GHQ), Rosenberg Self Esteem Questionnaire, Eating Attitude Test, interviews derived from Darlington Family Assessment Schedule (not reported in article).

Results: (1) No children were significantly below norms on DDSI. (2) No significant maternal psychological disturbances identified by GHQ. (3) Significant increases on all growth measures relative to general population, particularly for weight.

Notes: Authors suggest that the explicit focus on feeding patterns in reframing the mother and child's behaviours and relationship was the most helpful intervention because it enabled mothers to be rewarded by their success and be more successful caretakers in the future – though booster therapy sessions may be necessary.

Harling and Haines (1980)

SPECIALISED FOSTER HOMES FOR SEVERELY MISTREATED CHILDREN

Sample: 43 severely abused and neglected children aged between 2 and 7 years who have used the service to date. Referral (seems to be) on basis of developmental and emotional problems and placement problems. In most cases children have already been made dependents of the Juvenile Court.

Focus: Children's developmental functioning.

Objectives: To achieve permanent placement of children preferably in their original home.

Programme: Specialised foster homes that prepare severely mistreated children for permanent placement in a new family or for return to their original families. Prior physical, psychological, and psychiatric assessment. Plan of work negotiated between agencies, foster parents and birth parents. Homemaker provides practical support and advice, student volunteers act as siblings and role models for children and help to develop trust. Social worker co-ordinates service and support birth and foster families. Foster families must be non threatening to the birth parents.

Design: Post-test on treatment group.

Measures: Unspecified assessments of emotional and physical developments, age appropriate behaviours, ability to relate to peers and adults, leading to the achievement of permanent placements.

Results: Children improved on all measures, but few children were able to return to their birth parents. A later follow up indicated that there were few permanent substitute family placements.

Notes: Authors stress the importance of providing consistency and of involving all the different parties in the case plan and the child's progress.

Haynes et al (1984)

HOSPITALIZED NON ORGANIC FAILURE TO THRIVE: A SHORT TERM LAY HOSPITAL VISITOR INTERVENTION

Sample: 20 hospitalized children who failed to thrive. 80% of children less than 6 months old. Problem seen as due to a disturbed mother child relationship. Mothers reported that they had received inadequate care as children. Sample a mix of Spanish-American, Caucasian, and black families. Approximately half were on public assistance. Two comparison groups, (1) failure to thrive cases not receiving lay visitor service, (2) control group of 15 healthy children matched with treatment group except for parental histories and state of child.

Focus: Functioning of mothers and their children.

Objectives: To improve children's weight and intellectual development and the mother child interactions.

Programme: A lay hospital visitor service was provided for 6 months, with later follow up from social workers, visiting nurse, and paediatrician. Children often received physical therapy and stimulation. Also parenting classes for mothers.

Design: Repeated measures (pre and post-test) on treatment and control groups.

Measures: Cognitive development of children, weight of children, agency records of maintaining contact with services.

Results: No effect of lay visiting on cognitive and physical development compared to failure to thrive controls, though treatment mothers did keep more contact with services.

Notes: Article gives most emphasis to discussing the failure to thrive group as a whole, rather than the details of the evaluation.

Hornick and Clarke (1986)

A COST EFFECTIVENESS EVALUATION OF LAY THERAPY TREATMENT FOR CHILD ABUSING AND HIGH RISK PARENTS

Sample: 55 families in Calgary, given service over a one year period. 20 were cases of abuse and 35 were cases of high risk. Many were single unemployed parents. Sample divided randomly into control and treatment groups.

Focus: Functioning of parents.

Objectives: Remove emotional stressors, develop child care and home making skills.

Programme: Paid lay therapists offer 12 hours home contact and 5 hours telephone contact per month for a year. Therapist nurture parents, act as a parenting model, and teach homemaking. Also 3 hours social work time per month for parents. Therapists had caseload of 6 clients. Controls given 5 hours social work time per month and social workers had average case loads of 27.

Design: Repeated measures experimental design with random allocation to one treatment and one control condition.

Measures: Parental self reports of nurturing and parenting attitudes, affection and empathy to children, perceived ease of child care, and control of hostility and expressions of anger. Rating of parents' involvement with their children, discipline and control of children, and general parental adjustment.

Results: At 6 months, treatment group only significantly better than controls on 'ability to empathize with child' and 'expression of pleasure when with child'. At 12 months treatment group significantly better in believing that 'parents influenced children'. At 12 months there had been 26% and 50% drop out in the treatment and control groups respectively. No re-abuse recorded in either groups.

Notes: The article endorses the usefulness of the intervention, despite recording marginal effect and the treatment being three times as expensive to provide as the control.

Iwaniec et al (1985)

SOCIAL WORK WITH CHILDREN WHO FAIL TO THRIVE
AND THEIR FAMILIES

Part I of the study contrasted the psycho-social features of the sample compared to controls. Part II evaluated a behavioural social work intervention.

Sample: 17 children with non organic failure to thrive hospitalized for investigation and assessment, and their families, referred by hospital paediatrician to the paediatric social worker involved in the intervention in Leicester. Mothers evidence higher anxiety, depression, and lower self esteem than a control group of children with organic failure to thrive and other illnesses. In addition the families in the treatment group were often financially stressed and socially isolated thought not of particularly low socio-economic status. Marital disharmony was common and children showed behavioural difficulties, particularly at feeding. Mothers average age was 25 years (range 16 to 32) and the median age of the children was 27 months (range 3 months to 6 years).

Focus: Functioning of mothers, children, and mother-child interactions.

Objectives: Goals set for each family. Primary goals were improved feeding and eating patterns (100% of cases), mother-child social interactions (70% of cases), and child behaviour problems such as tantrums (70% of cases).

Programme: (1) Initial social work and behavioural assessment in the hospital and then at home. (2) Short term crisis intervention including day nursery for children to reduce stress on parents and provide stimulation for the children, practical and emotional support to parents and in some cases, desensitizing mother. (3) Longer term intervention in 3 stages, using instruction and behavioural techniques, such as modelling, as well as personal and developmental counselling in the context of task setting and problem classification. Stage 1: 6 weeks of twice weekly meetings for structuring feeding routines. Stage 2: Lengthening of agreed feeding and play sessions. Stage 3: final 2 weeks of intense interactions between mother, child and other siblings. Treatment terminated when goals achieved, which was approximately 13 months. Fathers worked with where practicable, and particularly if father-child interactions were considered problematic. Median length of intervention was 10 months.

Design: Repeated measures (pre and post-test) on treatment group.

Measures: Parents' assessment of child problems, workers' checklist of child behaviours and of parent behaviours, records of child weight gains, agency records of re-admissions of children to hospital.

Results: Change in feeding patterns reached goals of parents and clinician and therefore satisfactory 64%, some goals achieved moderate improvement 29%, not achieved 7% (n = 1). Change in child behaviour problems was satisfactory 44%, moderate 44%, not achieved 17% (n = 3). Change in mother child interactions was satisfactory 50%, moderate 33%, not achieved 17%. There was a single hospital re-admission, but this was for organic failure to thrive. Follow up of data suggest some loss of interactional gains, but maintenance of feeding routines.

Notes: Authors state that multicomponent nature of programme precludes specification of active components, but these were probably not consistent across cases. Further outcome data available in unpublished paper by first author.

Justice and Justice (1978)

EVALUATING OUTCOME OF GROUP THERAPY FOR
ABUSING PARENTS

Sample: 30 couples who completed group therapy in the period 1973–1977. Couples had been identified as responsible for child abuse by Child Welfare. In 75% of cases the children were in care and couples were given to understand that therapy would increase the probability of their child's return. The majority were middle and lower middle class, 60% white, 20% Mexican American, 20% black.

Focus: Functioning of the parents.

Objectives: To achieve changes in parents' behaviour and functioning so that they could provide a safe home for their children.

Programme: A maximum of 5 couples made up the group at any one time. New couples were introduced to the group and encouraged to trust and use the support of other members both within and outside the group. Couples completed a problem checklist which provided a goal and a contract for therapeutic work, a basis for assessing change, and a non threatening framework for discussing problems. Each parent also had in depth interviews with therapists. A variety of therapeutic techniques were used including Transactional Analysis, Rational Emotive Therapy, Parent Effectiveness Training, paradoxical intention, and relaxation training. The therapists did not have strict schedules of work and let the flow of the group determine the focus, but within the framework of the contracted goals of work. Common goals concerned isolation, talking and sharing, tension and temper, child development and management and employment. Average length of therapy was 5 to 6 months.

Design: Repeated measures (multiple baselines) on treatment sample.

Measures: Agreed goals were assessed by therapist and their attainment from –2 to +2 to produce a weighted composite Goal Attainment T score. A score of 55 was judged to be sufficient to state that therapy had been successfully completed.

Results: 22 couples completed therapy with 9 scores of over 55. High scores were achieved as improvement in one area would produce benefit in other areas. 4 couples dropped out and lost permanent custody of their children. 5 couples were still in the group. One of these had previously completed therapy, but experienced renewed marital conflict. A 6 month follow up showed that the scores of over 55 were maintained. Only one case of re-abuse was reported for the 22 couples.

Notes: The authors emphasize the benefits of using Goal Attainment Scaling to make the assessment of change more observable, confirmable, and so less subjective.

Kitchen (1980)

BREAKING THE VICIOUS CYCLE OF BATTERING

Sample: All those attending the family centre in Harrow since 1977 for physical abuse of children. Parents have poor self image and false expectations of child rearing.

Focus: Mainly functioning of parents.

Objectives: To care for parents so that they will be better able and encouraged to care for their own children. To help families to be more realistic about child rearing.

Programme: Family centre in a hospital. Families are collected from home up to 5 days per week and most attend between 6 and 12 months. 5 staff care for up to 8 families at a time. Day is unstructured except for a weekly parents' meeting to discuss problems. Appropriate child rearing is taught 'by example'. Staff encourage independence. Lunch is 'comfort feeding', and seen as symbolic meeting of emotional needs. A daily record is kept on all families and children are checked for injuries. Each family's progress is reviewed fortnightly by staff conference.

Design: Descriptive.

Measures: None

Results: None

Notes: Article discusses competition for care between parents and children, stigma of attending centre, access to specialist via hospital setting, and the anger projected by mothers on to the one male worker.

Kruger et al (1979)

GROUP WORK WITH ABUSIVE PARENTS

Sample: 5 women (from 15 selected), attending a parent education group and considered to be abusive or neglectful parents. Women were of low income and of different racial backgrounds.

Focus: Mothers.

Objectives: To help adult children interactions be more productive.

Programme: Weekly group discussions originally planned for 6 weeks, but half parents voted for a further 7 weeks. A particular topic was addressed each week, such as child rearing and birth control. Staff consisted of several students who encouraged discussion and sometimes role played interactions. Staff conferred before and after sessions to share feelings and compare observations.

Design: Post-test on treatment group.

Measures: Workers' assessment of group cohesion and the mother's self esteem and abilities to consider alternative means of discipline, and to cope with anger.

Result: Staff considered that there had been improvement on all measures.

Kunkel (1981)

SUCCESSFUL NURTUING IN RESIDENTIAL TREATMENT FOR ABUSED CHILDREN

Sample: Abused and neglected children in group homes run by a private agency (Rubicon) in California. Sample of 18 children discharged from the programme in 1979. Children have problems with trust, developmental delay, and emotional care. Average age of the children was 8 years.

Focus: Effects of abuse on children, functioning of the parents.

Objectives: To enable children to develop trust and non destructive forms of self expression. To form a bond between the mother and therapist. To nurture parents so that they can be better able to nurture the child.

Programme: Framework of 'relationship therapy', 'reality therapy', and 'social learning therapy'. Average stay is 18 months and children live in units of 6 children and 4 counsellors. The programme includes sporting activities when therapist gives 'endless positive strokes' and children can let out aggression and develop self control; play therapy with ventilation; working through of unmet dependency needs; a nurturing relationship; immediate consistent consequences for unacceptable behaviours. Therapists also develop nurturing relationship with the parents who visit Rubicon once or twice per week on an outpatient basis.

Design: Post-test on treatment sample.

Measures: Meeting treatment goals, the communication in the family, family social network, parents ability to take responsibility, permanency of post-treatment placement.

Results: 15 of the children went on to permanent placements in new families and were still there six months later though one child was having problems. At one year 14 children were still in placement and doing well. Parents showed improvements in marital and family relations, support networks, responsibility, and communication.

Notes: Article provides a good indication of the intervention, but less details about the sample and its evaluation. Authors stress the importance of the personal qualities and emotional maturity of the staff.

Land (1986)

CHILD ABUSE: DIFFERENTIAL DIAGNOSIS, DIFFERENTIAL TREATMENT

Sample: 89 clients of two programmes in agency servicing court ordered cases of child abuse (mostly physical abuse and neglect) where personality data on Minnesota Multiphasic Personality Inventory (MMPI) had been collected. 70% of the sample had abnormal MMPI scores (elevations for hypomania, schizophrenia, or paranoia, etc). No significant differences observed between the two agency groups.

Focus: Children and Parents.

Objectives: To produce improvements in child and parent behaviours and their interactions. Article interested in relative efficacy of different intensities of treatment.

Programme: Supervised parent and child interaction plus various therapies such as modelling and group and family milieu therapy in order to build relationships and skills. Also home visits and social support. Low staff client ratios, and often more than 12 hours contact per week and easy access to staff. Variable length of time in programme. One of the two programmes had a residential nursery for diagnosis and treatment of children.

Design: Post-test on treatment sample. Analysis of relationship of length of involvement in programmes and intensity of service with outcome.

Measures: Ratings by programme administrator not directly involved in treatment of global measures of, (1) improvements of both parent and parent-child relations, (2) partial improvement, (3) no improvements.

Results: Approximately 11% improved, 43% improved partially, and 46% did not improve. Those in treatment for longer than 4 months (n = 48) showed significantly greater levels of improvement (by Chi Square) compared to those with shorter programme involvement. Similar significantly greater improvements were found for those receiving more than 12 contact hours per week, compared to those receiving less. Even with less intense level of treatment, there was still a significant effect from length of time in programmes. No differences between comparison groups in race, MMPI scores or types of abuse.

Notes: Article emphasises severe problems of families. Few details of actual treatments.

Lane and Van Dyke (1978)

LAY THERAPY-INTIMACY AS A FORM OF TREATMENT FOR ABUSIVE PARENTS

Sample: All 27 families treated in the first 22 months of programme. Range from potential to severe cases of physical abuse. Main criteria for programme were unmet dependency needs and willingness of parents and social worker to participate. Severe emotional illness screened out.

Focus: Functioning of parents.

Objectives: To nurture parents' emotional growth and the establishment of natural and ongoing support system using relationship with therapist and a model.

Programme: Home visits and telephone calls to maintain contact and companionship. More specific help in areas of assertion, selfcare, housekeeping, planning leisure activities, allowing negative expressions to therapist. Child related help included counselling re parent-child communication, discipline, parental expectations, child's expression of feelings, use of behavioural techniques. Training and continual back up for lay therapists.

Design: Post-test on treatment group.

Measures: Therapists' measures of marital status, employment, address, illness, placement of children.

Results: Few changes in marital status or placement of children. More changes in illness, employment and family address. Lay therapy ended in 14 cases for various reasons.

Notes: Article provides detailed descriptions of service rather than evaluation. Authors stress that lay therapy is only one component of treatment and that the use of lay therapists avoids over dependence, the potential psychological regression of parents, and neglect of the child through pre-occupation with the parents' needs.

Larson et al (1987)

A BEHAVIOURAL FEEDING PROGRAMME FOR FAILURE TO THRIVE INFANTS

Sample: Three infants (2 male, 1 female) ranging in age from 4–21 months hospitalised for 3–6 weeks for treatment of chronic feeding disorders that had no known organised basis and had not responded to all other treatment attempts. All three were Caucasian from varied socio-economic backgrounds.

Focus: Young children with feeding disorders.

Objectives: To eliminate maladaptive feeding patterns and to promote normal eating behaviour.

Programme: Behavioural programme with feeding attempted 2 or 3 times per day by the nurse or mother for a minimum of 20 minutes over 2–6 days.

Two phases: (1) Fun time with music and play. The mother engaged in play activities with the infant. At the end of 10 minutes the music remained on, but the activities were discontinued and the infant was placed on a high chair. The aim was to enable the infant's mother to gradually fade in feeding time without unduly disrupting their interaction. (2) Music with feeding:– the mother offered the infant food while the music remained on. If food accepted, the infant had praise from the mother, but if food rejected a time out period ensured with four 'reprimand' components:– music immediately turned off, mother said 'NO' firmly, infant removed from high chair and put in crib, mother turned chair from infant and made no eye contact with infant. After 3 minutes, if infant was not crying, feeding was resumed by:– turning music on, picking up infant from crib, returning infant to high chair, a minute playing with infant, resumption of feeding. This programme was then recycled contingent upon infant's behaviour until the food had been consumed or 45 minutes had elapsed.

Design: An AB design with replication across the three infants. In order to evaluate the function of the music component, partial withdrawal probes were applied within the feeding sessions for 2 of the infants across feeding sessions for the third infant. All other treatment variables were held constant during these probes.

Measures: Feeding sessions were broken into percentage of spoonfuls of food accepted per session. An opportunity for feeding was defined as the placing of a spoonful of food on the infant's lips. The termination of the opportunity was signalled by return of the spoon (full or empty) to the food container. Food acceptance was defined as the opening of the infant's mouth and the taking in of one spoonful of food. Food refusal was defined by the infant pushing the spoon away with their hand, sliding down the chair and turning away from food, closing-covering their mouth to avoid food, screaming upon presentation of food, biting the spoon, or the infant gagging or vomiting.

Results: Upon implementation of the feeding programme all three infants demonstrated rapid increases in rate of food acceptance and reductions in rate of vomiting. Rate of food acceptance was found to increase or decrease in relation to presence or absence of music. (1) Infant 1: increased rate of food acceptance from 49% to 89%. During the probe session, eating was maintained when the music was on, and decreased when it was off. Within 3 days vomiting responses decreased from a baseline mean of 6 to nearly 0. (2) Infant 2: baseline of acceptance was highly variable, but this stabilised for 5 days at 95% acceptance on the programme. When music was withdrawn, eating decreased significantly, and rose again when the music was reinstated. (3) Infant 3: Within 8 sessions of the programme, the frequency of vomiting per feed was reduced from 4 to 0. Withdrawal of music increased vomiting to a mean of 3, but this disappeared on reinstatement of the music. Also qualitative changes in behaviour of all 3 children and informal follow up over 1 year later indicated that all children were continuing to thrive.

Notes: The authors conclude that the programme enables the infant to develop alternative adaptive repertoires to control the environment which were previously controlled by maladaptive behaviour. This results in the natural reinforcing characteristics of food 'taking over' and the mother infant interactions becoming mutually satisfying.

Leeds (1984)

EVALUATION OF NEBRASKA'S INTENSIVE SERVICES PROJECT

Sample: 37 families newly referred to Child Protection Service because there was risk of child being placed in alternative care. Exclusion criteria of sexual abuse, psychosis, psychopathy and mental retardation, in order to avoid chronic multi problem cases. Main single problem was child neglect. Families were often poor, single or cohabiting, and had moderate to severe problems in interpersonal and family functioning. 86% of families were white. The cases were the first year's intake of a new service.

Focus: Parental and family functioning.

Objectives: To service 35–40 cases in first year, to prevent out of home placement in 75% of cases, to meet case goals and close case within 6 months in 60% of cases, to be cost effective. To achieve this by increasing parents' self esteem, self sufficiency, ability to cope with conflict and depression, home management skills and general parenting skills.

Programme: Direct work in home by social worker with reduced caseloads. Work included coaching and counselling, parent education and training, co-ordination of other resources and services, and service programme planning. Also homemaker services and a 24 hour crisis and counselling service, there were 4 workers, 3 at Lincoln and 1 at McCook.

Design: Repeated measures on treatment group.

Measures: Self report of achievement of goals, social workers' assessments of case-goals, agency records of long term placement, and case status of open or closed.

Results: Objectives of servicing 35–40 cases and preventing placements met. Only 43% of cases success-

fully closed and average time was 6 months. Severity of problems in Lincoln families lessened, but if anything increased in McCook families. Factors related to success included no previous placements or mental health problem, and two parent families.

Notes: Article discusses aim of short term goals handicapped by a few multi-problem referrals. Also outcomes at McCook due to inadequate preparation, staffing, and support for the one worker. Article gives details of sample and outcomes, but less on the actual service provided than service goals.

Lines (1986)

THE EFFECTIVENESS OF PARENT AIDES IN THE TERTIARY PREVENTION OF CHILD ABUSE IN SOUTH AUSTRALIA

Sample: 36 mothers in programme within first 5 years of operation. Cases of physical abuse and neglect referred and accepted as suitable for service.

Focus: Mothers.

Objectives: To nurture, support and advise mothers.

Programme: Aides were experienced volunteer mothers, given a one week training, followed by fortnightly sessions. Aides offered home counselling, telephone contact, and had meetings with primary workers. Total of approximately 32 hours per month per client with no more than 2 clients per aide.

Design: Post-test on treatment sample.

Measures: Reports of successful outcome by mothers, parent aides, and primary workers. Abuse reports on child abuse register. Aides fulfilling initial commitment to work for 2 years in programme.

Results: 10 cases had successful outcomes. In 10 other cases the parent aide visits were terminated at the mothers' requests. In 10 further cases aide visits were terminated for other reasons (for example parents moving away). At end of five years, 6 cases were still active. In total there was only one reported case of re-abuse in three to eight years from termination of programme. This is a rate of 3% which compares with 8% for all abuse cases locally.

Notes: Author very positive about results of programme and its cost effectiveness. Also emphasises need to assess subjects' suitability for the programme and to have good publicity about the service because of the high turnover of social workers.

Moore (1982)

PROJECT THRIVE: A SUPPORTIVE TREATMENT APPROACH
TO PARENTS OF CHILDREN WITH NON ORGANIC
FAILURE TO THRIVE

Sample: 28 babies who failed to thrive, hospitalized
over a 16 month period in 1979/80. Selection made
by the paediatric social worker screening hospital
admissions. Cases of parental psychosis, cultural
behaviour, hard drug use, or other forms of child
abuse excluded. Article describes general characteristics of parents of infants who fail to thrive, such as
depression, anxiety, and guilt.

Focus: Mothers.

Objectives: To work with mothers so that the children gain weight and there is no necessity for
re-hospitalization.

Programme: Cases allocated to social work students
who developed individual treatment plan. Whilst
child is in hospital workers provide transport,
and encourage caring role for parents. At home,
workers support, nurture, provide role model, help
with medical visits, encourage and mobilize use of
social network, make referrals to other agencies,
and monitor the child's welfare. Case examples
illustrate the use of modelling through cuddling
child, verbal reinforcement of care behaviour, and
parent counselling. Treatment lasts between 3 and
9 weeks with an average of 7 weeks.

Design: Pre and post-test on treatment sample.

Measures: Workers' assessments of family progress,
agency measures of child's physical development,
re-hospitalization.

Results: Increases in infants weights. No cases of re-
hospitalization. All families perceived to be doing
well and half did not require referral to other agencies at end of the programme.

Parish et al (1985)

DEVELOPMENTAL MILESTONES AND A FAMILY ORIENTED
APPROACH TO THE TREATMENT OF CHILD ABUSE

Sample: Clients of family development centre attached
to a children's hospital in the area of Cincinatti.
Criteria for admission included child being between
$2\frac{1}{2}$ and 5 years, physical abuse being reported
within the last year, allocated case worker, and
parental acceptance of treatment. Some children
had delays in fine motor, language and social skills
and some were thought to have had suffered central
neurological damage. Intervention and pre and post-
tests achieved on 53 children. There were roughly
equal numbers of black and white subjects.

Focus: Parents, children, and parent-child interactions.

Objectives: Improving social, language and motor skills
of children, and the parenting skills of the parents.

Programme: Pre-school class for children, classroom
participation for parents with children, group work
with parents, teaching anger control to parent
group. There were twice weekly sessions for up
to a maximum of six months.

Design: Repeated measures (pre and post-test) on treatment group of children.

Measures: Blind assessment of social competence, and
language and motor skills. Tests were developed
from 'Learning Accomplishment Profile'. Two indices developed of 'months of gain' beyond the
expected (MG) and a gain quotient (GQ) that was
the average gain on four skills divided by the time
in the programme.

Results: Highly significant result of 79% of children
sowing a GQ greater than one. Social skills showed
the lowest improvement. MG scores showed improvements on fine motor and language skills, but these
were not significant. There was no correlation
between length of treatment and improvement.

Notes: Results need to be interpreted in light of 28%
sample drop out. Article also discusses various other
factors that effect interpretation.

Paulson et al (1974)

PARENTS OF THE BATTERED CHILD: A
MULTIDISCIPLINARY APPROACH TO LIFE THREATENING
BEHAVIOUR

Sample: 54 parents fearful of admitting, or charged
with, neglect or maltreatment of 32 children. Injuries included bruises 39%, bruises plus fractures
35%, skull fractures 16%, and permanent injury to
organs including brain damage 13%. Parents were
aged between 17 and 40 years; 45% of the parents
were fathers with an average age of 28, 55% were
mothers with an average age of 24 years. Female
children accounted for 40% of the child sample and
were aged from 1 to 7 years with an average of
1 year. Male children accounted for 60% of the child
sample and were aged from 1 to 10 years with an
average of 2 years. The sample was predominantly
white, two parent families, of lower than average
social economic status.

Focus: Functioning of parents.

Objectives: To encourage the sharing of feelings and
emotional growth in parents and prevent further
child abuse.

Programme: Group psychotherapy using an eclectic psycho-dynamic approach of intervention and understanding.

Design: Descriptive outcome of treatment sample.

Measures: Therapists' assessment of improvement and measures of re-abuse and of family membership.

Results: 52% of children who were in care were returned home. None of the initially abused children were reported as being re-abused. In one family, in therapy, a sibling was abused. In 2 families that had left therapy, a sibling was abused.

Notes: The authors do not see this as a formal evaluation but an experimental encounter and a biography of human failures in child rearing.

Peters and Carswell (1984)

PARENTING EDUCATION PROJECTS IN ALABAMA

Sample: 717 less serious child protection cases in several counties in Alabama (involving 1751 children) assessed by workers as amenable to parent education. In some counties participation is mandated condition for return of child from foster care.

Focus: Parents.

Objectives: To develop parenting skills, awareness of children's needs. To reduce social isolation and enhance self esteem, home management skills and use of community resources. To prepare for return of children from care.

Programme: Classes on children's needs, discipline, stress management, homemaking skills, and making use of community resources. Modelling of parenting skills. Classes meet home economist once a week for 6 to 10 weeks. Also home visits by parent assistants once a week for 6 to 12 months. Parent assistants negotiate a contract with clients and there is an emphasis on teaching of household skills and modelling general parenting skills.

Design: Descriptive outcome of treatment sample.

Measures: General assessment of parents competence, self esteem, self development, and possibility for children to remain and/or stay at home. The establishment of similar parent education projects.

Results: Improvements on all items reported.

Notes: Little outcome data. Much detail provided on homemaking skills.

Press-Rigler et al (1990)

PARENT AIDES: AN INTERVENTION PROGRAMME IN CASES OF CHILD ABUSE AND NEGLECT

Sample: Child abuse and neglect cases in Los Angeles.

Focus: Parents.

Objectives: To provide emotional supports and increase parental functioning in order to modify the social and psychological circumstances that produce abuse.

Programme: Parent aide service twice per week in the home. Aides offered practical support of transport and baby-sitting plus advocacy.

Design: Description of case series.

Measures: Descriptive.

Results: The programme seemed to make a difference to the overall interaction processes of the families.

Prodgers and Bannister (1983)

ACTIONS SPEAK LOUDER THAN WORDS

Sample: 8 mothers chosen from amongst those attending a family centre of National Society for the Prevention of Cruelty to Children (NSPCC). The mothers had physically abused their children or lived with men who did, were aged between 19 and 32 years, had poor self esteem, and were isolated. Mothers chosen for their willingness to participate. There was a deliberate strategy of mixing the composition of the group. For example, variation in the women's level of guilt/responsibility, dependency or ability and articulate views/feelings, more and less articulate and more guilty and more dependent clients. Sample notable for the high level of abuse, including sexual abuse suffered by the women in their own childhoods.

Focus: Functioning of the mothers.

Objectives: To increase self esteem, insight and self help. To provide opportunities for catharsis and women to test out less damaging forms of behaviour. To enable clients to become helpers as well as 'the helped'.

Programme: A psycho-drama group. Initial contract for regular meetings with client was to focus on mother-child relations. First half hour in preparation and eating of a meal, then physical warm up and relaxation, then role play and sculpting. Sculpting involved positioning people to represent and explore their relationship. Lastly sharing and empathy of issues raised, and the exploration of new patterns of behaviour. Group provided a holding environment with nurturing by whole group and therapist acting only as an enabler.

Design: Description of case series.

Measures: Therapists' report of clients' self esteem, insight into how past experiences relate to their present difficulties with children.

Results: The therapist reported increased self esteem and insight.

Notes: A treatment description rather than evaluation. The authors stress the importance of the mix of participants in the success of this method.

Ramey et al 1975

NUTRITION, RESPONSE – CONTINGENT STIMULATION, AND THE MATERNAL DEPRIVATION SYNDROME

Sample: 9 infants for whom data is available from 12 identified (from 44 screened) as meeting criteria of being between 6 and 24 months of age, below 3rd percentile for height and weight for age, no organic basis for failure to thrive (FTT), evidence of apathy or developmental lags, evidence of inadequate mothering in the medical history, absence of common metabolic abnormalities. Mean age of 94 months. Study in Detroit Metropolitan area.

Focus: Infants responses as control of stimulation received as secondary prevention of FTT.

Objective: To provide social stimulation, in order to improve infants response contingent stimulation and hence increase the stimulation received from environment, particularly mothering.

Programme: Five phases: (1) Pre-test I: 5 days hospitalized assessment. (2) Food delivered to infant's house 3 times per day, 7 days per week for 4 weeks, by food aide who remained until child fed. Uneaten food weighed. (3) Pre-test II: Repeat of hospitalized assessment, (4) Children assigned to experimental and control groups. Both groups continued to receive daily food deliveries for 5 days per week for 3 months. Experimental group received in addition a one hour per day individual home tutoring session by child development specialist that focused on experiences promoting child's awareness of how actions could control external stimulation in 4 areas of competence (language, gross motor, exploratory behaviour, social development). (5) Post-test: Repeat of hospitalized assessment.

Design: Repeated measures (2 pre-tests, and 1 post-test) experimental design with random allocation to 2 treatment conditions (n = 4 in food only group, n = 5 in food plus tutoring group).

Measures: (1) Height and weight. (2) Bayley Scales of Infant Development. (3) Test of rate of acquisition of instrumental responding in a free operant task. Infant placed in situation where their vocalizations could control the onset and donation of brightly coloured patterns on a screen. Four conditioning sessions during each of the hospitalized tests periods. Rate of vocalizations recorded.

Results: (1) From pre-test I to pre-test II mean weight gain of 42 ounces which is 2.7 times expected gain, mean height gain of 2.66 cm compared to 2.0 cm expected. From pre-test II to post-test weight gain near double expected; height gain as expected, but no differences between treatment conditions for either weight or height. (2) From pre-test I to pre-test II a statistically significant increase in both mental and psychomotor developmental age scores. At post-test the tutoring group had greater scores on both mental and psychomotor age scores but the differences only significant for the psychomotor scores. (3) At pre-test I very little increase in baseline rate of vocalizations recorded. At pre-test II a non significant increase, in vocalizations recorded. At post-test the food only group showed a non significant increase but the tutoring group showed a significant increase in rate of vocalizations. Also baseline rate of vocalizations of food only group significantly lower than tutoring group.

Notes: Authors suggest that both the quality of nutrition and the opportunity to receive increased response contingent stimulation contribute to the remediation of non organic developmental retardation. Authors remark that all infants seemed to lose their marked apathy over the course of the intervention programme.

Rogowski and McGrath (1986)

UNITED WE STAND UP TO PRESSURES THAT LEAD TO ABUSE

Sample: 4 parents admitted abuse and 4 were considered at risk but 2 denied this. Families experienced poverty, bad housing and unemployment.

Focus: Parents.

Objectives: To provide understanding of structural pressures, mutual support, and the breaking down of isolation. To alleviate pressures and provide advice on housing and welfare. Emphasis was on the present and future rather than the past, and on increasing parental self respect.

Programme: A 10 week discussion group with attendance by Welfare Rights Officer, Housing Manager, Social Service Manager. Discussion focused on material stress and relief, and agency responses. Group met for 6 weeks after worker involvement.

Design: Post-test on treatment group.

Measures: Self report questionnaires on satisfaction with project including practical gains, change in role behaviour, increase in self confidence, mutual support, understanding of stress and of the child protection and agency systems.

Results: Parents reported increased confidence and general satisfaction with the group, increased knowledge of the system and their own rights, and better understanding and ability to cope with stress (3 fully, 5 partially). Two couples became mutually supportive, outside the group.

Notes: Emphasis on enabling and on consumer understanding and reaction to agency systems rather than treatment.

Stempler and Stempler (1981)

EXTENDING THE CLIENT CONNECTION: USING HOMEMAKER-CASEWORKER TEAMS

Sample: Case study of a Puerto Rican family with 5 children between the ages of 3 and 11 years who were reported for neglect and emotional abuse. Previous short term improvements achieved by homemaker but client-worker relationship broke down. Children 'acting out' and mother had ill health and reacted to stress with hysteria.

Focus: Functioning of parents and family.

Objectives: To meet parents' needs and enable them to be self determining so that foster placement of the children can be avoided.

Programme: Homemaker and caseworker acted as a team. Homemaker provided a model for housework activities, and coping with stress and communication in the family, by the use of 'supportively confronting' areas of difficulty. Caseworker met with homemaker and family weekly. The joint meetings prevented divisions occurring between the two workers and any client manipulation. Team acted as advocates for the family to other agencies such as doctors and public assistance. Contact of 40 hours per week for approximately 2 years and then reduced to 3 half days per week.

Design: Case description.

Measures: Workers' assessment of parental self determination, parental involvement in housework, child response to improved parental model, and parental relationship.

Result: Increased independence of parents who could negotiate with other agencies. Better marital rela-

tions and no hysterical attacks by mother. She became more involved in housework chores, which offered model to children who helped with the work. The trust developed between families and workers was the basis for changing mothers' hysteria, but created difficulties in terminating the service.

Notes: Article emphasizes use of team of 2 workers, but some aspects of their roles not clear.

Stephenson (1977)

REACHING CHILD ABUSERS THROUGH TARGET TODDLERS

Sample: Child abuse and neglect cases in Child Protection Service in Vancouver approached about a special pre-school programme called Project Toddler. A quarter of those approached refused to participate. 24 families recruited and divided into treatment and control groups. 10 families dropped out and were replaced. Families were deprived, had multiple problems and children with developmental delay. Children mostly aged between 18 and 30 months.

Focus: Functioning of children and parents.

Objective: Not specified.

Programme: Programme run by pre-school teachers and volunteers. Enrichment programme for children's groups. Adults taught and encouraged in self esteem, medical care, nutrition, budgeting. Each teacher assigned 2 to 3 families and acted as general advisers and advocates for the families. Controls receive the routine Child Protection Services.

Design: Repeated measures experimental design with allocation to one treatment and one control condition.

Measures: Test of cognitive development, teachers' assessments of psychological functioning, and social competence. General indicators of family networks and family functioning and organisation.

Results: Significantly greater increases in cognitive scores for treatment groups. Also impression of improvements in children's functioning after only 3 months involvement. Marked changes in family functioning and employment status for most in the programme for more than one year.

Notes: Length of treatment seems to be important. Use of teachers allowed small caseloads and more intense work. Few details about objectives and methods. Article discusses problems of borderline cases where intensive work may be damaging. Also control group did better than expected.

Sturm and Drotar (1989)

PREDICTION OF HEIGHT AND WEIGHT FOLLOWING
INTERVENTION FOR FAILURE TO THRIVE

Sample: 59 children who completed programme from total of original 80 children meeting non organic failure to thrive (NOFT) criteria of: decrease in weight from normal limits at birth to below 5th percentile, absence of significant organic conditions, normal growth potential, weight gain in hospital. Also extra study criteria of age between 1 and 9 months, absence of child abuse, geographic proximity, parental consent. Sample recruited from children hospitalized for NOFT at 7 Cleveland hospitals. 39 male, 20 females; 32 Black, 24 White, 3 Hispanic; majority of families economically disadvantaged with average annual income of $6,000; average maternal age of 22 years; average onset of NOFT at 3.3 months with duration of 1.7 months to study intake.

Focus: Weight gain of failure to thrive infants.

Objectives: To improve children's weight/height ratios to normal limits through a time limited outreach intervention.

Programme: One of 3 time limited intervention plans conducted for an average of 12 months in the home: (i) Family centred (n = 19) weekly sessions directed at family coping skills and support of the mother to enhance the child's nurturing. (ii) Parent centred (n = 20) weekly sessions with supportive education for mother to enhance her nutritional management and relationship with the child. (iii) Advocacy (n = 20) of emotional support and assistance for mother in securing resources from community agencies through 6 home visits and telephone contact.

Design: Repeated measures (pre-test and 5 follow up tests at 6 monthly intervals from 12 months to 36 months post intake) experimental design with random allocation to three intervention groups.

Measures: (1) Pre-test only: age of onset of below 5th percentile, duration from onset to study intake, parental income at intake. (2) Pre-test to 1st follow up: growth velocity standardized against population weight norms. (3) Pre-test and follow ups: (a) Home Inventory for Measurement of the Environment (HOME); (b) Height for weight of child's weight as a percentage of typical weight for a given height, classified as degrees of wasting of mild (80–90% of typical weight), moderate (70–79%), and severe (below 70%).

Results: (1) Outcome of total sample including case drop outs: number of children with no wasting increased from intake of 13% to 66% at 12 month, and 68% at 36 month follow up. Severe wasting decreased from 52% at intake to 6% and 7% at 12 and 36 months respectively. Reduction in wasting was significant from intake to 12 months but not from 12 to 36 months. (2) Predictor variables identified by multiple regression: NOFT characteristics such as weight gain accounted for more of variance of weight at 36 months than environmental factors such as income or HOME scores. Controlling for age of onset, duration of NOFT prior to intake was also predictive of 36 month weight. (3) No significant differences found between treatment conditions.

Notes: Authors argue that children presenting with chronic NOFT who do not show good weight gain in the months following treatment may be at long term risk.

Tracy and Clark (1974), Tracy et al (1975)

TREATMENT FOR CHILD ABUSERS

Sample: 37 black urban families in Philadelphia characterized as lacking parenting skills. Two thirds were single. Most children under 3 years of age. Three quarters at least at risk of abuse, one quarter physically abused. Families referred from hospital and from the community.

Focus: Mothers.

Objectives: Improve the skills and functioning of the mother and therefore also improve her abilities as a parent.

Programme: Initial behavioural assessment based largely on interviews and some observations. Parents then introduced to the outreach workers who are middle aged black women from the same communities, who have been given some training. Work is in the home and includes behavioural techniques such as modelling and positive reinforcements, practical steps to reduce life stresses, and advocacy on behalf of the parents. Work is based on negotiated and contracted plans and practical and advocacy, rather than emotional support and friendship. An average of 46 home visits were made.

Design: Repeated measures (pre and post-test) on treatment group.

Measures: Workers' assessment of frequency of target behaviours clustered into areas of concern such as household management and these then rated as categories of improvement or deterioration. Also self reports of parenting skills and general functioning.

Results: For 129 goals, 84% of families were 'improved' or 'very improved', 9% were 'worse' or 'same', and 7% were unknown.

Notes: Authors stress the important continuity, yet distinction, between the hospital and community work.

Zastrow (1981)

Self Talk: A Rational Approach to Understanding and Treating Child Abuse

Sample: A case of physical abuse to a 4 year old and a case of sexual abuse to a 15 year old.

Focus: Fathers.

Objectives: To promote in the fathers an understanding of their 'self talk and to change it, so that their parental behaviour also improves.

Programme: Use of 'Rational Therapy' to explain self talk to the clients.

Design: Description of case outcomes.

Measures: Therapists' descriptions of what the father had learned.

Results: In the case of physical abuse, the father learned to challenge and change his self talk which led to emotional outbursts of anger. In child sexual abuse case, the father came to see how his thinking has led to incest.

Notes: Few details given of how self talk was challenged and changed. Few details about whether there were changes in behaviour particularly as children were in care.

Zimrin (1984)

Do Nothing But Do Something: the Effect of Human Contact with the Parent on Abusive Behaviour

Sample: 20 mothers of children hospitalized following physical abuse. Families are from low socio-economic status groups in part of Israel. Controls are similar but receive routine social work.

Focus: Mothers.

Objectives: To improve mothers' behaviour to children using non professional workers and 'more human contact'.

Programme: Young women volunteers from same social class as the mothers, without a professional education, act as friends rather than therapists. They provide social control, re-attention to strengthen parental self image, and practical help such as housework to ease stress.

Design: Repeated measures (pre and post-test) experimental design with allocation to one treatment and one control condition by stratified random sampling (controlled for severity of abuse, level of education, ethnic origin, socio-economic status).

Measures: Volunteers and social work ratings of mother-child interactions, general coping, and emotional capacity. Inter rater reliability of 83%.

Results: At post-test 9 of the experimental group showed improvement and 11 no change, whilst only one case improved in the control group. This is a highly significant difference. At 3 months follow up, all but one of all 40 mothers had reverted to previous behaviour.

Notes: Article concludes that intervention worthwhile despite short term nature of effects because, (1) other approaches have such limited success, (2) it is a useful strategy in emergencies, and, (3) volunteers are a readily available and cheap resource and may benefit from the work.

CHAPTER NINE
Multi Component Intervention

Background

Many of the special interventions that have been developed for child abuse do not use a single method, but apply a range of services. These are often individually funded demonstration programmes, with resources to provide a wide range of intensive services.

One reason for this breadth of provision, is that child abuse is seen as having multiple causes and often occurs in families with multiple problems. The logic is, that in order to produce change, it is necessary to deal with a large proportion of these problems at the same time. Another argument for multi-component services is that it enables inter-agency co-operation, which is often considered to be an essential part of case management, but there have been many concerns that this co-operation is not achieved in practice. (DHSS, 1982, Hallet and Stevenson, 1980; Brent, 1986; Greenwich, 1987; Department of Health, 1991; Hallett and Birchall, 1992). Multi-component teams are thought to facilitate inter-disciplinary work, because members can develop personal relationships, a knowledge of each others work and the responsibilities, priorities, and pressures that determine each others' actions. If these professionals can concentrate purely on child abuse work, they can further develop a specialism and expertise in this particular area. A rather more basic reason for multi-component services is that child abuse cases have been found to be so intractable, and the negative effects of failure are so dangerous to children, that all the interventions at our disposal should be utilised to increase the likelihood of at least one component being a success. Special demonstration projects provide an opportunity for concentrating a wide range of resources and expertise.

Research Studies

As the multi-component programmes are the largest special projects and demonstrations of what can be achieved with high levels of funding, it is not surprising that they have attracted a great deal of research. Both the scale and the cost of the programmes invite interest as to the relative efficacy of these models of work, partly because the programmes are special innovatory services and so require evaluation, and partly because the high costs involved make it necessary for the efficacy to be demonstrated or confirmed in some way. It may even be a requirement of future funding that an evaluation takes place. Furthermore, the projects are often set up or staffed by those concerned with research and development in child abuse, who then also undertake the research studies.

As the projects are multi-component, they involve at least an equal number and range of interventive approaches as were considered in the previous chapter on special projects. The difference here is, that the approaches are integrated in one programme. In practice this is a question of degree. Many of the projects discussed in the previous chapter had several components. It is simply that the projects reviewed in this chapter were more overtly multi-component in form.

Many of the multi-component projects overlap in the services that they offer, and there are so many possible combinations of services, that the programmes are not easily classified or contrasted with each other. It is also difficult to generalize from the findings of studies with so many types of intervention and outcome. For this reason, comparatively short descriptions of the studies are given in the text of the chapter and the reader is advised to refer to the full summaries of the studies provided at the end of the chapter.

The studies (listed in Table 9.1) can be crudely divided according to the emphasis they put on individual or group work. There are several examples of the more individually based programmes. Baher et al (1976) considered the impact of long term individual casework, the Bowen Centre described their work with fifty five families, Moore et al (1981) described a programme of task centred casework and Green et al (1981) reported on a service providing counselling and psychotherapy. Magura and colleagues (Magura and Derubeis, 1980; Willems and Derubeis, 1981) undertook a controlled experimental evaluation of an intensive specialist child protection service, and Lutzker (1984) reported on an eco-behavioural programme involving up to fifteen components.

Two projects evaluated residential services. McBogg et al (1979a) studied a three to six month residential programme in Denver. Lynch and Roberts (1982) examined the outcomes of three week residential treatment with after care support. Both of the residential programmes were concerned with particularly serious cases where the children were at risk of being permanently removed to care.

Being multi-component many of the projects also had communal or group aspects. For example, the studies by Green et al (1981) and Lightfoot et al (1983) involved parents groups in addition to individual counselling. The residential treatment reported by Lynch and Roberts (1982) also included group therapy. The residential setting in a children's hospital allowed the groups to be introduced to different clients such as parents of handicapped or chronically ill children. Parents of the abused children were thus able to reflect and gain insight into the types of problems experienced by other parents. Magura and colleagues argue that groupwork is important not just in terms of direct therapeutic effect on families but in the opportunities it provides for workers in understanding the dynamics of the families that they are treating.

Other projects took a more definite group approach. West and West (1979) examined an out patient psycho-therapy group and a monthly marital group provided in a psychiatric hospital. Similarly Bean (1971) and Dougherty (1983) examined groupwork. In the Dougherty study parents attended the project twice per week. Their days started with general social interaction and moved on to group therapy and to parenting classes. Children were provided with a therapeutic nursery.

The study by Laughlin and Weiss (1981) concerned a community centre programme for child protection service cases. This was not specifically group work based, but the philosophy of the programme was to counter the social isolation of the families and help to foster new relationships. In order to reach out to families the project initially would discuss material needs with families and avoided negative attributions about child abuse.

Two of the largest research studies ever undertaken in child abuse contrasted a range of multi-component demonstration projects in the United States. The first study (Berkeley Planning Associates, 1977) compared eleven projects and the second nineteen (Berkeley Planning Associates, 1983; Daro, 1987).

The first study assessed the progress of 1,724 clients and found that the less professionally based and significantly cheaper programmes involving lay counselling and Parents Anonymous, were the most strongly associated with positive client outcomes of improved individual and family functioning, and an assessment of reduced propensity for further abuse. These lay services required intensive professional training and support, but indicate that broadening the base of therapeutic services, may make them more effective, more acceptable to clients, and more economical.

The second study covered 986 cases in a similar manner to the first study, although the sample contained very few cases of physical abuse. The nineteen

TABLE 9.1

Multi Component Programmes Research Studies

Study	Programme	Sample/ Size	Population	Design	Main Measures
Baher et al (1976)	Denver House: weekly nurturing & mothering group	n = 25	Physical abuse	RPM	Parenting & marital relationships, child injuries
Bean (1971)	Parents Center Project	n = 23	Physical abuse	Descriptive	Therapist assessments, abuse
Berkeley Planning Associates (1979)	11 Demonstration projects	n = 1274	Physical abuse/ neglect	RPM + C	Case work quality, progress, re-abuse, costs
Berkeley Planning Associates (1983) Daro (1987)	18 Demonstration projects	n = 986	Sexual abuse/ adolescent abuse	RPM + C	Progress, re-abuse, costs
Bowen Centre (1975)	Multi disciplinary teams	n = 35	Neglect	Descriptive	Family relationships, aggression
Dougherty (1983)	Holding environment	n = 30	Neglect/risk of abuse	Descriptive	Parenting relationships
Fontana and Robinson (1976)	Residential treatment	n = 62	Abuse & neglect	RPM	Stress, child development, child placement
Green et al (1981)	Brooklyn Family Centre	n = 79	Physical abuse	RPM	Parental insights, child care
Laughlin and Weiss (1981)	Milieu therapy	n = 80	CPS cases	? + C	Client engagement, abuse, child placement
Lightfoot et al (1983)	PACT	n = 83	Violence, neglect, isolation	RPM	Progress, abuse, child development
Lutzker (1984) Lutzker and Rice (1984, 1987)	Project 12 Ways: Eco behavioural treatment	n = 50/352	CPS cases/single poor mothers	RPM + C	Goal attainment, abuse
Lynch and Roberts 1982)	Parke Hospital: residential treatment	n = 40	Physical abuse	RPM	Child development, care environment, parental health
Magura and Derubeis (1980) Willems and Derubeis (1981)	Hudson County Project: intensive support	?	Neglect	RPM + C	CLLS, family functioning, goal attainment
McBogg et al (1979a)	Circle House Residential treatment	n = 23	CPS severe cases	POST	Child placement
Moore et al (1981)	Basildon Treatment	n = 28	Violence, scapegoating	PRPM	Marital relationships, violence
West and West (1979)	Psychiatric day hospital	n = 50	Child abuse, psychiatric illness	POST	Re-abuse
Wood (1981)	Residential treatment	n = 29	CPS referrals	POST	Child placement, use of services.

Design

POST = Post-test only; RPM = Repeated Measures including pre-test; PRPM = Repeated Measures post-test only;

+ C = Control or comparison group; + PC = Control or comparison group but at post test only;

CLS= Childhood Level of Living Scale; CPS = Child Protection Service; CLS = Childhood Level of Living Scale projects applied a variety of treatment methods differentially to different cases. The analysis was therefore of the methods applied to individual cases within the total research sample. The services found to be the most strongly associated with improvements in client functioning and reduced propensity for abuse, were group counselling and educational classes. The highest rates of success were for cases of child sexual abuse. Another major predictor of positive outcome, was client compliance. It may be that clients who accept that they have a problem, and are prepared to comply with the services, are the most likely to improve. Alternatively it may be that compliant clients receive a halo effect, whilst difficult clients are categorised as irresponsible and uncaring parents (abusers) leading to bias in clinical assessment of change.

The first comprehensive study (Berkeley Planning Associates 1977) did not include many direct services for children, but these were included in the second large study (Daro 1987). This study found that the direct services were associated with gains in all areas of functioning and this supports the encouraging results for children discussed in Chapter Eight. Therapeutic day care was seen as being particularly effective.

Discussion

The studies suffered from the same methodological weakness described in other chapters. In particular a lack of sample specification, of treatment specification, of independent measures, and relevant experimental controls. There was also the tendency for studies to report mixed outcome results. Often this was presented in a manner which emphasised the intractability of some of the cases seen, rather than suggesting that the treatment should be questioned or that another method should be preferred. In some studies authors emphasised the importance of specific components, but this was usually on the basis of clinical impression rather than strong research findings. The consequence was, that even where experimentally controlled research designs were employed, it was not possible to distinguish which components were responsible for any success reported – whether the reported success was due to specific components or the total multi-component package.

The problems of differentiating the cause of any reported effects, is exaggerated by the manner in which most studies are set up to evaluate the success or otherwise of a single project. Even if the data was collected independently to avoid observer bias, and the design was experimentally controlled to limit the effect of potentially confounding variables, it is still not possible to determine which of the multi-components (or combinations of them) had the required effect. Sample sizes are usually too small to allow multiple variate analysis and the studies are usually not sufficiently well defined (particularly according to sample definitions) to allow comparisons across studies. The consequence is that the results of the studies of individual demonstration programmes become isolated pieces of information which are difficult to apply to service planning.

The only studies that could overcome these obstacles were the very large American studies. These have produced provocative and interesting results. Their findings support very low cost effective services that have not been well developed in Britain, despite some moves toward the use of self help, community help and groupwork (particularly in child sexual abuse cases).

There are, however, difficulties in interpretation of these large scale studies. The main problem is that the outcome measures are based upon clinical judgement which is almost certainly open to bias. For example, lay therapists or members of Parents Anonymous may be more emotionally involved with the service and empathise more strongly with the clients. It would therefore not be at all surprising, if they were more optimistic about client improvement. This would be particularly true for those in longer term treatment and the studies do find a co-relation between longer treatment and positive outcomes, except for treatment of 18 months or more. The negative association with very long treatment could simply be due to bias in the distribution of cases. The most complex and intractable cases may use long term case work with little success, but this does not necessarily mean that it is not the most effective treatment available. This illustrates a wider problem of the confounding effects from the service component selected for different clients. Lay services may be offered in less serious situations which have a better likelihood of improvement even if case type and case severity are controlled. Similarly, the reported success with child sexual abuse cases, may be due to the nature of that form of abuse, rather than the treatment per se. Despite these reservations, the demonstration projects do point to more use of lay services, of group counselling, and of direct services to children. These two large scale studies also included an assessment of the relative costs of services and found that the most effective were usually the cheapest. Lay services, group counselling, and educational classes are all cheaper than the more usual individual or family therapy. The one expensive and effective services was direct work with children.

The general findings of the studies are similar to those reported in the previous chapter on more narrowly focused intervention projects. There did not seem to be a positive or negative interaction effect, from the combination of services available in the multi-component demonstration projects. The large American multi-component studies therefore provided no support for the concept of multi-component services. Other studies have reported interaction effects. For example, Dodds et al (1978) found that behavioural treatment for children with conduct disorders was more effective when there was also parent support training, but only where there was marital discord. Multi-component projects are usually aimed at whole families with services for individuals, pairs and the whole family group. They therefore offer great potential for the type of effects reported by Dodds which could be further explored in future studies.

The positive effects reported by multi-component studies are encouraging, but these only referred to improvements in functioning and reductions in propensity for future abuse. A more negative aspect of the results was that there was re-incidence of abuse during treatment in between 30% and 47% of cases (Daro, 1987). If treatment successes are so low, then policies for deciding which families have a future together may be open to question.

The main strength of the research reports considered in this chapter is the description of the development of innovative multi-component services for cases of child abuse. The way in which the research is organised, makes it difficult to single out specific effects but the studies are valuable because they spread the expertise of child abuse specialist, working in special programmes, to a wider audience. The question is, whether this is best achieved in terms of both cost and communicative effect, by research studies attempting relatively unsuccessfully, to isolate hard data on the efficacy of programmes and their sub components.

Summary

1.   A series of studies were identified that evaluated multi-component therapeutic interventions for child abuse. The components of these interventions were similar to those in more narrowly focused projects discussed in other reactive interventions described in this volume.

2.   The multi-component nature of the projects added to the methodological problems discussed in the previous chapters. These problems were heightened by the greater number of variables involved in multi-component interventions.

Only very large scale studies are able to use multivariate methods to distinguish the interacting effects of different intervention components.

3. The size of the two large North American research studies allowed the statistical comparison of the effects of different project components, although the results were limited by the use of clinical outcome measures.

4. The results of the two American large scale studies supported the use of lay therapy services, group counselling, educational groups, and direct services for children.

5. The studies did not report positive interaction effects between the components of the large programmes. This is worthy of further study as it is one of the main potential benefits of multi-component projects.

6. Although the studies reported encouraging treatment effects including a reduced propensity for abuse, the actual outcomes were not encouraging. There were still re-incidence rates of between 30% and 47%.

7. Small scale specialist multi-component interventions often attract research interest. These studies have value in describing specialist work, but are often not effective in determining the efficacy of different interventions. These studies might be more productive if they concentrated on analysing the processes of intervention rather than attempting and failing to assess their efficacy.

Chapter Nine   Research Summaries

Baher et al (1976)

At Risk: an Account of the Battered Child
Research Department.

Sample: 25 families treated and evaluated over 36
months from 1970 to 1974 for whom there was
sufficient data for inclusion. 14 cases involved severe
physical abuse, 2 moderate abuse, and 4 minor
abuse. 2 children died, 3 had permanent injuries and
one had brain damage. In 4 cases there was evidence
of physical neglect. Nearly all the children were
depressed, withdrawn, and anxious and showed
developmental delays particularly in speech. Most
children were under 3 years of age with half under
one year. Half were boys and half were girls. Parents
were mainly in their mid to late twenties and all
were married or cohabiting. 52% had a single child.
Parent's problems included unrealistic expectations
of children, lack of empathy, poor marital relations
and maternal support, maternal depression and low
self esteem, health problems. Most fathers were
in employment though there were some financial
problems, poor housing and social isolation. Pregnancies were often unplanned and stressful with
poor child birth experiences. Half of parents had
themselves suffered from emotional abuse. Referrals of pre-school abused children to programme
were solicited from hospitals and general medical
practitioners from 3 London Boroughs. Over half
the cases were referred by hospitals and a quarter
from other health facilities.

Focus: Functioning of parents.

Objectives: To nurture or mother parents in order to
meet their dependency needs and so improve their
general functioning and their capacity for the care
of their children.

Programme: Long term casework with an emphasis on individual therapeutic relationships and
psycho-analytical derived concepts of nurturing
and mothering. (1) In first 3 months emphasis of
casework on caring and acceptance. Also provision
of practical help day care, and bringing in help of
other agencies. (2) From 4 to 12 months emphasis
on increasing self esteem through praise and on
relaxing those with a punitive approach. (3) From
13 to 24 months work was more directive. (4) From
25 to 36 months clients were encouraged to be more
independent and assertive. Client contact was twice
weekly in first few months reduced to monthly by
third year when 16 cases were still in treatment, the
rest having been referred on to other agencies.

Additional services included 3 mothering aides in 8
cases, drop-in foster mothers for crisis relief, mothers' group for discussion and sharing, general socializing from attendance at centre, day care providing
stimulation and warmth, psychiatric treatment for
some parents and children. Main staff were 7 social
workers, a nursery nurse, a consultant psychiatrist,
and mothering aides.

Design: Repeated measures on case series.

Measures: Coding of mothers into 'accessible', 'ambivalent', or 'resistant' during initial casework. Analysis of case records at 18 to 21 months into treatment. Descriptive assessments of cases at end of
the project. Authors' coding include warmth of handling and rejecting attitudes towards children; marital contact and extent of mutual support; parental self esteem, mood swings and depression; records of housing adequacy; social work assessment
of changes in paternal drinking and employment,
and maternal and family social isolation.

Results: Significant increases in paternal work satisfaction, adequacy of housing, contact in marriage,
mutual marital support; decreases in maternal isolation. There was no change in drinking, employment,
or isolation from extended family. Similar results
found at follow up at end of project although 10 out
of 25 marriages had ended. By end of project 12 out
of 22 children had sustained unexplained injuries, 2
of which were serious, and there were also injuries
to 7 siblings. Some behavioural improvements but
only made 8 satisfactory developmental progress.

Notes: The lack of improvement in parent-child relations leads the authors to conclude that treatment
goals should be more conservative. Authors state
that more direct services for children would have
been helpful. Authors discuss many practical treatment issues and the organisational context of their
work including the difficulties of combining the legal
and therapeutic roles.

Bean (1971)

The Parents Center Project: a Multi-service
Approach to the Prevention of Child Abuse.

Sample: All 23 families treated by Centre in the first 22
months of operation. Criteria for admission to service included the incidence of physical abuse, parents being amenable to help and willing to attend

group therapy, and living locally. Alcoholic, psychotic and mentally retarded parents excluded. Age of the children in the first year of operation was between 6 months and 4 years. Centre was located in low to middle class area.

Focus: Functioning of Parents.

Objectives: To work with parents who have personality problems and difficulty in controlling their behaviour towards their children, but where removal of children would be more harmful than helpful.

Programme: Weekly group therapy with 6 families and a male and female co-therapist. Discussions, sharing of experiences and ventilation including the discussion of own abusive tendencies. Children attend day care as example of a good care environment and as a relief for the parents. Parents also to participate to learn age appropriate expectations of children, consistency in their child care, and to encourage togetherness of parent and child. Medical care fo children.

Design: Description of case series.

Measures: Therapists assessment of improvements in functioning of children. Agency records of incidence of re-abuse.

Results: The author reports improvements in the functioning of the children and that no children were re-abused.

Notes: Author discusses the practical issues of the operation of the Centre.

Berkeley Planning Associates (1977)

CHILD ABUSE AND NEGLECT DEMONSTRATION PROJECTS, 1947–1977.

Sample: 1724 adults participating in 11 demonstration projects. Specific admission criteria varied between projects and most were able to be selective about the clients served. Two offered programmes to all protective services in the county. Case types for the total sample were: 28% potential abuse or neglect, 14% emotional maltreatment, 4% sexual abuse, 31% physical abuse, 20% physical neglect, 3% physical abuse with neglect. In 31% of cases there was only one adult per household. Less than 10% of cases were taken to a Court Hearing or involved a child being received into care.

Focus: Parental/family functioning.

Objectives: Most projects were concerned with improving parental and family functioning in order to minimize the chances of recurrence of abuse. In addi-

tion some projects offered direct services to children in order to mitigate the effects of abuse or impoverished environments. Other objectives were the developments of child protection services, community awareness, and community resources.

Programme: Most projects employed a wide range of services and approaches directed at children, adults, families, welfare agencies, and the community. There was variation between projects in both the specific components employed and in the proportion of time directed to different activities. Time for direct services to clients ranged from under 40% to over 60%; time for community activities from less than 10% to nearly 30%. In three of the four projects offering direct services to children, the time varied from 23% to 63% of the total.

Design: Internal comparisons both between projects and within total sample. Descriptive data recorded under the study areas listed in Measures section.

Measures: Most data gathered by site visits using interviews, examination of agency records, and use of special research record forms. Separate data collected for the different study components.
   (1) General Process: Case studies of planning and programmes.
   (2) Project Goals: Unique project goals developed with each project, and their attainment assessed by research staff using interviews and examination of project records.
   (3) Cost Analysis: Monitoring of expenditure and income of different components and of whole projects.
   (4) Development of criteria for quality of case management. Coding of quality achieved by interviews with staff and examination of case records.
   (5) Project Management and Worker Burnout: Interviews and questionnaires to project staff.
   (6) Community Systems: Repeated measures of interviews with other agencies plus project records of activities.
   (7) Children: Repeated measures of children's problems using research records completed by project staff.
   (8) Adult client: Repeated measures of demographic data, nature of maltreatment, services received, improvements in functioning, propensity for future maltreatment, and of maltreatment during treatment. Standard research records completed by project staff.

Results: The results from the 12 volumes of the study report, which are listed below do not include the many descriptive results on project development.
   (1) Worker Burnout: significantly associated with worker variables of having a supervisory role, having worked in the agency for between 1 and 2 years, having poor leadership, poor communication, little or no opportunity for innovation, poor staff

support, minimum levels of involvement in decision making, little orientation, little job autonomy, poor job clarity, and medium and high levels of role observation.

(2) Quality of case management: at intake or overall was significantly associated with worker contact on day of receipt of report, use of multidisciplinary team, use of outside consultants, case manager handling case intake, referral source contacted for information, manager same ethnicity as client, manager professionally trained, manager trained more than once in child abuse, manager working with child abuse for more than 2 years, client interested in or responsive to treatment, length of time in project, the number of follow up contacts with client after end of service.

(3) Re-occurrence: of abuse during treatment was 30% and was significantly associated with the seriousness and type of original maltreatment. It was highest in the most serious cases of sexual abuse, and in cases of physical abuse with neglect. Also more common if treatment programmes of specialised counselling included lay services.

(4) Improvements: in at least one third of clients' problems were reported for 62% of cases, and in two thirds of problem for 21% of cases. Not much variation between types of problem though general stresses and behaviour towards child improved most often and general health least often.

Improvements in problem areas were significantly associated with different services as follows: (a) Lay services: self esteem. (b) Lay services or social work: general living stress. (c) Lay services or group work: sense of child as a person, adults' sense of independence. (d) Lay services, group work or parent education: understanding of self. (e) Lay group, or specialised counselling services: reactions to crisis situations. (f) Specialised drug or alcohol counselling: general health. (g) Couples and family counselling: negative association with anger management. Improvements were also associated with treatment longer than 6 months. The case types most likely to show improvement were physical abuse with neglect, emotional maltreatment, and severe household situations.

(5) Propensity for future maltreatment: at termination of services reductions in propensity was judged to have occurred in 42% of cases with rates varying from 25% to 56% between projects. Across the study those clients receiving lay therapy services were significantly more likely to be judged as having reduced propensity for abuse. The single exception was for cases of physical abuse where factors such as length of time in treatment were more important than the model of service. No client effects (including seriousness of maltreatment) were significantly associated with judged propensity for future maltreatment. There was also no association with judged quality of case management, years of experience of caseworkers, or whether the case-

worker approached the referrer for information. The only positive association was between the size of worker caseload and reduced propensity for maltreatment. Lay services, including Parents Anonymous and/or parent aide counselling were overall the most effective. No strong interaction effects between combinations of programme components were observed. Frequency of service was also not predictive of outcome, except for individual counselling.

(6) Children: were observed to have many and various developmental problems including eating problems, hyperactivity, tics and twitches, excess crying, aggression, apathy poor sense of self. Cognitive and language development was poor but not to the extent of the social and behavioural measures. For children receiving specialised services improvements were judged to have occurred through treatment. Most improvements reported in eating patterns, malnutrition and physical growth, pain dependent behaviour, apathy, affection, sense of self, and interactions with adults and peers. Greater improvements were reported in the least serious cases.

(7) Costs: of similar service packages. Cost efficiency was significantly associated with larger projects, with fewer supervisors and levels of management, and clarity of work procedures. These factors were not positively associated with job satisfaction. The cost per client of different services (in 1978 U.S. dollars) varied form $190 for parent education, $299 for Parents Anonymous, $377 for other lay therapies, $546 for group therapy, $767 for individual counselling, $882 for couples counselling, $1105 for individual therapy, to $1560 for family counselling. The cheaper services were also judged to be the most effective. Costs per successful outcome were calculated as $2,590 for lay therapies, $4,801 for group work, $4,462 for social work. Costs were dependent on the length of services offered.

Notes: The authors stress that the multi-component treatment projects evaluated, were chosen because of the interesting services provided, rather than because they were representative and so the results may not have general application. The authors also stress that there are no experimental controls and therefore the results must be interpreted with care. Many of the outcome measures are based on clinical judgement by project staff and are therefore not independent of the services provided. This is not totally mitigated by the reliability and validity measures employed in the study. In addition, it is important to note that not all of the measures are independent of each other. For example, one of the factors on which quality of case management was judged was the time between case referral and caseworker – client contact. The reported finding of a positive association between these measures is therefore not surprising.

Berkeley Planning Associates (1983), Daro (1987)

THE NATIONAL CLINICAL EVALUATION STUDY

Sample: 986 families served by 19 demonstration projects for the treatment of child abuse and neglect for which research forms were completed between October 1979 and October 1981. (1) 4 projects focused on cases of sexual abuse (26% of study sample). (2) 4 projects focused on adolescent maltreatment (29% of study sample), (3) 3 projects on substance abuse, (16% of sample), (4) 4 projects on remedial services for maltreated children (14% of sample), (5) 4 projects on child neglect (16% of sample). The average family included 1.3 adults and 1.7 children. The number of children per family differed according to type of abuse: families receiving remedial services had 1.1 children on average, families involved in sexual abuse or adolescent maltreatment had 1.5 children on average, and neglect families had an average of 2.6 children.

Focus: Child and family functioning.

Objectives: (1) Sexual abuse projects: 3 projects aimed to change behaviour and family functioning while the 4th emphasized stabilizing the situation so that treatment could occur. (2) Adolescent projects: 3 projects aimed to change behaviour and family functioning while the 4th aimed to make parents more effective. (3) Substance abuse projects: all 3 projects aimed to change individual and family functioning and behaviour. One of the projects was mainly concerned with the adolescent victims of abuse. (4) Remedial services: all 4 projects aimed to enhance the children's welfare and development through direct work and through the enabling of parents. (5) Child neglect: 3 projects aimed to provide services to support parents in their parenting role, while a 4th focuses directly on changing family functioning.

Programme: (1) Sexual abuse projects: methods included social support, with individual and group therapy, family counselling, modified Alcoholics Anonymous programme, social casework with sexual therapy and educational services, supportive psychotherapy and symptom relief during disclosure. (2) Adolescent projects: temporary shelter, stress relief and treatment and skills training to develop individual and family coping, family casework, counselling, psycho-dynamic family systems therapy. (3) Substance abuse projects: structural family therapy and direct treatment of victims. (4) Remedial Services: direct remedial work with children, therapeutic pre-school with education, skill training and psychotherapy for children, parent education and skills training and family systems therapy. (5) Child Neglect Projects: use of professional and lay services providing parents with

emotional support, education, problem resolution, therapy based on social learning and family systems theories, specialised medical and social work services, referral to community services.

Design: Repeated measures to allow univariate descriptions, analysis of bivariate association and multiple variate regression analyses controlled for non service factors.

Measures: Demographic data on clients and clinical judgements of client's problem areas, the severity and type of abuse, acknowledgement of abuse and compliance in treatment. Data on length and nature of services, staff characteristics, legal measures, and reasons for service termination. Clinical judgements (some by independent raters) of progress of children, adults, and families, were noted in a variety of problem areas as well as, difficulties in treatment, recurrence of abuse in treatment, and reduced propensity for future abuse defined as somewhat or very unlikely to occur. Most measures taken at case referral and at service termination. Some cases artificially terminated for purposes of the study. Data and results reported both in terms of families and individual members.

Results: The correlations between the main outcome measures were: Overall Progress to Reduced Propensity 0.46; Overall progress to Lack of Re-occurrence of abuse 0.44, Reduced Propensity to Lack of Reincidence 0.27. Potential for future maltreatment was influenced by the fact that only 40% of all the sample children were residing in the same household and with the same caretaker as at intake.

(1) Neglect Cases: (a) Overall Progress in 53% of cases. Positively associated with client compliance, and receipt of family counselling. Negatively associated with substance abuse. 16% of variance explained by service variables, 8% by problems in intake. (b) Reduced Propensity in 30% of cases. Positively associated with compliance, receipt of group or family counselling. Negatively associated with substance abuse, service variables, client compliance, and problems at intake which all accounted for between 7% and 8% of the variance. (c) No Re-occurrence of abuse in 34% of cases. Positively associated with some types of maltreatment. Negatively associated with less than 12 months treatment of individual group counselling. Service variables accounts for 7% of the variance and maltreatment characteristics for 9%.

(2) Emotional Maltreatment Cases: (a) Overall Progress in 54% of cases. Positively associated with compliance. Negatively associated with less than 12 months treatment. Service variables explained 13% of the variance and compliance 5%. (b) Reduced Propensity in 27% of cases. Positively associated with compliance, receipt of group counselling. Negatively associated with less than 6 months treatment, some

types of maltreatment, client age between 21 and 30 years. Service variables accounted for 9% of the variance, and maltreatment characteristics for 10%. (c) No Recurrence of abuse in 25% of cases. Positively associated with number of types of maltreatment. Negatively associated with less than 12 months treatment, and receipt of group treatment. Maltreatment characteristics accounted for 14% of the variance, service variables for 10%, and problems at intake for 9%.

(3) Sexual Abuse Cases: (a) Overall Progress in 69% of cases. Positively associated with compliance, some types of maltreatment, receipt of group counselling. Negatively associated with receipt of support services, less than 6 months treatment, client age between 31 and 40 years. Service variables explained 16% of the variance, and compliance 30% of the variance. (b) Reduced Propensity in 64% of cases. Positively associated with compliance. Negatively associated with number of types of maltreatment. Compliance accounted for 17% of the variance, and maltreatment characteristics for 10%. (c) No Re-occurrence of abuse in 81% of cases. Positively associated with female adult clients, and some maltreatment types. Maltreatment characteristics accounted for 15% of the variance, and service variables for 9%.

(4) For Adolescents: (a) Overall Progress was negatively associated with emotional maltreatment and neglect, the receipt of medical services, being aged between 11 and 13 years. (b) Reduced Propensity was associated with emotional abuse or neglect, moderate or severe harm from abuse, some types of treatment, casework counselling. Negatively associated with being aged between 11 and 13 years, the number of socio-emotional problems, and physical abuse. (c) No Re-occurrence was associated with neglect or emotional abuse, severe harm, number of types of maltreatment, personal skill development classes. Negatively associated with receipt of temporary shelter, less than 18 months treatment.

(5) For children: (a) Overall Progress was positively associated with therapeutic day care, supervised parent child interactions, individual or group counselling, treatment of between 7 and 12 months. Negatively associated with emotional abuse, number of socio-emotional problems, less than 6 months treatment. (b) Reduced Propensity was positively associated with receipt of therapeutic day care. Negatively associated with number of socio-emotional or health problems, neglect or emotional abuse, some types of abuse. (c) No Re-occurrence was positively associated with emotional abuse, neglect, number of types of abuse, socio-emotional or health problems, receipt of medical services. Negatively associated with less than 12 months treatment, receipt of therapeutic day care, number of developmental problems.

(6) For Infants: (a) Overall Progress negatively associated with treatment of less than 6 months. (b) Reduced Propensity positively associated with

physical abuse cases. Negatively associated with cognitive development problems, some types of abuse. (c) No Re-occurrence positively associated with some types of abuse, receipt of medical services. Negatively associated with physical abuse cases.

(7) The costs in thousands of dollars per 100 cases provided with a full therapeutic multi-component service varied as follows. (a) Individual counselling: Sexual abuse $798, Adolescents $1,079, Substance abuse $948, Neglect $988. (b) Family Counselling: Sexual abuse (with individual counselling) $934, Adolescents $806, Substance abuse $816, Remedial Services $914, Neglect $978. (c) Individual Counselling plus children's or youth services: Adolescents $1,342, Neglect $1,017. (d) Family Counselling plus children or youth services: Adolescents $1,069, Remedial Services $1,453, Neglect $958. (e) Group counselling: Sexual abuse $794. (f) Family plus Group Counselling: Remedial Services $1,035, rising to $1,575 with children's services.

Notes: Outcome data on physical abuse cases not included as small sample size. The authors stress that by controlling for non service factors, the results became conservative with respect to the impact of different services on similar client groups. Reliability measures were adopted but the use made of clinical judgements for data collection can not rule out confounding of independent and dependent variables. Also it is not possible to assess the long term validity of assessments of progress or propensity for future maltreatment.

Bowen Centre (1975)

A Demonstration in Child Protective Services

Sample: 35 families of 30 adults and 162 children served by the project in its first 6 years. Referrals of the most socially and emotionally deprived cases of child neglect. No referral refused on basis of severity of problem. Families characterised as having frequent crises, marital problems, mental illness, child developmental delay and previous failed involvement with agencies.

Focus: Functioning of total family.

Objectives: Improved parental functioning so that children can remain at home. Enable children to develop appropriately.

Programme: Multi-disciplinary team with social workers as key workers and a major contribution from student volunteers. 25 staff served 35 families, providing multiple services for over at least one year and sometimes for 3 or 4 years. Casework: to assess, involve and plan other services, included material help, medical care, and intensive advocacy for use of community services. Health Care: to motivate families to use facilities. Day Care: to provide children with specially designed treatment and learning programmes. Group Work: for children (and later adults) for social, academic, and manual skills. Pupil Support: tutoring and visits to school to motivate children towards schools. Educational Therapy: intensive work for older children at risk of delinquency. Also Emergency Shelter Care, Foster Care, and Homemaker services.

Design: Descriptive outcomes on case series.

Measures: Descriptive accounts of parent, child, and family progress in quality of relationships, control of aggression, general functioning, and family stability at 4 year follow up.

Results: Many examples of general improvement in the families' functioning and child development. Improvements maintained in all families followed up.

Notes: Report gives detailed descriptions of clients and services provided.

Dougherty (1983)

THE HOLDING ENVIRONMENT: BREAKING THE CYCLE OF ABUSE.

Sample: 30 families indicating neglect or risk of physical abuse, involved in a family multi-component programme in the first ten months of its operation. 18 of the families remained in treatment, dropout seemed to be related to the extent of problems. Children were all pre-school with a modal age of 4 years. They displayed high levels of anxiety, clinging and withdrawn behaviour and usually had at least 6 months developmental delay. Most referrals were from social services, but also from education, housing and medical agencies and 25% were self referrals. Parents were predominantly single, of lower than average socio-economic status, socially isolated and with a history of bad or abusive relations with their own parents; 50% were white and 50% black.

Focus: Functioning of mothers and their children.

Objectives: To provide a holding environment for the family based on Winnicott's work on problems of children arising from poor object relations, where parents perceive child as a need satisfying object. Holding environment aims to increase parents' self esteem and improve their understanding and parenting; to provide children with a consistent, safe structured environment and so promote growth; to achieve greater individuation and self reliance; to produce better parent child relations, and a less abusive caretaking situation.

Programme: Families attended programme twice per week. Self reliance in transport encouraged. Day started with short playtime of parents with children for interaction and observation. Then parents attended discussion group which developed into (1) group therapy with the therapist enabling the exploration of parents' feelings in a safe environment with some limit setting of acting out behaviour and, (2) parenting class, where problems seen as principally emotional rather than lack of factual knowledge. Also task mastery groups to develop self esteem, independence, and problem solving and to counter greed and hostility through successful accomplishment of tasks and activities. Lunch was provided to help gratify oral dependency needs and encourage socializing. Children had a therapeutic nursery with generous physical contact and opportunities for regression, acting out of feelings, development of self control by simple classification and consistency. Parents spent some time in nursery to learn new discipline techniques through role modelling and from learning by doing. Reference also made to home visits and to individual therapy for children and parents.

Design: Descriptive outcomes on case series.

Measures: Therapist ratings of children's' sociability, willingness to share, and impulse control. Therapist ratings of parents' relationship with children, use of physical punishment, awareness of role as mother, use of physical care and spontaneous affection.

Results: 12 out of 18 families in the programme made significant improvements on all variables. Slower improvement in mothers' awareness of children being separate people with separate needs. Quickest improvements in physical care. Children reported as improving in concentration, participation and cooperation with staff and peers, verbal skills, and general social behaviour.

Notes: Although the outcome measures are not independently assessed, the author provides much detailed description of the case outcomes. Few details provided of families that did not remain in treatment.

Fontana and Robinson (1976)

A MULTI-DISCIPLINARY APPROACH TO THE TREATMENT OF CHILD ABUSE.

Sample: 62 abusive and neglectful mothers referred by Child Welfare and treated in first 2 years in project at New York Foundling Hospital. All were single and most had abusive backgrounds. Psychiatric descriptions included dependency, depression in 18 cases, passive aggression in 16 cases, sociopathic in 6 cases, schizophrenic in 7 cases. Precipitating factors to abuse included drugs, alcohol, marital problems, unemployment, financial problems, and mental illness.

Focus: Functioning of mothers.

Objectives: Providing services to keep family together and to offer ongoing support where this is not possible. Sub-objectives to provide sympathy, encouragement, and general emotional support; reduce demands and stressors on mothers; model appropriate child handling skills; develop human network of support, particularly for times of crisis.

Programme: 3 to 4 months residential treatment followed by up to a year's after care in the home for up to a year. 8 to 10 mothers with children in residence at any one time. Thorough psychosocial evaluation to produce individual treatment plan. Emphasis on modelling and supportive interaction. Social work assistant acted as a friend and a link to community services. Group mother acts in a similar way to a homemaker, and provided an appropriate role model. Psychiatrist offered individual and group therapy. Video taping to provide feedback to parents in training. Psychologist offered stimulation and encouraged positive mother-child relations. Children received play therapy. After care involved weekly visits by a nurse and twice weekly by social work assistant to the home. Also weekly group therapy.

Design: Repeated measures on case series.

Measures: Parents' view of helpfulness of programme, and whether improvements in their relationship with their partner. Measures of reductions in stress factors and of children's motor and speech development. Changes in height and weight. Placement outcomes.

Results: 40 out of 62 families remained intact and this contained relatively more dependent depressive mothers than average. 44 mothers felt they had been helped and 30 of these maintained custody of their children. 12 mothers felt they had not been helped of which only 5 kept custody. 20 families moved into improved housing, 7 became employed, 9 showed improved family relations. Child care, patience, and self control were considered the most useful component skills and the most important factor in achieving these was relationship to the social work assistant. All the children showed growth and development within weeks of admission.

Green et al (1981)

FACTOR ASSOCIATED WITH SUCCESSFUL AND UNSUCCESSFUL INTERVENTION WITH CHILD ABUSIVE FAMILIES

Sample: 79 parents in cases of physical abuse cases who received more than 6 therapy sessions at the Brooklyn Family Centre. Parents were mostly women who had mean age of 28 years, were 57% black, 21% Hispanic and 20% white, and were socially and economically deprived. 55 given psychiatric diagnosis: 44% personality disorder, 8% neurosis, and 12% psychosis. Personality factors seen as a primary cause of abuse in three quarters of the sample Nearly half had a history of being abused themselves. Half of households were single mothers. Children had a mean age of 5 years and had been seriously abused, as measured by degree of child protective action by legal and welfare agencies. A third had physical, developmental, or psychiatric problems. A quarter had been sexually abused. Only a few neglect cases.

Focus: Parental functioning.

Objectives: Improving the child care environment.

Programme: Parents received counselling, psychotherapy, telephone advocacy, and home visiting from parent aides, a psychologist, and social workers. Also a parents' group and counselling and individual psychotherapy for the children. Majority of service provided by graduate social work students.

Design: Repeated measures on case series.

Measures: Therapists assessments of parental self awareness and insight, inter-professional relations and empathy, enjoyment of child and degree of role reversal and misperception of child, scapegoating, child care, household management.

Results: Significant improvements on most measures. Improvements not significant for decrease in child abuse and scapegoating, depression, nor for increases in general parenting and interpersonal relations. 40% improved slightly, 28% appreciably. Degree of improvement significantly related to parents receiving over 12 months of treatment, having entered treatment voluntarily, acceptance of problem, and use of the extra home based services available. Improvements less likely where physical abuse more serious, where there had been a previous history of abuse and where there had been a history of abuse and where there were inappropriate expectations of the child.

Notes: Authors suggest that the results are consistent with the findings of the large U.S. demonstration studies showing greatest improvements for those receiving lay services. Also the policy suggestion that most effort should be directed at parents somewhere between the well motivated and the incorrigible. Article does not explore the optimum length of treatment seeming to be more than 12 months but less than 18 months. Authors provide discussion of client profiles and amenability to treatment.

They acknowledge methodological shortcomings of subjectivity of ratings, lack of experimental controls and no follow up outcome data.

Laughlin and Weiss (1981)

AN OUTPATIENT MILIEU THERAPY APPROACH TO TREATMENT OF CHILD ABUSE AND NEGLECT PROBLEMS.

Sample: The evaluators of the 2 year programme consulted 80 project cases from an annual total of 900 Child Protection Service (CPS) cases. Not clear how many CPS cases were referred to project in the 2 years and how the research sample of 80 was selected apart from being 'worst cases'. Sample was poor and isolated families.

Focus: Social isolation of parents.

Objectives: Overall goal couched in terms of improving service delivery rather than change in families. Specific goals were to strengthen bonds in dysfunctioning families and to create support systems around them.

Programme: A community centre programme with an emphasis on countering isolation by fostering new relationships. Article stresses resistance of families and thus initial focus on outreach once they are referred. To establish a relationship with family workers the project (a) focused on material needs, (b) avoided talk of abuse, (c) was open and non-judgemental to the families, (d) re-defined troubles as those of isolation and insufficient resources. At intake, transport provided which enabled client worker relations. Later families were encouraged to use public transport with costs being reimbursed. Little detail given of the family and group therapy, but approach was to 'connect' family members to each other and to other families. Craft group for developing enriching skills and also to learn about sexualization. Mothers encouraged to organise their own social activities. Children's' centre for stimulation of children and relief of parents as well as to train mothers as volunteers aides, with lessons in child development and group supervision of child handling, and the award of certificates after successful training. Some families of 2–3 year old children had Family Home Child Programme for mother/child. The child and craft groups were often used as enticement in recruiting families into therapy.

Design: Control group of 89 non project CPS cases. Not clear how selected. Not stated whether samples were followed prospectively, or whether their records were selected and investigated retrospectively.

Measures: Client engagement rate, child removal rate, re-abuse rate.

Results: Client engagement: 85% for treatment, 25% for those CPS cases referred to other treatment services. Child removals 22% for treatment, 37% for controls. Re-abuse: 10.8% for treatment 26.9% for controls.

Notes: Few details about treatment methods particularly group therapy and "Family Home Child Programme" or about case characteristics. Interesting insights into approaches to the client such as ways of initially engaging the client, children's nursery as enticements to therapy, and training mothers as volunteer aides as a positive method of parent education. Ordinary parenting classes focus on parents' own children and so necessarily focus on parental inadequacy.

Lightfoot et al (1983)

THE PARENT AND CHILD TREATMENT PROGRAM (PACT)

Sample: All 83 families served by PACT in the first 2.5 years of operation in New York City. Families were from the minority unemployed urban poor. Under a fifth of famlies were white. There were a variety of relationship problems including marital violence, social isolation, addiction in 63 cases, mental illness in 26 cases. Over half were married or cohabiting. All had at least one child under 7 years. In 25% of cases children were subject to moderate or severe physical chastisement and 21% were injured in some other way. A recently referred group of children in the sample were mostly subject to deprivation although most children experienced some form of neglect. Cases were referred from child care agencies and legal and health agencies as well as the PACT parent organisation of the New York Medical Colleges Centre for Comprehensive Health Practice (CCCHP).

Focus: Functioning of children and parents including problems of substance abuse as tertiary prevention of child abuse.

Objectives: Intervention targets specified for each case. Predominant targets were family relations 98%, health 93%, substance abuse 88%, education and work and income 75%, housing 63%, legal involvement 58%, friendship and leisure 83%. Child focused targets were health 84%, nutrition 76%, development 84%, discipline 69%, peer interaction 51%, school 39%, clothing 27%.

Programme: Initial screening interviews followed by medical care, substance abuse treatment of counselling and sometimes detoxification, counselling in all target areas, parent group to discuss child rearing, structured play for children to remedy behaviour problems, and guided parent child interaction for particularly dysfunctional dyads. Average attendance in treatment was 1.6 times per week. Average length of treatment 56 weeks. Staff included PACT psychiatrists and social workers and specialists from CCHP.

Design: Repeated measures (pre and post test) on case series.

Measures: Codings of problems at intake, life event stresses during treatment, re-occurrence of abuse. Repeated assessment of children's' development. Outcome measures of therapist codings of problems in finance, social isolation, substance abuse, inter adult interaction, child control, parent-child role reversal.

Results: Some reduction in rates of abuse. Most re-occurrence for emotional abuse, followed by neglect and physical abuse. Re-occurrence was often of serious abuse, particularly for physical abuse. More re-occurrence in cases with initially serious physical abuse and with multiple types of abuse. In targeted problems there was greater negative than positive change. Negative changes in residence such as moving into substandard housing was correlated with re-abuse. High levels of service utilization was correlated with less serious levels of re-abuse. There was no correlation between type of initial abuse and type of substance abuse. In single parent families maltreatment was correlated with the number of children in the house.

Notes: Authors attribute lower rates of re-occurrence of physical abuse to its greater specificity over neglect and emotional abuse. They also suggest that the lack of improvement in targeted areas was partially due to lack of training for workers in family intervention. Authors optimistic about impact of programme despite limited improvements in sample. Article discusses organisational and confidentiality issues arising in negotiations with the Child Protection Service.

Lutzker (1984), Lutzker and Rice (1984, 1987)

PROJECT 12 WAYS: AN ECO BEHAVIOURAL TREATMENT PROGRAM.

Sample: (1) From 1984 papers: 50 randomly sampled cases from the 150 served in first year of operation and terminated prior to January 1981. All cases referred by Southern Illinois Department of Child and Family Services (DCFS). Two distinct referral criteria, (a) Child Protection Service clients because of actual risk of abuse/neglect. (b) Single young mothers who fall below the poverty line. In Fiscal year 1980 the treatment cases consisted of 45% prevention cases, 40% neglect, and only 15% other more direct forms of abuse. Not stated how many of the prevention cases were the single young mothers, though all of sample was poor and rural, predominantly female. In the year of this evaluation all 27 counties of Southern Illinois provided referrals. In 1981 it was just 9 counties. DCFS were the only source of referrals and the articles suggest that the agency refers most of its difficult cases. Control group of 47 child protection cases not served by the project, matched by field offices in order to reduce geographical bias in case types.

(2) From 1987 paper: All 352 families who had completed Project 12-ways services from July 1979 to June 1984, plus a comparison group of 358 families receiving standard child protection services.

Focus: Functioning of mothers.

Objectives: Child abuse prevention. Philosophy of treatment is that (1) child abuse is multi-determined and needs a variety of treatment approaches. (2) Assessment and treatment need to go beyond home to the different settings where children are found. However, in 1980 only 11% got 'multiple setting' behaviour management.

Programme: An 'In House' eco behavioural treatment programme with 15 different components of training and behaviour modification. Main components: (1) Parent training (42% clients). (2) Reinforcements, time out, use of token economies. For parents with children older than 8, token reinforcement programmes. Parents of children less than 3 years of age received less structured training. (3) Basic skills training for children. In 21% of cases this was to aid lagged development, e.g. toilet training, shoe tying. Useful in demonstrating to parent that change can be effected with children. (4) Stress reduction, assertiveness and self control (27% of cases). (5) Preventive services for single parents up to 1st four months of baby's life. Education (including didactic materials), stress reduction, money management and job finding. (6) Multiple setting training most frequently involving teachers in operating reinforcement systems.

In 1981, house safety, health training, money management, job finding, social support groups became major components, In addition to above, DCFS often provide other services such as homemakers. Project operated by counsellors who are students and graduate staff of the Behaviour Analysis and Therapy Programme at the Southern Illinois University. The reinforcement and stress reduction component has been evaluated separately by single case studies.

Design: (1) 1984 papers: Repeated measures matched controlled design. (2) 1987 paper: Repeated measures with comparison group.

Measures: Incidents of abuse known to Illinois State Central Registry. Frequency of services received. Number of project goals attained.

Results: (1) 1984 papers: Project 12 ways cases had one incident of abuse during treatment, and 4 post treatment, totalling 10% of sample. Recidivism negatively correlated with the number of Project 12 goals achieved. Comparison group had 5 incidents during treatment period and 5 post treatment, totalling 21% of control sample. Result statistically significant at 5% level. Analysis of covariance shows that field offices served by project had significantly fewer cases of child abuse. Also a highly significant negative correlation between frequency of neglect and number of client hours of Project 12 services in different field offices. Prevention cases had only one reported incident in a minimum 16 month follow up of all cases served in fiscal year 1980.

(2) 1987 paper: Recidivism for Project 12-Ways families was consistently lower than that of comparison families for treatment years 1980, and 1982 to 1984, but about equal for 1981. Overall recidivism was 21.3% for Project 12-Ways, and 28.5% for comparison families, which is statistically significant. The differences between project and comparison group recidivism seems to decline over time.

Notes: 1st arricle isolates factors which are thought to have contributed to success. There were high levels of compliance with treatment regimes – clients found the social friendship aspect of programme rewarding and compliance leads to quick termination of CPS status. No long term follow up by agreement with clients, because total invasiveness of programme might undermine subsequent ability to cope on their own. Successes are attributed by article to: (1) project relations with DCFS at all levels (state, region, field. (2) Project functions within the Behaviour Analysis Programme at the Southern Illinois University with well trained and supervised staff. (3) Behavioural approaches which are suitable for clients, many of whom are not verbal and appreciate action oriented treatment. (4) In-home service.

It is noted that clients do best when offered only 1 or 2 components at a time, despite large numbers of components available. Both 1984 articles use case studies to help provide detail of the many treatment components. Second article cautions interpretation of results because of possible referral bias. Little data provided on the characteristics of the control sample. 1987 paper concentrates on recidivism data.

Lynch and Roberts (1982)

CONSEQUENCES OF CHILD ABUSE.

Sample: Total sample of 42 abused children and 27 siblings from 40 families admitted to project between 1966 and 1974 at the Park Hospital in Oxford. The children were aged between 1 month and 3.5 years. Most were under one. They had experienced serious physical abuse in 23 cases and moderate abuse in 19 cases according to the classification of NSPCC child abuse registers. Half the children had been in serious life threatening situations and half displayed frozen watchfulness. Infants were often discontented and fussy. Older children were often aggressive and attention seeking. 49% were developmentally delayed particularly in speech. 18% showed growth retardation. Parental age varied from 16 to 36 years. The average age for mothers was 24 and for fathers was 26. Over half of the mothers had experienced emotional illness since the birth of their child and even more had earlier problems. Difficulties in all areas of life were prevalent including health and marital and sexual relations. 20% lived in substandard housing and the sample was of lower than average socio economic status although not particularly deprived. The majority of families were white though there was a Chinese family and 5 mixed marriages.

Focus: Individual and family functioning and relationships.

Objectives: To provide total family care, to improve disturbed family relationships and to promote parent child relationships. To provide a safe place of escape from normal pressures, to help improve parents' social relationship skills and their enjoyment of interacting with others.

Programme: Residential unit with links to the main hospital to which families are admitted for an average of 3 weeks. There is provision for 30 hospital inpatients and abuse families are only a proportion of these. Full assessment at intake. Family provided with total care within an undemanding routine and an informal atmosphere. Individual psychotherapy and marital therapy is provided in order to focus on disturbed family and marital relations. Group therapy focuses on socialization. Groups may also include parents of handicapped or chronically ill children and provide abuse parents with a relative view of their own problems. Practical support with child care also given. Children provided with play therapy, sometimes in the presence of parents, which enables children to have positive enjoyable experiences and for parents to learn to play with their children. Where parents, unable to care for their children they are supported in adjusting to alternative child placement. A follow up support service with a 24 hour hotline is provided and can continue for years after discharge from unit. Emphasis on a therapeutic relationship with the Unit rather than with particular professionals and members of staff.

Design: Outcome study of case series with an average of a four year follow up.

Measures: Formal test of linguistic and intellectual development. Medical assessment of physical growth and of neurological functioning. Ratings by hospital staff and children's teachers of behaviour disturbance and maladjustment. Parental interview to ascertain health and psychological problems. Assessment by research staff of the general child care environment. Also measures of re-abuse, social circumstances, family relations, social activities.

Results: 9 children in long term care, 16 under some form of compulsory order, 8 children were re-abused – one seriously. Half the parents reported medical and psychological problems. There were poor ratings of the home child environment in 13 of the 33 homes where the abused child was not in care, but 70% of these families had at least one 'problem free' child. 23% of all the abused children and 51% of siblings were problem free. Half of the school aged children showed no class room disturbances. Many parents had made good progress in their general life management. Factors significantly related to problem free children were uncomplicated pregnancy and birth, no prematurity, admission of child less than 2 years of age, high levels of language and intellectual abilities, fewer placements away. There was also a non significant association with small families. Siblings who were born after the abusive incident did best.

Notes: Book discusses the specific needs of the children that are often overlooked including language, learning and medical problems. Also stresses organisational aspect such as alternative placements, as children do badly when these fail. Overall the children who had established basic trust did best and this was not associated with any particular family characteristics.

Magura and Derubeis (1980), Willems and Derubeis (1981)

EFFECTIVENESS OF INTENSIVE PREVENTIVE SERVICES FOR ABUSED NEGLECTED OR DISTURBED CHILDREN – THE HUDSON COUNTY PROJECT.

Sample: Selected from clients referred to the Department of Youth and Family Services (DYFS). Screening by DYFS and by project staff to identify those at risk of reception into care within next two years. Used protocol that addressed (1) unmet needs of child and actual or potential harm experienced, (2) reasons for these, (3) family, community, agency resources available to deal with problems. Various exclusion criteria including current or planned placement. Sample considerably socio-economically disadvantaged but data do not suggest extreme dysfunction in family. Most common problems were neglect related.

Focus: Environmental stress of families at risk of children being taken into care.

Objectives: (1) Reduced frequency and length of placements away from home. (2) To improve social functioning and personal well-being of children and their parents to reduce family stress and preserve family integrity. Appendix lists 32 specific objectives relating to this. (3) Decrease length of agency involvement. (4) Achieve cost effectiveness. Project focused on environmental factors rather than psychosocial factors.

Programme: Programme of intensive, supportive services to multi-problem families. Most emphasis on environmental stresses, though parental inadequacies and client problems also addressed. Main features were low caseload, a special fund, legal advocacy, referral to other services and various types of groupwork.

Essential elements: Low caseload preventive services unit. Local expenditure fund with money for emergency fund (considered particularly useful). A materials fund for project activities. Legal advocacy for clients. Client groupwork. Development of community service resources. Work with clients based on establishing specific realistic goals and verbal contacts. Use of homemaker services, day care, adoption where necessary. Staff trained in group work methods. Adolescent and work enrichment group for girls; young mothers group; play/art therapy group for pre-school children; boys' activity and discussion group; and groups for acting out pre-teen youngsters which differed from others in being verbal and introspective rather than activity oriented. Caseworker spent much time in being a 'broker of services'.

Design: Repeated measures (pre and post-test) experimental design with random allocation to one experimental and one control condition.

Measures: The Childhood Level of Living Scale and another formal instrument for family functioning. Therapists views of case goals attainment. Clients satisfaction with service. Some measures only applied to experimental group. Agency records of placement and of case closure.

Results: At case closure experimental cases scored significantly higher than controls on measures of case goal achievement. For the experimental cases there was a statistically significant improvement in 11 of 13 problem areas in family functioning. Group differences in type rather than numbers of alternative placements. Treatment group in less statutory settings. More likely to be with relatives and with returns planned. Control group with less planned and less successful placements. Project cases had mean goal attainment score of 7 care goals at closure. Experimental families reported much higher rates of satisfaction with their worker. Correlations between client characteristics and outcomes were not statistically significant. Clients, goal achievements, and family functioning were related.

Notes: Article discusses (1) Use of existing Hudson County Staff. (2) Verbal contracts favoured over written. (3) Advantages of groupworker in leading to a better understanding of family dynamics through observation in a social setting and from workers learning about a greater number of families. (4) Team approach + group decision making with all workers having partial responsibility for clients of co-workers. (5) Staff training a crucial element of project. (6) Brokerage and advocacy role of caseworkers. (7) Project suffered from being over ambitious and from high staff turnover. (8) Evaluation suffered from gross outcome measures; could not distinguish project's strengths and weaknesses. However, project seen as successful.

Moore et al (1981)

EMOTIONAL RISK TO CHILDREN CAUGHT IN VIOLENT MARITAL CONFLICT – THE BASILDON TREATMENT PROJECT.

Sample: All 28 maritally violent couples with 66 children, comprising the case load of the project to date. Parents were on average in their early 30's and of lower than average socio-economic status. Average age of children 7 years. 45% of boys displayed anxiety and aggression and 37% of girls were under achieving at school. Parents scapegoated children as part of their own marital disputes.

Focus: Marital problems.

Objectives: To improve marital relationship in order to prevent further child abuse. To provide direct services to children to help mitigate the impact of abuse.

Methods: Specialised social work casework primarily in the home. Eclectic approach including task centred work with goal setting, time limited contracts with parents, and psychodynamic casework. Also play and painting for children and a play therapy group to help them ventilate their problems. Sequence of work: (1) joint interview with parent where it is explained that the worker's main client is the child. (2) Individual sessions with each parent. (3) Joint sessions with both parents to identify target areas and contracts. (4) Individual work with children.

Design: Description of case series with internal comparisons of multiple baselines.

Measures: Unspecified assessments of quality marital relationships and the incidence of violence.

Results: 7 families had further outbreaks of violence, 6 because separated or divorced, 26 displayed improvements in marital relationship and a decrease in marital violence.

Notes: No outcome data on children.

McBogg et al (1979a)

CIRCLE HOUSE RESIDENTIAL TREATMENT PROGRAMME.

Sample: 23 families involved in the residential programme between 1974 and 1977. Cases referred when abuse had occurred and foster care required. Probably the worst local Child Protection Service cases. 7 families resident for 6 months, 10 families for 3 months or less (because of high costs), 6 families participated with day attendance of adults and residence of children (as a further cost cutter).

Focus: Functioning of whole family.

Objectives: (1) To stop abuse through the provision of a safe environment where parents available but not directly responsible, (2) enhance bonds by avoiding separation, (3) provide intense milieu therapy with nurture, (4) improve child rearing. Diagnostic function of program is stressed.

Programme: Circle House in Denver offered residential treatment to abusive families. Children and parents lived in separate rooms. Meals provided an important occasion for intervention in parent child interactions. Main treatment components of nurturing milieu, models of communication, and excellent child care – latter considerably oriented to building self pride in children. Medical care used as opportunity to help parents be better parents by involving them in diagnosis and treatment. Parents took part in a variety of activities, children had play therapy and day care. Several other therapies and counselling groups for individuals and parent-child dyads to examine and vent feelings. Staff included para-professionals as well as secretaries, all of whom modelled relationships.

Design: Outcomes of case series.

Measures: Child placements away from home.

Results: 13 families reunited. 5 had parental rights terminated. 2 adoptions. 2 moved out of the state. No data provided for one case.

Notes: Authors suggest results are impressive given that 'worst cases'. For all children permanent plan made, and in a shorter time than would be normal in ordinary system. However, authors also state that residential care is most feasible as a diagnostic rather than treatment tool. Diagnosis is useful in planning and an opportunity to form therapeutic relations; constant interactions enable quick learning of interpersonal skills, living skills, and child care. Disadvantages of residential work is the effect of over concentration on faults rather than strengths. Also too many staff confuse families, and may undermine nurturing of child, and make consistency of approach harder to maintain. Greatest disadvantage seen is cost.

West and West (1979)

CHILD ABUSE TREATED IN A PSYCHIATRIC DAY HOSPITAL

Sample: 50 parents who were on at risk register for abuse but who had been referred primarily for psychiatric illness by doctors and psychiatrists. Data also provided on a sample of 50 non abuse children with 30 healthy mothers referred to the day hospital. Abusers were younger, had more family violence from childhood onwards, more unplanned pregnancies and were of lower intelligence. No differences reported in perinatal pathology, EEG's, verbal intelligence or social class, though more abusers lived in council housing.

Focus: Mothers.

Objectives: To determine how abusive parents differ from other psychiatric patients and healthy mothers and to use this information in a therapeutic setting to prevent abuse.

Programme: Day attendance at psychiatric hospital plus help in the home. Twice weekly group psychotherapy including behavioural methods. Parents meet children at lunchtime. Also 2 hour sessions a week when 'required to be with children'. Regular meetings with staff to 'thrash out' nursery problems. Staff children and less disturbed patients, provided role model of parenting behaviour. Monthly 'marital group'. 3 monthly developmental check of children by doctor. Liaison with health visitor and social worker. Case conferences held at centre to remind parents of seriousness of concern for children. Non attending abuse cases followed-up by visit if distressed, with practical help from health visitor, social worker or nurse. Family aides for some families.

Design: Outcome of case series.

Measures: Recurrence of abuse.

Results: No serious injury in treatment or follow-up. In whole 4 year period 4 'minor traumata' which equals an 8% re-abuse rate. Children taken into care from 2 families.

Notes: Few details of aims and methods of treatment such as group psychotherapy. Article discusses how findings differ from other studies. Psychiatric morbidity is seen as less important, and no difference found in perinatal pathology compared to control. Low re-abuse compared with other studies is attributed to extensive long term support and to the early referral due to the psychiatric illness. Families with long previous involvement with social work showed least success. This plus the social class distribution suggests to authors that they are seeing different parts of a spectrum of child abuse cases. The importance of health visitors and family aides in prevention is also discussed. Seen as crucial in focusing services on abusers who do not attend and avoid the hospital based services.

Wood (1981)

RESIDENTIAL TREATMENT FOR FAMILIES OF MALTREATED CHILDREN.

Sample: 29 cases referred by Child Protective Services and placed in programme in the first two years of operation. Most seem to be families with children temporarily in care.

Focus: Child, adults and child/parent dyads.

Objectives: To (1) increase parent-child intereaction by teaching discipline methods and increasing bonding, (2) help with parents personal/interpersonal problems, (3) reduce negative child behaviours.

Programme: A residential treatment home for abusing families. 5 families stay at a time and have a regime of activities, classes, and day care, focusing on improving parent-child interaction. Social services seem to use the facility mainly for rehabilitating families where children currently in care. Each family has private apartment and is assigned keyworker parent aide. Eating and recreation communal. Fathers expected to share child care. Parents have variety of activities in and out of the centre, as well as counselling/psychotherapy and 'quality time' with children. Extensive psychological assessment in the 1st week. Also skills classes and adult education class. Day care for children to help their development, but also to give parents an opportunity to observe and learn about their age-appropriate behaviour. Parents encouraged to take their children with them on outside activities. Confrontation/reinforcement of negative/positive behaviours respectively.

Design: Outcome of case series.

Measures: Agency records of placement of child and continuity of use of services.

Results: Out of 14 families completing programme 8 received no services after treatment. The 14 families completing programme had 9 children in care before, but only 4 families had children in care after programme. For 15 families not completing programme, data not given re number of children in care before program but 25% of their 30 children not at home at termination of treatment.

Notes: It is difficult to interpret whether the stated objectives of the programme were achieved. Firstly the reasons for the termination of services is unclear. Secondly, the families not completing the programme do not constitute a clear comparison group.

CHAPTER TEN

Routine Services and Special Service Initiatives

Background

The majority of studies considered in this review are concerned with the evaluation of a particular method of intervention. These are normally individual projects, which are new or innovatory in some way. The aim of the research is to examine and assess the efficacy of the method as a tool in treatment or prevention. There has been much less research attention directed at the routine child protection services. This situation has now begun to change as child protection systems become more developed and used to managing continuing large numbers of suspected child abuse cases. Child abuse is no longer a new phenomena where only experimental or demonstration programmes are of interest. Researchers and policy makers now realise the importance of studying the processes and outcomes of the systems that have been developed, are in routine use, consume considerable resources, and effect a large number of children and families.

This chapter reviews the few early outcome studies on routine child protection plus the more recent studies some of which are only just being completed. A few special intervention projects are also considered here, because their purpose is the development of service delivery, rather than the application of particular therapeutic techniques.

The usefulness of examining routine services is clear. Most cases of child abuse, or risk of abuse, are served by local professional staff, rather than by a special unit, or project. It might be argued that the research focus should be on special programmes where new therapeutic techniques can be tried, so that they can be adapted and employed by local routine services. But there are several reasons why this is not a sufficient research strategy.

First, the techniques developed in special programmes may rely on particular resources that are not typically available on a local basis. These may include physical facilities, certain staff-client ratios, or simply the potential to employ professionals from different disciplines within the same organisational framework, thus producing an inter-professional team that is not tenable in other contexts. Alternatively, it may be that a programme depends upon particular staff expertise, that may only have developed, from working in a specialist team.

Certain aspects of a project might produce general lessons which can be modified from a specialist to a routine service. However, there would still be a need for systematic study of the routine service, to see if the transition was successful. It is important to ensure that the techniques developed in specialist centres have been modified and applied appropriately to more routine casework. It is also necessary to test whether the techniques are still effective in their new context.

A related question is, whether users of special interventions are representative. Cases seen by the routine services provide a baseline: they make up the majority of child protection work and so define the nature of the problem. Child protection cases are by definition the cases that child protection services are dealing with and so must offer a better definition of the problem than an unknown sub-sample of cases referred to specialist services. A more fundamental baseline would be the range of relatively appropriate and inappropriate child care environments in the population, but virtually the only information currently available on the wider population is derived from retrospective recall studies on adults. The extent that there are unidentified cases of maltreatment in the community is, of course, important and studies of how child protection cases are identified, referred, and investigated should help to clarify this issue.

There are several other reasons why our knowledge of routine services is relevant to child abuse treatment interventions. Firstly, the procedural and legal systems and the policies within which they operate, provide the context for routine casework, and may make a larger impact on outcomes than any particular style or type of casework. Our knowledge of the efficacy of interventions in special centres, could then be seen as relatively unimportant, even if we improved the methodological bases of the studies considered in other chapters, and the quality of their reported results.

Secondly, the very ability to improve the quality of these evaluative studies, may depend on better information about routine work. This information could be used to clarify the conceptual confusion about definitions of child abuse and child protection which hampers the development of the evaluative studies. For example, the specification of research samples is often confused, and relies on operational definitions of abuse at different levels of child protection work such as placement on a child abuse register, the initiation of child care proceedings, or referral to a specialist agency.

Previous chapters in this volume, have reported that studies of special interventions do not often specify the nature of their sample, beyond demographic features and very general statements about the type of abuse involved. It is even more rare for these studies to specify, in any detail, the way in which their cases differ from, or are representative of, the local authority child protection caseloads. Even when studies specify the criteria for acceptance into a special programme, the authors and the project staff may simply not know the details of the population from which the sample is drawn, beyond knowing that referrals are relatively extreme or mild cases of child abuse and risk of abuse. Typically, special programmes control acceptance of clients – whether to accept referrals, rather than being able to actively choose cases from the wider population of child protection cases in a local community. There is, therefore, no basis for assuming that the cases in special programmes are at all representative of child abuse cases in social service teams, and that studies on their efficacy have any relevance to routine practice. Dingwall (1989) argues that for strategic reasons, one local child protection service in Britain referred less obviously serious cases to the local special child abuse unit. The special unit was valued for its ability to make powerful use of limited evidence in court rather than for the therapeutic services it offered to the more clear cut extreme cases of abuse (1989, p 41).

Another aspect of the importance of studying routine practice is the specification of appropriate outcome measures. Routine casework could be used to explore the main objectives of interventions, which could help to clarify the important parameters of change. This is not a trivial or simple issue. In child protection there are many competing rights and needs within families. Even if the best interests of the children are explicitly put first, it is not at all clear what these should be. They could be best served by keeping a child within the family of birth and maintaining the security of long standing emotional bonds or they could be best served by giving priority to physical safety at the expense of emotional needs, or by maximising social and development scores, as measured by standard psychological tests.

A related issue is the content of treatment programmes. The major issue for child protection work, is the process of assessment: does a child have a future in the birth family or does the child need to be placed with a substitute family on a permanent basis? Deciding between support of the child in the family of origin versus an alternative placement, is obviously problematic, because it is such a fundamental choice with so little middle ground. However, it is not usually a single one off decision. Casework management plans may have to be frequently changed as new events occur in the family or as certain legal child care actions succeed, fail, or are not attempted because of the poor quality of the evidence available, even if there are apparent high risks to the child. Casework decisions in this area are extremely complicated: firstly, because we do not have the technical knowledge to predict how a child's circumstances will develop following different placement decisions, and secondly, because there is little clarity in our society about the implicit cultural and moral values involved in these decisions. Research on such questions and on the outcomes for the child, are obviously central to the development of child protection work.

Complex decisions have also to be made about more immediate or short term risks. The low level of accuracy now possible in assessing such risks, and the opposing costs for children of being at risk of further maltreatment, or of losing their family, puts the professionals in an unenviable position. Only research on the decisions and outcomes for the vast majority of cases, will provide the context for critical judgement of professional casework: when children known to be at risk are left at home, as in the case of Jasmine Beckford, or when children are suddenly removed from their homes as happened for many suspected cases of child sexual abuse, in Cleveland.

The efficacy of therapy is obviously part of the decision making process. If a therapy proves to be highly effective, then this will alter the cost benefit equation in temporary and permanent placement practice. Furthermore, statutory child protection services provide the setting in which therapy is offered. This is acknowledged implicitly by studies that discuss compliance with treatment and the power of threat of legal proceedings. This aspect may positively or negatively effect the impact of the more therapeutic components of the service. On the other hand, the practical tasks of child protection work may leave little or no time for direct therapeutic work. The professional workers may spend the majority of their time managing the child protection system by making assessments, removing children into care, and liaising with foster parents and professional colleagues.

Research Studies

First, early studies of routine child protection services are described. This is followed by more recent studies examining the factors related to client outcomes, and then recent studies on decision making and the processes of case management. Finally, reference is made to a few studies exploring different roles or developments of routine services. Studies of the identification of cases and the social policy issues of child abuse definitions are not considered here. Interested readers are referred to Bacon and Farquar (1983), Dingwall et al (1983), Giovannoni and Becerra (1979), Gough et al (1993), Nelson (1984) and Parton (1985). The studies described in this chapter are listed in Table 10.1–10.4.

Early Studies

Early work on routine child protection is described by Stone and Stone (1983), Hensey et al (1983), Heap (1984), Lawder et al (1984), Magura and Moses (1984), King and Taitz (1985), Rivara (1985), Corby (1987), Gough et al (1987, 1993). A more recent study, mostly concerned with risk assessment, but with some outcome data on placement has been reported by Pritchard (1991).

The studies tend to give a few details about the services offered, the decision making process, or the characteristics of clients. Instead, they typically concentrate upon describing the outcomes in terms of the functioning of clients and of placement decisions. The studies provide information on the general outcomes of cases and these are often quite poor. Hensey et al (1983) found that 19 out of 26 children returned home from care had at least one major functional problem. The lack of

TABLE 10.1

Routine Services: Early Studies

Study	Programme	Sample/ Size	Population	Design	Main Measures
Corby (1987)	Social work casework	n = 25	Child abuse	Descriptive	Worker interviews/ client records
Gough et al (1987, 1993)	Routine casework	n = 202	Preschool child protection	Descriptive	Case records
Heap (1984)	Post crisis support	n = 14	Abused children	RPM	Appropriateness of service, child outcomes
Hensey et al (1983)	Child protection	n = 50	Physically abused children	POST	Children's development, re-abuse
King and Taitz (1985)	Routine services	n = 95	Child protection cases	RPM	Child height & weight
Lawder et al (1984)	Social work casework	n = 101	Multi problem families	PRPM	Case progress
Magura and Moses (1984)	Child protection casework	n = 250	CPS clients	POST	Client satisfaction, progress
Pritchard (1991)	Routine services	n = 60	Physical abuse/ neglect	Descriptive	Case records, placement
Rivara (1985)	Children in Crisis Centre	n = 71	Physical abuse	POST	Progress, attendance, re-abuse
Stone and Stone (1983)	Foster care	n = 64	Children RIC due to abuse	RPM	Placement, success

CP = Child protection; CPS = Child Protection Services; CPT = Child Protection Team; LFF = Levels of Family Functioning
POST = Post-test only; RPM = Repeated Measures including pre-test; PRPM = Repeated Measures post-test only

resolution of problems is also confirmed by Lawder et al (1984). They found that resolution was particularly difficult when there was a lack of compliance and agreement with the workers. Need of material assistance was the most easily resolved issue. Rivara (1985) reported taht only 13% of families made good progress and that in 30% of cases the children were re-abused. Magura and Moses (1984) were more encouraging, as clients reported satisfaction and positive results from the service provided, even though problems often remained for the family.

The information provided by studies on the proportion of children being received into long term care and the differential outcomes in child functioning and progress, is particularly relevant to the development of policy. The conclusion from several early studies was that children received into care and placed in substitute families do better even though these may be the most serious cases (Hensey et al, 1983; King and Taitz, 1985). Children returned home from care did particularly badly (Hensey et al, 1983). It would be simplistic to deduce that children fare better in foster care and that this option should therefore be preferred. Without more detailed case information it is not possible to rule out other hypothesis. It may for example be that children received into long term care, are clear victims of extreme physical abuse. Less straightforward cases may have more negative emotional overtones and produce worse outcomes for children, as well as having less chance of leading to a successful alternative family placement.

A few of the studies looked in more detail at the management process. Heap (1984) assessed the appropriateness of services provided and concluded that after one year most families were still receiving assistance, but that it was not appropriate. Heap also examined the degree to which care plans were carried through. A similar approach was used by Corby (1987) and Gough et al (1987, 1993) who examined the broad nature and length of child protection work as well as the placement outcomes achieved. The study by Stone and Stone (1983) also provides descriptive information about placements and reports high rates of placement breakdown.

Corby (1987) and Gough et al (1987, 1993) found that most of the intervention work was provided directly by social services departments or by facilities and organisations under their control. There was little use of psychological, psychiatric, or paediatric services. This corrects an impression of the high involvement of these professions, from the literature on special interventions. For social workers child protection is a main part of daily work and of their statutory responsibilities. Special projects are more likely to involve psychological and medical experts who have developed a particular interest in the field, but the interest of these medical and psychological experts are neither representative of their professions. Nor are their cases representative of the main bulk of child protection casework.

Corby reported that nearly a quarter of the children in his sample were removed into permanent alternative care. These were cases where there was initial serious abuse or reoccurrence of abuse. In Gough et al's study the sample was the total caseload of new pre-school cases children on the local abuse register over a 15 month period. The sample was drawn from the most deprived part of the community, with many incidents of parents being unable to cope with their child care responsibilities. Gough et al reported that 10% of cases went to permanent alternative care, although this took a long time to be achieved and followed concerns about general ability of the original parents to cope with the care of their child. Rarely was it due to actual serious abusive assaults, even if that had been part of the original referral. The alleged perpetrators had often moved away from the home, and even if they had not, the children remained or were returned home. The result was that most of the children who were permanently removed from their homes came from single mother families who were perceived as failing.

This section is entitled early studies because they represent some of the earlier attempts to describe child protection practice. Policy makers and managers are now aware that they need more regular information on practice and what were simple registers of abuse cases are now becoming child protection management information systems (Gough, 1992, Social Work Services Group, 1992), which will slowly lead to more sophisticated research on routine work. This process is developing in North America, Britain and Australia, and is a component of some of the studies considered in the section on decision making, particularly the study by Thorpe (1991) which was part of a pilot project to develop a routine information system (see section on Decision Making).

Predicting Outcome

A few recent studies have attempted to predict the factors associated with the outcome of child protection services. The research focus can be the effects of different types of provision, the effects of different types of case presentation, or preferably, the complex interaction between services and children and families.

A study by Murphy et al (Murphy et al, 1991; Jellinek et al, 1992) was concerned with the outcomes of cases where there was a history of substance abuse. The sample were 206 consecutive child protection cases referred to the juvenile court, excluding sexual abuse cases. Alcohol or drug abuse was documented in a third of mothers and half of the families. The families were predominantly poor single parent families and most of the cases were of neglect.

Neither demographic variables or type of maltreatment were associated with alcohol or drug abuse. Substance abuse was associated with previous court or social service histories and current outcomes of non compliance with court ordered services. Nearly all the families (97%) who did not comply with services had their children removed into permanent alternative care. The probability of non compliance

TABLE 10.2

Routine Services: Predicting Outcome

Study	Programme	Sample/ Size	Population	Design	Main Measures
Famularo et al (1989)	Court ordered treatment	n = 136	Child maltreatment	POST	Substance abuse, treatment compliance
Gibbons, Gallagher and Bell (1992)	Routine casework	n = 170	Child protection cases	RPM + C	Agency records, interviews/tests of parents and children
Murphy et al (1991) Jellinek et al (1992)	Child protection	n = 206	Neglect/physical abuse, treatment compliance		Substance abuse, risk assessment

Design

POST = Post-test only; RPM = Repeated Measures including pre-test; PRPM = Repeated Measures post-test only;

+C = Control or comparison group; +PC = Control or comparison group but at post-test only

was even higher if the Court Investigator rated the risks to the child as high (80% of those with substance abuse and high risk rating rejected services compared to 57% of total substance abusers). The authors conclude that treatment of substance abuse may not ensure better case outcomes, but that attempts to assist the family are doomed to failure if the problem of substance abuse is not addressed. They also argue that the extensive prior child protection histories indicate that the families had been given many, may be too many, previous chances by the system. Whatever the truth of this, the 97% rate of permanent child removal subsequent to non compliance indicates a firm line being taken by the courts.

The authors also report on the time taken for permanent decisions to be taken on the placement of the children. The cases took an average of nearly three years from first official report of mistreatment to arraignment in court and then several more years until permanent arrangements had been made for those children permanently removed.

Famularo et al (1989) also report on the outcome of cases referred to juvenile court. Of 136 cases 87% received a treatment order, but compliance varied depending on the service required. Compliance rates for individual, family, or marital therapy varied from between 42% to 61%. Compliance for substance abuse treatment was only 21%. Substance abusers as a group had a compliance rate for treatments of any kind of 42% or only 34% if they abused multiple drugs, compared to a compliance rate of 62% for others. Compliance rates for cases of physical and sexual abuse were low, but were quite high (69%) for neglect cases. As compliance rates were lower for substance treatment facilities than for substance abusers as individuals (i.e. complying with other services), the issue of compliance is affected by the services or their perception rather than just the case type. As compliance seems to be so closely related to placement outcome for the child it is important that both case presentation and service response are examined by future research.

The argument for examining both services and case types is strengthened by research by Crittenden in Miami (1992, listed under special initiatives, Table 10.4). She found that many child protection case plans were not implemented within six weeks of being accepted by the courts and that failings on the service delivery side were more common than failure of families to take up services. In 33% of cases the caseworkers were too busy to make the referral, in 32% of cases the treatment facility had a waiting list, and in 29% of cases there was failure of family uptake. Crittenden also argues that even in the cases where there was lack of uptake of a service, this was often because of the treatment plans not taking sufficient account of the families' practical difficulties in attending appointments, finding carers for their children, or simply their ability to achieve or understand the treatment plans created for them. Crittenden's views are supported by Heap's (1984) earlier finding that most case plans were not appropriate or not implemented.

The most comprehensive outcome of child protection identified by this review is a ten year follow up of all 170 children placed on two English child protection registers in 1981 (Gibbons, Gallagher, and Bell, 1992). Other studies have examined the long term outcome of cases, but the focus has been predominantly on the long term consequences of abuse. The study by Gibbons et al was concerned with the interplay of child, family, and service variables on the long term outcomes for these cases. A group of comparison families was also recruited in order to assess how typical or atypical were any adverse outcomes in the registered group.

Findings of the study showed that both the registered and comparison children performed worse than population norms on measures such as child behaviour. No differences between the registered and comparison groups were reported for social class, ethnic background, children's abstract reasoning, children's fears and depressions, or general physical development. In general, however, the registered children had worse outcomes than the comparisons. Registered children were less likely to live with both biological parents, more likely to be economically disadvantaged. Registered children were generally unhappy, unpopular, aggressive, and disobedient. Girls were more antisocial and boys were more neurotic. They reported more use of and fear of physical chastisement in the home, and reported that mothers were less available to them and that fathers were less likely to keep their promises.

Baseline risk factors derived from features of the abuse, the child, and the family failed to predict the later outcome for registered children, including whether or not they were subsequently reabused. A quarter of children were known to have been reabused and this was also not related to general outcome.

Baseline risk factors were related to the length of social work service and whether legal measures of protection were invoked. Social work consisted of keeping in regular contact with the child and carer for long periods, monitoring the situation, liaising with other services, and providing practical help with frequent marital, financial, and housing crises. As also previously reported by Corby (1987) and Gough et al (1987, 1993), there was little use of more specialist therapeutic services. The only aspect of the social work or legal child protection service that was statistically related with outcome was that short intensive intervention was associated with better outcome, even after controlling for level of baseline risks. Referral to adult psychologist or psychiatrist was also related to better outcome.

Nearly a third of the children were in long term care but these children had no better outcomes despite having much improved material circumstances. These children did have slightly greater baseline risks, but the new parents were also more punitive than other parents of registered children. Gibbons et al suggest that it should not be assumed that the new parents are perfect carers, particularly if they are caring for children they perceive as difficult.

The general findings of the study are that registered children do have worse outcomes than controls but it was difficult to find aspects of the child abuse cases or of the child protection interventions that had any relation to later outcome. Outcome was, however, related to some variables across both the registered and comparison groups. Lack of parental warmth, violent methods of child control, children feeling that they could not rely on their mothers for help and could not trust parents to keep their promises were all related to poorer outcome scores. Gibbons et al were unable to find a general model to predict poor outcome but these few statistical associations suggest that it maybe the higher rate of continuing adverse parenting conditions that produced the poorer outcomes in the registered group rather than anything to do directly with the abuse and its consequences.

Decision Making

In the last few years there has been an increasing interest in examining professional decision making. In the United States there have been a number of studies concerned with child abuse referrals and their screening by child protection services. Much of this research has consisted of vignette studies where workers are presented with short descriptions of referrals and asked what disposal they would recommend. The studies are a development from Giovannoni and Becerra's (1979) original vignette studies on what situations people consider to be abusive to children.

Recently a few studies have been undertaken on actual practice. Sedlak (1992, 1993) has undertaken secondary analysis of the 1988 National Incidence Study of Child Abuse and Neglect in the United States. The incidence study surveyed a wide range of professionals to identify instances of child maltreatment known to them. Sedlak reported that certain features of these cases were more common than families in the general population. The cases were more likely to involve children from poorer families, older children, females for sexual abuse allegations, older female children for physical neglect allegations, older Black and Hispanic children for physical neglect allegations, father only families for sexual abuse allegations and for physical neglect allegations concerning older female children. The important finding is that the associations between the different variables differed considerably between different types of maltreatment and for different age children. Poverty was

TABLE 10.3

Routine Services: Decision Making

Study	Programme	Sample/ Size	Population	Design	Main Measures
Cleaver and Freeman (1992)	Routine services	n = 583	Child abuse investigations	Descriptive	(1) Case files (2) Client interviews
English and Aubin (1991) English (1992)	Routine CP	n = 1,604	CP referrals	Descriptive	Case type, re-referrals
Farmer (1993) Farmer and Owen (1991)	Routine casework	(1) n = 120 (2) n = 44	Child protection	Descriptive	(1) CC observation (2) Client & workers interviews
Gough (1990) Gough and Sutton (1991)	Children's Hospital	n = 107	Sexual abuse	Descriptive	Physical examinations, referral routes
Sedlak (1992)	Routine services	n = 2,235	Abuse cases	Multivariate +C	Casetype, CPS investigation
Thoburn (1991) Thoburn et al (1991)	Family participation in child protection	(1) n = 200 (2) n = 35	Child protection cases	POST	Client & worker perceptions of CP intervention
Thorpe (1991)	Routine CP	n = 672	Abuse investigations	Descriptive	Case type, services
Waterhouse and Carnie (1990, 1992)	Routine CP	n = 51	Sexual abuse investigations	Descriptive	Case records, worker interviews
Wells et al (1989)	CPS screening of referrals	Macro study	CPS referrals	Descriptive	State laws & policies, case types, screening decisions

CC = Case conference; CP = Child protection; CPS = Child Protection Services
POST = Post-test only; +C = Control or comparison group

the only strong universal feature of these cases and the association between single parent households and maltreatment disappeared when income was controlled for.

Sedlak (1992) then examined which of these cases of maltreatment known to professionals had been investigated by child protection services. She found that there was no greater chance of investigation of cases involving low income families despite their high rate of identification in the survey of community professionals. There was an increased likelihood of CPS investigation of sexual abuse if there was evidence that the child had actual harm, but for physical abuse there was only an increased chance of investigation for inferred injuries and known serious injuries in female children. Cases involving young children were only more likely to be investigated if they concerned (i) male children with physical abuse, neglect, or emotional abuse allegations, (ii) black children for sexual abuse allegations, or (iii) non white children for educational neglect allegations. Family structure was not related to whether the case was investigated except that physical abuse allegations were more likely to be investigated in father only households. The chance of case investigation varied considerably between community professionals. Cases already known to CPS or known to medical services or law enforcement were much more likely to be investigated by CPS than cases known to schools.

Sedlak was unable to determine whether the lack of an investigation by CPS was due to non referral of cases or due to CPS screening the cases out as not urgent or not appropriate. She does conclude, however, that it is of concern that certain groups such as physically neglected poor children and sexually abused minority group adolescents were at high risk of being thought to have been maltreated yet had a lower than normal chance of having these allegations investigated by child protection services.

Wells et al (1989) have directly studied how child protection workers in the United States screened initial referrals to decide whether or not to investigate. Screening was previously not specifically allowed, but laws and policies are changing because of the very large numbers of referrals being received and the belief that some referrals probably do not require investigation. The issue then becomes one of how such decisions are made and on what basis. Some referrals are clearly outside the remit of child protection cases, but for those considered to be within the remit, Wells et al found that reports of child maltreatment, child injury, sexual abuse, alleged victim under two years of age, and referral received from mandated reporter were all associated with higher rates of investigation. Some agencies were found to be screening out over 70% of referrals. The finding of greater rates of investigation of referrals from other professionals supports the finding of Dingwall et al (1983) that action was more likely to be taken in possible child abuse cases if the information was 'not contained' and known to other professionals. Wells et al (1989) argue that much greater clarity is required about the criteria for screening and the effects that such criteria have on cases screened in and screened out.

English and Aubin (English and Aubin, 1991; English, 1992) conducted a study that examined both screening, CPS risk rating, and re-referral of cases (within six months of initial referral) to child protection services. They found that over a quarter of cases were screened out on the basis of referral information and 13% of these were re-referred within six months. These cases were more likely to concern poor single mother households, neglect cases, or cases with previous CPS histories. The cases screened in and rated low risk had a 21% re-referral rate and these were more likely to be single mother households. The cases with the lowest rate of re-referral (12%) were those initially screened in as high risk but re-evaluation after investigation as low risk. The cases re-evaluated at low risk tended to involve physical abuse referrals, referrals from professionals, prior CPS history, or not poor families. For all cases re-referrals were more common for low income, prior CPS contact, two or more children, and female headed households.

Re-referrals were at much higher risk of child placement away from their family. Although there were high numbers of re-referrals only 3% of all original referrals were re-referred with confirmed actual harm.

Wolok and Mumm (1992) reported a re-referral rate to child protective services of 25%. They found that re-referral was signifcantly more likely if the families were substance abusers, had three or more children, received government financial support for dependent children, were Black or Hispanic, or scored poorly on a range of scales of stress, mental state, and child behaviour. Multivariate analysis isolated substance abuse, government financial support, and three or more children as the three main predictors of re-referrals (accounting for 22% of the variance). The use of agency services was not related to outcome.

Thorpe (1991) in a pilot study of a child protection management information system in South West Australia reported a re-investigation rate of 10%. Two thirds of the re-investigated cases had originally been closed because of lack of substantiation and some of these were subsequently substantiated. Thorpe also found that 13% of substantiated cases (at initial investigation) received no service, whilst in 15% of cases the children were removed to substitute care. For those families receiving services, neglect cases were predominantly offered material and practical assistance, whilst physical and sexual abuse cases were predominantly offered advice, guidance, or treatment.

In Britain, the Department of Health funded a series of studies on child protection case work in the late 1980's which have just begun to report initial findings.

Cleaver and Freeman (1992) examined the parent and professional perspectives in the very early stages of case referral and investigation. They report that only a third of investigations result in placement on the child protection register, though the other cases may receive social work support or continue to be monitored informally. Registration was more likely if there had been police involvement in the investigation, the alleged abuser being the male parenting figure or an outsider, sexual abuse referrals, family history of abuse, criminal behaviour, or the family being chaotic or joined by a person with a history of violence or abuse. The parents reported high levels of shame, anxiety and continuing negative effects upon then from the investigation even if it did not result in registration. Also the relationship between parents and professionals were often affected by misunderstandings in the highly charged anxious atmosphere as well as by hidden agendas not revealed by families or professionals.

Farmer and Owen (Farmer and Owen, 1991; Farmer, 1993) have conducted a study of child protection in two local authority areas in England. One authority employs child protection coordinators to chair case conferences and advise on child protection matters. Conferences chaired by the coordinators were clearer about the distinctions between assessing risks to the child and case conference decisions such as registration. The coordinators also treated parents differently at case conferences. In the other authority, the normal line managers chaired the conferences. The line managers were more cordial to parents than the coordinators. They seemed to be working within a welfare model of care. Coordinators, on the other hand, were more formal and treated the parents as more equal providers of evidence to the conference. To enable further analysis of the eighteen months of longitudinal data collected on the families, Farmer and Owen distinguish cases according to the parents agreement with the social worker as to who had abused child, the culpability for this abuse, and future risks to the child.

In another study Thoburn et al (Thoburn, 1991; Thoburn et al, 1991) have been investigating family participation in child protection work. Despite studying cases in seven social work teams stating a wish to involve parents, in only 21% of cases did parents attend the whole of all case conferences, though a further 40% attended part of the conference. Professionals from other agencies are known to be wary of parental attendance, but Thoburn et al report that the social work staff who have moved towards greater participation have not regretted these changes.

Case conferences are often large, being attended by a range of professional disciplines and large numbers of social work staff (Gough et al, 1987). It is therefore not surprising therefore that there are difficulties, particularly if the parents feel that they can have no influence on the outcome of the proceedings or are not treated with respect. Professionals from other disciplines may also be concerned about discussing the families with the families present, which has resulted in some case conferences having an initial fact finding session with parents only being invited to the following discussion and decision making session (Lonsdale, 1991). Involvement of parents may have also resulted in an increasing wish to have case strategy discussions (advocated in Department of Health guidance, 1991) prior to initial case conferences and often prior to parents being informed of the professional concerns about the care of their child (Gough, 1992).

The final two studies of child protection case management funded by the Department of Health in the late 1980's are being undertaken by Hallett and Birchall at Stirling and by Jones, Aldgate and Sharland in Oxford, but at the time of writing both these studies had yet to report their findings. Hallett and Birchall are examining interprofessional work in child protection (Hallet and Birchall, 1992). Jones. Aldgate, and Sharland are examining investigations and early intervention of child sexual abuse referrals. Their early results indicate that approximately half of the investigations concern extrafamilial abuse and that the investigations are relatively well received by parents even if the cases concern intrafamilial abuse. Most parents found the process difficult but understood that it was necessary. Parents were less happy about the first contact with social services and the way in which the possibility of sexual abuse was first raised. Parents in extrafamilial cases also complained about the lack of follow up support. Families felt that they were provided with little information about the process of investigation, often did not realise that there had been a formal child protection investigation, and were unsure if the social workers would or would not be calling again (Jones and Sharland, personal communication).

Few other studies have been focused on routine child protection work in child sexual abuse. An exception is the study of sexual abuse investigations in four regions of Scotland by Waterhouse and Carnie (1990, 1992). The cases were predominantly teenage women alleged to have been touched and fondled by males related to them by role or biology. Social workers rarely confronted these men directly but relied on the police officers who were mostly male, older, and with more experience of child abuse investigations. Social work decision making was concerned primarily upon criteria of future risk concerning child care and secondly upon criteria about the quality of disclosure information. Although having different roles and responsibilities social workers and police usually worked together within a collaborative model. In a few cases there was only a minimalist model of cooperation, very rarely was there full integrated team work. Although police and social work were nearly always both involved in the cases, medical involvement was extremely variable between cases and between geographical areas.

The role of medical involvement was examined more directly by a survey of suspected cases of sexual abuse seen at the main children's hospital in Glasgow (Gough, 1990; Gough and Sutton, 1991). In a twelve month period there were one hundred and seven suspected cases with an average age of seven years, much younger than the social work based study of Waterhouse and Carnie. In a third of the cases neither police nor social work (or education) were involved in the referral and investigation even though the majority of the children were given formal physical examinations for sexual abuse. Furthermore, although police were involved in half of the cases seen at the hospital, they were only involved in 3% of cases that social work and health were both involved.

It seems that there is a lack of communication about cases in both directions between health and other agencies. It is also likely that these agencies are seeing slightly different types of cases. The 'health services only' cases were younger and the referrals often arose because of some aspect of the child's physical state, whereas referrals that came through the police often arose because of allegations made by the child or someone else in the community. These results have implications for practice, but are also important for research which often assumes that cases are similar whatever the agency sampling source. The evidence suggests, however, that different types of cases are identified in different ways and than referred along different referral pathways with different outcome choices at each decision point and with probably different decision making criteria being applied. Future research needs to assess the extent of these variations in case type, referral pathway, decision making, and outcome.

In ninety per cent of cases actually seen in the hospital (in the Gough and Sutton study), the children were formally physically examined for sexual abuse. This is a very contentious area of work because other agencies, the courts, and the public at large look to medical doctors for evidence that abuse has taken place, but there is often no conclusive evidence even if possible physical signs are present. Until recently, the medical profession had not made a priority of studying the range of ano-genital development in children. In the last few years more studies have begun to appear, focusing upon (i) children in the general population not thought to have been victims of abuse, (ii) children thought to have been abused, or (iii) controlled comparisons between abused and thought not to have been abused children. There have been very few studies on what is actually occurring in daily practice. Gough and Sutton found that in over two thirds of the cases no physical signs were identified. In 13% of cases there were possible signs and in 11% of cases there were significant or even diagnostic signs. For the cases with strong signs of abuse there was already a strong indication that abuse had taken place from other data. In 41% of the physical examinations there was strong referral data on abuse but no physical signs found. In four fifths of these cases the doctors continued to believe that the children had been abused, suggesting that the examination is primarily to determine if there is evidence to support the allegations of abuse, rather than to find evidence to disprove the hypothesis of abuse. The study also found that there was minimal use of laboratory examinations to test for signs of sexually transmitted diseases, which is of concern for two reasons. First it is important for the child's health. Secondly, although such diseases may not be common in British cases, when they are discovered they are a very strong indication that the child has experienced sexual contact.

Special Initiatives

The final group of studies looked at several special initiatives for enhancing routine services. There are many descriptive studies of this type in the literature. Only a few studies are included here as examples of this approach.

Berger (1981) studied a programme in which staff and clients spent time together in the less formal treatment or case management setting of a series of residential weekends. Workers and clients rated the weekends a success and reported long term positive effects on staff-client relations and on clients' social isolation. Without more independent measures this is difficult to confirm.

Harper and Irvin (1985) also examined staff-client relations. They concluded that mandatory reporting of abuse had a positive effect. One of the purposes of this study was to convince other professionals, that reporting cases would not have the extreme negative effect on their relationship with clients that they seemed to fear. This raises a much wider question about the use of authority and its effects on

TABLE 10.4

Routine Services: Special Initiatives

Study	Programme	Sample/ Size	Population	Design	Main Measures
Bailey et al (1984)	Nursing Officer's role	n = 15	Health Visitors	RPM	Satisfaction/use of service
Berger (1981)	Residential weekends	n = 7	Child abuse	POST	Family functioning/ parenting
Burt and Balycat (1977)	Emergency servcies	n = 1349	Abuse/neglect	RPM	Re-abuse, child placements, costs
Corry and Breathwick (1987)	Family Resource	n = 1	Physical abuse	Descriptive	Worker assessments
Crittenden (1992)	Miami CPT	n = 281	CPT cases	RPM + C	LFF, outcomes of new CPT policy
Harper and Irvin (1985)	Mandatory reporting	n = 49	Neglect	RPM	Client-worker relationships
Krell et al (1983)	Worker support groups	n = 9	Child protection workers	RPM + C	Worker coping, insight, skills
Magura (1982)	Intensive CPS	n = 34	Abuse/neglect	POST + C	Client satisfaction, progress.
McBogg et al (1979b)	Foster care enrichment	n = 8	Child abuse/neglect	Descriptive	Child placement, client satisfaction
Mouzakatis and Golstein (1985)	Multidisciplinary team	n = 2	Neglect	Descriptive	Workers' attitudes, abilities, treatment compliance

LFF = Level of Family Functioning; CPT = Child Protection Team; CPS = Child Protection Services
Design
POST = Post-test only; RPM = Repeated Measures including pre-test; PRPM = Repeated Measures post-test only;
+C = Control or comparison group; +PC = Control or comparison group but at post-test only

treatment. It has already been noted that client compliance is regularly interpreted as a major factor positively associated with outcome, but there are serious questions as to how much such results are contaminated by coding bias. The studies by Berger (1981) and Harper and Irvin (1985) are particularly useful in presenting staff-client relations as a major issue.

McBogg et al (1979b) studied the use of the resource of foster placements, to improve treatment. They found that the special foster care programme increased the quality of placements and reduced the number of fostering breakdowns. Burt and Balycat (1979) examined the impact of a new crisis intervention system, that offered emergency home makers and foster families. They saw a marked decrease in permanent placements of children away from home, and improved inter-professional cooperation. In another study Magura (1982) measured the effects of more intensive social work combined with lower staff-client ratios, and reported increased client satisfaction. Corry and Breathwick (1987) described the use of a local authority family resource centre to provide residential assessment and task centred casework with families in danger of losing their children into care.

The remaining studies in this group were concerned with developing supports for workers. Bailey et al (1984) described the success of employing specialist nursing officers to support Health Visitors in child protection work. Mousakitis and Goldstein (1985) reported on the quicker implementation of child care plans following the introduction of monthly inter-professional meetings for case discussion.

Krell et al (1983) report on a controlled study of support groups for professionals working with cases of child abuse. The intervention groups demonstrated considerably greater improvement on questionnaires of coping skills and insights into working with child abuse cases.

Finally, Crittenden (1992) reports on an attempt to implement a new local child protection policy to reform the many problems in the child protection service of Miami. Problems included lack of time spent with families, lack of focus to assessment and intervention, and lack of compatibility between treatment plans, intervention in practice, and the clients' needs and potential for change. New staff had to be trained, because those already located within a discipline had difficulties in accepting some part of the new programme. The difficulties depended upon the discipline from which they came. Social workers were not comfortable with using assessment protocols, nurses did not like the high focus on family functioning, and psychologists were unhappy about undertaking home visits. The new programme aggravated previous inter agency difficulties and was unable to achieve the necessary changes in practice before a higher level political and bureaucratic reform of the service was undertaken. Crittenden states that the political bureaucratic changes put an end to the new programme yet did not begin to address the fundamental problems of the original service that the experimental programme had been attempting to reform. Crittenden's conclusion is that one should only attempt limited reforms unless it is possible to change the fundamentals of the macro political systems in which the local child protection systems have developed.

Discussion

Studies in this chapter, were not so subject to the methodological problems referred to in other chapters, because most of the studies were not attempting to assess the efficacy of a particular treatment but to describe and analyse the process and outcome of routine work. This is in line with the approach taken by recent studies of child care in Great Britain (DHSS, 1985; DOH, 1991). Despite the absence of the standard methodological problems, the descriptive studies were difficult to interpret because they are so limited in scale and number.

Information on routine child protection has improved in the last few years as researchers in the United Kingdom and United States have begun to conduct studies on routine practice. These studies, however, had to start from a very low base. There is still very little data available on the number of children in different parts of the child protection system. The most comprehensive figures are available on child protection referrals and substantiated cases in the United States and child abuse registration figures in the United Kingdom. In the United Kingdom it has only been in the last few years that registration figures have become available and there is hardly any data on the number of referrals or case investigations (for England, see Department of Health, 1992; for Scotland, Gough, 1992). Statistics exist on legal child care measures and criminal prosecutions, but these statistics are not collected in a way that allows for child protection cases to be easily separated out.

In the American research literature which, like Britain, concentrates on specialist interventions there is often only brief mention of the existence of child protection service (CPS) workers. In many instances references to CPS is simply a mention of sources of case referral or that children and families are using CPS services in addition to special projects (the same is true for some British centres such as in the report by Bentovim et al, 1988). What is missing from the research literature are descriptions and evaluations of the CPS work. The studies by Wells et al (1989) Sedlak (1992), English and Aubin (1991), and Wolok and Mum (1992) are just a beginning.

The conclusion is that there is only a limited understanding of the context of routine child abuse case work in either this country, or in America. The research that has been undertaken shows that there is considerable variation in practice between screening by different American child protection teams (Wells et al, 1989), in the management of English case conferences (Farmer and Owen, 1991; Thoburn et al, 1991), in the compliance of clients to court ordered interventions (Famularo, 1989; Jellinek, 1992), and in the outcomes achieved for the children and families. Despite the enormous literature on special interventions for child abuse cases, it seems that routine child protection does not even usually include referral to local psychological or psychiatric services (Corby, 1987; Gough et al, 1987; Gibbons et al, 1992) or even the use of therapeutic techniques such as family therapy or counselling by social workers (Gibbons et al, 1992). This is despite the fact that many children are removed permanently from their homes after protracted attempts to maintain them at home or return them home from temporary care (Gough et al, 1993; Jellinek et al, 1992). Maybe specialist services might assist permanency planning decisions in these cases.

There is little information on the efficacy of routine child protection. It is difficult to undertake such studies because effects may only reveal themselves in the long term, yet research has to contend with considerable numbers of other intervening variables including variation in case types and interactions with treatment modalities. These effects may become masked in the soup of variables that must be taken into account. It is therefore difficult to interpret the findings of Gibbons et al (1992) on the long term outcome of a population of registered cases. Few effects of case presentation or agency intervention were identified and even reception into care did not produce better outcomes for the children. As Gibbons et al suggest, it may be the continuing adverse and positive factors in the children's lives that are more important than any aspect of child abuse or child protection. Gibbons et al's conclusion is that intervention may be more productively focused on these adverse factors. Child mistreatment would then be seen as just one of many factors contributing to the psychosocial development of children.

Child protection systems will continue to be necessary, whether or not they are a subset of other services to children and families. The research base on child protection, therefore needs to be substantially further developed. The current state of the literature does not allow for proper comparative evaluation of different organisational policies. Further research could help to make these distinctions more explicit and inform policy development. This process could also be helped by more sophisticated studies of the benefits of small service initiatives. Crittenden (1992) has demonstrated the difficulties in achieving macro changes in service delivery. Even if such major changes are sometimes indicated, there is much scope for also exploring more subtle changes in service delivery.

Summary

1. There have been few studies which examine the efficacy of routine casework or simply describe the content, process, and outcome of this work.
2. There is a great need for this data for at least the following reasons: (a) To provide information on current practice and its effect on case outcomes. (b) To understand the context and influence of procedural and legal systems on therapeutic interventions. (c) To clarify the definitions, and processes of child protection work for the development of more coherent studies of therapeutic interventions. If these are not clear, it is unlikely that research hypothesis can be articulated and tested out.
3. The descriptive data available on routine practice, reveals that there is little use of specialist social work or of referral to other disciplines such as child psychology, psychiatry or paediatrics. Any additional services are provided directly by social work departments or through resources under their control.

This contrasts with the fact that most research effort has been invested in evaluating specialist services.

4. Descriptive studies reveal that many abused children are removed into long term care and that this is a protracted exercise. Most of the children received into care come from families in deprived areas without the physical or emotional resources to cope unaided with child care responsibilities. Non compliance with court ordered services is associated with removal of children into care.

5. Studies of case outcome have suggested that outcome can be predicted from case presentation, such as substance abuse by the parents. Other studies indicate the importance of examining both service and case variables in predicting outcome.

6. Child protection cases have relatively high rates of re-referral. There is little evidence that child protection services improve outcomes for children or reduces re-referral rates (except when children are permanently removed). Abused children have worse long term outcomes than control children, but this may be due more to continuing adverse aspects of their lives rather than specific attributes of the abuse or child protection responses.

7. Systems to provide routine child protection management information are in their infancy, but confirm significant variation in practice. These new systems offer much potential for providing feedback to professionals and policy makers and to provide data to inform future micro studies of practice.

8. A few studies have examined the effects of special developments on routine services. These report encouraging results, but their methodological limitations restrict them to being mostly descriptions of innovatory practice.

Chapter Ten   Research Summaries

Bailey et al (1984)

THE NURSING OFFICER'S ROLE.

Sample: 15 Health Visitors.

Focus: Health Visitors.

Objectives: To provide staff support to enable Health Visitors to develop appropriate service to cases of child abuse and neglect.

Programme: In two sections of a district health authority, a specialist nursing officer was appointed on a temporary basis for 6 months, to provide advice and support to health visitors with child abuse cases. Officer provided assistance in preparation for case conferences (12 cases), alleviated anxiety by crisis support (12 cases), offered a relief service in home visiting and case conference attendance (2 cases), and was accessible at all times (14 cases). The service corresponded to the 5 greatest needs of Health Visitors.

Design: Repeated measures (pre and post-test) on Treatment Group.

Measures: Pre-test: questionnaire to Health Visitors to determine their needs in abuse cases. Post test: questionnaire on use of service and rating of satisfaction.

Results: Satisfaction with each aspect of service used by each Health Visitor was 100%. Pre-test views of usefulness of service were 50% and this rose to 73% at post-test.

Berger (1981)

RESIDENTIAL WEEKENDS FOR CLIENT FAMILIES AS AN AID TO CASE MANAGEMENT

Sample: 7 child abuse cases of an Australian Social Work Unit.

Focus: Client-worker relationships.

Objectives: Improving client-worker relations and thereby case management. Other case objectives included reducing clients' social isolation, ability to enjoy a respite from normal pressures, involving parents more in activities with child, to demonstrate appropriate handling of child behaviour problems, allow workers extended observation of parent-child interactions.

Programme: A series of 3 residential weekends, developed in style and content with client feedback. It is the last weekend with 7 clients that is evaluated. There were high staff-client ratios and clients were encouraged to suggest activities. There were team and musical games, treasure hunts, and craft work. Parents spent time alone together, especially in the evenings. Mutual support was encouraged.

Design: Post-test on treatment sample.

Measures: Worker and client questionnaire on outcomes specified in results section.

Results: Workers' assessed that there were short and long term improvements respectively, achieved in the following areas of social isolation (5/5, 3/5), staff-client relations (4/5, 4/5), improved child handling (3/3, 2/3), promotion of father-child interaction (1/4, 0/4), development of new experiences (5/5). Client assessment were, that they enjoyed the weekend, being in a group, and finding that the workers were 'human'. There were thought to be enough activities but 3/3 would have preferred more therapeutic input. Parents were relieved at their children's behaviour. An unexpected result was an improvement in marital relations.

Notes: Article reports the development of the project over the 3 weekends. By the third weekend a balance had been achieved between aimless freedom and over-structuring of activities. Group discussion of parents' problems was dropped because of a wish to escape from their problems. Workers were relieved to relate to clients on a different basis, but boundaries to intimacy were still necessary. Article discusses aspects of the weekend considered most useful.

Burt and Balycat (1977)

A COMPREHENSIVE EMERGENCY SERVICES SYSTEM FOR NEGLECTED AND ABUSED CHILDREN.

Sample: 1981 families with 4,845 children referred in first two years of system in Nashville. 1349 families received emergency services and there were 295 suspected cases of abuse.

Focus: Reaction of Emergency services to abused children.

Objectives: To re-organise services to reduce the numbers of children removed precipitously from their homes or put through the legal system unnecessarily. To plan orderly placements for children who must be removed from home. To set goals for children who come into emergency care, with decisions to return home being made quickly and preferably within a month. To develop placements that better meet the needs of children who must remain in care.

Programme: Development of a new emergency service that included (1) 24 hour service, (2) emergency caretaker service to provide a caretaker in the home in cases of parental absence/abandonment, (3) emergency homemaker service for children at home with parents, (4) emergency foster homes, (5) outreach and follow up services, (6) emergency shelter facilities, (7) a new Protective Services Unit operated by the local courts.

Design: Cross sectional repeated measures (pre and post-test).

Measures: Agency records of numbers of court cases, of recidivism of abuse measured by repeat petitions to the courts, of delinquency, of children placed away from home. Measures of cost effectiveness. Also achievement of service level changes.

Results: (1) 56% drop in court petitions, despite increased case referrals. Result explained in terms of better education and liaison between Child Protection Service, Juvenile Courts, and the police. (2) 51% drop in temporary placements away from the parental home. (3) Drop in recidivism rate of court cases. (4) No cases of delinquency in children in court cases. (5) System was cheaper than previous arrangements. (6) Only 34% of fosterd children still in foster care at 2 years, previously 94% were still so placed. (7) Improvements in co-ordination of services. This evolved informally under the new structures provided.

Clever and Freeman (1992)

PARENTAL PERSPECTIVES IN SUSPECTED CHILD ABUSE AND ITS AFTERMATH

Sample: (1) Extensive study: a survey of 583 cases using agency files from social services, police, health visitors, hospitals, and probation case records in one geographic area. (2) Intensive study of 30 families suspected of child abuse.

Focus: Suspected perpetrators' views on agency interventions.

Objectives: Not specified – objectives of routine services involved in child protection – but the 1989 Children Act and the accompanying guidelines introduce the concept of parental responsibility and emphasise the need to work in partnership with families wherever possible. Agencies involved in child protection work must balance the need to protect children from abuse or neglect with allowing parents reasonable opportunities to present their points of view.

Programme: Routine social work, probation, police, health visiting and hospital services involved in early stages of child protection cases.

Design: Descriptive survey at two levels of detail.

Measures: (1) Extensive study: examination of case files in all agencies involved in child protection work in a specific geographical area in one year. (2) Intensive study: interviews with parents, children (if over 9 years), other key family members following the agency's investigative interview. Re-interviews over the next 18 months at regular intervals and after critical events; analysis of records and all minutes of meetings.

Results: (1) Extensive study: showed that different cases follow different routes in the career of suspicion. Two thirds of abuse situations are disclosed by the child, close family members or a neighbour, while others come to light during an agency's regular work or as the result of an unrelated event.

Social services become involved in most investigations at some stage. Less than one third of investigations result in the child being placed on the child protection register, although the suspicion usually lingers with cases being monitored informally (as 28,000 children are registered in England, approximately 84,000 investigations may have been involved).

Registration was more likely if (a) social services or police involvement (b) the suspected perpetrator being either the male parenting figure or an outsider, (c) the suspicion involving sexual abuse, (d) the family having a record of child abuse or criminal behaviour, (e) the family being chaotic and dysfunctional and joined by an outsider with a record of child abuse or violence.

However, there is a danger in over simplifying the complex processes that lead from the first suspicion to eventual registration or even the removal of a child. Many of the variables associated with a child's placement on the child protection register are inter-related. Nevertheless, three aspects of a child abuse inquiry seem to influence, both independently and in combination, the likelihood of the child being placed on the protection register. Initially important are the characteristics of the child and the circumstances which led to the referral. Secondly, the type of family from which the child comes and finally, the way in which the abuse comes to light influence the decision to register the child.

(2) Intensive study: preliminary results/issues identified: (a) suspicion influences behaviour so that parents may behave guiltily even when telling the

213

truth, whilst professionals may judge responses as deceptive when they are honest. (b) Suspicion engenders high levels of anxiety. Parents' fears result in them frequently being unable to assimilate information given by professionals during an investigation, and misunderstandings are common. Professionals are anxious because every investigation is a potential child abuse scandal. (c) Hidden agendas of individuals and agencies, for example, an agency being punitive because of previous involvement with the family. (d) In terms of outcome, we would suggest that how parents are handled during the early stages of an investigation influence the later stages. The majority of parents felt violated and ashamed by the investigation and some isolated and vulnerable families felt too embarrassed to seek help and support from relatives or neighbours. In addition, welfare agencies were increasingly viewed with deep suspicion. (e) Suspicions of child abuse disturbed parents profoundly, whether or not suspicions were founded. Family relationships rarely returned to their previous situation. Many were still reviewing what had happened to them 18 months later and few wished to see a social worker again, despite benefits which could clearly accrue from social service intervention.

Notes: This summary is based on preliminary results of a study nearing completion.

Corby (1987)

WORKING WITH CHILD ABUSE.

Sample: 25 cases of mostly physical abuse and neglect considered to be representative of the middle to serious end of child abuse work, although the parents often denied the allegations and there was rarely any formal evidence of abuse. Most of the families were already known to social services for various reasons. A wider comparison group was formed by analysing retrospectively 99 case records chosen randomly from 1983.

Focus: Decision making and case outcome in routine cases.

Objectives: Family support and child protection.

Programme: Social Work casework provided principally through home visits which in 17 cases were at least fortnightly within the first six months. Casework included financial and material help, monitoring of children's welfare, and several types of counselling, social skills, and marital work. Psychodynamic casework was mentioned in 9 cases.

Design: Two year prospective study with multiple measures on treatment group with a comparison group identified retrospectively from case records.

Measures: Descriptive analysis of case decision making and the progress of cases through interviews with social workers and the analysis of agency case records.

Results: In 5 cases there was minimal intervention with cases closed within six months and no reports of re-abuse. In 2 of these cases the household circumstances had changed considerably. In 7 cases there was some continued concern over a longer period. There were no known further instances of injury or neglect, but the case workers felt a need to monitor the cases and provide support if necessary. In 7 cases there was re-abuse. In 4 of these cases the children were allowed to remain at home whilst in the other 3 the children were removed into permanent alternative care. In 6 other cases where there was initial evidence of serious abuse, the children were removed into care and only 3 of these were later returned home under supervision orders. Few families received specialist psychological or psychiatric services.

Notes: The book reports on many aspects of practice and procedure of child abuse casework by social workers.

Corry and Breathwick (1987)

THE RESIDENTIAL TREATMENT OF AN ABUSING FAMILY

Sample: Two teenage parents and a five month old baby. They were deprived, lived in a homeless family unit and had severely distorted perceptions of their child. The baby was admitted to hospital after an alleged fall from her mother's lap – an examination revealed a pattern of fractures and bruising, consistent with non-accidental injury.

Focus: Family functioning.

Objectives: (1) General: To prevent family breakdown, or if this has occurred, to promote family rehabilitation, to avoid the drift of taking children into care and to avoid separation of family and child. The intervention must support and strengthen and not undermine the parents' responsibility for their behaviour to the child. (2) Specific to family: To ensure the child's safety, to assess the viability of this family as a unit and recommend what support they may require in the future, to help the family with coping skills within and outwith the family situation, and to help the family maintain links with their extended family.

Programme: Local Authority Family Resource Centre which consists of a residential wing with accommodation for 10 residents, a flat for an independent living unit and the rest of the building for group therapy and play. The framework of intervention was drawn from task-centred work, Reid and Epstein, 1972; Vickery, 1982. Three stages: (1) Ten week residential assessment with almost constant supervision of child. The parents were responsible for the every day care of their child and for seeking any support required. They were allowed access to their records and to discuss them with staff. (2) Parents care for their child in the centre's independent flat. (3) Parents care for their child in the community.

Design: Case study – follow up (fortnightly for twelve months).

Measures: Staff assessments through: (1) Daily meetings of family with care staff (3 times daily). (2) Weekly meetings of family with the key workers. (3) Weekly meetings of family with other residents of the centre. (4) Inter-professional case conference discussions.

Results: (1) Stage 1 Assessment in centre: The family felt as though they were in a 'goldfish bowl' and the staff were apprehensive about the child's safety as she could not be constantly supervised. The parents explored their own relationship, made contact with their extended family and the father traced his own natural father whom he had not seen since he was a toddler. The mother became more confident and assertive, and the father developed a more positive attitude towards the baby. (2) Stage 2: In independent flat initial pleasure followed by feelings of separation and isolation, but family then became settled. (3) Stage 3 in the community: Initial anxiety and separation reflected in child being cold, dirty and uncared for. After further support from the centre, the family settled again, so the staff decreased their input. (4) Follow-up: the baby became a healthy toddler, the mother continued to attend a weekly group in the centre and received fortnightly home visits from centre staff. The mother's own family became more supportive. Although the marital relationship seemed unsteady, the workers believed that further abuse of the child was unlikely.

Crittenden (1992)

The Social Ecology of Treatment

Sample: 281 maltreating families seen by Miami Child Protection Teams (CPTs) and 111 comparison families with similar income levels. Total sample were Black 42%, Hispanic 26%, White 25%, Haitian 9%. Study also examined general child protection services available in Miami.

Focus: Child protection services.

Objectives: Provision of coherent and appropriate child protection services.

Programme: (1) Routine child protection services. (2) New programme of (a) family assessment in the home in contrast to routine service of interviews with child and sometimes mothers in hospitals or offices. (b) Standardized assessment procedures to increase CPT time with families from original level of 11% and to decrease time spent with CPT and other colleagues (originally 29% and 20% respectively), (c) more in-depth work on frequent cases that are resistant to change and most damaging to children, (d) written treatment plans (e) more specific matching of needs to treatment.

Design: Cross sectional analysis of intervention sample and local service provision contrasted with comparison group. Longitudinal follow up (2 and 6 week) of intervention sample. Description of outcome of new CPT policy.

Measures: Level of Family Functioning (LFF): assessment of families into 5 levels of functioning/current and future ability to care for their children.

Results: (1) Differences between CPT and comparison families: (a) No differences between groups in mothers' age, age at first pregnancy, family moves, or income (controlled for family functioning scores). (b) Differences between groups in the number of partners of mothers, marital status, stressful life experiences, (c) family coping strategies, maternal depression, physical neglect, and conflict tactics. (c) Descending linear trend with more adverse factors in families assessed at worse on LFF.

(2) CPT cases (a) Protective service workers classified services available in Miami as appropriate to 'Vulnerable to Crisis' families 51%, 'Restorable' families 28%, and for 'Supportable' families 16%. (b) Estimate by CPT workers of proportion of family case types were 'Vulnerable to Crisis' 20%, 'Restorable' 40%, 'Supportable' 30% and 'Inadequate' 10%. (c) Researchers' coding of 281 families into case types: 'Vulnerable to Crisis' 24%, 'Restorable' 48%, 'Supportable' 24%, 'Inadequate' 3%.

(3) Service provision: (a) Less than 50% of recommended services implemented within 6 weeks of courts' acceptance of the plan. Reasons of: professional too busy to make referral 33%, waiting list at receiving agency 38%, family uptake of service 29%. Analysis of cases of no uptake by family indicated practical problems of transport, providing care for siblings, ability to achieve schedule of appointments, and treatment plans often confusing to parents. (b) Lack of evidence of improvements in the home often led judges to keep children in temporary care for longer than federal guidelines (averaged 53 months in care in early 1980s). Provision for parental access to children in care rarely included in treatment plans.

(4) Outcome of new CPT policy (a) Micro systems: Resistance of staff to (i) visiting clients in home (ii) working outside of normal hours, (iii) use

of standardized protocols, (iv) producing written reports. Staff resigned, replacement staff sought but psychology trained uncomfortable with home visits, social work trained uncomfortable with assessment protocols, and those with nursing background uncomfortable with emphasis on family functioning. Few had sympathy or understanding for cultural environmental context affecting families. Solution was hire younger staff and provide training. (b) Mesosystem (subsystems): Previous problems of inter-disciplinary cooperation became more fraught with perceived threats to status quo of status/hierarchies and methods of working. (c) Exosystem (bureaucratic structures): Political pressure on CP services from media attention to CPT deficiencies and deaths of several children. Bureaucratic response of changing administrators and ending of new programme. The more fundamental deficiencies in CP policies and practice that new programme was beginning to expose were not addressed.

Notes: The author argues that the new CPT programme did not take a sufficiently strategic approach. The underlying problem with the CP services were rooted in the political system. It is necessary either to change the macrosystem or to attempt more limited changes that do not disrupt the interlocking micro and mesosystems.

English and Aubin (1991), English (1992)

OUTCOMES FOR CHILD PROTECTIVE SERVICES CASES RECEIVING DIFFERENTIAL LEVELS OF SERVICE

Sample: 1,604 cases of alleged abuse randomly (block) selected from 3,825 total allegations meeting study criteria of referred in one of 4 sites in Washington State between June 1988 and May 1989, alleged perpetrator living with child. Two of the case recruitment sites included experimental community based services, one urban, one rural. The two further sites were selected by matching the demographic characteristics of the 2 experimental sites. Sub-sample of 88 screened in cases selected for telephone survey on quality of service.

Focus: Assessment and intervention in routine Child Protection Services (CPS).

Objectives: Vary with disposal of referral: Programme 1: CPS screen out case as not appropriate for investigation on basis of referral information. Programmes 2 and 4: Routine CPS for low risk cases. Programme 3: A community based alternative service (ARS) to help support the family and so prevent maltreatment of the child.

Programme: Referral and re-referral of four types of cases: (1) 455 cases screened out by CPS on basis of referral information and so received no service.

(2) 427 cases classified at referral as low risk and received CPS services. (3) 404 cases classified at referral as low risk and referred to community services offering assessment, counselling, parent education, and material support. (4) 318 cases classified as high or moderate risk at referral but downgraded to low risk after investigation and received CPS service.

Design: Six month repeated measures natural experiment on 4 types of case.

Measures: Analysis of case records for demographic data, previous agency contact, source of referral or re-referral, type of abuse alleged, alleged perpetrator, whether alleged abuse confirmed as having occurred. Telephone survey on perception of services.

Results: (1) Screened out: (a) original referrals were 43% single child, 56% single parent mothers; (b) 13% re-referred & more likely than original referrals to be single mothers, on public assistance, prior CPS contact, 2+ children in family, a neglect allegation; (c) after investigation 27% of re-referrals rated as moderate or high risk, 23% of re-referrals confirmed as abuse, re-referral rate higher for neglect than physical abuse cases, confirmation more likely than original referrals to be low income, 2+ children, prior CPS contact, referral from community; 3 re-referrals concerned actual harm to the child, 1 from physical abuse, 2 from medical neglect.

(2) Screened in low risk CPS: (a) original referrals often children under 5, low income families, allegation of neglect from lack of supervision; (b) 21% re-referred & re-referrals more likely than original referrals to be single mothers, other adults in household; no effects from children's age, ethnicity, economic status, or referral source; neglect allegations mostly about inadequate food; (c) after investigation 35% of re-referrals rated moderate/high risk, 1/3 cases confirmed as abuse with confirmation highest for physical abuse (41%) and neglect (34%); 4 children had actual harm & 2 allegations of sexual abuse were confirmed.

(3) Screened in low risk ARS cases: (a) half of original referrals were children under 5 years, 71% were neglect allegations; (b) 17% re-referred & more likely than original referrals to be single mothers, low income, and with unrelated adults in household; no effect from child age, gender, ethnicity, type of parent, type of alleged perpetrator, or type of abuse; (c) after investigation 35% of re-referrals rated moderate or high risk. Approx. 40% cases confirmed as abuse, with alleged neglect being twice as likely to be confirmed at re-referral than at original referral (47% rather than 19%); actual physical harm in 8 cases and sexual abuse confirmed in 1 case.

(4) Cases screened in as moderate or high risk but reassessed as low risk: (a) cases more likely to be referred by a professional alleging physical abuse by a male; (b) 12% re-referred & more likely than

original referrals for the new alleged victims to be siblings for there to be unrelated adults in the household; no effect from children's age, gender, ethnicity, family economic status, family type, source of referral, or alleged abuse; (c) after investigation 18% of re-referrals rated as moderate or high risk, a third of cases confirmed, confirmation rate for neglect 43% and for physical abuse 24%; 3 cases of actual physical harm.

(5) Within site comparison of cases screened as low risk with those screened as higher risk but then reassessed as low risk: (a) those initially screened higher risk were more likely to be allegations of physical abuse by a male caretaker; the neglect allegations were often referrals alleging imminent harm, lack of medical care, coloured children; (b) those initially screened as higher risk were less likely (than those initially screened as low risk) to be re-referred and if re-referred then less likely to be confirmed as abuse or to be given a high risk rating.

(6) In total less than 3% of the original cases received re-referrals concerning actual physical or emotional harm or sexual abuse within 6 months of the original allegation. All re-referrals were at signifcantly greater risk of child placement than original referrals.

(7) Comparison of low risk cases who received CPS or ARS: In urban sites ARS physical abuse cases had higher economic status and more ethnic minority children; neglect cases more likely to involve coloured children, be professional referrals, less previous agency contact. In rural sites ARS physical abuse cases had less previous agency contact, no differences found for neglect cases. Re-referred ARS cases significantly more likely to have children placed than other re-referrals.

(8) Multiple regression analysis indicated 4 variables independently predicting higher risk rating at screening later reassessed as low risk: (i) physical abuse rather than neglect; (ii) referrals from professionals rather than the community; (iii) prior CPS contact; (iv) not a low income family. The variables of child age & family composition were significant only in bivariate tests.

(9) Multiple regression analysis indicated 4 variables independently predicting re-referral of cases; (i) economic status of low income; (ii) prior CPS contact; (iii) 2+ children; (iv) female head of household. The variables of geographical site, risk status, child age, referral source,type of abuse were significant only in bivariate tests.

(10) Qualitative data: Of 88 screened in cases selected 60% could not be contacted and 16% refused to participate. Data on the 24% responding to survey: 50% agreed with the CPS referral allegations, only a third of families received services after initial CPS contact, the majority of clients reported being satisfied with the service and their worker.

Notes: The authors argue that the results show the practicability of using a risk classification system

as those screened out or classified as low risk (according to the risk assessment guidelines) at intake were not significantly likely to be re-referred for serious abuse or neglect. They state that the results showed a tendency for physical abuse cases to be over rated as high risk with lower priority being given to cumulative harm neglect cases, but that this bias can be corrected by changing office policies and practice.

Famularo et al (1989)

PARENTAL COMPLIANCE TO COURT ORDERED TREATMENT

Sample: 136 cases of child maltreatment involving 218 parents seen at an urban juvenile and family court and taken into at least temporary state care.

Focus: Court ordered treatment.

Objectives: Not specified routine court determination of cases and referral for treatment.

Programme: Not specified routine court determination of cases and referral for treatment.

Design: Retrospective analysis of case outcome from agency records.

Measures: Analysis of court records for (a) type of maltreatment (b) parental substance abuse using 'Research Diagnostic Criteria' (c) court orders for psychological intervention (d) parental compliance rated as excellent if attended 75% of appointments, as compliant if attended 50% of appointments for at least half of the specified interventions.

Results: (1) Treatment order to 87% of parents. (2) Treatment required by court and compliance were (a) individual therapy 61% of whom 52% complied, (b) substance abuse 62% of whom 21% complied, (c) family therapy 29% of whom 45% complied, (d) marital therapy 9% of whom 42% complied, (e) psychiatric hospitalization 5% of whom 75% complied. Significant difference between low compliance rates for substance abuse therapy and individual, family or marital therapy. (3) Whatever the mode of treatment offered, substance abusers' compliance rate was 42% compared to 62% for others. Abusers of multiple drugs had lowest compliance rate of 34%. (4) Significant difference in compliance rate between different types of maltreatment: physical plus sexual abuse 22% compliance; physical only 40%; sexual, 44%; neglect cases 69%.

Farmer and Owen (1991), Farmer (1993)

DECISION MAKING, INTERVENTION, AND OUTCOME IN CHILD PROTECTION WORK.

Sample: (1) 120 initial child protection case conferences attended in 2 local authorities. (2) 44 cases that could be included in detailed study from 73 cases registered at the 120 case conferences (CCs). 19 registered cases not included due to non consent from families, 10 not included for other reasons. Approximately equal numbers of physical abuse, sexual abuse, and emotional/neglect cases.

Focus: Routine child protection.

Objectives: Not specified – routine child protection.

Programme: Not specified – routine child protection.

Design: Prospective longitudinal follow up of intervention sample.

Measures: Observation of initial CCs, interviews with parents, social workers, and older children after initial CCs and 18 months later.

Results: Preliminary findings from initial CCs and first interviews. (1) CCs chaired by line manager in one local authority (LA) and by non line managers (child protection coordinators) in the other. Independent line manager associated with clearer distinctions between assessments of risk and decisions about registration and criteria for these decisions. Also clearer differentiation of stages of conference. (2) Most parents invited to CC and independent chairs treated parents formally and asked them to submit their views to the meeting. Line manager chairs treated parents more cordially but according to a welfare model. (3) In both LAs registration used as a tariff: not registering could be warning that might be registered in future, registering could be seen as a stage towards care proceedings. (4) Most of CC time spent assessing risk, then in deciding on whether to register. Least time spent on future plans or monitoring and these were specified vaguely even though they were the basis for the agenda of review CCs. CC decisions put few limits on case workers' intervention. (5) Events can make plans become quickly outdated. Also review CCs attended by fewer other professionals allowing social workers to alter any previous plans they disagree with. (6) Difficulties occur because of divergences of views between parents and professionals at CC, and parental feelings of being coerced, stigmatized, and unable to put their views at CC. (7) (a) In 8 cases parents agreed with social workers about who had abused child, culpability for this and future risk; 7 of these were sexual abuse by others, one was self referral by mother for sexual abuse; (b) in 6 cases parents agreed about who abused child and culpability but disagreed that there was any future risk; (c) in 15 cases parents agreed about who abused child but disagreed on culpability and future risk. The parents did not perceive the actions as abusive in the circumstances; (d) in 15 cases parents disagreed on how

injuries (or other) occurred, blame for this and future risk. (8) Early actions by workers affect the possibility of constructive cooperation between parents and workers. Mishandled there were dangers of parents being unable to accept assistance and of the family re-forming in a way that excluded or endangered the child, especially if the bond between the non abusing parent and child had not been strengthened.

Notes: These are preliminary findings of an on-going study.

Gibbons, Gallagher and Bell (1992)

A FOLLOW UP OF PHYSICALLY ABUSED CHILDREN

Sample: (1) All 170 children placed on child protection registers in 1981 in one city (n=75) and one shire county (n=95) of whom 144 were interviewed at follow up. Mean child age of 11 years; sex ratio 1.5 males to 1 female; at registration 16% had serious injuries, 30% moderate injuries, 53% slight injuries. Subject recruitment: 85% traced and interviewed in UK, 12% traced in UK but not interviewed, 2% emigrated, 1% deceased, 1% not traced. (2) Comparison group of children matched for sex, age, school and area of residence (excluding any children placed on registers or subject to any legal order). Majority identified through the school medical service, the remainder by direct approach to schools.

Focus: Routine child protection.

Objectives: Not specified – routine child protection.

Programme: Routine child protection.

Design: Retrospective prospective 10 year longitudinal case follow up.

Measures: (1) Agency records. Systematic extraction of data from agency files of (a) social work on contact with family, contact with other agencies, referral history, allocation history, structure of social work file, social work methods, social work services, referrals to specialist agencies, social work involvement prior to birth and prior to registration of index child, summary of social work contact, file contents; (b) medical from hospital and accident and emergency department on date, nature, and outcome of presentation and treatment. Also hospital notes, (c) health records from a range of community health services on types of contact, tests, vaccinations, injuries, other health and social information, file contents.

(2) Outcome measures: (a) interviews with child's main carer on social situation, social support, child's behaviour and management, health, affect, social life, care giver-partner relationship; family problem questionnaire; Malaise Inventory; contact with services; (b) interview with child on leisure, social support, peer and sibling relationships, relationship

with parents including their rules and control; a depression inventory; a fears inventory; (c) educational/cognitive assessment of child by Raven's Progressive Matrices, British Picture Vocabulary Scale, and parts of the British Ability Scale; (d) child physical development by height, weight, head circumference and a further 7 measures; (e) teacher questionnaire of Prosocial Behaviour questionnaire, Rutter B Scale for behavioural and emotional disorder, schooling history.

Results: (1) Social background. (a) lone parent households, index cases 35%, comparisons 23%; reconstituted households, index 23%, comparisons 16%; 2 adults both joint parents of all children in household, index 26%, comparisons 59%; (b) race: no significant differences in ethnic background; (c) social class: no significant differences, though affected by higher social class of adopting families; (d) poverty: on index of disadvantage index families scored worse than comparisons.

(2) Child behaviour: (a) parents' reports: no differences in emotional difficulties, but index children more likely to have conduct problems and be overactive. Effect more marked for girls; (b) teachers' reports: index children, particularly girls, more anti social than comparisons, index boys more neurotic than comparisons, index girls less pro social than comparisons. Scores of comparison groups worse than general population studies. Items that best discriminated index and comparison children included being unpopular, solitary, often miserable, unable to keep still, disobedient, aggressive and destructive; (c) children's fears and depressions: no significant differences.

(3) Academic performance and physical development: (a) abstract reasoning: few differences; (b) language and number skills: depressed performance in both groups with index significantly poorer than comparisons on all but word reading; (c) physical development: few differences.

(4) Outcome profiles: analysis of all scores identified 3 clusters of I) very poor, II) good, III) intermediate. Index children significantly over represented in cluster I and under represented in cluster II. A fifth of index children were high achievers, a fifth of comparison children had serious problems.

(5) Activities and self perceptions described by children themselves: (a) no relationship between group membership, involvement in organised activities, and outcome cluster; (b) friendships: index friendships seen as less satisfying and at more risk of quarrelling and getting bullied. However, level of friendships only related to outcome cluster for comparison group in which few friends were related to poor outcome (ie abused children did not have better outcomes if they had more friends, but comparisons did); (c) bad behaviour: no differences between groups but in whole sample, admission of stealing strongly associated with poor outcome; (d) siblings: no group differences but in whole sample difficul-

ties with siblings associated with poor outcome; (e) activities with mother: no group differences but few joint activities related to poor outcome; (f) pocket money: amount related to outcome within comparison group only; (g) discipline: index children more likely to report that smacked and more in fear of telling father of misdemeanours than comparisons. Children with poor outcomes more likely to see their parents' reactions as unpredictable and to report parents' use of smacking, shouting, and threatening; (h) parental availability: index more likely to say parents too busy for them and that fathers did not keep their promises. Poor outcomes in whole sample associated with not being able to rely on mothers for help, and parents not keeping their promises. Interviewers also rated lack of availability of parents more often in poor outcome children; (i) parental warmth: index children and poor outcome children rated parental warmth less than comparison and good outcome children.

(6) Current influences: data from parent interviews: (a) boys had more behaviour problems; (b) social class I and II children performed better on school performance tests; (c) self report depression and fears higher in lone parent families in comparison group; (d) level of current family problems seemed to have greater effect on outcomes in comparison rather than index group; (e) parenting style: non violent controls related to better outcomes and fewer behaviour problems, high parental involvement related to better school test performance.

(7) Outcomes for index cases: (a) same carers, 24% (3/4 include original abuser); one carer the same, 47% (37% of these include original abuser); new carers, 29%. For those who committed the abuse, father figures less likely to still be present compared to mother figures (22% vs 56%). No statistical relationship between outcomes and current household, or whether adopted/fostered, or whether abuser still present, except that better outcomes if with same siblings; (b) fewer school problems, fears and depression, from children in middle age group of 1 to 3 years of age of injury; (c) base line risk factors derived from features of the abuse, the child, and the family, fail to predict the outcome 10 years later. Neither the combination of physical abuse with neglect, nor the presence or absence of injury, were associated with outcome; (d) 24% of index children known to have been abused subsequent to registration, over 75% within 2 birthdays of registration. Subsequent abuse more likely for those registered as abused rather than as grave concern (25% vs 13%). 5% of children sexually abused post registration, mostly by different perpetrators to original physical abuse; (e) 76% of children had lived with siblings in follow up period and 6% of these siblings known to have been physically abused and 1% sexually abused. Total post registration abuse rate for index children and siblings residing in same family was 30% (including new adoptive families); (f) subsequent physical abuse only marginally related to

poorer outcomes, so neither abuse nor re abuse on their own very predictive of outcome. Subsequent sexual abuse not obviously related to outcome but small sample; (g) other injuries and also more than one hospital admission (for whatever reason) related to better outcomes; (h) no conclusive effect from number of changes of carer, but experiencing temporary or permanent separation from siblings was related to better outcomes. Living in families with few house moves related to worse outcomes; (i) nursery attendance: better outcomes associated with either no nursery attendance or attendance at 3 or more nurseries (but possible confounding by case type); (j) evidence of increased stability of families with time since registration in terms of life events of abuse, care giver changes, and school changes.

(8) Protective services in 5 year detailed follow up: (a) two thirds of children had one or two different social workers in follow up, who kept in regular contact with child and carer for long periods, providing practical help with the frequent marital, financial, and housing crisis, monitoring situation, and liaising with a wide array of agencies. Little referral for professional treatment or use of counselling, family therapy, or group work. More intensive and planned service and therapy when NSPCC was key agency; (b) length of social work service and likelihood of legal measures of protection significantly related to base line measures of risk; (c) short intense intervention was associated with better outcome (having control for base line risk category). Referral to adult psychologist or psychiatrist was only family support service related to good outcome.

(9) Substitute care: (a) 13% of children were removed permanently at registration, 12% removed during the follow-up after a failure of home care, 8% were removed for over 6 months but rehabilitated home, 18% had one or more short periods in care; (b) proportion of children received into care with good outcomes between 19% and 22%, except for those rehabilitated home of whom 31% had good outcomes; (c) significantly more children in long term care were in 2 parent families (97% vs less than 50% for those not in care), were in a higher social class, had fewer social disadvantages, and offered significantly greater parental involvement. However, the children in new families had slightly greater levels of base line risks and the adoptive parents used significantly more punitive methods of control (associated with poor outcome – see 6.e).

Notes: this summary was prepared from a draft report that is open to revision.

Gough et al (1987, 1993)

A LONGITUDINAL STUDY OF CHILD ABUSE IN GLASGOW

Sample: The total 202 children under 5 years of age placed upon the child abuse register of one British city over a 15 month period. The children came from 147 families; the majority were single or had relatively unstable, cohabiting relationships. Serious injury was uncommon and although many children had some bruising, most were suspected or at risk cases. The families were virtually all in receipt of public welfare benefits and under financial stress.

Focus: Decision making and case outcome in routine cases.

Objectives: Family support and child protection.

Programme: Social services casework.

Design: Two year prospective study with multiple measures on the treatment group.

Measures: Descriptive analysis of case decision making and case progress, using agency case records.

Results: 50% of the families had their children removed from the child abuse register within 10 months and 92% by 2 years. In 40% of the cases were referred to Children's Hearing System to obtain legal powers of supervision. 21% of cases the children spent some time in the care of the local authority and half of these children were still in care at 2 years post initial registration. Factors most associated with long term placement, were single parenthood and not coping with child care. Child injury or risks from cohabitees did not seem to be important factors. The services offered, were dominated by social services casework with few referrals to psychological or psychiatric services.

Notes: The authors also discussed other aspects of routine child abuse work. The report is part of a wider study on case decision making and family change in abuse cases.

Gough (1990), Gough and Sutton (1991)

HOSPITAL REFERRALS FOR SEXUAL ABUSE

Sample: 107 children (70% female) seen at Royal Hospital for Sick Children in Glasgow in 1989 where there were suspicions of child sexual abuse. Cases identified by 12 staff (predominantly paediatricians) particularly involved in cases of sexual abuse. Average age of children 6.9 years (range 0.25–15.25), 6.8 years for females and 7.1 years for males. In 21 cases the alleged perpetrator was thought to be less than 18 years. Some cases referred from part of city where special initiative between hospital paediatricians and police surgeons to conduct joint physical examinations for sexual abuse.

Focus: Routine and special initiative hospital paediatric work in sexual abuse.

Objectives: Non stated objectives of routine paediatric hospital work with cases of suspected sexual abuse.

Methods: Routine paediatric hospital work with cases of suspected sexual abuse including physical examinations, interviews with child and family, and consultation and advice to other professionals.

Design: Descriptive survey.

Measures: Standardized reporting forms completed by respondents for each case involving suspicions of sexual abuse.

Results: (1) Police involved in approximately 50% of referrals emanating from concerns of people in the community or from education staff and in 57% of cases emanating from child disclosure, but police involved in only 3% of referrals from social work or health. 36% of the referrals involved only health personnel and two thirds of these children physically examined for sexual abuse without reference to other agencies. Only health personnel were concerned in 65% of the cases arising from the physical state of the child. In only 3% of cases did the concern about possible sexual abuse emanate from a hospital paediatrician. Referrals from health visitors and general practitioners only concerned female children.

(2) Main work with cases were physical examination for sexual abuse (70%), interviews with children and/or families (10%), consultation/advice to other professionals (20%). Physical examinations more likely for referrals from police.

(3) For children physically examined 24% seemed distressed, 16% withdrawn, and 13% were resistant to the examination. In at least 76% of cases permission for examination was sought from child. Four children did not wish to be examined but one of these children was still examined.

(4) Police surgeons present at physical examination for 88% of cases referred by police, but at only 18% of examinations of cases referred from other sources. Police surgeons present at 85% of examinations of case from the special initiative area but at only 16% of cases from other areas of the city. Other data supplied by Strathclyde Police indicate that in 1988 before the special initiative of joint examinations 38% from this area were undertaken in hospital but this rose to 80% with the introduction of the initiative in 1989. Examinations for physical abuse, however, continued to be undertaken in police stations.

(5) For the 75 children physically examined doctors reported 8 cases of diagnostic or significant anogenital signs of abuse, 10 cases with some possible signs, and 57 cases with no signs. Laboratory tests included genital swabs in 21 cases, anal swab in 10 cases, pharyngeal swab in 4 cases, blood test in 2 cases. Doctors reported that in 8 cases referral data made them believe sexual abuse had occurred and this confirmed by diagnostic or significant signs; in 24 cases believed that abused from referral data and this view maintained although no significant physical signs found; in 7 cases believed that abused from referral data but became uncertain after no physical signs found in examination (though other possible influences on judgement).

Notes: The authors discussion includes the relevance of the different routes of case referral, the limited inter-disciplinary involvement before children are physically examined, the lack of laboratory tests, and the effects of the presence of physical signs on doctors belief as to whether abuse has occurred.

Harper and Irvin (1985)

ALLIANCE FORMATION WITH PARENTS.

Sample: 49 cases admitted to an inpatient child psychiatry psychosomatic service in one year, where there had been mandatory reporting for child abuse before, during, or after admission. Cases were mostly of neglect.

Focus: Professional-parent relationship in the context of mandatory reporting.

Objectives: To enhance clinical relationship and so improve parents' ability to work on child's behalf in alliance with the professional staff.

Programme: The use of mandatory reporting of child abuse and a range of 'clinical limit setting' tools to enlist the active co-operation of parents.

Design: Retrospective analysis of treatment sample.

Measures: Descriptive.

Results: Effects of mandatory reporting considered good, as 71% of the relationships improved; for 25% there was no change. One negative outcome occurred where inter-team differences led to premature discharge at the same time as child abuse was reported.

Notes: Context of the article is a general unwillingness of clinicians to report abuse. The authors believe, on the contrary, that reporting can be beneficial and the purpose of the study was to demonstrate this.

Heap (1984)

A Follow Up of Post Crisis Support.

Sample: 14 children admitted to a hospital in Norway for child abuse (n=4) and neglect (n=10). Children were aged from 6 months to 9 years.

Focus: Child protection system.

Objectives: Family support and child protection.

Programme: Day care, health visiting, counselling, psychiatric service, supervision orders, child care placements. 86 professionals had contact with the families, but social workers were still providing a service at the 3 year follow up.

Design: Repeated measures on treatment group.

Measures: At one, two, and three year follow up: researchers' assessment of whether service was appropriate. At 3 year follow up only: (1) Agency records and worker's views on the children's development and functioning; (2) whether there had been adherence to the original treatment plan, and (3) whether help was given to the families.

Results: At one year: cases receiving either no help (n=2), help but not appropriate (n=10), help and appropriate (n=2). At 3 years: cases with no help (n=5), cases with appropriate help (n=6). Two thirds of treatment plans were either discontinued or not implemented. Many of the children (n=9) had moderate or severe emotional problems and two were borderline psychotic. Not much evidence of the children receiving help.

Notes: Author states that inappropriate treatment characterized by (1) lack of inter-agency co-operation, (2) overemphasis on child injuries at expense of psycho-social factors (3) over identification with the parents (4) reluctance to use authority in relationship with child, (5) inappropriate case plans that often overlooked child needs (6) lack of time, support, supervision of caseworkers.

Hensey et al (1983)

Intervention in Child Abuse: Experience in Liverpool.

Sample: 50 children who presented at the Casualty Department of a children's hospital in Liverpool and who were subjects of case conferences and subsequently taken into care. 78% physical abuse, 22% severe neglect.

Focus: Children received into care because of risk of abuse.

Objectives: Providing a service for children at risk of abuse.

Programme: 25 children were in foster care for periods from 10 months to 5 years and returned home. 25 children remained in care with up to seven changes of placements. 36% of the sample had more than 2 placements.

Design: Post-test on treatment sample.

Measures: Workers' assessments of emotional disturbance, educational progress, re-abuse, physical and neurological development of the children. Outcomes including one major problem coded as unsatisfactory.

Results: Abnormal development in 7 cases including epilepsy, handicap, and failure to thrive (n=4). Emotional disturbance in 18 cases of which 12 were referred for specialist help. 11 children were behind in school progress. 5 children were re-abused. 26 (52%) of case outcomes coded as unsatisfactory. 19 of the 26 unsatisfactory outcomes were for the 25 children who were returned home. Outcome worst for those longest away before return home. Quality of outcome relative to assessment at placement. Those under 3 years had significantly better outcomes.

Notes: Authors emphasize importance of intensive support for children returned home. They note that the cases where return home was successful had major changes in family circumstances. The article does not give much indication apart from outcome as to the differences between the cases where children went home or remained away.

King and Taitz (1985)

Catch Up Growth Following Abuse.

Sample: 95 child abuse cases referred to a children's hospital in Sheffield, who were at some point subject to intervention by the child protection system. Children varied in age from 8 weeks to 12 years. 64 were at home, 11 were at home after short term fostering, 120 were in long term foster care. On average the children were one standard deviation below developmental norm and 38 children were two standard deviations below. No significant differences between the placement group at pre-test on weight, height, or age.

Focus: Child placements in cases of abuse.

Objectives: Child placement, case planning.

Programme: Various kinds of child placement. (1) Placement at home, (2) short term foster care (3) long term foster care.

Design: Repeated measures (pre and post-test) with between and within group comparisons, controlled for age by use of data expressed in terms of norms for age (i.e. standard deviations from the mean).

Measures: Height, weight.

Results: Significant increase in height and weight for whole group. The number severely retarded fell from 38 to 19 children. Between groups: height: 11% catch up whilst at home, 55% whilst at foster placement (extremely significant). Weight: 22% catch up at home, 50% in foster care (significant). The biggest changes occurred in the long term foster care group and only these showed a significant gain in weight compared to normal children.

Note: Authors speculate on reasons for different outcomes. In particular the poor outcomes of the mixed care group who possibly experienced a succession of short term placements.

Krell et al (1983)

CHILD ABUSE AND WELFARE TRAINING

Sample: The 9 participants in the last of six 6 monthly support groups for workers involved with child abuse cases. A comparison group of 14 participants of earlier support groups. A matched group of 9 workers who did not participate in the groups.

Focus: Workers involved in child abuse work.

Objectives: To increase workers' ability to cope with emotional burdens of the work, to provide them with skills for helping families and for working with colleagues, and to provide insights into job related feelings and behaviour. Also to provide model for inter-disciplinary communication, case planning, and team work, and to allow workers to examine their perceptions of other workers.

Programme: Weekly group for six months which was co-led by child psychiatrists experienced in working with abusing families and with the possible deep emotional reactions of workers that can influence their behaviour. Specific techniques included exploration of case management dilemmas, role modelling of expression of feelings, resolution of 'worst crises', consideration of alternative coping strategies, examination of influences on worker behaviour.

Design: (1) Repeated measures (pre and post-test) on treatment group and matched controls, (2) within group pre-test comparison of members of the last group (n=9) with members from earlier groups (n=14).

Measures: Self report questionnaire on insight into the work, on emotional coping skills, on skills with working with both families and colleagues.

Results: (1) Treatment group showed significantly greater increase in scores compared to the matched controls, but at pre-test the treatment group had lower scores and thus greater scope for improvement. (2) Pre-test scores of members in the last group were significantly higher than members of previous groups tested at the same time. Regression analysis showed this to be due to the effect of earlier participation in groups rather than other factors.

Notes: Article discusses the nature of the problem and usefulness of the groups used. Few details given on the research sample of workers or how the questionnaire responses relate to worker behaviour.

Lawder et al (1984)

HELPING THE MULTI-PROBLEM FAMILY: A STUDY OF SERVICES TO CHILDREN IN THEIR OWN HOMES.

Sample: 101 Multi-problem families referred either for the prevention of reception into care, or for children returning from care in the first 2 years of the service. Most families were single parent, black, with 2 to 3 children, on public assistance and living in poor housing conditions. Parents reported problems of child control, parenting skills, relationship with child. Workers perceived mental health and family communication as main problems and child behaviour as relatively minor.

Focus: Mothers as clients of caseworkers.

Objectives: Integration of child into family. Increasing insight and understanding of family and individual problems.

Programme: Mainly social casework involving a therapeutic relationship, engagement of client and involving them in the helping process, carried out through home visits, telephone contact, and practical help through contact with other agencies. 80% of cases referred to other agencies and nearly 25% to 4 or more agencies. Service was usually for more than 6 months and often for over a year. Home visits varied in rate from 0.25 to 12 per month with an average of 2.4 visits.

Design: Post-test of treatment sample.

Measures: Retrospective analysis of case records and the production of case summaries. 3 point scale of no change, partial change, and problem resolved. Scale applied to overall case and to all of the main problem areas identified. 28% rated by 2 coders with inter rater reliability from 79% to 83%.

Results: Overall: little or no progress, 27%, partial progress, 48%, problems resolved, 26%. Problems identified by clients and workers: most progress in resource assistance where only 10% unresolved. Worst was home management where 40% unresolved. Average for all problems was 35% unresolved. There were 'lower' rates of success with problems identified by the worker but not agreed by parent. Factors significantly related to outcome were (1), children home from care, (2) positive emotional climate in home, (3) higher parental ego function, (4) parental insight, (5) willingness to enter therapeutic relationship. All these factors were inter correlated, with relationship and insight being the best predictors.

McBogg et al (1979b)

FOSTER CARE ENRICHMENT PROGRAMME

Sample: 8 families with 10 children involved to date in the programme. Most were court ordered to attend, because of child abuse and neglect. Age of children at entry varied from 3 weeks to 9 years with a mean of 3.5 years.

Focus: Foster placements.

Objectives: To promote the development of the child and to determine a permanent plan within 3 months and work towards this. To prevent children drifting in foster care.

Programme: (1) Natural family: psycho-social evaluation followed by 'foster family service', lay therapy, weekly group therapy, social service casework. (2) Child: provision of safe, caring foster parents, developmental evaluation, 'appropriate' therapies, frequent and productive visits from natural parents. There was a 3 month diagnostic period in which a permanent plan was developed.

Design: Description of outcomes of treatment sample.

Measures: Descriptive.

Results: In 7 out of 8 cases plans were achieved or were in progress. No foster breakdowns and re-placements of the children. General satisfaction with programme by all concerned.

Notes: Programme grew out of awareness of problems in achieving permanency planning and foster parents desire for better communication with all parties. Article emphasises the importance of developing good relations between foster and natural parents.

Magura (1982)

CLIENTS VIEW OF OUTCOMES OF CHILD PROTECTIVE SERVICES

Sample: 34 abuse and neglect cases with risk of child placement away from home, allocated randomly to either the intensive or routine service of Child Protective Service. The cases represent 43% of those approached for the study. The others were unwilling to participate, but did not differ in type of family problems or case motivation from the research sample.

Focus: Child protection and functioning of parents.

Objectives: Child protection service to support families and remove children if and when at risk.

Programme: Intensive service with client worker ratio of 11 to 1 compared to the routine services ratio of 33 to 1. Also additional resources of client workshops and therapy groups. Both normal and routine services based on individualized counselling for the parents, counselling for children, age graded projects for children, material support such as housing allocation, and referral to other services as necessary.

Design: Post-test comparison of experimental (intensive service) and control (routine service) groups with random allocation to groups.

Measures: Interviews with parents about their current situation, what has improved over treatment, and satisfaction with service.

Results: Whole sample: 47% said things were 'much better', 23% 'somewhat better', 24% same, 6% worse. The proportion of sample reporting things to be much better, was higher in the intensive group. Main areas of importance were self confidence, coping, material improvements, child behaviour. Improvements were mostly attributed to individual counselling because of both emotional and practical supports and particularly the empathy and unconditional positive regard of the workers. Counselling seemed to be emphatic without being condoning and directive without being overbearing or in hostile conflict. High correspondence between level of client satisfaction and client ratings of improvement. Dissatisfaction of intensive group related to unwanted advice and to lack of skills. In routine group it was mainly to do with inaccessibility of services.

Notes: Article notes the positive client response to counselling in contrast to views of abuse clients being non verbal and unamenable to 'talking therapy'. Authors state that engaging families in group work was more difficult. Despite the experimental design there is relatively little data on the services provided or the differential outcomes of the groups.

Magura and Moses (1984)

CLIENTS AS EVALUATORS IN CHILD PROTECTIVE SERVICES

Sample: 250 clients from 4 agencies chosen to provide a naturally representative sample (U.S.A.). Clients had been receiving child protection services for a variety of forms of abuse, with at least one child at home, receiving the service.

Focus: Child Protection and functioning of parents.

Objectives: Child protection service to support families and remove children if and when at risk.

Programme: Predominant tool was casework counselling for parents on child disciplining and control, physical and emotional child care, child education, and sexual abuse. Children were counselled about their behaviour, education, symptomatic behaviour, and child sexual abuse. Also practical help with material problems, referral to other agencies, and advocacy in the educational system.

Design: Post-test on treatment sample.

Measures: Interviews with clients 5 months into casework on 11 areas of concern.

Results: Percentage of clients stating that the problem (if they had it) was diminished: child discipline 32%, child supervision 25%, living conditions 21%, finance 19%, physical care 18%, emotional care 26%, school adjustment 36%, child conduct 27%, child symptoms 15%, sexual abuse 60%, parental coping 23%. In all cases the problems remained after help, but 70% of parents expressed satisfaction with service. Only 25% disagreed fundamentally with service though most of sample had important areas of dissatisfaction with case handling and attitudes. Only 35% reported receiving assistance with material problems and only 10% of those with problems in living conditions.

Notes: Article discusses (1) deleterious effect of material stresses, often not mentioned in study responses, as help not expected. (2) Lack of variety of services for children, who mostly received counselling which did not solve their problems. No use of parent education or skilled trainees. (3) Child behaviour problems referred to other agencies with parental approval.

Mouzakatis and Goldstein (1985)

A MULTIDISCIPLINARY APPROACH TO TREATING CHILD NEGLECT.

Sample: Neglect cases in Baltimore. Two case examples of single parent families providing inadequate emotional and physical care for their children, where an impasse has arrived for the keyworker and a consensus is required about the children's future placement. Family 1 had two children (2 & 4 years), both emotionally deprived. Mother has material and emotional problems. Family 2 had a 6 year old child with encopresis and receiving therapy. Mother was alcoholic.

Focus: Case management.

Objectives: To assist workers in providing a service and to co-ordinate services and prevent the fragmentation of care. To increase inter-agency and inter-disciplinary communication. To identify and intervene in cases of neglect.

Programme: Team of 14 members from social work, paediatrics, school social work, psychiatric social work, child psychology, police. Team met once a month to discuss cases including outcome of earlier team recommendations. In the 2 case examples the team suggested the development of more focused, time limited, and contractual casework relationship. Team also discussed its own functioning.

Design: Descriptive.

Measures: Descriptions of workers' abilities, attitudes and morale. Descriptions of time taken to achieve outcomes in two case examples.

Results: In the 2 case examples the recommended case actions had been achieved within 8 months in contrast to the usual 18 to 24 months taken. Team thought to be definitely effective in improving workers' moral and functioning as professionals.

Notes: No data on more global goals of identification of cases, and co-ordination of services.

Murphy et al (1991), Jellinek et al (1992)

SUBSTANCE ABUSE AND SERIOUS CHILD MISTREATMENT

Sample: 206 consecutive child mistreatment cases involving children under 13 years and excluding sexual abuse cases referred to Boston juvenile court. Cases were 60% neglect, 17% physical abuse, 24% both physical abuse and neglect. 67% came from minority groups, 67% were single parent families, 56% primary income from financial aid, 66% SES V, 53% of families had rejected court ordered services, 81% had prior social services or court referral.

Focus: Court ordered child protection services.

Objectives: Not specified – routine child protection work of juvenile court.

Programme: Routine child protection work of juvenile court.

Design: Prospective analysis of intervention group only.

Measures: (1) Risk List (RL) questionnaire with 92 items on presence of risks to child plus overall subjective rating of risk/danger to the child completed by Court Investigator (CI) (only overall rating reported in this paper). (2) Analysis of court records (includes agency reports) for written reports concerning substance abuse. (3) Details of case presentation and outcome. (4) Socio-economic status (on mother and on father/male partner if he contributed financially) and other demographic variables.

Results: Risk of maltreatment ratings available on 194 of 206 cases: 25% very severe risk, 30% severe risk, 33% moderate risk, 12% slight risk. Very severe and severe grouped as 55% high risk.

(1) Substance abuse for mothers, fathers, and families respectively were for alcohol abuse 24%, 54%, 31%; for cocaine abuse 16%, 20%, 16%; heroin abuse 12%, 22%, 12% (fathers' data based on the 69 families with fathers). Cocaine and/or heroin in 24% of families. Half of the families and 40% of mothers had alleged or documented alcohol or drug abuse.

(2) Neither demographic variables nor type of maltreatment significantly associated with substance abuse, but being in receipt of financial family aid was related to substance abuse. Prior protective history significantly longer and court referrals significantly higher in alcohol abusing families.

(3) Prior court or social service record significantly associated with definite drug or alcohol abuse by either parent, definite alcohol abuse by mother only, and alcohol abuse by either parent. CI rating of high risk related to definite drug or alcohol abuse by either parent. Both rejection of court ordered services and permanent removal of child very highly related to definite drug or alcohol abuse by either parent, definite drug or alcohol abuse by mother only, or heroin or cocaine by either parent. Similar findings when data controlled for receipt of financial family aid.

(4) 80% of families with both substance abuse and high CI risk rating rejected services. This was significantly higher than the 57% rejecting services who had either substance abuse or a higher risk rating. This in turn was significantly higher than the 23% rejecting services who had neither factor. Similar findings for outcome of permanent removal of children except that the difference in percentage

between both factors and either factor not quite significant.

(5) Failing to comply with court recommendations led to permanent removal of children in 97% of cases compared to 67% for complying parents (highly significant).

(6) 31% of parents had a documented DSM III psychiatric diagnosis, a further 11% had historical or behavioural evidence suggesting psychiatric disorder, though not formally documented. Neither type or severity of disorder predicted either compliance with court ordered services or permanent removal of child.

(7) Mean length of time from official report of mistreatment to arraignment in court took an average 2.7 years. Time from arraignment to deposition in the juvenile court took an average further 1.4 years. Cases not dismissed at the juvenile court then took an average further 1.6 years to final placement at probate court. For all cases (not all of which proceeded to the end of the court system) the average time to final placement was 4.9 years.

(8) Outcome of cases at 30–54 months after filing child protection petition: (a) awaiting decision from the juvenile court 6% (average initial age of child over 9 years, 2 foster placements, in care for over 3 years); (b) juvenile court dismissed case, child returned to parents: 31% (average initial age 4.2 years, 2 foster placements, 1.4 years in care); (c) juvenile court removed children permanently and placed with other parent or relative: 15% (took only 1.3 years to final placement, significantly less than average of 2.6 years for others); (d) juvenile court removed children permanently and referred to probate court for adoption: 39% (on average initial age 9.5 years and in temporary care 3.5 years); (e) children adopted: 10% (average initial age of 17 months, in court system for total of 2.2 years, longer history of social services involvement and this often due to mistreatment of older siblings). In the 2 years since 63 cases dismissed by juvenile court, 29% had further substantiated official reports of abuse or neglect and slightly over half of these (16% of dismissed cases) were re-referred to court.

Notes: Author's suggestions include (a) that the longer prior protective histories and reports of child mistreatment for substance abusing parents (particularly alcohol) indicate that they are given more chances by the system but also that substance abuse was but one of many problems in these families; (b) treatment of substance abuse may not solve child mistreatment, but failure to address the substance abuse is almost to guarantee a failure of other intervention attempts; (c) tightening procedures and inter agency cooperation and emphasising the importance of permanency could significantly reduce the time taken through the courts; (d) judges should be given feedback as to the outcomes of their decisions.

Pritchard (1991)

FAMILIES ON THE AT RISK OF ABUSE REGISTER

Sample: 60 child protection cases made up from the first 20 cases formally closed in each of three areas of Hampshire Social Services after January 1987. Majority of cases involved physical abuse and/or neglect concerning a child under 2 years. Families had many negative social characteristics, 85% had long term unemployment.

Focus: Routine child protection services.

Objectives: Not specified, but would include child protection, support of parents to enable to care for child, removal of child if necessary to ensure welfare.

Programme: Routine child protection by local authority social service department.

Design: Descriptive.

Measures: Analysis of case records.

Results: All cases closed (sample criteria). For 68% of families the children had remained at home with no known recurrence of abuse; for 22% children were in care temporarily; for 7% the children were in foster care with no plans for return home; 3% of cases had moved out of the area.

Notes: Much of this study concerned assessing case risk characteristics and not summarized here.

Rivara (1985)

PHYSICAL ABUSE OF CHILDREN UNDER TWO: A STUDY OF THERAPEUTIC OUTCOMES.

Sample: 71 cases referred from Centre for Children in Crisis to mental health centres where the child was less than 2 years and the problem was physical abuse.

Focus: Parents of physically abused children.

Objectives: To develop parenting skills, relationships, and change attitudes in the family. To reduce stresses on the family.

Programme: Group teaching of parenting effectiveness, individual insight orientated therapy, marital counselling, general counselling and casework, placement of child where necessary. Contents of services varied across clients.

Design: Post-test on treatment sample.

Measures: Agency records of attendance for treatment, re-abuse of children, general progress and stability of family, reduction of family stressors.

Results: Only a third of sample complied with recommendations to receive treatment, 30% of children re-abused, half of families deemed unstable, only 13% thought to have made good progress in counselling. 59 children removed from home at some point and at follow up 40% were no longer with either parent. Little impact of service on socio- economic stresses. No correlation between re-abuse of children and compliance with treatment.

Notes: Author suggests that lack of compliance may be due to: lack of aggressive outreach; that insight therapy may be ineffective with low IQ parents; that personality treatment may be irrelevant as perhaps no psychopathology; that training in parenting skills may be less important than parental sensitivity; all treatments ineffective if socio-economic stressors not addressed.

Sedlak (1992)

RISK FACTORS FOR CHILD ABUSE AND NEGLECT AND THE LIKELIHOOD OF OFFICIAL INVESTIGATION

Sample: 2,235 children identified as abused or neglected in 1986 in a nationally representative sample of 0.24% of the United States child population by the Second National Incidence Study of Child Abuse and Neglect (1988). Children identified as abused by a wide range of community professionals including child protection services (CPS). Criteria of 'Harm Standard' definition where child usually required to have experienced demonstrable harm from maltreatment. Control group of 3,798 nationally representative non maltreated children from 1986/87 census.

Focus: Maltreatment identified by community professionals.

Objectives: Non specified objectives of community professionals and CPS.

Programme: Non specified programmes of community professionals and CPS.

Design: Multi-factor logistic analysis of survey data to contrast (i) cases of maltreatment identified by community services compared to controls (ii) cases of maltreatment known to community professionals by whether investigated or not by CPS.

Measures: Evident from results section.

Results: In these results 'WHB' represents 'Whites, Blacks, and Hispanics', 'No independent association

227

means that any association disappears when other variables are statistically controlled.

1. Survey of community professionals identified 2,235 cases of maltreatment equivalent to a national estimate of 931,000 maltreated children in the United States for 1986. Fifty four per cent of the cases were identified by schools.

2. The following variables were associated with greater risk of child maltreatment:

(a) Child's sex: for physical abuse, no association; for sexual abuse, females generally at greater risk; for emotional maltreatment, no association; for physical neglect, 15–17 year old females; for educational neglect, no association; multiple maltreatment, females generally.

(b) Child's age: for physical abuse, older children, especially Blacks and Hispanics and with both parents present; for sexual abuse, older children for WHB and for father only households; for emotional maltreatment, older children generally; for physical neglect, older females and father only families; for educational neglect, older children when both parents present; for multiple maltreatment, older WHB children at greater risk.

(c) Race: for physical abuse, older for Blacks and Hispanics; for sexual abuse, Whites, Blacks, and Hispanics, as age progresses; for emotional maltreatment, non WHB children generally; for physical neglect, no independent association; for educational neglect, Whites and Blacks; for multiple maltreatment, Whites at older ages.

(d) Family income: lower income families at greater risk for every type of maltreatment.

(e) County Metropolitan status: for physical and sexual abuse and emotional maltreatment, no association; for physical neglect, large urban counties at higher risk; for educational neglect and for multiple maltreatment, urban generally.

(f) Number of children in household: for physical abuse and for educational neglect, only one child; for sexual abuse and for multiple maltreatment, no association; for emotional maltreatment and for physical neglect, no independent association.

(g) Family structure: for physical abuse, two parent families for children over 5 only; for sexual abuse, father only families for older children; for emotional maltreatment, no association; for physical neglect, father only families for 15–17 year olds only; for educational neglect, both parent families for older children only; for multiple maltreatment, both parent or mother only compared to father only families.

3. For all those identified as maltreated by community professionals the following variables were associated with greater likelihood of investigation by CPS:

(a) Child's sex: for physical abuse, females for severe injuries or for older ages; for sexual abuse, no association; for physical neglect and emotional maltreatment, males below 6 years, females above 6 years; educational neglect, no independent association.

(b) Child's age: for physical abuse, risk of investigation increases with age for Black children and decreases for male children; for sexual abuse, risk increases with age for Whites, decreases for Blacks and Hispanics; for physical neglect and emotional maltreatment, decreases with age for males only; educational neglect, risk increases with age for Whites and when other victims are suspected, decreases with age for Non Whites and for both parent and father only families.

(c) Race: for physical abuse, Blacks below 12.5 years only; for sexual abuse, Hispanics below 7 and Blacks below 8 years, Whites for older ages; for physical neglect and emotional maltreatment, Blacks and Whites; for educational neglect, Non Whites below 14, Whites above 14.

(d) Family income: for physical abuse, no association; for sexual abuse and for educational neglect, no independent association; for physical neglect and emotional maltreatment, income above $15,000.

(e) County Metropolitan status: no association for any type of maltreatment.

(f) Number of children: for physical abuse, unknown number of children; sexual abuse, no association; for physical neglect and emotional maltreatment, no independent association; for educational neglect, only one child in household.

(g) Family structure: for physical abuse, father only families; for sexual abuse, no association; for physical neglect and emotional maltreatment, no independent association; for educational neglect, less likely for those under 16 in mother only households.

(h) Recognition source: for physical abuse and for educational neglect, less likely if identified by day care, social services, or mental health; for sexual abuse, no association; for physical neglect and emotional maltreatment, more likely if identified by law enforcement or medical services.

(i) Other suspected victims in household; for physical abuse and for sexual abuse, more likely; for physical neglect and emotional maltreatment, more likely unless identified by day care, social services, or mental health; for educational neglect, more likely if over 9.5 years.

(j) Nature of harm: for physical abuse, sexual abuse, and educational neglect, no association; for physical neglect and emotional maltreatment, physical injury.

(k) Severity of harm; for physical abuse, fatal, serious, or inferred injuries for females only; for sexual abuse, less likely if no evidence of harm available; for physical neglect and emotional maltreatment, moderate and inferred harm; for educational neglect, no independent association.

(l) Perpetrator relationship: for physical and sexual abuse and educational neglect, no association; for physical neglect and emotional maltreatment, parents and parent substitutes.

(m) Perpetrator location: for physical abuse and for physical neglect and emotional maltreatment, no independent association; for sexual abuse, perpetrator not in child's home; for educational neglect, no association.

(n) Number of perpetrators: for physical and sexual abuse and educational neglect, no association; for physical neglect and emotional maltreatment, less likely if multiple perpetrators.

(o) Perpetrator sex: no association with any type of maltreatment.

3. Overall CPS investigated 57% of physical abuse, 65% of sexual abuse, 29% of physical neglect or emotional maltreatment, and 10% of educational neglect, as identified by the incidence study. The rate of CPS investigations for different sources of cases identified were: CPS own sources, 100%; Medical Services, 69%; Law Enforcement, 58%; Schools, 26%; Others, 33%.

Notes: Authors conclusions include: (1) low income families at greatest risk of maltreatment, older children also generally at greater risk, that risk was also related to many other factors but these varied with type of maltreatment with interactions among risk factors being common; (2) single parent households were only associated with greater risk of abuse if income was not statistically controlled; (3) Although low income families were at higher risk of being identified as maltreated, there was no greater chance that they would be investigated by CPS; (4) groups such as physically neglected low income, physically neglected 2 parent, physically or sexually abused minority adolescents were at greater risk of abuse yet were less likely to have their maltreatment investigated by CPS; (5) Schools were the source of over half of the cases identified by the survey of community professionals yet these cases had the lowest rate of investigation by CPS either because they were not reported or because they were screened out at intake.

Stone and Stone (1983)

THE PREDICTION OF SUCCESSFUL FOSTER PLACEMENT

Sample: 64 cases of child placements away from the family of origin, due to child abuse and neglect. Children were over $3\frac{1}{2}$ years with an average of 8 years. The sample consisted of all such placements made by 3 child welfare units in the area.

Focus: Child Placements.

Objectives: Placements as part of child protection service, providing shelter from immediate risks and sometimes a long term alternative home for the child.

Programme: Foster care placements.

Design: Retrospective analysis of case records. Stepwise inter-correlational matrix of all variables, identified factors with no predictive value discarded, stepwise multiple regression on remaining factors to a cut off of a 5% level of significance, multiple

regression with case worker variables excluded to identify best general predictors.

Measures: Successful placements defined as lasting more than 60 days without breakdown due to either disruptive child behaviour or non compliance by natural parents. Lack of detail on other measures.

Results: 48.5% of placements broke down within first 4 weeks because of child's behaviour. 11 variables significantly correlated with placement outcome. Strongest association was found for degree of contact, rapport building, energy expended by caseworker. Other significant variables were skills, motivation of foster parents, rapport between foster parents and welfare agency. Less aggressive and better socialized children did well. Chronically abused or neglected did worse.

Notes: Authors conclude that motivation and energy of worker and selection of foster parents are the most important. Article gives little detail as to how the case variables were rated.

Thoburn (1991); Thoburn et al (1991)

FAMILY PARTICIPATION IN CHILD PROTECTION WORK

Sample: (1) 200 consecutive child protection cases involving 380 children. Cases recruited at initial child protection case conferences in 7 social work teams in different parts of England. Teams chosen that espoused parental participation in case conferences (CCs). A third of teams routinely invited parents to all of all CCs, a third invited them to part of CCs, a third did not invite parents but attempted to involve them in other ways. (2) A random sub-sample of 35 cases studied in more depth.

Focus: Parental participation in routine child protection.

Objectives: Not specified routine child protection, but authors suggest 4 possible value positions regarding objective of parental participation: citizen's rights, effectiveness of service, therapeutic to parents, and placation and manipulation (though this last dimension not considered in this study).

Programme: Routine child protection of social work teams interested in achieving greater parental involvement.

Design: Prospective longitudinal (6 month) follow up on main and sub-sample. Analysis using Arnstein's Ladder of citizen participation and data source triangulation.

Measures: (1) Main sample: mini record and questionnaire for parents and social workers on: early contact, investigation, assessment, help or services offered, agency policy regarding intervention, personal views regarding participation. (2) Sub-sample: guided interview for parents, child, and social worker. (3) Researcher rating of successful engagement of family in child protection work and the outcome of this in terms of the child's interests.

Results: Tentative preliminary findings: (1) 51% of children allegedly abused placed on register on categories of physical abuse, 27%; sexual abuse, 17%; emotional abuse and failure to thrive, 8%; neglect, 12%; grave concern, 34%. 20% of children in care at time of initial CC. (2) Parental attendance at initial CC: attended whole, 21%; part, 40%; end only, 8%; invited but not attend, 19%; not invited, 13%. Workers and agencies that have moved towards greater participation have not regretted this and to date report no obviously damaging effects re care of children. (3) A number of other ways of involving parents are being identified. (4) Difficulties in participation identified include tokenism of attendance at CCs which can be counter-productive; the involvement of alleged abusers, particularly if they are excluded from the home; older children sharing social worker with parents; parental information re access to records and to complaints procedures.

Thorpe (1991)

PATTERNS OF CHILD PROTECTION INTERVENTION AND SERVICE DELIVERY

Sample: All 672 allegations of child abuse investigated by Department of Community Services, South West Australia, from 1st March to 30th June 1987.

Focus: Routine child protection services.

Objectives: Provision of child protection intervention and service delivery.

Programme: Not specified routine child protection.

Design: Retrospective analysis of case records.

Measures: see the results section for types of classification employed.

Results: (1) Allegations concerned physical abuse, 22%; emotional abuse, 2%; sexual abuse, 22%; neglect, 48%; unknown, 6%. Of these cases 34% were substantiated and 16% were labelled as at risk. (2) Contexts of the allegations: 6% custody/access disputes of which 21% were substantiated; 10% other conflict between family members of which 67% were substantiated; 4% conflict between neighbours of which 12% were substantiated; for 79% cases some other context. (3) 49% reports concerned single parent families, 18% reconstituted families, 27% families with both biological parents. 22% families were of Aboriginal origin with a substantiation rate of 68% compared to a rate of 45% for other Australian cases reported.

(4) Case career types were: substitute care from the beginning, 9%; became substitute care later, 6%; home based services only, 21%; substantiated but received no further action, 13%; not substantiated, 50%. Those in substitute care from the beginning were mostly cases of neglect, 37%; at risk, 30%; sexual abuse, 19%; or physical abuse, 12%. Those cases that became substitute care later were mostly neglect, 55%; or at risk, 34%. For Aboriginal families the children went into care at some point in 51% of cases, but the rate was only 21% for other Australian families.

(5) Home based services for at risk cases were material/practical assistance, 41%; advice/guidance/ treatment, 41%; surveillance/monitoring, 10%. Neglect cases mostly (72%) received material/practical assistance; physical abuse and sexual cases mostly (67% and 86% respectively) received advice/guidance/treatment. (6) In 6% of the substantiated or at risk cases care and protection applications to court were withdrawn. (7) Only 15% of allegations were open cases 52 weeks after the initial reports. Over a third of these open cases were in two of the state's twenty divisions. Of the closed cases 10% were re-investigated within 52 weeks of initial report and two thirds of these had been originally closed because of lack of substantiation. In the re-referred cases that were originally unsubstantiated a fifth were substantiated on second investigation. For re-referred cases originally labelled at risk, 31% were substantiated on second investigation. For re-refered cases case careers were similar to original investigations, though a larger proportion of physical abuse cases entered substitute care.

Notes: The project was undertaken to study the feasibility and develop a system for managing child protection information. Data on individual divisions within the state also presented. The author suggests that the withdrawn court applications were a tactic to safeguard children's welfare as the state has no supervision orders, only full wardship.

Waterhouse and Carnie (1990, 1992)

CHILD SEXUAL ABUSE: THE PROFESSIONAL CHALLENGE TO SOCIAL WORK AND POLICE

Sample: 51 consecutive cases of intra familial sexual abuse identified from child abuse registers of 4 local authority departments in Scotland in 1986/87.

Focus: Routine child protection investigations by police and social work.

Objectives: Unspecified objectives of routine child protection investigations.

Methods: Unspecified methods of child protection investigation.

Design: Descriptive survey.

Measures: Standardized recording form for recording details from social work records, standardized interviews with the front line social workers and police officers in each case.

Results: (1) 56% of sample females aged 12–16 years, 94% sample female. At least strong suspicion of abuse to siblings in 33% of cases. 50% of case records did not specify type of sexual abuse,but touching and fondling most commonly reported. 33% perpetrators biological father, 33% others in father role, 25% close male relatives. 60% of referrals emanated from those within or close to the family and the police or social work were the first referral point in only 10% of cases. Social work and police were both involved in most cases, whilst the rate of medical involvement varied from 0% to 70% depending upon the geographical region. Child disclosure was seen as particularly pivotal in triggering an investigation and determining child care outcomes and children rarely retracted these disclosures during early social work investigation.

(2) Police officers involved in cases mostly male, social workers mostly female. Police officers older and had more previous experience of abuse investigations than social workers. Social workers rarely confronted alleged perpetrators about sexual abuse, relying on police officers to do this. Internal checks on alleged perpetrators were automatic for police but only sometimes made by social work. Allegations could rarely be judged true or false due to lack of detailed evidence.

(3) Social work decision making based on evaluation of (i) risk to child based upon primary (child care) criteria including attitude of non abusing parent to alleged perpetrator, access of alleged perpetrator to child, type of abuse, age of child, attitude of alleged perpetrator to allegations, parental attitude to investigation; (ii) secondary (disclosure) criteria including belief/confirmatory information re child's disclosure, psychological symptoms of child, physical signs of abuse, child's attitude to remaining at home, criminal or psychiatric history of parents/caregivers.

(4) The most common model of inter-agency work was collaborative with close formal and informal consultation about progress and courses of action, a sizeable minority of cases followed a minimalist model communicated only according to the minimum required by formal procedures, very few cases followed an integrated model of joint work although this was the preferred mode of work proposed by both police officers and social workers. Mild confusion about responsibilities of both agencies apparent in most cases. Few police officers or social workers had received specialist training in sexual abuse work. Police officers in areas with specialist units felt that training should be primarily for these specialists whilst social workers wanted training for all workers. Social workers had great faith in training whilst police officers expected to learn through

experience. Police officers felt that supervision could provide them with specific information and advice, whilst social workers felt that it could help with their personal reactions to abuse, their professional responsibilities, and the dynamics of sexual abuse.

Wells et al (1989)

SCREENING IN CHILD PROTECTIVE SERVICES (CPS).

Sample: Five discrete surveys of (1) U.S. state laws and policies re the investigation of CPS referrals. (2) Screening and prioritization policies of 100 local county administrators and supervisors in 8 states. (3) On site study screening in 12 communities from 5 states. (4) Views of community agencies in the 12 communities. (5) Case registry follow-up of children who were CPS contacts in the study period.

Focus: Screening of CPS referrals.

Objectives: To determine which referrals require investigation.

Programme: Most state laws require citizens and professionals to report all cases of suspected child abuse and neglect to the local child protection services. CPS have limited resources and there are also public concerns about 'over investigation' of 'inappropriate' referrals. CPS have had to develop policies and practices in order to decide which cases to investigate and to what degree.

Design: Cross sectional descriptive study plus follow up on one variable.

Measures: (1) Examination of state laws and policies. (2) Survey of administrators of both written policies and practices. (3) Completion of form by workers on every referral received. (4) Views of referring agencies in community. (5) Repeat contacts at follow up.

Results: (1) State Laws and Policies. Screening decisions fall into three broad categories of (i) Classification of contacts; for example, does it fall within the laws mandating state intervention; (ii) Preliminary assessment: sometimes necessary on cases probably not requiring state intervention because of lack of precise information; (iii) Selection for Investigation: decision not to investigate bona fide report falling within mandate of law and policy.

Initial screening out of referrals has not been generally permitted in state laws, but is increasingly the subject of new laws and policies. For those states with provision for initial screening the allowable reasons for non investigation include: (a) Characteristics of the perpetrator are not within legal definition; for example: not identified, not a caretaker, a juvenile. (b) The complaint does not describe a specific act of abuse, for example, no injury specified, general domestic violence, homelessness. (c) Problem is the province of another agency; for example: delinquency, mental health of child or parent. (d) History of repeated unsubstantiated allegations. (e) Complaint is an obvious attempt to harass, for example, custody disputes. (f) Insufficient information to proceed. (g) Family already in receipt of service from Social Services or similar. (h) Case not within jurisdiction of the specific protection service contacted. (i) Information obtained which invalidates the report. (j) Other; for example, concerns about unborn children, insufficient risk.

(2) Local Screening Policies. Supervisors generally identified the following as reasons for screening: (i) Perpetrator not a caregiver, (ii) no specific act alleged – just general situations, (iii) problem not appropriate for CPS. Supervisors generally did not list (a) lack of injury, (b) injury not severe, (c) incident not intentional and injury minor, (d) incident long time in past, (e) perpetrator unknown, (f) parent or child could not be located, (g) repeated unsubstantiated allegations, (h) parent worried that might harm, but had not yet, (i) custody dispute.

Data on trends over time revealed that policies supported at supervisory level had most impact on reporting rates; (authors suggest because community becomes aware of policy and so do not report); that screening and prioritizing was associated with lower rates of increases in reporting, but no effect on substantiation levels; likely that the policies only have short lived impact on reporting (authors suggest because of inexorable rise in reporting).

(3) Screening Practices. 2,504 contacts studied in 12 sites. (a) Percentage of types of maltreatment of contacts similar to report of American Humane Association in 1986. 14% did not allege maltreatment, just general concern; 8% alleged unspecified maltreatment. (b) Investigation rate ranged from 26% to 97%. The average for unspecified allegations was 42%, for specific allegations, 66%. If child reported injured then 70% were investigated whether allegations specific or not. (c) Reason for investigating no maltreatment contacts included: child may still be at risk, 22%; specific act alleged, 20%; specifics not clear but referrer believable, 14%. Also other risks such as child had no place to stay. (d) Reasons for not investigating specific allegations included: no injury reported, 38%; child not at risk, 24%; no specific act alleged, 23%; responsibility of another agency, 18%; insufficient information, 13%; custody dispute, 7%; referral considered harassment of family, 5%. (e) Major variation between sites, but controlling for this, allegation of maltreatment and presence of injury were the strongest predictors of investigation. Severe injury 1.7 times more likely to be investigated controlling for all other factors. Also important were full data on study report form, presence of perpetrator in home, overload or lack of ability in parental child care, over harsh

parental discipline, child not teenager. Less likely to be investigated were contacts from perpetrator, non perpetrator parent, victim, other relatives and friends. Mandated reporters contacts most likely to be followed up. Similar results for subset of contacts alleging specific maltreatment, but increased investigations for sexual abuse, child under 2 years. Also less impact from parental problems and perpetrator in the home. Authors note that data on 12 sites may not be representative of all sites. Two sites were chosen because known to screen referrals and they were found to screen 70% of contacts. At time of project few agencies acknowledged any screening activity.

(4) Community Agencies' Views: The higher the percentage of respondents reporting a positive relationship with CPS the more likely that contacts would be screened but this may be explained by a confounding of positive relationship with neglect cases which had a high chance of being screened in.

(5) Follow Up: A greater chance of subsequent report on a child if a report occurred prior to original data collection, if previous report had been screened in.

Notes: Authors conclude that (1) approximately 9% of contacts are out of jurisdiction and 9 to 14% obviously not appropriate. (2) Few unwarranted investigations, but many bona fide allegations not being investigated, so maybe insufficient resources to investigate all relevant contacts. (3) Chance of the same maltreatment being investigated varied greatly between sites – suggesting a dimension of philosophy of CPS agencies with the 2 extremes of (i) broad approach including voluntary assessments and support, (ii) policy of only including most serious and clearly specify what is not within the CPS remit. (4) Practice that presence of an injury as indicator of seriousness, but not reflected in written policies. (5) Screening is a process with at least 3 levels. (6) There is a need for the development of policies on screening and monitoring of their effects. For example, the ability of workers to screen for risk and the use of often untested risk assessment systems.

Wolock and Mumm (1992)

PREDICTORS OF RE-REPORTS OF CHILD ABUSE AND NEGLECT

Sample: 401 families randomly sampled from cases reported to five offices of New Jersey Division of Youth and Family Services between December 1988 and October 1989, but closed after investigation due to lack of substantiation, lack of risk to children, or other reasons.

Focus: Routine child protection services.

Objectives: Routine child protection services.

Programme: Routine child protection services.

Design: Survey of routine cases.

Measures: Interviews with main caretaker on family functioning, services recommended by the agency and used, demographic variables. Data scored on 9 scales: Negative stressful life events (17 items); Emotional Well Being (14 items); Difficulty of Parenting (3 items); Family Conflict (4 items); Children's Psychological Problems (10 items), Children's Behavioural Problems (23 items); Financial Stress Scale (9 items); Social Isolation (6 items); Neighborhood Scale (7 items). Also recording of ethnicity, number of children, and whether evidence of substance abuse, time between initial report and any re-report.

Results: (1) 93% principal caretakers women, three quarters aged between 20 and 39 years. 54% Caucasian, 24% Hispanic, 22% Black. Number of adults per household ranged from 1 to 8 with average of 2.1. 29% were lone single parent families, 32% were single parents with other adults, 39% were two parent families. Total of 975 children, number per home ranging from 1 to 10, with an average of 2.4. A quarter of the children were under 3 years old, 65% were under 10. 26% of families had no adult employed, 43% had one adult employed, 31% two adults employed. Median monthly income of $1,310; 47% were below poverty line; 32% received ADFC assistance. Substance abuse apparent in 34% families.

(2) 25% had one re-report and 21% had two or more re-reports of abuse. Time ranged from 1 to 31 weeks post initial report, average of 10.5 months.

(3) Re-reports significantly associated with all variables except for families' use of community or recommended services. Re-reported families were more likely to be Black or Hispanic, to be receiving ADFC, to have three or more children, and to have worse scores on all 9 scales (see Measures section).

(4) Multiple regression analysis found that re-reports significantly associated with substance abuse, three or more children, ADFC as main income. These variables accounted for 22% of the variance. Being Black or Hispanic and believing that you lived in a poor neighborhood approached significance.

Notes: The authors discuss the importance of the findings that substance abuse, many children in the family, and financial stress are the best predictors of re-reports, whilst the use of agency services is unrelated to rate of re-reports. Belsky's ecological model of child abuse also discussed.

CHAPTER ELEVEN
Child Sexual Abuse

Background

The last ten years has witnessed an exponential increase in the numbers of identified child abuse cases. In the early 1980's there was not a category for sexual abuse on local child abuse registers in Britain and descriptive studies of local authority case management only identified two or three per cent of cases that had any identified sexual abuse component (for example, Gough et al, 1987, 1993). The number of sexual abuse cases on Child Abuse Registers held by the National Society for Prevention of Cruelty to Children in 1981 was only 27, but by 1986 this had risen by a factor of twenty to 527 cases (NSPCC 1988). Currently sexual abuse accounts for an estimated 16% of registrations in England and Wales (Department of Health, 1991) and 23% of registrations in Scotland (Gough, 1992).

More dramatic evidence of the high prevalance of sexual abuse has arisen from population surveys of adults' retrospective recall of childhood sexual experiences. Between 3% and 30% of males and between 6% and 62% of females report such experiences (see Peters et al, 1986; Siegal et al, 1987). The high variation in rates reported between studies may be due to differences between samples, but is more likely to be a function of differences in methodology in interviewing and in definitions of sexual abuse. Findings of one of the few British studies (Kelly et al, 1991) well illustrates the effect of definition. The study reported prevalence rates (for under 16 year olds) of 18% for men and 43% for women for all abusive experiences (including where there was no physical contact) with someone at least two years older than themselves. Using a five year age difference and limiting cases to those involving forced penetration or masturbation the rates were 2% and 4% for men and women respectively.

The most conservative estimates of the prevalance of sexual abuse in the population are extremely high and much greater than the approximately one per thousand children placed on child abuse registers for suspected sexual abuse. Although the population surveys differ in their reported rates of sexual abuse, they all agree that it is extremely common in western societies. Finkelhor argues that this fact is more important than determining the exact prevalence rates (Finkelhor, 1991). The problem is how best to intervene to prevent the abuse occurring. This will depend upon both one's analysis of the cause of the abuse and upon political considerations as to whom or what is responsible for achieving the necessary change.

The relatively short period of time within which there has been widespread awareness and acceptance of the extent of sexual abuse there has been limited time to undertake research. Despite this, the attention that it now receives has overshadowed work on other forms of abuse to the extent that some people use the terms child abuse and child sexual abuse inter changeably.

The concern to learn more about the nature of sexual abuse and appropriate methods of intervention has not always resulted in well organized and defined research studies. In many ways the literature on child sexual abuse is similar to the treatment studies on other forms of abuse. Most studies are not experimental tests of the efficacy of different treatment models, but are descriptive accounts of the various therapeutic innovations that have been attempted.

The authors of these studies are often deeply committed to, and positive about, the services that they describe and assess. Their commitment is probably beneficial to the quality of service provided, but the lack of independent data to support clinical reports means that possible bias in reporting can not be ruled out. Haugaard and Reppucci state that '. . . empirical work on the treatment of child sexual abuse is almost non existent . . .' (1988, p 183) and that 'the current literature is rife with authors' assumptions that are presented as truth or permanent knowledge . . .' (1988, p 376). Similarly, Jill Waterman states that 'Evaluating the outcome of treatment with sexually abused children has been woefully inadequate so far. Most results have been presented in terms of the therapists' opinion that improvement . . .' (1986, p 202). And for perpetrators a Canadian Government report stated that, '. . . no definite conclusions can be reached concerning the known or potential efficacy of correctional treatment programs for convicted sexual offenders' (Canadian Government, 1984, p 881).

Although the dearth of treatment studies is even more serious in child sexual abuse than other forms of child abuse, there are some aspects of the research into child sexual abuse, that are more advanced. A higher proportion of the literature is concerned with child protection practice, which in most cases, provides the context for any treatment intervention. There is an awareness that both legal measures and the procedures of health and welfare agencies for child protection, may have as great an impact on the family and its individuals, as any therapeutic regime. Why this should be given such attention within child sexual abuse and yet have a relatively low profile in the research literature on other forms of child abuse, is not clear. It may be, that child sexual abuse is a more sensitive issue, with identification and intervention resulting in greater social consequences for both victims, perpetrators, and other family members. Alternatively, it may be that child sexual abuse has arisen as an issue at a time when there is a greater awareness of the significant effect of legal practice and agency procedural systems, on defining cases and producing the context for therapeutic work. This explanation is supported by the recent growth in case management studies in child protection reported in Chapter Ten. Whatever the reason for the concern about legal and inter-professional management issues, it is a positive development in child abuse research.

There are further ways in which child sexual abuse studies differ from others in the child abuse field. It is evident from the studies reported in other chapters that the main focus of therapeutic interventions, has been upon helping parents to care better for their children. This has principally been to reduce poor child care strategies and behavioural routines or to develop new behaviours and skills. There was also some direct work to mitigate the effects of abuse on victims. In child sexual abuse research, there is a much greater emphasis on direct treatment of perpetrators, of victims, and of older survivors of earlier abuse.

Causes of Abuse

There are two related factors that may explain the increased attention on perpetrators, independent of the family or of parenting responsibilities. The first is, that child sexual abuse is not just seen as a failing to cope adequately with the problems of parenting. It is also perceived as a manifestation of deviant desires and practices. This is related to the second factor, which is that the concept of sexual abuse is not restricted to familial abuse. It also covers the abuse of children by non related adults. Perpetrators are thus more easily characterised as paedophiles, victimizing children within the community and requiring direct treatment. A view supported by the fact that many perpetrators of child sexual abuse have multiple victims (for example, Becker, 1991; Maletzky, 1991).

Much of the research on treatment is concerned with deviant sexual orientation, but this is only one explanation for acts of child sexual abuse. Finkelhor (1986) argues that there are four main types of factors contributing to the cause of acts of sexual abuse. These are: (1) the emotional gratification from such acts, (2) sexual arousal to children, (3) blocks to other forms of sexual and emotional gratification, and (4) why normal social inhibitions against such acts do not deter the abuse.

These four factors aim to explain individual behaviour, but they may be more or less likely to occur in different social and cultural contexts. For example, in different families or in different societies or sub cultures. This is well illustrated by the much higher rates of sexual offending by males than females. The four factor model therefore suggests possible individual, family, situational, and societal causal factors. Currently, the main division in causal explanations is between those that emphasize pathology in the offender, the family, or in other aspects of the immediate context, and those that emphasize the societal attitudes and power relations that encourage members of groups with more power to exploit those with less power. The latter argument being that offenders abuse women and children because they are able to behave in this way with little cost to themselves (see Gelles, 1983). This ideological divide about the responsibility for the cause of sexual abuse obviously has a major influence on what would be considered an appropriate method for intervening to prevent the recurrence of abuse to a child.

Many practitioners emphasize the treatment of children and adults in the family and of the family itself. If anything, there is a more overt focus upon the contribution of the whole family system to the occurrence of sexual abuse, than in writings on other forms of maltreatment (though child protection casework is predominantly concerned with families ability to care and protect their children; also some writers discuss family treatments, for example, coercive family interaction patterns by Nicol et al 1985, 1988; Patterson et al, 1975).

The assumptions of much family work have been criticized by gender/power theorists. MacLeod and Saraga (1988, 1991), for example, argue that family dysfunction explanations of abuse implicitly remove much responsibility from the offender (often the adult male) and place responsibility with the child and non abusing parent. They argue that this approach also leads to an over emphasis on maintaining the family as a functioning unit, and placing children at risk of further abuse. An emphasis on maintaining family units may, in practice, be the consequence of a family dysfunction model, but it is not necessarily so. A dysfunction model could also routinely diagnose families as having too poor a prognosis to hope for change (Bentovim, 1988), but may be the therapists have too much invested in believing that their methods of healing families are effective. In contrast, a report from the Canadian Government stated that a child centred service, which could result in temporary break up of the family, produced at least better short term benefits for the child victims (Canadian Government, 1984, p 635).

Gender/power explanations fit slightly better with interventions that attempt to treat, educate, or re-orientate the sexual interests of paedophiles. The view would be that all men are potential molesters of children and so that these interventions should be broadly based in society. Evidence supporting this view comes from sexual arousal studies on child molesters, where some control group male subjects display arousal to child stimuli. Those taking a more medical individual dysfunction view would only be concerned with the individuals displaying sexual deviancy.

Whatever the truth or importance of the gender/power relations arguments, there is still the issue of what to do about the specific individuals identified as having sexually abused children. Some may be found guilty of a criminal offence and temporarily imprisoned for purposes of deterrence and to mark society's disapproval, but they are then released and may have the opportunity to offend again. Many authors therefore advocate treatment or education of some kind.

A complication is the lack of information on the range and type of abusers. Most are male, and as many as a third of these are identified as abusers when they are themselves children (Becker, 1986; Johnson, 1988; Gough, 1990; Horne et al, 1991; Marshall et al, 1991; National Children's Home, 1992). Furthermore, many more male offenders admit to starting the abuse when they were children (Davis and Leitenberg, 1987). One American study reported that 58% of offenders committed their first sexual abuse offence as teenagers (Becker, 1991), another study reported a figure of 46%, but this was only for extrafamilial abuse, with only 8% of intrafamilial abuse occurring before age twenty (Marshall et al, 1991). There are also reports of female offenders, either aiding men or acting independently (particularly high figures have been reported in day care settings by Finkelhor et al, 1988), and some of the children who abuse others are female (Cavanagh Johnson, 1989).

Becker (1991) distinguishes sexual abusers of children into three broad categories of (i) those with major personality damage who commit abuse as just one of many anti-social activities, (ii) those who prefer consensual sex with adults but if this is unavailable will coerce adults or children into engaging in sex, (iii) those whose sexual orientation is towards children rather than adults, and (iv) a small number who have major psychiatric illness. Most of the patients seen in sexual abuse therapy programmes fall into the third category of paedophilia. Attempts have therefore been made to distinguish these abusers further on the basis of whether their victims are same sex, within the abusers family, and whether the victims have past puberty. Although these distinctions may be helpful clinically, it is difficult to determine whether victim patterns are due to an underlying typology of paedophilia or due to other factors such as availability of victims. Becker (1991), for example, argues that those who normally only abuse within the family will often also abuse other children if the opportunity arises.

Research into the treatment of paedophiles has a long history as part of a wider concern with all types of sexual offenders. Behavioural strategies have been particularly popular and, in a review of treatment studies, Kelly (1982) identified more than twenty different behavioural procedures that had been used to reorient the sexual desires of paedophiliacs. In a more recent 'therapeutic cookbook' Maletzky (1991) has described a range of techniques that might be involved in a behavioural treatment plan. These include:

1. Aversive Conditioning

Association between overt or covert (covert sensitization) deviant stimuli (for example, photographs of children) and aversive stimulus of electric shock, foul odour, foul taste, behaviour rehearsal (shame of being observed rehearsing the offensive acts), masturbating post orgasm, aversive imagery (of unpleasant consequences such as being caught or repulsion during abuse from vomit, gross genital infection, etc. on victim).

2. Positive Conditioning

Association between appropriate stimuli (for example, photographs of adults) and positive stimuli of masturbation up to and including orgasm, pleasant odours, other pleasant olfactory experiences such as amyl nitrate.

3. Fading

Overlap of positive and negative responses to stimuli so that a previously conditioned response is extended to cover a new stimulus. Method can be used either as an aversive technique (aversive conditioning but increase deviant stimuli and decrease aversive experience as arousal decreases) or as a positive technique to increase arousal to appropriate stimuli (present deviant stimuli and gradually fade in appropriate stimuli so that become associated with arousal). Also masturbatory fantasy change where masturbate to deviant thoughts but change to appropriate stimuli just prior to orgasm, then make the change over in fantasies progressively earlier during masturbation.

4. FEEDBACK

Biofeedback of level of sexual arousal by plethysmograph that measures changes in penile circumference. Feedback usually given to subject through series of coloured lights indicating different degrees of penile tumescence. Plethysmograph readings also used to assess arousal to deviant stimuli and to provide data for reinforcement of responses in operant conditioning paradigms.

5. DESENSITIZATION

Subject's anxiety/aversion to a particular experience reduced by initial relaxation of subject, presenting mildly threatening scenes and then gradually increasingly difficult scenes, whilst ensuring relaxation is maintained. Scenes can be in artificial/imagined (in vitro) or real (in vivo) experiences. Technique used predominantly to increase offenders' abilities to engage in appropriate social and sexual relationships; for example, being able to ask an adult woman out socially (so fits Finkelhor's category of blockage of normal social/sexual outlets). Technique can also be used to inhibit sexually deviant behaviour; for example, training subjects to become relaxed in situations where they may have previously become inappropriately sexually aroused.

6. OPERANT TECHNIQUES

Similar to classical conditioning paradigms but aversive or positive experiences dependent upon subject's response to stimuli. For example, electric shock only given if subject's penile circumference increases on presentation of deviant stimuli. Variable ratio schedules of reinforcement often used as shown to be more effective. Positive reinforcers may be in the form of tangible material rewards such as money, extra privileges within an institution, praise and extra time with the therapist. Negative reinforcers may be presented in an avoidance paradigm where a required behaviour, for example removing the deviant stimulus of a sexual picture of a child, will ensure the subject avoids the aversive experience of electric shock or foul odour.

7. ADJUNCTIVE TECHNIQUES

Behavioural approaches are often supplemented by other techniques either to assist the success of the behavioural techniques or because of their independent value to treating the offender. Examples provided by Maletzky include: trust building, social skills training, anxiety management training, assertiveness training, environmental change, marital and family therapy, cognitive therapy, group therapy, impulse control therapy, empathy training, paradoxical intention, deviant cycle awareness, substance abuse treatment, somatic therapy of medication to reduce male sexual arousal.

Maletzky (1991) argues that behavioural methods are unlikely to be successful if they do not take account of the idiosyncrasies of individual offenders and this may include the need for adjunctive therapies. The problem for service delivery in Britain, however, is the lack of facilities for any form of treatment and the difficulties in ensuring identification and referrals of cases to the facilities that do exist (see, for example, NCH, 1992).

Effects of Child Sexual Abuse

The increased attention to direct work with victims of child sexual abuse is easier to explain, at least superficially. It mirrors the focus on the emotional sequelae of child sexual abuse. This was first reported to occur clinically and was then supported by research studies (briefly described later in this section). In response there have been efforts to mitigate the effects of sexual abuse on child victims and to provide help for adult survivors of abuse. What is less easy to explain, is why there has been relatively less attention to the long term effects of other forms of abuse (though see Egeland, 1988; Oates, 1988; Gibbons et al, 1992). It may be that there has been a particular need to show that child sexual abuse has long lasting consequences and should be taken seriously as a human and social problem. The consequences of other forms of abuse such as physical injury may be more self evident. However, if it not necessary to argue against sexual abuse on the basis of the damage it causes. It is sufficient to argue that children have the right not to be involved in sexual acts to which they can not give informed consent (Finkelhor, 1979).

The evidence is, however, that sexual abuse is damaging to a large number of children (see Briere, 1992 and Kendall-Tackett et al, 1993, for reviews of studies). There can be serious physical consequences from the physical trauma of the abuse, from sexually transmitted infection including HIV infection, or from becoming pregnant. Alternately there may be serious social psychological consequences from the abuse. Nearly every psychological problem that a child could experience has been described at some point in the clinical literature on child sexual abuse (Berliner, 1991; Briere, 1992). Studies have shown that using standardized scales parents report significantly more behaviour problems for sexually abused children than for matched comparisons (for example, Conte and Schuerman, 1988; see also review by Browne and Finkelhor, 1986), but these differences have been more difficult to detect using child self report measures (Mannarino et al, 1991). Also, as many as 21% of children in the study by Conte, Berliner, and Schuerman (Conte and Schuerman, 1988) showed no symptoms on a 38 item check list.

Information on the adverse psychological effects of abuse comes mostly from clinical case descriptions of abused children and retrospective studies of adults abused as children. The retrospective studies are of at least three types. Firstly there are descriptions of the psychological difficulties of adults presenting for treatment who report histories of child sexual abuse. Second, there are investigations to determine the frequency of sexual abuse histories in clinical psychiatric populations (for example, Briere and Runtz, 1986, 1988; Palmer et al, 1992). Third, there are similar studies on non clinical populations (for example, Mullen et al 1988; Stein et al, 1988). Fourth, there are a few prospective studies (Bagley and McDonald, 1984; Bagley and Ramsay, 1986; Egeland, 1988). These studies report much higher rates of psychological symptoms in those who have experienced sexual abuse in childhood.

The research has also attempted to differentiate the types of abuse, age and sex of victim (see Hunter, 1991), and the type of abusive relationship that are associated with different adult outcomes. Wyatt and Newcomb (1990), for example, report that negative outcomes were associated with severity of the abuse, close relationship to the abuser, immediate negative response, self blame, and non disclosure of the abuse. Despite the value of these studies they mostly rely on retrospective data. There is little basis for arguing that the nature and quality of data is independent from current mental state. In other words, the variables may be confounded with each other. Also it is difficult to isolate the relative importance of abuse to other features of the childhood environment, particularly when sexual abuse seems to be so prevalent in society (Haugaard and Reppucci, 1988). Large scale prospective designs would be better able to identify the relationship between abuse, coping responses, and later outcome.

Factors found to be statistically associated with the experience of sexual abuse in childhood include anger, sleep disturbance, disassociation (feelings that things are unreal), sexual difficulties (Briere and Runtz, 1988); anxiety, anger, guilt, depression, and substance abuse (Stein et al, 1988); eating disorders (Oppenheimer et al, 1985; Palmer et al, 1990), disrupted marriages, dissatisfaction with sexual relationships, not participation in religious activities, and to be more aware of current debates on sexual abuse (Finkelhor et al, 1989).

Some authors (for example, Wolfe et al, 1989) argue that many of these negative effects can be subsumed within the model of Post Traumatic Post Disorder (PTSD), an accepted psychiatric diagnosis for a set of symptoms associated with violent traumatic experiences as in war. Finkelhor (1988) argues, however, that although there may be some common symptoms in some cases of child sexual abuse and PTSD, this is not sufficient to indicate that the same conceptual model is applicable. Instead, Finkelhor and Browne (1986) propose a Four Traumagenic Dynamics model consisting of four main trauma causing factors of traumatic sexualization, stigmatization, betrayal, and powerlessness. For each of these they describe examples of the dynamics of how the trauma occurred, its psychological impact on the child, and its behavioural manifestations. Briere (1992) stresses the stages of the impact of abuse on the individual. Firstly, initial reactions to victimization. Secondly, accommodation and coping with ongoing abuse. Thirdly, long term elaboration and accommodation to these experiences and their effects. Briere classifies the psychological difficulties frequently encountered in victims into: PTSD; Cognitive Distortions such as powerlessness, poor self esteem; Emotional Effects of anxiety, depression, dissociation; Impaired Self Reference; Disturbed Relatedness in aggression, sexuality, and the belief in an adversarial world; and Avoidance through mechanisms such as substance abuse, suicide, obsessive behaviour, and eating disorders.

Research Studies

As most of the emphasis on child sexual abuse has been on process, there have been very few studies of the impact of different therapeutic interventions. Many intervention models have been described, but few have been evaluated in any formal sense. There are a number of special service initiatives/demonstration programmes with process and outcome evaluations not included in this review (see for example, NYCN, 1993; Patton, 1991). The studies included in this review are listed in Tables 11.1 to 11.3.

Perpetrators

The main approach to treatment of perpetrators that has been evaluated by research is the re-orientation of the sexual arousal pattern by behavioural conditioning. The research has therefore concentrated upon only one of the four causal factors listed by Finkelhor (1986). Virtually all of the studies have concerned only male offenders (studies listed in Table 11.1).

The literature contains several case studies which powerfully illustrate the nature of behavioural treatment interventions (see Kelly, 1982, for a review of many of these studies). Earls and Castonguay (1989), for example, described the treatment of a 17 year old male with a history of aggressive sexual assaults against children. Treatment involved twenty sessions of olfactory aversion to audio tapes of violent adult child interactions. Treatment reduced sexual arousal to aggressive stimuli but not for consenting sex with children.

Case studies can illustrate behavioural interventions but they are less useful at establishing the relative efficacy of different intervention techniques. The literature does contain many large sample studies, but these are mainly retrospective outcome

TABLE 11.1

Sexual Abuse: Offenders Research Studies

Study	Programme	Sample/Size	Population	Design	Main Measures
Barnett et al (1989)	Group therapy	n = 6	Imprisoned female offenders	RPM	Distorted beliefs, client records
Becker et al (1988)	Sexual Behaviour Clinic	n = 24	Adolescent male offenders	RPM	Sexual arousal
Bradford and Pawlak (1987)	Chemotherapy	n = 1	Male imprisoned for homosexual paedophilic murder	RPM	Sexual arousal, hormone levels
Chaffin (1992)	Group psychotherapy	n = 36	Male incest offenders	RPM	Treatment compliance, therapist ratings, personality
Earls and Castonguay (1989)	Olfactory aversion	n = 1	Imprisoned male offender	RPM	Sexual arousal
Kahn and Chambers (1991)	10 different programmes	n = 221	Juvenile male offenders	POST	Reconvictions for abuse
Maletzky (1980)	Covert sensitization	n = 100	Adult male offenders	RPM	Sexual arousal, attendance
Maletzky (1991)	Behavioural abuse clinic	n = 2865	Adult male offenders	RPM	Sexual arousal, re-abuse
Marshall and Barbaree (1988)	Behavioural treatment	n = 68	Adult male offenders	RPM + C	Sexual arousal, re-abuse
Prentky and Burgess (1990)	Massachusetts Treatment Centre	n = 129	Adult male offenders	POST	Re-offense, costs
Quinsey et al (1980)	Biofeedback +/− signalled punishment	n = 18	Adult male offenders	RPM + C	Sexual arousal
Rice et al (1991)	Aversion therapy	n = 136	Adult male extra familial offenders	POST	Sexual arousal, re-abuse

FACES = Family Adaptability & Cohesion Sales; PTSD = Post traumatic stress disorder symptoms;
CCSATP = Comprehensive Child Sexual Assault Treatment Program
Design
POST = Post-test only; RPM = Repeated Measures including pre-test; PRPM = Repeated Measures post-test only;
+ C = Control or comparison group; + PC = Control or comparison group but at post-test only

studies of subjects released from treatment facilities such as psychiatric hospitals, or from prisons over a period of years. Details of the treatment interventions are often lacking and the follow up is often of variable length within the same sample and dependent upon official records of new sexual offences. The evidence from these and other types of studies for all types of sexual offenders has been extensively reviewed by Furby, Weinrott and Blackshaw (1989). They provide a detailed analysis of the methodological shortcomings of the research and find it difficult to provide any firm conclusions from the studies. One of the few conclusions that they were able to draw was that 'we can at least say with confidence that there is no evidence that treatment effectively reduces sex offence recidivism' (1989, p 25). On the other hand, they were able to find some evidence that recidivism rates for paedophiles are lower than for other sexual offenders (1989, p 27).

More optimistic results for treatment of offenders are reported by detailed studies concentrating on paedophile offenders and often with smaller samples than the retrospective outcome studies. Maletzky (1980), for example, reported a study where homosexual paedophiles were presented with increasingly arousing stimuli of deviant acts. When the paedophiles became aroused, they were presented with aversive stimuli of an unpleasant odour and of unpleasant experiences occurring during deviant acts (for example being caught by a friend or colleague). Subjects also had homework assignments that included thought control and changing the environments and situations that they created for themselves in their daily lives. The main outcome measures were reports by subjects, by significant others, and physical measures of arousal to deviant stimuli by plethysmogaph recording of penile tumescence. Maletzky reported significant improvements on all measures that were maintained at long term follow up with regular booster therapy sessions. The external validity of the physical measure was supported by the high correlations observed between it and the self report data. No significant difference was found in the degree of improvement between court and self referred subjects. There may have been a ceiling effect, but the author argues that at last court ordered referrals should not be seen as counter indicative for this type of therapy.

More recently, Maletzky (1991) has reported on the outcome of all 5,000 subjects who have been treated with a range of behavioural methods at the Sexual Abuse Clinic in Portland, Oregon, 75% of whom were paedophile offenders. No effect of treatment was evident for the first six weeks, but between six and sixteen weeks there were significant reductions in the subjects covert and overt deviant sexual behaviours. After 10 months of treatment, heterosexual offenders displayed only 10% penile tumescence to deviant stimuli (defined as producing 80% tumescence at pre-test); after 16 months homosexual offenders displayed 30% arousal to deviant stimuli. Recidivism rates were extremely low, 1.3% and 1.4% for hetero and homosexual paedophiles respectively. Using a broader definition of treatment failure these figures rose to 5% and 14% and to 24% for the subjects who had both male and female victims. Failure was statistically associated with having more than one victim, not knowing the victim well or at all, the use of force, denial of the offences, and high pre-test arousal to deviant material.

Another evaluation of a behavioural intervention for perpetrators is described by Quinsey and colleagues (1980). They examined the relative efficacy of biofeedback for arousal to deviant stimuli with the efficacy of biofeedback plus signalled punishment in the form of a mildly painful electric shock. Non deviant stimuli of adults were presented and penile plethysmograph readings were used to calculate a sexual preference ratio of arousal to adult stimuli compared to child stimuli. Quinsey and colleagues found that the addition of signalled punishment significantly increased the efficacy of the intervention. The study also found that the age preference ratios could distinguish those who were later found to have committed new offences. The six who were known to re-offend had significantly worse post-test scores than other subjects.

Maletsky's (1991) finding of a relationship between pre-test deviant arousal and outcome has been supported by a follow up study of 136 subjects in a maximum psychiatric institution by Rice, Quinsey, and Verson (1991). Their results show that after treatment only half the subjects displayed any change in their sex age preferences; over half were also involved in some later offence (31% of total were involved in later sexual offences). In agreement with the review of outcome studies by Furby et al (1989), case outcome was not associated with having received treatment. Outcome was, however, associated with more previous offences, admissions to correctional institutions, never having married, personality disorders, and greater arousal to deviant stimuli at pre-test.

Marshall and Barbaree (1988) using a repeated measures design showed significantly less recidivism in treated compared to untreated cases (though not random allocation), but outcome was not related to pre or post-test measures or changes over treatment in deviant arousal patterns. Marshall and Barbaree also reported that unofficial records identified 2.4 times more recidivism than official records.

The success of behavioural methods for adolescent offenders, has also been reported by Becker et al (1988) using a broadly based intervention package. They have developed a programme that includes verbal satiation of deviant sexual material, role playing the victim, social skills training, anger control training, education about sexual development and relationships, and relapse prevention (Abel et al, 1984). The efficacy of the programme was demonstrated by significant reductions in the physical arousal to deviant sexual material, but only with offenders against male victims. There was considerable variation in the responses for offenders against female victims, so the poor result could be due to a few non responsive subjects who happened to be in this group. Further research using larger samples should clarify this.

In another case outcome study, Kahn and Chambers (1991) examined what factors were associated with recidivism of 221 juvenile sexual offenders treated in eight outpatient and two inpatient treatment centres in Washington. A range of eclectic treatments were used and only occasionally did these involve behavioural reorientation of sexual arousal patterns. Subjects had a history of crime in 47% of cases and of sexual crime in 5% of cases. At least 7% were subsequently convicted for another sexual offence, 7% were convicted for violent crimes, and 45% for any crime. Subsequent sexual offences were related to denial of original offences, blame of victim, and use of verbal threats. There was a trend for outpatient treatment to have better outcomes than inpatient treatment, but it is unclear the extent that this could be explained by pre-test differences between subjects.

Prentky and Burgess (1990) attempted to assess case outcome on the basis of the cost efficacy of offender treatment. They reported a post treatment recidivism rate of 25% and contrasted this with Marshall and Barbaree's (1988) non treatment recidivism rate of 40%. They argue that treatment is cheaper than imprisonment and that this cost efficiency is greatly enhanced by the lower recidivism rates of treated subjects. This argument depends, of course, upon transferring the results from one study to another in a field known for great variability in reported results.

Most studies in the literature are studies of behavioural treatment or are general outcome studies on cases receiving a broad range of interventions. Many non behavioural treatments have been proposed for perpetrators of child sexual abuse; some of these are part of multicomponent programmes for whole families and their members (considered in a later section). The literature contains descriptions of other forms of practice such as group work, counselling and individual psycho-therapy outside the family programmes, but few evaluation studies. The same lack of evaluation is true of the chemical therapies reported to reduce all sexual desires, including paedophiliac fantasies (see Kelly, 1982). An exception is the study by Bradford and Pawlak (1987) which found a decrease in testerone levels and sexual arousal subsequent to administration of cyproterone acetate.

Two studies of group work with perpetrators have been reported in the literature. Chaffin (1992) has reported on the outcomes of long term group psychotherapy for father – daughter/stepdaughter offenders diagnosed as regressed. Outcome measures depended upon personality and stress schedules and therapist ratings of improvement on several dimensions. Completion of therapy and improvement on therapist ratings was associated with less personality disturbance. Those with personality disturbance showed particularly poor improvement on therapist ratings of empathy for victim.

The second study of group therapy was the only study identified evaluating treatment for female offenders. Barnett et al (1989) examined six subjects imprisoned for their offences enroled in a time limited group led by two female therapists. Subjects showed significant improvements on a scale of distorted beliefs and the therapists and subjects reported improvement on measures of insight into the causes, the effects, and their responsibility for the offences.

Victims and Survivors

CHILDREN

There are few good studies on the effects of direct treatment for victims of child sexual abuse (see studies for child and adult survivors listed in Table 11.2). Group work seems to be preferred, because it allows for sharing of experiences and the development of self esteem which may have been badly damaged by the abuse. Delson and Clark's (1981) study describes a programme, where young female victims are, amongst other things, encouraged to discuss the abuse and the responses of the legal system and how best to cope with the stresses this creates.

Furniss and colleagues (1988) report on a group for sexually abused adolescent girls that aims to help them rebuild their self esteem and ability to control their lives, to rebuild their inter personal relationships and learn appropriate intergenerational boundaries and models of parenting, and to distinguish the offender responsibility from their own self blame. The results based upon staff and client ratings showed, with a couple of exceptions, improvements on most measures of self esteem and behaviour.

Borgman (1984) reports on another model for group discussions and activities which explicitly avoids dwelling upon the topic of child sexual abuse. The danger of emphasizing the experience of the sexual abuse is that it might encourage a deviant self image of being a victim, and so handicap children further from developing positive self images and from acting positively upon the world. Similar approaches are taken by groups that encourage the development of creative skills and attitudes. For example, activities like dancing or acting which can involve self expression, non sexual touching, and positive feedback and rewards.

TABLE 11.2

Sexual Abuse: Victims/Survivors Research Studies

Study	Programme	Sample/ Size	Population	Design	Main Measures
Alexander et al (1989, 1991) Follette et al (1991)	Interpersonal transaction group vs process group	n – 65	Women abused as children	RPM + C	Mental state, marital/ social adjustment, FACES
Borgman (1984)	Residential treatment	n = 16	Female children abused by known males	Descriptive	Client & workers reports of relationships
Deblinger et al (1990)	Cognitive behavioural treatment	n = 19	Female children abused by known males	RPM	Social competence, anxiety, PTSD
Delson and Clark (1981)	Group therapy	n = 5	Female children abused by fathers	Descriptive	Case progress
Furniss et al (1988)	Group orientated group	n = 10	Female children abused in family	Descriptive	Workers & clients assessments
Jehu (1988, 1989)	Marital sexual dysfunction clinic	n = 51	Women abused as children	RPM	Mental state, marital and sexual relationships
Kolko (1986)	Social cognitive skills training	n = 1	Male child offender/victim	Descriptive	Social skills/behaviour
Sullivan et al (1992)	Psychotherapy	n = 72	Children abused at school for deaf	RPM + C	Child Behaviour Checklist

FACES = Family adaptability and Cohesion Scales PTSD = Post Traumatic Stress Disorder

Design

POST = Post test only; RPM = Repeated Measures including pre-test; PRPM = Repeated Measures post-test only;

+ C = Control or comparison group; + PC = Control or comparison group but at post-test only

Borgman's approach is in stark contrast to individual behavioural treatment reported by Deblinger et al (1990), where sexually abused female children are exposed to abuse related stimuli. The aim is to reduce the anxiety experienced from abuse related stimuli and from innocuous stimuli that have become associated with this anxiety. The purpose was not to devalue the reactions to the abuse, but to prevent the women becoming long term victims of the behavioural associations of the abuse to which they had been subjected. The children and young women were given training to help them to cope with the emotions generated and to aid them in managing abuse related memories. General child sexual abuse preventive training was also provided and non offending parents received training on their reactions to the behaviour of their child. At post test, the children/young women had significantly reduced depression and anxiety scores and parental ratings of behavioural problems. The authors report that at post-test none of the cases met the diagnostic criteria for PTSD, though this had been a criteria for initial acceptance into treatment.

There are various accounts in the literature of individual work with clients. Kolko (1986) used training through modelling, feedback and coaching in new cognitive constructions, to develop social competence and other positive behaviours to displace the negative behaviour displayed by a sexually abused and abusing child psychiatric inpatient. The use of very specific measures allowed the study to record the significant improvements in behaviour achieved. Such descriptions of individual work provide useful insights into therapeutic issues, though they offer less information about the relative efficacy of different interventions. That the case studies are predominantly about intrafamilial abuse suggests that victims of extrafamilial abuse may have been rather overlooked in terms of both service provision and research.

Sullivan et al (1992) assesses the outcome of a broad based psychotherapeutic intervention for children sexually abused by staff and older pupils at a residential school for the deaf. The study showed that children with hearing impairments subject to sexual abuse do exhibit more behavioural problems than their peers and that these problems do improve in response to treatment. Behavioural scores for boys improved generally, but for girls there was greater improvement on the more withdrawn/internal types of behaviour problems. Girls with more external aggressive behaviours improved less. The authors note that female children disclosing abuse are less likely to be believed if they act delinquently, though these behaviours may be a response to the abuse.

Other more descriptive reports in the literature (not summarized in the chapter appendix) include experiences of developing a group for young victims (Kitchur and Bell, 1989; Walford, 1989), groups developed specifically for sexually abused boys (Friedrich et al, 1988), the use of parallel groups for children and their caregivers (Nelki and Watters, 1989), and groups just for parents and caregivers (Clark et al, 1989).

A comparative study of family network treatment with and without group work by Monck (1991, see Multicomponent section of this chapter) found that depression scores improved for children in both treatment groups. Less encouraging preliminary results (not summarized in chapter appendix) are reported by Berliner (1992) who contrasted group work at the Sexual Assault Center in Seattle with group work plus cognitive behavioural treatment of stress innoculation and gradual exposure to thoughts of abuse. Berliner (1992) reports little improvement in either treatment group in the children's scores on fear and anxiety and other measures.

ADULTS

Treatment for adult survivors is less developed (see studies for adult and child survivors listed in Table 11.2). There are direct services for adults who experience psychological problems and are referred to psychological and psychiatric services on the bases of these problems, rather than on the basis of history of sexual abuse. There are also self help groups, and counselling for survivors, set up by other survivors or by professionals. Often these resources develop out of incest crisis or other telephone line services. For example, in Leeds, the National Children's Homes started a telephone counselling service for victims of child sexual abuse (Touchline) with the offer of a more intensive service of family therapy where appropriate. In 1987 (personal communication) many of the callers were young adult women wishing to talk about the sexual abuse they experienced a few years earlier, rather than from children currently being abused.

Survivors' groups can be based on many different theories and involve different ideas about membership, length, and specific techniques. Many professionally led groups are time limited to avoid a negative dependency.

Bagley (1988) reports a project in Canada, where 'voice therapy' is used by survivors in small groups to reconstruct their internal cognitive system. The aim is to change the 'voices' from the past that have led to hostile thoughts and feelings which may be damaging self esteem and causing depression. Coping techniques are taught for dealing with stress and previous clients act as 'buddies' to provide long term social support. The project is not aimed at clients already suffering from chronic depression or other psychiatric illness. The project aims to prevent these problems occurring (or recurring) in those just able to cope. This approach is based upon other work (cited by Bagley, 1988), which claims that self esteem enhancement, problem solving skills, and social support are effective in preventing the onset of depression. The programme is being evaluated in an experimental study with a wait list control (Bagley, 1988).

Alexander and colleagues (Alexander et al, 1989; Follette et al, 1991) have completed one of the few experimental studies of treatment. They contrasted two forms of group treatment. The first was an interpersonal transaction group with paired and group discussions of feelings related to the experience of abuse. The second was a less structured process group where interactions within the group were used to explore how participants related to each other and to others outside the group. Both groups showed improvement compared to wait list controls on independent measures of depression, psychological symptoms, and a self report scale of a range of fears. No major differences were reported between the two groups, though there was a trend for those who had some experience of therapy to benefit more from the less structured process group. Individual predictors of poor outcome included a history of oral/genital abuse, pre-treatment distress/depression, and being married rather than single. Duration of abuse, whether the offender was biological or step father, and functioning of present family were not related to outcome. The researchers suggest that the more structured transaction group is probably more suitable for those who experienced more extreme abuse that they have not disclosed before. Also that couples therapy may be indicated for married women, particularly if they have not disclosed the abuse to their partner.

Jehu (1988, 1989) reported on the outcome for women sexually abused as children, treated at the Manitoba Sexual Dysfunction Clinic. Individual or couple therapy focused on specific presenting problems including mood disturbances, interpersonal problems and sexual dysfunctions. Major improvements were found in rating scales of distorted beliefs, depression, and to a lesser extent for self-esteem. Improvements also reported for the few cases where interpersonal relationships were the main focus of intervention. Jehu used two case studies to illustrate the complex difficulties the women experienced in sexual relationships and how these improved with treatment. These case studies have been criticized by Kitzinger (1992) for the manner in which a lack of interest in having sexual relations with men is considered pathological.

Most of the literature concerns the use of group therapy for adult women who were victims of sexual abuse as children, but there are some reports of services for male victims (for example, Friedrich et al, 1988), though no formal evaluations of such interventions were found in this review.

The literature also contains a few exploratory studies attempting to examine in more detail the varying nature of adults who were victims. Kendel-Tackett (1991), for example, examined the factors associated with time taken before the adults sought treatment. She found that victims who were abused at an early age, for a short duration, experienced fewer sexual acts, and who did not disclose the abuse to law enforcement agencies, took longer before seeking treatment. The author cautions against assuming that these late seekers of help experienced less serious abuse, because often the short duration abuse involved oral/genital penetrative acts and included the use of force. What the study can not reveal, however, is the characteristics of child victims who are never known to have sought treatment.

Another important issue raised in the literature is the evidence that some therapists develop sexual relationships with their clients (Armsworth, 1990). Although some therapists apparently justify these acts in terms of assisting their clients, it is more likely that they are using their position in order to satisfy their own needs. They are thus mirroring and repeating the original sexual exploitation experienced by their clients in childhood.

Multicomponent/Families

The Comprehensive Child Abuse Treatment Program developed by Giaretto in California (Giaretto 1976, 1982; Kroth 1979) became well known in Britain following it being advocated as an effective and appropriate method by the report of a symposium funded by the Ciba Foundation (Porter, 1984). The programme has four main components; professional counselling of individuals, dyads and families; volunteers providing companionship and support; self help groups for parents and children; and a community awareness programme. Giaretto and Kroth have reported very high rates of success with the programme. Victims are reported to become symptom free and to increase their social skills, parents to have improved marital and sexual relationships, and perpetrators acknowledging their responsibility for the abuse and not repeating the offences.

TABLE 11.3

Sexual Abuse: Multi Component

Study	Programme	Sample/ Size	Population	Design	Main Measures
Furniss (1983), Furniss et al (1984)	Goal orientated group treatment	n = 10	Female children abused in families	RPM	Client & worker ratings
Bentovim et al (1988)	Structural family therapy + group worker	n = 274	Families where abuse to children	Descriptive	Case records, progress, family composition
Giaretto (1976, 1982), Kroth (1979)	CCSATP	n = 51	Families where abuse to children	RPM	Client reports, agency records
Monck et al (1991)	Family Network +/− Group treatment	(1) n = 99 (2) n = 47	Children abused in families	RPM+C	Mental state, behaviour, progress
Woodworth (1991)	Family Project; groupwork	n = 15	Families where abuse	POST	Mental state, relationships

FACES = Family Adaptability & Cohesion Scales; PTSD = Post traumatic stress disorder symptoms;

CCSATP = Comprehensive Child Sexual Assault Treatment Program

Design

POST = Post-test only; RPM = Repeated Measures including pre-test; + C = Control or comparison group

There were two problems with the suggestion that the Giaretto treatment model be replicated in Britain. Firstly, the suggestion was based on an optimistic view of the research evidence in support of the model. Secondly, those who attempted to adopt the model only implemented parts of the programme and therefore did not do full justice to the comprehensive nature of the model proposed by Giaretto.

The evaluation of the Giaretto programme depended on an outcome measure of self reports by parents about children and their adjustment to the incidence of child sexual abuse and of any recurrence of abuse (this and other studies listed in Table 11.3). Given the complex nature of child sexual abuse in terms of family relationships and secrecy, self reports are not an ideal measure. The second problem is, that Giaretto stresses the importance of the total package and particularly the self help components of Parents United, Daughters and Sons United, and Adults Molested as Children United. These have all grown to be large organisations with Chapters (or branches) across the United States. Each Chapter is the self help component of a statutory controlled treatment programme (Gillies, 1991). Equivalent organisations do not exist in the United Kingdom. Programmes that do not include this self help component can not become replications of the Giaretto model. Giaretto's emphasis on self help is supported by the United States demonstration research projects, which found lay support to be highly associated with successful outcome in physical abuse and neglect cases (see Berkeley Planning Associates, 1977, Op. Cit.).

The original service for cases of sexual abuse developed at Great Ormond Street Hospital for Sick Children in London was largely influenced by the Giaretto model. Since then, however, the child sexual team have developed their own distinctive service. The treatment offered is in addition to those services already provided by the social work department in the community. The extra service has two components. The first is family work (now called Family Network Treatment) through a system of assessment, case plan, and continuous review, which aims to clarify the origins of the abuse, responsibility for its occurrence, and what is required to convince the therapists (and the courts) that the child's future safety is secure. The second component of the treatment is group work for different members of the family. Direct treatment for the children is provided as necessary. The overall framework is based on assessing whether the family, with the current or different composition can be a viable unit to adequately protect and care for their child. A preliminary evaluation of the project (Furniss, 1983; Furniss et al, 1984; Bentovim et al, 1988) reported that the community professionals rated 61% of victims to have improved. In 76% of cases there was a change in the composition of the household. Only 14% of victims continued to be at home despite only 43% of perpetrators remaining at home.

A more formal evaluation of the programme has contrasted outcomes for children and mothers from cases receiving only family network treatment with those cases also attending treatment groups for different family members (Monck, 1991). The findings show children in both samples to have improved on measures of depression, but not for self esteem or psychological symptoms. The children said that the treatments were effective in preventing re-abuses and removing their feelings of guilt, but had not been effective in helping them understand why the abuse had occurred. Mothers also reported that the treatment had reduced the risk of re-abuses, but relatively few felt that treatment had helped them relate better to their child, to the offender, or to the family, or had helped them in plan for the future. It was only the clinicians' ratings that indicated differences between the treatment groups. Clinicians reported that cases receiving group work improved to a greater degree than those receiving family network treatment alone.

Woodworth (1991) has reported a follow up study of 15 of the 22 families who had attended the Family Project in St. Paul Minnesota from 1980 to 1986. Most offenders, mothers and previous victims, reported that therapy had been helpful, but nearly a third of offenders and mothers expressed dissatisfaction with the treatment. Many of the family members had sought further clinical treatment and nearly a quarter of victims and mothers had used informal support groups. Nearly all victims were still in contact with the offender and no families reported recurrence of abuse, though 42% of victims still felt uncomfortable in the presence of the offender.

Finally, the National Clinical Evaluation Study (Berkeley Planning Associates, 1983; Daro, 1987; both Op. Cit.) included some cases of sexual abuse. The researchers reported progress in 69% of cases, reduced risk of abuse in 64% of cases, and no re-abuses in 81% of cases. Progress and reduced risk was associated most with treatment compliance, but data dependent upon official records and workers' ratings.

As with all aspects of intervention in sexual and other forms of abuse, the literature contains many helpful discussions of treatment issues (for example, Furniss, 1991), but relatively few formal evaluations. The research studies that do exist often rely upon clinical ratings of improvement and also lack control or comparison groups to rule out the possibility of spontaneous recovery. Monck's (1991) study is one of the few to adopt a full experimental design and it is disappointing that she and her colleagues found no differences between two treatment interventions. At present, therefore, it is necessary to rely on clinical expertise, rather than research evidence, to choose between treatments. The descriptive studies are useful, however, in providing basic data as to how many children were removed from their families and the proportion of families that continued to contain the person who had sexually assaulted the child.

Routine Services

The basic descriptive data on case outcome provided by informal evaluations of treatment is just beginning to be supplemented by basic descriptions of what services are available (see Keller et al, 1989, on the United States; Afnan and Smith, 1992, on the United Kingdom; and Kettle, 1990, for services for young victims and young offenders in England and Wales) and prospective longitudinal studies of the process of routine case management of routine cases (see, for example, Chapter Ten on Waterhouse and Carnie, 1990, 1992; Gough, 1990; Gough and Sutton, 1991). More detailed studies of just some aspect of intervention are also being reported. Goodman et al (1989, cited in Becker, 1991) report that children called to give evidence in court concerning sexual abuse showed more short term distress, but no greater long term distress than those not called, as long as they were not required to make repeated appearances in court. There are also consumer studies of what was considered most and least helpful aspects of agency intervention (Armsworth, 1989).

Retrospective studies of short term outcome are starting to be undertaken. Faller (1991) reports on outcome of cases after three years since initial identification. She found that nearly two thirds of the children had been removed from the families and the majority of these remained in care but without permanency as to their future caregivers. Also, more than half of the original families had experienced other membership changes. In a quarter of cases there had been subsequent re-referrals for child mistreatment.

Further information on the removal of children into care is provided by Jaudes and Morris (1990), who attempted to examine what factors were statistically associated with a change in the children's custody by the courts. Despite examining a large number of factors including severity of abuse and perpetrator access to the home, the only factor found to be associated with change in custody was the nature of the case identification. Initial 'outcry by child' was associated with removal from home.

The authors therefore question whether there is any consistency or underlying basis to the decisions made by the courts.

Another study by Pellegrin and Wagner (1990) did identify factors that were associated with the decision to remove the child at least on a temporary basis. A number of factors including duration and severity of abuse were related to the decision to remove, but the two primary factors were maternal compliance (attendance at appointments) and maternal belief that their child had been abused. The authors also suggest that the 67% maternal compliance and 74% maternal belief in the whole sample shows that the majority of mothers are supportive of their children in these situations.

Pellegrin and Wagner's results are supported by a study by Hunter et al (1990) that found that maternal support of the child was the only significant predictor of both removal of child and placement over time. Temporary removal was predicted by the presence of the offender in the home, but this was not a predictor of later placement. The high rate of long term removal of children (73% of this sample) leads the authors to suggest that greater attempts should be made to assist the mother to support the child so that the child might be able to remain at home.

Discussion

Offenders

Of all the approaches to the treatment of child sexual abuse reviewed, the treatment of perpetrators has been the subject of the most research and has the most evidence supporting its efficacy. The impression, though, is that treatment services are not widespread and are often limited to special initiatives (see for example, Knopp, 1988; Kettle, 1990; Mezey et al 1991; Afnan and Smith, 1992).

Many of the studies report positive effects of behavioural intervention on rates of recidivism, but only one of these studies (Marshall and Barbaree, 1988) had any form of comparison group. It is therefore difficult to be sure that any changes are due to the treatment applied rather than other aspects of the offenders' situation. Furthermore, the study by Rice et al (1991) found no difference in outcome between treatment and no treatment groups, just as reported by Furby et al (1989) for outcome studies on all types of sexual offender.

The second problem with these studies is the measure of recidivism. Sexual behaviour, even if when it is appropriate and legal, is particularly difficult to monitor and official records of reoffending are likely to be a small proportion of all new offences. Marshall and Barbaree (1988) reported that they identified 2.4 times more offences than officially recorded, but this is still likely to be an underestimate. This would not be of particular concern from a research point of view if the rate of non identification was evenly distributed between offenders, but it may well be that certain offenders are more likely to be caught reoffending than others.

The studies reporting significant reductions in sexual arousal are more convincing in that the changes are relatively large considering the timescale of treatment and because the measure seems more rigorous and able to be more consistently applied than recidivism. There are, however, two difficulties with the measure. First, there is evidence that some offenders do not respond at all to the deviant stimuli during testing. Maletzky (1991) reports a rate of non response of 29% and similar figures have been reported elsewhere (Marshall et al, 1986, 1988). The non response may be due to subjects controlling their reactions to the stimuli or in other ways manipulating their response or the physical measure of recording. Measures of sexual arousal are therefore a useful way of monitoring individual therapy including feedback and response contingencies in operant paradigms, but they have some deficiencies as an independent measure of outcome in evaluation studies.

The second limitation of sexual arousal measures is that the relationship between arousal and offending is unknown. Some studies reported a relationship between pre-test arousal and recidivism (Maletzky, 1980; Rice et al, 1991), but others did not (Marshall and Barbaree, 1988). Also, if it is a predictive measure, then post-test arousal should be related to recidivism rates, but this association was only reported by Quinsey et al (1980). The positive results reported by the behavioural studies can, therefore, be questioned on the basis of the validity of their outcome measures. However, these measures have advantages in being more easily specified and more reliably recorded than other seemingly more valid measures. Furthermore, the validity of the physical measures gain support from the positive correlation with self report measures found by Maletzky (1980). Further support is offered by a study by Avery-Clark and Laws (1984). They found that the penile plethysmograph measures could distinguish aggressive and violent offenders from other offenders. Both types of subject displayed arousal to non consensual acts, but only those with histories of violence and aggression were aroused by non consensual violent acts. Freud et al (1982, cited in Haugaard and Reppucci, 1988, p 252) report that normal male college students showed more sexual arousal to pictures of naked female children than to pictures of naked male children or of landscapes. The conclusion is that differential rates of response to different stimuli can still be effectively used to assess the outcomes of treatment, even if the physical response to deviant stimuli is widespread in our societies. The need therefore is to specify in more detail the nature of the variation in the relationship between the two variables of arousal to deviant stimuli and abusive behaviour.

The majority of studies on offender treatment have concentrated on inappropriate sexual arousal rather than other possible causal factors in child sexual abuse. Physical attraction to children is just one of the four factors described by Finkelhor (1986) and few studies have examined the other three factors of emotional congruence, blockage from other and appropriate sexual outlets, and the lack of social inhibitions against deviant sexual acts. There is particular scope for increasing the ability of perpetrators to develop adult sexual relationships. Several studies confirm that child molesters have social skill deficits. Laws and Serber (1975, cited in Kelly 1982, p 400) found that paedophilic patients had difficulties in both verbal and non verbal communication in a role play of 'picking up a girl at a party'. Similarly, Overholser and Beck (1986) report that child molesters are afraid of negative opinions. They are seen as '. . . socially inept, unassertive, and overly sensitive about their performance with women . . . .' (1986, p 686). This suggests much scope for studies of causal factors beyond sexual attraction to children. Some of these other factors are taken on board by the treatment services offered in wider child sexual programmes, but the very breadth of these programmes has made it difficult for the impact of the individual treatment components to be evaluated.

Victims and Survivors

The situation concerning treatment for victims and survivors is more uncertain. It is encouraging that treatment for these groups has been taken seriously in child sexual abuse work, particularly as it is so neglected for other types of abuse. It is only recently, that overviews of the range of treatments have begun to be published (for example Bagley and Thurstone, 1988; Haugaard and Reppucci, 1988; Briere, 1992), but these texts provide a useful basis for future research hypotheses. It is important that specific and relatively narrow hypothesis are examined. The need is less for demonstrations of the possible, but to determine which techniques and therapies are relevant for which cases and in which circumstances.

The strong evidence of the long term negative sequelae of child sexual abuse, provides both a strong reason to pursue evaluative studies as well as offering many specific hypotheses to explore in such studies. Special attention should be given to the victims of extrafamilial abuse. It is thought that the consequences of extrafamilial abuse are less damaging, but this seems to have led to a neglect of the needs of these victims (Haugaard and Repucci, 1988).

Research has not really started to evaluate the relative impact of the treatment strategies that are being developed. These treatments raise many questions, such as: should boys and girls be treated together or separately in groups, does focusing on the problems of abuse help the child to deal with the reality of their sexual molestation or does it create an identity for them as a victim, to what extent does the treatment deal with the events of the abuse, the consequences of the abuse or its disclosure, or other aspects of the children's lives? Similar questions about the efficacy of different forms of treatment can be raised about the therapies and other supports offered to adults who were assaulted sexually in childhood.

A crucial issue is the extent that different individuals require different forms of assistance. Most studies have only been concerned with distinguishing victims by the severity, age, and duration of abuse, and relationship to the offender. The literature, on the other hand, contains many discursive papers on the differential effects of abuse and the studies on child placement indicated that child disclosure and maternal support to the child were important determinants of outcome. Future studies on treatment efficacy could, therefore, productively examine factors such as the means by which the abuse was disclosed, how the child (and may be later adult) coped with the abuse, and how all the individuals concerned coped with the disclosure, and the reaction of others to the disclosure including any social work, health, and legal interventions by the courts. One first step in this process is the finding by Maletzky (1991) and Goodman (1989, cited by Becker, 1991) that court involvement is not contra-indicated for work with either perpetrators or victims. This does not mean, however, that court involvement can be ignored as a variable in further research. Only a small percentage of the cases of sexual abuse identified by retrospective population studies were disclosed to any government agency, let alone taken through the civil or criminal courts.

Multicomponent and Routine Services

Multicomponent intervention programmes for sexual abuse have reported dramatic improvements as measured by rates of recidivism (for example, Giaretto, 1982; Berkeley Planning Associates, 1983; Daro, 1987). On the other hand, behavioural treatment studies of paedophiles also report high levels of success using totally different methods of intervention. The similarity in results may be because all these forms of intervention are equally effective. Either perpetrators are highly receptive to treatment or all the treatments have been particularly powerful, well focused, and well executed. If this were true, then there would be no great need to invest more research resources and it would be more productive to provide wider coverage of the cheapest intervention model available. Unfortunately, there are other explanations for the coincidence in results. It may be that the results of one or both types of study have been contaminated by bias. The broadly based programmes are particularly vulnerable, as they are currently dependent on clinical or self report outcome data. Alternatively, the results may relate to different populations. The behavioural studies typically concern paedophilic patients who have offended against related or non related children. The wider treatment programmes typically involve families where incest has occurred. It may be that paedophiliacs have inappropriate sexual age preferences which are open to behavioural treatment and that perpetrators of intrafamilial sexual abuse are best served by the range of treatments offered by the broadly based programmes. Furthermore, the treatment of incest takes place within a very different context, with strong social and legal pressures for compliance and for successful outcome. In both the Santa Clara programme (Giaretto, 1982) and the Great Ormond Street project (Bentovim et al, 1988) there is a requirement that parents accept responsibility for the abuse, and that the child must not be blamed.

Another major issue is the use of volunteer self help groups. The Santa Clara Programme (Giaretto, 1982) has had a major influence on the development of British thinking (Porter, 1984), but the central component of self help groups have not been developed in this country. In the United States there are many Parents United Chapters. The Chapters are not independent self help groups and they can only operate as the self help components of a professional sponsoring agency, with the capacity to provide treatment that is viable and recognised by local Child Protective Services, by Law Enforcement agencies and the Courts (Parents United 1987, Gillies, 1991). The encouraging results reported by Giaretto (1982) and Kroth (1979) on the Santa Clara Programme, the reported efficacy of volunteer support in other areas of child abuse treatment, and the cost efficiency of self help, all suggest that this is an approach worth examining in more detail in Britain.

This review has concentrated on studies that have attempted to evaluate the impact of intervention programmes. There are many articles which suggest interesting innovatory approaches to treatment, but without a firm research base to inform service provision. The problem is partly that there are few studies, partly it is that the studies that are available often read as statements of belief rather than independent objective evaluations. The one study that did implement a controlled experimental design (Monck, 1991) did find improved depression scores for the children in the families, but no differences between the two contrasted methods of intervention.

The problem of individual views and beliefs also extends to the general texts in child sexual abuse. Texts are mostly written by committed clinicians working in specialist centres, and it is understandable that the reviews reflect their own approach and expertise in treatment. Recently more widely based reviews have appeared and mention has already been made of three of them. Briere (1992) has reviewed the evidence on the effects of abuse and suggested strategies of therapeutic intervention. Haugaard and Repucci have outlined the main therapeutic issues involved in the treatment of child sexual abuse (1988, p 181–312). Bagley and Thurston (1988) have produced critical summaries of approximately 210 key articles on many aspects of child sexual abuse research (not just treatment or formal outcome studies). Bagley and Thurston cover many of the issues discussed by Haugaard and Repucci but in the form of more detailed summaries of separate research reports. The texts provide a starting point for research in this area to move forward and become more productive.

Finally, the literature on child sexual abuse has given considerable attention to the problems of intervening with and without legal powers and the effects of this intervention on all the family participants. There has also been considerable research interest in children's abilities to disclose information about abuse (see for example, Smith, 1992) and to provide testimony in court (see Myers, 1992). Descriptive process studies of both special and routine interventions, however, are in their infancy. Further such studies are necessary in order to identify the relevant variables to include in more complex evaluations of therapeutic interventions.

Summary

1.   Research studies have reported that some interventions have been associated with improved scores on research measures at post-test, but the lack of many

controlled studies or comparative studies limits the conclusions that can be drawn.

2. The research data that are available, differ in emphasis from data for other forms of child abuse. There is a greater focus on individual treatment for perpetrators, on group treatment for victims and adult survivors, and on the causative effect of certain family systems. There is also more explicit regard for the effects of the statutory child protection process.

3. Four causal factors have been described for perpetrators of sexual abuse. There is evidence that one of these, inappropriate sexual orientation, has been successfully treated by behavioural interventions. The studies can be criticised for their reliance on measures of sexual arousal and recidivism, but the results are relatively strong compared to most child abuse intervention studies and the methodology can be commended for testing of specific hypotheses.

4. There are indications that other factors regarding perpetrators including sexual blockage, emotional congruence and social inhibitions, are suitable for treatment and could provide a basis for future research.

5. There is an impression that treatment for perpetrators is one of the least available services, despite having the strongest empirical support for efficacy.

6. Research data on treatment for victims and survivors is very limited. There is some research support for the benefits of groups and of some individual therapies, but little data to suggest that one approach is superior to another or that a particular approach is indicated for particular types of case. There are few research reports on interventions with male victims or on extra compared to intra familial abuse.

7. Multicomponent programmes for whole families in cases of incest, report high rates of success, but there are uncertainties about the independence of the outcome measures used. Evaluation is particularly complex because, (a) many treatments are used in parallel and (b) the interactive effects of routine field services, child protection agencies, and the criminal justice system.

8. The reported success of multicomponent programmes in reducing recidivism, is similar to the success reported by behavioural programmes for perpetrators, despite very different methods of intervention. This may be due to equal efficacy, experimental error, or different client populations. Neither finding is supported by large scale retrospective outcome studies of all sexual offenders.

9. Future research is unlikely to be productive unless individual studies limit themselves to testing narrow hypotheses regarding specific treatments and/or specific agency and legal processes. The current literature is well able to provide details of the individual issues that this research could address. Many approaches to treatment are suggested by (a) the clinical work reported in the literature and detailed in recent reviews, (b) new studies of the process and outcome of routine case management, and (c) the sequelae of child sexual abuse indicated by clinical records and retrospective studies, and recently confirmed by prospective studies.

Chapter Eleven Research Summaries

Alexander et al (1989, 1991); Follette et al (1991)

A COMPARISON OF GROUP TREATMENTS OF WOMEN SEXUALLY ABUSED AS CHILDREN AND INDIVIDUAL PREDICTORS OF OUTCOME

Sample: 65 adult women abused by fathers/stepfathers recruited via the media and not in therapy. Cases of psychosis, severe substance abuse, or serious suicidal feelings excluded. 65 women recruited but 7 did not complete treatment, 3 because they became suicidal during treatment and requested hospitalization. Average age of 36 years (range 23 to 55), average years of education of 14 years (range 2 to 21); 39% single, 36% married, 20% divorced; 76% Caucasian, 24% Black. Average length of abuse 7 years (range 1 month to 16 years); onset of abuse before age of 6 for a third, from 6 to 11 years for half, and in adolescence for the remaining women. A third experienced fondling, 15% oral/genital contact, and over half sexual intercourse. Approximately two thirds were abused by natural fathers, a third by step fathers, and a tenth by other male relatives.

Focus: Functioning of adult women sexually abused when children.

Objectives: Treatment to ameliorate the effects of sexual abuse in childhood.

Programme: Two types of group. Both types met for 1.1/2 hours per week for 10 weeks. Groups led by pairs of advanced female doctoral students supervised by experienced clinical psychologists using videotapes of groups.

(1) Interpersonal transaction group (IT): Focused on topics common to the experience of incest (feelings of helplessness and being different, trust, family secrets, ambivalence towards parents). New topics introduced each week and group split into pairs for about 4 minutes and then rotated to a new partner. The dyadic discussions used to prime subsequent whole group discussion with leader asking 'bridging' questions to elicit recognition of relevance of topic by group members. Weekly topics became more intimate over life of group.

(2) Process group format group (PF). In the first few sessions members shared their goals and expectations and abuse histories. Then focused on each member interactions with group in order to examine what behaviours were problematic (and perpetuated 'victimisation') and to explore new ways of relating to people. Therapists led and focused groups but actual topics decided by group members.

Design: Repeated measures (pre and post-test and 6 month follow up) with near random allocation to two treatment conditions and one wait list condition. Four groups in each of the two treatment conditions making 8 groups in all. Subjects assigned as they were recruited to one group at a time except for 2 subjects assigned to wait list who felt unable to wait for treatment. Each pair of group leaders conducted groups in each condition to control for differential competence and match between the leaders.

Measures: (1) Beck Depression Inventory (BDI), a 13 item shortened version. (2) Social Adjustment Scale (SAS) by experimentally blind raters viewing videotape of SAS structured interview. (3) Symptom Check List (SCL), self report of psychological symptoms, revised version. (4) Modified Fear Survey (MFS), self report of various fears. (5) Family Adaptability and Cohesion Scales (FACES-II). (6) Traditional Family Ideology Scale (TFI). (7) Locke Wallace Marital Adjustment Scale (MAS).

Results: 1. Group results: (a) Repeated measures (pre and post-test) MANOVA with individual groups nested within group type conducted on all 4 measures. Significant effect for time, but no significant main effect for treatment type, groups within treatment type, or interaction of Groups Within Treatment Type x Time. (b) Univariate analysis showed improvement over time on BDI, MFS, & SCL. (c) Some Treatment x Time interactions with mostly significant improvements on BDI, SAS, & SCL for IT and PF groups and no change for wait list control group. Exceptions were (i) that improvements on SAS for IT group was only a trend, (ii) that wait list controls actually deteriorated on SAS. (d) MANOVA including follow up data also showed a significant effect for time, but no significant effect for treatment, Treatment x Time, or Groups Within Treatment x Time. However, there was a significant effect of time and univariate analysis showed linear effects on BDI, MFS, SAS, and SCL. (e) The 7 failing to complete treatment did not differ significantly from completers on a range of demographic or abuse variables or on 6 study outcome measures, except that they reported significantly less fearfulness at pre-test.

2. Individual factors associated with poor outcome were (a) history of oral-genital abuse or penetrative abuse, (b) high levels of pretreatment distress and depression, (c) currently married rather than single, (d) non significant trend for those with previous therapy experience to benefit more from less structured process group.

3. Individual factors not associated with outcome: (a) duration of abuse; (b) family cohesion, adaptability, and paternal dominance; (c) level of marital satisfaction; (d) whether abuse by father or step father.

Notes: Authors conclude that results show:

(1) Effectiveness of groups and maintained at follow up, but that no difference between the types of group.

(2) Robust nature of effects and not highly dependent on vagaries of group composition as no variability between individual groups.

(3) Although groups helpful many women (some of whom had not previously disclosed) sought further therapy.

(4) Women with severe abuse experiences who had never disclosed and with less education or confidence about participation in groups likely to benefit more from structured groups and may also need concurrent individual therapy.

(5) Married women had worse outcomes so couple therapy may be useful particularly for those not disclosing abuse or participation in group to spouse.

Barnett et al (1989)

GROUP TREATMENT FOR WOMEN SEX OFFENDERS
AGAINST CHILDREN

Sample: 6 women sex offenders who were serving terms of imprisonment of 2 to 4 years for sexual offences against children. All had been accomplices of other perpetrators. 2 co-offenders with males, 2 with males and females, 2 with males plus they also offended on own. Their average age was 35.5 years (range 23–47 years). All were married or divorced and all but one had children. Only one woman had been a victim of child sexual abuse herself. All had extensive experience of males who sexually abused children with their first sexual relationships being with abusers. There were 8 victims, aged from infancy to fifteen years. Their abusers had been their own mothers (n=6), their sister (n=1), or family friend (n=1). Co-offenders were natural fathers (n=4), stepfathers (n=2), natural mother (n=1), client's cohabitant (n=1), brother-in-law (n=1), friend of family (n=6). Sexual abuse included manual and oral stimulation, insertion of objects into vagina and anus, participation in making of pornography, accomplice to anal or vaginal penetration by co-offender.

Focus: Deviant sexual behaviour of women offenders.

Objectives: To examine the client's feelings, attitudes and beliefs, and to reduce the risk of clients reoffending. For clients to examine and change their offending behaviour to protect children.

Programme: Ten $1^{1}/_{2}$ hour sessions led by two female therapists. Session (1) basic group rules of confidentiality, openness and honesty, mutual trust, and group identity. Each client had a private book in which to express her ideas and feelings which could be shared with the others if she wished.

(2) Session covered naming of body parts in street and conventional terms, discussing the offences, accepting responsibility for the offences and examining their denials and justifications and the factors that triggered the abuse. Role-plays were used to confront their abusive behaviours with the client performing as perpetrator and child.

(3) & (4) Discussion of context of abuse with role play of alternative actions in potentially abusive situations (e.g. refusing to participate, leaving, removing child and seeking help).

(5) Clients traced their family tree to identify happy and unhappy life events plus role play of police investigation interview.

(6) Brain-storm on effects of sexual abuse. Also watched a video sharing personal accounts of victims.

(7) & (8) Review plus assertiveness training.

(9) Implications of their offences for the future, and two clients disclosed further acts of abuse.

(10) Review and evaluation, praise and encouragement and a cream cake tea.

Design: Repeated measure (pre and post-test) on treatment sample.

Measures: (1) Therapists records of sessions. (2) Clients completed evaluation sheets at the end of every session. (3) The Cognitions Scale (Abel et al, 1984) completed by clients before and after the therapy sessions to measure distorted beliefs held by sex offenders to justify their abuse of children.

Results: Scores on the Cognition Scale improved significantly (5%, 1 tailed Wilcoxon). Clients and therapists reports indicated improvement on clients' understanding of causes of the abusive behaviour and possible alternative behaviour, their responsibility for it, the negative effects of the abuse on them and on the children, empathy with the victims, and assertive rather than aggressive or passive methods of coping.

Notes: The authors acknowledge the potential bias from subjects falsely representing their cognitions. Also difficulties in assessing if any impact on recidivism. Authors still consider intervention worthwhile as: clients said helpful; seems to have changed their beliefs and attitudes; an innovative intervention and evaluation.

Becker et al (1988)

Sample: 24 males aged between 13 and 18 years treated at the Sexual Behaviour Clinic of the New York State Psychiatric Institute. The cases were referred for 'hands on' consensual sexual activity with victims under 13 years of age by the use of verbal and physical coercion. Most subjects were referred from the criminal justice system and it was usually the first arrest for a sexual crime, although 22 subjects had previous non sexual crime arrests. Two thirds of subjects were black, one third Hispanic, and one subject was Caucasian. There was virtually no history of psychiatric hospitalization in the sample.

Focus: Deviant sexual behaviour of teenage males.

Objectives: To teach the adolescent sexual offender control over his deviant sexual interest pattern and so prevent future multiple, life time offences, which are known to be common in this type of subject.

Programme: Assessment through structured clinical interview regarding demographic characteristics and history of deviant sexual acts, a battery of psychological tests, and a psycho-physiologic test of deviant interest patterns by measuring penile response to various audio taped stimuli. Treatment had seven components

(1) Verbal satiation: 30 minutes of continual repetition of a deviant phrase relevant to the subject, whilst he views slides of deviant target of a young boy or girl. Following satiation, subjects are orientated towards learning more appropriate sexual responses.

(2) Four weekly group sessions of 75 minutes. The therapist role plays the offender, while the offender role plays the victim, the victim's family or legal staff. In role play the offender confronts own rationalization of deviant behaviour as role played by the therapist.

(3) A 75 minute group session and eight 15 minute individual sessions of covert sensitization. Offenders imagine and verbalise the antecedents of a deviant act and immediately bring to mind the negative consequences of such acts.

(4) Four 75 minute sessions for social skills training.

(5) Four 75 minute sessions of anger control training through role playing.

(6) Education about sexual development and appropriate sexual values and behaviour.

(7) Two 75 minute sessions of relapse prevention. Subjects identify areas of weakness to develop skills for coping with deviant anger that may appear in the future.

Design: Repeated measures (pre and post-test) on case series producing multiple baselines.

Measures: Penile erection response to deviant audio material of verbal coercion, physical coercion, and sadism used to achieve sexual access to victims plus a tape of non sexual physical assault.

Results: For the 4 subjects who used verbal coercion on male victims, level of response to the deviant audio stimuli fell from pre-test to post-test, as follows: to the verbal coercion tape, 77% to 17%; physical coercive tape, 73% to 34%; sadism tape, 53% to 32%; non sexual physical assault, 37% to 3%.

For the subjects who used physical coercion on male victims, the changes in response were: to verbal coercion tape, 18% to 15%; physical coercion, 40% to 21%; sadism, 36% to 6%; non sexual assault, 21% to 7%.

For the 12 subjects who used physical coercion on female victims, the change in response were: to verbal coercion tape, 31% to 16%; physical coercion, 38% to 20%; sadism, 41% to 24%; non sexual assault, 19% to 14%.

For the one subject who used verbal coercion on female victims, the changes in response were: to verbal coercion, 42% to 85%; physical coercion, 80% to 33%; sadism, 23% to 95%; non sexual assault, 0% to 28%.

The changes in the psycho-physiological response to treatment, was statistically significant for offenders against male victims, but not for offenders against female victims. Standard deviations were high in the female victim group, indicating variability in subject response to treatment.

Notes: The authors discuss the possible explanations for the less successful result for the female victim group, as well as methodological issues. A fuller account of the treatment programme is reported in Abel et al (1984).

Borgman (1984)

Sample: 16 sexually abused girls receiving treatment in a residential home for abused and neglected children, who had been victims of serious sexual abuse, including physical genital contact and penetration. At placement 5 victims were pre-adolescent and 11 were aged 12 to 15 years. Perpetrators were 7 fathers, 3 stepfathers and 6 other known males. Many of the families were excessively violent and a few parents were alcoholic, mentally ill or involved in crime, and came from lower than average socio economic groups.

Focus: Functioning and development of female children subject to sexual abuse.

Objectives: To prevent children developing negative self images and to help them to develop positive self images.

Programme: Group discussions of both knowledge and sexuality and clarification of current feelings and future intentions. Teaching of skills such as cooking. Various activities including acting as volunteers for the elderly, part time employment, drama and ballet as a normal forum for any exhibitionist and sexually provocative or aggressive tendencies. Encouragement of nurturing others such as siblings. No attempt was made to change the long standing motivations and life perceptions of the children. Discussion of sexual abuse was discouraged apart from clarification of emotional feelings and future relationships, because of danger of encouraging a deviant self image and of developing a repertoire to avoid what needed to be faced.

Design: Report of case series.

Measures: Self reports of relationships with adults and peers. Therapists' reports of self image and sexual activity.

Results: Six cases showed improvements in relationships with adults and peers, self image, and levels of sexual activities and aggression. Two further cases showed similar improvements but regressed on reunion with their families. Three cases showed little change in self image or levels of sexual activity but this became more discrete and age appropriate. Five cases showed no change or refused to accept treatment.

Bradford and Pawlak (1987)

SADISTIC HOMOSEXUAL PAEDOPHILIA: TREATMENT WITH CYPROTERONE ACETATE SINGLE CASE STUDY

Sample: 23 year old male imprisoned at age 16 for homosexual paedophilic murder. Abnormal sexual arousal patterns unchanged by a variety of behavioural techniques over a 5 year period. Man had a history of significant prenatal insult, brain damage, epilepsy, and aggressive behaviour since early childhood. He had an IQ of 70, exhibited irritable behaviours, and complained of sadistic sexual fantasies including the rape, torture, and murder of his sister. His sex hormone profile was within normal limits.

Focus: Deviant sexual arousal patterns of aggressive male paedophile.

Objectives: Reduction in deviant sexual arousal.

Programme: Two levels of dosage of Cyproterone Acetate (CPA): 50 mg. per day for 6 weeks followed by dosage of 100 mg. per day for 4 weeks.

Design: ABA case study design of (A) 4 weeks baseline, (B1) treatment at lower dosage, (B2) treatment at higher dosage, (a) repeat follow up testing at 22 weeks.

Measures: All measures taken twice with subject under and not under the influence of alcohol. (1) Multiple measures of sex hormone levels. (2) Sexual arousal (penile tumescence) to audiotaped stimuli of consenting and non consenting homosexual paedophilic sexual interactions, and heterosexual and homosexual adult-adult sexual interactions. Audiotapes presented twice with instructions to suppress or be aroused to stimuli. Paedophilic Index (P1) calculated to indicate ratio of arousal to non aggressive paedophilia to adult consenting hetereosexual intercourse. Paedophilia Aggressive Index (PA1) calculated to indicate the ratio of arousal to aggressive paedophilia to consenting paedophilia. (3) Subject's rating of his sexual response to audio stimuli.

Results: (1) Significant correlation between CPA dosage and levels of testosterone, but not with levels of other hormones. Significant correlation between testosterone and sexual response to both violent and non violent paedophlic stimuli.

(2) Reduction in sexual arousal to both non violent paedophilic stimuli for both treatment dosages and mostly maintained at follow up. No change or increased arousal to consenting homosexual and heterosexual adult sex and to non sexual physical assault of male child.

(3) Alcohol nearly completely suppressed arousal to adult heterosexual stimuli resulting in an increase in the Paedophilic Index, but this was reduced during treatment. However, The Paedophilic Aggressive Index with alcohol, increased during treatment.

(4) Significant positive correlations between self report and measured arousal for all stimuli except for consenting adult homosexual sex and for non sexual physical assault on male child.

Notes: Authors suggest CPA helped subject to control his sexual arousal and that this was due to cognitive components. The maintenance at follow up may be due to the treatment interrupting the conditioned behavioural response of sexual arousal. Authors conclude that treatment effective in case with worst prognosis.

Chaffin (1992)

TREATMENT COMPLETION AND PROGRESS AMONG INTRAFAMILIAL SEXUAL ABUSERS

Sample: 36 consecutive father-daughter/stepdaughter sexual abusers referred to an outpatient treatment programme by child protective services or by the criminal justice system (25 subjects attended as requirement of parole). Criteria for acceptance into the programme included absence of schizophrenia, psychosis, mental retardation, antisocial personality, dementia, or delirium; admission of the abuse; agreement between initial interviewer and clinical consultant that subject regressed paedophile according to Groth's 1978 typology. Cases not included in study if non completion due to transfer to other treatment or imprisonment. Average age of 37 years (range 22–55 years), average IQ of 96. History of childhood physical abuse, 33%, sexual abuse, 39%.

Focus: Sexual abuse by regressed male paedophiles.

Objectives: To treat regressed intrafamilial sexual abusers in order to prevent their reoffending.

Programme: Long term (2 year) outpatient group psychotherapy. Groups consisted of 6 to 8 men, and one male and one female therapist. Groups open and informally structured. Therapeutic target areas included detailed admission, acceptance of responsibility, motivation for abuse, modifying cognitive distortions and rationalizations, sexuality, impact upon the victim, stress management, relapse prevention. Brief problem focused individual, marital, or family therapy provided where necessary. Also participation for some in outside substance abuse programme.

Design: Repeated measures/outcome of case series.

Measures: (1) Completion of programme; (2) Attendance; (3) Therapist ratings at post test of emotional congruence (EC), sexual arousal (AR), blockage (BL), internal inhibition (IN), acceptance of responsibility (R), and victim empathy (EM). (4) Derogatis Stress Profile (DSP) at pre and post test. (5) Minnesota Multiphasic Personality Profile (MMPI) at pre test with the MacAndrew Addiction Scale (MAC).

Results: (1) No meaningful differences between criminally charged and not charged subjects at pre-test.

(2) Programme completion rate of 64% significantly related to low score for personality disturbance and trend suggesting related to court ordered attendance.

(3) Trend that attendance rate (of those who completed) better for higher MAC addiction scores.

(4) Post-test therapist ratings high for Responsibility and Empathy for Victim, but very low for Blockage of sex/relationships with adults.

(5) High post-test ratings significantly related to less personality disturbed on MMPI. Less personality disturbance and criminally charged both significantly related to Victim Empathy ratings. Of those with personality disturbance it was only the criminally charged who reached criterion for Victim Empathy.

(6) Trend for high score on personality disturbance to be associated with poor outcome on internal inhibitors.

(7) Significant group improvement on stress scores, but no association of pre-treatment or improvement in scores with personality disturbance or whether criminally charged.

Notes: Author argues that

(1) personality profiles of dubious value in identifying sexual abusers, but useful for predicting completion and outcome of therapy.

(2) Group may have been too threatening or not sufficiently intensive for more personality disordered subjects.

(3) Small effect from whether criminally charged may be because most were attending as part of juvenile court service plans, but at least criminal charges did not seem to hinder benefits from therapy.

(4) Concern that personality disturbed improved so little on Empathy for Victim rating.

Deblinger et al (1990)

COGNITIVE BEHAVIOURAL TREATMENT FOR SEXUALLY ABUSED CHILDREN SUFFERING POST-TRAUMATIC STRESS

Sample: 19 girls aged 3 to 16 years (mean 7.8) who suffered contact sexual abuse by anyone at least 5 years older than themselves and met DSM-III-R criteria for post-traumatic stress disorder (PTSD). 68% suffered oral-genital and/or penile penetration, 26% suffered genital touching and/or digital penetration. Perpetrators were fathers or stepfathers, 53%; other male relatives, 21%; other male trusted adults, 21%; and one child was abused by a stranger.

Focus: Psychiatric state of child victims of sexual abuse.

Objectives: To assist the sexually abused child in

(1) disconnecting the association (classical conditioning) frequently made between anxiety, shame and abuse related thoughts;

(2) disrupting the association (instrumental conditioning) between avoidance of innocuous abuse related stimuli and the reduction of anxiety;

(3) training parents so that they can assist children learn more functional social behaviours.

Programme: 12 individual structured treatment sessions for child and his/her non offending primary caretaker.

(1) The child is gradually, but repeatedly, exposed to abuse related stimuli until anxiety decreases. (a) Coping/modelling: 2 sessions of skills training for dealing with emotions raised by therapist and encouraging full disclosures. (b) Gradual exposure: 6 sessions using flexible methods giving child choice and sense of control to identify and confront

abuse related memories; therapist provides education and therapeutic feedback. (c) Education/prevention training 2 sessions on clear communication, body ownership, the touch continuum, secrets, etc.

(2) The parents are taught skills for responding to their child's behaviour difficulties (a) Education/coping: 2 sessions on own emotions and their influence on child. (b) Guidelines for effective parent-child communication (2 sessions). (c) Behaviour management: 6 sessions: on principles for altering their interactions with their child and hence the dysfunctional behaviour.

Design: Repeated measures (2 pre-tests 2–3 weeks apart and one post-test).

Measures: (1) Interviews with parent and child on demographic data, history of abuse, other trauma, school performance, social performance with peers, family support networks. Also family psychiatric history and symptoms of PTSD. (2) CBCL parent report measures on social competence of children of 4–16 years. (3) STAIC self report state and trait anxiety scale. (4) CDI a 27 item self report depression inventory.

Results: (1) Significant improvements (paired t tests) on PTSD subcategories including re-experiencing phenomena, avoidance behaviour, and arousal symptoms. Continuation of some symptoms, but no children met criteria for PTSD at post-test.

(2) No changes between 1st and 2nd pre-tests but significant improvement from pre-test to post-test on CBCL (both externalizing and internalizing subscale), CDI, and STAIC (trait and state). Note that half the children did not complete CDI or STAIC as too young.

(3) One way ANOVA found no significant differences in change scores across age groups, abuser groups, duration or time since last abuse. Experience of oral-genital sex or intercourse showed more change on CBCL subscales.

Notes: Authors note that despite improvement the child subjects CDI scores indicated mild depression at post-test.

Delson and Clark (1981)

GROUP THERAPY WITH SEXUALLY MOLESTED CHILDREN

Sample: 5 girls aged between 6 and 11 years in child play therapy group following sexual molestation by their fathers.

Focus: Functioning and development of female children sexually molested by fathers.

Objectives: To mitigate the effects of child sexual abuse. To help the children develop their own abilities and

self respect, to prevent an intergenerational cycle of abuse by teaching new skills and providing new role models.

Programme: Discussion groups, art therapy groups, role plays to create a new structure for 'regressive experiences', body contact to promote positive self image and respect for own bodies. Role plays included court appearances and caring for babies. Body contact such as back rubbing provided non sexual and non threatening experiences of physical nurturing. The therapy group met weekly for 16 weeks and had 2 therapists. The therapy group was one component of a programme for families modelled on Giaretto's work (op cit).

Design: Case series description.

Measures: Author's description.

Results: Author's conclusion that the treatment was 'likely' to mitigate the redevelopment of repression and denial in the children.

Notes: The authors discuss the girls' desire for 'happy endings' in their role plays and their attribution of powerfulness to social worker. The authors also note the slowness of healing of the children and suggest empowering victims to reach out for help and support in the future. Strong initial parental resistance to the group was reported.

Earls and Castonguay (1989)

EVALUATION OF OLFACTORY AVERSION FOR A BISEXUAL PAEDOPHILE

Sample: 17 year old white single male in a maximum security psychiatric hospital consisted of molesting (mutual masturbation and fellatio) a 12 year old boy. Also two years previously convicted of sexual aggression (intercourse) against a 9 year old girl. Both offences involved high levels of aggression on victims at least 5 years younger than himself. No history of drug, alcohol, or psychiatric problems. Only frequent sexual fantasies involving children.

Focus: Inappropriate age-sex fantasies/behaviour of young male.

Objectives: To reduce deviant sexual arousal.

Programme: 20 treatment sessions (2 to 4 per week) lasting between 30 minutes to an hour. Stimulus materials were eight 7 minute audio tapes of violent and non violent adult–child interactions. One violent and one non violent tape presented per session with subject instructed to inhale from bottle of ammonia crystals if he began to feel aroused. In practice subject inhaled ammonia after arousal (>75% penile tumescence), so on 7th session he was instructed to inhale when the polygraph indicated 20% tumescence. The client self administered the aversive stimuli an average of 9 times per session. Initial target behaviour was responses to male children and once this had been reduced to 20%, the target was shifted to female children.

Design: Repeated measures (multiple baseline including 2 pre-tests 6 months apart, 1 week post-test, and 2 year follow up) on single case study.

Measures: Penile tumescence in response to different stimuli: (1) pre-tests: adults and children, audiotapes of violent and non-violent adult-child interactions, sexually neutral newspaper articles. (2) Baseline and weekly throughout treatment: audio tapes of 15 episodes constructed from client's fantasies. (3) One week post-test and follow up: photographic slides and some of pre-test audio tapes.

Results: (1) Baseline: full erection in response to all stimuli.

(2) Treatment re male children: gradual decrease to 20% response to males over 4 weeks but response to female stimuli maintained.

(3) Treatment re female children: response decreased and remained below 30% throughout treatment. Response to male children remained low. Response to adult females remained high except for weeks 2 and 5.

(4) Pre-tests to audio stimuli: near maximum responses to all except neutral stimuli across both pre-tests.

(5) Post-test to audio stimuli: low levels of arousal response except for sex with consenting (33%) and non consenting (38%) male child, consenting sex with a female child (73%), and sex with adult females (100%).

(6) Follow up to audio stimuli: low levels of arousal except for consenting sex with male child (43%), consenting sex with a female child (38%), adult female (92%), adult male (87%).

(7) Response to visual stimuli of females. Pre-test showed a moderate response to female children aged 1 to 7 (41%) and near full response for all other female children and female adults. At post-test response to female children aged 1 to 12 was below 25% but a full response to females aged 13 to 17 and adults. Similar findings at follow up except response to 13 to 17 year olds moderate at 46%.

(8) Response to visual stimuli of males: Pre-test showed a response to male children aged 1 to 7 of 61%, aged 8 to 12 of 83%, aged 13 to 17 of 16%, and adult males of 15%. At post-test and follow up responses to all males was below 16% and 25% respectively.

Notes: Authors note: (1) lack of change between pre-tests in the absence of treatment.

(2) Considerable generalization across stimuli which were varied to prevent habituation.

(3) Variability in the client's responses to adult female stimuli during treatment.

(4) It seems as if treatment does not generalize across class of deviant arousal, i.e. between male and female children.

(5) Poor results for consenting sex with children and that client refused further treatment on this.

(6) Client encouraged to use ammonia on own to control fantasies but the capsules not allowed on his home ward.

(7) Unclear relationship between reductions in deviant arousal and re-offending.

Furniss (1983), Furniss et al (1984), Bentovim et al (1988)

A THERAPEUTIC APPROACH TO CHILD SEXUAL ABUSE

Sample: Families served by child sexual abuse team at The Great Ormond Street Hospital for Sick Children in London. Main sample data from intake history on 274 families referred between 1980 and 1986 with 411 child victims and 362 siblings. Outcome data on 120 families referred between 1981 and 1984 with 180 child victims and 226 siblings. Outcome data recorded on all 1986 cases, with variation in length of follow up.

Referrals were predominantly (78%) from social workers in the community, requesting assessment and treatment because of concern about future risk, or needing advice replacement decisions. Requests also for diagnostic services; approximately a fifth of referrals due to suspicious symptoms in children. Criteria for intake included case being problematic for local services and parents accepting at least some responsibility for the situation.

Fondling had probably occurred in 47% of cases, partial intercourse in 20%, full intercourse in 17%, and anal intercourse in 11% of cases. The victims were 77% female with one victim per family in 65% of cases. The age of onset of abuse was equally distributed between 3 and 14 years. The abuse lasted less than 12 months in 44% of cases, one to two years 21%, two to four years 15%, five years plus 20%. Perpetrators were parents in 46% of cases and step parents in 27%; 96% were men. Family types were nuclear 39%, step families 23%, single 19%, cohabiting 11%, and foster families 4%. The majority of families had been together for more than five years. Common family problems included violence, marital problems, sexual problems and to a lesser extent, unemployment. Previous histories of sexual abuse, psychiatric problems and chaotic families and violence, were not common for perpetrators and were more commonly recorded for other adults in the family.

Focus: Functioning of family system in which sexual abuse had occurred.

Objectives: Protection of child by assessing whether the family can provide a viable, caring family unit. If this is a possibility, treatment provided to enable family to operate in less dysfunctional ways. Sub-objectives include breaking the taboo of secrecy about sexual matters, enhancement of self esteem and assertiveness, to restructure rigid and enmeshed family patterns and assist perpetrators cope appropriately with their sexual drives.

Programme: Cases receive individual counselling and support from social workers in the community who retain legal responsibilities for child protection. The treatment programme provides assessment followed by treatment through group work, with regular review meetings with family and community social workers.

Assessment involves a range of techniques including direct and circular questioning and detailed observation of the family. Also individual interviews with children. Assessment based upon present situation and history provided by child interview, and an initial hypothesis of the patterns of family relationships and dysfunction. Potentials for child care particularly based upon parental concern for needs of child and the taking of responsibility for abuse. Scapegoating and evidence of hostility to child very significant.

General approach to treatment based upon structural family therapy to change dysfunctional patterns, and to clarify the family history and individual responsibility for the abuse. Treatment of the family systems taking place in the context of child protection, the legal child care, and criminal systems. Families are enabled to change and so convince these other systems that, for example, they are able to care and to protect their children.

Treatment groups with a range of ages for children of both sexes, for mothers, for perpetrators, for parents, and for various workers. The groups run weekly for one hour, for five months, and each group has a leader and trainee leader. Although treatment is the main goal, the groups are psycho educational in approach, with training in social skills, forms of touching and sexuality, protection against abuse. Groups allow peer support and sharing and confrontation of issues to accelerate learning, increased self esteem and clarification and open communication about sexual abuse, its causes, and the responsibility for its occurrence.

Treatment was offered to 87% of cases. 46% completed a course of treatment, 36% attended some sessions. 47% of victims attended children's groups and a further 27% attended some meetings. 10% were provided with some individual treatment. 29% of parents attended mothers' and fathers' groups.

Design: Case series.

Measures: Community social workers' assessments of change. Therapists' ratings of social workers' support for children and of children's sexualized behaviour and of changes in family functioning. Agency records of changes in placement and family status and recurrence of abuse.

Results: Community professionals reported improvement in 61% of victims and 25% of siblings. Therapists felt that community professionals' support for children was sufficient in 74% of cases.

Changes in households since intake in 76% of cases and in marital status in 50%. Only 14% of victims were with both parents, 40% with one parent, 27% in care, and 20% had grown to independent adulthood. 43% of perpetrators remained at home, 15% of whom had been sent to prison and returned home. 61% of perpetrators were prosecuted and 91% of these were found guilty.

Victims were reported to have marked or moderate sexualised behaviour in 21% of cases compared to 38% of the intake sample. Other emotional disturbances were seen in 49% of cases compared to 75% in the intake sample. Recurrence of abuse reported in 16% of cases and possibly a further 15%. Risk of abuse considered to be high in 7% and moderate in 25% of cases. Families reported as worse 3%, no change 19%, improved due to structural change and some relationship changes 70%.

Notes: The treatment programme has developed over time and so the sample was exposed to slightly different services. The publications make detailed comments about the practice of treatment and clinical impressions of success and outcome. Published information supplemented by personal communication from Dr. Bentovim. See also summary of Furniss (1988) for case series of girls group, and Monck et al (1991) for controlled evaluation of whole programme.

Furniss et al (1988)

GOAL ORIENTATED GROUP TREATMENT FOR SEXUALLY ABUSED ADOLESCENT GIRLS

Sample: 10 girls aged 12 to 15 years, who had attended the group in previous 2 years. All had been victims of sexual abuse (mostly penetrative) by fathers (n=5), stepfather (n=4), or brother (n=1). All perpetrators sentenced to prison after admitting abuse. Most girls subject to child protection orders. Girls displayed a range of psychiatric and behavioural symptoms. Common features of families were male alcohol abuse, a history of violence, sexual abuse of siblings, poor marital relationships and maternal depression.

Focus: Functioning of victims based on a model of sexual abuse as a symptom of family disturbance.

Objectives: Girls group part of an integrated treatment programme for sexually abused children and their families. Specific objectives of group to provide direct help for the girl in her own right independent from other family members. (a) Individual: to help girls find a language to communicate about the abuse, to teach normal sexual development that unexpectedly ignorant of, rebuild self esteem, to develop a sense of choice about lives. (b) In relation to family: non abusing or threatening adult male and reliable trustworthy yet firm adult therapist to provide appropriate intergeneration boundaries plus a different model of parenting to that experienced in their own families. To help girls distinguish the abusing parent's responsibility from their own self blame. (c) In relation to peers: to overcome by isolation by sharing experience with peers, to rebuild normal adolescent relationships to desexualize inter personal relationships.

Programme: Weekly group of one hour for 7 months to 2 years. Maximum of 6 girls per group. Initial sessions more structured and focused on finding the language and breaking the secrecy of abuse, later sessions less structured and guided by issues raised. Sessions included therapists interpretations, active physical intervention to prevent dangerous acting out and provide firm limit setting, teaching child care and sexual development, drawing to encourage non verbal self expression, and role play and video feedback to develop social skills and self assertiveness. The group ran parallel to family groups and therapists checked with girls about issues they did or did not want raised at family sessions.

Design: Clinical case series plus independent follow up.

Measures: Therapists' reports of girls progress. For follow up, questionnaires to girls, their families, and wide range of professional staff involved both at hospital and local services.

Results: (1) Post treatment: (a) All children less anxious and exhibited less sexualized behaviour. (b) Increase in trusting relationship expressed by trust and expression of anger to therapists. (c) Improved self esteem evidenced by ability to say felt not wanted, dirty, etc. and no recurrence of suicidal or self mutilating behaviour. (d) Increase in self assertiveness and confidence with other family members. (e) Less pseudo mature behaviour and more appropriate adolescent behaviour and relationships.

   (2) At follow up (on n=9) improvements for 7 girls in behaviour, social adjustment, relationships with peers, family communication and relationships, with no emotional, behavioural, or psychiatric problems, and no recurrence of abuse. One girl showed some improvement but still had low self esteem, and was in relationship with younger immature boy. Another girl still had low self esteem, over sexual behaviour, withdrawn and isolated, and vulnerable to re-abuse. Improvements in family relationships

did not necessarily mean family re-union: one father or stepfather returned home permanently, four girls lived with their mothers, three lived independently, one lived with friends.

Notes: Authors discuss the challenging behaviour of the girls and the importance of the sex of the therapist, linking in with work with family, and close co-operation with local social worker. See also summary of Furniss (1983), Furniss et al (1989) and Bentovim et al (1988) for case series evaluation of whole programmes. See summary of Monck et al (1991) for controlled evaluation study.

Giaretto (1976, 1982), Kroth (1979)

A COMPREHENSIVE CHILD SEXUAL ABUSE TREATMENT PROGRAMME

Sample: 51 cases of intrafamilial child sexual abuse drawn cross sectionally from 3 different treatment stages of the programme in 1978. The majority of victims were female with an average age of 12 years and had been molested for more than 6 months, usually by fondling rather than penetrative sex. Perpetrators had an average age of 36 years and more of them were stepfathers than natural fathers. At intake half of the victims manifested psychosomatic symptoms and the parents reported themselves to be near a state of breakdown. Families had slightly higher than average incomes.

Focus: Family relations and child functioning.

Objectives: Treatment of families through support, growth of self esteem, and harmonizing family systems to achieve self growth and actualization to, (1) enable families to remain together and, (2) to minimize trauma of the victims and the non abusing parent. Also to repair damage to child victims by developing self esteem social skills, and preventing subsequent self destructive behaviours. Incest seen primarily as symptoms of distorted family relationships. Therapy aim to rebuild family around the essential core of mother-daughter care.

Programme: Four Components,
   (1) Professional Counselling of individuals, dyads, and family including crisis counselling for children.
   (2) Volunteers acting like older siblings providing companionship and physical and emotional support. Volunteers usually counselling students.
   (3) Self help groups (a) Parents United including group therapy and practical support (b) Daughters and Sons United with age graded groups with play therapy and particular support for children separated from parents and companionship and support for court appearances.
   (4) Community Awareness Programmes to encourage referrals to treatment programme. The pro-

gramme is not judgemental and emphasises need for support. Many perpetrators prosecuted and programme works closely with the Criminal Justice system. Perpetrators commonly sentenced, paroled, or on probation with required attendance in programme. Rehabilitation of family only attempted if parents do not continue to blame child for crisis.

Design: Three stage cross sectional design with no external controls. Treatment groups matched on ten variables including age of victims and perpetrators, education level of parents, and duration of abuse. Groups recruited at treatment stage of 2 to 3 weeks, 5 months, and near termination at about 14 months into treatment.

Measures: Self reports by parents of marital and parent child relationships, feelings of responsibility for abuse, self esteem, guilt, feelings of being in control, self destructive behaviour of children, recurrence of abuse, and perception of treatment programme. Agency records of referrals to programme.

Results: Data shows victims only received an average of 9.8 counselling sessions and 7.5 Sons and Daughters United meetings and most of both of these were in the first 5 months of treatment. Figures for parent counselling and Parents United were 18 to 19 meetings. Significant results were

(1) victims becoming symptom free, increasing social skills, relationships with father (not significant for mother);

(2) parents having improved marital and sexual relations;

(3) perpetrators reported increased acceptance of responsibility for abuse, increased self esteem and mastery, particularly in sexual relations, and no recidivism reported by families. Negative results included a slight increase in a reluctance to report further molestation, persistence of symptoms in non molested siblings, 24% of couples still had serious sexual problems at termination. Agency records show 40% annual increase in referrals to programme.

Notes: Kroth suggests that the attention of the criminal justice system may explain the lack of recidivism and that programme referrals are a better indicator of success. Giaretto states that there has been no recidivism in 600 cases receiving at least ten hours of treatment. All of the results, except case referrals, limited by the lack of independence of self report data.

Jehu (1988, 1989)

Beyond Sexual Abuse: Therapy With Women Who Were Childhood Victims

Sample: 51 women sexually abused as children who received treatment at the University of Manitoba Sexual Dysfunction Clinic.

(1) 90% aged between 20 and 39 years, 47% married, 51% had tertiary education, 76% Caucasian and 19% native Americans.

(2) The abuse started before 6 years of age in 45% of cases, before 10 years in 86%. The abuse lasted for more than a year for 92%, and for more than 3 years for 78%. 66% were abused more than 100 times. Abuse stopped by age 13 for 47%. Selection criteria included some form of genital contact and in 63% of cases this involved penile-vaginal intercourse.

(3) 94% of perpetrators were male, 30% were fathers of some sort, 28% brothers of some sort, and 25% male acquaintances. Selection criteria required the perpetrator to be known to the victim and be at least 5 years older for victims under 12, and 10 years older for victims over 13 years.

(4) The perpetrators methods of inducing participation in abuse included adult authority, 78%, threats, 67%, and force, 59%, representing activities as special/games, 59%, attention and affection, 55%, bribery, 51%, promise of sexual gratification, 33%, 'sex education', 27%, proclamation of love, 23%.

(5) 96% of victims kept the abuse secret for some time for reasons including fear of disbelief/anger/blame by third party, violence from offender, loyalty to offender, attention/affection. 51% did disclose by age 17 and the reactions were predominantly negative including shock/horror, denial, conflict of loyalties between victim and offender, and anger/hostility towards victim.

(6) Families often had marital conflict, frequent changes in membership, a milieu of abandonment for the child, poor supervision, and male supremacy. Fathers were often ineffective/non nurturing parents, had limited social skills, were psychologically absent from the family, and were violent. Mothers often had limited social skills, were overdependent, ineffective, and oppressed.

(7) Subjects were referred by themselves (39%) or by agencies/professionals. Over half had previously received some form of psychological treatment.

Focus: Psychological adjustment of women sexually abused as children.

Objectives: Negotiated with each subject.

Programme: Initial assessment and planning included a preliminary interview, initial assessment interview, negotiation of treatment goals, further formulation of target problems, developing a treatment and evaluation plan. The general context of treatment included attention to the therapeutic relationship, prognostic expectancy (clients expectation of receiving effective help), empathy and acceptance and support, sharing understandings of cause, repeated exposure to issues of the abuse in a safe environment, assisting clients in use of other resources.

The main treatment format was individual or couple therapy including specific treatment approaches:

A. Mood Disturbances: cognitive restructuring using well timed questions to induce the victim to see issues differently. Sequence of explaining rationale of approach, identifying belief systems, recognizing distortions, and exploring alternatives. Common are (i) self blaming beliefs of victim responsibility and offender exoneration, and (ii) self denigrating beliefs of worthlessness/badness, difference from others, stigmatizing, inadequacy and inferiority, and subordination of rights.

B. Interpersonal Problems: (1) Communication training, problem solving, and anger control through feedback, coaching and modelling. (2) Situation/Transition (S/T) group for partners (n=8) met 2 hours weekly for 15 weeks to alleviate feelings of isolation/being different, provide mutual aid/support, assist acceptance/adaptions. (3) Assertiveness training group (n=5) of 2 hour weekly sessions for 10 weeks with a male and female therapist. Follow up session 6 weeks later.

C. Sexual Dysfunctions. (1) Coping skills training involving relaxation training, thought and image stopping, coping plans, guided self dialogue, imagery rehearsal, role playing, in vivo exposure (graded series of sexual assignments from self examination to mutual genital pleasuring and maybe intercourse). (2) Cognitive restructuring.

Design: Repeated measures (pre and post-test and follow up) on treatment sample plus case histories and descriptions of issues raised in therapy.

Measures: The process of treatment involved continuing assessment and evaluation procedures including reconstructive techniques of instant replay, remote recall, role play, induced imagery, recording by clients, card sorts. More formal measures included interviews; medical examination; Hudson Index of Self Esteem (ISE); Beck Depression Inventory (BDI); Belief Inventory (BI) for distorted beliefs including self blame and denigration; Marital Relationship Questionnaire (MRQ); Dyadic Adjustment Scale (DAS) on satisfaction, cohesion, consensus, and affection; Target Complaints Scale (TCS) a 5 point scale of disturbance felt on each identified problem; Index of Sexual Satisfaction (ISS); Sexual Arousal Inventory (SAI) only for females; Sexual Relationship Questionnaire (SRG); Sexual History Form (SHF).

Results: Only main findings summarized.

A. Mood Disturbance, (n=36 as 11 not treated/completed, 4 not followed up). Significant improvement in beliefs, depression, and self esteem from pre-test to post-test. Distorted beliefs were clinically significant for 94% at pre-test, 13% at post-test, and 5% at follow up. The sequence for clinically significant depression was 58%, 8%, and 5%. For self esteem 86%, 53%, and 40%. 31 of the clients (who did not receive treatments B or C) reported satisfaction with the treatment.

B. (1) Interpersonal Problems identified in therapy: (a) Relationship with men of fear, mistrust, avoidance of commitment, subordination, promiscuity, anger/hostility. (b) Feelings of partners: vicarious victimization, loss of control and communication in relationship, anger, negative self concept and depression. S/T group rated as helpful by partners but half did not complete due to feelings and memories raised, (c) Relations with women: feelings of anger, disparagement, and distrust, and some uncertainty about sexual orientation. (d) Relations with offspring: two thirds reported that inadequate care or physically abusive to offspring at some time. (e) Relations with family of origin and offender: continuing feelings of anger and grief yet also loyalty and idealization and difficulty in achieving proper separation and individuation from family.

   (2) Assertiveness: (n=5) from pre-test, post-treatment, and follow up the number of victims with clinical problems were (a) Expressions of opinions feelings and beliefs: 5, 2, 1. (b) Saying no: 4, 3, 1. (c) Understanding/accepting personal rights: 4, 2, 1. (d) Discomfort with assertiveness: 5, 2, 3. (e) Four of the 5 women significantly increased in the likelihood of making an assertive response. (f) Clients stated that group met their needs. Also satisfied with group structure and with presence of male therapist.

C. Sexual Dysfunction. Two case studies. (1) Alison and Michael: clinically significant sexual dissatisfaction. Alison found sexual situations stressful, with negative emotional reactions and feelings of helplessness as in the abuse and coped by avoidance and dissociation. Significant marital discord. Therapy on sexual dysfunction from weeks 54 to 143 of treatment with follow up at week 155. Satisfaction with marital sexual relationship (TCS) improved from 'could not be worse' to 'little' at post-test. Sexual satisfaction problems highly clinically significant at pre-test and borderline at follow up. Alison's scores on SAI reduced but still many aversive features of sex. Post-test SRQ showed defensiveness to be mostly within the normal range. At interview the couple expressed satisfaction with the situation accepting limitation in their sexual relationship.

   (2) Amanda and Steve: Amanda lacked sexual motivation with impaired arousal and sexual dissatisfaction and phobia. After 22 weeks treatment on mood disturbances client discovered phobia of own body secretions. Phobia treated for 13 weeks with a 16 week follow up. At follow up Amanda reported improvement in communication and sexual and general relationship with husband.

D. Consumer evaluation (n=41). Only one victim's responses were negative on CSQ. Beneficial aspects reported of information on sexual abuse, acquisition of skills to be one's own therapist, alleviation of self blame, classification re feelings re abuse/perpetrator/family of origin, participation of partner in therapy, meeting other women who had been abused, relationship with therapist.

Notes: A major part of the 1988 book includes discussion of approaches to therapy with this client group with extensive case discussion and case illustration. The 1989 article summarized part of the data from the 1988 book.

Kahn and Chambers (1991)

ASSESSING REOFFENSE RISK WITH JUVENILE OFFENDERS

Sample: 221 juvenile sexual offenders who entered one of 10 treatment programmes between March and October 1984. Male:female ratio of 20:1. Median age of 14.7 years (range 8–12 years but 65% between 13 and 15). 79% white, 5% black, 6% other, 10% unknown. 83% lived at home with at last one biological parent at time of offence (46% mother, 20% both parents, 15% fathers), 6% in foster home, 4% with relations, 1% no fixed address, 6% unknown. More than 75% were in school or vocational training, but histories of disruption (53%), truancy (30%), learning disabled (39%). Also histories of substance abuse (37%), and victims of physical (47%) and sexual (42%) abuse. 35% of siblings sexually abused by person other than subject. Previous criminal history for 47% of subjects and previous sexual crime for 5%.

Focus: Juvenile sex offending.

Objectives: To prevent juvenile sex offenders from continuing to abuse children.

Programme: 10 treatment programmes: 8 outpatient programmes (7 juvenile court sponsored, 1 university based) and 2 institution based correctional treatment programmes. Range of eclectic methods using individual, group, and family therapy of confrontation, sex education, anger management, social skills training, victim empathy development, and, occasionally, behavioural reorientation of deviant sexual arousal. Median number of treatment sessions 27 (range: under 10 to 110). Treatment termination usually at end of court supervision/sentence and only 25% subjects had satisfactory treatment completion.

Design: Retrospective outcome of case series.

Measures: (1) Demographic characteristics.
(2) History of abuse and family dysfunction.

(3) Sexual offence characteristics.
(4) Response of juvenile justice system.
(5) Responses of offender to treatment.
(6) Location and type of treatment.
(7) Reason for treatment termination.
(8) Number/type of previous convictions.
(9) Reconvictions for sexual or other crimes. Follow up until 18th birthday or 1st October 1987 if earlier. Average follow up of 28 months but incarceration resulted in average time at risk of offending being 20 months.

Results: (1) Subsequent convictions: any offence 45%, violent crimes 7%, sexual crimes 7%.

(2) More total subsequent convictions statistically related to more previous convictions, to institutional rather than community treatment (trend only), younger age at first sexual offence, school behaviour problems, school truancy, diversion rather than formal adjudication by court.

(3) Subsequent sexual offences statistically related to use of verbal threats, blame of victims, and denial of initial sexual offences.

(4) Non significant trend for more subsequent sexual offences to be related to institutional rather than community treatment, initial offence against non related child, therapist rating of deviant sexual arousal, therapist rating of risk of reoffending.

Notes: Authors conclusions include: (1) for many juvenile offenders sexual offending is part of wider offending behaviour, which is more prone to recidivism than sexual offending; (2) diversion from formal adjudication related to higher reoffending yet outpatient treatment as effective as incarceration for treatment. Authors explain that they direct two of the treatment programmes in the study and that the actual research was undertaken by Donna Schram and Wendy Rowe.

Kolko (1986)

SOCIAL COGNITIVE SKILLS TRAINING WITH A SEXUALLY ABUSED AND ABUSIVE CHILD PSYCHIATRIC INPATIENT

Sample: An anxious and withdrawn 11 year old boy with developmental delay and coordination difficulties diagnosed as having an adjustment disorder with mixed emotional features. Prior history of maternal neglect, sexual abuse by maternal uncle, and 18 months in foster care at age of 9 years. Current study based on the second period of hospitalisation following his sexual abuse of a 6 year old girl.

Focus: Mental health and development of child.

Objectives: Training child by reducing negative behaviours and developing social competence, cognitive abilities, and positive behaviours. Overall objective of treating adjustment disorder.

Programme: Training by modelling, role play, nurses' and psychiatrist's feedback during training and by others during unit activities. Coaching in new cognitive constructions with video feedback didactic discussions.

Design: Case Study.

Measures: Percentage of skills exhibited in 30 minute sessions of lunch and free play including measures of eye contact, voice quality, physical gestures, and verbal content. Several measures of socio-emotional behaviour such as cheerfulness and participation in activities, routinely rated by duty staff. Weekly blind ratings of pre-social activity, and adjustment. Several general measures of social skill and pro-social adjustment recorded prior to intake, at midpoint of training, and one week post training. Pre-test by mother and one year follow up by foster mother on Child Behaviour Checklist (CBCL). Matson Evaluation of Social Skills of Youngsters (MESSY). Foster mother also completed a long term follow up questionnaire on the child's social skills and adjustment.

Results: Improvements in voice quality, eye contact, physical gestures and verbal content followed training on each skill, with evidence of generalization to behaviour in lunch period and unit activities. Significant increase in the average scores of non targeted pro-social behaviours, and these were maintained post-test except for sharing with others. At one year follow up, there was a statistically significant decrease in overall problem behaviour ratings, which was confirmed by the foster mother's questionnaire and her reports of improved peer relations and no reports of deviant physical contact/sexual behaviour.

Maletzky (1980)

SELF REFERRED VS COURT REFERRED SEXUALLY DEVIANT PATIENTS: SUCCESS WITH COVERT SENSITIZATION

Sample: A total of 100 patients, 38 were homosexual paedophiles 15 of whom were self referred and 23 of whom were Court referred. 62 were exhibitionists, 30 of whom were self referred, and 32 of whom were Court referred. The definition of Court referral included conditions of probation (62%), conditions of parole (7%), release under condition of receiving treatment (9%), direction by attorneys to obtain treatment prior to a Court hearing (22%). The last category does not strictly represent Court referrals and so data from these cases analysed separately at first. Other intermediate cases where there was overt pressure from friends and relatives to attend therapy were not included. Homosexual paedophiles were included because of their greater

frequency of self referral compared to heterosexual paedophiles. Between a third and a half of the homosexual paedophiles were married, whereas two thirds of the exhibitionists were married. Age range of patients was from 17 to 63 years with an average age of approximately 33 years. Average length of education was approximately 11 years. No significant differences found between the 4 groups on demographic data.

Focus: Deviant behaviour of four types of sexual offender.

Objectives: The aim for all cases was to reduce the deviant sexual behaviours. For some cases this was exhibitionism and for others it was homosexual paedophilia. Most of the homosexual paedophiles wished their interest in all homosexual acts to be eliminated, but 13 patients only wished for change in their paedophiliac behaviour.

Programme: Covert sensitization. Patients were encouraged to relax and then to imagine a series of increasingly arousing sexual deviant acts, that were paedophiliac or exhibitionist, depending on the client group. When the patients were aroused they were presented with an aversive odour of decaying tissue and an aversive image. The aversive images were of extremely unpleasant experiences, whilst performing deviant acts. Three sets of aversive stimuli were presented during each weekly session. Also homework assignments of environmental manipulation, thought and masturbatory fantasy change, and covert sensitization using tape records. Exhibitionists also received three aversive behaviour rehearsal sessions. Main treatment phase of 6 months followed by three monthly booster sessions up to a total of 3 year. Treatment provided by author (65%) or by psychiatric technicians under his supervision.

Design: Repeated measures (pre and post test plus follow-up at 12, 18, 24, and 30 months) on all 4 experimental groups.

Measures: Self reports of frequency of deviant urges and deviant acts. Penile plethysmograph measures. Correlation between self reports and physical measure of tumescence. Reports of improvement by significant others of patients. Attendance record. Legal records of deviant acts.

Results: Significant improvements for all groups on most measures and maintained at follow-up. No significant differences between the four experimental groups in the degree of improvement. No differences found between the patients directed by attorneys to attend treatment and the officially Court referred cases.

Notes: The author briefly discusses some of the methodological problems in interpreting the results, including reported bias from patients and significant others and the possible fallibility of the plethysmogaph measures. Also questionable validity of legal records, as known that sexual crimes are under reported. Main conclusion is that Court referred cases, are potential candidates for treatment despite a general belief that involuntary referrals are not sensitive to treatment. Author notes that there are pressures for many patients to attend therapy whether Court ordered or not.

Maletzky (1991)

DATA GENERATED BY AN ABUSE CLINIC

Sample: All 2,865 heterosexual (57.3%) and 855 homosexual (17.4%) paedophiles (classified by main diagnosis) consisting of 74.4% of total of 5,000 male sex offenders seen at the Sexual Abuse Clinic in Portland Oregon from 1973 to 1991. Fifteen females also referred to clinic but data not included. Heterosexual paedophiles were 32% of referrals in 1978, but 68% in 1988–1990. Most referrals from probation/parole officers or from lawyer after subject charged with offence. For all offenders: average age 35 (range 13–79 years); 45% married, 12% living with a woman, 21% divorced, widowed 1%, never married or lived with woman 23%; 76% employed; non sexual psychiatric diagnosis, 29%; prior legal charges 35% of which 76% sexual only, 11% sexual and non sexual, 13% non sexual only. 27% of total sample had relatives who had offended sexually. 29% of sexual offenders had been victims of sexual abuse in childhood. Homosexual paedophiles had significantly longer duration of symptoms than all other offenders and a significantly more victims than heterosexual paedophiles. Maletzky (1980, Op. Cit.) previously reported a study on a subset of this sample.

Focus: Deviant behaviour and sex age preferences of sexual offenders.

Objectives: Elimination of deviant sexual arousal in the sexual offender so that they do not repeat sexual offences.

Programme: Sexual abuse clinic with six locations. Percentage of hetero and homosexual paedophiles respectively receiving different therapies: electric shock aversion (92%, 100%), foul taste aversion (78%, 90%), covert sensitization (100%, 100%), aversive behaviour rehearsal (57%, 48%), plethysmographic feedback (96%, 93%), masturbatory reconditioning (92%, 94%), desensitization (46%, 90%), amyl nitrate conditioning (62%, 74%), empathy training (67%, 85%), social skills training (55%, 87%), assertiveness training (24%, 47%), impulse control training (31%, 57%), marital/family counselling (37%, 17%), group therapy (4%, 7%), depo-Provera medication (1%, 1%).

Design: Repeated measures/outcome on case series.

Measures: (1) Subject self report of covert and overt deviant sexual behaviours. (2) Plethysmograph recordings of penile circumference. (3) Observers rating of subject progress and compliance with treatment. (4) Legal records of arrest, charge, and conviction for sexual offences. (5) Treatment success defined as completion of treatment, under 20% penile response to test stimuli at discharge, no arousal to deviant stimuli at annual follow up tests, self report of no overt/covert deviant arousal, no charges/arrests/convictions for deviant sexual activity even if not substantiated. If not treatment success, then classed as treatment failure.

Results: (1) For total sample, little reduction in overt and covert deviant behaviours in first 6 weeks of treatment, but very marked reduction by 16th week.

(2) Penile responses declined from 80% tumescence (criteria for test deviant stimulus) to deviant stimuli at pre-test to average of under 10% after 10 months for heterosexual paedophiles and to under 30% after 16 months for homosexual paedophiles. Correlation between average of self report and penile response data 0.63 for hetero sexual and 0.53 for homosexual paedophiles.

(3) Significant others reported progress and compliance scores of approximately 3 out of a possible 4.

(4) 1.3% of heterosexual and 4.1% of homosexual paedophiles apprehended during treatment or follow up. At treatment termination their penile responses to deviant stimuli were on average 9.5% and 17.3% of full tumescence respectively.

(5) Follow up on 76% of total sample for between 1 and 17 years. Preliminary data on all offenders show significant association between treatment failure and not living with victim, more than one victim, offender not well known to victim, offender denial of crime, denial of need for treatment, high pretreatment deviant arousal, use of force in offence, multiple paraphilias, unstable employment history, history of unstable social relationships. No statistical association found for offender being a victim as a child, duration of offending greater than 5 years, or frequency of offending of more than 10 times per year.

(6) Follow up data on paedophiles showed treatment success (up to last follow up) of 95% for heterosexual, 86% for homosexual, and 76% for the 112 subjects who had both male and female victims.

(7) Rape offenders had the highest failure rate of all sexual offenders.

Notes: The author argues that despite the methodological limitations of the case series study the results indicate that the majority of sexual offenders can be treated with behavioural methods, that this need not necessarily be prolonged or expensive, that most but not all offenders can be treated safely on an outpatient basis, and that success in treatment can be reliably measured.

Marshall and Barbaree (1988)

THE LONG TERM EVALUATION OF A BEHAVIOURAL TREATMENT PROGRAM FOR CHILD MOLESTERS

Sample: 126 Child molesters who presented to the Kingston Sexual Behaviour Clinic, who met the criteria of admitting the problem, agreement to participate in treatment, had no evidence of psychosis or brain injury. Sample consisted of two groups: 68 men who completed treatment, and 58 men not treated. Reasons for non-treatment were (a) that they lived too far away from the clinic or (b) they were imprisoned (n=24) and decided against treatment when released. Most of non treated group did receive some form of treatment. Offenders modal age between 30 and 40 years. Offences were against natural or step children (n=48), non familial female (n=49), or non familial male (n=29) children. 30% to 40% included genital contact.

Programme: Evolved over time. Major elements are to normalize sexual preferences and enhance social functioning, and, more recently, cognitive distortions.

(1) Sexual Preferences: (a) electrical aversion, that originally used individually tailored fantasy sequences, but later used visual stimuli in a simple classical conditioning paradigm. (b) Masturbating reconditioning, by masturbating to orgasm to image of appropriate partner followed by masturbatory satiation to deviant fantasies, originally in the laboratory but later more use of home practice. (c) Self administration of smelling salts contingent on deviant thoughts/urges in order to prevent deviant thoughts in other settings.

(2) Social Functioning: targeting of skill deficits of conversational skills, social anxiety, assertiveness, conflict resolutions, and constructive use of leisure time. Also control of behaviour when intoxicated with alcohol. Deficits dealt with in individual therapy of (a) providing information, (b) challenging dysfunctional assumptions, for example, that not liked or must be liked by everyone (c) modelling, role play, and role reversal of more effective social interchanges, (d) cue controlled relaxation and flooding therapy if anxiety a problem.

Design: Repeated measures (pre and post-test and follow up) on 3 treatment and 3 untreated comparison groups.

Measures: (1) Intelligence by Ravens Progressive Matrices, (2) Sexual arousal by mercury in rubber strain gauge plethysmography. Stimuli of colour slides of nude males or females aged from 3 to 24 years in sexually explicit poses. Percentage of full erections used to calculate deviancy quotients. (3) Official and unofficial reports of recidivism and re-offences (dichotomous and continuous variables respectively).

Results: (1) Pre-test between group differences: treated molesting parents targeted significantly more older children and had tendency to have higher deviancy scores than corresponding untreated group. Also a tendency for treated molesters of non familial girls to have higher IQs and lower deviancy quotients than did untreated comparison group.

(2) Post-test: a between groups repeated measures analysis of variance showed a significant effect of treatment. No significant interactions between subgroups and time indicating improvement for all 3 types of treated case.

(3) Follow up: (a) Significantly lower recidivism rates (1 tailed, Chi Square) and significantly fewer offences (ANOVA) in treated compared to untreated cases. (b) Significant increases for all groups in both recidivism and number of offences with time (since treatment or since assessment for untreated group). Differences between treated and untreated groups in the effects of time was only significant for recidivism after 4 years, therefore the effect of treatment on re-offending held constant over time since treatment. (c) For treated group age of molester under 40 years and genital-genital abuse were significantly associated with recidivism (untreated sample data not presented), but not associated with pre-test or post-test or change in deviancy quotients.

Notes: Authors raise many issues including (a) nature of comparison group and the relative value of different methodological compromises in this difficult area, (b) that unofficial records revealed 2.4 times more recidivism than official records, (c) wished to also offer group treatment, but lacked resources, (d) poor prognosis for young offenders committing genital-genital abuse, (e) that deviant arousal may be a necessary but not sufficient condition as not directly related to re-offending and so arousal not a sufficient research outcome measure.

Monck et al (1991)

TREATMENT OUTCOME IN CHILD SEXUAL ABUSE

Sample: Families treated at tertiary referral clinic (Gt. Ormond Steet Hospital for Sick Children). Subjects recruited from the 25% of referrals (99 children in 24 families) in a descriptive study of clinic cases, (many cases excluded as only referred for consultation). Approximately half of the descriptive study cases met further criteria for treatment study resulting in sample of 47 children in 39 families. Criteria were disclosure within last 12 months, episode of abuse within last 2 years, and that sexual abuse intra familial or household. 1% refusal rate. Children aged 4 to 16 years with 75% approximately evenly spread between 6 and 14 years. Approximately equal numbers in two treatment groups.

Focus: Whole family and all individual members re effects of abuse, future functioning, and future protection of children.

Objectives: Generally to treat effects of abuse, to prevent re-abuse, to manage cases in association with local social services. More specifically to increase:

(1) Effective communication between abused child and caring parent.

(2) Appropriate allocation of blame and guilt.

(3) Self esteem of abused child and non-abusing parent.

(4) Improving the opportunities for disclosure of any subsequent abuse.

(5) Reducing self-reported depression in abused children and non-abusive parents.

(6) Improve relations between abused child and peers.

Programme: Children and families received either Family Network Treatment (FNT) only or FNT plus group treatment (FNT & G).

Family Network Treatment: developed from previous work of clinic (see summary of Furniss and Bentovim et al, 1988). Therapy to change dysfunctional family patterns, and to clarify the family antecedents and the individual responsibility for the abuse. Treatment of the family exists in the context of the community social workers child protection system and the legal child care and criminal systems. Families are enabled to change and so convince these other systems that, for example, they are able to care and protect their children. Treatment is provided for the abused children to enable them to recover from the trauma of abuse and re-establish family relationships; adult family members are given help in understanding the origins of abuse, and encouraged their care and protection of all the children in the family. The younger children have groups lasting only 6 or 8 weeks.

Treatment groups: various sex/age groups of children, for mothers, for perpetrators, for parents, and for various workers. The groups run weekly for five months and each group has a leader and a trainee leader for an hour. Although treatment is the main goal the groups are more psycho educational in approach with training in social skills, forms of touching and sexuality, protection against abuse. Groups allow peer support and confrontation of issues to allow accelerated learning, increased self esteem and classification and open communication about sexual abuse, its causes, and the responsibility for its occurrence.

Design: Repeated measures (pre and post-test after 10 to 12 months) with random allocation to two treatment groups.

Measures: (1) Depression/anxiety: child, Children's Depression Inventory; mother/carer, 28-item General Health Questionnaire. (2) Self-esteem: child, ICH self-perception inventory; mother/carer, ICH Adult Self-Perception profile. (3) Behaviour in school: teachers' rating on Rutter 'B' Scale. (4) Health and Behaviour of child in home during previous month: child and mother's reports. (5) Clinicians' view of progress for child. (6) Children's views as to efficacy of treatment in understanding origins of the abuse, prevention of further abuse, removing guilt. (7) Various consensual ratings derived from the interviews such as mother/carers warmth and criticisms of child.

Results: (1) Clinicians' rated greater progress for children in the FNT & G programme.

(2) Children's depression: improved for both programmes.

(3) Children's self esteem and symptoms: no improvement in either programme.

(4) Mothers' self esteem symptoms: improved for both programmes.

(5) Children's views of efficacy of treatment: majority felt that treatment had been effective in preventing reabuse (79%) and removing guilt (67%). Fewer (40%) felt it effective for understanding origins of abuse.

(6) Mother/carers had less positive reports than the children of the helpfulness of treatment: about two thirds felt treatment would help them prevent further abuse, and about half said treatment offered them support or clarification of their role. Less than a third felt treatment helped them relate better to the family, the perpetrator or the child, or plan effectively for the future or understand the origins of the abuse.

Notes: Authors conclude that the results provide low support for the hypothesis that the FNT + G programme produced a better outcome. See also two summaries of publications by Furniss and colleagues for case series evaluations of girl victims groups and whole treatment programme.

Prentky and Burgess (1990)

REHABILITATION OF CHILD MOLESTERS: A COST BENEFIT ANALYSIS

Sample: 129 child molesters treated at the Massachusetts Treatment Center and discharged between 1960 and 1985. 94% Caucasian, 6% Black. Average IQ of 97 and school grade level of eight. 31% had juvenile penal record, 90% an adult penal record.

Focus: Perpetrators for tertiary prevention of sexual abuse.

Objectives: To treat offenders so that they are less likely to repeat sexual offences against children.

Programme: No details in paper but reference to other article in press.

Design: Follow up of case series.

Measures: (1) All criminal charges for sexual offences involving physical contact with victim. (2) Estimate of costs of investigation, treatment, legal process, and imprisonment.

Results: 25% reoffense rate within 5 years. Reoffense costs of investigation, trial, 7 years incarceration (expected term for reoffense), and parole, estimated at $169,000. Victim related costs of social services, medical, victim evaluation, witness services, and one year of treatment, estimated at $14,000. total expense of $183,000. If risk of reoffense for treated cases is 25%, then expected cost per offender is $46,000. Marshall and Barbaree (1988) report reoffense rate of 40% for untreated case, so expected cost per offender of $73,000. Cost differential between treatment and no treatment even greater because costs of commitment to Treatment Center for 5 years for first proven offence $118,000 compared to $159,000 for 5 years in prison for first offence.

Notes: Authors argue that the reoffense rate for untreated offenders would have to be as low as 3% for this strategy to be cheaper than the reported reoffense rate of 25% for treated offenders. This, however, seems to depend upon attendance at a treatment centre being cheaper than the cost of imprisonment.

Quinsey et al (1980)

BIOFEEDBACK AND SIGNALLED PUNISHMENT IN THE MODIFICATION OF INAPPROPRIATE SEXUAL AGE PREFERENCES

Sample: The criterion for inclusion of subjects in the programme were: (a) history of sexual contact with a child less than 13 years when subject was over 16 years of age and at least 5 years older than the child, (b) record of inappropriate sexual age preferences at baseline, (c) consent to treatment. 18 patients resident in a mental health centre were recruited to the study. 15 of the patients were diagnosed as personality disordered, 4 as retarded, and one as psychotic. The average age was 27 years and the average length of residence in the centre was 26 months, 16 were held in the maximum security division.

Focus: The treatment of deviant sexual age preferences of perpetrators of child sexual abuse.

Objectives: To reduce the sexual arousal to children and increasing the sexual arousal to adults of known perpetrators of child sexual abuse.

Programme: Treatment of biofeedback and biofeedback in association with signalled punishment. Each treatment session contained 20 slide presentations. Slides were presented individually for 30 seconds with a 60 second interval between slides. The slides acted as sexual stimuli and half were of children and half were of adults. Biofeedback was presented by a red light for an above criterion sexual response to a child slide and by a blue light for an above criterion response to an adult slide. The same procedure was used for biofeedback with signalled punishment, except that an arousal response to a child slide produced the risk of a mildly painful electric shock. A shock was delivered in 40% of the 5 second intervals in which the response of the subject to a child slide was above the set criterion. The physical arousal responses were measured by a penile plethysmograph. The criterion levels were set for each subject at baseline assessment, and then raised for the child stimulus and lowered for the adult stimulus, as the subject progressed. Each treatment contained 10 sessions and most subjects received both types of treatment.

Design: Repeated measures (pre and post-test) for each treatment session providing multiple subject baselines. 12 subjects received biofeedback as the first treatment and 8 of these received a second treatment of biofeedback with signalled punishment. 6 patients received the biofeedback with signalled punishment as the first treatment and 2 then received biofeedback alone as a second treatment. One of these patients received a third treatment of biofeedback with signalled punishment.

Measures: Psychophysiological measurement of penile response to visual sitmuli as in the treatment sessions, except that neutral stimuli such as landscapes also used. Age preference ratios were calculated by dividing the raw response to the adult stimulus by the raw responses to the child stimulus.

Results: In the first treatment group, there was a significant improvement for 4 of the 12 subjects receiving biofeedback, and for 5 of the 6 receiving biofeedback with signalled punishment. In the second treatment group there was a significant improvement for 5 of the 8 receiving biofeedback with punishment, after 4 of these 5 subjects had shown no significant improvement to biofeedback alone, in their first treatment. In sum there was significantly more improvement recorded from biofeedback with signalled punishment, than biofeedback alone.

Notes: The analysis did not examine order effects in treatment. The authors note the success of biofeedback with signalled punishment was greater than that reported in a previous study of classical conditioning using aversion therapy. The authors also stress the need for follow-up data on larger samples.

Rice et al (1991)

Sexual Recidivism among Child Molesters Released from a Maximum Security Institution

Sample: 136 extra familial child molesters from a total of 153 released from a maximum security institution between 1972 and 1983. Cases excluded on basis of refusal to consent/understand psychiatric assessment or because data lost. Two thirds sent to institution for pre-trial psychiatric assessment, a fifth after being certified mentally ill, 6% after not guilty verdicts on insanity pleas, 5% for other reasons. 50 subjects participated in sexual preference change behavioural programme plus regular institution treatments, 11 subjects received the regular treatment regimes only, the remainder not treated. Average age at discharge approximately 31 years (S.D. 10 years).

Focus: Deviant sexual behaviour of child molesters.

Objectives: To alter sexual age preferences of molesters in order to prevent them reoffending by sexually assaulting children.

Programme: Laboratory based aversion therapy. Patient received an average of 20 one hour sessions of one or more of three paradigms each involving slide presentations of adults and children: (1) Classical conditioning (n=18) of electric shock to arm in the last seconds of 80% of child slides; (2) Biofeedback (n=32, but 4 subjects only received this paradigm) of different coloured lights if penile circumference exceeded preset criteria for deviant and appropriate slides; (3) Signalled punishment (n=28) of electric shock on a random basis to deviant slides where penile circumference exceeded preset criteria – also feedback of coloured lights. Some subjects received heterosocial skills training (n=16) and sex education (n=26).

Design: Repeated measures/outcome of case series.

Measures: (1) Data from records on personal characteristics, psychiatric and criminal history including sexual convictions/misbehaviours.
(2) Sexual assessment measures of (a) penile circumference change in response to standard array of slides of males and females of different ages, explicit heterosexual activity, and landscapes; preference to children index of highest average response to an adult minus highest average response to a child; (b) Rank ordering of preference for photographs of persons of varying age and sex. (c) Bentler Inventory of heterosexual Activity.
(3) Recidivism: (a) Convictions for sexual offences; (b) Violent failure of arrest or return to the institution for a violent offence; (c) Any arrest or return to the institution. Follow up time calculated from freedom to possibly offend averaged 6.3 years (S.D. approximately 33 months).

Results: (1) Treatment significantly altered sexual age preferences of one half of subjects. (2) Recidivism 31% for sexual offence alone, rising to 43% if violent failure included, and rising to 56% if any offence/return to institution included.
(3) Sexual offence recidivism significantly related (multiple discriminant function analysis) to previous history of more sexual offences, more admissions to correctional institutions, to have never married, to be personality disordered, and to have more inappropriate sexual preference rating (from penile responses) at pre-test.
(4) Neither behavioural treatment nor progress in treatment related to recidivism. Matching treated and untreated subjects for previous convictions, arrests, and penile response to child stimuli was possible for 29 pairs, but this revealed no difference for sexual offence recidivism or time before these reoffences occurred. Similar findings when 18 successfully treated cases matched with untreated cases.
(5) No effect found for extra therapies received by behavioural treated subjects.

Notes: Authors suggest that (1) finding of association of prior history with recidivism yet no association between progress or outcome of treatment and recidivism are in line with other studies, but relationship reported between initial sexual preference rating and recidivism is new.
(2) High recidivism rates compared to other studies may be due to severity of cases, that only extrafamilial abuse, and that no follow up treatment in the community.
(3) Study limitations of non random allocation to treated and untreated group, many pre-test between group differences, untreated group received some institutional interventions, interventions received post discharge unknown.

Sullivan et al (1992)

The Effects of Psychotherapy on Behaviour Problems of Sexually Abused Children

Sample: 72 children (51 male, 21 female) aged 12–16 years at a residential school for the deaf who experienced sexual abuse by staff or older students. Abuse ranged from witnessing sexual abuse, forced fondling, oral/digital penetration, and anal and vaginal intercourse.

Focus: Psychological functioning of hearing impaired children subjected to sexual abuse.

Objectives: Alleviation of guilt, treatment of depression, appropriate and productive expression of anger. Education/discussion about sexuality and relationships, sexual preferences, maltreatment, self protection. Development of meaningful stable identity, emotional independence and ability to form lasting physical and emotional relationships, a personal value system, and appropriate vocabulary for emotions and feelings.

Programme: Individual psychotherapy by three trained individuals with expertise in the psychology of deafness and fluent in sign language. Two hours of therapy per week for 36 weeks.

Design: Repeated measures (pre-test at one year from start of therapy) experimental design with non random allocation to one treatment and one control condition. Allocation was on basis of parental agreement to treatment at no financial cost. Only half of each sample given pre-test assessments to test for bias from repeated measures scored by school staff.

Measures: Child Behaviour Checklist (CBC) with three composite scales of Total, Internal and External plus sub-scales.

Results: (1) No significant pre-test differences for girls, but treatment group boys had higher scores on the Internal, Somatic, Schizoid, Uncommunicative, and Obsessive scales, and lower scores on the Aggressive scales than the no treatment boys.

(2) Significant treatment effect for boys on all scales except for Schizoid and Obsessive (non significant effect for these two scales which were significantly higher for treatment group at pre-test).

(3) Significant treatment effect for girls on scales of Total, External, Depressed, Aggressive, and Cruel.

(4) Treatment by pre-test interaction and pre-test main effect non significant except for a pre-test difference for girls on the Aggressive scale.

Notes: Authors state that study indicates:

(1) sexually abused hearing impaired young people have greater than normal behaviour problems;

(2) treatment effective and no evidence of bias from raters (possibility of bias raised as some staff had denied the children's accusations that sexual abuse had been occurring in the residential home);

(3) differential effect of therapy with a broad effect on boys and more effect on internal behaviour problems in girls. Authors also note that delinquent behaviour in girls is sometimes used to discredit their allegations of abuse, yet delinquent behaviour in abused girls seems more resistant to treatment. Findings for girls tentative due to small sample.

Woodworth (1991)

EVALUATION OF A MULTIPLE FAMILY INCEST TREATMENT PROGRAM

Sample: Attempts were made to interview all 22 families who had completed treatment in the Family Project in St. Paul, Minnesota, between 1980 and 1986. At least one member of 15 of the families (73%) agreed to be interviewed, 5 families refused, and 1 could not be traced. The proportion of different family members agreeing to the interviews were victims 42%, mothers 65%, offending fathers/stepfathers 63%, siblings 8%. At intake to project the typical victim was aged 13, white, female, with well educated parents with a family with employment and a median income of $19,000.

Focus: Functioning of families in which incest had occurred.

Programme: Family Project works with entire families in order to effect lasting change in family systems that previously supported incest. Therapy in multiple family groupings and with multiple therapists giving family members opportunities to experience both mutual support and challenge from others facing the same issues. Also peer groups for men, women, couples, and children, plus individual, couple, and family therapy.

Design: Outcome on case series.

Measures: Two part interview. (1) Group interview for whole family, or part there of, with non threatening questions on background, needs, use of services, The Family Project. (2) Self administered questionnaires on employment, housing, relationships within and outside the family, mental and physical health, positive and negative effect, recurrence of sexual abuse, the Family Project. (3) Clinical information from project staff.

Results: (1) Assertiveness: mothers and offenders reported that mostly resistant to peer pressure, victims reported that open to peer pressure, but would say no to unwanted sex. No recurrence of abuse reported but difficult to confirm this.

(2) Nearly all the victims (12 of 13) were still in contact with the offenders and 42% (n=5) still felt uncomfortable in presence of offender.

(3) Most respondents only thought about the sexual abuse occasionally or seldom, but 2 mothers and 1 offender thought about it more often.

(4) Relationship with friends and boyfriends seemed comparable to general population except some greater contact than expected with people, alcohol or drug problems.

(5) Most families reported few problems re education and employment.

(6) Up to half the respondents had sought out further clinical treatment, others reported using informal support groups (23% of victims and mothers), friends (half of parents) and relatives (a third of parents).

(7) 88% offenders strongly satisfied and 83% felt that very helpful to them.

(8) 83% of mothers felt that therapy helpful, but 30% dissatisfied with treatment.

(9) 75% of victims felt therapy personally helpful, but 31% dissatisfied with treatment.

(10) Respondents reported that the project helped them learn about themselves and the causes of the abuse, provided emotional support, and enhanced self respect. They appreciated the support from other participants and the counsellors. Suggestions for improvement included smaller groups, more focus, and confrontation of perpetrators.

Notes: Authors report that respondents' views feedback to develop project by increasing structure and control of groups and by lessening emphasis perceived by mothers of support given to offenders. Less successful had been attempts to develop a mother-daughter group and to involve siblings more.

CHAPTER TWELVE
Overview of Research Issues

Background

A wide range of studies have attempted to evaluate the impact of child abuse interventions. The variation would have been relatively straight forward, if based purely upon the techniques employed. However, they also varied in the level of analysis, ranging from micro analyses of sexual drive to macro analysis of changing attitudes or relative power within society. Within each level, the focus varied between different individuals and groups, such as victims, perpetrators and other adults. Within each client group, strategies varied from primary, to secondary, to tertiary prevention and mitigating the effects of abuse.

The literature contains a large number of studies, though many of these are descriptive containing limited outcome data. Enough data is presented to illustrate the potential benefits of a service, but this is not sufficient to determine its efficacy relative to other services. Nor is there sufficient to allow readers to themselves set up a similar service (as Maletzky, 1991, advocates in his book providing a 'cookbook' approach to the treatment of sexual abuse offenders).

There are more thorough evaluative studies in the literature but these tend to be concentrated in specific areas of research, particularly those involving behavioural interventions. Behavioural work is usually highly focused and includes routine systematic collection of objective behavioural data. This makes behavioural interventions highly amenable to research evaluation. The danger is that other interventions not so amenable to study or undertaken by those less concerned or aware of research evaluation may not be adequately assessed. One consequence may be that ineffective interventions may continue unnecessarily. An alternative consequence is that useful and effective interventions are overlooked because they lack adequate research data to support their development.

The separate chapters of the review have examined particular areas of research and these have already been summarized at the end of each chapter and do not require repeating here. Instead, this chapter addresses some of the general research issues relevant to the different intervention studies, in particular, the common difficulty in providing clear evidence for or against the various treatment services.

The lack of adequate research base has limited the ability of the research literature to give clear policy guidelines for the development of services. These issues are addressed, in order to inform future studies, so that they may be more productive in guiding policy. Two main issues are considered. The first is the existence of gaps in the literature on interventions. The second is the appropriateness of the methodologies used by the evaluative research studies.

Gaps in the literature

For each of the types of child abuse intervention considered in the main chapters of the report, there are a host of specific research issues requiring attention. The concern here is with the more fundamental gaps, where whole services or major themes have not been sufficiently covered by the outcome studies. There is potential for considerably more work on:

A. Primary and Secondary Prevention

1. Child education for types of abuses other than child sexual abuse. Sexual abuse of children is of obvious concern, but there is a need for research on prevention of other negative child experiences such as physical and emotional abuse, neglect, bullying, and sexual assault by 'normal' adolescent peers as in date rape. These suggestions may be considered unacceptable by some because they more directly challenge societal assumptions about age, gender, power, and rights that can be avoided in discussions of child sexual abuse, where there is a clearer sense of perpetrators as abnormal, criminal or both.

2. Preventive education for adolescent males who are potential perpetrators (Bagley and Thurstone, 1988). There is considerable evidence that many sexual abuse offenders start to assault children when they are themselves children. Attempts should be made to prevent these abnormal behaviours developing and to intervene to treat them as soon as they can be identified.

3. Adult and community education about child abuse and child protection. Child protection services depend on the local community in many ways. Child protection might therefore be more effective if the community participated in and better understood the role and the policies of child protection services.

B. Tertiary Prevention

1. Most American and British research on intervention is concerned with evaluating specialist services which account for a small minority of work in this field. An individual psychologist or psychiatrist might work full time on child abuse, but the numbers of cases that these individuals see is very small indeed compared to the number of cases seen by social services. We invest in special resources and their evaluation, whilst knowing little about the content or impact of routine casework on, for example families with children placed on child abuse registers in Britain, or the caseloads of the Child Protection Service in the United States. The last few years has seen some improvement in this situation (such as the programme of research funded by the Department of Health considered in Chapter Ten), but there is still a need for much further work on the many specific areas of child protection intervention.

2. The relation of these specialist programmes to routine services. In some cases these programmes provide additional service and case management contributions to routine services (as for example in Bentovim, 1988). In others, the special programme may take on total responsibility for case management, even if local services remain involved. Many research reports on specialist services hardly mention the existence of child protection workers and agencies, but if specialist interventions have something to offer then they need to do so within the context of child protection services.

3. The influence of health welfare and legal processes on preventive and reactive interventions, including the laws for child protection, child care, and prosecution for offences against children in the criminal justice systems. It is only in the child sexual abuse literature, that this figures as a major issue for evaluating the impact of intervention services.

4. Services for victims other than of child sexual abuse. Services directed at children suffering from other forms of abuse seem to be highly effective yet do not seem to be generally available or be the focus of much research interest. For many, the term child abuse seems to have become synonymous with child sexual abuse and there is less interest in helping other sorts of victims.

5.	Services for victims of extrafamilial child sexual abuse. Most projects and their evaluations involve cases of intrafamilial abuse and female victims rather than male victims.

C. *All Forms of Intervention*

1.	Variable receptivity of different clients to services (Stevenson, 1986). For example, in Chapter Two it was suggested that those most at risk of child sexual abuse, benefited least from preventive education.

2.	Acceptability of the service to the clients. Customer satisfaction is one important measure of success and can also affect uptake of services offered. It is complicated by the legal powers involved in much child protection work, but there is no reason why professionals and clients can not have a positive respectful relationship even if the clients or their children are subject to some form of legal control. In fact, the studies that describe difficulties between parents and professionals are often discussing cases where there are no legal powers of intervention.

3.	Clients compliance with treatment. It is evident that many clients do not comply even if this results in them being imprisoned or losing their children into care. Little data is available on who are the least likely to comply or which programmes are the least likely to be complied with. It may be that there is an interaction effect with some clients being particularly suitable or unsuitable for different interventions. Outcome studies that simply examine the percentage of clients with positive outcomes are unlikely to identify these subtleties.

4.	The possible negative consequences of various interventions on different clients. Research reports are largely enthusiastic about the interventions they describe and not very informative about the possible disadvantages that may arise, but there is evidence that interventions can disrupt people's lives even when simply providing social support.

5.	The relative efficacy of different forms of voluntary services, including the impact of similarity of experience and background of workers and clients (Thoits, 1986). There is evidence that subjects improve more from voluntary than statutory involvement. Also services based within local communities may be less likely to cause the disruptive social effects mentioned in (3).

6.	The relative efficacy of the use of children to help other children as in the work of Fantuzzo et al (1988) discussed in Chapter Eight (see also Foot et al, 1990). Fantuzzo's use of peers to help withdrawn children initiate social interactions is also a good example of the efficacy of interventions when provider and client are similar, as in (5).

7.	Cost/benefit ratios of programmes to compare and contrast direct and indirect gains and losses attributable to interventions (Schopler, 1987).

8.	Financial cost efficiency, as different strategies may vary considerably, in both the costs of the services and in the monies saved by the intervention (Daro, 1987; Dubowitz, 1987).

Some of these gaps in research are due to there being no service to evaluate. On the other hand, there are instances where there is the research but little in terms of services. For example, in Britain it is difficult to find services for the treatment of perpetrators of child sexual abuse, although several American studies have shown the power of this type of work.

The most fundamental weaknesses in the literature relate to the failure to examine routine casework and the impact of the child protection systems on interventive treatment services. The relevance of the results of studies of special interventions to policy development is likely to be judged against the efficacy of routine work.

The contribution of the child protection system is crucial. The whole concept of child abuse is based upon responsibility (usually parental) for adverse child experiences (Gough et al, 1987). Thus reactive intervention in cases defined as child abuse, are likely to be concerned with perceptions of the parent's adequacy to care and protect the child, even if the alleged perpetrator is no longer involved with the child. The monitoring and assessment of whether a child is sufficiently cared for and protected, is a major component of child abuse work, as it can lead to a child being legally removed to another family and/or an adult being prosecuted for an offence against a child. These issues provide the background for child abuse interventions and the actual processes by which they are achieved (for example monitoring of child care, access visits, court appearances), provide an often time consuming practical aspect of child abuse work. This probably takes up more client and professional time than more therapeutic work. That most of the outcome studies give only passing reference to the realities of child protection, seriously limits the applicability of the studies, and raises questions about the context in which the special services were provided.

Finally, it is important to reiterate the point made in the introduction that child abuse research, and sometimes child protection services (Stevenson, 1992), are artificially separated from other research and practice on helping children and families. Rutter (1989) argues that adverse experiences in childhood are probably a necessary if not a sufficient condition for later poor parenting. Child abuse is only one form of adverse experience in childhood and it is also only one form of poor parenting. Child abuse is therefore only one symptom of individual and inter personal difficulties and should not be artificially be separated off from other areas.

Methodological problems

Most of the studies included in the review were coded according to set questions about the sample, research focus, objectives, method of intervention, research design, research measures, and results. This offered a systematic method of understanding the content of the research studies. The aim was not to judge the studies, but to understand them within their own terms, and within their categories, from samples through to results.

The summaries of the studies are not intended to be critical as it is not always clear under what circumstances individual studies are carried out, and data on outcome may be a small component of a larger and different research project. Similarly, some limited data on outcome may have been accessible within a project which did not include a formal research component, but where it was considered worthwhile to share this data with others in a publication. Such reports can be of considerable value. They can describe innovative projects, indicative positive and negative aspects of these new interventions, and create a dialogue between professional workers, policy makers, and researchers. In addition, the actual process of undertaking even limited research can help professional workers to clarify various aspects of interventions.

Arguments for publishing studies that do not fulfil all the requirements of a formal evaluation of the impact of an intervention on outcome, concern individual studies. However, problems arise if the majority of published studies do not fulfil these requirements. This is the situation with the studies on reactive (treatment) intervention reviewed. No over critical assessment of experimental method or statistical analysis was necessary to observe this.

SAMPLE

Many studies described their sample in terms of demographic data, but few gave details of the population of child abuse cases from which they were drawn. The type of abuse was sometimes discussed, but with little information about the criteria for the definition of abuse or the representativeness of the sample to other local identified cases. It may be that the special projects simply did not know. They may have power to refuse or accept case referrals, but have no power or knowledge concerning other cases seen by local services. The consequences for the integrity of the research are immense. Without more knowledge about the sample who are receiving the intervention, it is impossible to sensibly interpret the results, however well controlled the study is in other respects. Quite apart from not knowing the nature of the problems of those receiving the intervention, it is unlikely that the sample is homogenous. Child abuse is itself a form of outcome variable. It is a grouping based upon interpretations of the social circumstances of child adversity rather than of the cause of child care and family problems, or an assessment that they require a certain form of therapeutic intervention. There is therefore little basis for assuming that cases will be similar to each other, even within one category of abuse, such as physical abuse or neglect.

FOCUS AND OBJECTIVES

The focus of the different studies was not explicitly stated but was usually implicit in the report of the study. Study objectives were also implied but were less clear. This was a serious fault because it is the objectives that determine what are relevant methods of intervention and how the outcomes should be assessed.

METHODS OF INTERVENTION (PROGRAMMES)

Methods were often stated in broad terms but not in sufficient detail to allow a study to be replicated, or for results to be compared and contrasted with other studies. Global terms such as casework and group work were common. The value of the recent studies of routine child protection has been in telling us more about what the term casework actually means in practice. Little is known about variations in content and style of such practices.

DESIGN AND MEASURES

The design was often but not always implicit in the study report. Measures were frequently well specified, although it was not always necessarily evident how these related to the objectives and the methods of intervention, particularly in respect to formal measures and to global ratings of improvement. The exception was behavioural studies which are much more disciplined about specifying what they are trying to do and why, and most importantly, how. Many studies did not use independent measures relying instead upon the clinical judgement of the workers involved and thus open to bias. In other cases, professional or legal records were used to identify recurrence of abuse (recidivism), with all the problems of uniformity of definition that this involves.

RESULTS

The results and conclusions were mostly well presented. It was less clear how the conclusions were derived from the results. It was not common for all the alternative interpretations of the data to be explored.

The criticisms of the methodology of the studies is, to repeat, not a criticism of individual studies which may all have served useful purposes as previously described. The criticism is against the total body of research into child abuse. It can be characterised as the study of unspecified measures of outcome. It is not simply that it is difficult to have confidence in the study results. It is also that there is virtually no basis for assuming comparability across studies so that it is impossible to compare and contrast their findings.

There are some important exceptions to their criticisms. Some narrowly focused studies examined one small area in some detail using well specified experimental designs. Examples of such studies can be found in Chapter Two on preventive education, in Chapter Seven on behavioural interventions, and in Chapter Eleven on behavioural work with perpetrators of child sexual abuse. The narrow focus of the studies had disadvantages, like laboratory based outcome measures with questionable external validity (such as sexual arousal in sexual offenders), but there is no reason why this should not be overcome by testing the validity of the measures or by developing new measures. A more fundamental problem was the limited applicability of the results of studies, but this is outweighed by the increased reliance that can be placed upon these results compared to the wider focused and less well specified studies.

The very large American studies of demonstration projects are broadly based and not particularly well defined in terms of their samples and objectives nor in the independence of their outcome measures, but their breadth and size undermines many of the criticisms of other studies. The samples are so large, that more reliance can be put on them as being representative of a wider population of child abuse cases. Furthermore, the sample size allows the use of multi variate analysis to isolate the contribution of different factors to the reported variance in outcome. The studies could benefit from improvement in their internal specification, but they do provide a powerful addition to the more narrowly focused studies.

Britain has not undertaken such large scale projects, but the one large outcome study reported by Gibbons et al was more focused than the American projects, used independent measures of outcome, and was in a better position to draw conclusions about the efficacy of case intervention. There is enormous scope for further outcome studies of this kind but following up more specific hypotheses suggested by all the previous less focused research and attempting to do this over relatively short time periods. What is required is systematic enquiry by a series of studies (at the same time or sequentially) focused on specific issues. Currently there are still too many one off studies that produce equivocal results that are not followed up and so do not lead anywhere.

Future research

Criticism of research studies, does not in itself, improve future research. The rest of the chapter examines some of the reasons that underlie the research problems, and suggests more productive options for the future.

It must be acknowledged that there are severe practical difficulties in undertaking even relatively narrowly focused studies of behavioural projects (Smith et al, 1984). For reasons such as the sensitivity of child abuse cases, the ethical problems of confidentiality, and the requirement for worker and client cooperation during a time of great stress, there are considerable obstacles in gaining access to subjects. Researchers are often restricted to the few cases seen by an individual project of agency team, and the researcher may even be one of the professionals within that team. As the most beneficial interventions available must be made to ensure improvements within the family and protection of the child, there is little possibility of using placebo or waiting list controls. During the period of therapeutic intervention, there may be considerable sample drop out, because of a breakdown in worker or client cooperation, the removal of the child into care, the death of the child or a family member, the imprisonment of a parent, or because the family moves, out of the geographical area of research.

There are also major methodological problems in evaluating the impact of any psychological therapy, as can be seen from the history of psychotherapy research (see reviews of Kazdin, 1986; Van den Bos, 1986). These problems have been known for a long time, yet child abuse research does not seem to have benefited from the experience of such related work. This may be because of the way the research arises. In many cases the special intervention precedes a plan to conduct research: a special programme is developed and thoughts of evaluation follow. The programmes may offer a range of specialist services which are unlikely to test any narrowly focussed hypotheses or assessments of the relative efficacy of particular techniques. The aim of evaluation is then simply to assess whether the broad programme of work is effective and justifies the concentration of funds and expertise required.

The unfocused nature of these evaluations has several consequences. Firstly, the broad programmes act against the possibility of a focused research design. Instead, the researchers attempt to cover the diversity of the programme by using multiple baseline and outcome measures. The multiple measures mirror the multiple therapy perspective of many programmes based on the belief that child abuse has multiple causes and requires multiple interventions. Secondly, research is unlikely to be a priority for the programme, and will probably not influence practice relevant to an evaluation, such as control of case referrals or narrowness or uniformity of service provision. Thirdly, this approach seems to encourage the study of special projects in isolation from community agencies from which cases would have been referred, and plays down the contribution of any continuing routine services. There is also a tendency to ignore the procedural and legal child protection contexts within which therapeutic work takes place. Fourthly, there is little reference to research on therapeutic practice similar to the programme under study, but not involving child abuse cases.

It is ironic that many studies attempt to use control groups in order to be more scientific in their programme evaluations. Without sufficient specification of the sample or more narrowly focused research questions, it is unlikely that the control groups will increase the reliability of the study results. The research designs are simply unable to answer the required questions. This is not to argue that the study reports are of no value, but it is possible, that more would be achieved by not attempting clinical trials that fall short of the standards required for meaningful results.

There are many appeals in the literature for controlled treatment trials as there is a need to ensure that treatments are effective (for example, Smith et al 1984). This is a particularly important consideration, when exaggerated claims are made for interventions on the basis of slim empirical evidence. There is little point in using a control group if the research study is then unable to specify the nature of the samples or if the study outcome measures are not independent of the intervention. There are many examples in the literature of authors investing considerable energy in recruiting control cases and then relying on therapist ratings to evaluate outcome. However, the move towards better case sampling and use of independent outcome measures has been so slow, that it is probably preferable to encourage controlled treatment trials only when the planning and research conditions are favourable. This might improve the present situation, when most studies are neither successful clinical trials nor illuminating process studies. There are probably many reasons why in the current climate, clinical trials, however limited in design, seem to be preferred to other forms of research. In the first place, there is a widespread acceptance of the medical model (Parton, 1985) which has proved successful in many medical studies. Then there is the view, that child abuse is synonymous to a medical condition or syndrome (Gough et al, 1982) which underestimates the heterogeneity of cases. Similarly the treatment of abuse may be seen merely as a technical issue, which is potentially soluble with sufficient technical knowledge, instead of regarding better technical knowledge as an aid to value based case planning which is central to child protection work.

A second and related reason why it may be difficult to dissuade researchers from incomplete controlled treatment trials, is the credibility that they provide for the programmes under study. The fact that the efficacy of a programme is or has been subject to an evaluation, increases its perceived importance. These studies rarely report negative effects of the interventions. Usually a few positive results can be found as empirical support for a project, amongst many non significant results which undermine their statistical relevance. It is not likely that such pressures can be avoided. However, it may be possible to move the focus of studies away from unsatisfactory and incomplete clinical trials and towards more achievable goals. These studies could still fulfil their justificatory role yet be more enlightening and contribute more to the development of a service. The awareness that research is often inadequate because it is underfunded, can lead to the view that expensive treatment trials are the only real research option. There is considerable potential for small scale studies including single case designs by individual practitioners (Sheldon, 1984). The research effort could be more productively invested to examine the process of intervention, to describe how therapy works in practice and the problems or negative results that need to be avoided. Simply recording the process of intervention can be useful to clarify the nature of therapeutic work. It can also reveal practical information about the realities of an intervention. For example, Stevenson (1986) reports that an attempt to increase teacher-child contact in a nursery school had no impact on the actual levels of adult-child contact as there was a corresponding decrease in nursery nurse to child contact. Another strategy to be developed, is action research, where researchers continuously feed back their data to professional staff, in order to help further specify and develop a programme.

Although it is not productive to attempt clinical outcome trials when they cannot be achieved, it is still necessary for proper trials to be undertaken. This requires greater specification of the research questions and all aspects of the studies from samples through to outcome measures.

This is an aim more likely to be achieved by studies which are modest in the number of questions they address, rather than attempting too many and answering none of them. The behavioural studies included in this review demonstrated that limiting the number of uncontrolled variables offers a greater chance of success. There is no shortage of issues generated by obvious gaps in the literature, questions that arise from previous studies, and from different forms of research, such as intervening variables in the long term sequelae of abuse. In addition, the limitations of the focused studies provide many research questions about the value and validity of the results for other cases in other situations.

The narrow focus proposed, is a strategy of incremental development of knowledge, as advocated in psychotherapy research (Basham, 1986; Kazdin, 1986). Multi-component programmes can still be the subject of study, but only when their application and evaluation is clearly specified and closely controlled. Classic placebo control studies or use of waiting list controls are inappropriate because both are contrasting limited, or no treatment, with a multi-component programme. It would be more useful to contrast slight variations in the multi-component service to fine tune service provision (Basham, 1986). This also avoids the ethical issue of withholding treatment on a random basis, although Haugard and Reppucci (1988, p 184) cite studies by Klein and by McCord which found that waiting list controls and pure controls achieved better outcomes than the main treatment groups.

The incremental approach using comparative designs, differs from normal control trials in that it attempts to identify the relative, rather then the absolute effects, of clinical interventions (Basham, 1986). This is not such an immediate issue in child abuse work, where there is not the luxury to consider absolute effects. Agencies have no choice but to intervene and the development of services is the refining of what might be termed 'the art of the possible' and this makes relative efficacy the central issue. There are also some specific advantages of comparative designs: they focus attention on what are the real differences between various therapeutic practices (Kazdin, 1986); differences that might be taken for granted when practice is allowed to develop behind global descriptions such as social casework or family therapy.

The comparative approach makes it easier to have well controlled and focused studies, but does not avoid the need to specify the research goals and their components in some depth. Particularly, as the comparison of similar treatments increases the difficulties in isolating an experimental effect, so that studies may require greater control or variables and larger sample sizes, to be effective (Kazdin, 1986). However, the narrow focus may also make the differential effects relatively stark as in Quinsey et al's (1980) comparison of signalled feedback versus signalled feedback plus punishment in the treatment of perpetrators of child sexual abuse. There are many possible comparisons that would benefit the development of services and ideas for such productive studies can easily be gleaned from papers on practice issues or from the research literature (for example in this review and in the reviews by Daro, 1987; Dubowitz, 1987; Bagley and Thurstone, 1988; Haugaard and Reppucci, 1988). Comparisons should not be restricted to the relative effectiveness of different interventions, but could include the influence of different procedural and legal contexts on outcome.

Finally, it is worth noting two areas of research that would provide essential background data for developing hypotheses for treatment studies. The first is descriptive data on the prevalence and outcome of adverse child care environments in the community. This is not a simple counting exercise of the number of children who are victims of different types of abuse, as there are no significant policy implications of knowing exactly how many children are, for example, sexually abused in the community (Finkelhor, 1991). But more important questions would concern the specific contexts in which the abuse took place, the strategies children took to avoid or cope with the abuse and the outcomes related to these different circumstances. Such information would lead to more sophisticated targeting of preventive and reactive interventions.

Secondly, there is need for more descriptive data on normal and special services, including the legal and procedural contexts in which they operate. There is little scope for developing services coherently without information on how they operate at present. In particular, the relation between child protection services and general health, welfare, and education services needs to be understood. Furthermore, therapeutic work in child abuse is connected to varying degrees of state child protection intervention. Currently we are unaware of what proportion or type of cases is subject to these different levels of intervention and over what periods of time. A major development in this area is the introduction of computerized management information systems. These are able to provide information on the clients of child protective services, the service response they receive, and the outcomes achieved. Such data can often exceed the detail provided by previous single research grant funded studies of practice. These information systems have the potential for dramatically increasing our understanding of child protection practice and informing more sophisticated evaluations of child abuse interventions.

Summary

1. The literature evaluating the efficacy of child abuse interventions covers a wide range of techniques applied at different levels, theories and strategies of work.

2. Several gaps in the literature exist and these often relate to gaps in service provision. There is also still a relative lack of reference to routine child protection services and the legal and procedural aspects of child protection which constitute the context of reactive interventions. a distinction needs to be made between studies of the dynamics of child maltreatment and the processes and outcomes of child protection interventions.

3. The majority of studies were limited by their lack of reference to a wider research and practice base of related but non-child abuse work: for example, the research literature and service developments in family support programmes.

4. Most studies were limited by methodological problems arising from a lack of specification of their sample, focus, objectives, methods, design, measures and results, and the inter-relationship between them.

5. Despite methodological weaknesses, many of the studies provided useful descriptions of the process of the innovative interventions. It is suggested that the studies would therefore be more productive if this analysis of process were the main initial purpose, rather than a by-product of unsuccessful outcome studies.

6. The most successful studies were narrowly focused evaluations of specific interventions where research was primary, or at least equal to the service, component.

7. Other successful studies were large demonstration projects with large enough sample sizes to allow multivariate analysis. The expense of these studies restricts their general use.

8. Treatment outcome studies are necessary but should only be attempted with highly specified research designs. Narrowly focused designs have been the most successful to date and provide the most sensible model for future research. This results in an incremental model for developing research knowledge and will probably be best achieved by comparative research designs.

9. Related research would also contribute to the study of the efficacy of child abuse interventions. This could include studies of the natural history of childhood adversities in the population; the description of routine child protection practice and outcome; and related, but non-child abuse, health, welfare and educational services.

10. The development of computerized service management systems, particularly child protection management information systems, should have a dramatic impact on our knowledge of the content and outcome of service provision.

Appendix

This appendix lists the main authors of the studies considered and summarized in Chapters Two to Eleven. The full references for these studies can be found in the references section which follows.

Adams (In preparation) *Chapter Two*
Adams and Llewellyn (1991) *Chapter Two*
Alexander et al (1989, 1991) *Chapter Eleven*
Argyles (1980) *Chapter Eight*
Armitage (1989) *Chapter Two*
Armstrong & Fraley (1985) *Chapter Six*
Armstrong (1981) *Chapter Six*
Baher et al (1976) *Chapter Nine*
Bailey et al (1984) *Chapter Ten*
Baker et al (1981) *Chapter Four*
Barnard et al (1988) *Chapter Five*
Barnett et al (1989) *Chapter Eleven*
Barth (1989) *Chapter Four*
Barth (1991) *Chapter Five*
Barth et al (1983) *Chapter Seven*
Bean (1971) *Chapter Nine*
Becker et al (1988) *Chapter Eleven*
Behaviour Associates (1977) *Chapter Eight*
Bell et al (1983) *Chapter Eight*
Belluci (1972) *Chapter Eight*
Bentovim et al (1988) *Chapter Eleven*
Berger (1981) *Chapter Ten*
Berkeley Planning Associates (1979) *Chapter Nine*
Berkeley Planning Associates (1983) *Chapter Nine*
Binder and McNeil (1987) *Chapter Two*
Blumberg et al (1991) *Chapter Two*
Booth et al (1989) *Chapter Five*
Borgman (1984) *Chapter Eleven*
Borkin and Frank (1986) *Chapter Two*
Bowen Centre (1975) *Chapter Nine*
Bradford and Pawlak (1987) *Chapter Eleven*
Breton (1979) *Chapter Eight*
Brown (1985) *Chapter Eight*
Brunk et al (1987) *Chapter Eight*
Bunyan (1987) *Chapter Seven*
Burch and Mohr (1980) *Chapter Eight*
Burt and Balycat (1977) *Chapter Ten*
Chaffin (1992) *Chapter Eleven*
Chapman and Reynolds (1982) *Chapter Five*
Cleaver and Freeman (1992) *Chapter Ten*
Conger et al (1981) *Chapter Seven*
Conte et al (1985) *Chapter Two*
Corby (1987) *Chapter Ten*
Corry and Breathwick (1987) *Chapter Ten*
Cox et al (1990) *Chapter Four*
Crimmins et al (1984) *Chapter Seven*
Crittenden (1992) *Chapter Ten*
Crow (1985) *Chapter Three*

Crozier and Katz (1979) *Chapter Seven*
Culp et al (1987) *Chapter Eight*
Dachman et al (1986) *Chapter Five*
Daro (1987) *Chapter Nine*
Dawson et al (1986) *Chapter Eight*
De Bortali-Tregerthan (1979) *Chapter Seven*
Deblinger et al (1990) *Chapter Eleven*
Del Castillo (1985) *Chapter Three*
Delson and Clark (1981) *Chapter Eleven*
Denicola and Sandler (1980) *Chapter Seven*
Doherty and Barrat (1989) *Chapter Two*
Dougherty (1983) *Chapter Nine*
Earls and Castonguay (1989) *Chapter Eleven*
Elmer (1986) *Chapter Eight*
English and Aubin (1991) *Chapter Ten*
English (1992) *Chapter Ten*
Famularo et al (1989) *Chapter Ten*
Fantuzzo et al (1987) *Chapter Eight*
Fantuzzo et al (1988) *Chapter Eight*
Farmer (1992) *Chapter Ten*
Farmer and Owen (1991) *Chapter Ten*
Feldman et al (1986) *Chapter Eight*
Feldman et al (1992) *Chapter Eight*
Follette et al (1991) *Chapter Eleven*
Fontana and Robinson (1976) *Chapter Nine*
Fryer et al (1987a, 1987b) *Chapter Two*
Furniss (1983) *Chapter Eleven*
Furniss et al (1984) *Chapter Eleven*
Furniss et al (1988) *Chapter Eleven*
Gabinet (1979) *Chapter Five*
Galdston (1971, 1975) *Chapter Six*
Giaretto (1976, 1982) *Chapter Eleven*
Gibbons and Thorpe (1989) *Chapter Four*
Gibbons, Gallagher and Bell (1992) *Chapter Ten*
Gilbert et al (1989) *Chapter Two*
Gough et al (1987, 1993) *Chapter Ten*
Gough (1990) *Chapter Ten*
Gough and Sutton (1991) *Chapter Ten*
Gray E. et al (1983) *Chapters Three and Five*
Gray J.D. et al (1977, 1979) *Chapter Five*
Green (1978) *Chapter Eight*
Green et al (1981) *Chapter Nine*
Hamilton (1989) *Chapter Two*
Hanks (1987) *Chapter Eight*
Hanks et al (1988) *Chapter Eight*
Harling and Haines (1980) *Chapter Eight*
Harper and Irvin (1985) *Chapter Ten*
Harvey et al (1988) *Chapter Two*
Haynes et al (1984) *Chapter Eight*

Hazzard et al (1991) *Chapter Two*
Heap (1984) *Chapter Ten*
Hensey et al (1983) *Chapter Ten*
Hornick and Clarke (1986) *Chapter Eight*
Howlett et al (1985) *Chapter Six*
Hutchings et al (1981) *Chapter Seven*
Iwaniec et al (1985) *Chapter Eight*
Jehu (1988, 1989) *Chapter Eleven*
Jellinek et al (1992) *Chapter Ten*
Jones (1990) *Chapter Two*
Justice and Justice (1978) *Chapter Eight*
Kahn and Chambers (1991) *Chapter Eleven*
King and Taitz (1985) *Chapter Ten*
Kitchen (1980) *Chapter Eight*
Kolko (1986) *Chapter Eleven*
Kolko, Moser, and Hughes (1989) *Chapter Two*
Kraizer et al (1988) *Chapter Two*
Krell et al (1983) *Chapter Ten*
Kroth (1979) *Chapter Eleven*
Kruger et al (1979) *Chapter Eight*
Kunkel (1981) *Chapter Eight*
Land (1986) *Chapter Eight*
Lane and Van Dyke (1978) *Chapter Eight*
Larson C.P. (1980) *Chapter Five*
Larson K.L. et al (1987) *Chapter Eight*
Laughlin and Weiss (1981) *Chapter Nine*
Lawder et al (1984) *Chapter Ten*
Lealman et al (1983) *Chapter Five*
Leeds (1984) *Chapter Eight*
Lieber and Baker (1977) *Chapter Eight*
Lightfoot et al (1983) *Chapter Nine*
Lines (1986) *Chapter Eight*
Lutzker (1984) *Chapter Nine*
Lutzker and Rice (1984, 1987) *Chapter Nine*
Lynch and Roberts (1982) *Chapter Nine*
Magura (1982) *Chapter Ten*
Magura and Derubeis (1980) *Chapter Nine*
Magura and Moses (1984) *Chapter Ten*
Maletzky (1980) *Chapter Eleven*
Maletzky (1991) *Chapter Eleven*
Marshall and Barbaree (1988) *Chapter Eleven*
Mastria et al (1979) *Chapter Seven*
Mayes et al (1991a, 1991b) *Chapter Two*
McAuley (1980) *Chapter Seven*
McBogg et al (1979a) *Chapter Nine*
McBogg et al (1979b) *Chapter Ten*
Miller et al (1984, 1985) *Chapter Four*
Miltenberger and Thiesse-Duffy (1988) *Chapter Two*
Monaghan and Buckfield (1981) *Chapter Five*
Monck et al (1991) *Chapter Eleven*
Moore (1982) *Chapter Eight*
Moore et al (1981) *Chapter Nine*
Mouzakatis and Golstein (1985) *Chapter Ten*
Murphy and Davies (1979) *Chapter Seven*
Murphy et al (1991) *Chapter Ten*

Nicol et al (1988) *Chapter Seven*
O'Connor et al (1980) *Chapter Five*
Olds et al (1986a, 1986b, 1988) *Chapter Five*
Ounstead et al (1974) *Chapter Six*
Ounstead et al (1982) *Chapter Five*
Owen Scott et al (1984) *Chapter Seven*
Palfreeman (1982) *Chapter Six*
Parish et al (1985) *Chapter Eight*
Paulson et al (1974) *Chapter Eight*
Peraino (1990) *Chapter Two*
Peters and Carswell (1984) *Chapter Eight*
Philips et al (1981) *Chapter Six*
Pillai et al (1982) *Chapter Six*
Poche et al (1981) *Chapter Two*
Poche et al (1988) *Chapter Two*
Prentky and Burgess (1990) *Chapter Eleven*
Press-Rigler et al (1990) *Chapter Eight*
Pritchard (1991) *Chapter Ten*
Prodgers and Bannister (1983) *Chapter Eight*
Quinsey et al (1980) *Chapter Eleven*
Quitiquit et al (1986) *Chapter Five*
Ramey et al (1975) *Chapter Eight*
Reid et al (1981) *Chapter Seven*
Resnick (1985) *Chapter Six*
Rice et al (1991) *Chapter Eleven*
Rivara (1985) *Chapter Ten*
Roberts et al (1977) *Chapter Six*
Rogowski and McGrath (1986) *Chapter Eight*
Rosenstein (1978) *Chapter Four*
Roth (1985) *Chapter Six*
Sandford and Tustin (1973) *Chapter Seven*
Sandler et al (1978) *Chapter Seven*
Sankey et al (1985) *Chapter Eight*
Scaife and Frith (1988) *Chapter Six*
Schellenbach and Guerney (1987) *Chapter Six*
Schinke et al (1986) *Chapter Six*
Schultz et al (1979) *Chapter Eight*
Scott (1986) *Chapter Six*
Sedlak (1992) *Chapter Ten*
Siegal et al (1980) *Chapter Five*
Sigurdson et al (1986) *Chapter Two*
Smith and Rachman (1984) *Chapter Seven*
Soumenkoff et al (1982) *Chapter Five*
Stempler and Stempler (1981) *Chapter Eight*
Stephenson (1977) *Chapter Eight*
Stevenson and Bailey (1988) *Chapter Five*
Stillwell et al (1988) *Chapter Two*
Stone and Stone (1983) *Chapter Ten*
Sturm and Drotar (1989) *Chapter Eight*
Sullivan et al (1992) *Chapter Eleven*
Suphi (1990) *Chapter Two*
Swann et al (1985) *Chapter Two*
Szykula and Fleischman (1985) *Chapter Seven*
Taylor and Beauchamp (1988) *Chapter Five*
Telleen et al (1989) *Chapter Six*

Thoburn (1991) *Chapter Ten*
Thoburn et al (1991) *Chapter Ten*
Thomasson et al (1981a, b) *Chapter Six*
Thorpe (1991) *Chapter Ten*
Tracy and Clark (1974) *Chapter Eight*
Tracy et al (1975) *Chapter Eight*
Van Der Eyken (1982) *Chapter Four*
Waterhouse and Carnie (1990, 1992) *Chapter Ten*
Welbourne and Mazuryk (1980) *Chapter Six*
Wells et al (1989) *Chapter Ten*
West and West (1979) *Chapter Nine*
Whiteman et al (1987) *Chapter Seven*
Willems and Derubeis (1981) *Chapter Nine*
Wolfe and Sandler (1981) *Chapter Seven*
Wolfe et al (1981) *Chapter Seven*
Wolfe et al (1982) *Chapter Seven*
Wolfe et al (1986) *Chapter Two*
Wolfe et al (1988) *Chapter Seven*
Wolock and Mumm (1992) *Chapter Ten*
Wood (1981) *Chapter Nine*
Woodworth (1991) *Chapter Eleven*
Wurtele (1990) *Chapter Two*
Wurtele et al (1986) *Chapter Two*
Wurtele et al (1987) *Chapter Two*
Wurtele et al (1989) *Chapter Two*
Wurtele et al (1991) *Chapter Two*
Wurtele et al (1992) *Chapter Two*
Zastrow (1981) *Chapter Eight*
Zimrin (1984) *Chapter Eight*

References

Abel, G.G., Mittelman, M.S., and Becker J.V. 'Sexual offenders: results of assessment and recommendations for treatment' in H.H. Ben Aron et al (eds.) 'Clinical Criminology', M. & M. Graphics, Toronto, 1985.

Abel, G.G., Becker, J.V., Cunningham-Rathner, J., Routeau, J., Kaplan, M., and Reich, J. 'The Treatment of Child Molesters: A Manual', Unpublished manuscript, University of Columbia, 1984.

Adams, M.J. 'Taking Care with Toby and the Puppet Gang: Prevention and Treatment Package and Manual', Birmingham Health Authority, in preparation 1991.

Adams, M.J. and Llewellyn, A. 'A puppet video to prevent sexual abuse in young children', Newsletter of the Association for Child Psychology and Psychiatry, Vol. 13, 1991.

Affleck, Tennen, H. Rowe, J. Roscher, B. and Walker, L. 'Effects of formal support on mothers' adaptation to the hospital to home transition of high risk infants; The benefits and costs of helping', Child Development, 60, 488–501, 1989.

Afnan, S. and Smith, J. 'Working together? A survey of current child sexual abuse practice', Newsletter of Association of Child Psychology and Psychiatry, 14, (1), 11–16, 1992.

Ainsworth, M.D.S. 'Attachment in child abuse' in G. Gerber, C.J. Ross, and E. Sigler, (eds.) 'Child Abuse Reconsidered: An Agenda for Action', Oxford University, New York, 1980.

Alexander, D.C., Neimeyer R., Follette, V.M., Moore, M.K., and Harter, S. 'A comparison of group treatments of women sexually abused as children', Journal of Consulting & Clinical Psychology, 57, (4), 479–483, 1989.

Alexander, P.C., Neimeyer, R.A., and Follette, U.M. 'Group therapy for women sexually abused as children. A controlled study and investigation of individual differences', Journal of Interpersonal Violence, 6, (2), 218–231, 1991.

Allen, I. 'Education in sex and personal relationships', Policy Studies Institute Research Report No. 605, London, 1987.

Alloway, R. and Bebbington, P. 'The buffer theory of social support – a review of literature', Psychological Medicine, 17, 91–108, 1987.

Antonucci, T.C. 'Social support: theoretical advances, recent findings and pressing issues' in I.G. Sarason and B.R. Sarason (eds.) 'Social Support: Theory, Research and Applications' Martinus Nijhoff, Dordrecht, 1985.

Argyles, P. 'Attachment and child abuse', British Journal of Social Work, 10, 33–42, 1980.

Armitage, J. 'A Study to Evaluate the Effectiveness of a Puppet Show Video Designed to Prevent Child Sexual Abuse in Nursery Children', Unpublished. Undergraduate Thesis, Aston University, 1989.

Armstrong, K. and Fraley, Y. 'What happens to families after they leave the program?' Children Today, May–june 1985, 17–20, 1985.

Armstrong, K.A. 'A treatment and education program for parents and children who are at risk of abuse and neglect', Child Abuse and Neglect, 5, (2), 167–175, 1981.

Armsworth, M.W. 'A qualitative analysis of adult incest survivors' responses to sexual involvement with therapists', Child Abuse and Neglect, 14, (4), 541–554, 1990.

Armsworth, M.W. 'Therapy of incestor survivors: abuse or support?', Child Abuse and Neglect, 13, (4), 549–562, 1989.

Association of Child Psychology and Psychiatry 'Health Visitor based services for preschool children with behaviour problems', Report of study group, 1990.

Avery-Clark, C.A. and Laws, D.R. 'Differential patterns of sexual child abusers to stimuli describing activities with children,' Behaviour Therapy, 15, 71–83, 1984.

Bacon, R.J.E. and Farquar, I.C. 'Child Abuse in an English Local Authority. A descriptive and interpretative study,' Report to DHSS, London, 1983.

Bagley, C. 'Depression, suicidal behaviour and impaired self-esteem as sequels of childhood sexual abuse: Evaluation of group counselling for vulnerable women' in G. Cameron (ed.) 'Family Violence: New Directions in Theory and Research, Erlbaum Associates, New Jersey, Forthcoming.

Bagley, C., and McDonald, M. 'Adult mental health sequels of child sexual abuse, physical abuse and neglect in maternally separated children, Canadian Journal of Community Mental Health, 3, (1), 1984.

Bagley, C., and Thurston, W. 'Prevention and treatment of child sexual abuse: Critical review of the research literature', paper prepared for the Calgary Society of the Prevention of Child Sexual Abuse, June 1988.

Bagley, C. and Ramsay, R. 'Disrupted childhood and vulnerability to sexual assault: long term sequelae with implications for counselling', Social Work and Human Sexuality, 4, 33–48, 1986.

Baher, E., Hyman, C., Jones, C., Jones, R., Kerr, A., and Mitchell, R. 'At Risk: An Account of the Battered Child Research Department, NSPCC', Routledge and Kegan Paul, London, 1976.

Bailey, J., Ramm, K. and Warner, U. 'The Nursing Officer's role', Nursing Times (Community Outlook), March 14th, 1984.

Bailey, V. 'A controlled trial of post-natal mothers' groups as psychosocial primary prevention', summary of spoken paper, Association for Child Psychology and Psychiatry Newsletter, 8, (1), 34–36, 1986.

Baker, B., Grant, J., Squires, J., Johnson, P. and Offermann, L. 'Parent aides as a preventive intervention strategy', Children and Youth Services Review, 3, 115–125, 1981.

Ballew, J.R. 'Role of natural helpers in presenting child abuse and neglect', Social Work, 30, (1), 37–41, 1985.

Barker, W. and Anderson, R. 'Response to critique of the CDP's Evaluation Document 9, The Psychologist, 11, 483–485, 1991.

Barker, W. and Anderson, R. 'The Child Development Programme: an evaluation of process and outcomes', Early Child Development Unit, University of Bristol, 1988.

Barnard, K.E., Maguary, D., Sumner, G., Booth, C.C., Mitchel, S.K. and Spieker, S. 'Prevention of parenting alternations for women with low social support', Psychiatry, 51, 248–253, 1988.

Barnett, S., Corder, F. and Jehu, D. 'Group treatment for women sex offenders against children', Practice, 2, 148–159, 1989.

Barrera, M. 'Distinctions between social support concepts, measures and models', American Journal of Community Psychology, 14, 413–445, 1988.

Barth, R. 'Evaluation of a task centred child abuse prevention programme,' Children and Youth Services Review, 11, 117–131, 1989.

Barth, R.P. 'An experiential evaluation of an in house child abuse prevention service', Child Abuse and Neglect, 15, (4), 363–375, 1991.

Barth, R.P., Blythe, B.J., Schinke, S.P. and Schilling II, R.F. 'Self-control training with maltreating parents', Child Welfare, 52, (4), 313–323, 1983.

Basham, R.B. 'Scientific and practical advantages of comparative design in psycho-therapy outcome research', Journal of Consulting and Clinical Psychology, 54, 1, 88–94, 1986.

Bean, S.L. 'The Parents' Center Project, A multi-service approach to the prevention of child abuse', Child Welfare, 50, 277–282, 1971.

Becker, J. 'Working with perpetrators', in Murray and Gough, 1991, Op. Cit.

Becker, J.V., Kaplan, M.S., and Kavoussi, R., 'Measuring the effectiveness of treatment for the aggressive adolescent sexual offender', Annals of the New York Academy of Sciences, 1988.

Becker, J.V., Kaplan, M.S., Cunningham-Rathner, J., and Kavoussi, R., 'Characteristics of adolescent incest sexual prepetrators: preliminary findings', Journal of Family Violence, 1, (1), 85–79, 1986.

Behaviour Associates, 'Parents anonymous self-help for child abusing parents', Project Evaluation Report for Period May 1, 1974–April 30, 1976, Parents Anonymous National Office, California, 1977.

Bell, C.A., Casto, G. and Daniels, D.S. 'Ameliorating the impact of teen-age pregnancy on parent and child', Child Welfare, 62, (2), 167–173, 1983.

Beller, E.K., 'Early intervention programs' in J.D. Osofsky (ed.) 'The Handbook of Infant Development', Wiley, New York, 1979, (1st edition).

Bellucci, M.T. 'Group treatment of mothers in child protection cases', Child Welfare, 51, (2), 110–116, 1972.

Bentovim, A. 'Who is to blame', New Statesman and Society, 5th August 1988.

Bentovim, A., Elton, A., Hildebrand, J., Tranter, M. and Vizard, E. (eds.) 'Child Sexual Abuse within the Family, Assessment and Treatment', John Wright, Butterworths, London, 1988.

Berger, V. 'Residential weekends for client families as an aid to case management', Child Abuse and Neglect, 5, (3), 309–315, 1981.

Berkeley Planning Associates 'Evaluating child abuse and neglect demonstration projects 1974–1977', Vols 1 to XII, Prepared for National Center for Health Services Research, December 1977.

Berkeley Planning Associates 'Evaluation of the clinical demonstration projects on child abuse and neglect', Vols I to IX, prepared for National Center on Child Abuse and Neglect, June 1983.

Berliner, L. 'Treating the effects of sexual assault' in Murray and Gough, 1991, Op. Cit.

Berliner, L. 'Treating fear and anxiety in sexually abused children: preliminary results.' Paper presented at Ninth International Congress on Child Abuse and Neglect, Chicago, September 1992.

Berliner, L. and Conte, J.R. 'What victims tell us about prevention', unpublished manuscript, 1989.

Berrick, J.D. 'Sexual abuse prevention education, is it appropriate for the preschool child?', Children and Youth Services Review, 11, 145–158, 1989.

Berrick, J.D. and Gilbert, N. 'With the Best Intentions', Guildford Press, 1991.

Binder, R.L. and McNeil, D.E. 'Evaluation of a school-based sexual abuse prevention program: Cognitive and emotional effects', Child Abuse and Neglect, 11, (4), 497–506, 1987.

Blumberg, E.J., Chadwick, M.J., Fogarty L.A., Speth, T.W., Chadwick, M.W., Fogarty, G.A., Speth T.W., Chadwick, D.L. 'The touch disrimination component of sexual abuse prevention training: unanticipated positive consequences', Journal of Interpersonal Violence, 6, (1), 12–28, 1991.

Booth, C.L., Mitchell, S.K., Barnard, K.E. and Spieker, S.J. 'Development of maternal social skills in multiproblem families: Effects on the mother-child relationship', Developmental Psychology, 25, (3), 403–412, 1989.

Borgman, R. 'Problems of sexually abused girls and their treatment', Social Casework, 65, (3), 182–186, 1984.

Borkin, J. and Frank, L. 'Sexual abuse prevention for preschoolers: a pilot program', Child Welfare, 55, (1), 75–82, 1986.

Boss, P.G., 'Family Stress Management', Sage, Beverley Hills, 1988

Bowen Centre, 'The Bowen Center Project, A Report of a demonstration in child protective services', Juvenile Protective Association, Chicago, Il, 1975.

Bowlby, J. 'Child Care and the Growth of Love', Penguin, Harmondsworth, 1972.

Bowlby, J. 'Attachment and Loss, Volume I, Attachment', Hogarth, London, 1969.

Bowman, F. 'Help at home for parents under stress', The Scottish Child, 1, (2), 11–12, 1987.

Bradford, J. McD.W. and Pawlak, A. 'Sadistic homosexual pedophilia: treatment with cyteporone acetate: a single case study', Canadian Journal of Psychiatry, 32, 22–30, 1987.

Brent, London Borough and Health Authority. 'A Child in Trust', The Report of the Panel of Inquiry into the death of Jasmine Beckford, Brent, 1986.

Breton, M. 'Nurturing abused and abusive mothers: the hairdressing group', Social Work with Groups, 2, (2), 161–174, 1979.

Briere, J.N. 'Child Abuse Trauma: Theory and Treatment of the Lasting Effects', Sage, Newbury Park, 1992.

Briere, J. and Runtz, M. 'Suicidal thoughts and behaviours in former sexual abuse victims', Canadian Journal of Behavioural Sciences, 18, 413–423, 1986.

Briere, J. and Runtz, M. 'The Trauma Symptom Checklist (TSC-33). Early data on a new scale', Journal of Interpersonal Violence, 4, (2), 151–162, 1989.

Briere, J. and Runtz, M. 'Multivariate correlates of childhood psychological and physical maltreatment among university women' Child Abuse and Neglect, 12, 51–59, 1988.

Biere, J. and Runtz, M. 'Post sexual abuse trauma' in Wyatt and Powell, 1991, Op. Cit.

Brown, G.W. 'Joining two social institutions to counter rural Alaskan child abuse', Child Abuse and Neglect, 9, (3), 393–388, 1985.

Brown, H. and Craft, A. 'Thinking the unthinkable. Papers on sexual abuse and people with learning difficulties', Family Planning Association Education Unit, London, 1989.

Browne, A., and Finkelhor, D. 'Initial and long term effects: a review of the research' in D. Finkelhor and Associates, 1986, Op. Cit.

Browne, K.D. and Saqi, S. 'Parent-child interaction in child abusing families: possible causes and consequences' in P. Maher (ed.) 'Child abuse: an educational perspective', Blackwell, Oxford, 1987.

Browne, K.D., & Saqi, S., 'Mother – infant, interaction and attachment in physically abusing families', Journal of Reproductive and infant psychology, 6, (3), 163–182, 1988.

Brunk, M. Henggeler, S.W. and Whelan, J.P. 'Comparison of multisystemic therapy and parent training in the brief treatment of child abuse and neglect', Journal of Consulting and Clinical Psychology, 55, (2), 171–178, 1987.

Buchanan, D.G., Aitken, K. and Bechofer, J. 'Groups for parents with difficult under fives – An evaluation study', Newsletter of the National Children's Bureau Scottish Group, No. 12, 21–23, November 1986.

Budin, L.E. and Johnson, C.F. 'Sex abuse prevention programs. Offenders attitudes about their efficacy', Child Abuse and Neglect, 13, (1), 77–88, 1989.

Bunyan, A., 'How I can't cope with my child – A behavioural approach to the treatment of a conduct disordered child within the natural homesetting', British Journal of Social Work, 17, 237–256, 1987.

Burch, G. and Mohr, V. 'Evaluating a child abuse intervention program', Social Casework, 61, (2), 90–99, 1980.

Burt, M.R., and Balycat, R.R., 'A Comprehensive Emergency Services System for Neglected and Abused Children', Vantage Press, New York, 1977.

Callard, E.D. and Morin, 'P.E. PACT Parents and Children Together. An Alternative to Foster Care', Department of Family and Consumer Resources, Wayne State University, Detroit, 1979.

Canadian Government, 'Sexual Offences Against Children', Report of the Committee on Sexual Offences Against Children and Youths, Ottawa, 1984.

Centers, K.L., Jump, J.L., Murray, S.E., and Sarra, D.W., 'Preventing child abuse through systemic reform: a grass roots approach', Paper presented at Eighth International Congress on Child Abuse and Neglect, Hamburg, 1900.

Chaffin, M. 'Factors associated with treatment completion and progress among intra-familial sexual abusers', Child Abuse and Neglect, 16, (2), 251–264, 1992.

Chapman, S. and Reynolds, E. 'Postnatal group for mothers with serious mothering problems', Health Visitor, 55, 461–466, 1982.

Cichetti, D. and Carlson, V. (eds.) 'Child Maltreatment. Theory and research on the causes and consequences of child abuse and neglect', Cambridge University Press, Cambridge, 1989.

Clark, A., Durrani, L., Barnett, B. 'Group work with parents and care givers after child sexual abuse', Newsletter of Association for Child Psychology and Psychiatry, 11, (6), 14–17, 1989.

Clarke, A.D.B. and Clarke, A.M. 'Constancy and chance in the growth of human characteristics', Journal of Child Psychology and Child Psychiatry, 25, (2), 191–210, 1984.

Cleaver, H. and Freeman, P. 'Parental perspectives in suspected child abuse and its aftermath', Personal communication from authors at Dartington Social Research Unit, 1992.

Cochran, M. 'The parental empowerment process: building on family strengths,' in J. Harris (ed.) 'Child Psychology in Action: Linking Research and Practice', Croom Helm, London, 1985.

Cohen, S. and Warren, R.D. 'Preliminary survey of family abuse of children served by United Cerebral Palsy Centers', Development Medicine and Child Neurology, 29, 12–18, 1987.

Cohn, A.H. and Daro, D. 'Is treatment too late: What ten years of evaluative research tell us', Child Abuse and Neglect, 11, (3), 433–442, 1987.

Conger, R., and Lahey, B., 'Behavioural intervention for child abuse', The Behaviour Therapist, 5, 49–53, 1982.

Conger, R., Lahey, B. and Smith, S. 'An intervention program for child abuse. Modifying maternal depression and behaviour', Paper presented to Family Violence Research Conference, University of New Hampshire, Durham, N.H., 1981.

Conte, J., and Schuerman, J.R. 'The effects of sexual abuse on children: a multidimensional view', in Wyatt and Powell, 1988, Op. Cit.

Conte, J.R. and Fogarty, L. 'Sexual abuse prevention programs for children', Paper prepared for a special issue of Education and Urban Society, May 1989.

Conte, J.R. and Schuerman, J.R. 'Factors associated with an increased impact of child sexual abuse,' Child Abuse and Neglect, 11, 201–211, 1987.

Conte, J.R., Rosen, C. and Saperstein, L. 'An evaluation of a program to prevent the sexual victimisation of young children', Child Abuse and Neglect, 9, (3), 319–328, 1985.

Conte, J.R., Wolf, S. and Smith, T. 'What sexual offenders tell us about prevention strategies', Child Abuse and Neglect, 13, (2), 293–301, 1989.

Cooper, P.J., Murray, L. and Stein, A. 'A Postnatal depression in A. Seva (ed.) 'European Handbook of Psychiatry', 1991.

Corby, B. 'Working with Child Abuse', Open University Press, Milton Keynes, 1987.

Corry, M. and Breathwick, 'The residential treatment of an abusing family', Journal of Social Work Practice, 38–49, 1987.

Cox, A.D., Puckering, C., Pound, A., Mills, M. and Owen, A.L. 'Newpin: The evaluation of a home visiting and befriending scheme in South London', Report to Department of Health, London, 1990.

Crimmins, D.B., Bradlyn, A.S., St. Lawrence, J.S. and Kelly, J.A. 'A training technique for improving the parent-child interaction skills of an abusive-neglectful mother', Child Abuse and Neglect, 8, (4), 533–539, 1984.

Crittenden, P.M. 'Family and dyadic patterns of functioning in maltreating families' in K.D. Browne, C. Stratton, and P. Davies (eds.) 'Early Prediction and Prevention of Child Abuse', Wiley, Chichester, 1988.

Crittenden, P.M. 'The social ecology of treatment: case study of a service system for maltreated children', American Journal of Orthopsychiatry, 62, (1), 22–34, 1992.

Crittenden, P.M. and Ainsworth, M.D.S. 'Child maltreatment and attachment theory' in D. Cichetti and V. Carlson. (eds.) 'Child Maltreatment', Cambridge University Press, New York, 1989.

Crow, G. 'A study of community responses to child maltreatment: protocol development', Report for the Coalition for Community Action on Child Abuse, Second Edition, Melbourne, October 1985.

Crozier, J. and Katz, R.C. 'Social learning treatment of child abuse', Journal of Behavior Therapy and Experimental Psychiatry, 213–220, 1979.

Culp, R.E., Richardson, M.T. and Heide, J.S. 'Differential developmental progress of maltreated children in day treatment', Social Work, 497–499, Nov–Dec, 1987.

Cutrona, C.E. and Troutman, B.R. 'Social support, infant temperament, and parenting self efficacy; a mediational model of post partum depression' Child Development, 57, 1507–1518, 1986.

Dachman, R.S., Alessi, G.J., Vraza, G.J., Fugua, R.W., and Kerr, R.H. 'Development and evaluation of an infant-care training program with first-time fathers', Journal of Applied Behaviour Analysis, 19, (3), 221–230, 1986.

Dadds, M.R., Scwartz, S., Sanders, M.R. 'Marital discord and treatment outcome in behavioural treatment of child conduct disorders', Journal of Consulting and Clinical Psychology, 55, (2), 171–178, 1987.

Dangel, R.F. and Polster, R.A. (eds.) 'Parent Training. Foundations of Research and Practice', Guildford Press, New York, 1984.

Daro, D. 'Confronting Child Abuse, Research for Effective Program Design', The Free Press, McMillan, New York, 1987.

Daro, D. 'Public attitudes and behaviours with respect to child abuse prevention 1987–1991', National Committee for Prevention of Child Abuse, Working Paper no. 840, Chicago, April, 1991.

Davenport, C., Browne, K., and Palmer, R. 'A vignette study of child sexual abuse: opinions on traumatic effects', submitted for publication, 1991.

Davis, G.E. and Leitenberg, H. 'Adolescent sex offenders', Psychological Bulletin, 101, (3), 417–427, 1987.

Davis, J.A., Richards, M.P.M. and Robertson, N.R.C. (eds.) 'Parent-Baby Attachment in Premature Infants', Croom Helm, Beckenham, 1983.

Dawson, B., de Armas, A., McGrath, M.L. and Kelly J.A. 'Cognitive problem-solving training to improve the child-care judgment of child neglectful parents', Journal of Family Violence, 1, (1), 209–221, 1986.

De Bortali-Tregerthan. 'A behavioural treatment of child abuse: a case report', Child Behavior Therapy, 1, 287–293, 1979.

De Panfilis, D. 'Clients who refer themselves to child protective services', Children Today, 11, (2), 21–25, 1982.

de Young M. 'The Good touch/bad touch dilemma' Child Welfare, LXVII, (1), 60–68, 1988.

Deblinger, E., McLeer, S., and Henry, D. 'Cognitive behavioural treatment for sexually abused children suffering post-traumatic stress: preliminary findings', Journal of American Academy of Child Adolescent Psychiatry, 29, (5), 747–752, 1990.

Del Castillo, M.L.T. 'Neighbourhead protective strategy for children with special reference to the Phillipines', Child Abuse and Neglect, 9, (4), 565–569, 1985.

Delson, N. and Clark, M. 'Group therapy with sexually molested children', Child Welfare, 60, (3), 175–182, 1981.

Denicola, J. and Sandler, J. 'Training abusive parents in child management and self-control skills', Behavior Therapy, 11, 263–270, 1980.

Department of Health and Social Security, 'Child Abuse: A Study of Inquiry Reports 1973–1981'. HMSO, London, 1982.

Department of Health and Social Security, 'Child sexual abuse: Survey report on interagency co-operative in England and Wales', Social Services Inspectorate, London, 1988.

Department of Health and Social Security, 'Social Work decisions in care: recent research findings and their implications'. HMSO, London, 1985.

Department of Health and Social Security. 'Child abuse-working together'. A draft guide to arrangements for interagency co-operation for the protection of children. April 1986.

Department of Health 'Child Abuse: A Study of Inquiry Reports 1980–1989', HMSO, London, 1991.

Department of Health, 'Working Together under the Children Act 1989', HMSO, London, 1991.

Department of Health, 'Patterns and Outcomes in Child Placement', London, 1991.

Department of Health, 'Children and Young Persons on Child Protection Registers Year Ending 31 March 1991 England', Personal Social Services Local Authority Statistics A/F91/13, prepared by Government Statistical Service, London, 1992.

Dingwall, R. 'Problems of prediction in child abuse research', in O. Stevenson (ed.) 'Child Abuse: Public Policy and Professional Practice', Harvester Press, Brighton, 1989.

Dingwall, R., Review of N. Parton 'Governing the Family (1991), Child Abuse Review, 1, 1992.

Dingwall, R, Eekalaar, J., and Murray, T. 'The Protection of Children. State intervention and family life', Blackwell, Oxford, 1983.

Doherty, N. and Barratt, W. Personal safety programme', Report to Cambridgeshire County Council in cooperation with Huntingdon Health Authority, 1989.

Dougherty, N. 'The holding environment: breaking the cycle of abuse', Social Casework, 64, (5), 283–290, 1983.

Dowling, S. 'Health for a change. The provision of preventive health care in pregnancy and early childhood', Child Poverty Action Group, London, 1983.

Drotar, D. Eckerle, Satola, J. Pallota, J. and Wyatt, B. 'Maternal interactive behaviour with non organic failure to thrive infants: A case comparison study', Child Abuse and Neglect, 14, (1), 41–52, 1990.

Dubowitz, H. 'Child maltreatment in the United States. Etiology, impact, and prevention'. Paper prepared for the Office of Technology Assessment, United States Congress, May 1987.

Earls, C.M. and Castonguay, L.G. 'The evaluation of olfactory aversion for a bisexual pedophile with a single-case multiple base-line design', Behaviour Therapy, 20, 1237–146, 1989.

Egan, A.G. 'The Acorn Club after six years – A participant observer's evaluation of the processes involved in a preventive intervention', Revised version of paper presented at Sixth International Congress on Child Abuse and Neglect, Sydney, Australia 1986.

Egeland, B. 'Breaking the Cycle of Abuse' in K. Browne, C. Davies and P. Stratton, 'Early Prediction and Prevention of Child Abuse', Wiley, Chichester, 1988.

Eliot, S.A. 'Psychological strategies in the prevention and treatment of postnatal depression' in Balliere (Ed.), Clinical Obstetrics and Gynaecology, 3, (4), 1989.

Elliot, M. 'The Kidscape Programme for the Prevention of Sexual Assault on Children', Kidscape, London, 1986.

Elmer, E. 'Outcome of residential treatment for abused and high-risk infants', Child Abuse and Neglect, 10, 351–360, 1986.

English, D.J. 'Prediction in child protection: Research results from two studies,' paper presented at Ninth International Congress on Child Abuse and Neglect, Chicago, September 1992.

English, D.J. and Aubin, S. 'Impact of investigation outcomes for child protective services cases receiving differential levels of service' Children's Services Research Project, Department of Health and Social Services, Washington State, 1991.

Ennew, J. 'The Sexual Exploitation of Children', Polity Press, Cambridge, 1986.

Faller, K.C. 'Polincestuous families. An exploratory study', Journal of Interpersonal Violence, 6, (3), 310–322, 1991.

Faller, K.C. 'What happens to sexually abused children identified by child protective services?' Child Abuse and Neglect, 15, 101–111, 1991.

Famularo, R., Kischerff, Bunshaft, D., Spivak, G., and Fenton, D. 'Parental compliance to court ordered treatment interventions in cases of child maltreatment', Child Abuse and Neglect, 13, (4), 507–514, 1989.

Fantuzzo, J.W., Jurecic, L., Stovall, A., Hightower, A.D., Goins, C., and Schachtel, D. 'Effects of adult and peer social initiations on the social behaviour of withdrawn, maltreated preschool children', Journal of Consulting and Clinical Psychology, 56, (1), 34–39, 1988.

Fantuzzo, J.W., Stoval, A., Schactel, D., Goins, C. and Hall, R. 'The effects of peer social initiations on the social behaviour of withdrawn maltreated preschool children', Journal of Behaviour Therapy & Experimental Psychiatry, 18, (4), 357–363, 1987.

Farmer, E. 'Protection or violation – the impact of child protection interventions on parents and children', in L. Waterhouse (ed.) 'Child Abuse and Child Abusers: protection and prevention', Research Highlights in Social Work, Jessica Kingsley, London, 1993.

Farmer, E. and Owen, M. 'Decision-making, intervention, and outcome in child protection work', Paper presented to Department of Health Child abuse Research Seminar, Dartingto Hall, October, 1991.

Feldman, M.A., Case, L., Garrick, M., MacIntyre-Grande, W. and Carnwell, J. 'Teaching childcare skills to mothers with developmental disabilities', Journal of Applied Behaviour Analysis, 25, (1), 205–215, 1992.

Feldman, M.A., Towns, F., Betel, J., Case L., Rincover, A., and Rubino, C.A. 'Parent Education Project II. Increasing stimulating interactions of developmentally handicapped parents', Journal of Applied Behaviour Analysis, 19, (1), 23–37, 1986.

Finkelhor, D. 'Abusers: special topics' in D. Finkelhor and Associates, 1986, Op. Cit.

Finkelhor, D. 'The scope of the problem' in Murray and Gough, 1991, Op. Cit.

Finkelhor, D. 'The trauma of child sexual abuse: two models' in Wyatt and Powell, 1988, Op. Cit.

Finkelhor, D. and Associates. 'A Source book on Child Sexual Abuse, Sage, Beverly Hills, 1986.

Finkelhor, D. and Browne, A. 'Initial and long term effects: a conceptual framework' in D. Finkelhor and Associates, 1986, Op. Cit.

Finkelhor, D. and Strapko, N., 'Sexual abuse prevention education: A review of evaluation studies' in Wills D.J., Holder E.W., Rosenberg M., (eds.) 'Child Abuse Prevention', Wiley, New York, 1992.

Finkelhor, D., 'What's wrong with sex between adults and children?', American Journal of Orthopsychiatry, 49, (4), 1979.

Finkelhor, D., Hotaling, G.T. and Yllo, K. 'Stopping Family Violence', Sage, London, 1988.

Finkelhor, D., Hotaling, G.T., Lewis, I.A., and Smith, C. 'Sexual abuse and its relationship to later sexual satisfaction, marital status, religion, and attitudes', Journal of Interpersonal Violence, 4, (4), 379–399, 1989.

Finkelhor, D., Hotaling, G.T., Lewis, I.A., and Smith, C. 'Sexual abuse and its relationship to later sexual satisfactions, marital status, religion, and attitudes', Journal of Interpersonal Violence, 4, (4), 379–399, 1989.

Finkelhor, D., Williams, L.M., with Burns, N. 'Nursery Crimes, Sexual Abuse in Day Care', Sage, Newbury Park, 1988.

Follette, V.M., Alexander, P.C. and Follette, W.C. 'Individual predictors of outcome in group treatment for incest survivors', Journal of Consulting and Clinical Psychology, 1991.

Fontana, V. and Robinson, E. 'A multidisciplinary approach to the treatment of child abuse', Pediatrics, 57, 760–764, 1976.

Foot, H.C., Morgan, M.J. and Shute, R. (eds.) 'Children Helping children', Wiley, Chichester, 1990.

Fosson, A. 'Family Stress' in S. Fisher and J. Reason 'Handbook of Life Stress, Cognition and Health', Wiley, Chichester, 1988.

Fraiberg, S., Adelson, E. and Shapero, V. 'Ghosts in the nursery', Journal of the American Academy of Child Psychiatry, 14, (3), 387–421, 1975.

Friedrich, W.N. Berliner, L., Urquiza, A.J., and Beilke, R. 'Brief diagnostic group treatment of sexually abused boys', Journal of Interpersonal Violence, 3, (3), 331–343, 1988.

Fryer, G.E., Kraizer, S.K. and Miyoshi, T. 'Measuring children's retention of skills to resist stranger abduction. Use of the Simulation Technique', Child Abuse and Neglect, 11, 181–185, 1987b.

Fryer, G.E. 'The efficacy of hospitalization of non organic failure to thrive children: A meta analysis', Child Abuse and Neglect, 12, (3), 375–382, 1988.

Fryer, G.E., Kraizer, S.K. and Miyoshi, T. 'Measuring actual reduction of risk of child abuse: A new approach', Child Abuse and Neglect, 11, 173–179, 1987a.

Furby, L., Weinrott, M.R., and Blackshaw, L. 'Sex offender recidivism: a review', Psychological Bulletin, 105, (1), 3–30, 1989.

Furniss, T. 'Family process in the treatment of intra familial child sexual abuse', Journal of Family Therapy, 5, 263–278, 1983.

Furniss, T., Bingley-Miller L., and Elburg, A. 'Goal-orientated group treatment for sexually abused adolescent girls', British Journal of Psychiatry, 15, 97–106, 1988.

Furniss, T., Bingley-Miller, L. and Bentovim, A. 'Therapeutic approach to sexual abuse', Archives of Disease in Childhood, 59, (9), 865–870, 1984.

Gabinet, L. 'Prevention of child abuse and neglect in an inner-city population, II, The program and the results', Child Abuse and Neglect, 3, 809–817, 1979.

Galdston, R. 'Preventing the abuse of little children: the Parent's Center Project for the Study and Prevention of Child Abuse', American Journal of Orthopsychiatry, 45, 372–381, 1975.

Galdston, R. 'Violence begins at home. The Parents' Center Project for the Study and Prevention of Child Abuse', Journal of American Academy of Child Psychiatry, 10, (2), 336–350, 1971.

Garbarino, J. 'A preliminary study of some ecological correlates of child abuse: The impact of socio-economic stress on mothers', Child Development, 47, 178–185, 1976.

Garbarino, J. 'Brief communication: children's response to a sexual abuse prevention program: a study of the Spiderman comic', Child Abuse and Neglect, 11, (1), 143–148, 1987.

Gelles, R.J. 'An exchange/social control theory' in D. Finkelhor, R.J. Gelles, G.T. Hotaling, and M.A. Straus (eds.) 'The Dark Side of Families', Sage, Beverley Hills, 1983.

Gelles, R.J. 'Child abuse as psychopathology: A Sociological critique and reformulation', American Journal of Orthopsychiatry, 43, 611–621, 1973.

Gelles, R.J. and Cornell, C.P. 'Intimate Violence in Families', Sage, Beverley Hills, 1985.

George, C. & Main, M. 'Social interactions of young abused children: approach, avoidance, and aggression', Child Development, 50, 306–318, 1979.

Giaretto, H. 'Humanistic treatment of father-daughter incest', In: R. Helfer and C. Kempe (eds.), Child Abuse and Neglect: The Family and the Community, Ballinger, Cambridge, 1976.

Giarretto, H. 'A comprehensive child sexual abuse treatment program', Child Abuse and Neglect, 6, 263–278, 1982.

Gibbons, J. 'Purposes and Organization of Preventive Work with Families', HMSO, London, 1990.

Gibbons, J. and Thorpe, S. 'Can voluntary support projects help vulnerable families? The work of Home Start', British Journal of Social Work, 19, (3), 189–201, 1989.

Gibbons, J., Gallagher, B., and Bell, C. Report of the Family Health and Development Project. A Follow Up of Physically Abused Children', Draft report to the Department of Health, January 1992.

Gilbert, N., Berrick, J.D., Le Prohn, N. and Nyman, N. 'Protecting Young Children from Sexual Abuse. Does Preschool Training Work?', Lexington Books, Masachusetts, 1989.

Gilgun, J.F. and Gordon, S. 'Sex education and the prevention of child sexual abuse', Journal of Sex Education and Therapy, 11, (1), 46–52, 1985.

Gillies, E. 'Parents United Programmes', in Murray and Gough, 1991, Op. Cit.

Giovannoni, J.A. and Becerra, R.M. 'Defining Child Abuse', Free Press, New York, 1979.

Goldberg, E.M. and Connelly, N. (eds.), 'Evaluative Research in Social Care', Heinemann, London, 1981.

Goldberg, E.M. and Sinclair, I. 'Family Support Exercise', National Institute for Social Work Research Unit, London, 1986.

Gottlieb, B. 'Theory into practice: Issues that surface in planning interventions which mobilize support' in I.G. Sarason and B.R. Sarason (eds.), 'Social Support: Theory Research and Applications', Martinus Nijhoff, Dordecht, 1985.

Gough, D.A. 'Scottish child abuse statistics 1985–1986' Unpublished report prepared for Association of Directors of Social Work, 1987.

Gough, D.A. 'Scottish Child Abuse Statistics 1987', Report for Association of Directors of Social Work, June, 1988.

Gough, D.A. 'Child Sexual Abuse Referrals to the Royal Hospital for Sick Children, Glasgow, 1989', Unpublished report, November 1990.

Gough, D.A. 'Survey of Scottish child protection registers' in Directors of Social Work in Scotland 'Policy, Practice, Procedures, and Protection. An Overview of Child Abuse Issues and Practice in Scotland', HMSO, Edinburgh, 1992.

Gough, D.A. 'Prevention' in L. Waterhouse (ed.) 'Child Abuse and Child Abusers: protection and prevention', Research Highlights in Social Work, Jessica Kingsley, London, 1993.

Gough, D.A. and Boddy, F.A. 'Family Violence' in G. Horobin (ed.) 'The family context or clients', Kogan Page, London, 1986.

Gough, D.A., Boddy, F.A., Dunning, N. and Stone, F.H. 'Research problems in understanding non accidental injury families'. Paper presented at International Congress in Child Psychiatry, Dublin, 1982.

Gough, D.A., Boddy, F.A., Dunning, N. and Stone, F.H. 'A Longitudinal Study of Child Abuse in Glasgow, Volume I, the Children who were Registered', Report to Social Work Services Group, Scottish Office, 1987.

Gough, D.A., Boddy, F.A., Dunning, N. and Stone, F.H. 'The Management of Child Abuse: A Longitudinal study of child abuse in Glasgow,' Scottish Office Central Research Unit Papers, Edinburgh, 1993.

Gough, D.A., Taylor, J. and Boddy, F.A. 'Child Abuse Interventions: A Review of the Research Literature', Report to Department of Health, 1988.

Gough, D.A. and Sutton, A. 'Hospital referrals for sexual abuse', unpublished paper, 1991.

Gray, E. and colleagues. Final Report, Collaborative Research of Community and Minority Group Action to Prevent Child Abuse and Neglect. Volumes 1 to 3, National Committee for Prevention of Child Abuse, Chicago, 1983.

Gray, E. et al 'Close to home: a television mini-series for parents', in Vol 3 of E. Gray, 1983. Op Cit.

Gray, E. et al 'Project network: Child abuse prevention in inner city Atlanta', In E. Gray et al, 1983, Op Cit.

Gray, E. et al. 'Blackfeet child abuse prevention project: Community awareness on an Indian Reservation', in E. Gray et al, 1983, Op. Cit.

Gray, E. et al. 'Inter-act: street theatre for parents', in: Vol. 3 of E. Gray et al 1983, Op Cit.

Gray, E. et al. 'Pan Asian parent education project: Parenting education for Asian immigrant families', in Vol 2 of E. Gray et al, 1983, Op Cit.

Gray, E. et al. 'Perinatal positive parenting', in Vol 1, 31–86, of E. Gray et al 1983, Op Cit.

Gray, E. et al. 'Primary prevention partnerships: Education, information and referral in North Western Washington', In E. Gray et al 1983, Op Cit.

Gray, E. et al. 'Project C.A.N. prevent: A comprehensive program for young Mexican-American families', in Vol 2 of E. Gray et al, 1983, Op Cit.

Gray, E. et al. 'Rural family support project: A systems approach to preventing child abuse', in Vol 1 of E. Gray et al, 1983, Op. Cit.

Gray, et al. 'Pride in parenthood: family friends for high-risk parents', in Vol 1, Part 3, of E. Gray et al 1983, Op Cit.

Gray, J.D., Cutler, C.A., Dean, J.G. and Kempe, C.H. 'Prediction and prevention of child abuse and neglect', Child Abuse and Neglect, 1, (1), 45–58, 1977.

Gray, J.D., Cutler, D.A., Dean, J.G. and Kempe, C.H. 'Prediction and prevention of child abuse and neglect', Journal of Social Issues, 35, (2), 127–139, 1979.

Green, A. 'Psychiatric treatment of the abused child', Journal of the American Academy of Child Psychiatry, 17, 356, 1978.

Green, A.H., Power, E., Steinbook, B. and Gaines, R. 'Factors associated with successful and unsuccessful intervention with child abusive families', Child Abuse and Neglect, 5, (1), 45–52, 1981.

Greenwich, London Borough of, 'A Child in Mind', Report of the Commission of Inquiry into the death of Kimberley Carlile, London Borough of Greenwich, 1987.

Hallett, C., and Stevenson, O. 'Child Abuse: Aspects of Interprofessional Co-operation', George Allen and Unwin, London, 1980.

Hallett, C. and Birchall, L. 'Coordination and Child Protection. A review of the literature', HMSO, London, 1992.

Hamilton, S. 'Prevention in Child Sexual Abuse – An Evaluation of a Programme', MSc Dissertation, University of Edinburgh, 1989.

Hanks, H. 'Failure to Thrive: Tales about failure to thrive infants and children', Child Abuse Review, 1, (7), 12–13, 1987.

Hanks, H.G.I., Hobbs, C.J., Semour, D. and Stratton, P. 'Infants who fail to thrive: An intervention for poor feeding practices', Journal of Reproductive and Infant Psychology, 6, 101–111, 1988.

Hardiker, P., Exton, K. and Barker, M. 'Policies and Practices in Preventive Child Care', Avebury, Aldershot, 1991.

Harling, P.R. and Haines, J.K. 'Specialized foster homes for severely mistreated children', Children Today, 9, (4), 16–18, 1980.

Harper, G. and Irvin, E. 'Alliance formation with parents: limit-setting and the effect of mandated reporting', American Journal of Orthopsychiatry, 55, (4), 550–560, 1985.

Harvey, P., Forehand, R., Brown, C. and Holmes, T. 'The Prevention of sexual abuse: Examination of the effectiveness of a program with kindergarten-age children', Behaviour Therapy, 19, (3), 429–435, 1988.

Haugaard, J.C. and Reppucci, N.D. 'The Sexual Abuse of Children: A Comprehensive Guide to Current Knowledge and Intervention Strategies', Jossey-Bass, San Francisco, 1988.

Haynes, C., Cutler, C., Gray, J. and Kempe, R. 'Hospitalized cases of non-organic failure to thrive: the scope of the problem and short-term lay health visitor intervention', Child Abuse and Neglect, 8, 229–242, 1984.

Hazzard, A., Webb, C., Kleemeir, C., Angert, L. and Pohl, J. 'Child sexual abuse prevention: evaluation and one-year follow up', Child Abuse and Neglect, 15, (1/2), 123–138, 1991.

Heap, K.K. 'Families with abused children: a follow-up of post-crisis support', Child Abuse and Neglect, 8, (4), 462–472, 1984.

Hensey, O.J., Williams, J. and Rosenbloom, L. 'Intervention in child abuse: experience in Liverpool', Developmental Medicine and Child Neurology, 25, (5), 606–611, 1983.

Hinde, R.A. 'Towards Understanding Relationships', Academic Press, London, 1979.

Hindman, J. 'Abuses to Sexual Abuse Prevention Programmes or Ways We Abuse our Children as we Attempt to Prevent Abuse', Alexandria Associates, (undated).

Hobbs, C.J. 'Failure to thrive: paediatric perspectives of emotional abuse', Child Abuse Review, 1, (7), 10–11, 1987.

Hobbs, C.J., Hanks, H.G.I. and Wynne, J. 'Child Abuse and Neglect. A Clinician's Handbook', Churchill Livingstone, Edinburgh, 1993.

Holman, B. 'Putting Families First', MacMillan, Basingstoke, 1988.

Hodgkinson, M. 'Behavioural parent training: cure all, palliative or token gesture?' Newsletter of Association for Child Psychology and Psychiatry, 13, (3), 6–9, 1991.

Horne, L. Glasgow, D., Cox, A.D., Callum, R. 'Sexual abuse of children by children: normal child experimentation or prognostic of adult offending', Journal of Child Law, 3, (4), 1991.

Hornick, J.P. and Clarke, M.E. 'A cost/effectiveness evaluation of lay therapy treatment for child abusing and high risk parents', Child Abuse and Neglect, 10, (3), 309–318, 1986.

Howlett, A., Lunan, S. and Symons, R. 'Aberdeen mother and child groups. Save the children Project 1981–1984', Unpublished report, 1985.

Hunt, J. McV. 'Reflections on a decade of early education', Journal of Abnormal Child Psychology, 3, (4), 275–230, 1975.

Hunter, J.A. 'A comparison of the psychosocial maladjustment of adult males and females sexually molested as children', Journal of Interpersonal Violence, 6, (2), 205–217, 1991.

Hunter, W.M., Coulter, M.L., Runyan, D.K., and Everson, M.D. 'Determinants of placement for sexually abused children', Child Abuse and Neglect, 14, (3), 407–418, 1990.

Huntingon, T.S. 'Supportive Programs for Infants and Parents' in J.D. Osofsky (ed.) 'Handbook of Infant Development', Wiley, New York, 1979 (1st Edition).

Hutchings, J., Jones, D. and Hughes, N. 'Children at risk: Working with the family', Community Care, July 23, 1981.

Iwaniec, D. 'Treatment for children who fail to grow in the light of the new Children Act', Newsletter of Association of Child Psychology and Psychiatry, 13, (3) 21–27, 1991.

Iwaniec, D., Herbert, M. and McNeish, A.S. 'Social work with failure to thrive children and their families Part 1: Psychosocial factors', British Journal of Social Work, 15, (3), 243–259, 1985.

Iwaniec, D., Herbert, M. and McNeish, A.S. 'Social work with failure to thrive children and their families Part 2: Behavioural social work intervention', British Journal of Social Work, 15, (4), 375–389, 1985.

Jaudes, P.K. and Morris, M. 'Child sexual abuse: who goes home?', Child Abuse and Neglect, 14, (1), 61–68, 1990.

Jehu, D. 'Beyond Sexual Abuse. Therapy with Women who were Childhood Victims', John Wiley, Chichester, 1988.

Jehu, D. 'Mood disturbances among women clients sexually abused in childhood: Prevalence etiology treatment', Journal of Interpersonal Violence, 4, (2), 164–184, 1989.

Jellinek, M.S., Murphy, J.M., Poitrast, F.M., Quinn, D. Bishop, S.J. and Goshko, M. 'Serous child mistreatment in Massachussetts: the course of 206 children through the courts', Child Abuse and Neglect, 16, (2), 179–186, 1992.

Jenkins, A. Text of paper presented at Fifth International Congress on Child Abuse, Montreal, September 1984.

Johnson, B.K. and Kenkel, M.B. 'Stress, coping and adjustment in female adolescent incest victims', Child Abuse and Neglect, 15, (3), 293–306, 1991.

Johnson, C.A. and Katz, R.C., 'Using parents as change agents for their children: A Review', Journal of Child Psychology and Psychiatry, 14, (3), 181–200, 1973.

Johnson, T.C. 'Child perpetrators – children who molest other children: Preliminary findings', Child Abuse and Neglect, 12, (2), 219–229, 1988.

Johnson, T.C. 'Female child perpetrators: Children who molest other children', Child Abuse and Neglect, 13, (4), 571–586, 1989.

Jones, C. 'The Effectiveness of a Video Taped Instruction in the Education of Junior School Children about the Identification and Management of Bullying

Situations', Unpublished Undergraduate Thesis, Wolverhampton Polytechnic, 1990.

Jones, D.P.H. 'The effectiveness of intervention' in M. Adcock, R. White, and A. Hollows (eds.) 'Significant Harm: it's management and outcome', Significant Publications, Croydon, 1991.

Justice, B., and Justice, R., 'Outcome of group therapy for abusing parents', Journal of Behaviour, 24, (1), 45–49, 1978.

Kadushin, A. and Martin, J.A. 'Child Abuse an Interactional Event', Columbia University, New York, 1981.

Kagan, S.L., Powell, D.R., Weissbound, B., Zigler, E.F. 'America's Family Support Programs, Perspectives and Prospects', Yale University Press, New Haven, 1987.

Kahn T.J. and Chambers, H.J. 'Assessing reoffense risk with juvenile sexual offenders', Child Welfare, LXX, (3), 333–345, 1991.

Kazdin, A.E. 'Comparative outcome studies of psychotherapy: Methodological issues and strategies'. Journal of Consulting and Clinical Psychology, 54, (1), 95–105, 1986.

Keller, R.A., Cicchinelli, L.F., and Gardner, D.M. 'Characteristics of child sexual abuse treatment programs', Child Abuse and Neglect, 13, (3), 361–368, 1989.

Kelley, S.J. 'Responses of children to sexual abuse and satanic ritualistic abuse in day care centres', Paper presented at the National Symposium in Child Victimization, Anaheim, California, April 1988.

Kelly, L., Regan, L., and Burton, S. 'An Exploratory Study of the Prevalence of Sexual Abuse in a Sample of 16–21 year Olds', Child Abuse Studies Unit, Polytechic of North London, 1991.

Kelly, R.J. 'Behavioural reorientation of pedophiliacs: Can it be done?', Clinical Psychology Review, 2, 387–408, 1982.

Kendall-Tackett, K.A. 'Characteristics of abuse that influence when adults molested as children seek treatment', Journal of Interpersonal Violence, 6, (4), 486–493, 1991.

Kendall-Tackett, K.A., Williams, L.M. and Finkelhor, D. 'Impact of sexual abuse on children. A synthesis and review of recent empirical studies', Psychological Bulletin, 113, (1), 164–180, 1993.

Kettle, J. 'Survey of treatment Facilities for Abused Children and of Treatment Facilities for Young Sexual Abusers of Children', National Children's Home, 1990.

King, J.M. and Taitz, L.S. 'Catch up growth following abuse', Archives of Disease in Childhood, 60, (12), 1152–1154, 1985.

Kitchen, M. 'Breaking the vicious circle of battering', Social Work Today, 11, (19), 8–9, 1980.

Kitchur, M. and Bell, R. 'Group psychotherapy with preadolescent sexual abuse victims: Literature review and description of an inner-city group', International Journal of Psychotherapy, 39, (3), 285–310, 1989.

Kitzinger, J. 'Sexual Abuse and the Violation of Childhood', in James A. and Prout A. (eds.) 'The Social Construction of Childhood', Oxford University Press, Oxford, 1990.

Kitzinger, J. 'Sexual violence and compulsory heterosexuality', Feminism and Psychology, 2, (3), 339–418, 1992.

Kleemeier, C., Webb, C., and Hazzard, A. 'Child Sexual abuse prevention: evaluation of a teacher training model', Child Abuse and Neglect, 12, (4), 555–561, 1988.

Knight, R.A. 'An assessment of the concurrent validity of a child molester typology', Journal of Interpersonal Violence, 4, (2), 131–150, 1989.

Kolko, D.J. 'Social-cognitive skills training with a sexually abused and abusive child psychiatric inpatient: Training, generalization, and follow-up', Journal of Family Violence, 1, (2), 1986.

Kolko, D.J., Moser, J.T., and Hughes, J. 'Classroom training in sexual victimization awareness and prevention skills: An extension of the Red Flag/Green Flag People Program', Journal of Family Violence, 4, (1), 1989.

Kopp, F.H. 'Remedial Intervention in Adolescent sex offences: nine program descriptions' Safe Society Press, Orwell, 1988.

Kraizer, S.K., Fryer, G.E. and Miller, M. 'Programming for preventing sexual abuse and abduction: What does it means when it works?', Child Welfare, LXVII, (1), 69–78, 1988.

Krell, H.L., Richardson, C.M., Lamanna, T.N. and Kairys, S.W. 'Child abuse and worker training', Social Casework, 64, (9), 1983.

Kroth, J.A. 'Child Sexual Abuse: Analysis of a Family Therapy Approach', Charles C. Thomas, Springfield, 1979.

Kruger, L., Moor, D., Schmidt, P. and Wiens, R. 'Group therapy with abusive parents', Social Work, 24, 337–339, 1979.

Kunkel, B.E. 'Successful nurturing in residential treatment for abused children', Child Abuse and Neglect, 5, (3), 249–251, 1981.

Land, H.M. 'Child abuse: differential diagnosis, differential treatment', Child Welfare, 55, (1), 33–44, 1986.

Lane, S. and Van Dyke, V. 'Lay therapy – intimacy as a form of treatment for abusive parents', Child Abuse and Neglect, 2, 233–241, 1978.

Larson, C.P. 'Efficacy of prenatal and post-partum home visits on child health and development', Pediatrics, 66, (2), 191–197, 1980.

Larson, K.L., Ayllon, T., and Barrett, D.H. 'A behavioural feeding program for failure-to-thrive infants', Behaviour Research Therapy, 25, (1), 39–47, 1987.

Laughlin, J. and Weiss, M. 'An outpatient milieu therapy approach to treatment of child abuse and neglect problems', Social Casework, 62, (2), 106–109, 1981.

Lawder, E.A. et al. 'Helping the multi-problem family, A study of services to children in their own homes', Childrens Aid Society of Pennsylvania, Philadelphia, 1984.

Lealman, G.T., Haigh, D., Phillips, J.M., Stone, J. and Ord-Smith, C. 'Prediction and prevention of child abuse – An empty hope?' The Lancet, June 25th, 1983.

Leeds, S.J. 'Evaluation of Nebraska's Intensive Services Project', National Resource Center on Family Based Services, University of Iowa, 1984.

Leventhal, J.M. 'Research strategies and methodologic standards in studies of risk factors for child abuse', Child Abuse and Neglect, 6, 113–123, 1982.

Leventhal, J.M., Fearn, K. and Stashwick, C.A., 'Clinical data used by pediatric residents to assess parenting', Child Abuse and Neglect, 10, 71–78, 1986.

Leventhal, J.M. 'Programs to prevent sexual abuse: what outcomes should be measured?', Child Abuse and Neglect, 11, (2), 169–171, 1987.

Leventhal, J.M. 'Can child maltreatment be predicted during the perinatal period: evidence from longitudinal cohort studies?', Journal of Reproductive and Infant Psychology', 6, (3), 139–161, 1988.

Leverton, T. 'Group treatment for depressed mothers of pre-school children', Maternal and Child Health, 16, (10), 332–336, 1991.

Lewis, M. and Schneffer, S. 'Peer Behaviour and Mother Infant Interactions in Maltreated Children' in M. Lewis and M.A. Rosenbloom (eds.) 'The Uncommon Child', Plenum, New York, 1981.

Li, C.K. 'Adult sexual experiences with children: a study of personal accounts' in C.K. Li, D.J. West, and T.P. Woodhouse (eds.) 'Sexual Encounters Between Children and Adults', 1991.

Lieber, L.L. and Baker, J.M. 'Parents anonymous – self-help treatment for child abusing parents: a review and an evaluation', Child Abuse and Neglect, 1, 133–148, 1977.

Lightfoot, H., Lippman, C. and Suffet, F. 'Final Report: The parent and child treatment program', Center for Comprehensive Health Care Practice, New York Medical College, New York, 1983.

Lines, D.R. 'The effectiveness of parent-aides in the tertiary prevention of child abuse in South Australia', Paper presented at the 6th International Congress on Child Abuse and Neglect, Sydney, Australia, 1986.

Long, P.J. and Jackson, J.L. 'Children sexually abused by multiple perpetrators. Familial risk factors and abuse characteristics', Journal of Interpersonal Violence, 6, (2), 147–159, 1991.

Lonsdale, G. 'A survey of parental participation at initial child protection case conferences' Child Abuse Review, 5, (1), 11–14, 1991.

Lutzker, J.R. 'Project 12-Ways: Treating child abuse and neglect from an Ecobehavioural Perspective', in R.F. Dangel and R.A. Polster (eds.), Parent Training, Foundations of Research and Practice, Guildford, 1984.

Lutzker, J.R. and Rice, J.M. 'Project 12-ways: measuring outcome of a large in-home service for treatment and prevention of child abuse and neglect', Child Abuse and Neglect, 8, 519–524, 1984.

Lutzker, J.R. and Rice, J.M. 'Using recidivism data to evaluate Project 12-ways: an ecobehavioural approach to the treatment and prevention of Child Abuse and neglect', Journal of Family Violence, 2, (4), 283–290, 1987.

Lynch, M.A. and Roberts, J. 'Consequences of Child Abuse', Academic Press, London, 1982.

MacLeod, M., and Saraga, S. 'Against orthodoxy', New Statesman and Society', 1st July 1988.

MacLeod, M. and Saraga, E. 'Clearing a path through the undergrowth: a feminist reading of recent literature on child sexual abuse'. in P. Carter, T. Jeffs, and M.K. Smith (eds.) 'Social Work and Social Welfare', Open University Press, Milton Keynes, 1991.

Magura, S. 'Clients view outcomes of child protective services', Social Casework, 63, (9), 522–531, 1982.

Magura, S. and Derubeis, R. 'The effectiveness of preventive services for families with abused, neglected and disturbed children', Second year evaluation of the Hudson County project, Division of Youth and Family Services, Bureau of Research, Trenton, New Jersey, 1980.

Magura, S. and Moses, B.S. 'Clients as evaluators in child protective services', Child Welfare, 53, (2), 99–112, 1984.

Maletzky, B.M. 'Treating the Sexual Offender', Sage, Newbury Park, 1991.

Maletzky, B.M. 'Self referred vs court referred sexually deviant patients: Success with covert sensitization', Behaviour Therapy, 11, 306–314, 1980.

Maluccio, A.N., Fein, E., Olmstead, K.A. 'Permanency Planning for Children'. Tavistock, London, 1986.

Mannarino, A.P., Cohen, J.A., Smith, J.A., and Moore-Motily, S. 'Six and twelve month follow up of sexually abused girls', Journal of Interpersonal Violence, 6, (4), 494–511, 1991.

Marneffe, C. Plenary presentation, Third European Congress on Child Abuse and Neglect, Prague, 1991.

Marneffe, C., and Soumenkoff, G. 'Evaluation en prevention primaire: Un must, II, Le point de 3 vue pedo-psychiatrique', Child Abuse and Neglect, 10, (1), 53–61, 1986.

Marneffe, C., Soumenkoff, G., Laruelle, C., Gellen, P. and Buekens, P. 'Outcome of children after a 4 year program of antenatal care', Paper presented at Sixth International Congress on Child Abuse and Neglect, Sydney, Australia, August, 1986.

Marshall, W.L., Barbaree, H.E. and Christophe, D. 'Sexual offences against male children; sexual preferences for age of victim and type of behaviour', Canadian Journal of Behavioural Science, 18, 424–439, 1986.

Marshall, W.L., Barbaree, H.E., and Butt, J. 'Sexual offenders against male children: sexual preferences', Behaviour Research and Therapy, 26, (5), 383–391, 1988.

Marshall, W.L. and Barbaree, H.E. 'The long term evaluation of a behavioural treatment program for child molesters', Behaviour Research & Therapy, 26, (6), 499–511, 1988.

Marshall, W.L., Barbaree, H.E., and Eccles, A. 'Early onset and deviant sexuality in child molesters', Journal of Interpersonal Violence, 6, (3), 323–335, 1991.

Mastria, E.O., Mastria, M.A. and Harkins, J.C. 'Treatment of child abuse by behavioural intervention: a case report', Child Welfare, 58, (4), 253–261, 1979.

Mayes, G.M., Gillies, J. and Warden, D. 'An evaluation of the 'Kidscape' safety training programme', Report to Scottish Education Department, 1991a.

Mayes, G.M., Gillies, J. and Warden, D. 'An evaluative study of a child safety training programme', Report to Economic and Social Research Council, 1991b.

Mezey, G., Vizard, E., Hawkes, C. and Austin, R. 'A community treatment programme for convicted sex offenders: a preliminary report', Journal of Forensic Psychiatry, 2, (1), 11–25, 1991.

McAuley, R. 'Success and failure in applying behavioural analysis', Social Work Today, 11, (25), 15–17, 1980.

McBogg, P., McQuiston, M. and Alexander, H. 'Circle House residential treatment program', Child Abuse and Neglect, 3, 863–867, 1979a.

McBogg, P., McQuiston, M. and Schrant, R. 'Foster care enrichment program', Child Abuse and Neglect, 3, (2), 515–519, 1979b.

McCurdy, K. 'Providing treatment services for abused children', National Center on Child Abuse Research, Working paper 853, Chicago, 1991.

McGrath, P., Wiseman, D., Allan, B., Khalil, N. and Capelli, M. 'Teacher awareness program on child abuse: A randomized controlled trial', Child Abuse and Neglect, 11, (1), 125–132, 1987.

McIntosh, J. 'A Consumer perspective on Health Visiting', Report to Scottish Home and Health Department, Scottish Office, 1986.

Melton, G.B. 'The improbability of prevention of sexual abuse' in D.J. Willis, E.W. Holden, and M. Rosenberg (eds). 'Prevention of Child Maltreatment: Development and Ecological Perspectives', Wiley, New York, 1992.

Miller, J.L. and Whittaker, J.K. 'Social services and social support: blended programs for families at risk of child maltreatment', Child Welfare, LXCII, (2) 161–175, 1988.

Miller, K., Fein, E., Howe, G.W., Gaudio, C.P. and Bishop, G.V. 'Time-limited, goal-focused parent aide service', Social Casework, 65, (8), 472–477, 1984.

Miller, K., Fein, E., Howe, G.W., Gaudio, C.P. and Bishop, G. 'A parent aide program: record keeping, outcomes and costs', Child Welfare, 54, (4), 407–419, 1985.

Millham, S., Bullock, R., Hosie, K. and Haak, M. 'Lost in Care – the problems of maintaining links between children in care and their families', Gower, Aldershot, 1986.

Mills, M. and Pound, A. 'The Newpin Project, Changes 4, (2), 199–203, 1986.

Milner, J.S. and Chilamkurti, C. 'Physical child abuse perpetrator characteristics. A review of the literature', Journal of Interpersonal Violence, 6, (3), 345–366, 1991.

Miltenberger, R.G. and Thiesse-Duffy, E. 'Evaluation of home-based programs for teaching personal safety skills to children', Journal of Applied Behaviour Analysis, 21, (1), 81–87, 1988.

Monaghan, S.M. and Buckfield, P.M., 'Obstetrics and the family: identification of mothers at risk for parenting failure, and methods of support', Child Abuse and Neglect, 5, (1), 27–32, 1981.

Monaghan, S.M., Egan, T.G., Muir, R.C., Gilmore, R.J., Clarkson, J.E., and Crooks, T.J. 'Prenatal screening and intervention in the maternity hospital – Final results of a ten year study from Queen Mary, Child Care Unit. Paper presented at Sixth International Congress on Child Abuse, Sydney, Australia, August, 1986a.

Monaghan, S.M., Gilmore, R.J., Muir, R.C., Clarkson, J.E., Crooks, T.J., and Egan, T. 'Prenatal screening for risk of major parenting problem: Further results from the Queen Mary Maternity Hospital Child Care Unit', Child Abuse and Neglect, 10, (3), 369–375, 1986b.

Monck, E., Lewin, R., Sharland, E. and Goodall, G. 'Treatment outcomes in child sexual abuse', Paper presented at First National Congress on the Prevention of Child Abuse & Neglect, Leicester, September, 1991.

Moore, J.B. 'Project Thrive: a supportive treatment approach to the parents of children with non-organic failure to thrive', Child Welfare, 61, (6), 389–399, 1982.

Moore, J.G., Galcius, A. and Pettican, K. 'Emotional risk to children caught in violent marital conflict – The Basildon Treatment Project', Child Abuse and Neglect, 5, (2), 147–152, 1981.

Morreale, S. 'The Ontario Centre for the prevention of child abuse', presented at Sixth International Congress on Child Abuse and Neglect, Sydney, 1986.

Moss, P. 'Child care in the early months', Thomas Coram Research Unit Occasional Paper No. 3, University of London, Institute of Education, London, 1986.

Mousakitis, C.M. and Goldstein, S.C. 'A multidisciplinary approach to treating child neglect', Social Casework, 66, (4), 218–224, 1985.

Mullen, P.E., Romans-Clarkson, S.E., Walton, V.A., and Herbison, G.P. 'Impact of sexual and physical abuse on women's mental health', Lancet, 16th April, 1988.

Mullender, A. 'Group work as a response to a structural analysis of child abuse', Children and society, 3, (4), 345–362, 1989.

Murphy, A.D. and Davis, S.O. 'Modification of a mother's verbal abuse', Child Abuse and Neglect, 3, 1087–1092, 1979.

Murphy, M.J., Jellinek, M., Quinn, D., Smith, G. Poitrast, F.G., and Goshko, M. 'Substance abuse and serious child mistreatment: prevalence, risk, and outcome in a court sample', Child Abuse and Neglect, 15, (3), 197–212, 1991.

Murray, K. and Gough, D.A. (eds.) 'Intervening in Child Sexual Abuse', Scottish Academic Press, Edinburgh, 1991.

Murray, L. 'The impact of postnatal depression on infant development', Journal of Child Psychology and Psychiatry, 33, (3), 543–561, 1992.

Myers, J.E.B. 'Legal Issues in Child Abuse and Neglect', Sage, Newbury Park, 1992.

National Resource Center on Family Based Services. 'Annotated Directory of Selected Family-Based Service Programs', Fourth Edition, School of Social Work, University of Iowa, 1986.

NCH 'The Report of the Committee of Enquiry into Children and Young People who Sexually Abuse Other Children', National Children's Home, London, 1992.

NYCN 'Treatment Programs for Child Sexual Abuse Victims in Canada', National Youth in Care Network, Ontario, 1993.

Nelki, J.S. and Watters, J. 'A group for sexually abused young children: unravelling the web', Child Abuse and Neglect, 13, (3), 369–378, 1989.

Nelson, B.J. 'Making an Issue of Child Abuse. Political agenda setting for social problems', University of Chicago Press, Chicago, 1984.

Nelson, M. and Clark, K. 'The Education Guide to Preventing Child Sexual Abuse', Network Publications, Santa Cruz, 1986.

Nelson, K.E. Landsman, M.J. and Deutelbaum, W. 'Three models of family-centred placement prevention services; Child Welfare, LXIX, (1), 3–21, 1990.

New South Wales, Department of Education'; Ideas for teaching about non violent relationships', Personal Development Unit, Sydney, 1984.

Newson, J. and Newson, E. 'Seven Year Olds in the Home Environment', Allen and Unwin, London, 1976.

Ney, P.G., Johnstone, I.D., and Herron, M.A., 'Social and legal ramifications of a child crisis line', Child Abuse and Neglect, 9, (1), 47–55, 1985.

Nicol, A.R., Mearns, C., Hall, D., Kay, B., Williams, B. and Akister, J. 'An Evaluation of Focused Casework in Improving Interaction in Abusive Families', in J.E. Stevenson (ed), 'Recent Research in Developmental Psychology, Pergamon Press, Oxford, 1985.

Nicol, A.R., Smith, J., Kay, B., Hall, D., Barlow, J., and Williams, B. 'A focused casework approach to the treatment of child abuse. A controlled comparison'. Unpublished report, 1988.

O'Connor, S. et al 'Reduced incidence of parenting inadequacy following rooming-in', Pediatrics, 66, 176–182, 1980.

Oakley, A. 'The Captured Womb', Blackwell, Oxford, 1984.

Oates, K. 'Consequences of intrafamilial child abuse', plenary paper, International Congress on Child Abuse, Rio de Janeiro, 1988.

Oldershaw, L., Walters, G.C., & Hall, D.K. 'Control strategies and noncompliance in abusive mother-child dyads: an observational study', Child Development, 57, 722–732, 1986.

Olds, D., Henderson, C.R., Tatelbaum, R. and Chamberlain, R. 'Improving the delivery of prenatal care and outcomes of pregnancy: A randomized trial of nurse home intervention', Pediatrics, 77, (1), 16–28, 1986b.

Olds, D. Henderson, C.R., Chamberlain, R. and Tatelbaum, R. 'Preventing child abuse and neglect: a randomized trial of nurse home visitation', Pediatrics, 78, (1), 65–78, 1986a.

Olds, D.L. and Kitzman, H. 'Can home visitation improve the health of women and children at environmental risk', Pediatrics, 86, (1), 108–116, 1990.

Olds, D.L., Henderson, C.R., Tatelbaum, R., and Chamberlain, R. 'Improving the life-course development of a socially disadvantaged mothers: a randomized trial of nurse home visitation', American Journal of Public Health, 78, (11) 1436–1445, 1988.

Oppenheimer, R., Howells, K., Palmer, R.L. and Chaloner, D.A. 'Adverse sexual experience in childhood and clinical eating disorders: a preliminary description', Journal of Psychiatric Research, 19, (2/3), 357–361, 1985.

Ounsted, C., Oppenheimer, R. and Lindsay, J. 'Aspects of bonding failure: the psychopathology and psychotherapeutic treatment of families of battered children', Developmental Medicine and Child Neurology, 16, 447–465, 1974.

Ounstead, C., Oppenheimer, R., and Lidsay, J. 'The fourth goal of perinatal medicine', British Medical Journal, 284, 879–882, 1982.

Overholser, J.C., and Beck, S. 'Multimethod assessment of rapists, child molesters, and three control groups in behavioural and psychological measures', Journal of Consulting and Clinical Psychology, 54, (5), 682–687, 1986.

303

Owen Scott, W., Baer, G., Christoff, K.A. and Kelly, J.A. 'The use of skills-training procedures in the treatment of a child-abusive parent', Journal of Behavior Therapy and Experimental Psychiatry, 15, (4), 329–336, 1984.

Palfreeman, S. 'Mother and toddler groups among 'At Risk' families', Health Visitor 55, 455–459, September, 1982.

Palmer, R.L., Oppenheimer, R., Dignon, A., et al, 'Childhood sexual experience with adults reported by women with eating disorders: an extended series', British Journal of Psychiatry, 156, 699–703, 1990.

Palmer, R.L., Chaloner, D.A., and Oppenheimer, R. 'Childhood sexual experiences with adults reported by female psychiatric patients', British Journal of Psychiatry, 160, 261–265, 1992.

Pardeck, J.T., and Nolden, W.L. 'An evaluation of a crisis intervention center for parents at risk', Family Therapy, 12, (1), 25–33, 1985.

Parents United, 'Chapter development packet', Parents United International, San Jose, California, 1987.

Parish, R.A., Myers, P.A., Brander, A. and Templin, K.H. 'Developmental milestones in abused children and their improvement with family-oriented approach to the treatment of child abuse', Child Abuse and Neglect, 9, (2), 245–250, 1985.

Parton, N. 'The Politics of Child Abuse', McMillan, Basingstoke, 1985.

Patterson, G.R., Reid, J.B., Johnes, R.R., and Conger, R.E., 'A Social Learning Approach to Family Intervention in Families with Aggressive Children', Castalia Publishing, Eugene, Oregon, 1975.

Patton, M.Q. (ed) 'Family Sexual Abuse', Sage, Newbury Park, 1991.

Paulson, M.J. et al. 'Parents of the battered child. A multidisciplinarian group therapy approach to life threatening behaviour', Life Threatening Behavior, 4, (1), 18–31, 1974.

Pecora, P.J., Fraser, M.W. and Haapala, D.A. 'Client outcomes and issues for program design' in K. Wells and D.E. Biegal, Op cit. 1991.

Pellegrin, A. and Wagner, W.G. 'Child sexual abuse: factors affecting victims' removal from home', Child Abuse and Neglect, 14, (1), 53–60, 1990.

Peraino, J.M. 'Evaluation of a pre-school antivictimization prevention program', Journal of Interpersonal Violence, 5, (4), 520–528, 1990.

Perkins, E.R. 'Education for Childbirth and Parenthood', Croom Helm, London, 1980.

Peters, M.L., and Carswell, M.S. 'PEP in Alabama', Children Today, 13, (4), 27–29, 1984.

Peters, S.D., Wyatt, G.E., and Finkelhor, D. 'Prevalence' in D. Finkelhor and Associates, 1986, Op. Cit.

Phelan, J. 'Family Centres: A Study', The Children's Society, 1983.

Phillips, N.K., Gorman, K.H. and Bodenheimer, M. 'High-risk infants and mothers in groups', Social Work, 26, (2), 157–161, 1981.

Pillai, V., Collins, A. and Morgan, R. 'Family Walk-in Centre – Eaton Socon: Evaluation of a project on preventive intervention based in the community', Child Abuse and Neglect, 6, (1), 71–79, 1982.

Poche, C., Brouer, R. and Swearington, M. 'Teaching self-protection to young children', Journal of Applied Behaviour Analysis, 14, 169–176, 1981.

Poche, C., Yoder, P., and Miltenberger, R. 'Teaching self protection to children using television techniques', Journal of Applied Behaviour Analysis, 21, (3), 253–261, 1988.

Porter, R. (ed.) 'Child Sexual Abuse within the Family', Tavistock, London, 1984.

Pound, A. 'The Development of Attachments in Adult Life – The Newpin Experiment', Paper presented at a meeting of The Association of Child Psychotherapy in honour of Dr. Bowlby's 80th Birthday, London, February, 1987.

Pound, A. and Mills, M. 'A pilot evaluation of Newpin', Association of Child Psychology and Psychiatry Newsletter, 7, (4), 13, 1985.

Prentky, R. and Burgess, A.W. 'Rehabilitation of child molesters: a cost benefit analysis', American Journal of Orthopsychiatry, 60, (19), 108–117, 1990.

Press-Rigler, M., Kent, J.T., Croot, P. and Finnila, M. 'Parent aides: An intervention program in cases of child abuse and neglect', Journal of the Association for the Care of Children in Hospitals, 8, (3), 64–68, 1980.

Pritchard, P. and Appleton, P. 'Home based behavioural interventions by a specialist Health Visitor', Health Visitor, 59, 35–37, 1986.

Pritchard, C. Levels of risk and psycho-social problems of families on the 'At risk of abuse' register: some indications of outcome two years after case closure', Research Policy and Planning, 9, (2), 19–26, 1991.

Prodgers, A. and Bannister, A. 'Actions speak louder than words', Community Care, July 28th, 1983.

Quinsey, V.L., Chaplin, T.C. and Carrigan, W.F. 'Biofeedback and signalled punishment in the modification of inappropriate sexual age preferences', Behaviour Therapy, 11, 567–576, 1980.

Quinton, D. and Rutter, M. 'Parental Breakdown: The Making and Breaking of Intergenerational Links', Gower, Aldershot, 1988.

Quitiquit, R., McPherson, S., Buckley, D. and Moore, D. 'Early identification of high risk families in the military', Paper presented at Sixth International Congress on Child Abuse & Neglect, Sydney, Australia, 1986.

Ramey, C.T., Starr, R.H., Pallas, J., Whitten, C.F. and Read, V. 'Nutrition, response-contingent stimulation, and the maternal deprivation syndrome: results of an early intervention program', Merrill-Palmer Quarterly, 21, (1), 45–53, 1975.

Rapoport, R., Rapoport, R.N. and Strelitz, Z. 'Fathers, Mothers and Others', Routledge and Kegan Paul, London, 1977.

Reid, J., Taplin, P. and Lorber, R. 'A social interactional approach to the treatment of abusive families', in R. Stuart (ed.) 'Violent Behavior: Social Learning Approaches to Prediction, Management and Treatment', Brunner/Mazel, New York, 1981.

Resnick, G. 'Enhancing parental competencies for high-risk mothers: an evaluation of prevention effects', Child Abuse and Neglect, 9, (4), 479–489, 1985.

Rice, M.E., Quinsey, V.L. and Harris, G.T. 'Sexual recidivism among child molesters released from a maximum security psychiatric institution', Journal of Consulting and Clinical Psychology, 59, (3), 381–386, 1991.

Richards, M.P.M. 'Effects on Development of Medical Interventions and the Separation of Newborns from their Parents', in D. Shaffer and J. Dunn (eds.) 'The First Year of Life', Wiley, Chichester, 1979.

Richman, N., Stevenson, J. and Graham, P.J. 'Pre-school to school: A behavioural study', Academic Press, London, 1982.

Riedel, R.R. and Harrington, M. 'Intensive placement prevention in a protective service agency', Protecting Children, 2, (1), Spring 1985.

Rivara, F.P. 'Physical abuse in children under two: a study of therapeutic outcomes', Child Abuse and Neglect, 9, (1), 81–87, 1985.

Roberts, J., Beswick, K., Leverton, B. and Lynch, M.A. 'Prevention of child abuse: Group therapy for mothers and children', The Practitioner, 219, 111–115, 1977.

Rogowski, S. and McGrath, M. 'United we stand up to the pressures that lead to child abuse', Social Work Today, 17, (37), 13–14, (May 26th) 1986.

Rosenstein, P.J. 'Family Outreach: a program for the prevention of child abuse and neglect', Child Welfare, 57, (8), 519–525, 1978.

Ross, A.O. 'Critical Commentary', Advances in Behaviour Research and Therapy, 6, 75–78, 1984.

Roth, H.J. 'Relationship between attendance at a Parents-Anonymous adult program and children's behaviour at the Parents-Anonymous child care program', Children and Youth Services Review, 7, (1), 39–43, 1985.

Royal College of Nursing. 'Thinking about Health Visiting', Discussion document from the Health Visitors' Advisory Group, Royal College of Nursing, London, 1982.

Rutter, M. 'Maternal Deprivation Reassessed', Penguin, Harmondsworth, 1981.

Rutter, M. 'Intergenerational continuities and discontinuities in serious parenting difficulties', in D. Cichetti and V. Carlson (eds.) 'Child Maltreatment. Theory and research on the causes and consequences of child abuse and neglect', Cambridge University Press, Cambridge, 1989.

Sameroff, A.J. and Chandler, M.J. 'Reproductive risk and the continuum of caretaking casualty', in F.D. Horowitz, M. Hetherington, S. Scarr-Salapatek, and G. Siegal (eds.), Review of Child Development Research, 4, 187–244, University of Chicago Press, Chicago, 1975.

Sandford, D.A. and Tustin, R.D. 'Behavioural treatment of parental assault on a child', New Zealand Psychologist, 2, 76–82, 1973.

Sandler, J., Vandercar, C. and Milhoan, M. 'Training child abusers in the use of positive reinforcement practices', Behaviour Research and Therapy, 16, 169–175, 1978.

Sankey, C., Elmer, E., Halechko, A. and Schulberg, P. 'The development of abused and high-risk infants in different treatment modalities: residential versus in-home care', Child Abuse and Neglect, 9, 237–243, 1985.

Saslawsky, D.A. and Wurtele, S.K. 'Educating children about sexual abuse: implications for pediatric intervention and possible prevention', Journal of Pediatric Psychology, 11, (2), 235–245, 1986.

Scaife, J. and Frith, J. 'A behaviour management and life stress course for a group of mothers incorporating training for health visitors', Child Care, Health and Development, 14, 25–50, 1988.

Schellenbach, C. and Guerney, L. 'Identification of adolescent abuse and future intervention prospects', Journal of Adolescence, 10, 1–12, 1987.

Schinke, S.P., Schilling, R.F., Barth, R.P. and Gilchrist, 'Stress-management intervention to prevent family violence', Journal of Family Violence, 1, (1), 13–26, 1986.

Schmidt, B.D. and Mauro, R.D. 'Non organic failure to thrive: An outpatient approach', Child Abuse and Neglect, 13, (2), 235–248, 1989.

Schopler, E. 'Specific and non specific factors in the effectiveness of a treatment system', American Psychologist, 42, 376–383, 1987.

Schultz, B., Houck, A. and Hollister, D. 'Parental Stress Center: A residential treatment program for abused infants', Child Abuse and Neglect, 3, 877–881, 1979.

Scott, J. 'And mother makes two', Youth in Society, No. 113, April, 1986.

Sedlak, A.J. 'Risk factors for child abuse and neglect and the likelihood of official investigation' Paper presented at Ninth International Congress on Child Abuse and Neglect, Chicago, September, 1992.

Sedlak, A.J. 'Risk factors for the occurrence of child abuse and neglect', Unpublished draft paper, 1993.

Seitz, V., Rosenbaum, L., and Apfel N. 'Effects of family support intervention: a ten year follow up', Child Development, 56, 376–391, 1985.

Senn, C. 'Vulnerable Sexual Abuse and People with Intellectual Handicap', Allan Rocher Institute, Toronto (undated).

Sheldon, B. 'Single case evaluation methods: review and prospects', in J. Lishman (ed.), 'Evaluation' Research Highlights 8, University of Aberdeen, 1984.

Siegal, J.M., Sorenson, S.B., Golding, J.M., Burnam, M.A., and Stein, J.A. 'The prevalence of childhood sexual assault. The Los Angeles epidemiologic catchment area project', American Journal of Epidemiology, 126, (6), 1141–1153, 1987.

Siegel, E., Bauman, K.E., Schaefer, E.S., Saunders, M.M. and Ingram, D.D. 'Hospital and home support during infancy: impact on maternal attachment, child abuse and neglect, and health care utilization', Pediatrics, 66, (2), 183–189, 1980.

Sigurdson, E., Strang, M. and Doig, T. 'What do children know about preventing sexual assault? How can their awareness be increased? A Review of the Effectiveness of Feeling Yes, Feeling No', Paper presented at Sixth International Congress, Child Abuse and Neglect, Sydney, Australia, 1986.

Simpson, V. 'Forum on maternity and the newborn', Conference report, Association of Child Psychology and Psychiatry Newsletter, 11, (4), 29–30, 1989.

Smart, E. and Hicks, B. 'The Parent support service (Australian Capital Territory)', Child Abuse and Neglect, 3, (1), 357–362, 1979.

Smith, J. and Rachman, S. 'Non-accidental injury to children – II – a controlled evaluation of a behavioural management programme', Behaviour Research and Therapy, 22, (4), 349–366, 1984.

Smith, J., Rachman, S. and Yule, B. 'Non-accidental injury to Children – III – methodological problems of evaluative treatment research', Behaviour Research and Therapy, 22, (4), 367, 1984.

Smith, M. 'Putting knowledge to practical use – an examination of the interview assessment model', in A. Bannister (ed.) 'From Hearing to Healing: Working with the Aftermath of Child Sexual Abuse', Longman, Harlow, 1992.

Soumenkoff, G. and Marneffe, C. 'Evaluation en Prevention Primaire: un obligation, I. Le point de vue obstetrical', Child Abuse and Neglect, 10, (1), 45–52, 1986.

Soumenkoff, G. Marneffe C., Gerard, M., Limet, R., Beekman, S.M. & Hubinont, P.O. 'A coordinated attempt for prevention of child abuse at the ante-natal care level', Child Abuse and Neglect, 6, (1), 87–94, 1982.

Social Work Services Group 'Child Protection in Scotland, Management Information' Report by a joint steering group, Scottish Office, March 1992.

Spaid, W.M. and Fraser, M. 'The correlates of success/failure in brief and intensive family treatment: implications for family preservation services', Children and Youth Services Review, 13, 77–99, 1991.

Spokes, D. and Digby, P. 'A community response to child abuse: protocol development', Paper presented at Sixth International Congress on Child Abuse and Neglect, Sydney, 1986.

Spungen, C.A., Jenson, S.E., Finkelstein, N.W., and Satinsky, F.A. 'Child personal safety: model program for prevention of child sexual abuse', Social Work, 127–131, March, 1989.

Stainton Rogers, W. and Stainton Rogers R. 'Taking the Child abuse debate apart', in W. Stainton Rogers, D. Hevey, and E. Ash, (eds.) 'Child Abuse and Neglect: facing the challenge', Batsford, London, 1989.

Stein, A., Gath, D.H., Bucher, J., Bond, A., Day, A, and Cooper, P.J. 'The relationship between postnatal depression and mother child interaction', British Journal of Psychiatry, 158, 46052, 1991.

Stein, J.A., Golding, J.M., Siegal, J.M., Burnam, A.M., and Sorenson, S.B. 'Long term psychological sequalae of child sexual abuse: The Los Angeles Epidemiologic Catchment Area Study' in Wyatt and Powell, 1988, Op. Cit.

Stempler, B.J. and Stempler, R.H. 'Extending the client connection: Using homemaker-caseworker teams', Social Casework, 62, (3), 149–158, 1981.

Stephenson, P.S. 'Reaching child abusers through target toddlers', Victimology, 2, (2), 310–316, 1977.

Stevenson, J. and Bailey, V. 'A controlled trial of post natal mothers' groups as psychosocial primary prevention. II: Evaluation of outcome', unpublished paper, University of Surrey, 1988.

Stevenson, J. 'A critique of the evaluation of the 'Child Development Programme', The Psychologist, 11, 480–482, 1991.

Stevenson, J. 'A feasible intervention in families with parenting difficulties: A primary preventive perspective on child abuse', Paper presented at Conference on Early Prediction and Prevention of Child Abuse and Neglect, Society for Reproductive and Infant Psychology, Leicester, March 1987.

Stevenson, J. 'Evaluation studies of psychological treatment of children and practical constraints on their design', Association of Child Psychology and Psychiatry Newsletter, 8, (2), 2–11, 1986.

Stevenson, O. 'Social work intervention to protect children: aspects of research and practice', Child Abuse Review, 1, (1), 19–32, 1992.

Stillwell, S.L., Lutzker, J.R. and Greene, B.F. 'Evaluation of a sexual abuse program for preschoolers', Journal of Family Violence, 13, (4), 269–281, 1988.

Stone, N.M. and Stone, S.F. 'The prediction of successful foster placement', Social Casework, 64, (1), 11–17, 1983.

Straus, M.A. and Gelles, R. 'Societal change and change in family violence from 1975 to 1985 as revealed by two national surveys', Journal of Marriage and the Family, 48, 465–479, 1986.

Stuart, R.B. 'Violent Behaviour. Social Learning Approaches to Prediction, Management and Treatment', Brunner/Mazel, New York, 1981.

Sturm, L. and Drotar, D. 'Prediction of weight for height following intervention in three year old children with early histories of non organic failure to thrive', Child Abuse and Neglect, 13, (1), 19–28, 1989.

Subramanian, K. 'Reducing child abuse through respite center intervention', Child Welfare, 54, (5), 501–509, 1985.

Sullivan, P.M., Scanlan, J.M., Brookhouser, P.E., and Schulte, L.E. 'The effects of psychotherapy on behavior problems of sexually abused deaf children', Child Abuse and Neglect, 16, (2), 297–307, 1992.

Sullivan, P.M., Vernon, M. and Scanlan, J.M. 'Sexual abuse of deaf youth', American Annals Deaf, 132, (4), 256–26, 1987.

Suphi, G. 'Production and Evaluation of a Puppet Video to Teach Nursery School Children about Prevention of Sexual Abuse'. Unpublished Masters Thesis, Birmingham University, 1990.

Sutton, C. 'Training parents to manage difficult children: a comparison of methods', Behavioural Psychotherapy, 20, 115–139, 1992.

Swann, H.L. Press, A.N. and Briggs, S.L. 'Child sexual abuse prevention: does it work?', Child Welfare, 54, (4), 395–405, 1985.

Szykula, S. and Fleischman, M. 'Reducing out of home placements of abused children – two controlled field studies', Child Abuse and Neglect, 9, (2), 277–283, 1985.

Taylor, D.K. and Beauchamp, C. 'Hospital-based primary prevention strategy in child abuse: a multi-level needs addressment', Child Abuse and Neglect, 12, 343–354, 1988.

Telleen, S., Herzog, A., Kilbane, T.L. 'Impact of a family support program on mothers' social support and parenting stress', American Journal of Orthopsychiatry, 59, (3), 410–419, 1989.

Thoburn, J. Family participation in child protection work', Paper presented to BASPCAN Conference, 1991.

Thoburn, J., Lewis, A., and Hemmings, D. 'Family involvement in child protection conferences', Discussion Paper 1, University of East Anglia Social Work Development Unit, 1991.

Thoits, P.A. 'Social Support and Psychological Well-Being: Theoretical Possibilities', in I.G. Sarason and B.R. Sarason (eds.) 'Social Support: Theory, Research and Applications', Martinus Nijhoff, Dordrecht, 1985.

Thoits, P.A. 'Social support as coping assistance', Journal of Consulting and Clinical Psychology, 54, (4), 416–423, 1986.

Thomasson, E., Berkovitz, T., Minor, S., Cassle, G., McCord, D., Milner, J.S. 'Evaluation of a family life education program for rural high-risk families: A research note', Journal of Community Psychology, 9, 246–249, 1981 (a).

Thomasson, E., Berkovitz, T., Minor, S., Cassle, G., McCord, D., Milner, J.S. 'Evaluation of a family life education program for rural risk families; unpublished report available from J.S. Milner, Western Carolina University, Cullowhee, North Carolina. 1981 (b).

Thorpe, D. 'Patterns of child protection intervention service delivery: Report of a pilot project', University of Western Australia Crime Research Centre, Research Report no. 4, April 1991.

Tipton, M. 'Cumberland county child abuse and neglect council prevention plan', presented to Sixth International Congress on Child Abuse and Neglect, Sydney, 1986.

Toro, P.A. 'Developmental effects of child abuse: A review', Child Abuse and Neglect, 6, (4), 423–431, 1982.

Tracy, J.J. and Clark, E.H. 'Treatment for child abusers', Social Work, 19, 338–342, 1974.

Tracy, J.J., Ballard, C.M. and Clark, E.H. 'Child abuse project: a follow-up', Social Work, 20, 398–399, 1975.

Trickett, P.K. and Kuczynski, L. 'Children's misbehaviours and parental discipline strategies in abusive and non abusive families', Developmental Psychology, 22, (1), 115–123, 1986.

Trudell, B. and Whatley, M.H. 'School sexual abuse prevention: Unintended consequences and dilemmas,' Child Abuse and Neglect, 12, (1), 103–114, 1988.

Van den Bos, G. 'Psychotherapy research: A special issue', American Psychologist, 41, 111–112, 1986.

Van der Eyken, W. 'Day nurseries in action: A national study of local authority day nurseries in England, 1975–83', Department of Child Health Research Unit, University of Bristol, 1985.

Van der Eyken, W. 'Home Start. A Four Year Evaluation', Home Start Consultancy, Leicester, 1982.

Van Meter, M.J.S. 'Isolating, Insulating or interfering: The many faces of the networks of abusive and neglectful families', paper presented at Sixth International Congress on Child Abuse and Neglect, Sydney, Australia, August, 1986.

Walford, G. 'Group therapy for sexually abused children: Setting up a service and preliminary follow up of the first twenty cases', Newsletter of the Association of Child Psychology and Psychiatry, 11, (6), 7–13, 1989.

Walker, H. 'Family centres', in P. Carter, T. Jeffs, and M.K. Smith (eds.) 'Social Work and Social Welfare', Open University Press, Milton Keynes, 1991.

Waterhouse, L., and Carnie, J. 'Child Sexual Abuse. The professional challenge to social work and police', Report to Social Work Services Group of the Scottish Office, May 1990.

Waterhouse, L., and Carnie, J. 'Assessing child protection risk', British Journal of Social Work, 22, (1), 47–60, 1992.

Waterman, J. 'Overview of Treatment Issues', in K. McFarlane et al 'Sexual Abuse of Young Children. Evaluation and Treatment', Holt, Rinehart and Winston, London, 1986.

Weiss, H.B. and Jacobs, F.H. 'Evaluating Family Programs'. Aldine de Gruyter, New York, 1988.

Wekerle, C. and Wolfe, D.A. 'Prevention strategies for child abuse and neglect: A review and critique', submitted, Autumn, 1991.

Welbourn, A.M. and Mazuryk, G.F. 'Inter-agency interventions: and innovative therapeutic program for abuse prone mothers', Child Abuse and Neglect, 4, (3), 199–203, 1980.

Wells, S.J., Fluke, J.D., Downing, J.D. and Hendricks Brown, C. 'Screening in child protective services, Executive Summary', American Bar Association, Washington, 1989.

Wells, K. and Biegal, D.E. (eds.) 'Family Preservation Services: research and evaluation', Sage, Newbury Park, 1991.

West, J.E. and West, E.D. 'Child abuse treated in a psychiatric day hospital', Child Abuse and Neglect, 3, 699–707, 1979.

Whiteman, M., Fanshel, D., and Grundy, J.F. 'Cognitive-Behavioural interventions aimed at anger of parents at risk of child abuse', Social Work, 469–474, Nov/Dec. 1987.

Whittaker, J.K., Kinney, J., Tracy, E.M., Booth, C. 'Reaching High Risk Families. Intensive family preservation in human services', Aldine de Gruyter, New York, 1990.

Willems, D.M., and DeRubeis, R. 'The effectiveness of intensive preventive services for families with abused, neglected or disturbed children', Division of Youth and Family Services, Bureau of Research, Trenton, New Jersey, 1981.

Winnicott, D.W. 'The Child, The Family and the Outside World', Penguin, Harmondworth, 1973.

Withey, V., Anderson, R. and Lauderdale, M. 'Volunteers as mentors for abusing parents: a natural helping relationship', Child Welfare, LIX, (10), 637–644, 1980.

Wolfe, D.A. 'Child Abuse. Implications for child development and psychopathology', Sage, Newbury Park, 1987.

Wolfe, D.A. 'Child abusive parents: An empirical review and analysis', Psychological Bulletin, 97, (3), 462–482, 1985.

Wolfe, D.A. and Sandler, J. 'Training abusive parents in effective child management', Behaviour Modification, 5, 320–335, 1981.

Wolfe, D.A., Edwards, B., Manion, I. and Koverola, C. 'Early intervention for parents at risk of child abuse and neglect: A preliminary investigation', Journal of Consulting and Clinical Psychology, 56, (1), 40–47, 1988.

Wolfe, D.A., MacPherson, T., Blount, R. and Wolfe, V. 'Evaluation of a brief intervention for educating school children in awareness of physical and sexual abuse', Child Abuse and Neglect, 10, (1), 85–92, 1986.

Wolfe, D.A., Sandler, J. and Kauffman, K., 'A competency-based parent training program for child abusers', Journal of Consulting and Clinical Psychology, 49, 633–640, 1981

Wolfe, D.A., Lawrence, J.S., Graves, K., Brehony, K., Bradlyn, D. and Kelly, J.A. 'Intensive behavioural parent training for a child abuse mother', Behaviour Therapy, 13, 438–452, 1982.

Wolfe, V.V., Gentile, G., and Wolfe, D.A. 'The impact of sexual abuse on children: a PTSD formulation', Behavior Therapy, 20, (2), 215–228, 1989.

Wolff, R. Plenary presentation, Eighth International Congress on Child Abuse and Neglect, Hamburg, 1990.

Wolkind, S., Dingwall, R., and Graham, P. 'Research Issues in Child Abuse', Social Science and Medicine, 21, (11), 1217–1218, 1985.

Wolock, I., and Mumm, A.M. 'Predictors of re-reports of child abuse and neglect: a longitudinal study', Paper presented at Ninth International Congress on Child Abuse and Neglect, Chicago, September 1992.

Wood, P.E. 'Residential treatment for families of maltreated children', Child Welfare, 60, (2), 105–108, 1981.

Woodworth, D.L. 'Evaluation of a multiple family incest treatment program', in M.Q. Patton, 1991, Op. cit.

Wortman, C.B. and Lehman, D.R. 'Reactions to victims of life crises: Social supports that fail', in I.G. Sarason and B.R. Sarason (eds.) 'Social Support: Theory, Research and Applications', Martinus Nijhoff, Dordrecht, 1985.

Wurtele, S.K., Saslawsky, D.A., Miller, C.L., Marrs, S.R., and Britcher, J.C., 'Teaching personal safety skills for potential prevention of sexual abuse: a comparison of treatments', Journal of Consulting and Clinical Psychology, 54, 688–692, 1986.

Wurtele, S.K., Marrs, S.R., and Miller-Perrin, C.L. 'Practice makes perfect? The role of participant modeling in sexual abuse prevention programs', Journal of Consulting and Clinical Psychology, 55, (4), 599–602, 1987.

Wurtele, S.K. 'School-based sexual abuse prevention programs: A review'. Child Abuse and Neglect, 11, (4), 483–496, 1987.

Wurtele, S.K., Kast L.C., Miller-Perrin C.L., and Kondrick P.A. 'Comparison of programs for teaching personal safety skills to preschoolers', Journal of Consulting and Clinical Psychology, 57, (4), 505–511, 1989.

Wurtele, S.K. 'Teaching Personal Safety skills to four year old children: a behavioral approach', Behavior Therapy, 21, 25–32, 1990.

Wurtele, S.K., Currier, L.L., Gillespie, E.I., and Franklin, C.F. 'The eficacy of a parent-implemented program for teaching preschoolers personal safety skills', Behaviour Therapy, 22, 69–83, 1991.

Wurtele, S.K., Gillespie, E.I., Currier, L.L., and Franklin, C.F. 'A comparison of teachers and parents as instructors of a personal safety program for preschoolers', Child Abuse and Neglect, 16, (1), 127–137, 1992.

Wyatt, G.E. and Newcomb, M. 'Internal and external mediators of women's sexual abuse in childhood', Journal of Consulting and Clinical Psychology, 58, (6), 758–767, 1990.

Wyatt, G.E. and Powell, G.J. (eds.) 'Lasting Effects of Child Sexual Abuse', Sage, Newbury Park, 1991.

Yarmey, A.D. and Rosenstein, S.R. 'Parental predictions of their children's knowledge about dangerous situations', Child Abuse and Neglect, 12, (3), 355–361, 1988.

Zastrow, C. 'Self-talk: A rational approach to understanding and treating child abuse and neglect', Social Casework, 62, (3), 182–185, 1981.

Zigler, E.G., Weiss, H.B. and Kagan, S.L. 'Programs to strengthen families: A Resource Guide', Yale University and Family Resource Coalition, Chicago, 1986.

Zimrin, H. 'Do nothing but do something: the effect of human contact with the parent on abusive behaviour', British Journal of Social Work, 14, 475–485, 1984.

Printed in the United Kingdom for HMSO
Dd296442 11/93 C20 G3397 10170